MAKING INDUSTRIAL PITTSBURGH MODERN

MAKING INDUSTRIAL PITTSBURGH MODERN

ENVIRONMENT, LANDSCAPE, TRANSPORTATION, ENERGY, & PLANNING

EDWARD K. MULLER AND JOEL A. TARR

UNIVERSITY OF PITTSBURGH PRESS

Published by the University of Pittsburgh Press, Pittsburgh, Pa., 15260

Manufactured in the United States of America
Printed on acid-free paper
10 9 8 7 6 5 4 3 2 1

Cataloging-in-Publication data is available from the Library of Congress

ISBN 13: 978-0-8229-4569-7
ISBN 10: 0-8229-4569-X

Cover art courtesy the Allegheny Conference on Community Development, Detre Library & Archives, Senator John Heinz History Center Pittsburgh, PA
Cover design by Joel W. Coggins

Dedicated to the memory of Moe Coleman,
devoted citizen of Pittsburgh

CONTENTS

III. ENERGY, THE ENVIRONMENT, AND THE MODERN CITY

IV. PLANNING THE MODERN CITY

MAKING INDUSTRIAL PITTSBURGH MODERN

INTRODUCTION

Making Industrial Pittsburgh Modern: Environment, Landscape, Transportation, Energy, and Planning contains writings about Pittsburgh that have been prepared over the past several decades by urban historical geographer, Edward K. Muller (Ted) of the University of Pittsburgh, and urban and environmental historian, Joel A. Tarr of Carnegie Mellon University. Writing about the history of Pittsburgh has been a joy for both of us. We have lived and worked in the city for many years and have experienced its periods of decline and renewal. Those familiar with the writing of the two authors will note that some familiar subjects such as wastewater issues, smoke control, and political changes are not covered separately but are integrated within various chapters. We chose which chapters to exclude primarily on the calculation that some of our writing is well known to scholars and easily accessed in other publications. The chapters in this volume include ones that were not easily accessed or ones for which the original publications needed updating with recent scholarship. Some chapters are new and unpublished. Those interested in our other writings on Pittsburgh will find them listed in the list titled Additional Works at the end of the book.

✦ ✦ ✦

Pittsburgh emerged as a modern American city after the mid-nineteenth century, sharing many characteristics with other contemporary cities. Before 1850 the city was small, compact, crowded, and largely focused on the waterfront of the Monongahela River's mudflat or wharf, with more limited development along the banks of the Allegheny and Ohio Rivers. Growth was complicated by the region's hilly topography and large rivers, which presented challenges in fashioning suitable industrial and residential sites and providing movement of goods and people. Still, city government and private enterprise, often working together, overcame these difficulties. In the late nineteenth and first decades of the twentieth century the city underwent explosive industrial growth. Pittsburgh burst into the national spotlight as an industrial juggernaut, a center of finance capitalism, and the headquarters of numerous national corporations. Manufacturing also grew in other cities, but none matched the extensive complex of iron, steel, and allied metals industries that became the hallmark of the Steel City along with its trademark pall of black smoke.

By 1900 Pittsburgh had a modern downtown of tall steel-frame office buildings (the first skyscraper, fittingly enough, was the thirteen-story Carnegie Building of 1895), magnificent department stores, and grand railroad terminals. Construction of networked infrastructures such as water and wastewater systems, improvements in transportation and communication technologies, and new energy sources both facilitated and shaped Pittsburgh's spatial growth. Working-class, immigrant, and racially segregated communities, middle-class neighborhoods, and elite enclaves radiated outward from downtown. Many mills and middle-class residents located beyond the central city to newly developing industrial towns and residential suburbs.

Government had played a vital role in city building, laying out, and lighting streets, constructing water and sewerage networks, and franchising transit, energy, and communications systems for use in the city streets. On occasion, as in many other cities, these activities were manipulated to the benefit of entrepreneurs and their political "ring" allies. Public-private collaborations, especially with voluntary organizations, made positive contributions and in many cases were an important factor in driving governmental reforms, infrastructure, and environmental improvements.

Largely, however, the profit-maximizing objectives of private enterprise did not meet the larger societal needs. The predilection of government and nonprofit organizations to minimally intrude on the private sector and ostensibly free markets contributed to the region's serious imbalance. In the first years of the twentieth century Pittsburgh was marked by smoky particulate-laden air, polluted water, untreated sewage, low wages, poverty, substandard housing, poor health outcomes, and political corruption. The Russell Sage Foundation's pioneering *Pittsburgh Survey* (1909–1914) highlighted these conditions, but reforms promoted by progressive forces were limited and difficult to achieve in a city dominated largely by industrialists, the business community, and their political allies.

Although seemingly still a major urban growth center, Pittsburgh had actually begun to recede from its high rate of industrial and population expansion before the First World War. The devastation of the 1907 flood and the financial crisis of the same year accelerated negative changes already underway. The slowing of growth and the specter of industrial decline demanded responsive city-building measures, but planning by nonprofit organizations and city and county governments was largely unsuccessful. The residential suburbs benefited in the 1920s at the expense of the central city after the public sector built highway, bridge, and tunnel access to facilitate automobile access to and from relatively undeveloped areas. In the 1920s most change occurred in regard to downtown development and transportation infrastructure, but other sectors in need of action, such as the environment and housing, were neglected.

The depression of the 1930s devastated Pittsburgh, especially because of its heavy dependence on the severely impacted iron and steel industry. Unemployment was high, and the city suffered badly. By the later years of the decade it was common to hear dire predictions regarding Pittsburgh's post–Second World War prospects. The city's powerful business and civic elites began to consider various strategies preparing for a postwar decline. Although defense spending temporarily reinvigorated its industries, Pittsburgh emerged from the Second World War with an aging and overspecialized industrial base, a battered housing stock, crumbling infrastructure, a shabby, congested downtown, and environmental contamination of air, water, and land. Major corporations began to question their commitment to the city as they faced the reluctance of professional personnel to relocate to Pittsburgh. A few considered transferring their headquarters to other metropolitan areas with brighter futures.

A rollercoaster of events marked the post–Second World War period through the end of the century. It began with Pittsburgh's commitment to becoming the first major industrial city to renew itself. The so-called Pittsburgh Renaissance—driven by a public-private partnership led by the Democratic mayor David Lawrence and Republican banker, Richard King Mellon, leader of the nonprofit Allegheny Conference on Community Development—undertook environmental, infrastructure, and redevelopment projects. Pittsburgh became a model throughout the nation for how industrial cities could recover from decline, often under the guidance of various nonprofit public authorities such as the Urban Renewal Authority, the Parking Authority, the Allegheny County Sanitary Authority, and the Port Authority Transit. These organizations led to successes in smoke control and sewage treatment, the construction of expressways and public parking garages, the consolidation of mass transit firms, an airport, and downtown redevelopment. The federal government contributed with a system of flood control dams in the city's watersheds, and the state aided with construction of Point State Park at the rivers' confluence. Other new parks and public entertainment facilities made the region more attractive. Public participation, authorization, and funding for these measures overcame political and legal opposition. Despite the successes and a palpable sense that Pittsburgh was overcoming its decades of inaction, the racial disparities, persistent unemployment, and shortages of low income housing remained intractable problems that were exacerbated by urban-renewal-type city-building efforts. In addition, although smoke pollution was reduced, the city still suffered from poor air quality.

By the 1960s the Renaissance had slowed, beset by a combination of economic, racial, and political issues. Efforts to diversify the economy had largely failed. Civil rights and neighborhood activism challenged the public-private partnership's agenda, especially its urban renewal projects. The partnership's two powerful leaders passed from the scene, and a new city administration under the direction of Mayor Peter Flaherty ruptured the Renaissance partnership. Retrenchment, cost cutting, scuttling of new infrastructure projects, continued racial tension, and general population loss marked the decade of the 1970s. The city's economy suffered, as the steel industry and allied manufacturing firms declined sharply. Despite some years of prosperity during the Korean and Vietnam Wars, the steel industry lost markets to foreign competitors and domestic mini-mills. The industry failed to employ new technologies or cut costs sufficiently; mill after mill banked its furnaces and closed. Unemployment soared during the late 1970s through the 1980s in the dramatic collapse of what had been at one time the nation's premier steel center. Other industries suffered as well. Pittsburgh was no longer the steel city.

Although seeds for a postindustrial economy had been planted before the 1980s, it required the coordinated efforts of governmental, nonprofit, and private entities in the decade to initiate a lasting economic transformation. A new mayor, Richard Caliguiri, revived the public-private partnership and the focus on enhancing downtown as a center for corporate offices and cultural amenities. The city and county once again upgraded public infrastructure. Simultaneously the universities, hospitals, local and state governments, and foundations designed a variety of programs to redevelop brownfields, create a flourishing "meds and eds" sector, and promote advanced technology firms. Pittsburgh today is often cited as the model of a city that has overcome the travails of deindustrialization and is on its way to becoming a booming high tech center bursting with new enterprises, a variety of cultural and educational activities, and low unemployment. Just as in the past, however, pockets of deprivation persist, and not all parts of the city and the region share equally in the positive postindustrial transformation as former industrial towns and minority communities struggle to find their footing in this new world.

✦ ✦ ✦

The sixteen chapters in this collection are studies of select aspects of Pittsburgh's city-building history as it emerged as a modern metropolis. They elaborate various dimensions of the urban experience whose legacy continues to influence its postindustrial transformation. In the first section, the chapters examine the shaping of the regional landscape by industry and natural resource exploitation. With scarce level land available, the search for large manufacturing sites served by transportation funneled industrial activity into corridors along the major river valleys that were also served by railroad lines. The resulting centrifugal movement of industry—more than residential suburbanization—led the expansive spatial growth of the metropolitan region before 1920. Many of the changes in the physical landscape resulted from efforts to either control or shape the natural environment of rivers, streams, and landforms to serve commerce, industry, and residential development. The transformation of the rivers from commercial arteries before the 1850s to their integration into the industrial economy was noteworthy, but it came at a cost of diminishing natural and recreational appeal. Their restoration and redevelopment, many decades later, turned them into environmental assets as part of an emerging postindustrial city.

The second section traces successive transportation innovations as Pittsburgh moved from the walking city to the networked city and finally to an automobile dominated metropolis. These chapters describe the shift from horsecars to cable and electric streetcars and automobiles. The changing modes of transportation profoundly facilitated the centrifugal movement of population and shifts in land use across the region. Mismanagement, progressively heavier traffic congestion, and fatal accidents attended each new mode, but the automobile's effects were the most dramatic as it came to dominate the city's streets. The section's final chapter describes the civic leadership's failed effort in the 1960s to establish an innovative rapid transit system called Skybus. Advocates had promised that it would alleviate congestion and boost the region's traditionally important railroad equipment industry. This chapter foregrounds the role of power and politics in building the city and coping with the consequences.

The focus of the next section is on energy issues and transitions. The coal industry famously powered Pittsburgh's industrialization, and it both shaped and devastated the landscape. (The city also had several decades as a major petroleum refining center, though this industry was sharply reduced by 1900.) Natural gas had a more lasting, if episodic, effect and played a critical role in the city's transitions from coal dependence. "Pittsburgh as an Energy Capital: Perspectives on Coal and Natural Gas Transitions and the Environment," provides an overview of these transitions and their impact on environmental, health, and economic issues as the city alternated between being identified as the Smoky City and as one with clean air. The next chapter, "Boom and Bust in Pittsburgh Natural Gas History: Development, Policy, and Environmental Effects 1878-1920," elaborates the story of the city's initial period of natural gas development and discusses its environmental effects from the perspective of those occurring with the contemporary Marcellus Shale boom.

The production of coke from bituminous coal was essential for the success of the iron and steel industry, but it also had severe impacts on air, land, and water. As discussed in "Searching for a Sink for an Industrial Waste: Iron-Making Fuels and the Environment," the transition from beehive ovens to by-product ovens shifted the pollution burden from the countryside to urban areas, presenting new public policy concerns. The final chapter in this section employs the ecological concept of an organism's metabolism to assess Pittsburgh's changing impact on the region's environment as it slowly moved to improve the quality of its air, water, and land.

Rapid industrialization and urbanization under the city's free market and laissez-faire governmental ideology resulted in the civic imbalance of environmental, health, social, and political factors that spurred reform-minded civic leaders to seek remedies. One such proscription was for public planning—which most Pittsburgh leaders viewed with suspicion and hostility. The last section explores planning initiatives from private endeavors to public-private partnerships and historical preservation ventures. The first chapter discusses a world of wealthy Pittsburghers at the turn of the century who engaged the prestigious Boston firm of Olmsted Associates to landscape their estates and plan their private housing developments and company town ventures. The resulting familiarity with the firm led the Smoky City's leadership to engage the planner and architect Frederick Law Olmsted Jr. to prepare Pittsburgh's first citywide plan. The second chapter explores several proposals before the 1980s for redeveloping the city's riverfronts, which largely did not materialize. The planning process, however, eventually laid the foundation for the celebrated postindustrial transformation of these lands. The riverfront history illustrates the slow evolution from largely private development to much more government involvement in city building in recent decades, as residential and environmental projects replaced industrial infrastructure.

Pittsburgh's Golden Triangle followed a similar trajectory from a privately developed nineteenth-century central business district to a modern, partially planned, and eventually postindustrial downtown characterized by public, private, and nonprofit collaboration (as discussed in the downtown chapter). The last chapter considers the struggle to preserve aspects of the region's industrial history. It explores the complicated and contentious issues involved in historical industrial preservation and how preservationists used the process to inspire residents of former industrial towns to envision a new future. In addressing the civic imbalances of private economic development and city-building, proposals for regulatory reform, planning, and municipal improvement projects encountered prevailing societal norms, high costs of change, and intense politics. Civic leaders had to be continually evolving a means to navigate the tensions built into American capitalism.

We would like to thank our coauthors who participated in developing several of these chapters, as well as the manuscript readers and editors of the University of Pittsburgh Press for insightful suggestions. Like all historians, we depend on the expert services of archivists and librarians who in this instance are far too numerous to identify, in part for fear of inadvertently leaving someone out of the list. Be assured, however, that we are grateful for their constant and enthusiastic assistance over the years. They work in relative obscurity to the public, but historians know full well their invaluable service in finding, preserving, curating, and suggesting historical materials.

I THE INDUSTRIAL FOUNDATION

For more than a century, heavily capitalized industry drove the growth of Pittsburgh and its metropolitan region. Before 1900 the iron and steel industry defined the region both locally and nationally. Several other industries, from railroad equipment and electrical machinery to glass, aluminum, and all manner of associated manufactures, also thrived throughout southwestern Pennsylvania. The coal and coke, oil and natural gas, sand, clay, and limestone industries provided essential raw materials and energy inputs. Transportation and communication networks connected the widely scattered parts of the sprawling industrial region. The omnipresent river system and complex hill and valley topography presented both opportunities and challenges for entrepreneurs. Industrial and natural resource firms manipulated, engineered, and abused land, water, and air in pursuit of industrial growth and financial success.

The first essay of this section explores the resulting complex landscape and environmental consequences of natural resource exploitation, industrialization, and urbanization. Many southwestern Pennsylvania residents accept the landscape around them as "natural" without appreciating how altered and dynamic it is. The second essay provides a brief overview of the region's industrialization and the emergence of industrial corridors of mills, factories, mines, and working-class communities along the waterways and railroads that threaded their way through the winding valleys. The third essay describes the decentralization of industries in search of suitable production sites for large operations and efficiencies of excellent transportation facilities. This centrifugal movement by the early twentieth century created a vast industrial region that in spite of its sprawling, dispersed character was strikingly interconnected by communication, transportation, and production linkages. The final essay focuses on the manipulation of the rivers and riverbanks for industrial ends, concluding with a brief discussion of the slow but tangible restoration of the rivers into environmental and recreational assets in the postindustrial phase of the modern city.

1 THE INTERACTION OF NATURAL AND BUILT ENVIRONMENTS IN THE PITTSBURGH LANDSCAPE

Edward K. Muller and Joel A. Tarr

> The capacity for being seen with the eye in the Large . . . is the birthright of Pittsburgh. Where from so many different points one sees the involved panorama of the river, the various long ascents and steep bluffs, the visible signs everywhere of movement, of immense forces at work,—the pillars of smoke by day, and at night the pillars of fire against the background of hillsides strewn with jets of light,—one comes to have the convincing sense of a city which in its ensemble is quite as real a thing as are the separate forces which go to make it up.
>
> —Robert A. Woods

There is probably no city in the nation that can match the dramatic landscape changes that have marked the city of Pittsburgh during the last two centuries. The natural environment itself provided a striking panorama of flowing rivers and streams, steep bluffs, and deep valleys that would shape the configuration of the built environment (see Figure 1.1). With nineteenth- and twentieth-century technology and the characteristic American disregard for the natural environment, however, Pittsburghers engineered and abused the landscape to accommodate the imperatives of industrial production, efficient transportation, communication, and city building such that it often became difficult to discern the land's original configuration. Early in the twentieth century, Pittsburgh elites became concerned with the perceived relationship between environmental degradation and a deteriorating civic culture and set in motion a countertrend toward consciously planning urban growth and controlling damages to the natural environment. In the decades after the Second World War, a publicprivate partnership made

Fig. 1.1 Doug Cooper etching and overview of Pittsburgh topography. The etching dramatically demonstrates the interaction of the Pittsburgh built environment with the region's topography (permission by Doug Cooper).

further attempts at restoration, driven in this case by fears of economic decline. Most recently, the collapse of the steel industry has again suggested possibilities for renewal, although the scope and quality of these endeavors are still open questions.

Many Americans have difficulty conceiving of an urban-industrial landscape because "landscape" conjures up images of natural scenery. For the geographer, however, the term "landscape" becomes the central organizing concept in contemplating both natural and built environments. It includes the physical properties of the land, flora and fauna, and climate as well as human-built features. The construction of an industrial city on a complex natural site produced a landscape that encapsulated inherent conflicts and tensions over issues of environmental quality and ecological protection.

We will explore some of these conflicts and tensions by examining Pittsburgh history over time, illuminating the city's impacts upon its physical landscape. Many of these changes were deliberate, resulting from the construction of a built environment designed to either control or re-form the natural environment of rivers, streams, and landforms. At times the forces of city building and industry were able to shape the rivers and landforms of the region to meet their needs, but at other times nature's forces surged out of control, wreaking havoc on the landscape.

ENCOUNTERING THE WESTERN PENNSYLVANIA REGION

In the eighteenth and early nineteenth centuries, westward-bound Euro-American settlers in Pennsylvania found themselves challenged by a massive mountain barrier, what the Native American populations called the "endless mountains"—the ridges and valleys of the Appalachian Mountains. After climbing the abrupt fifteen-hundred-foot-high Allegheny front that separated the mountain chain from the broad Appalachian Plateau stretching far to the west, they confronted two more ridges and a sea of hilltops as far as they could see. Descending down into that "sea," these pioneers encountered mature forests draped over a complex network of knobby hills and steep valleys. Small creeks, larger streams, and rivers further impeded their progress except where long floodplains offered some respite from the hills. The many small creeks flowing down steep grades to the larger rivers and streams cut a complicated pattern of sharply sloped narrow ravines. They were, in fact, traversing the eastern province of the great Appalachian Plateau.[1]

As the pioneers looked westward from atop the most western ridge, they might have noticed that most hilltops unfolding before them were nearly the same height. This uniformity, from roughly twelve hundred to thirteen hundred feet above sea level, is the plateau; the complexity of hills and valleys derives from the protracted erosion of this upland surface by the many streams and rivers. In short, the hill and valley character of southwestern Pennsylvania is really a dissected upland. Over millions of years fluctuating inland seas laid down layer upon layer of sedimentary rocks. When the seas periodically retreated, dense vegetation, peat swamps, and marshes emerged and flourished, only to be submerged again when the seas rose once more. The seas deposited strata of sand, mud, shells, and pebbles, which turned into layers of sandstone, shale, slate, limestone, and conglomerates. Under the increasing weight of this layering, the decomposed vegetation and peat became coal, petroleum, and gas intermingled with layers of sedimentary rock. Strata of clay—some soft, sticky, and unstable like the red-bed clays that make the region landslide prone—complete the profile. Compared to regions of the Appalachian Plateau to the west, the soils of this region are thin, sandy, rocky, and relatively acidic.[2]

Two more geological events shaped southwestern Pennsylvania's natural landscape. Buckling of the earth's crust thrust upward the two long parallel ridges—Chestnut and Laurel Ridges—running northeast to southwest across the region's eastern edge. Later, across the northern portion of the region north of a line from Beaver to Warren, glaciers covered the land and disrupted the original northward flow of the major rivers. They created the now familiar and distinctive three rivers geographical framework for the settlement and development of the region—the Allegheny River flowing southward to meet the northward-flowing Monongahela River to form the Ohio River, which courses generally westward to the Mississippi Valley. The glaciers also widened and deepened the Allegheny River valley, filling it with the sand and gravel detritus of glacial scouring action. After the glaciers retreated, the river cut into this sediment, leaving relatively broad fertile terraces and deep gravel deposits below the riverbed. All three rivers flow in broad sweeping meanders that create alternating arch-shaped floodplains on the inside of the curves and steep bluffs on the outsides.[3]

Given this geological history, southwestern Pennsylvania's potential for commercial agriculture paled in comparison to that of regions to the west or to the east in southeastern Pennsylvania, which possessed richer soils and flatter lands. However, the regional landscape still contained abundant resources to attract pioneer settlement. While eighteenth-century Euro-American explorers, traders, and trappers depended on the region's natural resources, they caused relatively minor and spatially concentrated impacts on the landscape, much like the Native Americans they encountered.

At the time of Euro-American contact, Native Americans only sparsely settled the region and the area was a crossroads for hunting and trading. This settlement pattern resulted from conflict between the powerful Iroquois, who claimed the land, and eastern tribes such as the Delaware and Shawnees, whom whites had forced to migrate westward.[4] Village sites, small crop plots, and overland trails were probably the most recognizable human imprints, though Native Americans sometimes burned forest undergrowth for hunting and agricultural purposes. Traders and trappers, trading for beaver and other animal hides, attached themselves to this pattern. In the 1760s the armies of Generals Braddock and Forbes constructed roads through the wilderness, probably having more of an impact on the environment than any Native American activity. Both of these roads became major overland routes in subsequent years.[5]

In the second half of the eighteenth century, major clashes for regional control occurred among Native Americans, French and British traders and troops, and American colonists. By the end of the century permanent Euro-American occupancy was assured, and regional development accelerated, thus beginning a dramatic transformation of the landscape.[6] Southwestern Pennsylvania settlers exploited the waters, forests, and wildlife of the region, and the primary rivers provided serviceable transportation routes during large portions of each year for migrants as well as access to slowly emerging markets.

Between the 1780s and 1830s, settlers carved farms out of the hills and valleys of southwestern Pennsylvania, wherever reasonably level or moderately sloped land permitted. Slowly they cleared the trees from arable land. The spreading market economy allowed farmers, self-sufficient at first, to add some cash crops, especially wheat and rye, and to make whiskey from grain for an especially marketable product. Compared to highly productive agricultural regions, however, southwestern Pennsylvania was not especially fertile or densely settled, and travelers frequently commented on the "rough and uncultivated" character of the land.[7]

Some observers, often from the more fortunate social classes, described the landscape in the picturesque terms that were fashionable after the first third of the century. A few eyewitnesses painted romantic views of the region's streams and countryside, while local painters of the Scalp Level School such as George Hetzel painted sublime landscapes of the western Pennsylvania wilderness in a manner derivative of the Hudson River School.[8] As Rina C. Youngner notes in her study of art and industry in Pittsburgh, local artists turned to nature at a time "when the city stood as an antithesis to pastoral values in its steady encroachment of the landscape along the three rivers."[9]

The growing commercial city of Pittsburgh presented a striking contrast with these wilderness and pastoral landscapes. Commercial activity focused on the busy Monongahela wharf, a mudflat stretching down to the river, while urban development spread across the point of land formed by the convergence of the Allegheny and Monongahela Rivers. Organized by a gridiron street plan that paralleled the rivers and the centering of trade around the wharf, the city featured artisan shops, inns and taverns, small offices, and residences, crammed densely into the confined space (see "Downtown Pittsburgh" in this volume). Only church spires and steamboat stacks broke the uniformly low skyline of two- and threestory brick and frame buildings. Small industries occupied the riverfronts around the edges of this settlement core. More rapid economic and population growth after 1830, especially with the opening of the terminal basins of the Pennsylvania Main Line Canal, pushed new manufacturing firms up both the Allegheny and Monongahela floodplains and across these rivers. Many settled in communities that Pittsburgh later annexed, such as Allegheny City on the north bank of the Allegheny River (annexed in 1907) and several smaller towns (annexed in 1872 and called Pittsburgh's South Side) on the south bank of the Monongahela River.[10]

Even in the initial decades of the nineteenth century, visitors remarked on the pall of smoke that lingered over the basin formed by the hills surrounding the city. As one visitor to the city noted in 1829: "After traveling for two weeks through white, clean, cheerful-looking villages and towns, to come all at once upon dirty streets and dark, filthy looking houses stretching away in rows continuously ahead and enveloped in an atmosphere of smoke and soot which blackened everything in sight, was not a pleasant transition."[11] Although covering only a land area of less than two miles in radius from the Monongahela wharf, this collection of several contiguous communities housed nearly eighty thousand residents at mid-century.

EMERGENCE OF THE INDUSTRIAL LANDSCAPE

Although Pittsburgh's massive industrialization occurred primarily in the second half of the nineteenth century, its identification with industry and industrial landscapes actually emerged at a relatively early time in its history. The rich diversity of minerals embedded in the sedimentary rock layers of the Appalachian Plateau supported the city's growth. Local manufacturers fashioned the region's clay into pottery wares and bricks. Others used local sand for making glass products, and Pittsburgh for a time was the nation's leading manufacturer of glass. Ironmasters refined the iron ore of Chestnut and Laurel ridges in nearby blast furnaces fueled with charcoal made from hardwood trees. The pig iron product of these country blast furnaces was usually sent to Pittsburgh foundries and rolling mills. Most important of all, however, was cheap energy, as outcroppings of coal or easily worked shallow drift mines provided fuel for local industries and residences.[12]

The focus on iron manufacture was so prominent that, as early as 1821, the British visitor George W. Ogden observed the city could be called the "Birmingham of America." Views of Pittsburgh painted by various artists before the Civil War also began to feature industrial scenes, as they felt less compelled to emphasize picturesque subjects. Especially striking, for instance, is Sherman Day's *Pittsburgh from the Northwest, 1843*, which highlights the smoke and industrial buildings that dominated the city when viewed from Mount Washington. William Schuchman's view of *Pittsburgh, Pa., 1859* also profiles industries such as ironworks, foundries, and cotton mills as well as riverfront activity.[13]

Much of Pittsburgh's industry up to the 1870s was concentrated either within the city or close to it in the neighboring city of Allegheny and in the South Side communities of Birmingham, East Birmingham, and South Pittsburgh. Otto Krebs's 1870s paintings, for instance, reflect the density of industry in these towns. In the late nineteenth century, as railroads increasingly penetrated the region and the rivers were made navigable through the construction of locks and dams (slack watered), large firms spread up and down the rivers, locating particularly in the river meanders (see "Pittsburgh's Industrial Corridors" in this volume). It is in this context that Pittsburgh's "meta-landscape" emerged, as is fully illustrated in representations of the industrial city in the major journals of the late nineteenth century.[14]

In his enlightening study, *Metropolitan Corridor: Railroads and the American Scene*, the historian John R. Stilgoe discusses the growth of what he calls the "industrial aesthetic" that emerged in the industrial zone outside cities east of the Rocky Mountains after 1880 or so.[15] One of the major features of these zones was the shift in the scale of enterprises. Even though Pittsburgh had had major industrial complexes before the late nineteenth century, they paled in comparison to those that emerged after this date, and the Pittsburgh region became renowned for presenting an unmatched urban industrial landscape to those that encountered it.

The most striking examples of the industrial aesthetic in the Pittsburgh region were its integrated steel mills.[16] These enormous complexes, each covering several hundred acres and sometimes both sides of the river, presented a chaotic assemblage of huge brick and metal sheds, towering blast furnaces, hot ovens, Bessemer converters, open-hearth furnaces, rolling mills, giant ore loaders and ore yards, all framed by river and rail. Most observers commented on fiery, dramatic displays of the converters and furnaces: "Particularly remarkable is the weird spectacle presented at night, with the furnaces fiercely gleaming, the fresh ingots smoking hot, the Bessemer converter 'blowing off,' the great cranes moving about like things of life, bearing giant kettles of molten steel." In a recent description, the writer

Laurie Graham captures the bewildering mass and complexity of a steel mill: "The view on approaching the mill was of another world—the looming plant sheds, the convoluted tubing of blast furnaces, the trusswork of ore bridges over mounds of reddish ore, the winding roads through hundreds of acres of buildings large and small, metal platforms and stairs, ductwork and railroad tracks, trucks and locomotives, torpedo and thimble and other types of railroad cars. . . . Plumes of water vapor rose from rooftops as steam issued into the cold winter air."[17] Many other industries, including glass and refractory brick makers, locomotive and railroad equipment manufacturers, carriage builders, metals fabricators, and electrical equipment firms, operated out of large brick multistoried structures that covered a full block or more, providing a solidity to the urban landscape.[18]

Stilgoe notes that travelers passing through the industrial zones found them "extraordinary, intriguing, beautiful places. Refineries, steel mills, locomotive plants, coal breakers, and mysterious factories combined . . . to make an awesome landscape of built forms." For many, the zone "hummed with enterprise," and these landscapes drew an appreciative response in trade journals, engineering magazines, and even more general circulation periodicals. Booster publications and materials prepared for Pittsburgh's many conference visitors proudly illustrated the industrial strengths of the city through facts and figures and multiple drawings and photographs.[19]

Whether the city was greeted with praise or blame, however, depended upon the perspective of the viewer. For Paul U. Kellogg, director of the Pittsburgh Survey, a "matrix" of pipelines, electric, telegraph, and telephone wires, mile-long river barge tows, and extensive railroad tracks had almost completely obliterated the natural features of Pittsburgh's rivers, hills, and valleys—in short, the industrial environment had replaced the natural environment.[20] Others, however, found it a fascinating landscape, reflecting the power and authority of dedicated human forces.

Critical to this industrial complex, of course, were the railroads that came to form a ubiquitous part of the Pittsburgh landscape.[21] The first railroad to enter Pittsburgh was the Pennsylvania & Ohio, which linked the city with Philadelphia in the east in 1852. This was soon followed by other major trunk line railroads including the Baltimore & Ohio from the south, the Allegheny Valley from the north, and the Pittsburgh & Lake Erie. By the First World War, the city was served by six major trunk lines and sixteen industrial and switching railroads.[22] In addition to the trunk line railroads, many short lines and feeder lines also honeycombed throughout the Pittsburgh region.

The railroads blanketed the city, tunneling through the hills, bridging the rivers and ravines, and usurping the riverbanks. Seeking flat land in order to run their tracks, they occupied both sides of river valleys and the bottoms of ravines. In some places two lines shared the same narrow shelf along the river. The Pennsylvania Railroad, which carried more passengers and freight than any other Pittsburgh line, was four-tracked throughout the city and much of the region. Until the first decades of the twentieth century, the railroads disrupted city traffic flows with numerous grade crossings; trains ran down Liberty Avenue through the middle of downtown to terminals at the Point until 1905.[23]

The railroads built massive freight and marshalling yards, roundhouses, and shops at convenient locations. The largest marshalling yard in the region until 1952, when the Pennsylvania Railroad established the Conway Yard, was the Pennsy's Pitcairn Yard, built in 1892 on a 250-acre site east of the city. On this site four major tracks fanned into thirty-six tracks to make possible the assembly of freight trains up to fifty cars long.[24] Other marshalling yards were scattered at points throughout the region, including sites close to the downtown.

The railroads established their presence downtown by locating their stations at important throats and disgorging thousands of commuting passengers into city streets every weekday morning (see "The Cable and Electric Streetcar Networks" in this volume). These architecturally prestigious stations furnished major landmarks in the city's downtown, surrounded by cabs, omnibuses, private vehicles, and horse-drawn drays, all competing for space. Railroad smoke formed a large fraction of the city's air pollution burden, creating especially bad conditions at locations such as marshalling yards, roundhouses, and terminals. Not until after the Second World War did diesel-electric engines replace the smoke-belching steam locomotives.[25] The shriek of the steam locomotive whistles pierced the Pittsburgh atmosphere day and night as they wended their way through the torturous Pittsburgh topography, hauling long trains of cars filled with coal, coke, and other goods.

FUELING THE INDUSTRIAL LANDSCAPE: COAL AND COKE

Without coal, Pittsburgh would have remained a relatively small commercial city for, as Willard Glazier wrote in 1883, all of Pittsburgh's industry was "rendered possible by the coal which abounds in measureless quantities in the immediate neighborhood of the city."[26] The rapid growth of steam railroads, steam-powered manufacturing plants, and the iron and steel industry, especially after mid-century led to a burgeoning demand for coal and the development of the bituminous coal and coke industry across the region.

Pittsburgh possessed a magnificent coal seam, which extended throughout southwestern Pennsylvania. Coal outcroppings and seams close to the surface in the city itself and in its outskirts were mined first, but as demand increased mining spread rapidly. Coal production in the four southwestern Pennsylvania counties of Allegheny, Westmoreland, Fayette, and Washington mushroomed from less than 0.5 million tons in 1850 to 5.5 million tons in 1870, 11.6 million in 1881, and 66.5 million in 1911.[27] By the early 1900s, coal mines and coke plants pockmarked the region's hills and valleys, existing uneasily with the earlier agricultural landscape in some areas and supplanting it in others.

The coal industry had major impacts on the landscapes of both the natural and the built environments. Coal mining scarred the natural environment wherever it took place, as men and technology ripped the coal out of the hills. As mining proceeded, huge heaps of mining waste or slate dumps (also called gob piles) accumulated near the mines and loomed over the patch towns. Debris from mining filled the streams and disrupted water supplies. Acid drainage from the mines turned the water in nearby streams rust colored and coated the hillsides with rivulets of orange- and rust-colored drainage, and land often subsided in areas where deep mines had been dug.[28]

Structures relating to mining were scattered over the landscape. The most recognizable structural feature of the mining complex was the coal tipple standing high above the landscape near the mine entrance or protruding from a riverbank. Depending on the age and size of the mine, other structures also stood nearby, including a head frame, hoist house, boiler house or powerhouse, fan house, repair shop, lamp house, and mine office.[29]

Near the mine complex, most coal firms built small company towns called "patches" or "patch towns." The companies owned and operated these patches in order to attract workers to inaccessible mine sites, have a stable labor supply, increase control over the workers, and turn a profit. Usually companies erected rows of identical cheaply built, wooden houses for workers and their families in a linear pattern along a road leading to the mine or on a grid plan rising up a hillside. The houses were generally two-story, semidetached structures on large lots equipped with double outhouses and coal bins in the backyards. Mine managers occupied more elaborate houses in a separate row. The largest building, mostly brick, was the company store. Streets and walkways were unpaved, except for rust-colored waste ("red dog") from the gob pile or coke ash that was spread on the surface to keep down dust.[30]

The towns presented a drab, monotonous, and temporary scene, for the companies believed the town would lose its utility when the coal was exhausted and the mine closed. Ironically, in the years after the Second World War when many mines were shut down, tenants often bought their homes, which they usually had upgraded with running water, indoor plumbing, and electricity. Those patches enveloped by urban development remained low-income housing and frequently deteriorated. In the rural areas, they evolved into residential pockets amid the countryside.[31] Many of the other physical remains of the coal industry, however, such as the large gob piles that loomed over the towns and streams tainted with mine acid, often remained as disfigurements on the landscape.

While much coal was shipped directly to markets, coal used for the coking process presented a different picture (see "Searching for a Sink for an Industrial Waste" in this volume). Carbon was a basic requirement of iron making, and for approximately the first half of the century iron manufacture took place primarily on charcoal iron plantations that drew on surrounding forest resources. After the 1850s coke made from bituminous coal increasingly substituted for charcoal as a source of carbon, making it possible to locate iron blast furnaces in the city. The best coking coal in the world—the so-called Connellsville Coke—was discovered in southwestern Pennsylvania in a narrow seam that ran approximately forty miles from northeast to southwest.[32]

From about 1850 to 1920, most coke was made by distilling bituminous coal in beehive coke ovens at high temperatures to drive out the volatiles (oils, gases, and tars) through holes at the top, leaving a high carbon residue that could be used in iron making (see "Searching for a Sink for an Industrial Waste" in this volume). Therefore, it made economic sense to process it near the mines and ship it to the city by river and rail.[33] Operators built rows of beehive ovens into the hillsides (called "bank" ovens) or in freestanding rows or blocks of fifty ovens, with some installations holding as many as three hundred ovens. The dome-shaped ovens had a base diameter of approximately twelve feet and rose to about seven feet in height. The coal cooked for between forty-eight and seventy-two hours and was then removed from the oven by laborers or, after 1900 or so, by mechanical unloaders.[34]

When demand warranted, the ovens operated around the clock. The coke plants themselves were dirty, noxious operations of several hundred ovens, busy railroad yards, and a proximate mine complex and gob pile, with cinders and ash everywhere. With thousands of ovens of several operators working in a relatively small area, the smoke, fumes, and ash cast a pall over the valleys. Muriel Sheppard captured the scene well:

> It depends on the wind and weather, the season, the time of day, and the coke market how much there is to see from the Chestnut Ridge lookout. Early on an autumn morning with a damp wind blowing up plumes of smoke traveling sideways, a violet curtain full of moving particles of soot blots out the valley. The spring smoke is apt to be whitish-blue, that of winter brown or gray, and any time of year it ranges from pinkish-lavender to gun-metal tinged with purple at evening. . . . It is a country of extremes, ugly by day with banks of coke ovens, tipples, sidings, and fields gnawed to the rock with strip-coal operations: luridly beautiful by night when the glare of the ovens paints the sky and works magic with head frames and sooty buildings.[35]

A regional urban network of towns arose to service the coal and coke industry, including administrative offices, repair facilities, and stores of machinery and parts. Estimates for 1910 suggest a population of more than one hundred thousand in the two major coke areas, including the urban centers. The railroads and, after 1900, interurban cars provided some connections within the region. And the rivers, railroads, and capital tied the whole area to Pittsburgh, which in ownership of the number of coal mines, coke plants, and coke ovens dominated the industry. In this manner Pittsburgh capitalists controlled the coke region, although considerable local fortunes were also made.[36]

In the years after 1910 the making of coke in by-product ovens began to emerge as an important alternative to beehive ovens. The by-product oven was a narrow slot oven constructed in batteries in which coking chambers alternated with heating chambers. Coal was charged through openings in the top of the oven, and the coke was pushed out by a powerdriven ram at the end of the combustion process, to be quenched outside the oven. The gas evolving from the coal supplied the heat required for distillation and was also used for other purposes throughout the mill. The by-product oven had the advantage of capturing the volatile elements such as coke oven gas, tar, and ammonia freed by the coking process as well as producing a higher coke yield per ton of coal than the beehive.[37]

While beehive coke ovens were customarily located close to the mines, by-product coke oven works were sited closer to the mills in or near urban areas. The various by-products such as coke gas could thus be utilized not only in the integrated steel mills but could also be sold to various users such as municipalities. US Steel opened the first full by-product coking plant in the region in 1916 at Clairton, twenty miles south of Pittsburgh on the Monongahela River. The plant occupied a riverfront site 5,200 feet long and

1,800 feet in width, the largest plant in the world at the time of its construction. The Clairton Works had fifteen hundred by-product ovens that consumed enormous amounts of coal, which was largely moved to the plant by river barge. Jones & Laughlin Steel (J&L) constructed a by-product coke oven between 1918 and 1920 at its Hazelwood complex (see "Searching for a Sink for an Industrial Waste" in this volume). While not as extensive as the Clairton Works, the location of the J&L plant within the city made it both highly visible and a producer of extensive air pollution and odor that plagued the nearby community. On a windy day, the odor of sulphur would carry far beyond the mill communities into middle-class neighborhoods.[38]

The by-product coke works, then, along with the iron and steel mills consumed huge amounts of land along the rivers, using the latter for purposes of cheap transportation and wastewater disposal as well as sources of process water. Their presence was indicated not only by the flaring of waste gases and columns of black smoke but also by plumes of white steam that rose as the red-hot coke was cooled with process and river water. Since the plants worked twenty-four hours a day, these plumes constantly appeared in the visible landscape. In addition, the companies constructed major networks of pipes to ship the coke oven gas to the linked steel mills and to other users, often running these pipes along the sides of hills of the river valleys. The plumes of steam and the pipelines provided additional visible evidence of the impact of industrialism on the landscape.[39]

THE RIVERS

The three rivers—and especially the point of land they form, which signifies the beginning of the Ohio River—have always been a defining feature of the Pittsburgh landscape. Although the rivers' relentless current makes them seem like the one constant amid the ever-changing man-made industrial landscape, the river landscape itself, in fact, also underwent significant changes. In the city's initial fifty years or so when its economy depended on being the "gateway to the West," river commerce dominated the urban scene. The city's street plan, merchant houses, and goods handling together focused on the busy Monongahela mudflat—that is, the city's wharf.

All kinds of craft, but mostly steamboats as the years went on, tied up at the wharf, which was a beehive of activity. The solid row of brick two- and three-story merchant buildings along Water Street at the top of the wharf was the city's face to the river and the world. Boatyards and factories claimed the riverfronts away from the wharf, and the riverbanks reverted to their natural state at the urban periphery, where the recreational activities of fishing, hunting, rowing, and picnicking took place.[40]

Industrialization changed the river landscape as profoundly as it did the rest of the urban area. Shippers, mine owners, and industrialists demanded greater control over the rivers' flow in order to enhance the shipping of resources, especially coal, essential to the region's burgeoning industries. Beginning with the Monongahela River in the 1840s, private and public construction of locks and dams successfully created slackwater pools between the dams on all three rivers. Slackwatering the river through the construction of dams and locks raised average water levels, narrowed their fluctuations, and thereby extended the navigation season. By the late nineteenth century huge rows of many barges lashed together (a "tow"), characteristically piled high with coal and pushed by powerful steamboats, plied the region's waters. Loaded barges were moored to enormous round piers or mooring cells, queued up for unloading or waiting for river conditions to be favorable for navigation.[41]

As railroads, mills, and factories spread for miles on every available floodplain, vegetation largely disappeared from the riverbanks, and the river edges became hardened with man-made structures. Industries built wood, brick, and concrete bulkheads; cranes towered over the river shorelines; industrial waste, sewage, and storm-water outflow pipes stuck through the banks; and mooring cells rose above the river surface near the shores. Some industries dumped fill beyond the river edges to extend the floodplain and then built bulkheads against erosion around the new land. The Pittsburgh municipal government raised the levels of many streets near the rivers with fill in order to diminish flood damage (see Figure 1.2).

Industrial and urban growth increased the release of toxic chemicals, effluent, and storm water into the rivers, and the water often took on a muddy brown color. Discarded rubbish and garbage littered the riverbanks along with abandoned barges and other debris stranded during high water episodes. At the same time, urban industrial development required the erection of numerous railroad and highway bridges over the rivers with their massive stone piers thrust into the channels. By the early twentieth century and for decades thereafter, the rivers became increasingly inaccessible to residents, unsightly and unnatural in both appearance and fact.[42]

CREATING A TECHNICAL NETWORK ABOVE AND BELOW GROUND: STREETS, STREETCARS, AND SEWERS

Much of the city building process took place above the surface of the ground with the construction of various networks—streets, transportation lines, along with electrical, telegraph, and telephone wires as well as buildings. By the late nineteenth century, canopies of wires shrouded the downtown

FIG. 1.2 Landslide damage, Shaler Street, June 17, 1920. Throughout its history Pittsburgh has suffered extensively from landslides (Pittsburgh City Photographer Collection, courtesy of the Archives Service Center, University of Pittsburgh).

streets, while steel tracks ran along the surface. At the same time, other construction activities took place below ground with the placement of water- and sewer-pipe networks as well as tunnels of various sorts. All of these features of the built environment had to cope with the constraints imposed by the natural environment.[43]

Pittsburgh's topography prevented a typical gridiron street pattern. Even without this constraint, however, streets were badly designed and poorly configured. Correspondent Ernie Pyle wrote, "Pittsburgh is undoubtedly the cockeyedest city in the United States. Physically, it is absolutely irrational. It must have been laid out by a mountain goat."[44] Nineteenth-century streets, aside from major corridors, were often narrow and poorly integrated with the street grid frequently having very steep grades. The municipality made major efforts in the first quarter of the twentieth century to widen streets, align them, reduce steep grades, and pave them. Beginning in 1899, city government constructed several boulevards, reflecting an attempt to improve communication between districts. In addition, because of the threat of flooding, the city raised a number of streets along the floodplain between eight and ten feet.

In the years after 1859 streetcar systems increasingly traversed the city streets, becoming a major element in the Pittsburgh landscape (see "The Omnibus, Commuter Railroad, and Horsecar" in this volume). Horsedrawn streetcars first appeared in that year, and by 1888 entrepreneurs had built fifty-six miles of track in Pittsburgh and surrounding towns, with their cars carrying twenty-three million passengers for the year. In the 1890s traction companies replaced the horsecars with electric streetcars and cable cars and extended their lines throughout the region (see "The Cable and Electric Streetcar Networks" in this volume). The replacement of the horsecar by the electric trolley was a great environmental improvement. It helped eliminate the manure, urine, and carcasses that dirtied the streets during the previous dependence on the horse.[45] By 1902, there were 469.5 miles of track linking city neighborhoods and regional towns and carrying 168,632,339 passengers for the year. Thus, the trolley became a constant feature of the urban landscape, occupying major streets, taking a large part in the downtown street congestion, and running precariously on trestles along the slopes of steep hills.[46]

Other aspects of the landscape and its alteration were related to the reshaping of the city's hydrological patterns. This change involved the physical transition from a hilly landscape cut by many streams to a landscape in which most streams were placed in culverts, becoming part of the sewerage system.[47] Initially the streams themselves were used to dispose of domestic waste and storm waters, but in the late nineteenth century the city began to develop an extensive combined sewer system. This system was based upon the natural drainage basins of the region and required the Pittsburgh Department of Public Works to culvert most of the city's streams. By 1910 the sewers drained over seven thousand acres of the city, discharging into the neighboring rivers. The outlets ranged in size from fifteen-inch terra-cotta pipes to twelve-foot brick sewers. Forty-seven public sewer outlets flowed into the Monongahela River, with another ninetyeight flowing into the Ohio and Allegheny Rivers. As of 1910 the four major streams that were still not culverted or only partially culverted—Nine Mile Run, Street's Run, Becks Run, and Saw Mill Run—became open sewers serving as the receptacles for sewage from both private and public sewers (see "The Metabolism of the Industrial City" in this volume).[48]

Urban development, therefore, created a need to dispose of both storm water and domestic wastes. This need transformed the hydrological landscape of the city from one marked by flowing streams and a healthy stream ecology into a site almost completely devoid of waterways except for the large rivers that transected it. The floodplains, valleys, and ravines where the runs had flowed were transformed into corridors for infrastructure, including sewer systems, railroads lines, and highways, as well as for industry. Increasingly, the untreated sewage and industrial wastes flowing into the rivers consumed their oxygen, destroyed their fish and plant life, and transformed them into open sewers rather than environmentally healthy natural bodies of water.

HILLSIDES AND VALLEYS

Dense development in the city was initially confined to the level lands of the river floodplains where the construction of infrastructure to provide for transportation and communication was not problematic. Expansion of settlement and infrastructure beyond the Point and low-lying areas of the sibling communities across the rivers often confronted the region's pervasive hills and valleys. Some adventuresome Pittsburghers attempted early on to move out of the flats. In 1843, for instance, traveler Mary Ann Corwin wrote in her diary that "the town with the surrounding hills and subberbs [*sic*], the roads winding up the hills, and houses up the sides of the hills, and on the top of some of them, [was] the grandest sight we have had."[49] As population grew, however, dealing with what the Department of Public Works called the city's "broken" topography was not easy. In his 1910 plan for Pittsburgh, Frederick Law Olmsted Jr. succinctly stated the problem: "No city of equal size in America or perhaps the world, is compelled to adapt its growth to such difficult complications of high ridges, deep valleys and precipitous slopes as Pittsburgh." Tributary stream valleys offered routes to many of the areas beyond the Point, but eventually the hills had to be climbed or breached, and the ravines bridged.[50]

The steep slopes of many hillsides not only presented a barrier to transportation but also meant that the hillsides were not usable for either commercial or residential purposes. Olmsted reported that "excessively steep hillsides [comprised] as much as 30 to 35 percent" of the Pittsburgh district outside of downtown and East Liberty. During the course of the nineteenth century, hillside forests were largely cut down for fuel and building materials. Acrid industrial and railroad smoke further harmed vegetation. The deforested hillsides eroded, gullies formed, earth slumped, and small landslides plunged to the valley floors.

Billboards sprouted up on some as if a new species was taking its place with the scrubby vegetation of secondary growth. People illegally and surreptitiously dumped trash and garbage on many hillsides. As Olmsted observed: "In far too many cases they [hillsides] are apt to be wholly uncared for and to become shabby, dirty, and altogether unsightly, depreciating adjacent property and contributing largely to the slatternly conditions in the midst of which so many of Pittsburgh's working people . . . are compelled to live."[51]

Building a road up a hill either was impossible or created a grade so steep as to be impractical. Nonetheless, a few incredibly steep roads such as Rialto Street to Troy Hill and Negley Avenue in the East End still exist today to intimidate the unwary driver. Local governments and private transportation companies turned to more elaborate engineering solutions to get around the hills. Although expensive tunnels provided the most direct route, in 1831 an 810-foot-long tunnel was dug to connect the Pennsylvania Main Line Canal from its tidal basin near the Allegheny River across the east end of downtown through Grant's Hill (later referred to as the Hump) to the Monongahela Wharf.[52] In the second half of the nineteenth century, railroad companies built many tunnels around the region. In 1899 a major tunnel penetrated Mount Washington (Coal Hill) for streetcar use, opening up areas beyond the bluff for settlement.

In the early twentieth century, public officials realized that an automobile tunnel through the escarpment of Mount Washington would, like the 1899 street railway tunnel, accelerate suburbanization of the South Hills. While consensus existed on the need for the tunnel, debate raged for years over its trajectory. Proponents for a lower-level tunnel into downtown won the political battle, and the 5,889-foot-long Liberty Tunnel (also known as the Liberty Tubes), the longest vehicular tunnel of its day, opened in 1925 at the cost of nearly six million dollars. The Liberty Bridge connecting the tunnels to downtown was completed three years later.[53] Two more tunnels for automobiles (the Squirrel Hill Tunnel and the Fort Pitt Tunnel) opened after the Second World War; together the three tunnels defined the commute to downtown. Despite the successful penetration of the hills, the tunnels functioned as bottlenecks in the flow of traffic during rush hours, with cars queued up in long lines behind the entrances. In contrast, the exits from both the Fort Pitt and Liberty Tunnels facing the Pittsburgh Point treated the motorist to dramatic views of the downtown landscape.[54]

Cuts across the sides of hills became the commonest means of getting around the hilly barriers. While the earliest roadways wended along valley floors, subsequent development and congestion in the valleys led to the placement of higher speed highways such as Bigelow Boulevard (1916) and the Boulevard of the Allies (1922) along the hillsides (see "The Automobile Comes to Pittsburgh, 1910–1935" in this volume). These cuts destabilized the slopes, especially when the red-bed clay strata were exposed. Because these strata are not porous, soils above them move along the slippery red clay and plunge downward at the cut. Although the secondary growth of vegetation on the hillsides enhanced stability, enormous retaining walls of wood, stone, or reinforced concrete provided the best deterrent of falling debris and landslides. In 1876 the city enacted an ordinance permitting the city's Bureau of Engineering to build on private property when grading streets. Many embankments extended for more than a mile. Along West Carson Street, for instance, on the city's South Side, the Bureau of Engineering constructed over 6,600 feet of reinforced concrete retaining walls from 13 to 17.5 feet high to buttress the hillside. Other parts of the city similarly required extensive construction of retaining walls, some of which were in need of constant reinforcement. Large sandstone blocks, which absorbed soot from smoke and turned black, were used for many and became an especially striking feature of the urban landscape.[55]

Smaller hills that obstructed traffic flows were sometimes simply lowered or removed. The most famous instance involved Grant's Hill, known as "the Hump," on the east end of downtown. Grant's Hill had been partially reduced in the first half of the nineteenth century, the dirt removed being used to fill in ponds in the downtown area, but it still posed difficulties since it had a steep enough grade to impede the smooth flow of traffic and discourage higher value retail and office development. Nonetheless, street, sewer, gas, water, and street railway infrastructure, as well as buildings, were already in place on the Hump. On the downtown edge of the Hump stood architect Henry Hobson Richardson's 1888 Allegheny County Courthouse, which some consider among his finest buildings. Across the street stood the industrialist Henry Clay Frick's 1902 skyscraper, designed by D. H. Burnham. Lowering the streets of this area would incur not only the considerable disruption and typical costs of excavation and street reconstruction but also the extraordinary expense of replacing infrastructure and the reimbursement for damages to the buildings. As a result, the Hump project remained the subject of debate for several years. Proponents, including Olmsted, argued for cutting the Hump and simultaneously widening the major streets in order to provide major routes to the city's rapidly developing East End neighborhoods. The director of the Department of Public Works in his 1912 annual report observed that the Hump cut was a "proposition of such magnitude and everlasting benefit . . . that the public will only realize its vast importance after . . . [its completion when] the city will be so greatly improved in appearance, convenience, and increased property valuation."[56]

Begun in 1912 with the funding of a council bond issue, the project involved an area of twenty acres, parts of eight streets, cuts as much as sixteen feet deep, and the demolition of many buildings. The entrances of extant buildings such as the courthouse and Frick Building had to be reconfigured to accommodate the new street levels. The total cost of the project to the city exceeded three million dollars at its completion in 1913. Today the rise eastward along the streets is very gradual; few people suspect that the Hump had ever existed.[57]

Although Olmsted aptly recognized that the steepness of many hillsides prevented residential development, numbers of Pittsburghers did build houses precariously sited on precipitous slopes. As development consumed the floodplains, people often turned to the hills for housing sites that were still within walking distance to factories and mills but also above the densest smoke. Many of these homes were owner built rather than constructed by professional builders.[58] Two-story and two-and-a-half-story row houses, built in party wall clusters or freestanding, climbed some hillsides along streets crossing the slopes at sharp angles or rose nearly straight up the slope along a stairway street. In some instances, houses sat isolated on hillsides. Others seemed to cling perilously to hilltop edges. Houses with two stories fronting on a street sometimes had a few more stories and/or outdoor terraces on the back side running down the hill. The slopes and instability of the hillsides forced these homeowners to build retaining walls made from a variety of materials to secure small yards, gardens, stairs, and driveways.

Over the years some of these hillside communities became affectionately embraced as emblematic of Pittsburgh's landscape, but heavy smoke pollution, scarred hillsides, and inadequate incomes during the industrial era rendered a less favorable residential landscape. In 1927 H. L. Mencken, Baltimore's renowned journalist, commented on this hillside residential landscape in his signature overheated style: "By the hundreds and thousands these abominable houses cover the bare hillsides, like gravestones in some gigantic and decaying cemetery. . . . On their deep sides they bury themselves swinishly in the mud. Not a fifth of them are perpendicular. They lean this way and that, hanging on to their bases precariously."[59]

Some residents of the hills could reach their homes and jobs by another man-made feature of the Pittsburgh landscape, the incline. The inclines were steep rail viaducts constructed along the hillsides to transport coal, freight, and passengers, and to open up hilly areas to settlement. Steam engines powered drums that operated endless cables pulling the cars. The Monongahela Incline, the first intended for passengers alone, was opened in 1870. Eventually, fifteen inclines operated in the city, hauling passengers and freight to and from hilly areas. The most inclines were on the city's

Fig. 1.3 Indian Trail Steps. Pittsburgh is renowned for its hundreds of wooden and concrete stairways. The city erected a wooden stairway up Mount Washington in 1909, along what had formerly been a Native American pathway (Pittsburgh City Photographer Collection, courtesy of the Archive Service Center, University of Pittsburgh).

South Side where the steep bluff of Mount Washington raised a formidable four-hundred-foot wall several hundred yards from the river shore, but they could be found in other parts of the city as well.[60]

Other steep slope residents had to reach their homes by traversing precipitous wooden and concrete stairways. Stairways began appearing in the nineteenth century, but the first year for which we have a measure of their length is 1937, when thirteen miles of stairways were recorded. By 1952 the total had reached twenty-nine miles, of now mostly concrete steps. In hundreds of cases, sets of these steps were legal streets, complete with street names, and they provided the only access to steep slope homes. During the nineteenth and the early twentieth centuries stairways were sometimes the only way that working-class families could access water supplies and privy vaults. The steps were the responsibility of the municipal Bureau of Steps and Boardwalks, part of the Public Works Department. In 1999 sixty-six of Pittsburgh's identified ninety neighborhoods possessed steps (see Figure 1.3).[61]

The valleys of tributary streams (usually named creeks or runs) to the region's primary rivers presented a different set of problems than did the hillsides. Early settlers established roads in these valleys or hollows, as they are often called. After the mid-nineteenth century, railroads appropriated space in the valley floors as well. Mines, factories, homes, and commercial enterprises soon followed. In the broader valley plains close to the mouths of the tributary streams, small neighborhoods or suburban, often industrial, towns occupied the level land. But the valleys narrowed and rose quickly toward the stream sources, forcing development into linear patterns with buildings aligned along road, rail, and stream. In search of space, some working families built homes on the lower portion of the adjacent hillsides, terracing upward for yard and garden space. The irregular placement of these houses contrasted with the linearity along the valley floor. Inadequate sanitary and storm sewers (if any at all), periodic flooding, bald hillsides, and the proximity of industry led to deteriorating and at times squalid environments. Municipalities placed many streams in culverts to contain the flow, and numerous small bridges crisscrossed them for access to homes and industry. Long high-level bridges passed overhead to connect developments on the adjacent hilltops with each other, bypassing the congested valleys below.

These linear valley or hollow settlements became isolated communities unto themselves. In 1909 the Pittsburgh Survey highlighted the dilapidated houses of Skunk Hollow, tucked out of the way below the Bloomfield neighborhood, as one illustration of the city's atrocious housing conditions for low-income families. In 1926 residents of a small Italian community, sometimes called Basso La Vallone (down in the hollow), inhabited a collection of wooden houses along a dirt road, Chianti Way, in a valley well below the large Italian Larimer neighborhood. The Meadow Street Bridge passed high overhead. Besides the dirt road, steps rose upward to connect the hollow residents with the Larimer community.[62]

Although picturesque in natural or park settings, countless small ravines were perceived as land that inhibited travel and defied development. The "useless ravines," as one engineer termed them in 1909, attracted illegal dumping of industrial waste and sewage and were candidates for filling with earth removed by excavations, rubble from construction and demolition, street sweepings, and a myriad of other sources.[63] Filled ravines created level, usable land. The filling of St. Pierre's Ravine in the years before the First World War illustrates the propensity to not just alter but obliterate this characteristic topographical feature of the region, even at substantial cost. It also reflects the elite's desire to manipulate the landscape for social and aesthetic goals, as well as economic ones.

St. Pierre's Ravine in the city's Oakland area was a small offshoot of two larger valleys that formed the western edge of the new major city park, Schenley Park. With the establishment of the park and Andrew Carnegie's library, Museum of Natural History, and concert hall in the 1890s, a developer, a public official, and an architect self-consciously set out to develop Oakland as a civic center in the current fashionable style of the City Beautiful movement. In addition to being a good investment opportunity, Oakland was to be a counterpoint to the haphazard and deleterious landscape of the industrial city. St. Pierre's Ravine commanded the key site at the entrance to Schenley Park and the front of the Carnegie Library. In recognition of this location, the city in 1898 erected at considerable expense a long stone arch bridge with balconies on each side for enjoying the view of the ravine.[64] But the increasing civic pride in the emerging civic center and blossoming park during the subsequent ten years sparked interest in a more formal design than the picturesque bridge and ravine presented. Partially at the request of Mayor William Magee, who apparently already had a plan before him on his desk, Olmsted advanced two proposals for the ravine; one that he favored involved filling the ravine and making it a grand plaza. Although some filling may have already occurred, the Department of Public Works directed thousands of loads of fill to the ravine in 1913 and 1914 (some of which reputedly came from the Hump cut project). Meanwhile, the city's Art Commission sponsored a competition for a plan of the filled site. With the bridge buried and the ravine filled, a plaza and a grander park entrance were ultimately completed in 1923.[65]

Few people today could imagine the site's original topography. The tension between development and conservation of the region's hilly topography continues today in the constant drive to flatten and extensively grade hills as well as to fill ravines and wetlands for new building sites. One critic of the plan to fill St. Pierre's Ravine captured this dilemma when he wrote in 1910: "Here in the foot hills of the mountains we possess a feature of natural beauty which we should appreciate and treasure—the ravine. Throughout this city the practical problems of transportation have demanded the filling up of ravines. . . . But here [St. Pierre's Ravine], in our little oasis, . . . why should the hand of man try to improve that refreshing slope, so restful to the eye of the jaded victim of the transportation system. . . . Shall we have beds of red geraniums and coleus in geometrical rows to mark the grave of our ravine?"[66]

Akin to the filling of ravines was the wanton depositing on the land of wastes of various sorts, including steel mill slag, coal mine debris, ashes, and garbage. These wastes have historically marked and shaped the landscape of the Pittsburgh region in the form of huge slag mountains or gob piles of coal wastes, filled-in wetlands, altered riverbanks, and open garbage dumps. These practices are well illustrated by the destruction of the beautiful valley of Nine Mile Run, which Frederick Law Olmsted Jr. identified as a perfect opportunity for a park but which, instead, was used by the steel industry as a dump for the waste product of slag from iron and steel manufacturing (for a discussion of development of Nine Mile Run as a green corridor after 2000 see "The Metabolism of the Industrial City" in this volume).

BRIDGES

The numerous rivers and streams in the region, along with the sharp valleys and ravines, created a particular need for bridges in the Pittsburgh region. As Allen T. Burns wrote in the *Pittsburgh Survey* in 1911: "No city in America, if in the world, has had such physical obstacles to overcome in securing free communication and access between its different parts. Not only the rivers, but also hills, gorges, cliffs, and precipices cut the land into separate districts."[67] Pittsburgh became known as the "City of Bridges," or a "bridge museum," spanned by many bridges of different styles.[68] Thus bridges, many of "great architectural and engineering skill and beauty," became a distinctive feature of the Pittsburgh landscape.

The first bridge built in Pittsburgh was the Monongahela Bridge, completed in 1818, followed by the Allegheny Bridge in 1819. Both were covered wooden toll bridges. Other bridges were constructed in subsequent years, three by the famous engineer John Roebling. By the 1850s five bridges crossed the Allegheny and two the Monongahela River. Perhaps the most striking was Roebling's Sixth Street Bridge (1859), which previewed his Brooklyn Bridge in its suspension cables and tall towers. All were private bridges aside from the suspension aqueduct that Roebling constructed in 1844 for the Pennsylvania Main Line Canal, the first bridge he ever built.

Entrepreneurs continued to build toll bridges of various styles over the rivers in the coming decades, but in the twentieth century, Pittsburgh bridges became public, free of tolls. Many reflected unusual styles, such as Gustav Lindenthal's Smithfield Street Bridge (1883), which featured a lenticular truss; the Point Bridge (1876) of Edward Hemberley, a suspension bridge that utilized pairs of Howe trusses as stiffening features; and George Richardson's George Westinghouse Memorial Bridge (1932) with the longest span in a reinforced concrete arch in the United States. By 1916 the city owned ninety bridges and was continuing to build new ones and replace deteriorating structures with more elaborate bridges.[69]

Railroad bridges are another type of structure that marks the Pittsburgh landscape. Within a few years of the railroad's initial entry into Pittsburgh in 1852, a dozen railroad bridges crossed the district's main rivers. These bridges were largely deck and through-truss bridges. An especially unique type of Pittsburgh bridge was the hot metal span, constructed to transport molten iron from blast furnaces on one side of the Monongahela River to Bessemer and open-hearth furnaces on the other. All rail bridges were designed to carry heavy loads, but the hot metal bridges had especially heavy construction. In addition to spans over water, the serrated Pittsburgh landscape required land bridges to connect sections of the city that were otherwise divided. Bridges crossed railroads, streets, ravines, and streams and were constructed and maintained by the city. In 1930 the city owned and maintained 149 land bridges, of which 33 were for pedestrian travel and 119 for vehicles. They ranged in size from spans of fifteen feet to half a mile in length.[70]

Allegheny County as well as the city of Pittsburgh constructed many bridges in the twentieth century. In the eight-year period between 1924 and 1932, the county built ninety-nine bridges.[71] Today the county claims to possess over two thousand bridges of more than eight feet in length, of which more than one-half are small single-span metal and masonry structures. These bridges reflected many types of design, including covered wooden, arch, cantilevered, suspension, and truss, with many design variations within these categories. Bridges, therefore, form a seemingly ubiquitous aspect of the region's landscape, taken for granted by residents but noticed by visitors.

RESHAPING THE LANDSCAPE IN THE TWENTIETH AND TWENTY-FIRST CENTURIES

By the early twentieth century many of Pittsburgh's elites were becoming concerned about the shabby appearance of their industrial city. In concert with the Progressive spirit of the times, they believed that a good natural and social environment not only boosted their city's economy but also uplifted the physical and moral health of the citizenry.[72] The Chamber of Commerce, the Civic Club of Allegheny County, the local chapter of the American Institute of Architects, and other voluntary groups entered into a public conversation about civic improvement, which by 1900 included, among many other issues, the beautification and civic design goals of the then fashionable City Beautiful movement. Although the city government had been developing a grand park system in the 1890s roughly following the principles of Frederick Law Olmsted Sr., it had not yet addressed the many design concerns of these advocacy groups. However, before the end of the decade the city adopted planning and beautification as part of its formal responsibility. This emerging partnership between private groups and government, though fluctuating in character over the century, has had a significant impact on the region's landscape.[73]

In 1904, for example, the Civic Club established a Forestry Committee that encouraged the municipality to protect and maintain the city's trees and that undertook a program to educate the public about the benefits of tree planting along the streets. In 1909 the city established a Shade Tree Commission within the Department of Public Works. The commission built a tree nursery, which by the end of 1914 had fifty-four hundred trees growing in it. In the first four years of operation, it planted over seven thousand trees along the city streets, which had to be regularly pruned, sprayed, watered, and replaced when vandalism, disease, and other factors such as pollution killed them. The commission optimistically viewed its ability to transform the landscape when it reported: "The coming generation will behold the wonderful transformation of the desiccated scarred hills of Allegheny County reverting to their former glory of forested crowns of green, and traversed not by wagon roads of former days but by miles of boulevards and broad avenues lined with symmetrical rows of fruit and shade trees."[74] The Shade Tree Commission assiduously continued to pursue its mission through years of fluctuating budgets. With improving air pollution conditions and the determined tree-planting program, the city's streetscape inevitably became greener in the later decades of the twentieth century. Pittsburgh is a reforested city.

If the urging of voluntary organizations succeeded in getting the city to undertake the greening of its streetscapes, their advocacy for the beautification of the shabby hillsides had much less success. Both the Chamber of Commerce and the Civic Club formed committees to study the proliferation of billboards at key intersections and on deforested hillsides. They tried to educate the public about the nuisance and to prod, without success, the city government to regulate the industry.[75] In 1910 Olmsted argued in his city plan that "the City ought to pursue a definitely active policy" in the case of shabby hillsides. It should "insist upon the maintenance of such vacant lands in a clean and orderly condition" and acquire some hillsides for return to "natural vegetation" and for views, terracing, walkways, and places to sit. Moreover, he recommended a number of designs based on European precedents for roads and even houses on those slopes not too steep for at least some development. Despite the new City Planning Commission's advocacy of "the beautification of the bluffs and hillsides," few of Olmsted's hillside recommendations were implemented in the following decades.[76] Three decades after Olmsted's recommendations, for example, a new nonprofit organization, the Greater Pittsburgh Parks Association, finally tackled the landscaping of the bald and unstable hillsides along one of the city's main boulevards. Bigelow Boulevard was opened in 1916 not only as a main artery to the East End but also as a parkway to Schenley Park in the manner of the famous designs of Frederick Law Olmsted Sr.[77]

Other design issues advocated by the private groups involved the refurbishment of downtown waterfronts, the creation of a civic center, and the rejuvenation of the Point, which had deteriorated into a rundown area of railroad yards, traffic congestion, warehouses, and other unsightly structures. Discussion of these concerns led to the mayor's appointment of the Pittsburgh Civic Commission, another voluntary elite organization that engaged Frederick Law Olmsted Jr. in 1910 to prepare a city plan. The decade-long conversation over environmental, social, and design issues along with the completion of the Olmsted plan resulted in the creation of the Pittsburgh City Planning Commission and an art commission in 1911 to plan for the long range physical development of the city. During the next three decades, the city and Allegheny County tackled an ambitious highway and bridge program. But, as with Olmsted's hillside recommendations, design plans for public spaces such as the Point infrequently left the drafting table, and few serious reforms of environmental problems materialized.[78]

Since the Second World War, however, two developments have markedly reshaped Pittsburgh's landscape. The first involved a reformulated public and private partnership that undertook a series of developments known as the Pittsburgh Renaissance. This partnership between the city government and an elite but corporate-dominated nonprofit organization attempted to reshape the city landscape in a number of ways both physically and environmentally. The most striking of these changes, which was essential for improving Pittsburgh in other ways, addressed the city's greatest environmental need, the elimination of the heavy smoke. Other major projects involving the environment included the erection of eight flood control dams (the first in 1941, the next seven after the war) by the US Army Corps of Engineers and the formation of the Allegheny County Sanitary Authority in 1946, with the mission to construct a regional sewage collection and treatment system.

Alterations of the built landscape under Renaissance programs involved the construction of new skyscrapers, downtown parks, automobile "parkways" along the rivers, and in the late 1940s and 1950s, the clearing of the structures and railroad tracks that desecrated Pittsburgh's historic Point. The latter action made possible the creation of Point State Park and the adjacent Gateway Center high-rise office complex. In the 1960s and 1970s two new bridges, a new stadium (Three Rivers Stadium), and a dramatic fountain at the Point joined the earlier redevelopment. Travelers entering the city from the west through the Fort Pitt Tunnel and bridge were presented with a striking view of the confluence of the rivers and downtown.[79]

Other significant landscape changes, often with less positive overtones, resulted from large-scale urban renewal projects. The most infamous one, the Lower Hill renewal, occurred in the 1950s. This project took place in what was one of the most densely inhabited areas of the city, adjacent to downtown. Residences and businesses involving over five thousand persons (80 percent African American) were demolished and replaced with the Civic Arena, a major sports arena surrounded by surface parking lots. A crosstown boulevard separated the renewal area from downtown. Two other massive demolition and renewal projects destroyed and reconfigured major neighborhood business districts of the city.[80] Thus, while the city's air and water were markedly improved in quality and its infrastructure greatly upgraded, changes to the built landscape largely replaced densely congested nineteenth-century areas with mid-twentieth-century modernistic, open, and geometrically designed spaces.

Renaissance II, which lasted from approximately 1978 to 1988, produced further landscape changes in the downtown. Most noticeable were major skyscraper additions to the city skyline, which further enhanced Pittsburgh's dramatic city entrance. The movement to preserve rather than demolish historic structures (which had begun in 1971 with the symphony's movement to Heinz Hall, a converted downtown movie palace) gained momentum. The growing recognition of the aesthetic quality and advantage of river locations resulted in the municipal construction of the Allegheny Landing and Sculpture Garden in 1984.[81]

Even as the municipality and its private partners labored to reshape the city, devastating changes to the region's economy dramatically affected the industrial landscape. Structural change in the national economy—most notably, deindustrialization—destroyed much of the region's manufacturing base, especially the major steel firms and allied manufacturing businesses in areas such as the by-product coking industry, machinery production, and railroad and electrical equipment. From approximately the mid-1970s through the late 1980s, mills and industries lining the riverbanks closed down, in the process eliminating many thousands of jobs; some closings continued into the 1990s. Thousands of acres of shuttered factories, rusting steel mills, abandoned rail yards, and vacant land contrasted starkly with the vibrant scene of decades earlier, described by John Stilgoe. Adjacent to the mills, city working-class neighborhoods and suburban towns sputtered, and their business districts began to deteriorate. The human cost was incalculable.[82] As the flow of investment capital shifted, the emerging brownfields of inactive industrial sites along the rivers contrasted markedly with the sprawling office parks, retail shopping centers, and residential developments sprouting up on suburban greenfields near the interstate highways on the urban periphery.

Clearing of the brownfield sites began slowly during the latter part of the 1980s and continued into the 1990s. The Urban Redevelopment Authority, which had coordinated much of the renewal of the Pittsburgh Renaissance, cleared sites in the city. Private salvaging firms and a regional nonprofit organization called the Regional Industrial Development Corporation (RIDC), working under the direction of county government, undertook redevelopment of brownfields around the county. The primary goals were to attract new tenants and provide for new taxes and jobs. This singleminded focus resulted in the sweeping destruction of the old industrial landscape and, except for a few isolated structures, almost a complete disregard for the history of the region.[83]

A new landscape began to emerge on the sites along the rivers, although only some of them took advantage of their river location. The Research and Development Park, a high-tech office project developed through the cooperation of the Urban Redevelopment Authority, Carnegie Mellon University, and the University of Pittsburgh on the former site of the LTV (formerly Jones & Laughlin Steel) integrated steel mill on the north bank of the Monongahela River near downtown, is designed as a suburban office park and makes only a limited attempt to take advantage of its river location. Although paying more attention to the river, the private Waterfront development on the mammoth site of the famous Homestead Steel Works on the Monongahela River southeast of Pittsburgh is a retail, entertainment, office, and light industrial complex seemingly designed to be more at home in a landlocked suburb than a river-based former mill town.[84]

In contrast to these brownfield redevelopments are several projects in the city and in a few former industrial towns that do recognize the opportunities of river locations.[85] The redevelopment of a former slaughterhouse and industrial site on Herr's Island—renamed Washington's Landing to distance it from its industrial past and tie it to the region's more distant history—uses proximity to downtown and great river views for housing, light industrial and commercial facilities, a marina, and a rowing club, along with space devoted to the public for biking, walking, and other recreational possibilities. The success of this project has helped to make city riverside real estate very attractive. The city reoriented its vastly expanded convention center in downtown to the Allegheny River and placed its two new sports stadiums on the opposite shore. The nonprofit Cultural Trust, enjoying the city's full cooperation, has expanded its orchestration of a downtown cultural district to include a linear park on the south shore of the Allegheny River. As a result of this focus on the Allegheny River, private firms are busily planning and erecting new projects in the river corridor. And another elite sponsored nonprofit organization, the Riverlife Task Force, has proposed a river park for the segments of the three rivers surrounding downtown with the imaginative concept of the rivers as the park's core.

In addition to these major redevelopment projects, the river landscape is changing in many smaller but no less profound ways. Despite the deteriorated conditions of Pittsburgh's industrial rivers they had remained a landscape of recreational interest and romance to some boaters and recreational boating grew in the years after the Second World War. A few marinas hugged the riverbanks, protected from powerful currents by proximate islands, or sought the calmer waters of tributary streams, where they widened near their confluence with the main rivers. In recent decades the improving environmental quality of both water and air and the collapse of "smokestack" industries have encouraged the proliferation of pleasure boating, boat tours, and cruises. Increasingly, they have replaced the diminishing number of commercial tows on the rivers. Marinas with lattices of docks occasionally dot the river shores; boat storage yards and launch facilities sit on the banks above the docks, although public access to the rivers is limited to only a few sites. Crews row past the new river-oriented stadiums, convention center, and restaurants of the city's core. Beyond this central area, riverbanks and edges are softening again with rapid vegetation regrowth, biking trails on former railroad track beds, and new community riverfront parks. Residences, office buildings, and even a shopping center are replacing the industrial character of riverfront land uses. Fishermen and picnickers again share the river shorelines with the blossoming flora and reviving fauna. Indeed, the river water more often is blue these days than the muddy brown that was the characteristic color of the industrial era.[86]

The former industrial riverfronts are not the only sites of renewal. Most striking, perhaps, are the developments of a regional shopping mall and an upscale housing complex on massive slag dumps. But, for every brownfield that has sprung back to life with new activity, many more await redevelopment. Suburban office and industrial parks still prove to be more attractive to businesses than settings in older industrial parts of the region. While industrial sources of air and water pollution have been largely eliminated, toxic residues remain in riverbeds and former industrial sites. Moreover, despite improving river conditions, the region still has nearly half of its days during the recreational season when sewage plunges water quality below acceptable levels.[87] Like other American cities that are dependent on fossil fuels for power and mobility, Pittsburgh constantly struggles to meet clean air standards, particularly during the hot and humid summer season.

Even though the distinctive industrial structures of the region's coal and steel days have largely disappeared from the built landscape, some river infrastructure and commercial, residential, and public buildings remain, along with the engineered river and land contours. Developers who propose new concepts for older areas frequently encounter a battle between those wanting to preserve the built landscape and those wishing to present a modern appearance free of the smoky past. This struggle over the city's image once again pits powerful public and private interests—informed by experts on both sides—against each other for control over shaping the landscape.

In the past, as today, average working-class Pittsburghers had little to say about the shape of the environment in which they lived. Low incomes, inadequate housing, and pedestrian mobility constrained workers in industrial Pittsburgh to live in noisy, congested, and smoky neighborhoods, while middle-class families rode streetcars to leafy, less crowded communities, which on certain days were still vulnerable to industrial soot and odors. While the upper class hired landscape architects to fashion plush gardens and grounds from the region's complex topography, working families had to make do with the industrialists' perceptions of a productive economic and social landscape in an individualistic, private society. But this does not mean that workers did not exercise agency in their landscape. Small vegetable and flower gardens, some with religious icons, represented only a small portion of the fashioning of ethnic and racial landscapes. Churches, fraternal societies, and small shops marked the neighborhoods more explicitly. Some workers trespassed onto industrial sites to fish and swim in the rivers; others by the 1930s became passionate hunters in the Pennsylvania mountains and golfers on local public courses. There is another landscape to be discovered and described, which existed outside that of the industrialists' world.

We have written in this chapter about the transformation of the Pittsburgh region's natural landscape by the creation of a built environment and the forces of industrial capitalism. Many of these changes were made to ensure and regulate the workings of the city—to guarantee that traffic would flow, that water would be available where needed, that wastes would be removed, and that streets would not flood. Urban civic leaders and experts such as engineers and planners competed with political interests (often unsuccessfully) in the attempt to shape the ideal of a more orderly and efficient urban system. The powerful currents of industrial capitalism also reshaped the landscape—but driven more by the imperative of productivity than by urban efficiency concerns. The two forces of the city-planned and efficient and the city-productive often clashed, even though there was considerable overlap in their aims. Over time the pendulum, driven both by conscious planning and by economic decline, has gradually swung toward coexistence with and regeneration of the natural environment rather than its mastery. How far these changes will be reflected in the landscape of the future has yet to be seen.

NOTES

Reprinted with permission from Joel A. Tarr, ed., *Devastation and Renewal: The Environmental History of Pittsburgh and Its Region* (Pittsburgh, PA: University of Pittsburgh Press, 2003), 11–40. The epigraph is from Robert A. Woods, the Pittsburgh Survey, 1909.

1. See Ben Marsh and Peirce Lewis, "Landforms and Human Habitat," in E. Willard Miller, ed., *A Human Geography of Pennsylvania* (University Park: Pennsylvania State University Press, 1995), 17–43; David Cuff et al., eds., *The Atlas of Pennsylvania* (Philadelphia: Temple University Press, 1989), 11–33. For a description of such a journey in the 1840s, see Jack D. Warren, ed., "A Young Woman's Vision of Western Pennsylvania: The Diary of Mary Ann Corwin, 1842–1843," *Pittsburgh History* 75 (Summer 1992): 91–107.

2. Henry Leighton, *The Geology of Pittsburgh and Its Environs* (Pittsburgh: Carnegie Institute, 1927).

3. Leighton, *Geology of Pittsburgh*, 37–43.

4. Fred Anderson, *Crucible of War: The Seven Years' War and the Fate of Empire in British North America, 1754–1766* (New York: Vintage, 2000), 18–24. See also Richard White, *The Middle Ground: Indians, Empire, and Republics in the Great Lakes Region, 1650–1815* (New York: Cambridge University Press, 1991); Daniel K. Richter, *The Ordeal of the Longhouse: The People of the Iroquois League in the Era of European Colonization* (Chapel Hill: University of North Carolina Press, 1992).

5. Solon J. Buck and Elizabeth Hawthorn Buck, *The Planting of Civilization in Western Pennsylvania* (Pittsburgh: University of Pittsburgh Press, 1938), 19–45.

6. See Buck and Buck, *The Planting of Civilization*, 19–45.

7. John Melish, *Travels in the United States of America* (Philadelphia, 1812), excerpted in John W. Harpster, ed., *Crossroads: Descriptions of Western Pennsylvania, 1720–1829* (Pittsburgh: University of Pittsburgh Press, 1938), 251. See also Jennifer Ford, "Landscape and Material Life in Southwestern Pennsylvania, 1798–1838" (PhD diss., University of Pittsburgh, 2001).

8. Paul A. Chew, *Southwestern Pennsylvania Painters: Collections of the Westmoreland Museum of Art* (Greensburg: Westmoreland Museum of Art, 1989). See, for instance: Eugene A. Poole, *River Landscape with Cows*; Jasper Lawman, *Trout Stream Landscape*; and William Coventry Wall, *River Scene at Sunset.*

9. Rina C. Youngner, "Paintings and Graphic Images of Industry in Nineteenth Century Pittsburgh: A Study of the Relationship between Art and Industry," 2 vols. (PhD diss., University of Pittsburgh, 1991), 1:4; published as Rina C. Youngner, *Industry in Art, 1812–1920* (Pittsburgh: University of Pittsburgh Press, 2006).

10. Verna L. Cowin, *Pittsburgh Archaeological Resources and National Register Survey* (Pittsburgh: Carnegie Museum of Natural History, 1985); Leland D. Baldwin, *Pittsburgh: The Story of a City, 1750–1865* (Pittsburgh: University of Pittsburgh Press, 1937).

11. Essay by Russel Errett in *Magazine of Western History* 7 (1887): 33–44, quoted in Harpster, *Crossroads*, 287–88.

12. For early manufacturing in Pittsburgh, see George Thurston, *Pittsburgh as It Is* (Pittsburgh: W. S. Haven, 1857); Catherine Reiser, *Pittsburgh's Commercial Development, 1800–1850* (Harrisburg: Pennsylvania Historical and Museum Commission, 1851). For iron and steel, see John N. Ingham, *Making Iron and Steel: Independent Mills in Pittsburgh, 1820–1920* (Columbus: Ohio State University Press, 1991), 21–46. For coal, see Howard N. Eavenson, *The First Century and a Quarter of American Coal Industry* (Pittsburgh: Privately printed, 1942), 155–204.

13. Rina Youngner and Emily Hetzel, "The Artist Looks at Industrial Pittsburgh, 1836–1993," (catalog, University of Pittsburgh Art Gallery, June, 1993); Youngner, "Paintings and Graphic Images," 74.

14. Youngner, "Paintings and Graphic Images," 144–202. See, for instance, G. E. Muller, "The City of Pittsburgh," *Harper's New Monthly Magazine* 62, no. 367 (1882): 49–68.

15. John R. Stilgoe, *Metropolitan Corridor: Railroads and the American Scene* (New Haven: Yale University Press, 1983), 81. See also David E. Nye, ed., *Technologies of Landscape: From Reaping to Recycling* (Amherst: University of Massachusetts Press, 1999).

16. For a discussion of the siting and development of these mills, see Kenneth Warren, *The American Steel Industry, 1850–1970: A Geographical Interpretation* (Oxford: Clarendon Press, 1973).

17. Reuben Gold Thwaites, *Afloat on the Ohio: An Historical Pilgrimage of a Thousand Miles in a Skiff from Redstone to Cairo* (Chicago: Way and Williams, 1897), quoted in Dan Hughes Fuller, "Roughing It on the River: Reuben Gold Thwaites in Western Pennsylvania," *Pittsburgh History* 79 (1996): 116; Laurie Graham, *Singing the City: The Bonds of Home in an Industrial Landscape* (Pittsburgh: University of Pittsburgh Press, 1998), 35.

18. "There are squares of great foundries, streets of machine shops and locomotive-works and engine-making establishments, besides huge shops that send wrought iron and steel bridges into the world. Muller, "The City of Pittsburgh," 62–63.

19. Stilgoe, *Metropolitan Corridor*, 78; also 96–97. George H. Thurston was a famous Pittsburgh booster who wrote a number of fact-filled books about the city in the nineteenth century. See, for instance, George H. Thurston, *Pittsburgh and Allegheny County in the Centennial Year* (Pittsburgh: W. W. Anderson, 1876), which contains chapters on the different industries. See also David Demarest and Eugene Levy, "Visualizing the Industrial Landscape: The Photographers of Pittsburgh's Westinghouse Air Brake Company, 1900–1960," *Pittsburgh History* 77 (Spring 1994): 4–21.

20. Quoted in Joel A. Tarr, "The Pittsburgh Survey as an Environmental Statement," in Maurine W. Greenwald and Margo Anderson, eds., *Pittsburgh Surveyed: Social Science and Social Reform in the Early Twentieth Century* (Pittsburgh: University of Pittsburgh Press, 1996), 172.

21. Some of the best discussions and images of the railroad landscape are in the illustrated volumes written by amateur railroad historians. See, for instance, Ken Kobus and Jack Consoli, *The Pennsy in the Steel City: 150 Years of Pennsylvania Railroad in Pittsburgh* (Kutztown, PA: Kutztown Publishing, 1996); Ken Kobus and Jack Consoli, *The*

Pennsylvania Railroad's Golden Triangle: Main Line Panorama in the Pittsburgh Area (Pittsburgh: Pennsylvania Railroad Technical & Historical Society, 1998); Howard V. Worley Jr. and William N. Poellot Jr., *The Pittsburgh & West Virginia Railway* (Halifax, PA: Witheirs Publishing, 1989). For a more detailed discussion of the effects of the railroad on the region, see David Hounshell, Mark Samber, and Joel Tarr, "Economic Impact of Rail Transportation in Western Pennsylvania, a Report to the National Park Service," Department of History, Carnegie Mellon University, Pittsburgh, August 1993.

22. Engineers' Society of Western Pennsylvania, *Pittsburgh* (Cramer Printing & Publishing, 1930), 113–19.

23. See the photograph in Stefan Lorant, *Pittsburgh: The Story of an American City* (Lenox, MA: Author's Edition, 1988), 264.

24. For the Pitcairn yards, see "PRR-Pitcairn Yard," at http://www.trainweb.org/horseshoecurve-nrhs/Pitcairn.htm; for the Conway Yard, see "Conway Yard," at http://home.swbell.net/jwacht/ambridge/id53.htm.

25. See Sherie R. Mershon and Joel A. Tarr, "Strategies for Clean Air: The Pittsburgh and Allegheny County Smoke Control Movement, 1940–1960," in Tarr, *Devastation and Renewal*, 143–75.

26. Willard Glazier, "The Great Furnace of America," quoted in Roy Lubove, ed., *Pittsburgh* (New York: Franklin Watts, 1976).

27. *Coal and Coke Resource Analysis: Western Pennsylvania and Northern West Virginia* (America's Industrial Heritage Project, Department of the Interior Washington, DC, 1992), Appendix A, 77; Carmen DiCiccio, *Coal and Coke in Pennsylvania* (Harrisburg: Pennsylvania Historical and Museum Commission, 1996), 37.

28. Kenneth Warren, *Wealth, Waste, and Alienation: Growth and Decline in the Connellsville Coke Industry* (Pittsburgh: University of Pittsburgh Press, 2001), 221–28.

29. DiCiccio, *Coal and Coke in Pennsylvania*, 113–14.

30. Companies sometimes put whitewashed wooden picket fences around the houses and encouraged tenants to plant vegetable and flower gardens. "Garden" competitions were often held in the towns. Margaret M. Mulrooney, *A Legacy of Coal: The Coal Company Towns of Southwestern Pennsylvania* (America's Industrial Heritage Project, Department of Interior, Washington, DC, 1989), 9–29; DiCiccio, *Coal and Coke in Pennsylvania*, 89–95; *Coal and Coke Resource Analysis*, 47–49.

31. David Demarest and Eugene Levy, "Touring the Coke Region," *Pittsburgh History* 74 (Fall 1991): 105–8.

32. Warren, *Wealth, Waste, and Alienation*, 11–24.

33. Jones & Laughlin broke from this pattern by constructing a major beehive installation (1,504 ovens) within the Pittsburgh neighborhood of Hazelwood between 1898 and 1903. See William L. Affelder, "Jones & Laughlin's Coke Plant." *Mines and Minerals* 29 (December 1908): 195–99.

34. John A. Enman, "Connellsville Coke: Catalyst and Victim of Change," in Dennis F. Brestensky, ed., *The Early Coke Worker* (Connellsville: Southwestern Pennsylvania Heritage Commission, 1994), 2–29.

35. Muriel Early Sheppard, *Cloud by Day: The Story of Coal and Coke and People* (Chapel Hill: University of North Carolina Press, 1947), 2. For a discussion of some of the environmental effects of coke production in beehive ovens, see Warren, *Wealth, Waste, and Alienation*, 221–28; Joel A. Tarr, ed., *The Search for the Ultimate Sink: Urban Pollution in Historical Perspective* (Akron: University of Akron Press, 1996), 388–91.

36. Warren, *Wealth, Waste, and Alienation*, 195–203.

37. M. Camp and C. B. Francis, *The Making, Shaping and Treating of Steel*, 4th ed. (Pittsburgh: Carnegie Steel, 1919), 101–29.

38. For environmental problems caused by by-product coking, see Tarr, *Ultimate Sink*, 385–412; Charles O. Jones, *Clean Air: The Policies and Politics of Pollution Control* (Pittsburgh, PA: University of Pittsburgh Press, 1975).

39. Joel A. Tarr, "The Plume Is Gone, but We Can't Forget Hazelwood," *Pittsburgh Post-Gazette*, May 27, 1998, A-13.

40. Cowin, *Pittsburgh's Archaeological Resources*; Reiser, *Pittsburgh's Commercial Development*, 124–40.

41. Leland R. Johnson, *The Headwaters District: A History of the Pittsburgh District, US Army Corps of Engineers* (Pittsburgh, PA: US Army Engineer District, 1979).

42. Edward K. Muller, "The Legacy of Industrial Rivers," *Pittsburgh History* 72 (1992): 64–75.

43. See Joel A. Tarr, "Infrastructure and City Building in the Nineteenth and Twentieth Centuries," in Samuel P. Hays, ed., *City at the Point: Essays on the Social History of Pittsburgh* (Pittsburgh, PA: University of Pittsburgh Press, 1989), 213–39.

44. Quoted in Albert W. Atwood, "Pittsburgh: Workshop of the Titans," *National Geographic Magazine* 96 (July 1949): 117.

45. Clay McShane and Joel A. Tarr, "The Centrality of the Horse in the Nineteenth-Century American City," in Raymond A. Mohl, ed., *The Making of Urban America*, 2nd ed. (Wilmington, DE: SR Book, 1997), 12–23. The electric streetcar, however, was not pollution free. Its demands for electricity contributed to the smoke burden produced by electrical generating plants.

46. Joel A. Tarr, *Transportation Innovation and Changing Spatial Patterns in Pittsburgh, 1850–1934* (Chicago: Public Works Historical Society, 1978), 6–21.

47. For a discussion of this issue, see Richard Pinkham, "Stream Restoration and Daylighting: Opportunities in the Pittsburgh Region," in Tim Collins, ed., *Three Rivers Second Nature Project Reports: Phase II 2001, Monongahela River Valley* (Pittsburgh: Studio for Creative Inquiry, June 2002).

48. Among the major culverted streams flowing into the Allegheny River were Negley Run, Haights Run, Cemetery Run, and Two Mile Run in the city's eastern end. On the city's North Side, Jack's Run, Butcher's Run, and Spring Garden Run also flowed into the Allegheny River and were culverted. Flowing into the Monongahela River from the city's eastern section were Soho Run and Four Mile Run, fully culverted, and parts of Nine Mile Run, partially culverted.

49. See Warren, "A Young Woman's Vision," 99, 105. Interestingly, Corwin made this observation in 1843 on the western leg of her trip from Philadelphia to Cincinnati. When she had passed through Pittsburgh going west in 1842, she noted that it was "the very dirtiest city that I ever saw in all my life, and as noisy as it can well be."

50. *The City of Pittsburgh and Its Public Works* (Pittsburgh, 1916), 21; Frederick Law Olmsted Jr., *Main Thoroughfares and the Down Town District* (Pittsburgh, PA: Pittsburgh Civic Commission, 1911), 93.

51. Olmsted, *Main Thoroughfares*, 109–10.

52. Cowin, *Pittsburgh's Archaeological Resources*, 73–74.

53. Steven J. Hoffman, "The Saga of Pittsburgh's Liberty Tubes: Geographical Partisanship on the Urban Fringe," *Pittsburgh History* 75 (1992): 128–41.

54. For images of Pittsburgh's downtown landscape, see Carnegie Library of Pittsburgh, "Photos and Scenes of Pittsburgh," at http://www.carnegielibrary.org/pgh/photos.html.

55. *Digest of the General Ordinances and Laws of the City of Pittsburgh* (Pittsburgh, 1938), 475; *The City of Pittsburgh and Its Public Works*, 29–31; Charles M. Reppert, "Recent Retaining Wall Practice," *Proceedings, Engineers Society of Western Pennsylvania* 26 (1910): 316–17.

56. Joseph G. Armstrong, "Annual Report of the Department of Public Works," *Annual Reports of the Executive Departments of the City of Pittsburgh, 1912*, 6.

57. *City of Pittsburgh and Its Public Works*, 26–28.

58. John Bodnar, Roger Simon, and Michael P. Weber, *Lives of Their Own: Blacks, Italians, and Poles in Pittsburgh, 1900–1960* (Champaign: University of Illinois Press, 1983), 153–80.

59. H. L. Mencken, *Prejudices: Sixth Series* (New York, 1927), 187–93.

60. Tarr, *Transportation Innovation*, 10. See also "Pittsburgh Incline Tribute," at http://members.tripod.com/riid/inclines.html.

61. Information on steps supplied to the editor by Bob Regan. Robert D. Regan, *Pittsburgh Steps: The Story of the City's Public Stairways* (Lanham, Md.: Rowman and Littlefield, 2015). See also "'Steptrek' Raises Profile of Pittsburgh's 700 Hillside Stairways," *Pittsburgh Post-Gazette*, March 22, 2000. For the burden imposed by steps, see F. Elizabeth Crowell, "Painter's Row: The Company House," in Paul Underwood Kellogg, ed., *The Pittsburgh District: Civic Frontage*, vol. 5 in the Pittsburgh Survey, 6 vols. (New York: Survey Associates, 1914), 132–33; S. J. Kleinberg, *The Shadow of the Mills: Working-Class Families in Pittsburgh, 1870–1907* (Pittsburgh: University of Pittsburgh Press, 1989), 90.

62. Florence Larrabee Lattimore, "Skunk Hollow: The Squatter's House," in Kellogg, *The Pittsburgh District: Civic Frontage*, 124–30; James Zanella, "From the *Paesi d'Italia* to the Village of Larimer: A Study of Pittsburgh's Forgotten Little Italy, 1920–1925" (unpublished paper, University of Pittsburgh, 2001), 5.

63. "Rapid Transit for Pittsburgh: A Discussion," *Proceedings: Engineers Society of Western Pennsylvania* 25 (1909): 468.

64. Ralph Brem, "341-Foot Stone-Arch Bridge Buried near Proposed Research Park," *Pittsburgh Press*, June 16, 1963.

65. Olmsted, *Main Thoroughfares*, 101–6; Barry Hannegan, "Schenley Plaza—Place of Dreams," *PHLF News* 144 (1996): 10–15.

66. Jessie Welles to Allen T. Burns, letter, February 1, 1910, in Papers of Frederick Law Olmsted, Manuscript Division, Library of Congress, Washington, DC, reel 200. For some decades the "Plaza" served as a parking lot but in 2006 a public-private coalition opened a redesigned Schenley Plaza as a welcoming public green space managed by the city and the Pittsburgh Parks Conservancy. See https://en.wikipedia.org/wiki/Schenley_Plaza.

67. Kellogg, *The Pittsburgh District: Civic Frontage*, 44–45.

68. For Pittsburgh bridges, see Walter C. Kidney, *Pittsburgh's Bridges: Architecture and Engineering* (Pittsburgh: Pittsburgh History & Landmarks Foundation, 1999); also "Bridges and Tunnels of Allegheny County and Pittsburgh, Pa.," at http://pghbridges.com/.

69. *The City of Pittsburgh and Its Public Works*, 38.

70. See Kidney, *Pittsburgh's Bridges*, 130, for the Monongahela Connecting Bridge. On land bridges, see Engineers' Society of Western Pennsylvania, *Pittsburgh*, 129–33.

71. Robert J. Gangewere, *The Bridges of Pittsburgh and Allegheny County* (Pittsburgh: Carnegie Library of Pittsburgh, 2001), 4.

72. Tarr, "The Pittsburgh Survey," 170–89.

73. John F. Bauman and Edward K. Muller, "The Olmsteds in Pittsburgh: Part II. Shaping the Progressive City," *Pittsburgh History* 76 (1993/1994): 191–205.

74. "Annual Report, Department of Public Works," *Annual Reports of the Executive Departments of the City of Pittsburgh, 1913*, 396, quoted in Roy Lubove, "City Beautiful, City Banal: Design Advocacy and Historic Preservation in Pittsburgh," *Pittsburgh History* 75 (1992): 30.

75. Kristin Szylvian Bailey, "Fighting 'Civic Smallpox': The Civic Club of Allegheny County's Campaign for Billboard Regulation, 1896–1917," *Western Pennsylvania Historical Magazine* 70 (1987): 3–28.

76. Olmsted, *Main Thoroughfares*, 106–12; "Annual Report of the Department of Public Works: City Planning Commission," *Annual Reports of the Executive Departments of the City of Pittsburgh, 1913*, 108.

77. M. Graham Netting, *Fifty Years of the Western Pennsylvania Conservancy: The Early Years* (Pittsburgh: Western Pennsylvania Conservancy, 1982), 67–68.

78. Bauman and Muller, "The Olmsteds in Pittsburgh: Part II"; and Roy Lubove, *Twentieth-Century Pittsburgh, Vol. 1: Government, Business, and Environmental Change* (New York: John Wiley and Sons, 1969), 87–105.

79. Lubove, *Twentieth-Century Pittsburgh, Vol. 1*, 63–78, 106–41; Sherie R. Mershon, "Corporate Social Responsibility and Urban Revitalization: The Allegheny Conference on Community Development, 1943–1968" (PhD diss., Carnegie Mellon University, 2000); Robert C. Alberts, *The Shaping of the Point: Pittsburgh's Renaissance Park* (Pittsburgh: University of Pittsburgh Press, 1980).

80. Lubove, *Twentieth-Century Pittsburgh, Vol. 1*, 142–77.

81. Roy Lubove, *Twentieth-Century Pittsburgh, Vol. 2: The Post-Steel Era* (Pittsburgh: University of Pittsburgh Press, 1996), 57–85; Shelby Stewman and Joel A. Tarr, "Four Decades of Public-Private Partnerships in Pittsburgh," in R. Scott Fosler and Renee A. Berger, eds., *Public-Private Partnerships in American Cities* (New York: Lexington Books, 1982), 95–99.

82. For the collapse of the regional steel industry and related impacts, see John P. Hoerr, *And the Wolf Finally Came: The Decline of the American Steel Industry* (Pittsburgh: University of Pittsburgh Press, 1988); William Serrin, *Homestead: The Glory and Tragedy of an American Steel Town* (New York: Times Books, 1992); Judith Modell, with photographs by Charlee Brodsky, *A Town without Steel: Envisioning Homestead* (Pittsburgh: University of Pittsburgh Press, 1998).

83. The Steel Industry Heritage Corporation (managing organization for the Rivers of Steel National Heritage Area) has played an active role in attempting to preserve structures, artifacts, and records relating to the steel industry region. See, for example, Jan Ackerman, "Steel Industry Preserved," at http://www. riversofsteel.com/articles/postgazette39.asp.

84. For case studies of these brownfield sites and their redevelopment, see the website of the Carnegie Mellon University Brownfield Center, at http//www.ce.cmu.edu/Brownfields/.

85. These developments are mostly reported in the newspapers. See, for example, Eve Modzelewski, "Rolling on the Rivers," *Pittsburgh Post-Gazette*, August 5, 2001; Tom Barnes, "Task Force Lays Out Grand Plan for Riverfronts," *Pittsburgh Post-Gazette*,

October 23, 2001; Tom Barnes and Dan Fitzpatrick, "Renaissance III," *Pittsburgh Post-Gazette*, March 22, 1998.

86. See, for example, Roxanne Sherbeck, "We're Rolling on the Rivers," *Pittsburgh Post-Gazette*, September 17, 2000.

87. Pennsylvania Economy League, *Southwestern Pennsylvania Water and Sewer Infrastructure Report* (Pittsburgh, 2002), 18.

2 PITTSBURGH'S INDUSTRIAL CORRIDORS

Edward K. Muller and Joel A. Tarr

For residents and visitors alike, the Pittsburgh industrial region seemed to be the home of Vulcan, the Roman god of fire and metalworking. The "pillars of smoke by day and at night the pillars of fire against the background of hillsides strewn with jets of light" heralded the great energy, power, and destructive force of this vast industrial complex built around its enormous iron and steel industry.[1] John Stilgoe observed that the awesome sight of the huge industrial plants clustered in the railroad corridors of America's metropolises provided an "industrial aesthetic."[2] No other city in the nation could provide a landscape more emblematic of this industrial aesthetic at the beginning of the twentieth century. "Particularly remarkable," wrote Reuben Gold Thwaites in 1897, was the "spectacle presented at night, with the furnaces fiercely gleaming, the fresh ingots smoking hot, the Bessemer converter 'blowing off,' the great cranes moving like things of life, bearing giant kettles of molten steel."[3] It is little wonder that artists at the turn of the twentieth century such as Aaron Henry Gorson in *Industrial Pittsburgh, Pittsburgh*, and Martin B. Leisser in *View of Mills on Mononaahela River, Pittsburgh* turned their gaze on these dramatic landscapes.

Already a center of iron foundries and rolling mills by the mid-nineteenth century, Pittsburgh became by 1900 the nation's foremost district of iron blast furnaces and mass steel production. As depicted by Otto Kuhler in *The Valley of Work* and Ernest Lawson in *Pittsburgh Mills, Monongahela River*, huge integrated iron and steel mills lined the valleys of the three rivers, with the largest concentration on the Monongahela River. The mills shared the floodplains with an array of specialized enterprises including sintering plants, bridge fabricators, barge builders, machine shops, and a host of other industries. Industry's astonishing growth depended on the development of coal mines and coke works scattered throughout southwestern Pennsylvania; a web of railroad tracks and marshaling yards; rivers engineered in the service of manufacturing; and an unusual concentration of investment capital, innovators, and fearless entrepreneurs.

Workers and their families from Europe, the surrounding countryside, and the American South flocked to this industrial cauldron where they labored under difficult conditions and fought with their employers. These men and women overcame harsh circumstances to raise their families and build strong communities in the shadows of the mills. The industrial aesthetic that thrilled visitors and inspired artists could not mask industry's devastating impact on its working families and the region's air, water, and land. In the nation's mind a smoky shroud that seemed to blot out the sun, portrayed by Harry Sternberg in *Forest of Flame*, often became synonymous with Pittsburgh. The river waters could barely sustain life, and the once verdant hillsides presented a barren and gullied aspect. Thus, although the art of industrial Pittsburgh captures the sense of industrial power and wonder that was present at the time, it barely considers the attendant social and environmental toll.

THE EARLY IRON INDUSTRY

With the establishment of the new nation in the mid-1780s, settlement flourished in southwestern Pennsylvania and the Ohio valley. The fledgling outpost of Pittsburgh, located at the head of the Ohio River, where the Allegheny and Monongahela Rivers flowed together to form the Ohio, experienced rapid growth as the natural transshipment point between this route to the new West and the arduous overland route through the Allegheny Mountains to the East. While Pittsburgh merchants worked to expand this commerce between the established eastern markets and the newly settled western country, they simultaneously invested in the local manufacturing of goods for passing migrants and the frontier markets. Artisans fashioned wood, leather, cloth, and metal products and joined manufacturers of textiles, glassware, wagons, boats—especially steamboats—and iron goods to produce a flow of commodities.

By the 1830s the manufacturing of iron products emerged as the young city's leading industry, with eighteen iron foundries and nine rolling mills in 1836. Despite another depression and a devastating fire in 1845, Pittsburgh continued to flourish. At the century's midpoint, approximately eighty thousand people resided in the several communities clustered on both sides of the rivers around the Point, the triangular area that was formed by the convergence of the three rivers. As the city's trade expanded throughout the burgeoning middle of the continent, local manufacturing kept pace. By the mid-1850s, the total number of foundries and rolling mills had more than doubled.

Pittsburgh had become a major center of the nation's iron industry. The ironmasters produced large amounts of merchant bar for frontier markets, along with iron sheet, boiler iron, nails, rivets, spikes, machinery parts, and household hardware. A few firms also turned wrought iron into batches of blister and crucible steel for the making of tools and agricultural implements. Overall, the city's iron firms remained relatively small, using labor-intensive batch processes that required skilled workers.

The coming of the railroads to Pittsburgh in the 1850s and their expansion to the Middle West extended the geographical range from which local ironmasters could assemble raw materials and where, in turn, they could sell their products. The railroad itself was a major market for iron goods. In addition, the Civil War dramatically increased the city's iron business. The resulting demand for large quantities and high quality pig iron exceeded the ability of the rural blast furnaces to supply the needs of Pittsburgh firms. In 1859 Pittsburgh's industry began to change when Graff Bennett and Company blew in the city's first blast furnace. Two years later the American Iron Works (later known as the Jones & Laughlin Steel Company) constructed its Eliza blast furnace. By the 1870s Pittsburgh's blast furnaces, growing progressively larger in size and technologically more modern, were on their way to becoming the nation's leading producers of pig iron.

THE ADVANTAGE OF CONNELLSVILLE COKE

The construction of blast furnaces in the city and the iron industry's continued growth required large quantities of high-energy fuels. After mid-century blast furnace operators west of the mountains began experimenting with coke made from southwestern Pennsylvania's rich deposits of bituminous coal. Coal from the Connellsville coke district produced a superior coke that gave nearby Pittsburgh ironmasters a great advantage over their competitors in other iron regions. The coal was mined from a narrow fifty-mile-long seam located about forty miles southeast of Pittsburgh. It was cooked for between forty-eight and seventy-two hours inside brick beehive-shaped ovens, each approximately twelve feet in diameter and six feet high, with the volatile gases escaping through a hole in the top of the oven. The ovens were arranged in single or double rows, usually in plants of about 250 ovens. The process left a uniform, porous, and crystalline silver gray coke that, because of its hardness and sturdiness, transported well and supported the load of iron ore and limestone in the blast furnace. The completion of the Connellsville and Pittsburgh Railroad in 1861 and the spread of rails throughout the coke district provided the transportation necessary for its exploitation.

The leading developer of the Connellsville coke fields was Henry Clay Frick, who began mining coal and producing coke in 1871 with the construction of 50 ovens. An astute capitalist and a tough manager, Frick relentlessly expanded his operations. In 1881 he formed an association with Andrew Carnegie in regard to their complementary coke and steel interests, later becoming a partner in Carnegie's steel empire. By 1890 H. C. Frick Coke Company owned 35,000 acres of coal land and operated 10,046 ovens.

The landscape of the Connellsville coke district was marked by coal tipples and breakers like that Ernest Fiene painted *in Coal Breaker, Pennsylvania*, banks of beehive ovens, small company towns where the workers lived (also called "patches"), miles of railroads, and a devastated natural environment. At the height of production in 1909 nearly 40,000 ovens cooked coal around the clock. Charles Richard van Hise, president of the University of Wisconsin and a geologist, described a trip he took through the region in 1910. He commented that if a traveler looked out of the train window they would "have seen long rows of beehive ovens from which flame is bursting and dense smoke issuing. By night the scene is rendered indescribably vivid. The beehive ovens make the entire region [by day] . . . one of dulled sky, cheerless and unhealthful."[4] The uncontrolled emissions of ash, fumes, and hydrocarbons vented from the ovens during the coal distillation process killed and stunted trees and crops and often left a layer of coal dust, ash, and particles on the surrounding fields. Oven operators heaped solid wastes such as coal wastes and ashes in huge gob piles or dumped them into nearby creeks or valleys, damming the flow, causing flooding, and damaging stream ecology. Environmental harm from abandoned coal mines can still be seen in the orange- and red-colored runoff of acid mine drainage and the subsidence problems caused both by old and new mining techniques.

RISE OF THE STEEL INDUSTRY

The increasing demand for iron after mid-century and the development of the new steelmaking technologies of the Bessemer and open-hearth furnaces that utilized Connellsville coke drove the expansion of Pittsburgh's iron and steel production facilities. Andrew Carnegie was the key figure taking advantage of the new technology in the development of Pittsburgh as the nation's steel manufacturing center. Carnegie, as is well known, was an immigrant boy from Scotland who worked his way up from telegraph boy to railroad manager, financial investor, and then steel magnate. He believed in the importance of "hard-driving," applied to both technology and to men, and in keeping costs low and production high. He noted that "Cheapness is in proportion to the scale of production. To make ten tons of steel a day would cost many times as much per ton as to make one hundred tons. Thus, the larger the scale of operation, the cheaper the product."[5]

After entering the iron business in the 1860s, Carnegie and a partner constructed in 1872 the seventy-foot-high Lucy blast furnace, while a group of competitors erected the equally imposing Isabella furnace. These two furnaces broke all records for iron smelting for both America and Great Britain, capturing much of the market for pig iron that was used in making steel rails. Carnegie subsequently acquired the Isabella furnace and in 1875 opened a new integrated steel rail mill at Braddock, Pennsylvania, that initially focused on manufacturing rails using the Bessemer process. He named the hugely successful works after J. Edgar Thomson, president of the Pennsylvania Railroad and an anticipated consumer of the rails.

Located between the junction of three railroads and the Monongahela River, the Edgar Thomson Works (ET) had a fiery ambience, operating blast furnaces after 1880 and steelmaking Bessemer convertors. Hot pig iron traversed by in-plant railway to the mixer and then to the Bessemer converters to become steel. Hot steel ingots, likely being poured in Aaron Henry Gorson's *Interior of a Steel Mill*, were cooled and transported on rollers to a massive rolling mill (a "three-high mill," with three rollers instead of the usual two rollers) to be worked into steel rails, then shipped out by both rail and river. The mill became the premier rail maker in the nation producing as much as three thousand tons of steel rails daily and close to a quarter of the national rail output. ET also pioneered the use of the open-hearth furnace in the United States, producing structural steel to serve the growing demand for steel-frame skyscrapers and bridges. The ET Works pointed the way toward the future of Pittsburgh's steel industry, involving steel's replacement of iron as the industry's main product, a massive increase in the size of the average mill and its productivity, and the growth of the region as the nation's major steel-producing area.

Carnegie acquired other major mills in the Monongahela Valley. In 1883 he purchased the newly built Homestead Works that used open-hearth furnaces to produce structural shapes, and in 1898 he acquired the Carrie blast furnaces on the opposite side of the river to provide iron for the open hearths. In 1900 Carnegie Steel erected a five-hundred-foot span hot metal bridge weighing fifty-five hundred tons to move ore, pig iron, and molten iron between the Carrie furnaces and the Homestead Works. In 1890 Carnegie acquired the Allegheny Bessemer Steel Works at Duquesne, about two miles upriver from Homestead. This plant featured the so-called continuous process, which involved running the steel ingots directly from the soaking pits through rollers that shaped them into rails and billets. This third acquisition gave the company control of the three largest integrated mills in the region.

During these years Carnegie also ensured his raw material sources. Because of his alliance with Frick, he was guaranteed an uninterrupted flow of the high quality coke so necessary to the making of steel. He also guaranteed the availability of supplies of high quality ore for fifty years from the Mesabi iron range in Minnesota.

By 1890 the demand for steel rails was increasingly matched by the growing market for structural steel shapes for which the innovative open-hearth furnace was especially suited. In the mid-1890s there were eighteen open-hearth furnaces in Pittsburgh, fifteen of which were at ET. With this new technology, portrayed in Cynthia Cooley's dramatic painting the *Furnace Door*, iron makers attempted to capture the market for higher quality steel, especially structural members for bridges, skyscrapers, and steel-frame factories. By 1899 mills in Allegheny County produced 64 percent of the nation's total structural steel production.

Andrew Carnegie was not the only steel entrepreneur to operate a successful integrated mill in the Pittsburgh region. At the outbreak of the Civil War the Jones & Laughlin firm (J&L) owned blast furnaces, rolling mills, finishing operations, and warehousing and distribution facilities. The firm used traditional iron puddling and rolling methods to produce wrought iron until the 1880s, when it installed Bessemer converters. J&L was located on both sides of the Monongahela River in Pittsburgh, with its Eliza blast furnaces and coke ovens on the north bank and its rolling mills on the south side. It connected them in 1887 with a hot metal rail bridge. Depicted by Annie Campbell in her painting of Pittsburgh's South Side, *Pittsburgh Aglow*, J&L went on to become a major producer of steel products, second only to Carnegie in Pittsburgh, and in 1907 built a new integrated mill at Aliquippa on the Ohio River a few miles below Pittsburgh.

Smaller firms in Pittsburgh continued to produce wrought iron, blister steel, and other specialized products, since markets persisted for iron products such as rolled merchant iron, nuts and bolts, wire nails, wire rods, and barbed wire. Many of these independent and specialized firms (thirty-one in 1920) continued to exist long after the formation of US Steel in 1901.

The giant US Steel Corporation evolved from the desire of the financier J. P. Morgan to bring order into the steel industry by removing Andrew Carnegie, the business's most ruthless competitor, from the scene. As Joseph F. Wall, Carnegie's biographer writes, "Carnegie was to Morgan what the Anabaptist had been to Calvin, the fanatical enthusiast who in an excess of fervor would destroy God's and Calvin's orderly plans for the universe."[6] In 1901 Morgan and his allies paid Andrew Carnegie $480,000,000 for the Carnegie Company, merging it with several other steel companies, including the Pittsburgh-based firms of the National Tube Company, American Steel & Wire Company, American Tin Plate Company, American Sheet Steel, and the American Steel Hoop Company. By 1906 the US Steel Corporation had 48 blast furnaces and 111 open-hearth furnaces within fifty miles of the city of Pittsburgh.

Because the new integrated mills demanded big sites, they increasingly spread up the length of the three rivers, with the Monongahela having the largest concentration, followed by the Allegheny and the Ohio. Eventually, as the demand for steel increased, the various steel mills, plus associated facilities and manufacturing firms, lined the riverbanks. The rivers provided easy access to the rich coal deposits in southwestern Pennsylvania and West Virginia and inexpensive water-based shipping. By 1910 over twenty-five separate iron and steel plants were located in the area from Allenport on the Monongahela, Kittanning on the Allegheny, to Beaver Falls on the Ohio.

Railroads were also key, and mills were usually sited between railroad and river, facilitating easy movement of goods in the region and to the East Coast and the expanding West. Thus, the railroads, rivers, and bridges were integral parts of the Pittsburgh scene, as Joseph Pennell pictured in 1908 in his *On the Way to Bessemer* (see Figure 2.1). The Pennsylvania Railroad (PRR), the Baltimore & Ohio (B&O), and the Pittsburgh & Lake Erie (P&LE) were the primary trunk lines serving the region. The PRR was the first to enter Pittsburgh, arriving in 1852 and growing rapidly in the next decades by merging regional and local lines into its national network. The B&O, chartered in 1828, developed extensive support facilities in the Pittsburgh region, strategically located near primary industrial areas. And in 1879 Pittsburgh industrialists organized the third major line, the P&LE, in an attempt to circumvent the high rates of the PRR. The P&LE eventually provided a line from Connellsville in the heart of the coke district through the Youghiogheny, Monongahela, and Ohio River valleys serving prime industrial real estate. In addition to the major roads providing national connections, numerous regional and local railroads, predominantly carrying coal, grew in the latter half of the nineteenth century, connecting blast furnaces and open-hearth furnaces with coal extracted from mines in the city's hinterlands.

The steel industry continued to make a number of changes in production processes at the turn of the century and in the first decades of the twentieth century, with the most significant shift being the introduction of by-product coking. Developed in Europe in 1893, this process rooted slowly in western Pennsylvania because of the heavy investment by coke companies and steel firms in beehive coking. By-product coking, however, had a number of advantages over the beehive process. It could utilize lower grade coal and still produce excellent coke, and the technology captured rather than wasted the gas and various chemical emissions. By-product coke plants, like the *Neville Coke Works* painted by Ron Donoughe, also shifted coke production much closer to the steel plants and blast furnaces in order to make possible the more efficient use of the gas and chemical products.

Both US Steel and J&L built large by-product plants along the Monongahela River near their Pittsburgh steelworks around the time of the First World War, including the immense US Steel Clairton By-Product Coke Works (1918). The Clairton plant occupied a riverfront site 5,200 feet long and 1,800 feet wide, filled with coke ovens, tracks, hoists, coal chutes, and processing units. Its by-product coke ovens consumed enormous amounts of coal, most of which moved into the plant by river barge. The plant began operations with 640 ovens producing as much coke as 4,650 beehive ovens and including equipment for the reclamation and processing of coking by-products; by 1923–1924 the plant had 1,134 ovens. Clairton supplied many US Steel works with tar, fuel oil, and coke oven gas as well as coke and even sold surplus gas to local mill towns. It provided a significant impetus to tightening the functional connections between previously independent and disconnected plants.

In 1920 the J&L Corporation built a by-product plant in the Pittsburgh neighborhood of Hazelwood on the north side of the Monongahela River, next to its Eliza furnaces. This plant actually replaced the largest beehive coke oven plant in the world, an installation of 1,510 beehive ovens that J&L had built between 1897 and 1901. In 1926 J&L added a by-product battery at its Aliquippa works on the Ohio River. By 1919 the amount of coke produced by the by-product process was higher than that produced in traditional coke ovens.

The development of huge integrated mass production iron and steel mills after 1875 had forced the companies to locate large sites along the river floodplains well beyond the city. The same condition faced other local industries that adopted mass production processes. Pittsburgh's glass manufacturers, for example, abandoned the South Side to develop mass production facilities in new industrial towns such as Creighton and Ford City on the Allegheny River and in Jeannette along the PRR tracks in Westmoreland County. Similarly, George Westinghouse erected enormous plants for his Air Brake and Electric Companies in the Turtle Creek valley, a few miles from the ET Works in Braddock. The Aluminum Company of America (ALCOA) also left its city works and built a massive modern complex up the Allegheny River in New Kensington. New regional manufacturers also constructed their plants in suburban locations rather than the city.

By 1920 Pittsburgh's riverbanks had become industrial "corridors," lined with railroad tracks, mills, docks, and wooden and metal "cells" designed to facilitate unloading of barges, while gantry and other cranes and hoists moved materials back and forth between processes in the mills, railroad tracks, and the rivers. The sight intrigued painters such as William J. Hyett in *River Scene* and Johanna Hailman in *Pittsburgh River Scene* and some observers such as Robert A. Woods in the *Pittsburgh Survey*, who wrote admiringly of the "involved panorama of the rivers, the . . . long ascents and steep bluffs, the visible signs everywhere of movement, of immense forces at work,—the pillar of smoke by day, and at night the pillars of fire against the background of hillsides strewn with jets of light."[7]

THE INDUSTRIAL LABOR FORCE

Pittsburgh's industrial growth required vast expansion of the labor force. Although migrations from the countryside and later by African Americans from the South were important sources of labor, the critical mass of ironworkers was provided by foreign-born immigrants, such as shown in Francis Komperda's portrait of his brother-in-law, *Portrait of Mike Kessel.* During the middle third of the nineteenth century, ironmasters recruited skilled workers from the British Isles; German and Irish immigrants met other labor needs. In this pre–mass production era, skilled workers exercised considerable control over production and working conditions. The adoption of mass production processes greatly expanded the demand for unskilled workers and diminished the roles of skilled workers. Southern and

FIG. 2.1 Joseph Pennell, *On the Way to Bessemer*, 1908 (etching on paper, 11 × 7 inches, courtesy of the Westmoreland Museum of American Art, Greensburg, Pennsylvania. Museum Purchase, 1977.32).

especially eastern European immigrants eagerly filled the unskilled laboring occupations.

Work in the region's iron and steel mills was harsh and precarious (see Figure 2.2). In settings like the plant interior drawn by Otto Kuhler, *Steel Pot (Teeming)*, unskilled workers in particular endured bone-wearying long hours; arduous manual labor; exposure to extreme heat, deafening noise, and dirty conditions; and the powerlessness of arbitrary and often repressive management rule, all for distressingly low wages. In the worst instances, some mill hands worked twelve-hour days, seven days per a week, and a twenty-four-hour stint at the turn of the shift. Work conditions in the coal mines and coke plants were no better, and these workers in their patch

Fig. 2.2 F. Frinka, *Open Hearth*, 1914 (charcoal on paper, 18 × 13 inches, courtesy of the Westmoreland Museum of American Art, Greensburg, Pennsylvania. Museum Purchase, 1983.87).

Fig. 2.3 Thomas Hart Benton (1889–1975), *Strike (Mine Strike)*, 1933 (lithograph on paper, 9 13/16 × 10 7/8 inches, courtesy of the Westmoreland Museum of American Art, Greensburg, Pennsylvania. Gift of the Women's Committee, 1999).

towns remained tied to their employers through the rental of housing with no shopping alternatives to the company stores.

Not surprisingly, workers grew restive under these brutal circumstances, and trade unions of skilled workers fought against increasing company power. A growing sense of injustice, radical politics, and even desperation eventually drew unskilled immigrant workers, who had often remained aloof from the fray, into the labor struggles. Strikes in the mines, mills, factories, and rail yards sometimes turned violent, as Thomas Hart Benton evoked in his lithograph *Strike*, but they frequently failed against brutal company tactics, unsympathetic police forces, repressive municipal policies abrogating basic civil rights, and the fragmentation of the workforce (see Figure 2.3).

Ethnicity, race, and occupational differentiation split the workers, and management manipulated these differences to its advantage. The violence associated with the 1877 railroad strike awakened the city to the emerging labor problem, and clashes between hired Pinkerton security forces and workers and their families in the 1892 Homestead strike at the Carnegie mill brought the Pittsburgh region's harsh labor relations to the nation's attention. The defeat at Homestead left the unions so weak that Carnegie Steel and many other iron and steel firms exercised nearly total control over their labor forces. Yet another failure for workers in the 1919 steel strike continued corporate domination over workers until the liberating Wagner Act of 1935, by which Congress and President Franklin D. Roosevelt provided a firm legal foundation for unionization.

Workers and their families lived near the mills in tightly crammed, cheaply built, and overcrowded homes exposed to smoke, din, and dirt, a scene that stirred Elizabeth Olds to paint *Steel Town, Pennsylvania.* The inadequate provision of running water or sewers and the prevalence of backyard privies and poorly drained streets created a muddy and unsanitary environment. Low wages, sporadic production downturns, strikes, and the prospect of injury to the breadwinners barely sustained families of unskilled workers. In *Madonna of the Mines* Mildred Olmes expressed the reality that wives worked as hard as the men to keep their families afloat, taking in piecework or caring for boarders to make ends meet. Children sacrificed their education to help with the chores and bring in additional money for the family. Churches, fraternal societies, local businesses, even taverns helped lighten the burdens of life, and "neighboring" with kin and other spouses sustained women throughout the ordeal.

THE DECLINE OF STEEL AND PITTSBURGH'S TRANSFORMATION

Ironically, the period of Pittsburgh's darkest smoke pollution might also be seen as the city's golden era. The pall created by industry, steam railroads, other businesses, and residences, all burning bituminous coal, gave the city its reputation as the Smoky City. However, between 1890 and 1920 the Pittsburgh region also reached its peak in its share of the nation's production of iron, steel, and coke. The region dominated many aspects of the steel industry, exploiting the hinterland's natural resources and extending its ecological footprint as well as its products into distant localities. The city itself had 588,000 inhabitants, and the metropolitan region with more than 1.3 million people was the sixth largest in the nation.

In view of the nation's rise to international economic prominence and Pittsburgh's critical role in that rise, it is little wonder that many artists saw in the region's integrated iron and steel mills the quintessential industrial operation and the era's archetype. The drama of this scene was not simply

Fig. 2.4 Last Vestiges of the Industrial Corridor, 2009 (photograph by Joel A. Tarr).

contained inside the mills; it was on display from outside for all to see and it drew artists like moths to flames. The spectacle was so awesome, so grand, that the environmental degradation inherent in the smoky pall, barren and eroded hillsides, polluted rivers, and drab neighborhoods merely became background or settings for artistic representations and workers appeared as small, impersonal forms against the industrial might. Progressive reformers raised concerns about the imbalance between industrial capital and social and civic life, but another decade would pass before the crisis of depression would set into motion any rebalancing.

The steel industry would persist as a power in the region, albeit reduced in its share of the national market, for another fifty years, but its era of remarkable growth had passed. New steelmaking technologies, rising labor and environmental mitigation costs, and foreign competition all inexorably weakened the large, older mills of the nation and the region (see Figure 2.4).

By the 1980s the industrial corridor that had generated such awe and creativity on the part of a host of artists exhibited mile after mile of shuttered mill and factory buildings. Although some steel is still manufactured (Edgar Thomson is still working, as are the Clairton Coke Works and

FIG. 2.5 Although activists tried to restart the Dorothy Six blast furnaces at US Steel's Duquesne Works, the furnaces were demolished along with the rest of the works, 1988 (photograph by Joel A. Tarr).

specialty steels have a special niche), a major epoch in American industrial history had come to an end (see Figure 2.5).

Pittsburgh today is a different type of city than it had been during the industrial period. Beginning in the late 1940s public and private leaders cooperated to orchestrate the Pittsburgh Renaissance, which aimed to revitalize the downtown, improve housing and transportation, and clean up the environment. While Renaissance had many successes, since the 1980s the city has struggled to combat urban decline, fighting to stem population loss and revitalize its economy through advanced technology, educational, and medical initiatives. City and county governments along with local foundations have focused their efforts on the region's cultural and environmental assets, constructing recreational facilities along the rivers, a regional trail network, new sports stadiums, a redesigned convention center, and a lively cultural district. Manufacturing continues to decline; today, the largest manufacturing employers are the University of Pittsburgh Medical Center and the institutions of higher education. Promising are advanced technology initiatives primarily stimulated by Carnegie Mellon University and the University of Pittsburgh's expertise in computer science, robotics, tissue engineering, and biotechnology. A vigorous movement is also underway to construct "green buildings" and make Pittsburgh a more environmentally sustainable city. The heritage of steel, however, has not been forgotten. The Rivers of Steel National Heritage Area works with museums and cultural societies to generate historical tourism, preserve ethnic traditions, and commemorate Pittsburgh's prodigious industrial past. Fortunately, the art of this exhibit forever enshrines the city's industrial power.

NOTES

Edward K. Muller and Joel A. Tarr, "Pittsburgh's Industrial Corridors," in Barbara L. Jones, ed., *Born of Fire: The Valley of Work* (Pittsburgh: University of Pittsburgh Press, 2006), 15–31. The paintings mentioned in the text are part of the collections of The Westmoreland Museum of American Art (reprinted with the permission of The Westmoreland Museum of American Art).

1. Robert A. Woods, "Pittsburgh: An Interpretation of Its Growth," *Charities and the Commons* 2 (1909).

2. John R. Stilgoe, *Metropolitan Corridors: Railroads and the American Scene* (New Haven: Yale University Press, 1983), 77. Read pages 77–103 for a description of what he means.

3. Reuben Gold Thwaites, *Afloat on the Ohio: An Historical Pilgrimage of a Thousand Miles in a Skiff from Redstone to Cairo* (Chicago: Way and Williams, 1897), quoted in Dan Hughes Fuller, "Roughing It on the River: Reuben Gold Thwaites in Western Pennsylvania," *Pittsburgh History* 79 (1996): 116.

4. C. R. Van Hise, *The Conservation of the Natural Resources of the United States* (New York: Macmillan, 1910), 28.

5. Harold C. Livesay, *Andrew Carnegie and the Rise of Big Business* (Boston: Little, Brown, 1975), 116.

6. Joseph Frazier Wall, *Andrew Carnegie* (New York: Oxford University Press, 1970), 784.

7. Woods, "An Interpretation of Its Growth."

3 INDUSTRIAL SUBURBS AND THE GROWTH OF METROPOLITAN PITTSBURGH, 1870–1920

Edward K. Muller

When the fieldworkers of the now famous Pittsburgh Survey arrived in Pittsburgh in the fall of 1907 to begin their investigations, they were already aware that the city was part of a much larger metropolitan district. From a compact urban area of fewer than 100,000 people in 1850, Pittsburgh had grown into a metropolitan area of more than a million. By 1920 the metropolitan region contained between 1.3 and 1.5 million inhabitants and sprawled thirty or forty miles from downtown into six counties. Even by the US Census's more restrictive measure, Pittsburgh ranked fifth among all metropolitan districts in the nation.[1] Writing in the Survey's initial report of its findings in 1909, Robert A. Woods (head of South End House, a Boston settlement house) aptly noted that Pittsburgh's extensive metropolitan area resulted from widely dispersed industrial development, not simply residential expansion. "Pittsburgh has grown into an industrial metropolis with outlying manufacturing towns reaching along the rivers and following course of all the railroads for a distance of thirty to forty miles. The time is soon coming when all the large industries will be eliminated from the city, and Pittsburgh proper will become simply the commercial and cultural headquarters of its district."[2] Residential dormitory suburbs contributed less than 10 percent of the total metropolitan population in 1920.[3]

Survey team members also recognized that the industrial activities of this metropolitan region were interconnected. Paul U. Kellogg, editor and mastermind of the Survey, described the physical linkages in his introduction to the Survey reports. "Again, there is a temptation to define Pittsburgh in terms of the matrix in which the community is set, and the impress of this matrix on the soul of its people no less than on the senses of the visitor. Pipe lines that carry oil and gas, waterways that float an acreage of coal barges, four track rails worn bright with weighty ore cars, wires surcharged with a ruthless voltage or delicately sensitive to speech and codes, bind here a district of vast natural resources into one organic whole."[4] In addition to these largely visible transportation and communication links, the dispersed communities of this sprawling complex were bound into a metropolitan region by capital, labor markets, and the division of labor in production processes.

In this chapter I argue that in the half century after 1870, tremendous growth in manufacturing and major reorganization of production under corporate capitalism drove the spatial extension of development far beyond the traditional urban core (see Figure 3.1).[5] During the middle third of the nineteenth century, industrial expansion occurred incrementally at the city's edges with establishment of new glass and iron plants. Beginning in the 1870s, however, large integrated steelworks sprang up well beyond these contiguous locations. Other capital-intensive mass production plants—in the electrical equipment and aluminum industries, for example, which often evolved from smaller incubator origins in the city—joined the movement of steel firms out of the city. While these events manifested the workings of the product cycle, new firms with modern factories and small, traditionally organized companies also proliferated at these metropolitan locations.

Other forces contributed to the extensive sprawl of industry. Topographical barriers prevented simple incremental spatial expansion during this period of rapid growth, and widely scattered natural resources further attracted new industrial development. Speculation in real estate suitable for industry prepared sites and hastened development, while minimal governmental oversight placed few obstacles in the way of developers and industrial firms. The construction of an extensive transportation network, composed of railroads, electric streetcars, and even interurban electric railways, facilitated this dispersal of manufacturing activity and the growth of related industrial communities well before automobiles and trucks affected the metropolitan geography.

This geographical process of city building, or geographical industrialization, was more than simply centrifugal expansion from the city and new

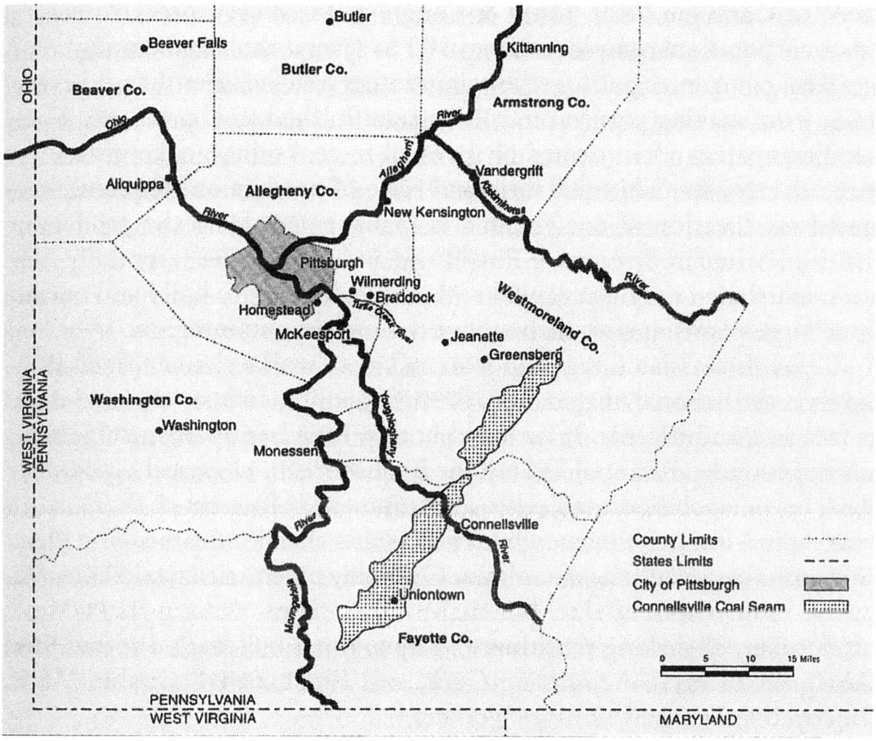

Fig. 3.1 The Pittsburgh Metropolitan Area map (courtesy of Temple University Press).

development in the suburbs. It involved the creation of a complex division of labor with multiple linkages among regional firms. Four industries formed localized production systems that, through their internal interrelationships, tied the spatially disparate regional parts into a metropolitan whole. The iron and steel, glass, and railroad equipment industries evolved into diverse complexes of large mass producers, specialized operators, subcontractors, suppliers, and servicers. This metropolitan growth of the Pittsburgh region eventually encompassed the extant Connellsville coke district, a fourth localized production system, which had initially been located beyond the metropolitan area.

PITTSBURGH BETWEEN 1850 AND 1870

By the beginning of the First World War, metropolitan Pittsburgh extended from thirty to forty miles beyond downtown, a process that had taken nearly five decades to unfold. Before this metropolitan expansion took place, new growth both increased density within already developed areas and pushed the urban margin outward a few miles. In 1850 the City of Pittsburgh was a small commercial city of around 46,000 inhabitants situated on the point of land formed by the convergence of the Monongahela and Allegheny Rivers. Hilly topography and the three rivers (the Ohio River is generally viewed as commencing at the confluence of the other two) fragmented urban development such that growth also occurred in politically distinct communities on the floodplains directly across the Monongahela and Allegheny from Pittsburgh. Vigorous iron, glass, and textile industries hugged the rivers' edges of these communities, where flat land and transportation were available. To the north across the Allegheny River, Allegheny City experienced a quickening of manufacturing after 1834, when the Pennsylvania Main Line Canal was opened within its municipal limits. In 1850 this sister city had a population of 21,262, nearly half that of the City of Pittsburgh. To the south across the Monongahela, three much smaller towns were showing signs of industrial growth, especially with coal being mined in the steep hillside that abutted their southern edges. Together South Pittsburgh, East Birmingham, and Birmingham contained only 7,239 residents. The entire urban complex formed a small compact area of approximately 75,000 residents.[6] The only urban industrial development beyond, but near, the Pittsburgh area occurred in four tiny communities along the Pennsylvania Main Line and Beaver Canals.[7]

Fueled by rapid growth in iron, glass, oil refining, and planning mill activities, the urban population doubled to more than 170,000 during the next two decades. Although larger plants and some new product lines such as blast furnaces for making pig iron were added, this round of investment did not transform the basic organization of production. Most rolling mills, foundries, crucible steelworks, and glass factories relied on long-standing craft practices, produced modest outputs, and expanded production more by addition than by technological innovation.[8] New plants were located farther away from Pittsburgh's central business district along the riverfronts. Andrew Carnegie and other ironmasters built their works eastward up the south bank of the Allegheny River, where the Pennsylvania Railroad shared the flat floodplain. In partnership with several associates, Carnegie controlled the Iron City Forge and Cyclops Iron Company (together better known as the Union Mills), which produced bar iron, railroad car forgings, plate, and structural iron shapes, the Keystone Bridge Company (customer of the Union Mills), and the huge new Lucy (iron blast) Furnace.[9] Across the Allegheny and curving down the Ohio River a short distance, Allegheny City nurtured a sizable and diverse manufacturing base.[10] Iron and glassworks multiplied along the south bank of the Monongahela River in the three communities that became the city's South Side in 1872. Henry W. Oliver and his partners operated one of the larger ironworks near Tenth Street, where they produced iron bars, plate, hardware, and wagon parts. A mile farther up the Monongahela, Benjamin F. Jones rebuilt the American Iron Works (later named Jones & Laughlin Steel) into an integrated iron mill during the 1850s and 1860s. The mill included blast furnaces across the river in Hazelwood, then an emerging suburb contiguous to Pittsburgh.[11]

Although Jones's move to integration foreshadowed events that would transform the metropolitan geography, the spatial expansion of industry before the 1870s was for the most part incremental and contiguous. Manufacturers found available land with access to water and rail transportation at the fringes of the urbanized area on the river floodplains. Plants were getting bigger but, significantly, land was not available in the topographically constrained and intensely congested commercial city without expensive acquisition and demolition costs. Even with this initial round of industrial expansion into the suburban edges, the urbanized area remained tightly clustered within three or four miles of downtown.

The adoption of steam railroads and horsecars in the 1850s and 1860s, respectively, also spurred some residential suburbanization, but there was only a little industrial development beyond the dense core of urban settlement. A few modest foundries, rolling mills, and glassworks operated at noncontiguous river sites as much as ten miles from Pittsburgh. Populations of the accompanying towns were thirty-five hundred or less. Scattered more widely around southwestern Pennsylvania were numerous small artisanal establishments and a few firms with more than twenty employees, which produced pig iron, rolled iron bars and sheet, made glass wares, or baked coal into coke.[12] Often trading in the Pittsburgh market, these operations were too far afield to be part of the urban area, however broadly conceived.

TECHNOLOGICAL CHANGE AND INDUSTRIAL SUBURBS

By the early twentieth century, capital-intensive mass production plants, often under corporately organized firms, replaced smaller traditional partnerships and craft factories as the dominant manufacturing form in the Pittsburgh area. This transformation of the region's industry and ultimately of its urban form began in the 1870s. Technological change, seen most clearly in the success of Bessemer steel production and unprecedented blast furnace outputs, introduced mass production to Pittsburgh's major industries, led to an enormous growth of manufacturing, and heightened the demand for large industrial sites. Integration of several manufacturing functions at one site, especially in the steel industry, exacerbated the pressure for land to the point that companies and real estate developers were speculatively buying up flat sites by the 1890s in anticipation of continued industrial suburbanization. Even though the search for suitable sites amid the region's rugged topography pushed industrial development well beyond the urban core, manufacturers generally concentrated along the transportation corridors of river and railroad service in a manner similar to the industrial patterns of other cities (see "Pittsburgh's Industrial Corridors" in this volume). The simultaneous development of clay, coal, and natural gas resources both hastened the spread of industry and accentuated the importance of transportation links between resources and industrial plants. The pace and pattern of this industrial metropolitanization was uneven, as different industries and resources experienced these changes at different times.

The railroad dispersed industry around Pittsburgh as much through its role as a market for iron and steel as through its being a means of enhanced accessibility. The burgeoning demand for rails, cars, equipment, and bridges after 1850 dramatically expanded the market for iron and eventually set off a search for a way to produce large quantities of inexpensive steel, especially to replace notoriously unreliable iron rails. In the 1850s and 1860s Pittsburgh ironmasters such as Benjamin Jones enlarged their ironworks so as to participate in this market, but with his close ties to the Pennsylvania Railroad, Andrew Carnegie entered the national competition to perfect the Bessemer steel process and manufacture steel rails. For the construction of an integrated Bessemer steel-rail mill, Carnegie chose in 1872 a greenfield site located nine miles from Pittsburgh at the junction of two railroads (one of them the Pennsylvania Railroad, which Carnegie anticipated would be a major customer) with the Monongahela River. The renowned Bessemer engineer Alexander L. Holley designed the works to fit the railroad so as to achieve a high-volume throughput. Within months of beginning production in 1875 the Edgar Thomson Works at Braddock became the model for the industry, pushing competitors to redesign their operations (see Figure 3.2).[13]

Although specialized and flexible batch-production operations always found niches in the regional metals industry, mass production works proliferated under the aggressive investing practices and careful coordination of Pittsburgh capitalists and financial institutions. Large plants—whether those of Carnegie Steel, Jones & Laughlin, Pittsburgh Steel, or Oliver's sprawling complex on the South Side, or several other corporations—employed from five hundred to several thousand employees. A few steel companies put together giant integrated facilities that did everything from making pig iron to rolling semifinished steel products. These same companies often owned or invested in coal mines, coke works, and iron ore reserves. This new form

Fig. 3.2 Andrew Carnegie's Edgar Thomson Steel Works (1875) was located in the mill town of Braddock and was one of the first major steelworks beyond the city and its contiguous built-up areas (photograph by Joel A. Tarr, 2010).

and scale of production frequently separated the location of ownership and management from the production site. Financiers in downtown Pittsburgh and other cities, notably New York, marshaled the huge capital resources necessary to build and operate these large plants at sites throughout the metropolitan region.

Although massive integrated iron- and steelworks characterized Pittsburgh in the national imagination, the metropolitan industrial complex was in fact vast and diverse. It included both a broad array of metalworking industries and substantial operations in aluminum, electrical equipment, glass, coke, machinery, and railroad equipment.[14] Capital-intensive mass production plants dominated in most of these industries. The plants of George Westinghouse's Air Brake and Electric Manufacturing companies and the Aluminum Company of America (ALCOA) rivaled the integrated steelworks in size, but many other firms, among them Mesta Machine (steelmaking machinery), Dravo (industrial contracting and boatbuilding), Pressed Steel Car (railroad cars), Armstrong Cork, and Pittsburgh Equitable Meter, employed a thousand or more workers.

The adoption of integrated works, mass production, and modern management led many Pittsburgh manufacturers to search for large sites with railroad and river accessibility. Some firms such as Carnegie Steel, Jones & Laughlin, and Westinghouse developed new locations beyond the city in order to modernize and expand their operations. They purchased land (usually floodplains along a waterway), designed plants to modern production standards, and sometimes built adjacent towns to house the workers. In 1890, for example, Westinghouse moved his railroad air brake factory from Pittsburgh to a site twelve miles away in the Turtle Creek valley, a tributary of the Monongahela River through which the main line of the Pennsylvania Railroad ran. Next to his modern factory and company headquarters, he built the town of Wilmerding for the workers. Four years later he moved his electrical manufacturing company from Pittsburgh into an enormous factory at a site a few miles downstream from the air brake plant.[15] In 1904 he constructed a foundry to supply castings for giant generators and an accompanying town (Trafford) immediately upstream from Wilmerding. With more than twenty thousand workers in these three plants in 1919, the Turtle Creek valley became known locally as the electric valley.[16]

In the half century since its formation before the Civil War, the Jones & Laughlin Steel Company (J&L) expanded, modernized, and reorganized its works on both sides of the Monongahela River in the City of Pittsburgh, but topography and city neighborhoods constrained further growth at these sites. Additional expansion and the construction of new mills for entry into markets not served by its Pittsburgh Works required the development of a new site. In 1905 J&L purchased a farm and dilapidated amusement park on the floodplain of the Ohio River several miles below Pittsburgh. There the company erected blast furnaces, open-hearth furnaces, and by the First World War tin, rod, wire, nail, and blooming mills. A subsidiary company laid out a town, built the houses, and sold them to J&L employees. By 1920 more than fifteen thousand people resided in the new communities of Woodlawn and Aliquippa adjacent to the Aliquippa Works.[17]

Investors attracted other firms to new communities begun as speculative industrial real estate ventures. For example, in 1894 a group of Pittsburgh investors purchased a farm on a floodplain nestled in a broad curve of the Monongahela River thirty miles south of the city. Although they correctly anticipated the expansion of the industry up the river, they resorted to financial inducements to get their development underway. Learning through personal connections that William Donner was considering moving his tin plate mill from Indiana to the Pittsburgh district, the group offered him twenty acres for free and a ten-thousand-dollar cash bonus. Donner's new plant opened in 1898, and five years later it was the largest tin plate mill in the nation. Meanwhile, the investment group formed the East Side Land Company to lay out and sell lots for an adjacent community. By the First World War their venture had become the city of Monessen (Essen on the Mon), home in addition to the tin plate mill to a foundry and machine firm, steel hoop plant, rod and wire mill, tube works, and a fully integrated steelworks employing thirty-five hundred workers in 1916. With more than eighteen thousand inhabitants, Monessen surpassed New Kensington and the county seat of Greensburg as the largest city in Westmoreland County.[18]

In some instances, the interests of the relocating firms and the real estate developers were closely allied. Originally nurtured in Pittsburgh's "strip district" along the Allegheny River adjacent to downtown (as Westinghouse and several other firms were), the Pittsburgh Reduction Company, later renamed the Aluminum Company of America (ALCOA), selected New Kensington in 1891 for the site of its modern aluminum plant. Located nearly twenty miles up the Allegheny River in Westmoreland County, New Kensington was the speculative real estate development of Pittsburgh-based Burrell Improvement Company. The new location provided access to natural gas and coal for the huge amounts of power required in aluminum manufacturing. An additional incentive for the struggling aluminum company came from Burrell Improvement, which offered four free acres of level land and a ten-thousand-dollar cash bonus. Instrumental in this deal were the Mellons, who were investors in both Pittsburgh Reduction Company and the real estate firm. Moreover, they advanced a loan to underwrite the costs of the move. In time New Kensington became the center of a small cluster of industrial towns that were home to a specialty alloy steelworks, a tin plate mill, a spring company, a window glass factory, and several smaller firms. By 1919 ALCOA alone employed twenty-four hundred workers, and the New Kensington area had grown to nearly eighteen thousand residents.[19]

While the move to mass production was the primary impetus for greenfield development at the turn of the century, management sometimes had social and political considerations as well. Pittsburgh had long been a center for the craft union movement, and the area experienced years of contentious labor relations. Some owners wished to remove plants and workers from this cauldron of labor politics by relocating to isolated communities where they could exercise more control. After a bitter strike in 1893, for example, the Apollo Iron and Steel Company relocated to a farm site almost directly across the Kiskiminetas River from its cramped Apollo Works. Here the Pittsburgh-owned company built a modern works that took advantage of the greater available space, but management also wanted to stabilize the labor force through the construction of a model industrial town, designed by Frederick Law Olmsted's well-known landscape architectural firm (see "The Olmsteds in Pittsburgh" in this volume). With an attractive plan and modern infrastructure, the company president, George G. McMurtry, hoped to encourage workers to become homeowners and turn their backs on the unions that had beleaguered the original works across the river. By 1892 more than twelve thousand people resided in the industrial communities of the Vandergrift area.[20]

Similarly, B. F. Jones Jr. and William Larimer Jones, partners and chief officers of J&L Steel, were influenced by Pittsburgh's social gospel reform movement and saw the advantage of the welfare capitalism then being instituted by their competitors such as the US Steel Corporation among others. They endeavored to establish both decent housing and a decent community for workers and their families by controlling the city-building process and dominating local institutions. Characteristically, however, such company domination of industrial communities became a two-edged sword; company policies often had both benign and pernicious effects. The police force of the Aliquippa Works, for example, worked closely with local police to enforce the company's vision of proper behavior and keep out "undesirable" people. The line between maintaining civil order and impinging on individual freedoms was blurred, and Aliquippa soon gained a reputation for being hostile to unions and union organizers.[21]

Carnegie's Homestead Works, the site of the famous violent 1892 Homestead Strike, exemplifies the political advantage of some suburban locations. A group of Carnegie's competitors originally built the mill in the early 1880s at a greenfield site along the Monongahela River in view of Carnegie's Edgar Thomson Works on the other shore, which they wished to challenge. However, poor management and a recession provided Carnegie the opportunity to buy the mill. Homestead was a short eight-mile train ride from the city. Control of the railroad station provided control over ingress and egress to the town, although management, the union, or the state militia could exercise this power, as strike events later proved. The steelworks, however, came to be located in adjacent Munhall, a municipality carved out by the company in 1910, where it built housing for management and controlled the government to its advantage. The workers mostly lived in Homestead without municipal control over either the plant or its tax revenues. Through the years both Munhall and Homestead depended on the company's largesse for many infrastructural improvements and annual maintenance.[22]

NATURAL RESOURCES AND METROPOLITAN DEVELOPMENT

Although the region's natural resources—timber, coal, iron ore, and clay—had been used since the beginning of the nineteenth century, the industrial transformation after 1870 led to the massive exploitation of coal beds, clay deposits, and oil and natural gas reserves. Small entrepreneurs, often indigenous to the resource's locality, leaped at the opportunities to supply the region's growing industries, especially with coal and coke. Large capital interests viewed these resources as one more factor of production to be controlled, exploited, or held for speculation. Pittsburgh investors such as Judge Thomas Mellon amassed hundreds of acres of coal lands throughout the metropolitan region and hired operators to mine them or left them undeveloped in order to realize profits from rising land values later.[23] Industrial firms such as Carnegie Steel, Oliver's iron and steel companies, and J&L sometimes developed their own "captive" mines, coke works, gas wells, or limestone quarries and integrated them closely with their manufacturing operations. Whether these facilities were owned by independent operators, speculators, or industrial firms, the intensive development of resource sites contributed to the sprawling character of the metropolitan region.

Clay, natural gas, and coal attracted manufacturers to sites widely scattered about the region. Clay deposits supported a sizable number of refractory brick manufacturers. Blast furnaces, various iron and steel furnaces, glass furnaces, beehive ovens for making coke, steam engines, and other high-heat apparatus all needed fire brick linings. By 1919 approximately three dozen plants employed a few thousand workers. Ceramic firms also capitalized on regional clay resources, building plants around the region to make pipe, tile, electrical fixtures, and tableware.[24]

Natural gas had its greatest impact on the glass industry. In 1880 Pittsburgh's nationally important glass industry remained concentrated on the city's South Side in fifty family owned, small batch-oriented factories. The city contained both a large number of skilled glassworkers and numerous equipment and supply firms. Beginning in the 1880s, the advantages of natural gas as a fuel and the adoption of mass production technologies led manufacturers to build large factories in the gas fields of southwestern Pennsylvania as well as beyond the metropolitan region (see "The Pittsburgh Region's First Natural Gas Boom" in this volume). In 1888, for example, prominent Pittsburgh glass manufacturers H. Sellers McKee and James Chambers purchased farmland twenty miles east of the city, where they could spread their new integrated window glass factory over thirty-five acres to accommodate continuous throughput production, enjoy access to the Pennsylvania Railroad's mainline, and obtain a steady fuel supply from nearby gas deposits. These entrepreneurs developed the property into the city of Jeannette, which with the addition of other firms grew into an important center of glass manufacturing and a community of more ten thousand in 1920. Many other sites for window, plate, and glassware manufacturing emerged around the metropolitan area. By one count, only fifteen plants remained in the city in 1902, while sixty-three plants operated in the metropolitan region.[25] Pittsburgh's last window glass factories closed in 1907, while the region retained 25 percent of the nation's capacity.[26]

Like clay and gas, coal spawned development at the site of the resource. In the first half of the century, mining occurred in Pittsburgh and the immediate environs as well as at sites scattered around the region. Most mines were small and not necessarily linked to Pittsburgh markets and capital. The situation changed dramatically after 1860. The rapid expansion of the city's iron industry in the 1860s overwhelmed the pig iron output of the rural, charcoal-fueled blast furnaces that traditionally supplied the city's rolling mills. In order to operate their own blast furnaces, Pittsburgh's ironmasters had to find a fuel other than wood charcoal, which would be chemically suitable and capable of transport to the city. Coke was already being manufactured near mines around the region, including some in Pittsburgh, for use primarily in foundries and forges because it had not proved feasible for blast furnaces. In 1860 Pittsburgh ironmasters discovered the superior qualities of coke made from coal found in a narrow forty-mile-long seam running parallel to the western front of the Allegheny Mountains between thirty and forty miles southeast of the city. This area became known as the Connellsville coke district. Connellsville area investors built 500–750 beehive ovens during the 1860s as the industry took its first tentative steps.[27]

Railroad construction into the Connellsville district and the emergence of the American steel industry, especially in Pittsburgh, transformed this rural area during the next three decades. In the 1870s the construction of huge blast furnaces in Pittsburgh to feed pig iron to the voracious Bessemer converters set off a coal rush and established the new coke industry.[28] Investors snapped up these special coal lands, opened dozens of mines, and erected thousands of beehive ovens, which baked the coal into coke and released unwanted gases into the air. More than twenty thousand ovens and ninety-four mines produced half of the nation's total coke output in 1900 (see "Searching for a Sink for an Industrial Waste" in this volume).[29]

Pittsburgh capitalists joined with indigenous Connellsville district investors to undertake and profit from the development, although the importance of Connellsville coke for American steel producers attracted capital from outside the region as well. H. C. Frick, for example, was living and working in the district when he initially entered the industry. With financial backing from Pittsburgh's Thomas Mellon and other city investors in the 1870s, he emerged as a powerful force in the coke district. A partnership with Andrew Carnegie, formed in 1881 after Frick moved his residence to Pittsburgh, provided capital to propel the H. C. Frick Coal and Coke Company to the dominant position in the coke industry. The leading figures of these two key regional industries were linked in an uneasy arrangement that led to Frick's appointment as president of Carnegie's steel empire, a position he held until the late 1890s, when they infamously parted ways.[30]

When the Connellsville coal resources began to show signs of exhaustion around the turn of the century, coal producers drifted a few miles west into the "Klondike" or Lower Connellsville area. In the peak year of 1910, operators from the two areas worked more than thirty-nine thousand beehive ovens and shipped nearly nineteen million tons of coke. Later coke operators crossed the Monongahela River to open mines with coal that could be made into suitable coke with the by-product retort technology that replaced beehive ovens.[31]

At the time of its initial exploitation around 1870, nearly thirty miles separated the Connellsville district from the Pittsburgh iron market. In subsequent decades, the development of a dense web of railroads, close capital and labor linkages, and steelworks in the middle Monongahela River valley drew the two areas tightly together both spatially and functionally. The Frick-Carnegie partnership symbolized this convergence. The Monongahela River was especially attractive to primary iron and steel producers because it knifed through the heart of the region's largest coal reserves and was close to the Connellsville district. By the First World War, iron- and steelworks occupied noncontiguous floodplain sites of this meandering river for almost thirty miles south of Pittsburgh's downtown. Monessen, for example, was as little as ten miles from the Connellsville district coke plants.

The massive development of coal and coke after 1870 spawned manufacturing opportunities in nearby towns and cities of Westmoreland and Fayette Counties. The small cities of Connellsville, Uniontown, and Greensburg thrived as centers of administration, capital, and supply for the coke district. Local foundries and machine shops produced and repaired mining cars and equipment, and a few even manufactured railroad cars for local coke firms. Railroads built spur lines throughout the coke district to service the local mines and coking plants. This rail network linked the coke areas into the Pittsburgh market and after 1880 supported the development of local metalworking firms making specialty alloy steels, steelmaking machinery, railroad equipment, pipe, valves, boilers, and plumbing supplies.[32]

THE METROPOLITAN GEOGRAPHY

Entrepreneurs in the other metropolitan counties of Beaver, Butler, and Washington similarly found market niches for their products. Together with Pittsburgh's manufacturers and those who left the city for, or originally built in, outlying industrial suburbs and satellites, they formed the nation's sixth largest urban manufacturing district in 1920 and fifth largest metropolitan area. The region's rugged hill and valley terrain inhibited simple incremental spatial expansion at the city's periphery and forced firms or investing groups to find suitable sites that were often not contiguous with the advancing edge of urban development. While Pittsburgh formed a dense urban core for the region, industrial towns and residential suburbs stretched linearly away from this core along the major meandering river valleys and the main railroads that snaked through smaller tributary stream valleys. A series of satellite cities in the surrounding counties and the industrial settings at the clay and coal resource areas completed the metropolitan pattern.

Between 1870, when the centrifugal movement of industries accelerated, and 1900 most industrial development occurred in Allegheny County. At the beginning of this period Pittsburgh had more than 90 percent of Allegheny County's population and by the most liberal definition of metropolitan 80 percent of the regional urban population.[33] In 1870 there were only six very small industrial communities outside the city in Allegheny County. By the turn of the century, there were twenty-one industrial towns and boroughs outside of Pittsburgh in the county. Another dozen or so communities in the county were residential suburbs, but they contained approximately one-quarter of the population of the industrial suburbs. Together these industrial and residential suburbs diminished the city proportion of the regional urban population to 58 percent in 1900.[34]

Industrial suburbanization burgeoned in the next two decades with an expansion of more than three hundred thousand in population. The number of industrial towns and cities with more than five thousand inhabitants nearly doubled from twenty-three to forty-five in 1920.

Seven of the cities were larger than twenty thousand. Large new steelworks opened at six towns in the Monongahela River valley, and four new ones were started in the Ohio River valley. New industrial towns with manufacturing plants established in the 1890s also grew rapidly during the early decades of the twentieth century. The aluminum and glass towns of the Allegheny River valley and the Westinghouse towns of the Turtle Creek

Table 3.1 Population Distribution of Metropolitan Pittsburgh, 1900–1920

	% Metropolitan Population	
Type of Community	**1900**	**1920**
City of Pittsburgh	58	45
Residential suburbs in Allegheny County	5	8
Industrial suburbs in Allegheny County	20	23
Industrial suburbs contiguous with Allegheny County	9	13
Satellite cities	8	11
Total metropolitan population*	**776,458**	**1,312,017**

Source: *Twelfth Census of the United States, 1900, Population* (Washington, DC, 1902), 1:329–49; *Fourteenth Census of the United States, 1920, Population* (Washington, DC, 1922), 1:586–601.

*Excluding coal-patch communities.

valley both exemplified this latter pattern. Overall, the City of Pittsburgh's share of the metropolitan population declined to 45 percent, while the proportion of population in industrial towns outside of Allegheny County rose from 17 percent to 24 percent. Although residential suburbs increased in number and size, they still were unable to match the growth of metropolitan industrial places. Dormitory suburbs made up approximately 8 percent of the metropolitan population. The complex topography notwithstanding, there was a discernible distance-decay pattern of development spreading outward from the city. The City of Pittsburgh contained 45 percent of the metropolitan population, adjacent industrial suburbs of Allegheny County added 23 percent, industrial towns contiguous to but outside Allegheny County had 13 percent, and the more distant satellite cities and towns had another 11 percent.[35]

The spatially extensive and complexly patterned geography of the Pittsburgh industrial district led to confusion among the Pittsburgh Survey fieldworkers, local politicians, and journalists as to what actually constituted the metropolitan region.[36] Were the many communities not contiguous with Pittsburgh and its adjacent urbanized areas part of it? Survey editor Paul U. Kellogg argued that "today, for most purposes, a city is a rapid transit proposition."[37] As a progressive reformer he was concerned with political consolidation for the sake of more efficient and effective municipal governance. His

Table 3.2 Town Size Distribution of Metropolitan Pittsburgh, 1900–1920

	Number of Towns	
Population Size	**1900**	**1920**
50,000+	1	1
20,000–49,999	2	7
10,000–19,999	4	6
5,000–9,999	6	21
Total number	**23**	**45**

Source: *Twelfth Census of the United States, 1900, Population* (Washington, DC, 1902), 1:329–49; *Fourteenth Census of the United States, 1920, Population* (Washington, DC, 1922), 1:586–601.

spatially restrictive perspective, one that apparently emphasized residential suburbanization, ignored the multifarious relationships that existed among the various parts of the industrial district.

METROPOLITAN INTEGRATION

What contemporaries and later historians often viewed simply as industrial decentralization in fact involved in many instances the creation or expansion of localized production systems. In Pittsburgh the rapid growth of iron and steel, glass, railroad equipment, and coke industries under corporate capitalism resulted in both integrated mass production plants and an increasing division of labor among firms, involving specialization, subcontracting, and services. As capital deepened and interdependence among firms grew, the number of participants increased, external economies from agglomeration accrued, and localized production systems formed around these industries. The flow of goods and services, capital, labor, and professional personnel through the dense transportation and communication networks among the many firms of these localized production systems tied the disparate sites of production and their communities into a metropolitan region without regard to spatial contiguity.[38]

The iron and steel industry was by far the largest localized production system of the Pittsburgh region. The seemingly self-contained character of the large integrated steelworks masked the persistence of older specialized batch producers, the division of labor, and the extent of linkages among firms. While the huge scale and dramatic technological spectacle of integrated steel mills at Braddock, Homestead, Duquesne, the South Side,

Monessen, and Aliquippa drew popular and later scholarly attention, the vast array of iron and steel activities emerged in relative obscurity. Independent mills producing wrought-iron products or mills that had switched to open-hearth steel production outnumbered and collectively outproduced the fewer integrated operations.[39] Hundreds of other firms supplied or serviced the basic iron and steel mills or used the semifinished products in their own operations. Foundries produced custom castings and steelmaking machinery. Machine shops made and repaired engines and custom-tooled machinery and parts. Other firms manufactured pipes, tubes, wire, fencing, tanks, barrels, plumbing supplies, hardware, barges, boats, and countless other items. Model and pattern makers, engineering firms, steel product distributors, scrap dealers, steel construction and fabrication firms, haulers, and many others were scattered throughout the region. The density of metalworking and metal-serving firms in the development of secondary specialties led to bridge-building and engineering firms among others of national renown. Corporate administrative offices, investment banks, and legal services took root in downtown Pittsburgh (see "Downtown Pittsburgh" in this volume). Membership in investment alliances and boards of directors overlapped and frequently changed in complicated patterns.[40] Even other local industries such as refractory bricks and the railroads were tied directly to the iron and steel complex, supplying goods and services or buying steel products.[41] The interrelationships of the numerous firms involved in this complex made up a metropolitanwide, localized production system just as surely as did the better known smaller scale garment districts of New York and Los Angeles.

The glass, railroad equipment, and coal and coke industries also displayed the scale and division of labor of localized production systems. Railroads were so pervasive throughout the region that one may easily overlook the substantial metropolitan railroad equipment and repair industry. The extension rail network involved the trunk lines of six major railroads, including the Pennsylvania and the Baltimore & Ohio; numerous feeder roads, particularly from coal mines; short lines between towns; and more than two dozen industrial switching railroads connecting separate plants of an individual firm or manufacturing plants with trunk lines. A dozen or more repair shops and switching yards, some quite large, operated around the region, employing forty-five hundred workers in 1902.[42]

This concentration of railroads, coal mines that used railroad technology, and metal manufacturers led to a sizable railroad equipment manufacturing sector. Besides the rails produced by iron and steel mills, companies in the region turned out locomotives, steel cars, air brakes, couplers, switches, signals, wheels, axles, frogs, and many other items. Both locomotive manufacturers and carmakers centered distinct clusters of suppliers in at least four locations in and outside the city, each of which employed thousands of workers. The H. K. Porter Company, for example, built narrow gauge locomotives for switching, mine hauling, logging, and other uses. Producing heavily for regional customers, H. K. Porter remained in the city along the Allegheny River, where rolling mills, wheel, spring, coupler, and other equipment makers (including Westinghouse's original companies) were concentrated. While approximately seventy-one hundred workers manufactured railroad equipment in this cluster in 1902, the Pittsburgh Locomotive Works was situated on the city's North Side amid a similar cluster of manufacturers employing nearly ten thousand workers.[43]

In 1919 more than four dozen glass manufacturers of various products operated within the region. Although many of Pittsburgh's glass firms had left for other metropolitan locations, or left the region altogether, the city continued to be important to their functioning in ways that suggest the intricate interrelations remained intact among the various components of the industry. Historian Richard O'Connor even found the city important to the window glass industry, which had entirely moved out. "Although window glass manufacturers abandoned the city proper, they found the environments of outlying areas hospitable. By locating their large, technologically advanced, firmly capitalized plants within the orbit of Pittsburgh capital, labor, and suppliers, they extended the city's sphere of influence without formerly redrawing its borders."[44]

Iron and steel as a localized production system encompassed the entire metropolitan area. Individual firms were connected physically by railroad, river, telegraph, telephone, and postal services. Capital also linked firms through emerging corporate organizations with interlocking boards, private investment banks (e.g., T. Mellon and Sons and the Union Trust Company), securities markets (e.g., the Pittsburgh Stock Exchange), and social institutions (e.g., prestigious business clubs such as the Duquesne Club and golf clubs).[45] These communication networks allowed administrative offices and investors to keep a close watch over the metropolitan plants. Owners and managers located at their plant sites also enjoyed easy access to downtown headquarters, business services, and entertainment opportunities. In 1922, in addition to electric trolleys and interurbans, 368 commuter trains ran daily between downtown Pittsburgh and the several satellite cities within a forty-mile radius, often making them less than an hour's ride from the city.[46] Even the network of trolleys tying coal patch towns of the Connellsville coke district together was linked to the broader metropolitan region through short direct routes to both McKeesport and Trafford, industrial towns only fifteen miles from Pittsburgh.[47]

Labors markets also manifested the systemic nature of regional industry. Employers and employees alike benefited from the concentration of firms in specific industries, employers from the reservoir of experienced workers and employees from the multiple job opportunities. The effects of these links were not always beneficial, however. Steelworkers feared blacklisting by employers, who commonly used the tactic to intimidate labor. Unions understood that part of their leverage lay in their ability to affect production at proximate and interconnected facilities. The 1892 Homestead Strike failed in part because Carnegie was able to keep his other local plants at Braddock, Duquesne, and Pittsburgh operating.[48] In 1916 Westinghouse Electric's striking machinists first attempted to close down other Westinghouse plants in the Turtle Creek valley and elsewhere in the region with some success. When they then marched down the valley, hoping to paralyze Carnegie's steelworks at Braddock, violence broke out. Because mill managers anticipated the strikers' strategy, the Braddock works thwarted the maneuver and production continued uninterrupted. Fighting the United Mine Workers at their own (captive) mines, US Steel justifiably feared that their miners would traverse the dozen or so miles to their Clairton steelworks to disrupt operations there.[49]

THE MODERN CITY

In his seminal 1933 study, *The Metropolitan Community*, sociologist R. D. McKenzie observed that the modern metropolitan region encompassed an unprecedented amount of territory and obtained "its unity through territorial differentiation of specialized functions," the speed and intensity of communication, and the interdependence of these functions.[50] He believed that the far-flung metropolitan community resulted from the regional integration provided by automobile and truck transportation and electronic communication in everyday life after the First World War. "Under present conditions of local transportation," he wrote, "the population residing within a radius of thirty to forty miles of a large city may be considered as within direct contact with its institutions and services and therefore in a sense might well be included as inhabitants of the city's metropolitan district."[51]

It is clear, however, that both the centrifugal spread of industry and the development of localized production systems between 1870 and 1920 created a sprawling and highly interdependent metropolitan region in parts of several counties of southwestern Pennsylvania before widespread adoption of motor vehicles. The Pittsburgh district, as contemporaries called it, presented a complex urban landscape with a large dominant central city surrounded by proximate residential suburbs, mill towns, small satellite cities, and hundreds of mining patch towns. Although ambiguities of census definitions and the realities of land use defy precise measurement, residential suburbanization certainly took a backseat to the centrifugal impetus of industry in forming Pittsburgh's metropolitan geography.[52] While commuters used steam railroads and horsecars to push the margins of contiguous urban development incrementally into the surrounding countryside, the region's financiers, speculators, and industrialists aggressively developed infrastructure, natural resources, and hospitable floodplain sites well beyond the city's limits (see essays of Section III in this volume). Between 1870 and 1900 their actions erected the outlines of a vast industrial metropolitan region, which would be filled in during the next few decades of sustained growth.[53] The city simply could not contain the requirements of the new industrial order of mass production, corporate organization, rapid communication and movement, and labor control. The region's distribution of natural resources and difficult topography accentuated the spatial sprawl of Pittsburgh's industrial development. Yet, as can be seen in other cities with simpler, more level topographies, the sheer magnitude of industrial growth and the profitability of speculative real estate development would still have created a complex metropolitan district that cannot be adequately described or explained by traditional views of suburbanization.

NOTES

Reprinted by permission of the publisher from Robert Lewis, ed., *Manufactured Suburbs: Building Work and Home on the Metropolitan Fringe* (Philadelphia, PA: Temple University Press, 2004), 124–42; with minor revisions from the *Journal of Historical Geography* 27, no.1 (2001): 58–73, by permission of Academic Press.

1. In 1920 the US Census Bureau defined a metropolitan district as follows: "In the case of each city having within its own boundaries 200,000 inhabitants or more, there has been delimited what may be termed a 'metropolitan district,' which includes, in addition to the city itself, only those sections of the adjacent territory [the suburban territory within ten miles of the city boundaries] which may be considered as urban in character." US Census, *Fourteenth Census of the United States, 1920, Population I* (Washington, DC: Government Printing Office, 1921–1923), 62–70.

2. R. Woods, "Pittsburgh: An Interpretation of Its Growth," *Charities and the Commons* 21 (1909): 531.

3. In this chapter the term "residential suburbs" refers to municipalities that are largely dormitory communities of Pittsburgh and part of the built up and contiguous urbanized area. "Industrial towns" are the municipalities centered on one or more manufacturing

firms within their boundaries or in adjacent municipalities. "Satellite cities" are industrial and commercial municipalities beyond the built up contiguous urbanized area.

4. P. Kellogg, "The Pittsburgh Survey," *Charities and the Commons* 21 (1909): 519.

5. The focus in this chapter is on the metropolitan dimensions of this urban industrial growth. For a discussion including the broader regional character of this growth beyond the metropolitan district, see E. K. Muller, "Metropolis and Region: A Framework for Enquiry into Western Pennsylvania," in S. Hays, ed., *City at the Point: Essays on the Social History of Pittsburgh* (Pittsburgh, 1989), 181–211.

6. Pittsburgh annexed the South Side communities in 1872 and Allegheny City in 1907.

7. J. Holmberg, "The Industrializing Community: Pittsburgh, 1850–1880" (PhD diss., University of Pittsburgh, 1981), and US Census, *Seventh Census of the United States, 1850: Manuscript Schedules of Manufactures: Allegheny, Beaver, Butler, Fayette, Washington, and Westmoreland Counties* (National Archives, microfilm).

8. J. Ingham, *Making Iron and Steel: Independent Mills in Pittsburgh, 1820–1920* (Columbus, OH, 1991), 21–46; H. Livesay, *Andrew Carnegie and the Rise of Big Business* (Boston, 1975), 77–90; P. Temin, *Iron and Steel in Nineteenth Century America* (Cambridge, 1964), 99–121; F. Couvares, *The Remaking of Pittsburgh: Class and Culture in an Industrializing City, 1877–1919* (Albany, 1984), 9–30.

9. J. Bridge, *The Inside History of the Carnegie Steel Company: A Romance of Millions* (1903; repr., Pittsburgh, 1991), 1–60; J. Wall, *Andrew Carnegie* (1970; repr., Pittsburgh, 1989), 227–306.

10. When Allegheny City, by far the largest of Pittsburgh's adjacent towns, was annexed by the city in 1907, it became known as the North Side.

11. Ingham, *Making Iron and Steel*, 30–32. While Hazelwood was then a suburb, its contiguity with Pittsburgh and annexation by the city in 1868 made it part of the pre-1870 industrial pattern. J. Tarr and D. DiPasquale, "The Mill Town in the Industrial City: Pittsburgh's Hazelwood," *Urbanism Past and Present* 7 (1982): 2; Henry Oliver Evans, *Iron Pioneer: Henry W. Oliver, 1840–1904* (New York, 1942), 22, 28–29, 33, 38–42; Ingham, *Making Iron and Steel*, 80–82.

12. Holmberg, "Industrializing Community"; J. Tarr, *Transportation Innovation and Changing Spatial Patterns in Pittsburgh, 1850–1934* (Chicago: Public Works Historical Society, 1978); US Census, *Ninth Census of the United States, 1870: Manuscript Schedules of Manufactures: Westmoreland County* (National Archives, microfilm).

13. Temin, *Iron and Steel*, 125–74; Wall, *Andrew Carnegie*, 307–30.

14. A. D. Chandler, *The Invisible Hand: The Managerial Revolution in American Business* (Cambridge, 1977), 258–69; Ingham, *Making Iron and Steel*, 47–95, 128–56; D. Meyer, "The Rise of the Industrial Metropolis: The Myth and the Reality," *Social Forces* 68 (1990): 731–52; J. Stilgoe, *Metropolitan Corridor: Railroads and the American Scene* (New Haven: 1983), 74–103.

15. The town that grew up around the Westinghouse Electric Manufacturing Company was named East Pittsburgh.

16. *The Third Industrial Directory of Pennsylvania, 1919* (Harrisburg, 1920), 527, 533; A. Warren, *George Westinghouse, 1846–1914: A Tribute* (n.p., 1914), 27–28.

17. D. Wollman and D. Inman, *Portraits in Steel: An Illustrated History of Jones & Laughlin Steel Corporation* (Kent, OH, 1999), 53–83.

18. M. Magda, *Monessen: Industrial Boomtown and Steel Community, 1898 to 1980* (Harrisburg, 1985), 3–16.

19. G. D. Smith, *From Monopoly to Competition: The Transformation of Alcoa, 1888–1986* (Cambridge, 1988), 30–32; C. Carr, *ALCOA: An American Enterprise* (New York, 1952), 42–43; G. Fitzsimons and K. Rose, eds., *Westmoreland County, Pennsylvania: An Inventory of Historic Engineering and Industrial Sites* (Washington, DC, 1994), 221–22; *Third Industrial Directory*, 1087–88.

20. A. Mosher, *Capital's Utopia: Vandergrift, Pennsylvania, 1855–1916* (Baltimore: Johns Hopkins University Press, 2004); A. Mosher, "'Something Better than the Best': Industrial Restructuring, George McMurtry, and the Creation of the Model Industrial Town of Vandergrift, Pennsylvania, 1883–1901," *Annals of the Association of American Geographers* 85 (1995): 84–107.

21. Wollman and Inman, *Portraits in Steel*, 64–79; D. Brody, *Steelworkers in America: The Nonunion Era* (New York, 1960), 123, 231.

22. P. Krause, *The Battle for Homestead, 1880–1892: Politics, Culture, and Steel* (Pittsburgh, 1992); M. Byington, *Homestead: The Households of a Mill Town* (New York, 1910), 12–32.

23. T. Mellon, *Thomas Mellon and His Times* (Pittsburgh, 1994).

24. E. Muller, "Westmoreland County Historical Overview," in Fitzsimons and Rose, *Westmoreland County*, 18–19: *Third Industrial Directory*.

25. These data were prepared by researchers at the Historical Society of Western Pennsylvania for a 1998 exhibit on glass manufacturing entitled "Glasstown, U.S. A."; Anne Madarasz, *Glass: Shattering Notions* (Pittsburgh: 1998).

26. R. O'Connor, "The Window Glass Industry and the Expansion of the Pittsburgh Metropolitan Area, 1880–1910" (unpublished paper, Pittsburgh, 1994).

27. K. Warren, *Wealth, Waste, and Alienation: Growth and Decline in the Connellsville Coke Industry* (Pittsburgh, 2001), 1–24.

28. Temin, *Iron and Steel*, 51–98; Warren, *Wealth, Waste, and Alienation*, 25–30.

29. J. Enman, "The Relationship of Coal Mining and Coke Making to the Distribution of Population Agglomeration in the Connellsville (Pennsylvania) Beehive Coke Region" (PhD diss., University of Pittsburgh, 1962); K. Warren, "The Business Career of Henry Clay Frick," *Pittsburgh History* 73 (1990): 3–15; Warren, *Wealth, Waste, and Alienation*, 263; F. Quivik, "The Connellsville Coke Region: A Report by the Historic American Engineering Record with Emphasis on H. C. Frick Coke Company" (Washington, DC, unpublished paper, 1992).

30. Livesay, *Andrew Carnegie*, 119–82; Wall, *Andrew Carnegie*, 478–536, 714–64; K. Warren, *Triumphant Capitalism: Henry Clay Frick and the Industrial Transformation of America* (Pittsburgh, 1996), 22–51.

31. Warren, *Wealth, Waste, and Alienation*, 263; Quivik, "Connellsville Coke Region."

32. Warren, *Wealth, Waste, and Alienation*, 195–203; Muller, "Westmoreland County Historical Overview," 5–7, 14–15.

33. The City of Pittsburgh's boundaries for these calculations are consistent with its 1907 boundaries after its last major annexation. The city added a few small municipalities in the 1920s. Despite active annexation between the 1840s and the early 1900s, the Pittsburgh region's central city remained a relatively small proportion of the metropolitan area in comparison to cities of similar sizes across the nation. This fact reflects both minimal annexations after 1907, when suburban communities refused to be absorbed, and the vast

extent of the city's industrial suburbs. See G. McLaughlin, *Growth of American Manufacturing Areas: A Comparative Analysis with Special Emphasis on Trends in the Pittsburgh District* (Pittsburgh, 1938), 129.

34. *Ninth Census*, 243–56; *Twelfth Census of the United States, 1900* (Washington, DC: Government Printing Office, 1902–1906), 329–49.

35. *Twelfth Census*, 329–49; *Fourteenth Census*, 586–601.

36. E. Muller, "The Pittsburgh Survey and 'Greater Pittsburgh': A Muddled Metropolitan Geography," in M. Greenwald and M. Anderson, eds., *Pittsburgh Surveyed: Social Science and Social Reform in the Early Twentieth Century* (Pittsburgh, 1996), 69–87.

37. Paul U. Kellogg, "The Civic Responsibilities of Democracy in an Industrial District," *Charities and the Commons* 21 (1909): 630.

38. E. Muller, "Industrial Complexes in Metropolitan Formation, 1870–10920" (unpublished paper, University of Pittsburgh, 1994); A. Scott, *Metropolis: From the Division of Labor to Urban Form* (Berkeley, 1988), 33–38, 61–63.

39. Ingham, *Making Iron and Steel*, 140–51.

40. J. Ingham, *Iron Barons: A Social Analysis of an American Urban Elite* (Westport, 1978); Ingham, *Making Iron and Steel.*

41. *Third Industrial Directory.*

42. D. Hounshell, M. Samber, and J. Tarr, "Technology and Transformation: The Railroad as a Shaper of Regional Space, Natural Resources, Industrial Practice, and Economic Development in Pittsburgh, 1830s–1920" (unpublished paper, Carnegie Mellon University, 1994), 25.

43. Hounshell, Samber, and Tarr, "Technology and Transformation," 47–54.

44. O'Connor, "Window Glass Industry," 28.

45. M. Samber, "Networks of Capital: Creating and Maintaining a Regional Industrial Economy in Pittsburgh, 1865–1919" (PhD diss., Carnegie Mellon University, 1995).

46. W. Schusler, "The Economic Position of Railroad Commuter Service in the Pittsburgh District: Its History, Present, and Future" (PhD diss., University of Pittsburgh, 1958).

47. Quivik, "Connellsville Coke Region."

48. Brody, *Steelworkers in America*, 50–79.

49. D. Jardini, "In the Footsteps of the Giant: Industrialization of the Lower Connellsville Coke Region" (unpublished paper, Carnegie Mellon University, 1994).

50. R. D. McKenzie, *The Metropolitan Community* (New York, 1933), 71.

51. McKenzie, *Metropolitan Community*, 45.

52. For the definition of yet another kind of suburban community in the period, including one in the Pittsburgh metropolitan area, see J. Borchert, "Residential City Suburbs," *Journal of Urban History* 22 (1996): 283–307.

53. After the Second World War, expressways, explosive residential and commercial growth, and corporate research and development campuses accelerated suburbanization into the 1960s when the region's metropolitan total population stalled and then began a long decline. Even with the population decline, suburbanization continued. See K. James, "Public Policy and the Postwar Suburbanization of Pittsburgh" (PhD diss., Carnegie Mellon University, 2005); Patrick Vitale, "The Atomic Capital of the World: Technoscience, Suburbanization, and the Remaking of Pittsburgh during the Cold War" (PhD diss., University of Toronto, 2013).

4 PITTSBURGH'S THREE RIVERS

FROM INDUSTRIAL INFRASTRUCTURE TO ENVIRONMENTAL ASSETS

Edward K. Muller and Joel A. Tarr
with Timothy M. Collins

Like most river cities in Europe and America, Pittsburgh has looked upon its three principal rivers—the Allegheny, Monongahela, and Ohio—as an invaluable natural resource to be used in support of economic development and everyday life. These urban rivers have always been as much a part of Pittsburgh's infrastructure as its roads, railroads, mass transportation lines, and electrical grids. For decades many of the natural aspects of these river systems vanished or were subsumed by human actions. Despite these dramatic changes, the natural systems adapted, survived, and now flourish once again as part of a new vision for the region's future.

Over the course of more than two centuries, the city has forged very different relationships with its rivers, corresponding with three distinct periods of economic life. During its initial one hundred years or so, Pittsburgh depended on the rivers for transporting the trade that was its lifeblood, but it only lightly and ineffectively attempted to manage them physically. The city's headlong embrace of industrialism, commencing around the mid-nineteenth century, radically transformed the rivers' hydrology and ecology. In order to serve the needs of rapid industrial and urban growth, Pittsburgh elites sought to regulate the rivers' flow, shape their banks, and augment the flat floodplain lands. They also used the rivers' water for both household and industrial consumption and waste disposal. In so doing, in this second period they conceived of the rivers as an integral part of the city's infrastructure. The rivers were harnessed, managed, and rationalized for the smooth functioning of the city and its industrial machine.

Turning the rivers into water infrastructure had negative consequences for their ecological systems as well as for public health and safety. A "second" or "industrial" riverine nature evolved as a result of the altered hydrology and massive pollutants that degraded water quality and greatly diminished the diversity and abundance of flora and fauna. In the first half of the twentieth century, progressive reformers sought through additional engineering and conservation measures to mitigate the most hazardous conditions for human existence resulting from water pollution and flooding. The subsequent improvements in water quality, especially after the mid-twentieth century, gradually awakened renewed interest in the possibilities of recreational and scenic uses of the rivers.

Federal water quality laws in the 1970s and the massive collapse of the region's traditional industries in the 1980s, however, provided the major factors making it possible for Pittsburgh, once again, to rethink its relationship to the rivers. Recognizing the recent and impressive revitalization of waterfronts in many American cities, Pittsburgh civic leaders came to view the rivers as providing valuable scenic and recreational amenities that could be part of a new regional development strategy. Others in the community have begun to advocate the restoration and preservation of a riverine ecology more like its preindustrial state. In this view the rivers, the river lands, and the air comprise a public commons, as they did before industrialization. Thus, even though amenity and restoration goals sometimes could come into conflict, together they promise an evolving third riverine nature as an environmental infrastructure for the region's future.

THE RIVERS BEFORE INDUSTRIALIZATION

Flying into Pittsburgh today, a traveler readily spots from the airplane the region's outstanding physical feature—the convergence of two broad rivers to form a third even larger river. At this junction, the tall buildings of Pittsburgh's downtown rise up from a small peninsula formed by the joining of the Allegheny and Monongahela Rivers. These skyscrapers stand like sentinels over the Ohio River, as it begins its journey westward for nearly one thousand miles to the Mississippi River.[1] Far to the south the sources of the Monongahela lie in the Appalachian Mountains of West Virginia. The Tygart and West Fork Rivers come down from the mountains and join at Fairmont, West Virginia, to form the Monongahela, which leisurely flows northward for 128 miles to Pittsburgh. In contrast, the more swiftly flowing Allegheny River begins in the mountains of north central Pennsylvania and flows briefly north and westward into New York state before turning southwest for 325 miles through western Pennsylvania for its meeting with the Monongahela. These three rivers and the point of land they create comprise the physical framework around which the Pittsburgh region developed. Three secondary rivers—the Beaver, Kiskiminetas, and Youghiogheny—as well as dozens of tributary streams, creeks, or runs augment this riverine structure.[2]

Before the invasion of Western Pennsylvania by French and English military expeditions, traders, and colonists, these rivers and their valleys were occupied at different times by various tribes of Amerindians, including the Delaware, the Shawnee, and several tribes from the Iroquois nation.[3] By the turn of the nineteenth century, settlers with the assistance of the US Army had largely pushed the various tribes out of the region's heart and taken over the land. The rivers, as they existed in nature, supplied the primary organizational framework for this new settlement, providing a transport corridor in drought-free years, an abundance of fish, and fertile land in the floodplains. Moreover, the location at the head of the Ohio River presented the young city of Pittsburgh the opportunity to be the commercial gateway to the newly settling midwestern frontier. Thus, the three rivers were both central to the city's economic function and aspirations and an integral part of people's everyday lives.[4]

Despite their critical role in supporting Pittsburgh's economy, the rivers presented serious impediments to commercial navigation. Water was an ideal surface to travel upon, but the fluctuations in flow, dangerous snags and boulders, treacherous riffles, and shifting sandbars all limited commercial uses. At the urging of politically connected local residents, both the state and federal governments funded modest attempts to clear the rivers of obstacles and deepen the channels. They contracted private companies to dynamite rocks in riffles, remove flotsam and jetsam, and establish small "wing" dams to ensure minimum depth for transport. However, these efforts to physically manage the rivers produced only minimal improvements by the end of the Civil War.[5] One solution was to create a network of canals that regulated water flow in separate, often parallel waterways. Among the many miles of canalized waterways constructed by the state, the most important was the 1834 Pennsylvania Main Line system, a combination of inclined plane, railroad, and canal extending from Philadelphia to Pittsburgh. For almost twenty years Pittsburgh's commercial life benefited enormously from this awkward system as it snaked into the city along the northern floodplain of the

FIG. 4.1 Water Street (Monongahela) Wharf in the 1890s, showing deforested Mount Washington across the river (Pittsburgh City Photographer Collection, courtesy of the Archives Service Center, University of Pittsburgh).

Allegheny River. The commercial value of Monongahela River traffic, especially coal, persuaded the state of Pennsylvania to commission the Monongahela Navigation Company in the mid-1840s to develop the first dams and locks between Pittsburgh and the West Virginia State Line. This modestly successful slack-water venture established privatized toll navigation.[6]

The rivers fulfilled essential functions for the young city, such as providing water for households and industry and a sink for municipal sewage, storm water, and the waste of commerce and industry. Pittsburgh residents used the rivers for recreation and coped annually with the cleanup required by spring and fall floods that inundated low-lying neighborhoods. As urban development emerged on the banks of the Allegheny and Monongahela across from the city at the Point, private companies erected bridges to replace the slower, less reliable ferries. As a result of the city's growth in the first half of the nineteenth century, the wooded banks of all three rivers gave way to wharves, docks, and other infrastructure that aided mercantile sales, commercial navigation, and early industries.[7] Nevertheless, the human impact on the natural ecosystem was still limited (see Figure 4.1).

THE TRANSFORMATION TO URBAN INDUSTRIAL INFRASTRUCTURE

When the Pennsylvania Railroad brought the first rail service to Pittsburgh in 1852, the role of the three rivers, as well as the civic leaders' conception of them, underwent a dramatic and long-term shift. Pittsburgh's commercial dream as a transportation gateway servicing westward migration and commerce via its canals and rivers was destroyed. The city, however, soon reinvented itself and its relationship to the rivers as part of the massive industrialization and concomitant rapid urban growth that transformed the region. Civic leaders increasingly conceived of the rivers as essential infrastructure for industrial production and urban development. As infrastructure, engineers shaped and controlled the rivers to fit the needs of industry and the city.

Industrialization supplanted the city's river-based mercantilism in the three-quarters of a century following the railroad's arrival. The most intensive development occurred in the iron and steel and regional coal and coke industries. After 1875 the explosive growth of the mass production steel industry most defined the city's industrial transformation. Industrialists sited their large mills on the broad river floodplains nestled within the sweeping river meanders with railroad tracks running along the landward side of the mill (see "Pittsburgh's Industrial Corridors" in this volume). Other capital-intensive mass production plants in glass, railroad equipment, aluminum, food processing, and electrical equipment industries, to name the most prominent, also spread out to sites stretching along the three rivers floodplain for thirty or forty miles from the Pittsburgh Point. By providing cheap transportation for fuel supplies from the region's coalfields and for other natural resources such as timber and oil, the rivers played a critical role in the region's industrialization.[8]

Although the total number of people and vessels engaged in commercial river traffic shrank steadily during the remainder of the century, the actual tonnage of goods shipped along the rivers increased dramatically. Bulk commodities, like oil, sand, gravel and especially coal, along with some finished iron and steel products, dominated this traffic (see Figure 4.2). With the end of the Civil War, the US Army Corp of Engineers took over management of the rivers from private interests and the state. Reshaping them into stable, manageable infrastructure systems had significant economic returns for commercial traffic since each additional six inches of channel depth allowed boats and barges to increase their cargo by seventy tons. Under pressure from Ohio valley business interests, Congress in 1875 authorized the construction of locks and dams for the Ohio River. Significant river traffic improvement resulting from the Davis Island Lock and Dam, located five miles below the Point, intensified political pressure for the "canalization" of the entire three rivers system. By the turn of the century locks had been completed down to

Fig. 4.2 Coal Barges on the Monongahela River near the Point, 1932 (Pittsburgh City Photographer Collection, courtesy of the Archives Service Center, University of Pittsburgh).

Marietta, Ohio, and up both the Allegheny and Monongahela Rivers. The Army Corps of Engineers finally completed the Ohio River system to Cairo, Illinois, in 1929. The now completely engineered rivers consisted of a series of pools with navigation channels maintained measuring from six to nine feet deep.[9]

Controlled river flow and the concomitant growth of industry along the riverfronts changed the river edges nearly as dramatically as the rivers themselves had been altered. The new "pools" permanently raised water levels, drowning previous mud flats and establishing new riverbanks. Industries constructed wooden and cement bulkheads for river terminals and flood control. They built large round mooring cells; sprinkled the banks with cranes, conveyor belts, and loading chutes; and added water intake and waste discharge pipes. Some companies extended and heightened the banks with extensive fill, much of it slag from the iron and steel mills, and even closed back channels to nearby islands. Boatbuilding firms erected launching facilities, and repair yards extended along the banks in several places. Shanty boats, sunken watercraft, and abandoned barges littered the river edges and banks. Railroads lined the riverfronts as well, and in many places steep hillsides narrowed the floodplains so that only the railroads occupied them.[10]

Both municipalities and industries used prodigious amounts of water. They pumped water for household consumption and industrial production and discharged wastewater contaminated with human and industrial wastes back into the rivers. Writing in 1912 N. S. Sprague, superintendent of the Pittsburgh Bureau of Construction, observed that, "Rivers are the natural and logical drains and are formed for the purpose of carrying the wastes to the sea."[11] No more succinct statement could be made about the attitude of most municipal officials and industrial leaders toward Pittsburgh's rivers for the years from 1850 to 1940. This position was codified into administrative law for Pittsburgh in 1923 when the Pennsylvania Sanitary Water Board created a classification system that designated streams into three categories for municipal and industrial users. This system classified streams as ones relatively clean and pure, streams in which pollution existed but could be controlled, and streams so polluted they could not be used as public water supplies without treatment or for fishing or recreational purposes. The latter streams could continue to be used for the discharge of untreated wastes—that is, as open sewers. Pittsburgh's three rivers fell into this last classification.[12]

Pollution flows into Pittsburgh's rivers were of three principal kinds: municipal sewage, industrial wastewater, and mine acid drainage. Cumulatively, they all degraded stream quality, although their effects differed somewhat in regard to public health and stream ecology. From the point of view of acute public health effects, municipal sewage had the most devastating effect.

Beginning in the second quarter of the nineteenth century, Pittsburghers drew their water supply largely from the nearby rivers, although some working-class areas continued to depend on groundwater and pumps into the twentieth century. By 1915 the City of Pittsburgh's system had grown to 743 miles of distribution pipes.[13] The provision of running water to households and the mass adoption of water using appliances such as sinks, showers, and water closets benefited households in many ways, but they also exacerbated the problem of wastewater disposal.

During most of the nineteenth century Pittsburghers placed household wastes and wastewater in cesspools and privy vaults, not in sewers. They continued this practice even after the availability of running water greatly increased the volume of wastewater. In 1881, for instance, about four thousand of the city's sixty-five hundred water closets were connected to privy vaults and cesspools with only about fifteen hundred linked to street sewers

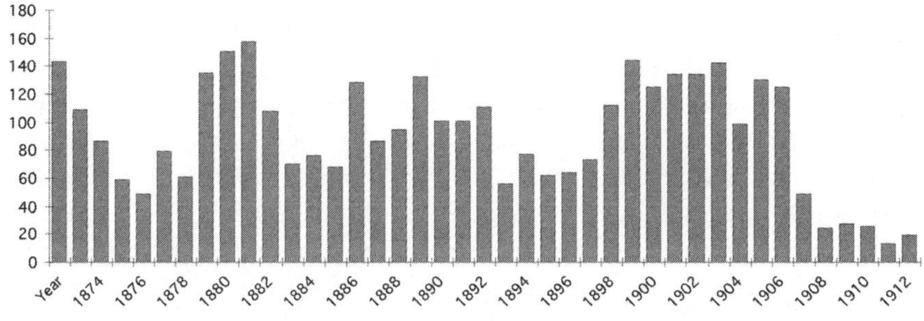

CHART 4.1 Typhoid Death Rates in Pittsburgh, 1870–1912 (Erwin E. Lanpher and C. F. Drake, *City of Pittsburgh: Its Water Works and Typhoid Fever Statistics* [Pittsburgh: City of Pittsburgh, 1930], 23–25).

that the city had begun constructing at mid-century. Overflowing privies were a constant nuisance, noted the Pittsburgh Board of Health, and presented the city with a major health issue.

Such conditions raised the possibility of epidemics from infectious disease and highlighted the need for improved sanitation and construction of a sewage system. Beginning in the 1880s a fierce debate ensued between engineers and physicians concerning whether the sewer system should be a separate system carrying only household and some industrial wastes or a combined system that could accommodate both wastewater and storm water in one pipe. The engineers triumphed, and the city began constructing a combined sewer system, building over 412 miles of combined sewers between 1889 and 1912. The design decision had large implications for future river water quality.[14]

Like other cities Pittsburgh discharged its untreated sewage from public sewer outlets (145 of them) directly into neighboring waterways, on the theory that running water purified itself and diluted and dispelled the wastes. Simultaneously, upstream communities were also building sewers and discharging their wastes into the same rivers. By 1900, more than 350,000 inhabitants in 75 upstream municipalities discharged their untreated sewage into the Allegheny River, the river that provided drinking water for most of the City of Pittsburgh's population. Even some of Pittsburgh's own sewers discharged into the river at locations above its water supply intake pumping stations. The resulting pollution gave Pittsburgh the highest death rate from typhoid fever of the nation's large cities—well over 100 deaths per 100,000 people from 1873 to 1907. In contrast, in 1905, the average death rate for northern cities was 35 per 100,000 persons (see Chart 4.1).[15]

Concerned over the growing typhoid mortality and morbidity rates, several professional groups and the Pittsburgh Ladies Health Protective Association formed a citizens' joint commission in the 1890s to study the question of water pollution and water quality. Their 1894 report found that Pittsburgh and Allegheny City water supplies were "not only not up to a proper standard of potable water but . . . actually pernicious" and recommended filtering the water supply of both cities. In 1896, following this report, the mayor appointed the Pittsburgh Filtration Commission, which made a similar recommendation. In December 1907 after several years of delay caused by political infighting and technical issues, the water department delivered the first filtered water to the city. Pittsburgh thus joined cities such as Philadelphia and Cincinnati that took their water from their neighboring rivers and filtered it, while cities such as Boston and New York chose to rely upon supplies from a protected watershed. Pittsburgh's typhoid rates immediately began to decline; and by 1912, after chlorination of the water supply, its typhoid death rate dropped to the level of the national average for large cities.[16]

Water filtration provided one safety net in regard to protection from polluted water, but many sanitarians and public health physicians believed that a second safety net—sewage treatment—was required for maximum protection. In 1905, responding to a severe typhoid epidemic, the Pennsylvania legislature passed the Pure Waters Act "to preserve the purity of the waters of the State for the protection of the public health." It forbade the discharge by new municipal systems of any untreated sewage into state waterways. While it permitted cities already discharging to continue the practice, it required them to secure a permit from the state commissioner of health if they wished to extend their systems.

In the beginning of 1910 Pittsburgh asked the Pennsylvania Department of Health to grant a permit allowing it to extend its sewerage system, thus creating a confrontation with the state agency. The department, then headed by Dr. Samuel G. Dixon, a follower of the New Public Health doctrine, responded by requesting a "comprehensive sewerage plan for the collection and disposal of all of the sewage of the municipality" before it would grant the permit. In addition, the department argued that, in order to attain efficient treatment, the city should consider changing from the combined sewer system to the separate system.

The municipality responded to Dixon's order by hiring the nationally renowned engineering firm of Allen Hazen and George C. Whipple to act as consultants to study the issue. In their 1912 report, Hazen and Whipple argued that a Pittsburgh sewage treatment plant would not free the downstream towns either from threats to their water supplies or from the need to filter them, since other communities would continue to discharge raw sewage into the rivers. The method of disposal by dilution in the rivers, they maintained, sufficed to prevent nuisances, particularly if storage reservoirs were constructed upstream from Pittsburgh to augment flow during periods of low stream volume. Thus rivers would continue to serve as sinks for urban wastes.[17]

Health Commissioner Dixon found the Hazen and Whipple report an insufficient response to his original request for a long-range plan for a comprehensive regional sewerage system, but most members of the engineering community agreed with its premises. The issue for them consisted of costs and the avoidance of nuisance, but for Dixon there was a larger question of developing "a campaign in order that the streams shall not become stinking sewers and culture beds for pathogenic organisms." Given the political context, however, and the financial limitations upon the city, Dixon had no realistic means by which to enforce his order. In 1913 he capitulated and issued Pittsburgh a temporary discharge permit, thus continuing the use of Pittsburgh's rivers as open sewers.[18]

While agitation for sewage treatment had been building, another major river pollutant, mine acid, escaped regulation. Other industrial pollutants were also problems, but the sulfuric acidic discharge from coal mines was the most ecologically damaging water contaminant in the industrial history of western Pennsylvania. Mine acid destroyed fish life, altered the flora along small streams and in major rivers, caused millions of dollars' worth of damages to domestic and industrial water users, and enlarged the costs of water and sewage treatment.[19]

The economic importance of coal production in southwestern Pennsylvania impeded attempts by government to counter the burden of acid mine drainage. The coal industry argued that no "suitable" method existed for the treatment of mine water. In addition, the courts had granted the industry legal protection in the infamous 1886 case of *Pennsylvania Coal Company v. Sanderson and Wife*, which concerned the destruction by mine acid of the water supplies of a farm near Scranton, Pennsylvania. In this case the Pennsylvania Supreme Court maintained that "the right to mine coal is not a nuisance in itself," and that the acidic substances entered the stream via natural forces that were beyond company control. The justices also noted the economic importance of the coal industry, arguing, "the trifling inconvenience to particular persons must sometimes give way to the necessities of a great community." In 1905, when the Pennsylvania legislature passed the Purity of Waters Act, it specifically exempted "waters pumped or flowing from coal mines," as it did again in 1937 in the Clean Streams Act.[20]

In general, therefore, as reflected in the failure to regulate sewage disposal and mine acid, the three rivers and their river valleys throughout the Pittsburgh industrial region had become and remained industrial infrastructure, both engineered and utilitarian. They had been so altered by the 1920s that few older residents would have recognized the rivers they had experienced a half century earlier.

REFORMING INDUSTRIAL NATURE

The rapid growth and unbridled development of the Pittsburgh region left in its wake a number of social, political, and environmental problems that many early twentieth-century Pittsburghers believed threatened the city's civic order and long-term economic welfare. As with the nation as a whole, local progressive reformers viewed improving the built and natural environments as a means to uplift the society's moral character and health conditions as well as to create a more efficient and successful business community. Although often emphasizing different aspects of the reform agenda, both voluntary citizens' groups such as the Civic Club of Allegheny County and business organizations like the Chamber of Commerce agreed on the importance of addressing problems associated with the rivers and the riverfronts. Never challenging the primacy of business prerogatives and private property rights, these reform efforts did represent a modification of the prevailing philosophy that the rivers were industrial infrastructure, which was consistent with progressive reform and the conservation movement then gaining power at the national level. Pittsburgh's elites increasingly participated in national networks where they encountered movements to conserve forest resources and watersheds, preserve land for parks, and adopt urban planning.

Following the disastrous flood of 1907 and the threat of another flood a year later (see Figure 4.3), the Pittsburgh Chamber of Commerce appointed the Flood Commission of Pittsburgh, chaired by an industrialist, H. J. Heinz, and comprised of representatives from local government, reform groups, and business organizations as well as men with engineering expertise. The commission hired an executive director who identified with national concerns for planned watershed development. In its massive technical report published four years later, the commission projected both locally pragmatic thinking and a regional conservation vision. Predicting that continued urban industrial development and clear-cut logging in the mountainous watersheds of the Allegheny and Monongahela Rivers would exacerbate the frequency and intensity of flooding, the commission called for building a flood wall to protect downtown, filling in back channels of islands near the

FIG. 4.3 The flood of 1907 was the most devastating in the history of the city to that time. (Pittsburgh City Photographer Collection, courtesy of the Archives Service Center, University of Pittsburgh).

city's center, creating seventeen regional impoundment reservoirs, and establishing forest preserves in the headwater areas. Although it had success in getting the federal government to purchase land for reforestation in the upper watersheds, mirroring President Theodore Roosevelt's and his chief forester Gifford Pinchot's forest conservation triumphs, the Flood Commission ran into a protracted struggle with Congress and federal agencies. In particular, the Army Corps of Engineers resisted broadening its mandate to manage inland rivers for more than navigational purposes. Only successive years of drought, economic depression, and the ruinous floods of 1936 and 1937 impelled local and federal leaders to prevail on Congress to authorize a comprehensive flood control program.[21]

At the same time as the Flood Commission tackled its work, civic leaders contracted with the landscape architect Frederick Law Olmsted Jr. to prepare a plan for Pittsburgh. His work focused primarily on issues of traffic congestion and future highway development, but in his 1910 report Olmsted also lamented the dilapidated condition of downtown riverfront lands and urged the city to rethink their possibilities (see "In spite of the river ought to be a Pittsburgh town-slogan: Riverfront Planning in Pittsburgh, 1900s–1970s" in this volume). He advocated modernization of the Monongahela Wharf cargo handling facilities, incorrectly predicting a resurgence of general merchandise business on the rivers, and he also envisioned the industrial rivers as a potential amenity for their picturesque qualities. Thus, with several European cities in mind, he pictured promenades and overlooks above the waterfronts, which would coexist with an expanded roadway to channel traffic rapidly around the periphery of the congested downtown. The Boston planner tapped into an ongoing discussion of recovering the land where the three rivers converged for a symbolic park and monument at this historical and geographical inception point of the city. Reminiscent of the various plans for the preservation of open spaces and river lands in Boston, Olmsted also suggested the preservation of several undeveloped tributary stream valleys for parks.[22]

For the next three decades Olmsted's successors in planning for Pittsburgh kept these ideas for the waterfronts alive in one form or another, but the industrial and infrastructural utility of the rivers and riverfront lands foreclosed their implementation. In 1923, for example, a subcommittee on waterways of the Citizens Committee on City Planning (CCCP), an elite voluntary group that put forth a city plan in six parts, summed up the business community's view of the rivers as infrastructure when it reported: "navigation interests have a prior right to the use of those portions of the City's water front which can be advantageously used for water transportation, and that no encroachments should be permitted thereon which will interfere with such activities."[23] The subcommittee recommended the development of several rail-to-river terminals on the waterfronts in and around downtown.

A few decades into the century, civic leaders still wished to manage the rivers for flood control and city planners envisioned the redesign of some riverfront lands, but other reformers and conservationists continued to worry about the disposal of waste in the rivers and the resulting public health questions. They refocused their energies on water quality issues. Although by 1934 the drinking water supplies of 80 percent of the state's population were treated, 85 percent of Pennsylvania waterways suffered from various degrees of degradation from raw sewage and industrial wastes. For instance, only 18 percent of the sewage was treated, from a population of 920,000 in the Allegheny River basin—the river from which the City of Pittsburgh drew most of its water supply. Sewage from Pittsburgh and other communities overwhelmed the oxidation capacity of the streams, creating offensive sights and smells on the rivers. Gross pollution levels in streams impacted the public health; and while water treatment had sharply reduced typhoid deaths, diarrhea and enteritis death rates remained elevated. Fish were absent from long dead stretches of the rivers, and chemical pollution fouled the taste of many drinking water supplies. In addition, mine acid drainage increased the costs of water filtration for Pittsburgh residents.[24]

By the end of the 1930s, these conditions had substantially increased the number of advocates of clean streams. Conservationists, notably outdoor sportsmen's groups, were especially active in demanding environmental improvements. In 1937 the Pennsylvania General Assembly passed the Clean Streams Act, giving the Sanitary Water Board power to issue and enforce waste treatment orders to all municipalities and most industries except for acid drainage from coal mines. In 1944 the Sanitary Board announced comprehensive plans to reduce pollution of Pennsylvania streams, requiring all municipalities to treat their sewage "to a primary degree." The following year the board issued orders to the City of Pittsburgh and 101 other municipalities, as well as to more than 90 Allegheny County industries, to cease the discharge of untreated wastes into the state waterways.

The state authorized the formation of the Allegheny County Sanitary Authority (ALCOSAN) in 1946, but negotiations dragged on for several years because of political complications. On October 1, 1958, ALCOSAN's centralized, activated sludge treatment plant located on the northern bank of the Ohio River below the Pittsburgh Point finally began treating the wastewater of Pittsburgh and eighty-one county boroughs and towns. A major step had finally been taken to improve the water quality of Pittsburgh's rivers.[25]

THE PITTSBURGH RENAISSANCE AND THE RIVERS

Despite Pittsburgh's economic revival during the Second World War, after years of depression, civic leaders feared that peace would return the city to the relatively declining industrial prospects, which it had experienced since 1920. These concerns for retaining existing firms and attracting new companies, especially ones that diversified the region's industrial base, dominated the postwar civic agenda. In 1945 Pittsburgh initiated a twenty-five-year redevelopment program, its so-called Renaissance, under the leadership of the civic leader Richard King Mellon, Mayor David Lawrence, and the newly formed Allegheny Conference on Community Development, a nonprofit civic organization dominated by the presidents of the largest corporations. Renaissance addressed issues of economic development, renewal of infrastructure, and downtown redevelopment. By 1960 the national media heralded the revitalization of the Smoky City. Even the three rivers received some attention from Renaissance. Besides completing sewage treatment facilities and flood control measures, the city cleared the railroad yards, warehouses, and last remaining dingy residences from the historic Point and undertook the construction of a state park there, which invited contemplation of both the beauty of the water and the historical significance of the three rivers' confluence. Moreover, recreational boating began to return to the city's waters.[26]

These steps toward the rehabilitation of the rivers, however, proved to be relatively small ones. The flood protection program only expanded management of the rivers, which had begun in the nineteenth century. Despite Olmsted's dreams, prewar plans of pragmatic planners to use downtown's waterfronts for highways and parking lots were completed during the Renaissance. The continued disposal into the rivers of industrial wastes, mine acid drainage, and sewage from the overflow pipes of the combined sewer system of Pittsburgh and other county municipalities kept the rivers from making a dramatic ecological recovery.[27]

In the 1970s the failure to exploit the ambient and public relations potential of the rivers for two major developments demonstrated the persistent grip of the industrial nature mentality on the perceptions of civic leaders. Despite its name and location across the Ohio River from the historic Point, the enclosed circular Three Rivers Stadium, which opened in 1970 and became a nationally recognizable sports venue because of the professional baseball and football teams' successes, did not even provide a view of either the rivers or the downtown. Similarly, the new Convention Center, opened in 1977, had its rear and loading docks facing toward the Allegheny River.[28] Even the region's principal conservation organization, which emerged in concert with the growing national movement for the preservation of wilderness lands, abjured the city's three rivers. The elite-sponsored Western Pennsylvania Conservancy, which became active and increasingly powerful after the Second World War, mostly protected river environments either well beyond the urban area or on the metropolitan fringe.[29]

Based on the Renaissance's successful smoke abatement program, new sewage treatment facility, flood control project, and preservation efforts beyond the urban region, the city proudly claimed the mantle of a leader of the national environmental movement in the 1960s. But a 1959 plan for the riverfronts belied this assertion, at least as far as the rivers were concerned. The planners noted that Renaissance had neglected the conservation of the rivers and riverfronts. They recommended several opportunities for riverfront parks and river-oriented recreational opportunities. Nevertheless, they still argued that "most of the flat land adjacent to the rivers must continue to be occupied by the industry and commerce which support the City." At best they hoped to "balance" the diverse interests in the rivers, because "the rivers can provide an additional opportunity for recreation without detracting anything from industry."[30] Thus, despite the dramatic post–World War Renaissance program, city leaders retained the long-standing conception of the three rivers as being engineered, infrastructural systems for industry and urban development. Conservation strategies since early in the twentieth century had only ameliorated the worst health consequences of this conception and marginally improved water quality and some riverfront lands.

REINVENTING THE RIVERS AS ENVIRONMENTAL INFRASTRUCTURE

The dramatic collapse of Pittsburgh's industrial base in the last quarter of the twentieth century forced a reconceptualization of the city's economic and social life, including the three rivers' role in that future. Although at the time it seemed as though civic leaders were slow to rethink the city's relationship to the rivers, in fact they began to develop a new understanding in little more than a decade. After initially scrambling to attract any job-providing businesses to former industrial sites, civic leaders, some developers, and community activists envisioned the rivers for scenic, recreational, and natural amenities that would give Pittsburgh a better quality of life and, thereby, make it more attractive to new businesses, especially advanced technology firms and the professionals they employ. This revised conception of the rivers repositioned them as a key component, once again, of the region's economic development strategy. But, as this view became generally accepted, a new tension surfaced between environmentalists and municipal boosters as growing appeals for the restoration and preservation of river ecosystems potentially conflicted with development that sought to exploit scenic and recreational possibilities.

In the late 1970s earlier predictions of absolute decline in Pittsburgh's industrial base began to come true. By the early 1980s older steel mills, factories, and coal mines were shuttered permanently, leaving the region in crisis. Seemingly all at once, thousands of acres of once industrially vital riverfront land turned into vacant and often polluted brownfields, commercial river traffic plummeted, and river infrastructure fell into disuse. Under intense pressure to replace the loss of many thousands of manufacturing jobs with new sources of employment, civic leaders cast about for all kinds of development opportunities and governmental support. Pittsburgh's weakened economy and rustbelt image, the real and perceived toxic condition of brownfields, the outdated character of the industrial areas' highway network, and the lack of any unified development strategy among the region's many local governments all stymied new investment, especially on the older industrial riverfronts.[31] This failure ironically saved these critical sites from

Fig. 4.4 Riverfront trail, new buildings, and construction on Washington's Landing, formerly industrial Herr's Island, 2005 (photograph by Joel A. Tarr).

the prospect of redevelopment without adequate consideration of the rivers' potential in the "new" Pittsburgh.

Although generally met with polite indifference by civic leaders, several studies by governmental agencies and nonprofit organizations in the 1980s explored the use of the rivers for raising the region's quality of life. Most Pittsburghers dismissed the recommendations of these reports as impractical and elitist because of the region's cascading under- and unemployment that spelled hard times for thousands of families. Nevertheless, a few new riverfront projects indicated that the rivers might become popular with the public and eventually investors, just as waterfront developments had already demonstrated in Baltimore, Portland (Oregon), and several other American cities. A small public boat launching ramp and linear park along the city's South Side riverbank attracted hordes of weekend boaters. The new high-profile annual River Regatta, punctuated by Formula One speed boat races, drew large crowds. A marina, riverfront park, and hiking and biking trail similarly enlivened the tired, small industrial city of McKeesport several miles south of Pittsburgh, while a water slide amusement park flourished

FIG. 4.5 Riverfront steps and recreational amenities of redeveloped central riverfronts, 2013 (photograph by Joel A. Tarr).

on the edge of a riverfront brownfield in rundown West Homestead, which formerly housed a massive industrial machinery works. Finally, a small sculpture park and office development called Allegheny Landing spruced up the riverfront across from downtown on that river's north shore.[32]

By the early 1990s the attitudes of investors and public officials toward the development prospects of the riverfronts for scenic and recreational opportunities had clearly shifted. The successful redevelopment of an old industrial island named Washington's Landing located a couple of miles above downtown in the Allegheny River—into a complex of offices, light industry, a large marina, and townhouses with a circumferential walking and biking trail overlooking the water—proved the point of those who promoted the importance of the rivers for the region's future (see Figure 4.4). Recreational boating replete with marinas and yacht clubs proliferated throughout the river valleys. The revival of rowing added another dimension to river participation, while river tours and commercial party boats attracted other clienteles. Most importantly, in direct contrast to the 1970s' neglect of the rivers, civic leaders grasped the idea of turning the north shore of the Allegheny River across from downtown into a signature development dependent on the river ambience (see Figure 4.5). The North Shore Corridor, as it has been called, featured two new stadiums (one each for baseball and football) now oriented toward the river with views of downtown. ALCOA built its new headquarters along the river. The city is currently supporting the development of offices, entertainment venues, retail shops, and residences there as well. On the south (downtown) bank of the Allegheny, the newly rebuilt and enlarged "green" Convention Center was reoriented to face the river scene. The adjacent Cultural District that has been emerging for over twenty years contributed to the North Shore Corridor with new buildings, signage, and lighting as well as a linear park along the river's edge. A group of civic leaders and foundations formed the Riverlife Task Force, which conceived of a Three Rivers Park of public spaces along the city's central riverfronts. The Riverlife Task Force takes it upon itself to steward the development of these public spaces, coordinating with private developers and public agencies as well as negotiating for appropriate designs.[33]

Not all development of riverfront brownfields, however, has taken advantage of their river location. For example, the new development on the former massive Homestead Steel Works, stretching nearly three miles along the Monongahela about eight miles from Pittsburgh, generally ignores the river despite its name as The Waterfront. The developers designed the complex as a suburban-style retail, restaurant, and office mall. Only a walking trail on the riverbank, some townhouses, and a few restaurants and office buildings face the river.[34]

The collapse of industry and the freeing of the rivers from many industrial uses, along with state and federal clean water regulations, have markedly improved both water quality and the river ecology. Biologists have determined that in the past "the Ohio River Drainage basin was so grossly degraded that these systems were [nearly] devoid of life."[35] The ecological recovery has been surprisingly rapid and extensive. Fish have returned to the rivers. In one recent study of fish in tributaries to the three rivers, twenty-nine species were discovered in streams flowing to the Allegheny, sixteen species in tributaries to the Monongahela, and thirty-two species in a tributary to the Ohio River. This significant recovery has sportsmen, environmentalists, and the Pennsylvania State Fish and Boat Commission employees cooperating to bring the first Bass Master Classic fishing tournament to Pittsburgh.[36]

The woody vegetation of the region's riverbanks was also severely degraded, but like the fisheries woody plants have vigorously returned to the once bare and eroded edges. A recent study of the Monongahela and Allegheny Rivers identified the existence of four native woody plant communities and one native herbaceous plant community typical of large rivers in North

America. It also determined that the frequency of invasive species decreases with distance from the city's Point.[37] This rapid regeneration of riparian vegetation has taken observers by surprise. Organizations concerned with riverine ecology such as the Friends of the Riverfront, the Pennsylvania Environmental Council, 3 Rivers 2nd Nature, and the Western Pennsylvania Field Institute have held several workshops on the rivers to discuss the creation of water trails and in the process have discovered local hotbeds of natural diversity. For instance, Sycamore Island, a large wooded island in the Allegheny River nine miles from downtown Pittsburgh, has few sycamores today but hosts a forest of silver maples of such significant girth and height that people seeing photographs taken in the middle of the grove assume the setting is in a national forest.

The ability of the rivers and streams to support life and the return of typical riparian vegetation reveal a natural potential that has been dormant for over a century and suggest the possibility for human intervention to aid the process. Planning for the restoration of riverine natural systems is appearing on several regional sites. The US Army Corps of Engineers, for example, is engaged in the process of restoring an urban stream, Nine Mile Run. The stream flows from creeks that have long been buried in sewer pipes and from springs in a city park, through a three-hundred-acre reclaimed brownfield site, and into the Monongahela River.[38] Additional plans and actions are underway to restore, conserve, and preserve natural systems. Recent river restoration studies by the US Army Corps of Engineers, river-island studies by the Fish and Wildlife Service, and river-land conservation by the Allegheny Land Trust reveal the gathering shift in thinking from the traditional conservation of the hinterlands to the conservation and restoration of land along the region's most industrialized waterways.[39]

Ecological restoration faces difficulties in spite of the remarkable recovery of natural systems. Riverine ecological systems encounter wet-weather water quality threats because of outdated sewage systems and the highest number of combined sewer outfalls in the country. Continued outbursts of mine acid also endanger ecological rejuvenation. Some of Pittsburgh's forested hills and slopes near the rivers are once again under consideration for rezoning for development. These proposals include the construction of an expressway through four Monongahela riverfront communities that would affect two miles of reforested waterfront, the longest contiguous natural edge in the central Pittsburgh pool. Clearly, the old development values still tug at Pittsburghers, even as natural systems have begun regenerating in the brief twenty-year respite from intense industrial use.

Despite these obstacles, the ecological recovery has spawned a growing interest in the aesthetics of river viewing. Public spaces with panoramic river views from vantage points such as walkways, bridges, hills, parks, or boats out on the water itself create highly desirable opportunities for looking at the rivers, their recovering banks and hillsides. Real estate developers are erecting townhouses on private property with a water view as a means to capture the increasing economic value created by this aesthetic. Thus, this panoramic aesthetic enhances the city's intention to be become known for the ability to play in, on, and along the rivers and riverbanks.

The postindustrial view of nature emphasizing preservation and restoration of riverine ecologies, however, clashes at times with development that leverages the rivers' recreational and scenic attributes. Intensive housing and office complexes, manicured landscaping of the banks, and noisy, high-speed boating roiling the river waters all contrast with the aesthetic of ecological preservation. Rowers and power boaters uneasily share the water, birdwatchers despair at the highly managed vegetation of developers' complexes, and commercial shipping still retains navigational priority.

The concepts of the environment as both an amenity and an ecological aesthetic depend on a physical, sensual relationship to place, appealing to fashionable values of youth and an active healthy life outside of work. Clean healthy rivers with green edges and trails, it is argued, help with a healthy lifestyle. Both concepts in their distinct ways depend on continued management of the three rivers. Both together, despite their inherent contradictions, have become critical environmental infrastructure that is essential for the Pittsburgh region to compete with other regions.

URBAN RIVERS

Throughout the city's history, Pittsburgh's civic leaders defined the rivers with respect to the three periods of its economic life. These three periods of the relationship between the city and its rivers conform generally with the experiences of other American river cities. Although the timing and specifics vary, Pittsburgh's river story also resonates with those of many European cities. The experiences of older industrial cities such as Newcastle upon Tyne in England closely parallel that of Pittsburgh, but even the relationship between Paris and the Seine River, as suggested by Isabelle Backouche, shares many of the same general characteristics.[40] Like Pittsburgh's three rivers, the Seine supported multiple functions and the "ordinary" life of Parisians until the late eighteenth century. After 1760 business elites and government officials increasingly regulated and reshaped this famous river in service of a "monofunctional" vision of it as a national trade artery in an industrializing economy. Slowly the Seine became a "stranger" to residents, writes Backouche, though not to tourists. Thus, in the minds of European and North American leaders who wielded decision-making power, rivers became highly regulated and engineered infrastructure in the service of urban industrial development. Completing the unlikely comparison between Pittsburgh and France's capital city, Parisian leaders in recent years have tried to reconnect the river to the lives of their citizens in the spirit of making the Seine part of public space once again.

In some ways the segments of rivers that flow through urban areas share many characteristics with their country cousins. Farmers, loggers, millers, and country merchants also looked upon rivers as natural resources that were critical to their economic enterprises; and, if need be, these rural entrepreneurs endeavored to regulate and manage them with, for example, dams or diversion canals. Managed as they may be, these rivers in the countryside generally were not as intensively managed and exploited as the urban segments, where greater waste loads, hardening of edges, and landfilling often drastically altered the natural systems.[41]

This intense intervention in urban rivers such as in the Pittsburgh region readily invites a historical interpretation that emphasizes the now familiar dichotomy between nature and culture.[42] While increasingly discredited in academic literature, this dichotomy existed in public perceptions. For most Pittsburgh residents up until recently, the highly engineered three rivers no longer seemed like "real" rivers. Just as Backouche so poignantly characterizes the Seine as becoming a "stranger" to Parisians, the three rivers became inaccessible and unusable to ordinary Pittsburghers. Humans—that is, business and political leaders—had so degraded both water quality and the flora and fauna in pursuit of their urban industrial vision that most citizens no longer thought of the rivers as part of nature. As infrastructure, the rivers might as well have been buried in culverts or concrete channels to do their job. In the search for nature's scenic and recreational amenities, Pittsburghers left the city for rural rivers or more distant water bodies. This industrial nature was "unnatural."[43]

Today the ecological rejuvenation of the three rivers and their rediscovery as part of the public commons depends ironically on the continued regulation and management by those with the power to make policy, effect development, and enforce laws. The return to the rivers' "natural systems" of the preindustrial era is, of course, no less a cultural construct than was the "second nature" existing during the industrialization of the rivers. As the environmental historian William Cronon noted, nature "is a profoundly human construction . . . the way we describe and understand [it] is so entangled with our own values and assumptions that the two can never be fully separated."[44] The return to preindustrial or so-called first nature will be only partially a return to that state. The continued existence of some aspects of the industrial river infrastructure such as the locks and dams, the legacy of other alterations such as dredging for sand and gravel or the hardened embankments, and the presence of invasive species will prevent the complete restoration of the earlier river hydrology and ecology. Further, the pressure for development, even some river friendly recreational and residential projects, will introduce highly managed landscapes. Nonetheless, the three rivers as conceived and shaped by humans will continue to be part of Pittsburgh's definition of itself.

NOTES

Reprinted with permission from Christof Mauch and Thomas Zeller, eds., *Rivers in History: Perspectives on Waterways in Europe and North America* (Pittsburgh, PA: University of Pittsburgh Press, 2008), 41–62.

1. Edward K. Muller, "The Point," in Donald G. Janelle, ed., *Geographical Sketches of North America* (New York, 1992), 231–34.

2. David J. Cuff et al., *The Atlas of Pennsylvania* (Philadelphia, 1989), 52–67. Some have questioned whether there are in fact three rivers, arguing that the Allegheny and the Ohio are one river, which the Monongahela joins. However, ever since Europeans explored this region, most people have viewed these as three separate rivers.

3. Paul A. W. Wallace, *Indians in Pennsylvania* (Harrisburg, 1993).

4. Leland D. Baldwin, *Pittsburgh: The Story of a City, 1750–1865* (Pittsburgh, 1937).

5. Shera A. Moxley, *From Rivers to Lakes: Engineering Pittsburgh's Three Rivers, a Report for 3 Rivers 2nd Nature* (STUDIO for Creative Inquiry, Carnegie Mellon University, Pittsburgh, 2001), 18; Leland R. Johnson, *The Headwaters District: A History of the Pittsburgh District, U.S. Army Corps of Engineers* (Washington, DC, 1978), 1–101.

6. Catherine Elizabeth Reiser, *Pittsburgh's Commercial Development, 1800–1850* (Harrisburg, PA, 1951); Richard C. Wade, *The Urban Frontier: Pioneer Life in Early Pittsburgh, Cincinnati, Lexington, Louisville, and St. Louis* (Chicago, 1959), 39–46.

7. See Edward K. Muller, "River City," in Joel A. Tarr, ed., *Devastation and Renewal: The Environmental History of Pittsburgh and Its Region* (Pittsburgh, 2003), 45–51.

8. John. N. Ingham, *Making of Iron and Steel: Independent Mills in Pittsburgh, 1820–1920* (Columbus, OH, 1991).

9. Moxley, *From Rivers to Lakes*, 10–25; Leland R. Johnson, *The Davis Island Lock and Dam 1870–1922* (Pittsburgh, 1985).

10. Muller, "River City," 51–56; Edward K. Muller and Joel A. Tarr, "The Interaction of Natural and Built Environments in the Pittsburgh Landscape," in Tarr, ed., *Devastation and Renewal*, 11–40, and in this volume.

11. Quoted in Joel A. Tarr and Terry F. Yosie, "Critical Decisions in Pittsburgh Water and Wastewater Treatment," in Tarr, ed., *Devastation and Renewal.* 10.

12. Tarr and Yosie, "Critical Decisions," 10.

13. Erwin E. Lanpher and C. F. Drake, *City of Pittsburgh: Its Water Works and Typhoid Fever Statistics* (Pittsburgh, 1930), 23–25.

14. Tarr and Yosie, "Critical Decisions."

15. Tarr and Yosie, "Critical Decisions."

16. Tarr and Yosie, "Critical Decisions."Allegheny City was a separate city directly across the Allegheny River from Pittsburgh until it was annexed by its larger sister city in 1907.

17. Tarr and Yosie, "Critical Decisions."

18. Tarr and Yosie, "Critical Decisions."

19. Nicholas Casner, "Acid Mine Drainage and Pittsburgh's Water Quality," in Tarr, *Devastation and Renewal*, 89–109.

20. Casner, "Acid Mine Drainage."

21. *Report of the Flood Commission of Pittsburgh, Penna* (Pittsburgh, 1912); Roland M. Smith, "The Politics of Pittsburgh Flood Control, 1908–1936," *Pennsylvania History* 42 (1975): 5–24.

22. Frederick Law Olmsted Jr., *Main Thoroughfares and the Downtown District* (Pittsburgh, 1911), 19–30; John F. Bauman and Edward K. Muller, *Before Renaissance: Planning in Pittsburgh, 1889–1943* (Pittsburgh: University of Pittsburgh Press, 2006), ch. 3.

23. Citizens Committee on City Plan of Pittsburgh (hereafter CCCP), *Waterways: A Part of The Pittsburgh Plan*, Report No. 6 (Pittsburgh, 1923), 13–15.

24. Tarr and Yosie, "Critical Decisions."

25. Tarr and Yosie, "Critical Decisions."

26. Roy Lubove, *Twentieth-Century Pittsburgh, Vol. 1: Government, Business, and Environmental Change* (1969; repr., Pittsburgh, 1995),106–41; Shelby Stewman and Joel A. Tarr, "Four Decades of Public-Private Partnerships in Pittsburgh," in R. Scott Fosler and Renee A. Berger, eds., *Public-Private Partnerships in American Cities* (Lexington, MA, 1982), 59–127; Sherie R. Mershon, "Corporate Social Responsibility and Urban Revitalization: The Allegheny Conference on Community Development, 1943–1968" (PhD diss., Carnegie Mellon University, 2000); Roland M. Smith, "The Politics of Pittsburgh Flood Control, 1936–1960," *Pennsylvania History* 44 (1977): 3–24; Robert C. Alberts, *The Shaping of the Point: Pittsburgh's Renaissance Park* (Pittsburgh, 1980).

27. Muller, "River City," 57–63.

28. Roy Lubove, *Twentieth-Century Pittsburgh, Vol. 2: The Post-Steel Era* (Pittsburgh, 1996), 201–2.

29. *50 Years of the Western Pennsylvania Conservancy* (Pittsburgh, 1982), 19.

30. Griswold, Winters, and Swain, *A Master Plan for the Development of Riverfronts and Hillsides in the City of Pittsburgh* (Pittsburgh, 1959), dedication, 3–5.

31. Edgar M. Hoover, *Economic Study of the Pittsburgh Region*, 3 vols. (Pittsburgh, 1963); John P. Hoerr, *And the Wolf Finally Came: The Decline of the American Steel Industry* (Pittsburgh 1988); Lubove *Twentieth-Century Pittsburgh, Vol. 2*, 5–23.

32. Lubove, *Twentieth-Century Pittsburgh, Vol. 2*, 5–23.

33. Riverlife Task Force, *A Vision Plan for Pittsburgh's Riverfronts* (Pittsburgh, 2001). See also www.riverlifetaskforce.org.

34. Muller, "River City," 62–63.

35. Robert Hoskins, Michael Koryak, and Linda Stafford, *Fishes of Small Tributaries to the Rivers of Allegheny County*, 2004 Water Quality Report, 3 Rivers 2nd Nature, STUDIO for Creative Inquiry, Carnegie Mellon University (Pittsburgh, 2004), Section II, a.

36. Robert Hoskins, Michael Koryak, et al., "The Impact of Above Grade Sewerline

Crossing on the Distribution and Abundance of Fishes in Recovering Small Urban Streams of the Upper Ohio River Valley," *Journal of Freshwater Ecology* 16 (2001): 594.

37. Susan Kalisz and Jessica Dunn, *3 Rivers 2nd Nature Terrestrial Report: Allegheny River Phase 3—2002, Riverbank Vegetation*, 3 River 2nd Nature, STUDIO for Creative Inquiry, Carnegie Mellon University (Pittsburgh, 2002), 1; Pennsylvania Economy League, *Investing in Clean Water: A Report by the Southwestern Pennsylvania Water and Sewer Infrastructure Project Steering Committee* (Pittsburgh, 2002). Attempts to resolve the mine acid problem included state and federal mine sealing programs, but they had only limited success. It would not be until state and federal legislation was passed requiring active mining operations to treat polluted water prior to discharge that conditions improved. See Casner, "Acid Mine Drainage"; J. Ackerman, "Mount Washington Residents Question Development Plans," *Pittsburgh Post Gazette*, May 29, 2003, http://www.posgazette.com/neigh_city/20030529hillsidec5.asp; T. Barnes, "Council OKs Mining Project as Precursor to Hays Development," *Pittsburgh Post Gazette*, July 31, 2003, 34.

38. L. Hawkins, *Nine Mile Run, Allegheny County, Pennsylvania*, US Army Corps of Engineers, http://www.lrp.usace.army.mil/pm/9mile.htm.e.com/neigh_city/2003 0731miningc2.asp.

39. US Army Corps of Engineers, *Ohio River Main Stem Systems Study (ORMSS) Interim Feasibility Report: Ohio River Ecosystem Restoration Program*(2000), http://www.lrl.usace.army.mil/pd/orms_eco_system/ecosystem_final_report/Appendix_G.pdf; US Fish and Wildlife Service, *Ohio River Islands, National Wildlife Refuge* (undated),

http://northeast.fws.gov/planning/ORI_WEB/chap1.htm; Allegheny Land Trust, *Allegheny Land Trust Acquires 212 Acre Riverfront Property* (2003), http://www.alleghenylandtrust.org/WhetzelPreserve.html.

40. Dieter Schott, "Rivers as Urban Environments: Cycles and Constellations in the Management and Perception of British Cities" (paper delivered at "The Making of European Contemporary Cities: An Environmental History," Third International Round-Table on Urban Environmental History of the Nineteenth and Twentieth Centuries, University of Siena, June 24–27, 2004), 89–96; Isabelle Backouche, "From a Parisian River to a National Waterway: Social Changes of the Seine River," in Christof Mauch and Thomas Zeller, eds., *Rivers in History: Designing and Conceiving Waterways in Europe and North America* (Oxford, 2005), 26–40.

41. For a comparison of rural and urban river development, see Susan Q. Stanching, *Susquehanna: River of Dreams* (Baltimore, 1993); Ari Kelman, *A River and Its City: The Nature of Landscape in New Orleans* (Berkeley, 2003). For an extreme example of an urban river, see Blake Gumprecht, *The Los Angeles River: Its Life, Death and Possible Rebirth* (Baltimore, 1999).

42. Eva Jakobsson, "How Do Historians of Technology and Environmental History Conceive Rivers," lecture delivered at "Rivers in History: Designing and Conceiving Waterways in Europe and North America," conference, December 4–7, 2003, German Historical Institute, Washington, DC.

43. Edward K. Muller, "The Legacy of Industrial Rivers," *Pittsburgh History* 72 (1989): 46–75.

44. William Cronon, "Introduction: In Search of Nature," in William Cronon, ed., *Uncommon Ground: Toward Reinventing Nature* (New York, 1995), 25.

II TRANSPORTATION AND THE RISE OF THE MODERN CITY

Throughout the history of Pittsburgh the city's inhabitants have utilized different forms of transportation. These choices were shaped by the technology that was available, policy decisions, topographical and socioeconomic variables, and value preferences. The period from approximately 1850 to 1900 was marked by rapid changes in the modes available as Pittsburgh changed gradually from a walking to a networked city. By the turn of the century networks providing water, sewage disposal, manufactured and natural gas, electricity, telephone, and telegraph as well as railed transportation systems were essential parts of the city's infrastructure. The first two chapters in this section focus on the development of transportation networks and explore their effects from the perspective of spatial change, population and housing growth and distribution, economic development, and topography. Increasingly after the first decade or so of the twentieth century, Pittsburgh was impacted by the development and spread of the automobile and the infrastructure devoted to its use. The third chapter in this section explores the changes produced by this technology, including its disruption of historical uses of streets by pedestrians as well as by other vehicles. The final chapter examines the attempt by the city's powerful public-private coalition in the 1960s to radically alter public transportation with the so-called Skybus innovation. Skybus was a driverless rubber-tired vehicle on an elevated concrete runway that would have run from downtown to the South Hills and simultaneously jumpstart a regional mass transportation industry. Political opposition blocked the innovation, however, leading to the present public transport system composed of buses, busways, and a light rail system that runs below ground in the downtown and above ground for most of the rest of its route.

In the past, as these chapters reveal, the city has been shaped by both construction and rejection of different forms of transportation innovations. Today the city is again debating various types of multimodal transportation infrastructure including autonomous vehicles, bus rapid transit systems, and proliferation of bicycle paths, The outcome of these debates may again present the city, as in its past experiences with changes in modes of transportation, with the prospect of a major reshaping of its built environment.

5 THE OMNIBUS, COMMUTER RAILROAD, AND HORSECAR

WALKING CITY TO NETWORKED CITY

Joel A. Tarr

Pittsburgh was originally founded as a frontier fort, and it served this function for both the British and the French empires in North America at different times in the eighteenth century. It was first incorporated as a city in 1816, and by 1850 it was a prosperous commercial and industrial center of 46,601 people. Seven contiguous towns surrounded it, the most important of which were Allegheny City, with a population of 21,262, and the boroughs of East Birmingham, Birmingham, and South Pittsburgh on the south bank of the Monongahela. The population of the Pittsburgh "metropolitan area" was over 80,000 in 1850.[1]

The region thrived economically. The Allegheny River enabled Pittsburgh to tap the trade of northwest Pennsylvania, the Monongahela River drew from northern Virginia and southern Pennsylvania, and the Ohio River supplied a direct inroad to the rich agricultural country of the Ohio valley. Because of its strategic location, Pittsburgh developed as a transfer station for goods carried from the east over the Allegheny Mountains. In addition, the city and the surrounding towns became manufacturing centers with the rivers providing cheap and convenient avenues of distribution. The rich beds of bituminous that underlay the region supplied cheap fuel for numerous factories of iron, glass, and textiles as well as for copper and brass foundries. Iron making was the city's chief industry and rolling mills, foundries, machine shops, and boiler yards employed about half of the region's working force (see "Pittsburgh as an Energy Capital" in this volume). Fahnestock's *Pittsburgh Directory* of 1850 valued "manufacturing and other business" at over $50,000,000 with iron products contributing nearly $6,500,000 of this total and glass over $1,000,000. The city itself had 8,368 manufacturing workers or 17.9 percent of the population.[2]

But if the Pittsburgh area qualified as a metropolitan area it differed from the present agglomeration by a lack of commuters who utilized either public or private forms of transit in their journey to work. Like other American cities of the time, Pittsburgh in 1850 was a walking city with a limited transportation system. The city's 46,601 people resided in an area of 1,130 acres (457 hectors). The original city was divided into four wards in 1833; a fifth was added in 1837; four more wards were added in 1845 and 1846 from towns to the east. Densities within the city ranged from 66.9 persons per acre in the wards that composed the original city to 24.1 persons in the fast-growing outlying wards.[3] Natural boundaries limited the area available for growth—the rivers stood to the north, south, and west of the city while the sharp escarpments of Herron Hill (paralleling the Allegheny River) and Boyd's Hill on the east (along the Monongahela) blocked expansion in these directions. Topography therefore prevented population spread except along the Allegheny River floodplain where the Northern Liberties or Bayardstown, a town annexed in 1837, attained a population density equal to the crowded city wards (see "The Interaction of Natural and Built Environments" in this volume).[4]

Most modern metropolitan areas (though there are exceptions) have a rising income curve as one moves from the central city to the fringe. Land uses are also usually separated into residential, commercial, and industrial purposes. This pattern, however, was not true of Pittsburgh in 1850 or of other "walking cities." In the walking city most members of the elite—merchants, professionals—lived in or close to the older core of the central city, which was devoted to mixed residential, commercial, mercantile, and industrial uses.[5] The most fashionable area of Pittsburgh was Penn Street in the Fourth Ward, but the First and Second Wards also had populations with a higher percentage of well-to-do residents than the remainder of the city.

Mixed with the luxurious homes of the elite were residences of the city's whitecollar workers, artisans, and unskilled workers.[6] In 1850, 78 percent (n = 516) of the city's bankers, merchants, manufacturers, and professionals lived in Wards 1–4; in contrast, only 36 percent (n = 1,288) of the city's unskilled laborers lived in this area and 48 percent (n = 1,425) of its skilled laborers.[7] Close to the residential areas were blocks devoted to industrial and commercial uses as well as churches and governmental buildings. Banks were concentrated along Fourth Street. Of the city's 814 manufacturing firms, 362 were located in Wards 3–4 and employed 3,364 of the 8,368 employees listed in the 1850 manufacturing census.[8] The Third Ward, although not the home of as many of the elites of the other older wards, was still the center of religious and governmental activity, housing twenty-four churches, the custom house, post office, courthouse, and jail.[9]

Further concentrations of foundries, iron- and machine works, rolling mills, glassworks, and warehouses existed around the upper and lower basins of the Pennsylvania Main Line Canal in the Sixth Ward and along the banks of the Monongahela and Allegheny Rivers in the Fifth and Eighth Wards. Boats that traversed Pennsylvania's unusual combination of canal and inclined-plane (the Pennsylvania Main Line Canal) brought goods and passengers from Philadelphia and other eastern points.[10] Many unskilled and semiskilled workers lived adjacent to the factories where they found employment. The Seventh and Ninth Wards were furthest from Pittsburgh's center; they had the lowest densities and populations almost entirely composed of laborers and artisans.[11]

Pittsburgh's economic activity centered in Wards 1–4, where 623 or almost three-quarters of the city's firms were located. In contrast, about half of the city's population lived in these wards. On the whole, firm size was small, with the number of workers per firm ranging from about three or four in the Seventh Ward to almost seventeen in the Eighth Ward. The citywide average size was just over ten (see "Downtown Pittsburgh" in this volume).[12]

The choice of the city's more affluent classes to live in crowded conditions under a pall of smoke and soot from industry is explained by their desire to have proximity to the urban center and by the absence of transportation to provide them with alternative living choices. Forced to walk to work or travel by horse on muddy streets, they preferred to live close to their places of employment, their churches, and the city's public buildings. Where alternatives were possible, however, they took advantage of them. In the 1850s, for instance, a substantial fraction of the elite had moved across the Allegheny River to Allegheny City where they lived in an emerging compact upper-class area. To reach downtown they utilized the toll bridges to cross the river (there were five bridges across the Allegheny by the end of the 1850s).[13]

THE CENTRALITY OF THE URBAN HORSE IN THE WALKING AND STREETCAR CITY

Horses played a critical role in the operations of the walking and streetcar cities. Pittsburgh's maximum horse population was about fourteen thousand, set in the late nineteenth century, although exact figures are lacking.[14] While a substantial number of horses were used for leisure activities such as riding and racing and personal transportation, most city horses were working horses. They hauled wagons carrying freight and pulled omnibuses and streetcars carrying passengers, and they furnished stationary power to drive treadmills, capstans, and whims that moved ferries, houses, and hoisted freight on the waterfront.[15] Pittsburgher George T. Fleming wrote a graphic image of horses at work on busy Smithfield Street at mid-century: "Drays were numerous and noisy. . . . The numerous wagons, hauling heavy pigs of iron and iron products, timber wheels with anywhere from six to fourteen horses from which huge and unwieldy vehicles hung castings of many tons weight; the clattering omnibus, the rattle of the mail wagons, drays . . . and other conveyances common to traffic and essential to the then modes of business" crowded the thoroughfare.[16] Improvements in intercity transport such as the Main Line Canal (1837) and the railroad (1852) advanced the city's commercial and industrial activities but also increased the dependence on the horse for intracity distribution of freight and passengers. In 1837 the city government issued 180 licenses for drays, wagons, and carts, while probably another 100 or so were unlicensed.[17] By 1880 the US Census counted over eleven hundred drayman, hackmen, and teamsters on Pittsburgh streets, many of them involved in moving goods between the city's several railroad stations and commercial and retail establishments.

The horses, as a critical source of urban power, required food (fuel), with their primary diet being hay and oats. Hay is a bulky material and difficult to transport economically for long distances; initially it was obtained locally from farms in Allegheny, Washington, and Westmoreland Counties. Farmers' wagons would transport the hay to markets in the city, one of which was located on Fifth and Liberty Avenues in downtown Pittsburgh and another in Hay Market Square, which stood opposite the Allegheny City Market House. City ordinances regulated the sale of commodities such as hay, and at the market official "weighers" used scales approved by the city sealer of weights and measures to ensure honest trade.[18]

The coming of the railroad and especially the development of the hay press transformed the local hay market. The hay press made it possible for hay to be transported long distances at a low cost, and increasingly it moved to cities by rail from midwestern farms to be sold from railroad cars, terminal warehouses and railroad warehouses.[19] In 1882 merchants organized the Pittsburgh Grain and Flour Exchange, which handled the sale of hay, oats, and flour in carload lots, clear evidence of a flourishing trade in these products.[20]

Numerous feed stores provided other evidence of the fuel requirements of the horse fleet. In 1857, for instance, Pittsburgh chronicler George H. Thurston noted that "the sales of hay, corn, chopped stuffs and such articles of horse and cow feed, consequent upon the great number of drays here, have given rise to a number of establishments called feed stores." By 1876, as both human and horse populations grew, the number of feed stores had grown to sixty-four. Retail businesses were scattered throughout the city, while wholesale establishments were concentrated in the Strip District along Liberty Avenue adjacent to the tracks of the Pennsylvania Railroad.[21]

The existence of a large urban horse population stimulated the growth of a number of horse-related businesses and industries serving both local and export markets. In 1880s, for instance, city directories listed forty-nine farriers, three express companies, forty-five harness makers, twenty-three carriage makers, and six wagon builders. Numerous retail stores provided carriage showrooms and displays of saddles, harness blankets, and items relating to horse fashion. By 1900 the city directory listed twenty-three carriage and wagon manufacturers, thirty-two firms making saddlery, forty-one harness makers, forty-three farriers, twenty-seven heavy haulers, forty-six livery stables, three whip makers, and two horse trainers. Pittsburgh was also the center of industries that manufactured products for the national horse market, and the city's industries produced various types of carriages, horse blankets, horseshoes, horse sheers, horse rakes, and other horse-related items to be sold throughout the nation.[22]

Owning a horse was expensive, and only members of the upper-middle and upper classes kept horses and maintained their own stables. Other city residents rented horses for occasional use from neighborhood livery stables (see Figure 5.1). Horseback riding was popular among the elite. In 1895 *Kelly's Handbook of Greater Pittsburgh* reported that "the sale of stock [horses] in Pittsburg [*sic*] since our parks have been opened, has assumed vast proportions."[23] The opening of large parks equipped with bridle trails in the 1890s undoubtedly encouraged horse recreational use. The Schenley Riding Academy on Bayard Street held horse shows, and in the late 1890s and early twentieth century the elite Schenley Matinee Club and the Crafton Club sponsored horse races on the half-mile Schenley Oval. A grandstand held three thousand spectators and the horse races attracted large crowds.[24]

FIG. 5.1 Livery stables served both the living and the dead (photograph by Joel A. Tarr).

Like humans, horses had to be housed. Stables were scattered throughout the city, with the streetcar companies possessing the city's largest. They were located largely in the downtown area, along the river floodplains where flatland and railroads were concentrated and at the end of horsecar lines on the urban periphery. During the 1890s, stable construction constituted between 5 and 7 percent of the city's new buildings, with 127 constructed in 1891 and 97 in 1895. The city's largest single horse barn was at the East Liberty Stock Yards and Horse Exchange.[25] Stable fires were frequent, and in 1906–1907 the Allegheny City fire department reported that stables had been responsible for a majority of their 376 alarms.[26]

As the city's human and horse populations grew, the number of livery and boarding stables increased. By 1892 there were eighty-two livery stables in Pittsburgh and Allegheny City. Some were elaborate, offering not only "good food" and careful grooming but also steam-powered clipping services, electric lighting, fans, and elevators.[27] A number of livery stables linked their livery operations with undertaking services. Funerals provided a substantial amount of livery stable business and often provided the margin between profit and loss. The Livery, Boarding, and Sale Stables of M. F. Leslie & Bro. in Lawrenceville, for instance, advertised that they made "Undertaking and Embalming a Specialty," and as undertakers supplied "every requite from the casket and mourning badge to the hearse, coaches, and opening of the grave, in fact take full charge of managing every detail in the performance of the last rites of the dead."[28] In 1892 twenty of the city's livery stables offered undertaking services.

Having so many horses in the city required various laws, and nineteenth-century city ordinances regulated matters such as traffic conditions, speed of travel, and the cost of hauling as well as requiring the proper shodding of horses and the licensing of vehicles.[29] Horses had an important role in maintaining public safety in the city, and the fire and police departments used them extensively. The fire department depended heavily on horse-drawn equipment until after the First World War.[30]

While the horse was vital to city operations, it also imposed many environmental and public health burdens on the city. The noise of horses' hoofs on cobblestone streets created a great din, but the largest environmental problem was horse manure. The average horse daily deposited about twenty-five or thirty-five pounds of manure and about two or three gallons of urine on the street daily. Farmers used the horse manure for fertilizer if they could obtain it, but city traffic often ground the manure and made it unusable. In 1890 the Department of Public Works purchased six two-horse sweepers in order to clean downtown streets and boulevards.[31] Besides littering the streets and making them difficult to cross, manure also provided a breeding ground for flies, the carriers of many acute diseases.[32]

Horses frequently died at work or were killed if they broke a leg, and their carcasses had to be hauled from the streets, usually by a special wagon. Cruelty to horses resulted in the founding of the Allegheny County Humane Society in 1874. The society's inspections found many streetcar horses and horses used for hauling freight were old, lame, and poorly shod, and they pulled overloaded cars and wagons. When they died the horse carcass was a commodity with a value and would be taken to a rendering factory to produce various by-products. When there were too many carcasses for processing, such as during the Great Epizootic (horse flu) of 1872, they could end up in the river.[33]

THE OMNIBUS

Horses were essential to the transportation innovations of the 1840s and the 1850s that facilitated the reshaping of land-use patterns and socioeconomic class distribution within the metropolitan area. The first use of horses to provide public transit involved the omnibus, a vehicle evolving from the traditional stagecoach. It possessed two revolutionary criteria: it had a fixed schedule and a predetermined route. Because of these characteristics it should be viewed as an instrument of partial urban modernization, combining a traditional means of power—the horse—with other novel characteristics. Originating in France, by the 1830s it had came into common use in New York, Boston, and Philadelphia. Entrepreneurs introduced the omnibus to Pittsburgh and Allegheny City in the late 1840s, and their city councils approved ordinances requiring the licensing of omnibuses, regulating fares, and determining routes.[34] The omnibus was usually drawn by two horses and carried between twelve and fifteen passengers over a fixed route of city streets. A coachman mounted on an elevated seat at the front of the vehicle collected the fares and drove the horses; the passengers entered through a door at the rear and sat on long seats along the inside of the omnibus.[35]

By the 1850s Pittsburgh had four regular omnibus lines. The busiest route was east along Penn Street to Lawrenceville on the level land along the Allegheny; another route traveled along Wylie Avenue east to the town of Minersville on Herron Hill; a third line ran east along Fifth Avenue to the community of Oakland; and the fourth crossed the Allegheny River to Allegheny City. In 1853 the Excelsior, the busiest line, ran buses every ten minutes from its depot on Fifth Avenue and Market Street to Lawrenceville, a distance of about three miles, where they connected with the ferry to Sharpsburg on the Allegheny northern bank. Omnibuses ran until ten o'clock in the evening for a fare of twelve cents. Rivalry among omnibus lines and competition for space in the heart of the city in the early 1850s caused the city council to pass an ordinance establishing an omnibus depot and requiring the vehicles to be "ranged in close order along the curbstone" while waiting for passengers.[36]

The omnibus raised issues of social conflict as it clashed with traditional mores. In 1794 Pennsylvania approved a Blue Law upheld by the courts that prohibited Sunday business. The omnibus companies challenged the Blue Law, claiming that their service was a "necessity" to city dwellers and exempt from the law. In 1853 the Sabbath Desecration Association brought charges against an omnibus driver, John Naser, for violating the law by conducting a "worldly business" on the Sabbath. Naser claimed that his omnibus service was a necessity for his patrons, frequently used by them to access church. The alderman who heard the case agreed that the service was a public necessity and could operate on Sunday. The *Pittsburgh Post* applauded the decision, arguing that, as "the poor man's carriage," the omnibus violated the law no more than did the rich who rode their carriages to church.[37]

Although the Pittsburgh lines claimed that they kept their fares low so that "everyone could ride the omnibuses," only upper and middle income groups could afford the fare.[38] Wages for unskilled laborers ranged from $0.75 to $1.00 a day, while iron puddlers received $16.25 a week and their helpers about $6.75.[39] While some skilled workers probably used the omnibus, advertisements in the Pittsburgh press for "country residences" for businessmen located near omnibus lines suggest that the well-to-do and growing middle class used them most extensively.[40] For those who could afford them, the omnibuses opened the possibility of a longer separation between residence and work so that they could avoid the "pent up and vitiated air of crowded cities" and experience the amenities of "suburban" living.[41]

THE COMMUTER OR ACCOMMODATION TRAIN

Another form of transportation innovation experienced in the Pittsburgh area during the middle of the nineteenth century was the commuter railroad, known more popularly as an accommodation train. While Boston had commuter railroad service in the late 1830s and New York and Philadelphia in the 1840s, the railroad did not enter Pittsburgh until 1851. In July the Ohio and Pennsylvania Railroad, which later became the Pittsburgh, Fort Wayne, and Chicago, completed its track going west from Allegheny City to New Brighton, a distance of about thirty miles; in December the Pennsylvania Central Railroad began running trains twelve miles east to Turtle Creek, with stops at East Liberty and Wilkinsburg. Late in the autumn of 1852, the Pennsylvania completed its through route from Pittsburgh to Philadelphia, and in 1856 the Pittsburgh, Fort Wayne, and Chicago opened a route to Chicago. That year also saw several other roads complete connections between Pittsburgh and other regional towns including the Allegheny Valley Railroad, the Pittsburgh and Steubenville (1854), and the Pittsburgh and Connellsville (1861).[42]

During the 1850s and 1860s, these railroads ran a number of accommodation trains. In 1857, for instance, the Pennsylvania Central ran six accommodation trains to the east, while the Pittsburgh, Fort Wayne, and Chicago ran four trains to the west, each train making seven stops. The Pennsylvania Central took fifty-four minutes to travel the approximately twelve miles from Pittsburgh to Walls Station just beyond Turtle Creek. The Pittsburgh and Connellsville and Allegheny Valley roads added accommodation trains to the south and north in the 1860s. Thus, by the end of the Civil War, commuter railroad service was available to the north, south, east, and west of Pittsburgh.[43]

By the 1860s, all of the railroads running accommodation trains had passenger stations within walking distance of the city's business center.[44] The original passenger cars were wooden and had a maximum capacity of forty persons, but improvements in the size and comfort of the cars, as well as the system's safety, were introduced in the 1860s and 1870s. In 1852 the round-trip from Pittsburgh to East Liberty on the Pennsylvania Railroad cost fifteen cents; to Wilkinsburg, twenty-five cents; and to Turtle Creek forty cents. The roads sold season tickets to commuters and family package tickets. Railroads also ran Sunday church trains as well as excursion trains to nearby towns.[45]

The development of the accommodation trains stimulated the growth of railroad suburbs, as commuter traffic developed between the urban core and outlying towns. In 1864 a "route book" of the Pennsylvania Central and the Pittsburgh, Fort Wayne, and Chicago Railroad boasted that in the town of Wilkinsburg, six miles from Pittsburgh, "the vicinity of the station is . . . thickly dotted with the suburban houses of the merchants and manufacturers of Pittsburgh," while a similar comment was made about Sewickley, twelve miles from the city on the Ohio River.[46] In Shadyside, about four miles from the city center, clusters of substantial homes were constructed within a five- or ten-minute walk of the station.

ADOPTION OF THE HORSECAR

In 1859 another form of transportation innovation far reaching in significance joined the commuter railroad—the streetcar, running on rails on city streets. Powered initially by horses and mules, then by cable, and ultimately by electricity, the streetcar dominated urban transport throughout the nation from the Civil War until the First World War. Horsecar lines were first introduced in New York City in the early 1850s and, by the end of the decade, had spread to Boston, Philadelphia, Baltimore, Chicago, Cincinnati, and Pittsburgh.[47] Horsecars were initially little more than omnibuses operated on rails laid in the city streets. New York and Philadelphia horsecars accommodated as many as sixty passengers, but those in Pittsburgh, because of the sharp grades, were often smaller carrying a maximum of twenty passengers. Two horses or mules pulled most cars (see Figure 5.2), although some lines had cars drawn by a single horse.[48]

Pittsburgh's rugged topography required that any transportation system that was to be developed without extensive tunneling had to follow natural corridors through the hills. Horsecar routes essentially used the same routes that had been used earlier by the turnpikes and omnibuses—those of least (travel) resistance. The first four Pittsburgh lines chartered by the city council, all of which commenced operations in 1859, followed routes that still remain important traffic arteries into the downtown. The original horsecar line, the Citizens' Passenger Railway Company, ran east on Penn

FIG. 5.2 Horsecars provided the city's first public transit system (Pittsburgh City Photograph Collection, courtesy of the Archives Service Center, University of Pittsburgh).

Street approximately parallel to the Allegheny River into the town of Lawrenceville. From Lawrenceville an omnibus line made connections with the town of East Liberty. The Pittsburgh, Allegheny, and Manchester Railway ran from St. Clair Street in Pittsburgh across the St. Clair Street Bridge and through Allegheny City to the town of Manchester. The Pittsburgh and East Liberty Passenger Railway Company made a loop in the downtown area and then ran east up Fifth Avenue roughly parallel to the Monongahela River to the town of Oakland; eventually the track was extended to East Liberty. The last of the original horsecar lines—the Pittsburgh and Birmingham—ran from downtown Pittsburgh, across the Monongahela Bridge, and along Carson Street parallel to the south bank of the Monongahela River through the industrial communities of South Pittsburgh, Birmingham, and East Birmingham.[49]

The running of cars on rails through city streets was a major technological breakthrough. Alexander Easton, the author of *A Practical Treatise on Street or Horse Power Railways* (1859), called streetcars the "improvement of the age." According to Easton, the horsecar provided advantages in space and time economy over the omnibus, prevented traffic jams, and eliminated "the nuisance occasioned by the rattling of omnibuses over the rough stones."[50] At a meeting held in support of street railways in Lawrenceville in 1859, one speaker noted that he had ridden a horsecar, and that "he never experienced anything as delightful in the way of a ride, except . . . a sleigh ride on ice." The meeting approved a resolution calling omnibuses "tardy and annoying" and maintaining that the horsecar was "in all points more desirable and in conformity with the spirit of this population, than other means yet devised."[51]

By 1863 the Pittsburgh area had over sixteen miles of horsecar track. In that year the four lines carried 3,960,009 passengers or an average of forty rides per year per inhabitant for the regional population. In 1871 the system had grown to over twenty-one miles, and passenger traffic had increased to 8,124,126 or fifty rides per inhabitant. Ridership increased steadily over the remainder of the horsecar period, approximately doubling during the decades of the 1870s and the 1880s. Rides per Pittsburgh inhabitant were approximately sixty-two in 1880 and sixty-eight in 1888, as the streetcar riding habit increased at a rate faster than population. In the latter year (the last of the horsecar era), the system had grown to almost fifty-six miles and carried 23,456,456 passengers, an increase in ridership of 558 percent since 1863.[52]

Pittsburgh rails, like those in Philadelphia, used a gauge measuring five feet two and a half inches. The city's recording regulator and the Committee on Streets were responsible for setting these gauges and overseeing construction. Steam railroads were unable to use this track, since their axels measured four feet eight and a half inches wide. Frederick Law Olmsted Jr., in his 1910 report on Pittsburgh planning, reported that the reason for using the wider gauge was so that other vehicles could run on the smooth track since pavements were frequently bad. Concerns about the risks presented by steam locomotives using the tracks on city streets may also have been a factor. While the use of the smooth tracks may have been an advantage for some vehicles, drivers often found it difficult to move from them, straining their horses and breaking axles. If wagons could not keep four wheels on the tracks, they often produced a deep trough in the ground next to the tracks.[53]

During the 1870s and 1880s the original four companies extended their routes, and entrepreneurs chartered and developed ten additional companies. Horsecar lines were extended to distances about five miles from the core of the city, with extensive feeder lines, crosstown lines, and competitive parallel lines. Although different companies had downtown loops, no single line followed a through route through the downtown area and across the bridges to another part of the region. The looping system and the lack of through lines caused congestion in the downtown section.[54] Although there were transfers between some lines, this privilege was not universal, resulting in passenger inconveniences. Fares varied from five to six cents, with two cents charged for transfers. The number of cars grew from 67 first-class (two-horse) and 12 second-class (one-horse) cars in 1863 to 134 first-class and 38 second-class in 1888.[55]

Horsecar riders often complained about irregular schedules and crowded cars, which were described in 1911 as "shabby, dirty, slow and uncomfortable."[56] Horses could be difficult to control, especially when startled, and accidents were frequent. Horses would leave piles of manure and urine on the streets, providing a breeding ground for flies and a nuisance from ground up and wind-blown manure. Horsecar tracks often hindered crosstown traffic, jarring the vehicles that attempted to cross them.[57]

Horses were not always dependable as power producers. They had a propensity to suffer from various diseases and were susceptible to roughly 200 of the 250 diseases that affect humans. When horses became sick or died in large numbers the city operations and their services could be severely affected. The 1872 epizootic, for instance, brought a number of eastern cities to a halt, and Pittsburgh newspapers traced the horse flu as it advanced. The city was not originally listed as suffering from the flu, and in late October the *Post* boasted that the city's horses were "exempt from the 'prevailing unwellness.'"[58] This optimism did not prevail, however, and by mid-November the *Post* was calling Pittsburgh a "Plague Stricken City," with only two street railways running, schedules cut, and travel suspended. Livery stables lacked horses to draw carriages or hearses, draught horses were unavailable to transport goods, and fire departments were hampered in their operations. Where available, oxen were used as horse substitutes.[59] By 1873 the horse epidemic had subsided, although its impact on Pittsburgh, as in other cities, emphasized the uncertainty of depending on animal power for urban operations.[60]

In addition to the surface lines, several inclined-plane passenger railways began operating in hilly areas on Mount Washington ("coal hill") to open them for settlement. Inclined planes had been used before the Civil War to transport coal from mines on the side of the mountain to the river, but the first passenger incline, the Monongahela, began operating in 1870. During the 1870s and 1880s, eleven more inclined-plane railways were built, seven on the south side of the Monongahela River, two in Pittsburgh, and two in Allegheny City. Data is not available for passenger traffic on all of these inclines, but in 1890 the five that reported to the Pennsylvania secretary of internal affairs recorded that they had carried over three million passengers in 1889.[61]

IMPACT OF THE HORSECAR AND COMMUTER RAILROAD ON RESIDENTIAL AND COMMERCIAL PATTERNS, 1859–1888

From 1860 to 1890, the population of Pittsburgh grew from 49,601 to 234,612. These figures are inflated, however, by Pittsburgh's 1868 annexation of a number of townships and boroughs to the east of the city and 1873 annexation of towns on the south side of the Monongahela River. These two areas added 75,000 inhabitants to the city and increased its land area from 1.77 to 27.31 square miles.[62] The city council made a major ward reapportionment after the 1868 annexation, and ward boundaries, except for the addition of new wards, stayed constant until 1907. Since governmental departments furnished demographic and building data on the basis of wards, this continuity makes possible comparisons from 1870 to 1900, the most dynamic period in terms of demographic, industrial, and spatial change in Pittsburgh's history.

In 1870 Pittsburgh had a population density of nearly 6 persons per acre. Densities, however, varied greatly throughout the city. The first four wards, which comprised the city's old core, had a density of nearly 48 persons per acre. Wards 5–12 covered a belt of land annexed in 1846, some of it very hilly, which extended between the rivers just east of the old city. These wards had an overall density of 54 persons per acre, although the Fifth Ward, on the fringe of the central city, was the city's densest, with 122.5 persons per acre. The most sparsely settled were Wards 13–23, the territory annexed in 1868, which had an area more than thirteen times that of the 1860 city. This vast section, much of it consisting of large estates, stretched between the rivers as they diverged; in 1870 its density was 2.25 persons per acre.[63]

By 1890 the city's density had increased to almost 15 persons per acre but population was spread more evenly. The density of Wards 1–4, the City Business District (CBD), had declined slightly to 45 persons per acre, with the sharpest drop in Ward 3, where a concentration of office buildings was developing, The group of wards within approximately three miles of the CBD—Wards 5–12, all served by horsecar lines—increased in density to nearly 70 persons per acre, while Wards 13–23, the eastern outlying wards, grew to 7.5 persons per acre. The South Side wards, which had had a density of about 12 persons per acre in 1870 when they were independent municipalities, now increased to just over 25, reflecting the growth of industry and employment opportunities in these neighborhoods.[64]

Commuter rail and horsecar transport improvements facilitated population distribution throughout the city and encouraged increasing commuter flows. As Robert J. Jucha notes in his study of the growth of the neighborhood of Shadyside, the "pattern of downtown residence for the middle and upper-classes began to break down with the introduction of the steam-power railroad." Towns such as Shadyside served by the steam railroad developed as railroad suburbs with houses on large lots.[65] The extension of the horsecar lines also furthered suburban development as routes that served areas less than an hour's ride from the downtown core grew. The appeal of the suburban ideal is reflected in a Pittsburgh land sale broadside of December 1860, which notes that the advertised property was "beautifully situated upon the Pittsburgh and East Liberty Passenger Railway [horsecar] and the said Railroad, in which the cars run at intervals of ten minutes to and from the city . . . [afford] a rare opportunity to those who wish to combine the advantages of City and Country Life."[66] In contrast, outlying wards requiring more than an hour on the horsecar to downtown saw only scattered development.[67]

More affluent commuters who lived in outlying areas as well as in suburban towns such as Wilkinsburg and Edgewood and who worked in the downtown probably utilized the faster commuter railroads. In the 1870s and 1880s, for instance, it could take one hundred minutes by horsecar from East Liberty (four miles from the core) but only twenty-eight minutes via the Pennsylvania Railroad. In 1883 the road ran 26 trains a day on this route and carried between 6,000 and 8,000 passengers at a cost of twenty-eight cents a round-trip. By 1890 the city's railroads ran 235 commuter trains a day and carried 2,698,633 passengers.[68]

Horsecars were much slower than the commuter railroads but more affordable for white-collar and skilled workers who found employment in the central city. The horsecar, with its five- or six-cent fare, was undoubtedly their method of commutation. Unfortunately, trip destination data is lacking for the streetcar lines, which makes it difficult to arrive at any but an educated guess as to what percentage of total ridership had a downtown or other workplace destination. We do know that the heaviest horsecar passenger flows were on lines with downtown destinations. While information is lacking for streetcar use by manufacturing workers, evidence from other cities suggests that few such workers used the streetcar in their journey to work, and they were usually walking.[69]

Aggregate passenger data show that in 1871, when there were 21.3 miles of streetcar track, the city's greatest passenger flows were on the East End lines, with a total of over 3,500,000 passengers; the North Side lines carried the second highest total, over 3,200,000 passengers; and the South Side line had 1,401,812 passengers. Nine years later in 1880, system mileage had nearly doubled and the passenger flow rose by over 80 percent to 61.7 rides per Pittsburgh inhabitant. In addition to the extension of existing lines, in 1880 a new company, the Pittsburgh and West End, was running cars from the Thirty-Sixth Ward on the Ohio River to the downtown. By 1888, the last year that horses alone were used as motive power, the four lines running from the east carried 44 percent of the total passenger traffic, and the three lines from Allegheny City carried 40 percent.[70] Not all of these riders were engaged in journey-to-work trips, since many undoubtedly used the horsecar for shopping or recreational purposes. In order to stimulate such trips and to encourage weekend usage many lines constructed amusement parks on the city's periphery.[71]

The extension of tracks in the eastern section of the city expanded the opportunities for housing development in this area. From 1870 to 1890, dwelling units in Wards 1–4 actually decreased; Wards 4–12, still part of the old city, saw an increase of 25 percent; Allegheny City had a rise of 143 percent; and the new eastern wards, annexed in 1867, witnessed a 221 percent increase in the number of dwellings.[72] Construction activity in the city as a whole accelerated during the 1870s and 1880s. From 1881 to 1888, over 13,000 buildings were constructed in the city (not counting Allegheny). The largest amount of building was again in eastern Wards 13–23, with the construction of 7,342 buildings at an average cost of $1,672. The other newly annexed area, the south side (Wards 24–36) saw 3,533 new buildings at an average cost of $1,260. The older areas of the city also witnessed a building boom as commercial structures replaced decaying residential structures and empty lots were filled. Wards 5–12 had 1,714 buildings constructed, many for industrial and commercial uses, at an average cost of $1,681.[73]

The city's original area was also the center of a great amount of construction. As the *Handbook to the Pittsburgh Exposition* noted in 1890: "Hundreds of costly business blocks, most of them stone, have taken the place of old soot covered structures in the lower part of the city."[74] From 1881to 1888, Wards 1–4 had 413 new buildings constructed at an average cost of almost $12,000. Building activity was especially intense toward the latter half of the 1880s. Up until 1887, Pittsburgh building permits supply only fragmentary information regarding a structure's function but these suggest that many of the five- and six-story buildings constructed in the 1880s were intended for use as offices.[75] The construction of stores, clubs, and warehouses accompanied the erection of office buildings as did the appearance of two new railroad terminals—one for the Baltimore & Ohio Railroad and one for the Citizens Traction Company. Noticeably absent among new buildings in the downtown were those intended to serve the basic needs of a residential population—dwellings, churches, and schools (see "Downtown Pittsburgh" in this volume).[76]

By 1888, therefore, primarily because of successive transportation innovations, Pittsburgh had begun to acquire the shape of a modern metropolis. In 1850, although the city had developed some "discrete districts segregated by function," land uses were largely unspecialized. But in 1888, because of the development of intraurban transportation, districts could more clearly be distinguished as residential, commercial, or industrial. In addition, residential districts began to form socioeconomic patterns, with elite groups moving out from the core and workers concentrating near or close to industry along the rivers.[77] In the industrial metropolis of 1888, the journey to work, carried on by public means of transit—the commuter railroad and the horsecar—assumed increasing significance. An outstanding characteristic of the downtown area and the outlying residential wards lay in the daily flow of people commuting to work and to shopping and then returning to their homes.[78]

But although zones of conflux and dispersion were evident in the 1888 city, factors such as topography, transportation costs, and the nature of the labor market still combined to influence the majority of unskilled and semiskilled workers to live within walking distance of places where employment was available. By the 1880s, industry was primarily located on the flat lands along the riverbanks, where there were concentrations of workers' housing within short distances of the factories (see "Industrial Suburbs and the Growth of Metropolitan Pittsburgh" in this volume).[79] Many other occupations, such as stogy-making or the production of "ready-made" garments, were found in home "sweatshops" or small stores located on the fringes of the CBD. The neighborhoods mixed in and adjacent to such "manufacturing" facilities were densely populated, mainly by the most newly arrived immigrants.[80] Employment within industrial and manufacturing facilities was often sporadic, making it necessary for workers to have easy access to a number of employment opportunities. Immigrant families frequently depended on the wages of all adult members of the family, which would have meant a multiplication of commuter fares if employment opportunities were beyond walking distance.[81] Therefore, most transit riders who used the commuter railroad and the horsecar in their journey to work were undoubtedly middle-class, white-collar workers rather than laborers moving from residence to factory.[82]

NOTES

Portions of this essay were originally published in Joel A. Tarr, *Transportation Innovation and Changing Spatial Patterns in Pittsburgh, 1850–1934* (Chicago: Public Works Historical Society, 1978), and Joel A. Tarr, "The Horse Era in Pittsburgh," *Western Pennsylvania History* 92, no. 2 (2009): 28–41. The essays were revised for this edition in 2017.

1. US Bureau of the Census, *Ninth Census (1870) Vol. 1: Population and Vital Statistics* (Washington, DC, 1872), 243–44. This census report includes data from 1850 and 1860, although it fails to note that the Pittsburgh wards in 1870 were not equivalent to those of 1850 and 1860.

2. Catherine Elizabeth Reiser, *Pittsburgh's Commercial Development, 1800–1850* (Harrisburg, 1951); Michael Holt, *Forging a Majority: The Formation of the Republican Party in Pittsburgh, 1848–1860* (New Haven, 1969), 17–22; US Manuscript 1850 Manufacturing Census for Pittsburgh.

3. Densities are computed from population statistics for 1850 in US Bureau of the Census, *Ninth Census (1870)*, 243–44, and annexation acreage in Bion J. Arnold, *Report on the Pittsburgh Transportation Problem* (Pittsburgh, 1910), 49. For growth of the city to 1850, see Erasmus Wilson, ed., *Standard History of Pittsburgh, Pennsylvania* (Chicago, 1898), 688–725; Leland D. Baldwin, *Pittsburgh: The Story of a City* (Pittsburgh, 1937), 202.

4. Baldwin, *Pittsburgh*, 202; Wilson, *Standard History of Pittsburgh*, 707–25; Richard C. Wade, *The Urban Frontier: The Rise of Western Cities, 1790–1830* (Cambridge, 1959), 9–12, 305.

5. William B. Meyer and Christopher R. Esposito, "Residential Patterns in the Pre-automotive American City," *Geographical Review* 104 (July 2014): 352–57.

6. Baldwin, *Pittsburgh*, 231–47. See the tables abstracted from the 1850 US Manuscript Census in Holt, *Forging a Majority*, 320–22, 333, 334; Wade, *The Urban Frontier*, 206. Peter Goheen notes that Toronto "was a jumble of confusion in 1860. Commerce, industry, and high class residential properties were tightly intermixed." See Peter G. Goheen, *Victorian Toronto, 1850–1900: Pattern and Process of Growth*, University of Chicago Geography Research Papers (Chicago: University of Chicago Press, 1970).

7. See "Numbers Belonging to Certain Occupational Types in Pittsburgh in 1850," Table 7 in Holt, *Forging a Majority*. 322.

8. Compiled from the US Manuscript Manufacturing Census for Pittsburgh (1850).

9. Holt, *Forging a Majority*, 31–32; Henry Oliver Evans, *Iron Pioneer: Henry E. Oliver, 1850–1904* (New York, 1942), 12–19; Reiser, *Pittsburgh's Commercial Development*, 129–31, 191–98; R. E. McGowin, "Map of the Cities of Pittsburgh and Allegheny" (1852), Pennsylvania Room, Carnegie Library, Pittsburgh.

10. Holt, *Forging a Majority*, 26–27; Baldwin, *Pittsburgh*, 236–39; McGowin, "Map of the Cities of Pittsburgh and Allegheny." For a discussion of the Pennsylvania Main Line Canal, see Reiser, *Pittsburgh's Commercial Development*, 85–111; Julius Rubin, *Canal or Railroad? Imitation and Innovation in the Response to the Erie Canal in Philadelphia, Baltimore, and Boston*, in *Transactions of the American Philosophical Society* 51 (Philadelphia, 1961), part 7, 15–62.

11. "Numbers Belonging to Certain Occupational Types in Pittsburgh in 1850," Table 7, in Holt, *Forging a Majority*, 322.

12. Compiled from the US Manuscript Manufacturing Census for Pittsburgh (1850).

13. *Pittsburgh Post*, November 7, 1851, April 19, 1859; James Borchert and Susan Borchert, "Downtown, Uptown, Out of Town: Diverging Patterns of Upper-Class Residential Landscapes in Buffalo, Pittsburgh, and Cleveland, 1885–1935," *Social Science History* 26 (Summer 2003): 321–24.

14. See Tarr, "The Horse Era in Pittsburgh." Many details regarding the horse in Pittsburgh not included here can be found in this article.

15. One source estimates that in 1840 animal sources of energy in the United States provided 52.4 percent of the total work output of which approximately half consisted of nonfarm or urban work animals.

16. George Thornton Fleming, *My High School Days: Including a Brief History of the Pittsburgh Central High School from 1855–1871* (Pittsburgh: Wm. G. Johnson, 1904), 12.

17. George H. Thurston, *Allegheny County's Hundred Years* (Pittsburgh: A. A. Anderson Sons, 1888), 244; *Harris' Pittsburgh Business Directory for the Year 1837* (Pittsburgh: Isaac Harris, 1837), 293.

18. Clay McShane and Joel A. Tarr, *The Horse in the City: Living Machines in the Nineteenth Century* (Baltimore: Johns Hopkins University Press, 2007), 143–44. On occasion owners fed their horses corn in an attempt to cut down on costs, but this often backfired because corn could not supply the niacin that horses required for energy.

19. McShane and Tarr, *Horse in the City*, 134–35.

20. J. M. Kelly, *J. M. Kelly's Handbook of Greater Pittsburg* (Pittsburg, 1895), 38. In 1894 the exchange transferred 7,520 cars of hay and 3,215 cars of oats from the railroads to local buyers.

21. George H. Thurston, *Pittsburgh as it is: Facts and Figures, Exhibiting the Past and Present of Pittsburgh—Its Advantages, Resources, Manufactures, and Commerce* (Pittsburgh: W. S. Haven, 1857), 183. For a discussion of the growing, shipping, and distribution of hay and oats, see McShane and Tarr, *Horse in the City*, ch. 5, "Nutrition: Feeding the Urban Horse," 127–48.

22. Richard Edwards, ed., *Industries of Pittsburgh, Trade, Commerce and Manufactures for 1879* (Pittsburg: Richard Edwards, 1879); Pittsburgh Chamber of Commerce, *The Mercantile, Manufacturing and Mining Interests of Pittsburgh, 1884* (Pittsburgh, 1884), 136–38; *Industries and Wealth of Pittsburgh and Environs, 1890* (New York: American Pub. & Engraving, 1890), 79, 105, 131, 146, 149, 156; US Census, *Twelfth Census of the U.S. (1900) Vol. 8: Manufactures, Part 2: States and Territories* (Washington, DC: US Census Office, 1902), 792–95.

23. Kelly, *Handbook*, 6.

24. W. W. Stevenson et al., *The Story of the Sesqui-centennial Celebration of Pittsburgh* (Pittsburgh: R. W. Johnston Studios, 1910), 346; Barbara Judd, "Edward M. Bigelow: Creator of Pittsburgh's Arcadian Parks," *Western Pennsylvania Historical Magazine* 58 (January 1975): 61; Francis G. Couvares, *The Remaking of Pittsburgh: Class and Culture in an Industrializing City 1877–1919* (Albany: State University of New York Press, 1984), 107–11; *Pittsburg Horse Show Given by the Riding Club in the Schenley Riding Academy* (Pittsburg, 1897).

25. David S. Rotenstein, "Getting Meat to the Big Apple: Samuel W. Allerton and the Rise of Urban Stockyards" (unpublished paper); "Hudson River Valley Cowboys: The Origins of Modern Livestock Shipping," *Hudson Valley Regional Review* 19 (2002): 1–15; *Kelly's Handbook*, 37. Originally constructed in 1863 by the Pennsylvania Railroad, the horse exchange covered twenty-five acres and accommodated 5,000 horses under a single

roof, as well as thousands of hogs, sheep, and cattle. The railroad gradually moved its facilities and abattoirs from East Liberty to Herr's Island in the Allegheny River. The Arnheim Live Stock Company operated another large sale barn with accommodations for 250 horses on Second Avenue and conducted a famous three-day event known as the Arnheim's Speed Horse Auctions. The Pittsburgh Horse Exchange was located on Duquesne Way.

26. Works Project Administration, *Story of Old Allegheny City* (Pittsburgh: Allegheny Centennial Committee, 1941), 107.

27. *Industries and Wealth of Pittsburgh and Environs*, 79, 105, 131, 146, 149, 156. For a map of Pittsburgh livery stables, see McShane and Tarr, *Horse in the City*, 108. There is a detailed discussion of Pittsburgh stables and horse dealers in David G. McDonald, "Historic Horse Sales Part of City's Story," and "Old Allegheny Was Once Gathering Place for Merchants Who Owned Finest Horses," *Pittsburgh Press*, January 6, 27, 1935. The H. J. Heinz Corporation maintained some of the city's most elaborate stables. In 1910 the firm issued a handsome illustrated brochure that proudly described the three-story fireproof building that housed its delivery horses. Electricity lighted the steam-heated structure and electric fans ventilated its screened premises. The horses were lodged on the second floor, wagons were parked on the first floor, and feed and bedding were kept on the third. The horse stalls were of open pipe, with cork block floors and swinging sides. Each manger had separate electrically controlled compartments for hay, grain, and water, and horses were fed automatically. Electric cleaning devices curried the horses, and a hospital stall was equipped with a Turkish bath stall and a footbath. The brochure boasted that the stables were "one of the most modern, practical and complete commercial stables in the world." "Heinz Stables—Main Plant," in *H. J. Heinz Company: Producers, Manufacturers and Distributers, Pure Food Products: "57 Varieties"* (Pittsburgh: H. J. Heinz, 1910), 19.

28. Edwards, *Industries of Pittsburgh*; McShane and Tarr, *Horse in the City*, 112–13.

29. An 1816 ordinance forbade the shoeing of horses in the street. An 1867 Pittsburgh ordinance gave the city the power "to prevent and punish fast or immoderate driving of horses." Since horses ate tree bark, an 1879 ordinance forbade the tying of horses, mules, or other animals to any tree. Later ordinances regulated the distance of stables from homes and from manure containers. Pittsburgh, *A Digest of the Acts of Assembly Relating to and the General Ordinances of the City of Pittsburgh from 1804 to Jan. 1, 1897* (Pittsburgh: W. W. Thomson, 1897), 313. Allegheny City had similar ordinances. See *A Digest of the acts of assembly relating to and the general ordinances of the city of Allegheny from 1840 to April 1, 1897* (Pittsburgh: Pittsburgh Printing, 1897), 32, 47.

30. In 1913 the New York Bureau of Research did a critical study of the various City of Pittsburgh departments. See Bureau of Municipal Research, *The City of Pittsburgh, Pennsylvania . . .* (Pittsburgh: Pittsburgh Printing, 1913), 71–127; Bureau of Horses, *City of Pittsburgh and Its Horses* (Pittsburgh, 1931); Allegheny County Board of Commissioners, *Bureau of Police: History of Organization and Report of Operations* (Pittsburgh: Board of Commissioners, 1935), 45.

31. Pittsburgh, Department of Public Works, *Annual Report 1890* (Pittsburgh: Best, 1891), 131–32.

32. In 1894, for instance, the chief Pittsburgh sanitary inspector reported 418 manure heaps in violation of the city ordinance.

33. Pittsburgh, *A Digest of the Acts of Assembly*, 245; McShane and Tarr, *Horse in the City*, 121. The Pittsburgh Grease and Oil Company, founded in 1882 by J. H. Czarniecki, used animal fats for all its products and acquired from twenty-five hundred to three

thousand dead horses a year from Pittsburgh and Allegheny. John William Leonard, *Pittsburgh and Allegheny Illustrated Review: Historical, Biographical and Commercial. A Record of Progress in Commerce, Manufactures, the Professions, and in Social and Municipal Life* (Pittsburgh: J. M. Elstner, 1889), 61–62. Czarniecki and his father were both veterinarians.

34. City of Pittsburgh, *A digest of the ordinances of the city of Pittsburgh: to which is prefixed a collection of the acts of assembly relating to the corporation* (Pittsburgh: W.H. Whitney, 1849), 154–56; City of Allegheny, *A digest of the ordinances of the corporation of the city of Allegheny and of the acts of assembly relating thereto: with notes and references to judicial decisions thereon* (Pittsburgh, 1854), 39, 118.

35. George Rogers Taylor, "Beginnings of Mass Transportation: Part 1," *Smithsonian Journal of History* 1, no. 2 (1966): 40; William Alfred James, "The History of Urban Transportation in Pittsburgh and Allegheny County with Emphasis upon the Major Technological Developments" (unpublished masters' thesis, University of Pittsburgh, 1947), 16–17.

36. *Pittsburgh Post*, November 1, 1850, January 5, 1852.

37. *Pittsburgh Post*, August 10, 1853. See also *Pittsburgh Gazette*, August 23, September 2, 8, 1853. For a similar conflict in Brooklyn over Sunday horsecar use, see McShane and Tarr, *Horse in the City*, 98–101.

38. *Pittsburgh Post*, July 8, 1854; Taylor, "Beginnings of Mass Transportation: Part 1," 48.

39. Holt, *Forging a Majority*, 30; George H. Thurston, *Pittsburgh as It Is*, 30.

40. See *Pittsburgh Post*, July 29, 1851, October 24, 1853, July 11, 1859; Taylor, "Beginnings of Mass Transportation, Part I," 48.

41. *Pittsburgh Gazette*, August 10, 1853.

42. William Kenneth Schusler, "The Railroad Comes to Pittsburgh," *Western Pennsylvania Historical Magazine*" 43 (September 1960): 251–66; John P. Cowan, "Beginning of Early Railroads in Pittsburgh," *Western Pennsylvania Historical Magazine* 12 (April 1929): 116–23; E. T. Whiter, "Pittsburgh and the Steam Railways," in *Pittsburgh and the Pittsburgh Spirit* (Pittsburgh, 1928), 307–9. For commuter railroads in other cities, see George Rogers Taylor, "Beginnings of Mass Transportation: Part 2," *Smithsonian Journal of History* 1, no. 2 (1966): 31–38; Charles J. Kennedy, "Commuter Services in the Boston Area, 1835–1860," *Business History Review* 36 (Summer 1962): 153–70.

43. *Pittsburgh Post*, April 15, October 10, 1856, June 15, 1857, August 15, 1862, July 19, 26, 1865; George H. Thurston, *Thurston's Route Book from Chicago to New York via the Pennsylvania Central Railroad and the Pittsburgh, Fort Wayne and Chicago Railroad* (Pittsburgh, 1864).

44. George Littleton Davis, "Greater Pittsburgh's Commercial and Industrial Development, 1850–1900" (PhD diss., University of Pittsburgh, 1951), 49. The locomotives of the Allegheny Valley Railroad were not allowed past Seventeenth Street; horses were used to pull the cars to the station at Pike and Eleventh. See *Pittsburgh Post*, November 3, 1860; Baldwin, *Pittsburgh*, 198.

45. William Kenneth Schusler, "The Economic Position of Railroad Commuter Service in the Pittsburgh District—Its History, Present, and Future" (PhD diss., University of Pittsburgh, 1959), 36–38; *Pittsburgh Post*, December 27, 1851, May 26, 1853.

46. Thurston, *Thurston's Route Book*, n.p. See also land sale broadside, "Subdivision of Larimer Farm," September 28, 1855, Western Pennsylvania Historical Society, Pittsburgh.

47. For a discussion of the origins of the horsecar and its operations, see McShane and

Tarr, *Horse in the City*, ch. 3, "Powering Urban Transit," 57–83; Taylor, "Beginnings of Mass Transportation: Part 2," 39–50.

48. Taylor, "Beginnings of Mass Transportation: Part 2," 39. Beginning in 1863, street railway companies furnished annual reports to the state containing information as to passengers carried, routes taken, equipment, revenues, and expenses. These reports, as well as comparative tables, are published in Pennsylvania, *Annual Report of the Auditor General . . . 1863–75* (Harrisburg, 1863–1875; hereafter Pennsylvania, *Auditor General*), and Pennsylvania, Department of Internal Affairs, *Annual Report, Part IV: Railroads, Canals, Navigation, Telegraph and Telephone Companies 1876–1910* (Harrisburg, 1876–1910; hereafter Department of Internal Affairs, *Annual Report, Part IV*).

49. Arnold, *Pittsburgh Transportation Problem*, 35–39. The company reports printed in Pennsylvania, *Auditor General*, contain route descriptions. See also James, "History of Urban Transportation," 18–23.

50. Alexander Easton, *A Practical Treatise on Street or Horse-Power Railways* (Philadelphia, 1859), 5–6.

51. *Pittsburgh Post*, January 24, July 11, 1859.

52. Passenger and mileage statistics are from the reports of the street railway companies printed in the Pennsylvania, *Auditor General*, and Department of Internal Affairs, *Annual Report, Part IV*. Rides per year per inhabitant were calculated by dividing population figures for Pittsburgh and surrounding towns from the US Census (1870–1890) into total ridership.

53. Pennsylvania, *Auditor General*, and Department of Internal Affairs, *Annual Report, Part IV*. Frederick Law Olmsted Jr., *Pittsburgh Main Thoroughfares and the Down Town District* (Pittsburgh: Pittsburgh Civic Commission, 1911), 31–33. See also McShane and Tarr, *Horse in the City*, 72–74.

54. Arnold, *Pittsburgh Transportation Problem*, 56; John P. Fox, "The Transit Situation in Pittsburgh," *Charities and the Commons* 21 (February 6, 1909): 838.

55. Information compiled from company reports in Pennsylvania, *Auditor General*, and Department of Internal Affairs, *Annual Report, Part IV*; James, "History of Urban Transportation," 23–25.

56. *Pittsburgh Post*, July 25, 1911.

57. McShane and Tarr, *Horse in the City*, 26–27, 63.

58. *Pittsburgh Post*, October 28, 1872.

59. "The Plague Stricken City," *Pittsburgh Post*, November 16, 1872.

60. McShane and Tarr, *Horse in the City*, 167–69.

61. For Pittsburgh inclines, see Margaret Pearson Bothwell, "Incline Planes and People—Some Past and Present Ones," *Western Pennsylvania Historical Magazine* 46 (October 1963): 311–46. For passenger traffic, see *Annual Report of the Secretary of Internal Affairs, 1890*, 836.

62. Population figures from US Census (1860–1900); acreage figures from Arnold, *Pittsburgh Transportation Problem*, 49.

63. Ward densities are given in US Bureau of the Census, *Eleventh Census (1890) Vol. 21: Vital and Social Statistics, Part II: Cities of 100,000 Inhabitants and Upward* (Washington, DC, 1896), 293–311.

64. Population and density statistics from US Bureau of the Census, *Eleventh Census (1890)*, 21:293–311; Howard V. Storch Jr., "Changing Functions of the Center-City: Pittsburgh, 1850–1912" (unpublished seminar paper, Department of History, University

of Pittsburgh, 1966), 15; John W. Larner Jr., "A Community in Transition: Pittsburgh's South Side, 1880–1921" (unpublished seminar paper, Department of History, University of Pittsburgh, 1961), 6–11.

65. Robert J. Jucha, "The Anatomy of a Streetcar Suburb: A Development History of Shadyside, 1852–1916," *Western Pennsylvania Historical Magazine* 62, no. 4 (October 1979): 302.

66. Broadside Collection, Historical Society of Western Pennsylvania.

67. See Pittsburgh Plat Maps for 1872, 1888, and 1889, Pennsylvania Room, Carnegie Library; *Pittsburgh's Industrial Exposition 1891* (Pittsburgh, 1891), n.p.; Pittsburgh Chamber of Commerce, *Mercantile, Manufacturing and Mining Interests of Pittsburgh, 1884*, 69; Homewood Board of Trade, *Official Souvenir Program, Mardi Gras Carnival and Fair* (Pittsburgh, 1902), n.p.

68. *Prospectus of the Pittsburgh East End Railroad, 1883* (Pittsburgh, 1883), 6–7; US Bureau of the Census, *Report on the Social Statistics of Cities, Eleventh Census (1890)* (Washington, DC, 1895), 50; Sven Hammar, "Wilkinsburg and Edgewood; Commuter Suburbs" (unpublished seminar paper, Department of History, Carnegie Mellon University, 1968), 1–16; William J. Rampon, "The Historical Geography of Swissvale, Pa." (master's thesis, University of Oklahoma, 1959), 35–51.

69. Theodore Hershberg, Harold E. Cox, Dale Light Jr., and Richard R. Greenfield, "The Journey-to-Work: An Empirical Investigation of Work, Residence and Transportation, Philadelphia, 1850 and 1880," in Theodore Hershberg, ed., *Philadelphia: Work, Space, Family, and Group Experience in the Nineteenth Century—Essays toward an Interdisciplinary History of the City* (New York: Columbia University Press, 1981), 17–25. Hershberg and his coauthors calculated that streetcar fare would have taken 13 percent of the daily wages for an average Philadelphia unskilled worker and almost 9 percent for skilled workers in the 1850s and in 1880. See Hershberg et al., "The Journey to Work," 146–47.

70. Statistics computed from company reports in Pennsylvania, *Auditor General*, and Department of Internal Affairs, *Annual Report, Part IV*.

71. Hershberg et al., "The Journey-to-Work," 17–25; Joel A. Tarr, "From City to Suburb: The 'Moral' Influence of Transportation Technology," in Alexander B. Callow Jr., ed., *American Urban History*, rev. ed. (New York: Oxford University Press, 1973), 202–12.

72. Information on dwelling units per ward is from the *Ninth Census (1870)*, 599, and *Eleventh Census (1890)*, 293–311.

73. For housing information see "Manuscript Pittsburgh Building Permit Records," Archives of Industrial Society, Hillman Library, University of Pittsburgh. The number of new buildings per ward from 1881 to 1890 and estimated costs are in Pittsburgh, *Third Annual Report of the Department of Public Safety* (Pittsburgh, 1891), 93–97. See also Walter Isard, "Transport Development and Building Cycles," *Quarterly Journal of Economics* 57 (November 1942): 90–112.

74. *Handbook and Guide of Pittsburgh Exposition 1890* (Pittsburgh, 1890), 50.

75. "Manuscript Building Permit Records," Wards 1–4, 1877–1888, Archives of Industrial Society, Hillman Library, University of Pittsburgh.

76. "Manuscript Building Permit Records," Wards 1–4, 1877–1888; Storch, "Changing Functions of the Center-City," 2–8.

77. See Pittsburgh Plat Maps for 1872 and 1882. For other cities, see Sam Bass Warner, *Streetcar Suburbs: The Process of Growth in Boston, 1870–1900* (New York: Atheneum, 1971), 153–66; David Ward, *Cities and Immigrants: A Geography of Change in Nineteenth*

Century America (New York, 1971), 105–43; Allan R. Pred, *The Spatial Dynamics of U.S. Urban-Industrial Growth, 1800–1914* (Cambridge, 1966), 197; Sam Bass Warner, *The Private City: Philadelphia in Three Periods of Its Growth* (Philadelphia: University of Pennsylvania Press, 1996), 177.

78. For other cities, see Ward, *Cities and Immigrants*, 94–102; David Ward, "The Industrial Revolution and the Emergence of Boston's Central District," *Economic Geography* 42 (April 1966): 164–71.

79. Edward B. Olds, "A Test of Four Hypotheses of the Urban Pattern Using Pittsburgh Data" (PhD diss., University of Pittsburgh, 1942), 71, 100; Ted C. Soens, "A Community in Transition: Hazelwood, 1890–1905" (unpublished seminar paper, Department of History, Carnegie Mellon University, 1969), 5–15. See Pittsburgh Plat Maps for 1882 and 1898; George H. Thurston, *Pittsburgh's Progress, Industries, and Resources, 1886* (Pittsburgh, 1886), 24; Thurston, *Allegheny County's Hundred Years*, 143–95.

80. Elizabeth B. Butler, *Women and the Trades: Pittsburgh, 1907–1908* (New York, 1911), 75–140, in Paul Underwood Kellogg, ed., *Pittsburgh Survey*, 6 vols. (New York, 1911); David Ward, "The Emergence of Central Immigrant Ghettoes in American Cities: 1840–1920," *Annals of the Association of American Geographers* 58 (June 1968): 343–59; *Eleventh Census (1890)*, 293–311.

81. Ward, *Cities and Immigrants*, 106–7; Josephine McIlvain, "Twelve Blocks: A Study of One Segment of Pittsburgh's South Side, 1880–1915," *Western Pennsylvania Historical Magazine* 60 (October 1977): 351–70.

82. McShane and Tarr, *Horse in the City*, 75–78.

6 THE CABLE AND ELECTRIC STREETCAR NETWORKS

Joel A. Tarr

The horsecar and the commuter railroad were important factors in stimulating residential out movement, the development of a core-oriented city with specialized land uses, and a daily flow of downtown commuters. Two transit innovations at the end of the 1880s—the cable car and the electric streetcar—greatly accelerated these changes. Both technologies were modifications rather than alterations in the basic streetcar technology of running cars on rails.[1] With both the cable car and the electric streetcar, however, the energy source was removed from the vehicle, making possible economies of power production.

The cable car preceded the electric streetcar, first appearing in San Francisco in 1873. It was powered by steam engines that turned large drums wrapped with an endless steel cable. The cable ran in either a concrete or a steel conduit between the streetcar rails. A grip engaged the cable through a slot at the top of the conduit and transmitted power to the wheels. The streetcar traveled at the speed of the cable, and drivers halted the cars by releasing the grip from the cable and applying the brakes (see Figure 6.1).[2]

After a delay of several years, other cities emulated San Francisco and constructed cable car systems: Chicago in 1882, Philadelphia in 1883, and Pittsburgh in 1888. In Pittsburgh, three lines operating from the CBD to

FIG. 6.1 Pittsburgh Traction Company downtown loop, 1888. Cable cars briefly replaced some horsecar routes and preceded electrified streetcars (Pittsburgh City Photographer Collection, courtesy of the Archives Service Center, University of Pittsburgh).

the east—Pittsburgh Traction, the Citizens Passenger Railway, and Central Traction—all changed from horse to cable operations between 1888 and 1890; by 1890, the city had 15.5 miles of cable car lines. The cable car was considerably faster than the horsecar. The Pittsburgh Traction Company, for instance, reported that speeds increased from an average of five miles per hour with the horsecar to an average of ten miles per hour with cable. The cable car reduced the five-mile trip from the CBD to East Liberty from one hundred to thirty-two minutes, and the cars carried twice as many passengers. Increased speed, larger cars, lower fares, and track extensions to new areas resulted in substantial ridership increases. The Pittsburgh Traction Company ran its first cable car from downtown east along Fifth Avenue to

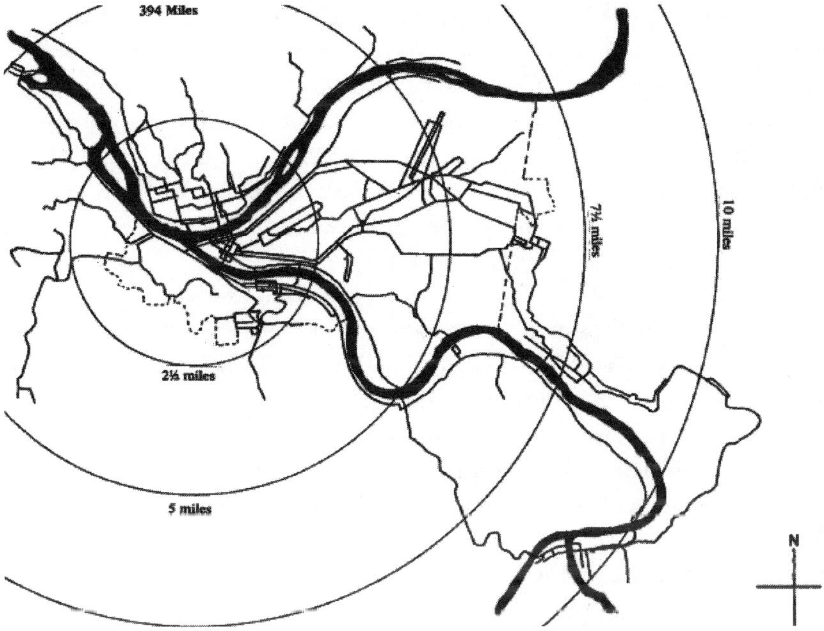

MAP 6.1 Electric streetcar lines in Pittsburgh and vicinity, 1902 (Joel A. Tarr, *Transportation Innovation and Changing Spatial Pattern in Pittsburgh, 1850–1934* [Chicago: Public Works Historical Society, 1978], 49).

East Liberty on October 8, 1888, and in 1889 passenger traffic increased 194 percent over that for 1888.[3] The other lines that converted to cable also underwent substantial ridership growth.[4] The importance of improved technology in increasing ridership suggests that there was a large latent demand for superior transit among the Pittsburgh population.[5]

The city's experience with electric traction reinforces this conclusion. Experiments in substituting electricity for horsepower as the motive force for streetcars had been conducted throughout the 1880s. Most of them had floundered on the technical problem of transferring current to a motor located on a vehicle that alternately changed speed, stopped, and started.[6] By the early 1890s, however, these problems had been solved by several inventors, primarily electrical engineer Frank Julian Sprague, and a number of Pittsburgh companies adopted his technology and converted to electricity.[7] The superiority of electricity as a means of propelling streetcars and its cost advantages caused the three lines that had previously installed cable to shift to electricity by the end of the decade.[8]

Expecting higher per capita earnings, entrepreneurs developed new routes and built parallel lines to already existing systems, with the result that total street length of track in the Pittsburgh region increased from 113 miles in 1890 to 337 in 1896.[9] Passenger traffic rose spectacularly. On the Pittsburgh, Allegheny, and Manchester Passenger Railway Company, for instance (which extended its track from 6 to 17.5 miles when it electrified), passenger traffic more than doubled, from 4,339,994 in 1888 to 9,648,946 in 1892. Traffic on the Pittsburgh & Birmingham line (which more than doubled its mileage from 7.5 to 16 miles in 1892 when it electrified) climbed from 3,000,000 in 1888 to almost 7,000,000 in 1892.

The Pittsburgh streetcar system rested on a number of franchises, originally secured through political and financial influence as well as bribery. As transit expert Bion Arnold noted in his 1910 analysis of the system, the public willingly accepted these manipulations because of its benefits. By 1902 the Pittsburgh Railways Company had acquired operating control of all the street railway companies, almost a monopoly.[10] Total mileage in the region had increased from 113 miles in 1890 to 469 miles in 1902, most of which was electrified. In these years ridership rose 264 percent from 46,299,227 passengers to 168,632,339, while rides per inhabitant more than doubled from 108 to 263. These spectacular advances were far ahead of the increase in the city's population. However, there were indications of overbuilding, as miles of track per 1,000 population increased and passengers per mile decreased. The majority of cities in the nation witnessed a different trend. In addition, the consolidated streetcar system had inherited financial obligations that increasingly weighed on its operations (see Figure 6.2).[11]

THE IMPACT OF THE CABLE CAR AND ELECTRIC STREETCAR ON RESIDENTIAL AND COMMERCIAL PATTERNS

The expansion and electrification of the traction system and the resulting ridership increases caused further regional spatial transformations. At its height, the Pittsburgh Railways Company was largely a radial system, with lines extending to city suburban neighborhoods such as Highland Park and Squirrel Hill; to outlying industrial towns such as Carnegie, Homestead, Turtle Creek, Wilmerding, and McKeesport via interurban routes; and a few local lines and shuttles. By 1919, the system had 600 miles of track, 1,630 passenger cars (953 double truck cars, 273 open cars, and 195 trailers) and 31 car barns. Before 1918, riders paid a nickel fare within the city and to closely linked towns and additional fares to more distant communities.[12]

Three trends that had begun during the horsecar era accelerated during the 1890s and the early twentieth century: the development of the CBD into a commercial, office, and shopping center; the stimulation of building activity both in the downtown core and in the residential areas; and the

Fig. 6.2 Liberty Avenue, 1919. As late as 1919 many horses still interacted on the streets with streetcars and automobiles (Pittsburgh City Photographer Collection, courtesy of the Archives Service Center, University of Pittsburgh).

movement of population into the outlying wards of the city, with a consequent lengthening of the journey to work for CBD employees. Population distribution in the city reflected these trends: from 1890 to 1900 population in outlying Wards 13–23 increased from 103,091 to 169,025 and density in the area climbed from 7.5 persons per acre in 1890 to 12.4 persons in 1900. For the city, density increased from 14.8 to 17.9 persons per acre. In contrast to the population growth in the eastern wards, the CBD (Wards 1–4) lost 35 percent of its population and 26 percent of its dwelling units, as commercial and business needs drove out the residential population. Wards 5–12, within three miles of the CBD and South Side Wards 24–36, both with growing industrial areas, had smaller percentage rises in population than the city.[13]

During the years of expansion and electrification of the transit system, the downtown core continued its transformation into an area used primarily for commerce and business rather than for residences.[14] From 1890 to 1900, population density decreased from 45 persons per acre to just over 29, while the number of dwelling units fell from 1,596 to 1,182. Other indices of the further decline of the first four wards as a residential area were the continued migration of churches from the area and losses in school enrollment.[15]

In the next two decades the building of a number of skyscrapers changed the CBD's profile. Construction activity proceeded at a high rate throughout these years except for a slowdown due to the panic of 1893 and the uncertainties created by the Spanish-American War in 1898. From 1888 to 1893, there were 428 buildings (largely of masonry) constructed in the CBD, none higher than nine stories. The development of the steel frame and the elevator, however, enabled the construction of taller structures, and in 1895 the city's first steel-frame building, the thirteen-story Carnegie Building, was completed. Increasingly, skyscrapers dominated the Pittsburgh skyline (see "Downtown Pittsburgh: Relentless Evolution," in this volume).[16]

Bankers and industrialists were the most important builders of office structures during the period from 1894 to 1906. From 1887 to 1893, nine new bank buildings were constructed including the eight-story German National Bank (1889) and the eight-story National Bank of Commerce (1889)—none, however, was yet a steel-frame skyscraper. In the remainder of the 1890s, six new banks appeared, none higher than three stories. Between 1901 and 1907, however, bankers constructed seven new buildings, and all of them were steel-frame skyscrapers. Among the most significant were the fifteen-story Keystone Bank Building (1901), the fifteen-story Peoples Bank Building (1901), the twenty-four-story Farmers Deposit National Bank Building (1902), the twelve-story Diamond National Bank Building (1904) and the twenty-one-story Union National Bank Building (1906). Most of these banks were located in the financial district (Pittsburgh's "Wall Street") bounded by Wood, Smithfield, Fourth, Fifth, and Sixth Streets in the Second and Third Wards.

Industrialists were also important builders of office structures. They constructed a number of masonry eight- and nine-story office buildings from 1888 to 1893. After 1895, however, the major new office buildings were multistoried steel-frame skyscrapers. Most important were the fifteen-story Park Building (1895), the twelve-story Empire Building (1899), the nineteen-story Frick Building (1902), the thirteen-story Bessemer Building (1902), the nineteen-story Frick Annex (Allegheny Building, 1905), the thirteen-story Fulton Building 1904), and the nineteen-story Benelux-Trees Building (1905).[17]

The construction of these large banking and office structures, as well as the appearance of several department stores, signified a sharp change in downtown land use patterns. What had been an area devoted to mixed industrial, commercial, and residential uses until the 1880s now became a section devoted almost entirely to commercial, industrial, and business purposes. The warehouses and factories that remained were concentrated in the

Point area and near the rivers. A number of other industries, pressured by rising land costs and the need for expansion, moved their manufacturing facilities out of the core, while maintaining their offices in the CBD.[18]

The financing of these new office buildings by industrialists points to the growth in the Pittsburgh region of mass production industries requiring specialized and differentiated administrative tasks. Such CBD transformation, however, would have been greatly restricted without the development of an effective mass transit system. This system made possible the daily movement into the CBD of white-collar workers who resided in outlying residential sections and who staffed the large office structures. Many commuters were male and female clerical workers who worked in the various corporate headquarters, a workforce that consistently grew.[19]

In 1909 streetcars with seating capacity for approximately 24,000 passengers and commuter railroads with seating capacity for 14,000 passengers left the CBD during the peak hour of the evening rush period. Of the streetcar passengers, 45 percent went to the east, 25 percent to the north, 16 percent to the south, and 14 percent to the west.[20] Nine years later, the Pittsburgh transit commissioner surveyed the travel pattern of 49,394 CBD workers (total employment was approximately 87,000) and showed a similar pattern of commuter flows into the CBD.[21] The report assumed that workers with less than a two-mile trip walked to work while those living more than two miles used public transit.[22]

New building activity in the outlying residential wards, stimulated by the cable and electric streetcar systems, paralleled the activity in the core. Much of this new construction was done in coordination with real estate development.[23] Building was heaviest in the eastern territory that had been annexed in 1868. The adoption of cable and electric power on the streetcars drastically cut travel time and enabled the extension of the lines to formerly unserved neighborhoods. From 1888 to 1893, Wards 13–23 saw 12,969 new buildings constructed.[24] Building activity slowed during the middle of the 1890s because of the depression of 1893 but then accelerated toward the end of the decade and into the twentieth century, with the greatest construction in the wards furthest from the downtown core. From 1899 to 1902, there were 1,498 new buildings constructed in the Twenty-First Ward, located on the city's eastern boundary. The Homewood Board of Trade, representing commercial interests in the area, noted that this "phenomenal growth" resulted from the development of "real rapid transportation to the East End."[25]

Residential development also took place in outlying towns served by commuter rail and electric streetcars. The commuter rail lines carried thousands of riders into the downtown from the outlying sections of the city and region. The Pennsylvania, the Baltimore & Ohio, and the Wabash Railroads had stations directly in the CBD, while the Pittsburgh & Lake Erie's station was located on the south shore of the Monongahela River across from the downtown. The Pittsburgh, Fort Wayne, and Chicago (controlled by the Pennsylvania Railroad) had a station in Allegheny City. The most heavily used station was the Pennsylvania Union Station (1904), which received commuters from city neighborhoods and towns in the eastern corridor. In 1917 over 62 percent of Pennsylvania Railroad commuters into the CBD arrived from the city neighborhoods of Homewood, East Liberty, Roup Station, and Shadyside.[26] Others came from suburban towns such as Wilkinsburg and Edgewood served by the Pennsylvania Railroad and streetcar lines. These two towns, for example, experienced substantial growth, with Wilkinsburg growing from a population of 1,529 in 1880 to 18,924 in 1910, and Edgewood from 218 to 2,596 in the same period. Other towns such as Sewickley on the Ohio River and Aspinwall on the Allegheny served by commuter railroads also grew substantially (see Appendix 6.1).[27] The population and building patterns within the core and in the formerly sparsely settled wards on the city's periphery all point to the further development of Pittsburgh into a modern metropolitan area characterized by a separation between residence and work and by daily commuter flows to the CBD. The separation of residence and work meant a longer journey to work in terms of distance, but not necessarily a time increase for commuters.[28]

Although the streetcar system made possible a greater separation between work and residence, many workers did not use the public transit system in their journey to work. A 1911 study based upon New York survey data concerning industrial location, residence, and workplace for industrial and clerical workers concluded that workers who worked long hours and were paid less were more likely to walk to work. Since most of the manufacturing workers in this study worked longer hours than did the white-collar clerical employees, they preferred close-in residential locations and were more likely to walk to work. White-collar employees, on the other hand, were heavier users of the public transit system.[29]

Similar conclusions about the relationship between residence and workplace appear warranted for Pittsburgh workers. Examination of Pittsburgh plat maps for 1872, 1882, and 1898 show row houses and houses with less than a thirty-foot front, which may be assumed to be workingmen's homes, located close to industrial districts.[30] More conclusive is the data for workers reported in the 1917 Pittsburgh transit commissioner's report. This report divided the city and nearby communities into 65 districts. It included a survey of the residence and workplace of 274,000 workers in the Pittsburgh district or approximately 70 percent of the total workforce. Of this sample, 44.6 percent lived within a mile of their place of work and another 25 percent within two miles. The report's compilers assumed that workers who lived less than two miles from their workplace walked to work. They based this assumption on evidence from trip surveys that showed that streetcar passengers traveled an average of three miles. In some city districts close to or incorporating large industrial plants the number of workers traveling under one mile to work was over 80 percent. Based upon the transit commissioner's report, therefore, one can assume that in 1917 at least a majority of the workers in the 270,000 sample walked to work.[31]

This pattern was characteristic of the steel industry, the largest single employer in the Pittsburgh region, where the seven-day and seventy-two-hour week was common. By 1917 integrated steel mills lined the Pittsburgh rivers to a distance of twenty miles from the city core and in the outlying mill areas as high as 80–90 percent of the workforce walked to work (see "Pittsburgh's Industrial Corridors" in this volume).[32] Beside the workers housing that clustered close to the mills, there were also densely packed residential areas on the fringes of the CBD. These were occupied primarily by unskilled and semiskilled immigrants who faced frequent changes in work location and sporadic unemployment. Proximity to the CBD provided numerous job alternatives. In addition, a number of small sweatshop-type industries, such as cigar-making, located in this area to take advantage of the labor supply, lower rents, and ready access to the CBD. For the most part, workers who lived in the neighborhoods that abutted on the CBD either worked at home or walked to the sweatshops that employed them.[33]

By 1910 the extensive Pittsburgh transit system had begun to suffer serious internal difficulties. The historian Mark Gallimore in his doctoral dissertation, "Business and Politics of Mass Transit in Pittsburgh," notes that the very success of the streetcar system in attracting riders "made the job of running, maintaining, and improving the trolleys harder, financially and politically."[34] Complaints increased by politicians and by the public about poor service, resulting in substantive studies of the Pittsburgh transportation problem but with little effect.[35] The transit expert Bion J. Arnold's 1910 *Report on the Pittsburgh Transportation Problem*, an analysis commissioned by the city council, was one of the most prominent of the studies. Arnold noted that the combined electric traction and commuter railroad system brought forth "insistent complaints from every section."[36] The problems he noted included overextension of lines to unprofitable areas, overcapitalization, insufficient amounts allocated for depreciation, and poor service. Arnold's major recommendations were for improved equipment on existing surface lines, better service and rerouting, construction of a CBD subway with branches under the rivers and through the hills, electrification of the steam rail lines, and a system of transfers between the surface traction, subways, and commuter railroads. Arnold also observed in his report that the construction of a rapid transit system would "create traffic," while "the failure to provide improved facilities will hold back the development of a community."[37]

In 1910 Pittsburgh ranked fourth among the nation's cities in terms of track mileage but sixth in terms of earnings, car miles, and passenger traffic. The city ranked third in expenses per car mile but eleventh in regard to passengers and earnings per car mile. Rugged topography explains some of the lower rankings, but the city was also considerably below the national average in terms of headway between cars and frequency of service. This data suggests that the Pittsburgh Railways Company had failed to allocate its resources in a manner most calculated to meet rising passenger demand. Rather than concentrating on improving service and developing short haul and transverse routes, it had extended lines into formerly untapped territory. Short-haul riders on the road paid the same nickel fare as long-haul riders who were essentially being subsidized by the former. Overcapitalization resulting from the consolidation of multiple streetcar lines, as its critics frequently noted, was perhaps the Pittsburgh Railways Company's most serious problem. Thus, in 1910, at a time when many big city traction systems were still relatively healthy, Pittsburgh's was already suffering severe difficulties.[38]

During the years after the publication of Arnold's report—although passenger traffic on the Pittsburgh Railways Company lines increased 21 percent from 204,755,471 in 1910 to 244,520,558 in 1916—the company's financial position disintegrated. It had paid little attention to maintenance or the purchase of new equipment, and in 1918 the Pittsburgh Railways Company went into receivership. In the following years, a number of reports were published recommending system improvements and the development of rapid transit lines as well as municipal ownership, but little of these recommendations were implemented. Although the system emerged from receivership in 1924 and some technical improvements were made in routing and equipment, no rapid transit system was ever constructed. Privately owned and operated public transit in Allegheny County, for the most part, came to an end in 1959 with the formation of the Port Authority Transit of Allegheny County and the consolidation in 1964 of thirty-three private companies.[39] To a large extent, however, the substantive impacts of

FIG. 6.3 Homestead and East Pittsburgh streetcar, 1917 (Pittsburgh City Photographer Collection, courtesy of the Archives Service Center, University of Pittsburgh).

public transit on Pittsburgh region spatial patterns had occurred long before this time.

CONCLUSIONS

From approximately 1890–1917, a series of transportation innovations radically changed residential, commercial, and industrial patterns within the Pittsburgh region. Whereas the 1850 city had been characterized by a large mixture of land uses within the core of the city, the twentieth-century metropolis had far more specialized patterns. Many of these patterns had emerged by the 1890s (see Figure 6.3).

Although the CBD in 1917 still contained a number of industries, the commercial, retailing, and central office functions were becoming increasingly important. To a large extent white-collar workers who used streetcars and commuter railroads to make a daily journey between residence and workplace staffed the growing commercial, retailing, and central office enterprises. Transportation improvements generated residential housing booms on the urban periphery as lines penetrated formerly untapped territory. This development made possible lower density living conditions with improved amenities for numbers of urbanites who had formerly lived in congested neighborhoods closer to their place of employment. Public transit, however, was limited in the changes it could accomplish in the travel patterns of industrial workers. Substantial numbers of industrial workers utilized the streetcar systems to separate residence and workplace, but large numbers of unskilled and semiskilled workers, perhaps a majority of industrial employees, could afford neither the time nor the fare required for commuting. Consequently, they lived within walking distance of their workplaces.

APPENDIX 6.1

Journey to Work, 1860–1910, for Bank Presidents

In 1860, out of a sample of eight bank presidents (all banks located in Wards 1–4), five lived within a half mile of their banks, two lived across the Allegheny River in nearby Allegheny City, and one lived in Oakland three–four miles from the core. In 1890 no bank president lived in Wards 1–4, five resided in the elite section of Allegheny, and five lived in neighborhoods near the city's eastern border, about five miles from the CBD. By 1910 Allegheny had been largely abandoned as an elite area, and some bank presidents were traveling from as far as Sewickley and Glen Osborne twelve miles down the Ohio River. Many of these bank presidents rode commuter trains to their banks.[40]

APPENDIX 6.2

Pittsburgh and Allegheny County Outlying Town Growth

Table 6.1 Pittsburgh and Allegheny County Demographic and Housing Patterns, 1870–1930.

City	1870	1880	1890	1900
Population	86,076	156,389	238,617	321,626
Density	5.82	8.8	14.82	17.9
Dwellings	14,224		37,725	51,024

Wards 1–4:				
Population	13,378	13,116	12,661	8,217
Density	47.9	46.9	45	29.1
Dwellings	2,245		1,596	1,182
Wards 5–12:				
Population	42,700	44,270	55,282	59,519
Density	54.05	56.04	69.98	75.34
Dwellings	6,629		8,275	8,094
Wards 13–23:				
Population	29,998	53,690	103,091	169,025
Density	2.25	3.9	7.59	12.4
Dwellings	5,350		17,604	28,278
Wards 24–36:				
Population	31,361	45,309	67,583	76,722
Density	11.7	16.9	25.2	28.6
Dwellings			10,250	11,891

TABLE 6.2 Population Growth of Selected Pittsburgh Suburbs, 1880–1920

	1880	1900	1910	1920
Wilkinsburg	1,529	11,886	18,924	24,403
Sewickley	2,053	3,563	4,479	4,955
Edgewood	218	1,139	2,596	3,181
Dormont			1,115	6,455
Aspinwall		1,231	2,592	3,170
Castle Shannon	305		2,353	
Penn Hills	3,291	3.407	6,201	8,342

NOTES

Portions of this essay were originally published in Joel A. Tarr, *Transportation Innovation and Changing Spatial Patterns in Pittsburgh, 1850–1934* (Chicago: Public Works Historical Society, 1978), and were revised in 2017.

1. Robert C. Post, *Urban Mass Transit: The Life Story of a Technology* (Baltimore: Johns Hopkins University Press, 2010), 14–64.

2. James, "History of Urban Transportation," 51; George W. Hilton, *The Cable Car in America* (Berkeley, 1971); Craig Semsel, "The Mechanization of Pittsburgh Street Railways, 1886–1897," *Pittsburgh History* 77 (Summer 1994): 54–66.

3. Semsel, "Mechanization, 59.

4. Citizens Passenger, which changed to cable at the beginning of 1889, boosted its ridership by 56 percent, from 6,952,131 in 1888 to 10,832,192 in 1889. Central Traction, which converted to cable in March 1890, augmented its ridership by 187 percent, from 1,062,235 in 1888 to 3,049,852 in 1890.

5. *Pittsburgh's Industrial Exposition, 1891*, n.p.; Homewood Board of Trade, *Official Souvenir Program, Mardi Gras Carnival and Fair* (Pittsburgh, 1902), n.p.; Lester A. Hoel et al., *Latent Demand for Urban Transportation* (Pittsburgh: Transportation Research Institute, Carnegie Mellon University, 1968), 1–4.

6. There were two early electrical experiments in Pittsburgh in the 1886–1888 period. The "Daft" system, which provided power through a small wheeled "Troller" running over an overhead electrified wire connected to a locomotive and cars below, operated in the South side, Knoxville, and Mount Oliver. In Allegheny City the Observatory Hill Passenger Railway Company began operating a "Bentley-Knight" system, which used underground electric wire to provide power. Semsel, "Mechanization," 59–60.

7. Harold C. Passer, *The Electrical Manufacturers, 1875–1900* (Cambridge, 1953), 216–17, 237–75; Charles H. Cooley, "Statistics of Street Railway Transportation," in Henry C. Adams, comp., *Report on the Transportation Business in the United States, Part I: Transportation by Land, Eleventh Census*, XVIII (Washington, DC, 1895), 688.

8. James, "History of Urban Transportation," 31–34; Arnold, *Pittsburgh Transportation Problem*, 41.

9. Arnold, *Pittsburgh Transportation Problem*, 41; J. M. Kelly, *Handbook of Greater Pittsburgh* (Pittsburgh, 1895), 55–59.

10. Semsel, "Mechanization," 60–66; Mark Gallimore, "The Business and Politics of Mass Transit in Pittsburgh, 1902–1938" (PhD diss., Lehigh University 2010), 71–76. The franchises often contained street maintenance obligations such as the paving and cleaning of some or all of the street around the rails.

11. See passenger and mileage statistics in Pennsylvania, *Annual Report, Secretary of Internal Affairs for 1888–1894* (Harrisburg, 1894–1895); Cooley, "Street Railway Transportation," 683–84; Gallimore, "Business and Politics of Mass Transit," 82.

12. Gallimore, "Business and Politics of Mass Transit," 79–81. See Gallimore's discussion of the characteristics of the transit fleet and improvements in the system between 1902 and 1918.

13. Population and density figures computed from *Eleventh Census (1890)*, 293–312, and *Twelfth Census (1900) Vol. I: Population, Part 1* (Washington, DC, 1901), 876.

14. See Edward K. Muller, "Downtown Pittsburgh: Relentless Evolution," in this volume.

15. Storch, "Changing Functions of the Center-City," 3–8, 25–27, 33.

16. "Manuscript Building Permit Records, 1888–1907," Archives of Industrial Society, University of Pittsburgh. Between 1894 and 1906, 356 new buildings were constructed in the CBD, many still of masonry.

17. "Manuscript Building Permit Records, 1888–1907."

18. Storch, "Changing Functions of the Center-City," 14–17; Olds, "Four Hypotheses of the Urban Pattern," 70–100; Kellogg, *The Pittsburgh District: Civic Frontage*, 16.

19. Storch, "Changing Functions of the Center-City," 17; Ileen A. DeVault, *Sons and Daughters of Labor: Class and Clerical Work in Turn-of-the-Century Pittsburgh* (Ithaca: Cornell University Press, 1990), 12, 144–45. DeVault analyzed the work careers of graduates of the Commercial Department of the Pittsburgh Public Schools and found that, in 1900, 70 percent of former students employed in office jobs worked in the CBD; by 1905 the percentage had grown to 81.

20. Computed from seating capacity maps in Arnold, *Pittsburgh Transportation Problem*, between pp. 86–87 and after p.160.

21. E. K. Morse, *Report of the Transit Commissioner to the Mayor* (Pittsburgh, 1917), 36, 62–64. The 1917 survey of 49,394 CBD workers showed that approximately 11 percent traveled from zero to one mile, 27 percent traveled from one to two miles; 16.5 percent, from two to three miles; 15 percent, from three to four miles; 11.5 percent, from four to five miles; 11 percent, from five to six miles; and 7.5 percent, more than six miles.

22. Computed from data in Morse, *Report of the Transit Commissioner (1918)*, 64.

23. Gallimore, "Business and Politics of Mass Transit, 83.

24. Pittsburgh, *Sixth Annual Report of the Department of Public Safety* (Pittsburgh, 1894), 66–72, gives building activity by ward with estimated costs from 1881 to 1893. See also Isard, "Transport Development and Building Cycles," 105–11.

25. Homewood Board of Trade, *Official Souvenir Program, Mardi Gras Carnival*, n.p. For fringe developments in other cities in response to transportation innovation in the period, see Warner, *Streetcar Suburbs*; Goheen, *Victorian Toronto*, 156–221; Homer Hoyt, *One Hundred Years of Land Values in Chicago* (Chicago, 1933), 88–231; David Ward, "A Comparative Historical Geography of Streetcar Suburbs of Boston, Massachusetts and Leeds, England: 1850–1920," *Annals of the Association of American Geographers* 54 (December 1964): 477–89; and John S. Adams, "Residential Structure of Midwestern Cities," *Annals of the Association of American Geographers*, 60 (March 1970): 37–61.

26. Morse, *Report of the Transit Commissioner (1917)*, 36, 62–64.

27. *Thirteenth Census of the U.S. Taken in the Year 1910, Statistics for Pennsylvania*, ch. 1, "Number of Inhabitants," 569. This census includes population of minor civil divisions from 1890–1910.

28. Morse, *Report of the Transit Commissioner (1917)*, 36, 62–64; Renee Reitman, "The Elite Community in Shadyside, 1880–1920" (unpublished seminar paper, Department of History, University of Pittsburgh, 1964), 5–10.

29. Edward Ewing Pratt, *Industrial Causes of Congestion of Population in New York City*, 116–88; Clay McShane, *Technology and Reform: Street Railways and the Growth of Milwaukee, 1870–1900* (Madison,: Wisconsin Historical Society, 1975), 38–39.

30. Pittsburgh Plat Maps, 1872, 1882, 1898, Pennsylvania Room, Carnegie Library, Pittsburgh, PA. For evidence from other cities that unskilled workers did not regularly use streetcar transit in the late nineteenth and early twentieth centuries, see Hoyt, *Land Values*

in Chicago, 311; Ward, *Cities and Immigrants*, 107–9, 120–21. For an opposite conclusion on ridership, see Goheen, *Victorian Toronto*, 184, 199–201.

31. Morse, *Report of the Transit Commissioner (1917)*, 57–66. See also "Residential Distribution of 274,083 Employees of Industrial and Commercial Establishments, Showing Location of Groups, Number of Employees, and Percentages of Totals Living at Various Distances from their Place of Employment," Table 6, Morse, *Report of the Transit Commissioner (1917)*. The report is confusing in its terminology. Its surveys recorded a large sample of pedestrians and streetcar passengers. However, it uses the terms "industrial" and "industries" when clearly many of those surveyed were not industrial workers.

32. Hershberg et al., "The Journey-to-Work," 25; David Brody, *Steelworkers in America: The Nonunion Era* (New York: Harper Torchbook, 1969), 37–40.

33. US Bureau of the Census, *Thirteenth Census (1910), Vol. III: Population* (Washington, DC, 1913), 609, gives a breakdown of ethnic groups by ward and number of dwellings per ward. See also Ward, *Cities and Immigrants*, 197; Kellogg, *The Pittsburgh District: Civic Frontage*, 87–138; John T. Holdsworth, *Report of the Economic Survey of Pittsburgh* (Pittsburgh, 1912), 47, 81.

34. Mark Gallimore, "The Business and Politics of Mass Transit in Pittsburgh, 1902–1938," (unpublished doctoral dissertation, Lehigh University, 1910), 107.

35. Gallimore, "The Business and Politics of Mass Transit," 142.

36. Arnold, *Pittsburgh Transportation Problem*, 3. See also Fox, "The Transit Situation in Pittsburgh,“ 834–40.

37. Arnold, *Pittsburgh Transportation Problem*, 1, 11–13, 78–85.

38. Arnold, *Pittsburgh Transportation Problem*, 123–39, 145; Gallimore, "Business and Politics of Mass Transit in Pittsburgh," 86–96.

39. The following is a list of the major transit reports for Pittsburgh and Allegheny County, made in the period from 1917 to 1967; [E. K. Morse], *Report of the Transit Commissioner to the Mayor* (Pittsburgh, 1917); Emil Swensson, *Report to the State Railroad Commission* [on Pittsburgh Railways] (Harrisburg: E. E. Aughinbaugh, 1910); CCCP, *Transit: A Part of the Pittsburgh Plan* (Pittsburgh, 1923); D. L. Turner and Winters Haydock, *Communication from the City Transit Commission to the Mayor and City Council Containing a Report on a Plan for Financing Initial Subway Construction in Pittsburgh* (Pittsburgh, 1926); W. S. Menden [Parsons, Klapp, Brinckerhoff, and Douglas], *Report on Pittsburgh Mass Transportation* (Pittsburgh, 1941); Philip Robinson [Allegheny Conference on Community Development], *Mass Transportation Study of Pittsburgh and Allegheny County* (Pittsburgh, 1949); Allegheny County, *Report of Allegheny County Mass Transportation Study Commissions* (Pittsburgh, 1953); Port Authority of Allegheny County, *Report of the Port Authority of Allegheny County on an Integrated System of Mass Transportation for Allegheny County* (Pittsburgh, 1961); *Pittsburgh Area Transportation Study*, 2 vols. (Pittsburgh, 1961, 1963); Parsons, Brinckerhoff, Quade, and Douglas, *Allegheny County Rapid Transit Study* (Pittsburgh, 1967); Transportation Research Institute, Carnegie Mellon University, *Application of a Rubber-Tired, Lightweight, Geometrically Flexible Transit Technology to a Rapid Transit System for Allegheny County*, 4 vols. (Pittsburgh, 1967).

40. Information on addresses of banks executives and employees was obtained from bank advertisements in various Pittsburgh city directories from 1850 to 1910.

7 THE AUTOMOBILE COMES TO PITTSBURGH, 1910–1935

Joel A. Tarr

Historians and urban scholars recognize that the chief transportation technology affecting the shaping of cities and metropolitan areas since the 1920s has been the automobile and the motor truck.[1] Several themes involving the impact of these vehicles on the Pittsburgh region during the initial decades of the automobile's adoption form the focus of this chapter. These themes include the effects of the automobile and truck on the city's built environment, journey-to-work patterns, traffic issues, and automobile and pedestrian safety. As in other metropolitan areas, Pittsburgh and its region sought to cope with the challenges presented by the new technology. Because of its unique topography, industrial development patterns, and trans-section by three rivers, Pittsburgh offered a sharp challenge to any attempt at a rationally organized metropolis. The introduction of the automobile into the city on top of an extensive street railway system compounded attempts by planners to create an "accessible city."[2]

The state of Pennsylvania did not adopt comprehensive regulations regarding automobile registration and operation until 1913. This law included requirements for licensing of automobiles, age limits for drivers, penalties for intoxicated drivers, and speed limits. The state legislature enacted additional regulations concerning automobile registration and operation in the

1920s.[3] No information is available regarding the exact number of automobiles in Pittsburgh until the 1920s, but inhabitants of cities such as Chicago, Boston, and Los Angeles appear to have adopted the vehicle much more rapidly than Steel City citizens. In 1910, for instance, Allegheny County had approximately one automobile to every 636 persons, and in Pennsylvania the ratio was one to every 136 (the national figure was one to 201). By 1920 the national figure was one automobile to 13 persons, and the Pennsylvania ratio was one to 15. By 1929 Allegheny County registration had reached almost one automobile to 7 persons (203,866 total), slightly below the national figure of one to 5 persons.[4] As was true in other cities, ownership and use of automobiles were unevenly distributed throughout the urban area.

In 1937 the Bureau of Business Research at the University of Pittsburgh published the Federal Works Project Administration's *Real Property Inventory of Allegheny County*.[5] This report provided a wide range of information regarding household characteristics such as utilities, plumbing facilities, fuel use, heating technology, and household rental and ownership values. In addition, and most pertinent for this study, it included statistics regarding automobile ownership, travel mode, and distance to work.

The *Real Property Inventory* showed that out of a sample of 220,461 Allegheny County "chief income earners," a little more than half owned automobiles. Automobile ownership was highest in the wealthier wards and suburbs. The Fourteenth Ward (Squirrel Hill), for example, had both the city's highest percentage of automobile ownership (almost all of the chief income owners) and the highest percentage of homes with a value of over ten thousand dollars (about three-quarters of the homes). At this time only 14.6 percent of all single family homes in Allegheny County had this value. The highest percentage of county automobile ownership outside the city (97 percent) was in the township of Mount Lebanon where 74 percent of the homes were valued at over ten thousand dollars. In contrast, Pittsburgh's Third Ward, where only 14.7 percent of the private dwellings were valued at over ten thousand dollars, had the city's lowest percentage of automobile ownership (8.7 percent); the mill town of Homestead where only one home was valued at over ten thousand dollars, had the lowest percentage of county automobile ownership (20.4 percent).[6]

There were, however, wards and county boroughs and townships that had relatively high automobile ownership in spite of lower home ownership and rental values. This suggests that people retained their automobiles in this Depression year either because they needed them for access to jobs or because automobiles were a luxury they were not prepared to surrender.[7] Generally, however, high automobile ownership was positively correlated with a high economic level, while low automobile ownership was correlated with low-income levels.[8]

THOROUGHFARE AND HIGHWAY DEVELOPMENT

From 1910 to 1930, a period in which the number of automobiles registered in Allegheny County increased from 1,601 to 205,905, Pittsburgh and the county attempted to design an effective system of automobile circulation. The growth in automobiles required a concomitant increase in smooth surfaced streets and roads, a process already begun in the late nineteenth century because of the demands of bicycle riders.[9] Before 1900 many of the city's streets were either unpaved or paved with cobblestones. Only a few of the streets in the city's road network led to its outlying areas, and no limited access roads existed that were free of streetcar tracks. The largely electric-powered streetcar network, however, was extensive and by 1902 had reached 469 miles of track and 263 rides per inhabitant. Many streetcar trips ended in the Central Business District (CBD), and riders included downtown workers, shoppers, and entertainment seekers.[10]

In 1909 Mayor George Gutherie had appointed the Pittsburgh City Commission (PCC) "to plan and promote improvements to civic and industrial conditions." In 1910 the PCC retained three prominent urban specialists, Bion J. Arnold, Frederick Law Olmsted Jr., and John R. Freeman, to develop an outline for a Pittsburgh city plan. Published as *City Planning for Pittsburgh*, the plan called for investigations into ten areas of municipal concern including steam railroads, water transportation, electric railroads, and street systems. Eventually only two reports appeared: one by Arnold, *Report on the Pittsburgh Transportation Problem*, and the other by Olmsted, *Pittsburgh: Main Thoroughfares and the Down Town District: Improvements Necessary to Meet the City's Present and Future Needs*.[11]

The architect and planner Frederick Law Olmsted Jr. viewed "the modern city as a mosaic of functioning parts." Over half of his study focused on the problem of downtown traffic congestion; the remainder discussed road issues outside this sector and beyond the city's boundaries. His recommendations included proposals to widen streets, plans for a new bridge and tunnel to the city's South Side, and boulevards and highways linking South Side to the downtown. Although not all of his proposals were enacted, others provided a plan that shaped street construction and highway building for decades to come.[12]

Improved connection with the downtown had actually begun before the growth in automobile ownership. In 1900 the city opened Grant Boulevard paralleling the Allegheny River for approximately three miles on Bedford

Hill. This boulevard extended from the downtown to Oakland where a new civic center was developing.[13] Grant Boulevard was originally planned as part of a twelve-mile drive through the city's eastern neighborhoods and parks for the exclusive use of carriages and other "light vehicles." In 1916 the roadway, which had been plagued by slides and steep grades, was widened and renamed Bigelow Boulevard and became a major route for automobiles into the downtown. A bridge connection with Baum Boulevard later extended the thoroughfare into the busy subcenter of East Liberty where it joined Penn Avenue near the eastern edge of the city linking into US Route 30.[14]

At the end of the First World War, the need for further street improvements and new thoroughfares was extremely pressing because of the rise in automobile and truck traffic. Downtown traffic had increased greatly since 1910, but Bigelow Boulevard remained the only restricted thoroughfare connecting it with the city. City planners such as Olmsted argued that automobile roadways were needed both to provide entry into the downtown and to open up some of the hilly and less accessible areas of the city and county to residential development.

An eastern thoroughfare along the Monongahela River, later named the Boulevard of the Allies, had been discussed since the beginning of the century. In 1913 the City Planning Department proposed a plan for a Monongahela Boulevard, but the city did not begin construction of the thoroughfare until 1919; completion occurred in October 1922. By 1924 the boulevard was carrying 9,387 inbound and outbound automobiles and trucks in a typical eleven-hour day. This traffic total compared with 15,406 for Bigelow Boulevard on the Allegheny side. In April 1927 the city council approved a further extension of the Boulevard of the Allies eastward into Schenley Park, opening direct access from the popular and developing Squirrel Hill neighborhood to the downtown.[15]

Another major arterial improvement completed in 1926 was a tunnel that penetrated the hilly escarpment Mount Washington that lined the Monongahela River.[16] The tunnel, which consisted of a 5,889-foot twin tube ventilated by fans to keep exhaust gases at a safe level, was completed in 1926. At the time it was constructed it was the longest automobile tunnel in the world. At its southern end, the Liberty Tunnel connected with West Liberty Avenue and eventually linked with Washington Road or US Route 19. This route connected the suburban areas of south Allegheny County with the city and opened them to settlement. Two years later, in 1928, the new Liberty Bridge was opened, tying the tunnel to the Boulevard of the Allies and to the downtown.[17]

These improvements were often not well coordinated as part of an overall county plan to accommodate the major growth in automobile traffic, especially in regard to downtown access. This problem is reflected in the fate of the recommendations of a major planning group, the Citizens Committee on City Plan of Pittsburgh (CCCP). The CCCP, formed in 1918, had an executive committee of prominent business executives and professionals. Under the technical direction of planners Harland Bartholomew and Frederick Bigger, the CCCP issued six reports on topics such as playgrounds, transit, parks, railroads, streets, and waterways. Their recommendations reflected the prevailing theory of Chicago urban sociologists Robert Park and Ernest Burgess of the city as a biological system. Streets, thoroughfares, and highways served as the city's vital arteries and veins, and the urban system had to provide, as the CCCP Major Street plan noted, a "general circulatory system, to secure the uniform flow and diffusion of traffic." Circulation of vehicles within this system had to be kept uninterrupted and traffic congestion avoided.[18]

To a large extent, however, in the 1920s, city and county officials ignored the recommendations of the CCCP and planning groups calling for comprehensive planning to meet the challenges of the expanding city and county. In 1924, for instance, the CCCP and its chief planner, Frederick Bigger, urged the city council to give priority to an Inter-District Traffic Circuit providing a crosstown expressway that would form part of a regional highway system. The proposed Inter-District Traffic Circuit would bypass the downtown and connect the south and north sides of the city. The CCCP referred the proposal to the City Planning Commission. The Commission officially adopted the Inter-District Traffic Circuit concept in 1925 but never took action to implement it.[19]

Another missed planning opportunity occurred when the county policy makers failed to adopt the Major Highway Plan produced by its Department of Public Works. This plan attempted to integrate the needs of the city's center and outlying areas of the county to improve traffic flows. Planning, however, conflicted with local political interests, and although parts of the Highway Plan including bridges and highways were constructed, the system was never completed.[20] These gaps were especially evident in the relationship of the automobile traffic to the CBD.

THE AUTOMOBILE'S IMPACT ON THE CBD

Rugged topography confined the Pittsburgh CBD or downtown (the "Golden Triangle") to the city's original location where the Monongahela and Allegheny Rivers met to form the Ohio. A sharp line of hills to the east prevented expansion in that direction, leaving 255 acres for development. In the late nineteenth century extensive construction transformed this site from a mixed commercial, industrial, and residential area to an office, retailing, and commercial center and railroad hub. By the first decade of the twentieth century approximately one hundred thousand people per working day entered the downtown for purposes of employment, shopping, and entertainment. A majority of the commuters traveled on the extensive electric streetcar system and commuter railroads.[21]

Limited access and an inadequate street plan accentuated the problem of funneling this many people into a relatively small area. All traffic coming into the downtown, except from the east, had to cross a river by bridge. Once into the downtown, steep grades, narrow streets, and sharp angle turns hampered traffic. Prior to 1904 there was no street or avenue wider than sixty feet except for Liberty Avenue, a major east–west thoroughfare much of which was occupied by the tracks of the Pennsylvania Railroad. Most streets (61.1 acres in total) were forty feet wide, while alleys were twenty feet. Besides their narrow width, many streets were occupied by streetcar tracks, which further impeded the flow of traffic.[22] In 1904 and 1905, faced by growing congestion, the city widened a number of downtown streets, and the Pennsylvania Railroad removed its tracks from Liberty Avenue. However, only Grant Boulevard (Bigelow Boulevard after 1916) served as a main thoroughfare from the densely populated East End.

The PCC had argued in 1909 that "inadequate traffic facilities in Pittsburgh . . . add to the cost of doing business and of living." Olmsted's *Pittsburgh: Main Thoroughfares and the Down Town District* discussed downtown traffic circulation improvements in detail. He advocated widening streets, eliminating steep grades, and removing traffic obstructions from street crossings. Although the major increase of automobiles and trucks in the downtown was in the future, Olmsted noted that they had already begun to contribute to traffic congestion. In 1917 the Pittsburgh transit commissioner reported that of the 30,205 vehicles entering the CBD during a normal summer business day (7:00 a.m.–7:00 p.m.) 9,911 were automobiles, 6,432 motor trucks, and 191 motorcycles; the remainder consisted of 8,370 horse-drawn vehicles and 5,301 streetcars. Adding to the congestion was the fact that almost one-fifth of downtown traffic was through traffic (see Figure 7.1).[23]

At the end of the war the city began acting upon some of Olmsted's and the transit commissioner's recommendations to reduce traffic congestion. In 1919 voters approved a twenty-million-dollar bond issue to support these projects. In the downtown, the major improvement involved widening streets

FIG. 7.1 Alternative modes of transportation, 1917 (Pittsburgh City Photographer Collection, courtesy of the Archives Service Center, University of Pittsburgh).

to accommodate four and six lanes of traffic.[24] Increases in traffic, however, overwhelmed the impact of these improvements. Between 1917 and 1920, the number of automobiles entering and leaving the CBD in a twelve-hour period increased from 9,811 to 32,416, and the number of motor trucks rose from 6,432 to 20,554. Horse-drawn vehicles decreased from 8,370 to 7,545.[25] The bond issue had included six million dollars for construction of a CBD subway, but political controversy blocked its development.[26]

In the period from 1920 to 1923, the CCCP continued its efforts to "give Pittsburgh an orderly, scientific, comprehensive program of city planning, producing a series of reports on various problems in the Pittsburgh region." The committee's overall report consisted of six parts: playgrounds, streets, transit, parks, railroads, and waterways. The report on streets, most pertinent to the issue of traffic congestion, recommended further street widening throughout the Pittsburgh region, the building of thoroughfares between business and industrial sections and residential areas, and the development of a downtown bypass. Although the committee maintained that the most serious cause of congestion was found "beyond the limits of the Triangle itself," it called for the improvement of downtown streets and the rerouting of through traffic. It also foresaw the eventual elimination of streetcars from the downtown in order to facilitate traffic flow.[27]

In 1922 the Pittsburgh City Council officially adopted the committee's street plan as a "guide in the expenditure of public funds," and the City Planning Commission endorsed it "as a measuring stick for further improvements." But although the planning report was accepted in principle, it was ignored in practice. Some isolated improvements were made, but no

FIG. 7.2 Congestion on Diamond Street (Forbes Avenue today), 1928—streetcars, delivery trucks, automobiles, and pedestrians typically crowd a downtown street (Pittsburgh City Photographer Collection, courtesy of Archives Service Center, University of Pittsburgh).

unified plan was undertaken. In 1929 Frederick Bigger, the chief technical advisor to the CCCP and a member of the City Planning Commission, complained that streets were still regarded as "isolated units undertaken spasmodically," and "therein lies our community stupidity, for piecemeal planning leads us no-where."[28]

The continued increase in cars and commercial vehicles in the downtown intensified the problems of congestion beyond any planner's expectations (see "Downtown Pittsburgh" in this volume). In 1924, in recognition of the traffic problem (see Figure 7.2), Mayor Magee appointed Burton W. Marsh as the nation's first full-time city traffic engineer.[29] Marsh had a major challenge facing him. From 1925 to 1930 the number of new car registrations for Pittsburgh was 128,864 and for the remainder of the county 64,090. In April 1927 there were 68,133 passenger automobiles, 22,623 trucks, 9,587 streetcars, 1,823 horse-drawn vehicles, and 504 buses that entered and left the CBD in a typical ten-hour day.[30]

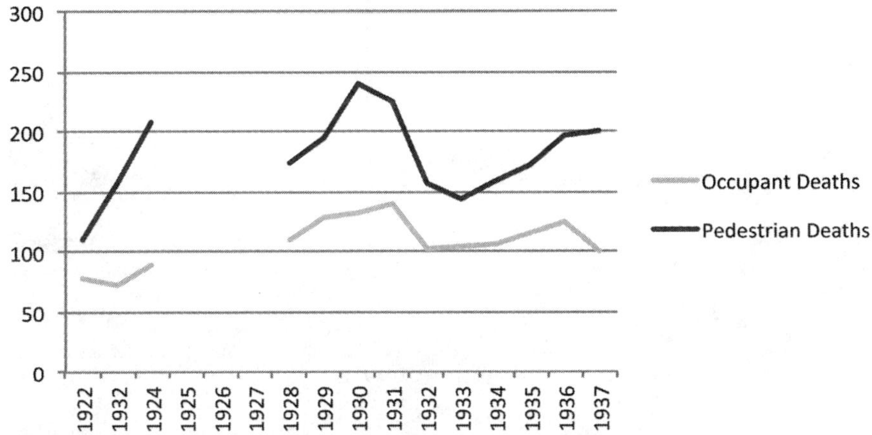

Chart 7.1 Deaths Related to Automobiles in Allegheny County, 1905–1935 (reproduction from "Recapitulation of Fatal Accidents Compiled by Coroner W. J. McGregor, M.D. 1906–1930," *Controller's 70th Annual Report . . . 1930* [Pittsburgh, 1930], 518).

AUTOMOBILE-RELATED DEATHS

The increase in the number of automobiles in the CBD and in the county as a whole resulted in dense traffic jams and a sharp rise in automobile and pedestrian accidents with related injuries and deaths. These increases were true of all American cities where automobiles, pedestrians, streetcars, and horse-drawn vehicles contested over street usage.[31] From 1915 to 1925, for instance, the US automobile death rate per one hundred thousand population increased from 6 to 17; in some cities, such as Detroit and Cleveland, the rate was approximately 25 deaths per one hundred thousand.[32] In the city of Pittsburgh in 1922 there were 81 automobile-related deaths, but by 1930 the total had reached 195; in Allegheny County outside the city the increase was from 101 to 201 in the same period. In total, from 1906 to 1930, there were 3,766 automobile related deaths in the county (see Chart 7.1).[33]

Pedestrian deaths were especially high. In 1922, for instance, automobiles killed 125 pedestrians in the county, which was double the number of automobile occupants (drivers and passengers) killed. Two years later, in 1924, automobiles killed 208 pedestrians, and the number of occupants killed reached 89. The high point for county automobile-related deaths was in 1930, with 240 pedestrian and 132 occupant deaths.[34] The Allegheny County coroner W. J. McGregor maintained that fatal accidents were highest in "the most congested districts of Pittsburgh" and resulted from the "inexplicable craze for speed, wanton carelessness and intoxication" on the part of

FIG. 7.3 Early attempts at traffic control (Pittsburgh City Photographer Collection, courtesy of the Archives Service Center, University of Pittsburgh).

drivers.[35] Children were especially vulnerable. In 1922 automobiles killed 59 children under the age of fourteen, and in 1930 the number was 67.[36]

Concern over pedestrian accidents focused on the downtown with its heavy vehicle and pedestrian traffic flows, although pedestrian deaths were also high outside the city and growing especially in new suburban areas (see Figure 7.3).[37] In 1924 Mayor William Magee, responding to the automobile and pedestrian crisis, formed the Better Traffic Committee (BTC) composed of city officials and citizens. Its task was twofold: to improve traffic flows and to enhance pedestrian safety. The BTC had four standing committees focusing on education, engineering, law enforcement, and traffic flow.[38]

In order to protect pedestrians the BTC and the city emphasized educating the public and especially children of the need for safety awareness. In 1927 the city held a Pedestrian Week sponsored by the BTC. It featured the distribution of pamphlets cautioning safe behaviors such as the need to observe road signs, crossing at proper intersections, and looking both ways at street crossings. The BTC also broadcast twenty-four radio addresses emphasizing pedestrian safety and established a "Court of Public Opinion" to discourage "jaywalking" (see Figure 7.4). So-called Undertakers distributed summonses to jaywalkers to attend the Court of Public Opinion to hear

Fig. 7.4 Jaywalking downtown, 1921 (Pittsburgh City Photographer Collection, courtesy of the Archives Service Center, University of Pittsburgh).

educational lectures on safe street-crossing behavior. Traffic experts later claimed that there was "no doubt that the continuous, coordinated educational program which has been carried on by various agencies has played a major part in accident prevention." Results were limited, however, since automobiles and pedestrians still contested for space on the same Pittsburgh streets.[39]

As a means toward greater and more efficient use of the streets, many American cities sponsored traffic surveys to better understand how automobiles were utilized. Traffic engineers recorded variables such as speed, turning patterns, curb parking, pedestrian activity, and accidents. In 1927 the BTC sponsored a CBD traffic survey conducted by seven hundred Boy Scouts and other volunteers under the direction of the City Bureau of Traffic Planning and the University of Pittsburgh traffic expert Lewis W. McIntyre.[40] These surveys became an annual event in the city, identifying dangerous street zones and bad driving practices such as high speed left turns and driving in the wrong lane, and the improper placing of traffic signals. The survey recommended the installation of a "flexible co-ordinated" electrical system in the downtown to replace police hand-operated semaphore signals used to control traffic and replacement of dummy or "silent policemen" intersection centerpoint markers. The report concluded that the new system would reduce time spent in traffic by at least 30 percent, cut accidents, allow pedestrians "to cross the roadway in an orderly and dignified fashion," reduce the number of traffic officers needed, and increase downtown business.[41]

In February 1928, the city council approved a bond issue of $125,000 for a traffic control system to cover most of the downtown. The system was designed to provide progressive traffic movement through approximately one hundred intersections. In addition, the system included a special cycle that informed pedestrians when it was safe or unsafe to cross the street. According to analysis of the system by the city traffic engineer Burton W. Marsh and the traffic planner Cornelius J. Lyons, the progressive lights had "certainly . . . prevented traffic accidents."[42] Other actions taken to reduce traffic and pedestrian accidents included installing standard traffic signs, adding signals outside the downtown, mapping accidents so as to identify problematic intersections, and extensive educational safety projects in the schools.[43]

In spite of these actions, the number of county automobile-related deaths (about half in the city and one-fifth of them children) soared in 1930 to almost 400, including 240 pedestrians. On July 9, 1930, the *Pittsburgh Press* ran a front page story on the city's "10 Deadliest Streets" and calculated that, between 1923 and 1930, 775 pedestrians had died in the city, more than half of whom were "jaywalkers" and about one-third pedestrians "who had the right of way."[44] In total, 1,150 Pittsburghers died in automobile crashes in this period.

During the years of increasing automobile-related accidents and death, as Traffic Engineer Marsh commented, the city had "aggressively tackled its traffic accident problem." Writing in 1930 he and the traffic accident analyst Cornelius J. Lyons noted the important steps toward accident reduction that had been taken. Some steps were institutional, such as the creation of the BTC and the Bureau of Traffic Planning. Others involved engineering innovations such as progressive signal systems and the development of maps showing high accident locations so preventive action could be taken. And another consisted of extensive educational work in and outside the schools including traffic essay contests, distribution of safety literature, and a safety speaker's bureau for school visits.[45] These innovations seem to have had a cumulative effect in reducing accidents, especially after a peak was reached in 1930, although totals began to rise again after 1935. Very possibly the recovery from the depression, the rise in automobile usage, and the end of prohibition were a causal factors in the increase.[46]

Pittsburgh was not unusual in the number of pedestrian and automobile deaths, as cities throughout the nation struggled to reconcile pedestrian rights and automobile traffic.[47] There were multiple causes of the high rate of automobile-related deaths. The complexity involved when vehicles and pedestrians shared the same streets was clearly a major factor. Although traffic expert Lewis W. McIntyre noted in 1928 that automobiles deserved no more "preference" than did pedestrians in the use of streets, it became clear over the years that facilitating automobile flows and reducing traffic congestion was the higher priority. As Peter Norton notes, the "city of the motor age was a new kind of city; a city redefined as hospitable to cars."[48] This preference was also reflected in the absence of facilities to deal with the victims of automobile accidents. Neither the police nor the hospitals had ambulances suited to traffic accidents, and victims were often transported in patrol wagons. Police investigations of accidents were superficial, and records were poorly kept. In addition, police traffic law enforcement was uneven, with few arrests.[49]

AUTOMOBILE IMPACTS ON RESIDENTIAL PATTERNS IN CITY AND SUBURB

From 1910 to 1930 Pittsburgh's population grew from 588,343 to 669,817 and the county population outside the city increased from 466,727 to 680,131. The streetcar and commuter rail system had stimulated the growth of peripheral urban wards and suburbs, and the automobile greatly accelerated these developments. City growth, however, also involved annexations of surrounding territory as well as natural increase and inmigration. The pattern in Allegheny County conformed to a national trend in which the rate of population increase in the suburban rings around the cities greatly outpaced population growth within the urban core.

From 1910 to 1930 the city wards situated on the city's edge grew most in population. These had not previously undergone development either because of difficulty of access or because the land had been held off the market for speculative reasons. From 1910 to 1920, a decade in which automobile ownership was increasing but was still limited, the fastest-growing wards were Ward 14, on the eastern periphery of the city (66 percent); Ward 15, an industrial ward along the Monongahela River (39 percent); Ward 26, on the northern fringe (35 percent); and Ward 19, on the south, a ward that extended from the section opposite the CBD to the southern boundary (30 percent). During this same period, the citywide increase was 23 percent. From 1920 to 1930, Ward 14 (85 percent) and Ward 19 (36 percent) continued their rapid growth and were joined by Ward 16, a South Side ward (24 percent); and North Side Ward 27 (20 percent). Wards 14 and 19 were on the periphery; they were served by thoroughfare routes and each had a high percentage of automobile ownership.[50]

The pattern of journey-to-work trips for attorneys provides a good example of this peripheral development. Attorney workplaces had tended to cluster in the CBD, but attorneys had been making a series of outward residential moves since the late nineteenth century. In 1850 thirteen of a sample of nineteen Pittsburgh attorneys lived within one-quarter mile of their places of work and no attorney lived more than three-quarters of a mile away. In 1905 out of a sample of 168 attorneys, only 2 resided within one-quarter mile of their offices, about half of them lived between three and six miles away, and about one-fifth lived beyond six miles away. The streetcar and the commuter railroad were probably their preferred transportation mode to work. By 1930, out of a sample of 136 attorneys, 82 lived between three and six miles from their offices, and 27 lived more than six miles away. Significantly, however, between 1900 and 1930, the percentage of attorneys residing in the eastern part of Pittsburgh increased from 39 to 49 percent. This increase undoubtedly reflected easy access by automobile from this desirable residential living area to the CBD via the Boulevard of the Allies and Bigelow Boulevard.[51]

Allegheny County differed from other urban areas in the extent to which industry had moved out of the city before the turn of the century.[52] By 1900 iron and steel mills lined the banks of the rivers to a distance of nearly twenty miles from the central city, while the Westinghouse Corporation spurred the industrial development of the Turtle Creek valley, approximately ten miles from the CBD. Mill towns developed around these industrial installations, with many of the workers living in company housing close to the works (see "Industrial Suburbs and the Growth of Metropolitan Pittsburgh" in this volume).[53] The automobile would have little initial impact on the spread of population in those sectors of the county with large mill town populations.

Those county townships and boroughs that had formerly been poorly served by public transit because of topographical barriers experienced the fastest rates of growth. Between 1920 and 1930, for instance, the townships south of the city that had access to the CBD via West Liberty Avenue and the Liberty Tunnel grew 57 percent (35,505 to 55,802). The northern townships also underwent rapid growth, increasing 30 percent in the same decade. In contrast, the eastern sector of the county did not experience any faster growth than the remainder of the county outside the city (19 percent). Hills blocked direct access to the region east of the Fourteenth Ward, the logical growth area, while other parts of the sector had already undergone industrial development.[54]

IMPACT OF THE AUTOMOBILE ON BUILDING PATTERNS

Building permits for Pittsburgh residential construction increased substantially in those areas on the city's periphery that had population rises. For example, Ward 14, which had the city's highest population increase from 1917 to 1930 and direct automobile connections with the CBD after 1922, had the greatest rate of building activity: over sixty-three hundred residential units or 24 percent of the city's total. South Side Ward 19, also extending to the periphery and benefiting from the Liberty Tunnel and Bridge, had an increase of over thirty-one hundred units in the same period. Wards 26 and 27, North Side peripheral wards, also had considerable building activity—10 percent of the city's total. More than half of the structures constructed in these four wards were single family homes. The automobile, therefore, by opening up previously poorly accessible areas, stimulated considerable building activity.[55]

The same pattern is observable for the county. Building permit data for the county is unavailable, but information does exist on the age of housing and lot subdivisions. Lot subdivision is essentially a speculative activity that occurs in anticipation of building demand. From 1910 to 1930 the number of recorded lots in Pittsburgh increased from 144,209 to 155,075, while the number in the county outside the city rose from 192,848 to 254,941.[56]

Townships had the largest numerical as well as percentage increase (32 percent) in recorded building lots in the outlying county in this period. The more urbanized boroughs and the industrial third-class cities had essentially been subdivided before 1910 or even before 1900. Those townships with access or potential access to highways that connected with the CBD underwent very active subdivision. Mount Lebanon, for instance, a township south of Pittsburgh that in the 1920s developed a connection directly with the downtown via the Liberty Tunnel and Bridge, underwent rapid subdivision as 92 percent of its land was subdivided into 5,238 lots. On the east, Penn Hills, which adjoined the city, divided up 50 percent of its land; on the north, Ross Township subdivided 51 percent; McCandless Township, even further to the north, subdivided 95 percent of its land. Since lot subdivision is an indication of anticipated population growth in an area, real estate speculators undoubtedly assumed that the automobile would permit the settlement of previously poorly accessible areas of the county.[57]

The data on the age of structures supports this conclusion. From 1910 to 1930, there were 64,778 houses built in the county lying outside the Pittsburgh city boundaries. This was over half of the total housing stock in that area as of 1934. During the same period, 34,366 new houses were constructed in the city, one-third of Pittsburgh's 1934 housing stock. For the county boroughs and townships as a whole, just over one-quarter of the 1934 housing stock had been built in the 1920s. But in the southern townships that led into the Liberty Tunnel and Bridge corridor, the rate of building was twice as high: 51 percent for Dormont, which lay on the city's boundary where 39 percent of the chief wage earners used the automobile to get to work, and 56 percent in Mount Lebanon where more than one-half of the chief wage earners used the automobile. The same pattern was true in northern and eastern townships such as Penn and Shaler, which experienced rapid building and high automobile use in the journey to work.[58]

CONCLUSIONS

The coming of the automobile and the motor truck to Allegheny County resulted in substantial changes in population, housing, and mode-to-work and journey-to-work patterns in the area. Some of these changes were a continuation of trends already begun by the streetcar and the commuter railroad; others could not have occurred without the flexibility offered by the motor vehicle, as the automobile opened up for residential settlement parts of the city and county that were underdeveloped. The building of improved road systems throughout the county facilitated these developments. In addition the motor truck enabled firms to migrate from the CBD and the river belts toward cheaper land on the urban periphery. The economy of the county benefited both from the demands of the motor vehicle industry upon local steel and glass production and from the growth of retail and wholesale businesses catering to the motor vehicle (see Appendix 7.1).

Automobile ownership and usage was largely a function of income level, with low working-class involvement. Automobile usage in the journey to work was also a function of economic level although access to alternative means of transportation was a factor. The 1934 data show that a relatively large number of automobile owners who had access to either streetcar or rail transport did not use their automobiles in their journey to work.

Although urban planners such as Frederick Law Olmsted Jr. and Frederick Bigger and city and county political decision makers attempted to provide a rational approach to dealing with automobile growth, the results were mixed. Both city and county attempted many infrastructure improvements, widening streets, building thoroughfares and highways, and constructing bridges. However, they often acted in an ad hoc fashion, and local political considerations frequently disrupted circulation plans for the larger region.

Much of the planning and construction focus was on improving downtown access for automobiles, reducing traffic congestion and chaos, and cutting pedestrian injuries and deaths. In addition to infrastructure improvements, the city instituted innovations such as eliminating left turns, installing "silent policemen," and constructing a system of timed electric traffic signals. Still, traffic flows in and out of the downtown remained snarled, and pedestrian injuries and deaths continued high until well after the Second World War.[59] Writing in 1930, the Pittsburgh traffic engineer Lewis W. McIntyre noted that the problems created by the automobile involved trying to fit "a very modern machine into a very obsolete place of operation."[60] In spite of sharply reduced pedestrian accident rates, this problem remains in contemporary Pittsburgh.

APPENDIX 7.1

Impact of the Automobile on the Pittsburgh Economy

Aside from the steel and glass that was produced in Pittsburgh and consumed in the automobile industry, the services required by the automobile had an important impact on the economy. From 1900 to 1929 the number of people employed in automobile factories (including a Ford Motor Company assembly plant) and repair shops, in servicing motor vehicles, and in maintaining and constructing highways increased from near zero to 17,896. Of these employees, 10,177 were employed in Pittsburgh and 7,719 in the county outside the city.

The automobile had its most substantial economic impact in retail business. In 1929 there were 102 automobile dealers, 167 garages, 225 filling stations, and 153 automobile accessory businesses in the city; there were 190 dealers, 302 filling stations, 215 garages, and 83 accessory stores in the remainder of the county. Automobile-related retail business constituted 9.4 percent of the total number of retail businesses in the county and 14.5 of county retail sales; in the city, retail auto activity constituted 7.6 percent of retail businesses and 12.6 percent of retail sales. Employees in automobile-related retail businesses constituted 9.8 percent (or 4,049) of the total retail workforce. In addition, there were 61 wholesalers of automotive products in Pittsburgh with 1,676 employees. When compared to other cities with more than a 300,000 population, Pittsburgh had fewer automotive-related retail sales and employees than the average. The large number of employees who walked to work and the heavy use of the streetcar system probably accounts for the smaller economic impact of the automobile on Pittsburgh.[61]

NOTES

Portions of this essay were originally published in Joel A. Tarr, *Transportation Innovation and Changing Spatial Patterns in Pittsburgh, 1850–1934* (Chicago: Public Works Historical Society, 1978), and were revised in 2017.

1. See, for instance, Mark S. Foster, *From Streetcar to Superhighway: American City Planners and Urban Transportation, 1900–1940* (Philadelphia: Temple University Press, 1982); Paul Barrett, *The Automobile and Urban Transit: The Formation of Public Policy in Chicago, 1900–1930* (Philadelphia: Temple University Press, 1983); Scott L. Bottles, *Los Angeles and the Automobile: The Making of the Modern City* (Los Angeles: University of California Press, 1987); Clay McShane, *Down the Asphalt Path: The Automobile and the American City* (New York: Columbia University Press, 1994); Christopher W. Wells, *Car Country: An Environmental History* (Seattle: University of Washington Press, 2012).

2. John F. Bauman and Edward K. Muller, *Before Renaissance: Planning in Pittsburgh, 1889–1943* (Pittsburgh: University of Pittsburgh Press, 2006), 14.

3. Sartaj S. Ajrawat et al., "Watch When You Walk: Pedestrian Safety in 20th Century Pittsburgh" (Pittsburgh: Carnegie Mellon University, History and Policy Project Course, fall 2006), 55–76, http://www.cmu.edu/hss/ehpp/documents/2006-Pedestrian-Safety.pdf.

4. Pennsylvania Bureau of Motor Vehicles, "Statement of Registration and Receipts by County, 1929" (typed ms., Carnegie Library, Pittsburgh), 1.

5. Bureau of Business Research, University of Pittsburgh, *Real Property Inventory of Allegheny County* (Pittsburgh, 1937; hereafter cited as *Real Property Inventory*).

6. *Real Property Inventory*, table 1, 62–68; table 30, 265–71. For a study of Mount Lebanon, see Steven J. Hoffman, "'A Plan of Quality': The Development of Mt. Lebanon, a 1920s Automobile Suburb," *Journal of Urban History* 18, no. 2 (February 1, 1992), 123–40.

7. New automobile registrations began to rise from 1931 to 1933. *Pittsburgh Business Review*, 1931. September 1933.

8. See *Real Property Inventory*, table 9, 118–24; for average rentals by census tract, see *Real Property Inventory*, table 10, 125–31.

9. Evan Friss, *The Cycling City* (Chicago: University of Chicago Press, 2015).

10. See, Tarr, *Transportation Innovation*, 24–28.

11. Bauman and Muller, *Before Renaissance*, 114–21.

12. Bauman and Muller, *Before Renaissance*, 72–75.

13. John Brunner, "The Grant Boulevard, Pittsburg [*sic*]," *Engineering Record* 45 (January 18, 1902); Nathan Schein, "Re-arrangement of a Business District: Changes in Recent Years in Pittsburgh, Pennsylvania," *Transactions of the American Society of Engineers* 92 (1928), 735–36.

14. "Bigelow Boulevard," at http://www.brooklineconnection.com/history/Facts/BigelowBlvd.html; "Edward Manning Bigelow," at https://en.wikipedia.org/wiki/Edward_Manning_Bigelow; Pittsburgh Department of Public Works, *The City of Pittsburgh and Its Public Works* (Pittsburgh, 1916), 31.

15. *Engineering News-Record* 83 (July 17, 1919), 138; *Pittsburgh Press*, November 1, 1928.

16. Bauman and Muller, *Before Renaissance*, 76–77. Olmsted had recommended a version of the bridge and tunnel in his 1910 report.

17. "Pittsburgh South Hills Tunnel and Earlier Projects," *Engineering News-Record*

83 (July 17, 1919), 138; S. L. Roush, "Liberty Tunnel Fan House, Pittsburgh, PA," *American Architect* 134 (July 5, 1928): 57.

18. Bauman and Muller, *Before Renaissance*, 136.

19. Bauman and Muller, *Before Renaissance*, 143, also 137–58.

20. Bauman and Muller, *Before Renaissance*, 193.

21. Citizens Committee on City Plan of Pittsburgh (CCCP), *A Major Street Plan for Pittsburgh* (Pittsburgh, 1921), 15; E. K. Morse, "Solution of the Transportation, Parking and Flood Problems of Pittsburgh," *Proceedings of the Engineers' Society of Western Pennsylvania* 40 (June 1924): 183.

22. Frederick Law Olmsted Jr., *Pittsburgh: Main Thoroughfares and the Down Town District* (Pittsburgh, 1910), 7–9; Schein, "Re-arrangement of a Business District"; Bauman and Muller, *Before Renaissance*, 166.

23. Morse, *Report of the Transit Commissioner (1917)*, 67–69.

24. Olmsted, *Pittsburgh*, 7–9; Schein, "Re-arrangement of a Business District," 735–36.

25. CCCP, *A Major Street Plan*, 15; Morse, "Transportation, Parking and Flood Problems," 183.

26. For the subway story, see Bauman and Muller, *Before Renaissance*, 169–78.

27. CCCP, *A Major Street Plan*, 28–34.

28. Roy Lubove, *Twentieth-Century Pittsburgh, Vol. 1: Government, Business, and Environmental Change* (Pittsburgh: University of Pittsburgh Press, 1996), 90–92.

29. "Traffic Engineer Is Named by Mayor," *Pittsburgh Post*, October 31, 1924.

30. B. W. Marsh and L. W. McIntyre, *Report and Recommendations of the Central Business District Street Traffic Survey* (Pittsburgh: Traffic Committee, 1927). The average passenger automobile in the CBD in 1929 carried 1.89 passengers; the average streetcar 32 passengers.

31. For studies of the history of automobile deaths and injuries in American cities, see David Blanke, *Hell on Wheels: The Promise and Peril of America's Car Culture, 1900–1940* (Lawrence: University of Kansas Press, 2007); Peter D. Norton, *Fighting Traffic: The Dawn of the Motor Age in the American City* (Cambridge, MA: MIT Press, 2008).

32. Miller McClintock, "The Traffic Survey," *Annals of the American Academy of Political and Social Science* 33 (September 1927): 6–18; Norton, *Fighting Traffic*, 25–29.

33. See "Recapitulation of Fatal Accidents Compiled by Coroner W. J. McGregor, M.D. 1906–1930," *Controller's 70th Annual Report . . . 1930* (Pittsburgh, 1930), 518 (hereafter cited as *Coroner's Report*, with the year). The *Coroner's Report* is included with the *Allegheny County Controller's Annual Report*. In 1930 the coroner W. J. McGregor wrote that he had interviewed many of the drivers involved in fatal accidents and that only a "low percent" of them made "an honest endeavor to assume responsibility" for their actions or evidenced "mental anguish."

34. *Coroner's Report, 1930*, 518.

35. *Coroner's Report, 1921* (Pittsburgh, 1921), 308; *Coroner's Report, 1923*, 271; *Coroner's Report, 1935*, 387.

36. *Coroner's Report, 1924*, 246. In his report the coroner bemoaned the public's indifference to the death of children.

37. In his 1933 report the county coroner noted that most suburban pedestrian fatalities occurred because the roads had "no provision for the safety of the pedestrian," such as sidewalks. *Coroner's Report, 1933*, 396.

38. "How Pittsburgh Is Reducing Its Traffic Accidents," *Nation's Traffic* (1928): 35; Burton W. Marsh, "Forms of Traffic Organization in Pittsburgh, Detroit, Washington, and Buffalo," *American City* 37 (January 1927).

39. Lewis W. McIntyre, "The Pedestrian-Education and Safety," *Engineers and Engineering* 4 (April 1929): 98–101. For national safety campaigns, see Norton, *Fighting Traffic*, 32–46.

40. McClintock, "The Traffic Survey," 6–18; Norton, *Fighting Traffic*, 133–34; Marsh and McIntyre, *Report and Recommendations*.

41. J. R. Stauffer and Burton W. Marsh, "Flexible Progressive Signal System Aids Traffic Movement in Downtown Pittsburgh," *Electric Railway Journal* (May 1930): 261–66. See also McShane, *Down the Asphalt Path*, 382; Norton, *Fighting Traffic*, 54–59.

42. Burton W. Marsh, "Pittsburgh to Install Flexible Progressive Traffic Control Signal System Covering 100 Downtown Intersections," *American City* 38 (April 1928): 79–83. See also Burton W. Marsh and Cornelius J. Lyons, "Traffic Accident Problem Receives Continuous Scientific Study," *American City* 42 (February 1930): 93–95; Clay McShane, "The Origins and Globalization of Traffic Control Signals," *Journal of Urban History* 25 (March 1999): 379–404.

43. Marsh and Lyons, "Traffic Accident Problem," 93–95; Burton W. Marsh, "Standard Traffic Signs for Pittsburgh," *American City* (April 1926): 429–32. The Better Traffic Committee focused considerable energy on education, including traffic essay contests in the public and parochial schools, school visits of traffic officers, the distribution of safety material, and a focus on pedestrian safety. See "It Pays to Educate," *Better Traffic* 3 (June 1932): 3.

44. Norton, *Fighting Traffic*, 65–102.

45. Marsh and Lyons, "Traffic Accident Problem," 93–96.

46. *Coroner's Report, 1936*, 441–42. In 1934 the new mayor, William N. McNair, removed the traffic engineer Lewis McIntyre from his position in the name of "economy." McNair's director of public safety, A. Marshall Bell, explained that he thought police traffic law enforcement would be more effective than that "by the traffic planning of competent engineers." See *Pittsburgh Post-Gazette*, October 14, 16, 1934.

47. In 1939 Pittsburgh had a traffic fatality rate of 13.6 per one hundred thousand, giving it a rank of seventh among the thirteen cities with a population of over five hundred thousand.

48. Norton, *Fighting Traffic*, 261.

49. Some police wagons would have first aid kits and first aid trained officers. See A. R. Foster, for the International Association of Chiefs of Police, Safety Division, "A Report on the Traffic Accident Prevention Program of the Bureau of Police, City of Pittsburgh, Pennsylvania" (Evanston, Illinois, 1939), 1:39. Norton noted that the police initially viewed the automobile as causing a new kind of disorder and guarded the right of pedestrians to the street. Norton, *Fighting Traffic*, 64. See also Andrew Simpson, "Transporting Lazarus: Physicians, the State, and the Creation of the Modern Paramedic and Ambulance, 1955–1974," *Journal of the History of Medicine and Allied Sciences* 68, no. 2 (April 2013), which illustrates the primitive state of emergency medical services in Pittsburgh before the late 1950s and 1960s.

50. *Real Property Inventory*, 62–64. In 1934, Ward 14 had the highest automobile ownership in the city, one auto to almost every five people. The overall percentage of automobile ownership in Ward 19 was not much above the citywide average, but the ward's

outermost census tracts had a ratio of one car to every eight persons. The ratio for the city in this Depression year was one car to every fourteen persons.

51. Large areas of the Fourteenth Ward lacked streetcar service. See CCCP, *Transit*, "plat 9," opposite p. 28. For attorneys' journey-to-work patterns, see Terry F. Yosie, "Journey-to-Work Patterns of Pittsburgh's Attorneys and Physicians, 1850–1920" (unpublished research paper, Department of History, Carnegie Mellon University, 1975).

52. Edward K. Muller, "Industrial Suburbs and the Growth of Metropolitan Pittsburgh, 1870–1920," *Journal of Historical Geography* 27, no. 1 (2001): 58–73.

53. American Historical Society, *History of Pittsburgh and Environs* (New York, 1922), 3:705–79.

54. Population densities are available from the US Bureau of the Census, 1910–1930.

55. Bureau of Business Research, University of Pittsburgh, *Real Estate Statistics for Allegheny County, Pennsylvania: Base Book* (Pittsburgh, 1936), 139–41.

56. Bureau of Business Research, University of Pittsburgh, *Real Estate Statistics*, 139–41.

57. Bureau of Business Research, University of Pittsburgh, *Real Estate Statistics*, 7–11.

58. Data on age of structure by census tract is available in *Real Property Inventory*, 9–75.

59. Bauman and Muller, *Before Renaissance*, 159–69.

60. *Report of the Better Traffic Committee* (October 1930), 1.

61. Bureau of Business Research, University of Pittsburgh, *Industrial Datebook for the Pittsburgh District*, 61–77.

8 SKYBUS

PITTSBURGH'S FAILED INDUSTRIAL TARGETING STRATEGY OF THE 1960S

Edward K. Muller with Morton Coleman
and David Houston

Pittsburgh like most large metropolitan regions in the past half century has undertaken a variety of economic development strategies, the most heralded and analyzed was the "Renaissance" that began in the late 1940s and extended into the 1960s. Renaissance emphasized redevelopment of downtown, cleanup of the environment, improvement of infrastructure, and reimaging as modern to make the city and region more attractive to businesses. The attention paid to these aspects of Renaissance has often overshadowed more specific efforts aimed at industrial development, which were also part of the Renaissance program. One strategy, for example, followed conventional lines of surveying the region's industrial base, determining companies' needs, inventorying available sites, and actively promoting the retention and attraction of companies. The Regional Industrial Development Corporation (RIDC) in 1955 and its successful industrial parks evolved from this approach.[1]

Another strategy was industry targeting. In the 1960s and early 1970s public and private leaders mounted a substantial effort to promote the Pittsburgh region's existing transportation industry as a center for the emerging urban rapid transportation equipment market. Industry targeting is a means to strategically plan economic development efforts and focus limited resources. Civic leaders identify and promote an industry in which their region may have a comparative advantage. They shape policies that develop the targeted industry and/or attract new companies of that industry, thereby expanding the economic base of the region. The selection of a targeted industry and the implementation of a program and policies to develop it inherently involve business, labor, and governmental interests, each with its own constituencies and goals. In addition to the methodological problems of selecting an industry, achieving consensus among interested parties, or at least enough consensus to enact and carry out expensive public programs, presents political minefields for policy makers.[2]

Selecting the rapid transit industry for targeting in the 1960s meant addressing two issues for the Pittsburgh region. Despite the national acclaim for its Renaissance redevelopment program, much more needed to be accomplished in the quest to reposition Pittsburgh for the second half of the century. In addition to improvements in housing and cultural facilities, economic diversification and mass transportation remained at the top of the civic agenda. Industrial development efforts had not substantially diversified the region's manufacturing base, which was recognized as late as 1963 to be still perilously concentrated on primary metals.[3] At the same time, and despite several new public parking garages, new parkways from fast-growing eastern and western suburbs to downtown had aggravated traffic congestion. Commuters fled a fragmented number of independent transit providers and the bankrupt streetcar system for the privacy of their automobiles. The metropolitan region begged for an effective mass transportation system.

With nearly twenty years of fruitful coordinated civic action, as well as being perceived as leaders in postwar American urban renewal, Pittsburgh's civic leaders did not hesitate to address the daunting transportation and persistent economic diversification problems. Rapid transit became a solution for both issues.[4] Corporate executives and public officials worked within the Renaissance public-private partnership to achieve their goals. Allegheny County became responsible for developing the rapid transit system; and nonprofit organizations with the backing of Richard King Mellon and the Allegheny Conference on Community Development undertook the promotion of the local industry. By the mid-1960s they had created a three-pronged transit strategy: (1) build an innovative rapid transportation system for Allegheny County, (2) use it as a showcase for testing and marketing rapid transit hardware developed by Pittsburgh-based corporations, and (3) promote the city as a center of the rapid transportation industry.

For the innovative system, they settled on Westinghouse's automated rubber-tired vehicle running on a separate, elevated, cement guide way, dubbed "Skybus." The public-private partnership assiduously pursued its rapid transit program through the 1960s, but by the early 1970s the Skybus proposal for Allegheny County was in trouble, and it soon lost critical state funding. With the program's demise the industry targeting strategy failed as well. The collapse of the winning Renaissance formula is noteworthy and instructive. The innovative character of Westinghouse's technology opened it to criticism, and a competitive technology advanced by another local corporation divided the business community at the moment when Richard K. Mellon's death removed his unifying leadership. The construction of a rapid transit system as the demonstration aspect of the strategy relied on local and state governments' decisions to incur public expense, subjecting the strategy to the vicissitudes of local politics. In the past the concentration of private and public power in two powerful figures (Mellon and Democratic party boss David L. Lawrence), their informal partnership, and the efficacy of their organizations simply bulldozed the political opposition to massive renewal programs and to behind-closed-doors top-down planning. By the late 1960s, however, the loss of this leadership (Lawrence died in 1966, Mellon in 1970) weakened the public-private partnership and rendered the public decisionmaking bodies vulnerable to new populist political sentiment. Galvanized by the riots in the aftermath of Martin Luther King's assassination, key politicians championed the interests of groups left out of the planning process and the benefits of the proposed system to undermine the necessary consensus for federal and state funding assistance.

This case study of industry targeting in Pittsburgh does not shed light on the process by which civic leaders selected the rapid transit industry. The literature of industry targeting typically focuses on approaches to industry selection. Writers lament the lack of studies on implementation experiences and outcomes. The Skybus experience in Pittsburgh bears out the essentially political nature of industry targeting. The successful outcome of a targeting program may well, as this Pittsburgh example suggests, depend more on effective leadership and local politics than on the quality of the selection process and the vigorous pursuit of traditional economic development strategies in support of the targeted industry.[5]

THE CONTEXT FOR INDUSTRY TARGETING IN PITTSBURGH

In 1960 Pittsburgh had just experienced fifteen years of redevelopment that established it as a dynamic city with a revitalized central business district, new pollution controls on water and air, expanded research capacity, a forward-looking business elite, a successful public-private partnership, and an increasingly positive public image within the nation.[6] Civic leaders had great confidence in their ability to effect change. Still, important changes in the political economy of the nation and region were making themselves felt locally.

The transformation of the national economy away from older smokestack manufacturing to service and technologically advanced industries was well underway. From the late 1940s Pittsburgh was experiencing early impacts of deindustrialization. Production workers in manufacturing declined 31 percent from 1947 to 1967, and the region's share of the national steel output declined steadily after 1950. The population of the region was growing slowly from 1930, and net migration had been negative in every decade since the 1920s.[7] The population of the City of Pittsburgh peaked in 1950. While it was not easy in 1960 for Pittsburghers to foresee how dramatic the changes in Pittsburgh's economy would be, it was apparent that unbridled optimism was not warranted. Civic leaders had for years called for diversification of the regional economic base in order to diminish the extreme impacts of recession years and wished to find a new growth industry.[8] Thus, a regional industry targeting strategy would be constrained by developments in both the national economy and the local economy, in which relative decline had already manifested itself and absolute decline was waiting impatiently in the wings.

The 1960s also brought forth many calls across America for solutions to the urban transportation problem. New expressways and steady increases in the use of automobiles coupled with decades of deteriorating public transportation led to unprecedented congestion and air pollution in the nation's cities. Expressway construction could not keep pace with America's love affair with the automobile, and increasing protests at the destructive impact of pushing expressways into cities threatened the construction of many planned projects. An obvious solution, it seemed, was to create modern, attractive, efficient public mass transportation that would encourage commuters to abandon their automobiles.

With hindsight the merits, or perhaps more accurately the practicality, of this approach seem weak. The powerful highway lobby—the auto manufacturers, oil companies, highway construction firms, government agencies, and sympathetic politicians—formed an immovable force against which mass transportation interests fought ineffectively. The consumer's attachment to the automobile also turned out to be stronger than many experts judged. Moreover, deteriorating social relations between middle-class whites and poor African Americans spurred suburban flight and the desire for privacy in residence and commuting. The unparalleled flexibility of the automobile (ignoring the congestion it caused) proved to be a virtue without peer. The rise of the automobile continued unabated.[9]

However, urban planners, many businessmen, a few politicians, and some of the citizenry understood the disadvantages of autocentric cities. They put mass transit on many public and civic agendas. Many experts believed that the nation was on the threshold of an enormous market for mass transit design, engineering, construction, and equipment.

Pittsburgh had suffered from traffic congestion for most of the twentieth century. The rugged topography constrained travel to narrow valleys and river floodplains. Numerous bridges and a few tunnels caused bottlenecks in traffic flows. The confining physical geography of the "Golden Triangle," the peninsular downtown crammed between the Allegheny and Monongahela Rivers where they meet to form the Ohio River, especially worsened downtown traffic conditions. Beginning with Frederick Law Olmsted Jr.'s plan in 1911, planners struggled throughout the years to provide an adequate highway network and simultaneously discussed mass transportation improvements.[10] Just as they had addressed longstanding environmental, redevelopment, and housing problems under the Renaissance banner, postwar leaders tried to solve the region's traffic problems. In addition to building new limited-access highways with tunnels, they wished to create an effective mass transportation system for Allegheny County.

The development of a public transportation system involves a complex network of intergovernmental arrangements among federal, state, and local governments. Differences in the political and bureaucratic objectives of these governmental units create problems, as does the strong tradition of local autonomy among municipalities. The pivotal governmental units for the Skybus rapid transit venture were Allegheny County, the City of Pittsburgh, and the Port Authority of Allegheny. Other governmental units, including federal, state, local, and judiciary ones, were important to the Skybus story.

Conflict between the City of Pittsburgh and Allegheny County, along with the added fragmentation of 129 other minor civil divisions within the county, always presented problems for regional initiatives. Between the 1930s and the 1960s the Democratic Party, centered in Pittsburgh, provided unity among the various elements of the City of Pittsburgh and Allegheny County governmental systems. The Democratic political machine informally coordinated and directed regional governmental policies. Party leaders managed conflict by brokering diverse interests of the various groups that brought rank-and-file Democrats into the coalition. Even so, the minor civil divisions remained alert and hostile to actions that might threaten their autonomy and lead to consolidation, which they called metropolitanism.

Political unity prevailed during the early stages of planning a new rapid transit system. When legislation passed to create the Port Authority Transit (PAT), David Lawrence, longtime Renaissance mayor and party boss, was the new governor of Pennsylvania. Close ally Joseph M. Barr was the newly elected mayor of the City of Pittsburgh. Dr. William D. McClelland chaired the Allegheny County Board of Commissioners with John D. McGrady the other Democratic commissioner and Blair F. Gunther the Republican minority member. McClelland had been a political opponent of the Lawrence organization since 1954. However, he eventually supported Pittsburgh's interest in a rapid transit system.[11] McGrady closely identified with the Lawrence/Barr organization, while even Republican Gunther supported the rapid transit strategy. Although the county commissioners were responsible for implementing rapid transit, city government under Mayor Barr and his staff was the principal contact with the business community and a driving force in the creation of the rapid transit system.

Since the Second World War, Pittsburgh business leaders under the auspices of Richard King Mellon strived to renew their smoky steel city. Through the Conference, Mellon and the presidents of the city's largest corporations worked with several nonprofit organizations to carry out planning, renewal, and development. The Conference exercised considerable influence over these diverse corporations and civic organizations through the power of the Mellon family interests in the business community and the interlocking appointments of corporate executives, nonprofit leaders, and public officials on various boards of directors. Mellon forged an informal partnership with Mayor David Lawrence as the leader of the Democratic Party, and together they oversaw the public-private partnership that implemented the various projects of Renaissance.[12]

Early in his administration Mayor Barr expressed his commitment to the private-public partnership and urban redevelopment that characterized the Lawrence years. In an article in the *Pittsburgh Post-Gazette* in December 1959, Barr stated: "There will be no let up, I assure you, on the part of the government, or on the part of civic agencies, whose contributions have been so essential to the past accomplishments."[13] The working relationship between the staffs of public and private entities primarily maintained the partnership during Barr's term. Aldo Colautti, executive secretary to Barr, can recall only two times when the mayor had personal meetings with Mellon. The Conference remained the key private agency setting the initiative for development.[14] Ed Magee, Conference executive director from 1959 to 1968, was a conservative man with a limited set of priorities for the development of the region. He had little or no concern about social issues.

His development agenda emphasized the continuation of the physical redevelopment started under Lawrence's administration. His interest in new programs centered on building an all-sports stadium, installing mass transit, and to a lesser extent refurbishing the city's zoo.[15]

Magee's major contact in the city administration was John Mauro, the mayor's urban renewal coordinator and later director of the city's Department of Planning and Development. Mauro began his career as a *Pittsburgh Post-Gazette* reporter and became the director of public relations at the chamber of commerce. After his work for the city, he moved on to roles as director of development for the Conference and finally the executive director of the Port Authority of Allegheny County. Mauro and Magee shared common concerns for physical development.[16]

The media helped to forge a broad public consensus around goals of economic revitalization of the region. The media rallied support for revitalization by dramatically making visible its accomplishments. In an interview years later Walter Giesey reflected on the media's public relations role in the Pittsburgh Renaissance: "Again, looking back, I think that the newspapers had some responsibility in the eventual degeneration [of Renaissance] in almost being too kind to the administration and to the Conference. If the Conference said this is good, it became automatically good. No one went out to find out whether everyone else thought it was good, that was the imprimatur and that was it, and so the *Pittsburgh Press* would say it was good and the *Pittsburgh Post-Gazette* would say it was good, and it was good."[17] The Conference assiduously promoted Renaissance's accomplishments with a multipronged public relations campaign. Much of the momentum for Renaissance resulted from "selling" an image—an illusion of redevelopment as a well-planned, fastidiously run, problem-free master operation. The same image was used to sell the rapid transit program.

SKYBUS AS PAT'S CHOICE FOR RAPID TRANSIT

After several studies since the Second World War, some conflict, and much indecision, the Conference reluctantly concluded that only a public agency could overcome the obstacles to creating a unified mass transit system. In 1956 the state legislature passed the second-class Port Authority Act, which created the Port Authority of Allegheny County. The Port Authority had the power to plan, acquire, construct, maintain, and operate facilities and projects for the improvement and development of the port district. Three years later the legislature amended the act enabling the Port Authority to purchase and operate mass transit facilities. The Allegheny County Commissioners appointed a Port Authority Transit Board; the commissioners

FIG. 8.1 Skybus vehicle on the South Park demonstration track (Harold Corsini Collection, courtesy of the Archives Service Center, University of Pittsburgh).

retained oversight of proposals made by the new body. The legislature directed that "the Authority, immediately upon its organization, shall commence its study of an integrated system of mass transportation within the service area."[18] This requirement set into motion the series of events that led to PAT's adopting an Early Action Program for rapid transit and subsequently led to an innovative but controversial rubber-wheel technology.

In 1960 PAT hired the engineering firm of Coverdale & Colpitts to conduct a feasibility study for an integrated system of mass transportation. The resulting plan, accepted by PAT in 1961 and amended and adopted by the county commissioners in 1963, recommended the consolidation of the Pittsburgh Railways Company (the streetcar system), two inclines on Mount Washington, and thirty bus companies into one operating system. The commissioners' decision came after considerable acrimony as to whether the issue of creating a countywide transit system should be put to a referendum and whether it was a step toward metropolitanism. Local municipal officials around the county, represented most vociferously by McKeesport mayor Andrew J. Jakomas and Bethel Park mayor Peter Page, feared the loss of autonomy. Still others perceived governmental intrusion on private enterprise and cried socialism. With county and federal funds PAT immediately began the implementation of this plan. As the acquisition of extant companies progressed, PAT was also considering futuristic designs and exclusive rights-of-way for carriers in order to provide rapid transit.[19]

In June 1963 PAT became a founding partner in the demonstration project for Westinghouse Electric Corporation's futuristic Transit Expressway System, that is, Skybus (see Figure 8.1). Responding to pressure from urban experts and civic leaders, the federal government and state counterparts had begun in the early 1960s granting financial assistance for upgrading local mass transportation systems as well as for experimental transit programs. In one of these initiatives, the Housing and Home Finance Agency, soon to become the Department of Housing and Urban Development (HUD), put up matching funds for the construction and operation of Westinghouse's innovative Skybus system in order to test its feasibility for medium density urban areas. The high capital and operating costs of conventional rail transit presumably prohibited its use in such markets.

Already under consideration for Tampa's airport, Westinghouse's technology offered, it was argued, advantages of modern comfort, lower operating costs, and route flexibility for Pittsburgh's rugged topography. Civic leaders may have already had Westinghouse's design concept in mind when the City of Pittsburgh, the Golden Triangle Association, and the Pittsburgh Regional Planning Association adopted the Golden Triangle Master Plan in June 1962, which included "recommendations for an automated rapid transit system serving areas to the east and south of the Triangle."[20] PAT joined HUD, the State of Pennsylvania, Westinghouse, and two dozen other corporations (many from Pittsburgh) in financing the five-million-dollar Transit Expressway Mass Transit Demonstration Project.[21]

Although HUD Secretary Robert C. Weaver did not dedicate the Skybus demonstration project until January 1966, Westinghouse initiated operation of its trains on the 1.77-mile demonstration loop in South Park in August 1965. The electric, automatically controlled (i.e., unmanned), and rubber-wheeled vehicles, operating individually or in trains, ran at speeds as high as fifty miles per hour along an elevated steel-frame, concrete-surfaced roadway. Together the vehicles and roadway were designed to provide the comfort and convenience necessary to attract commuters accustomed to their private automobiles. Skybus initially operated for ten months, covering twenty-one thousand vehicle miles and providing rides to the public during four days of the Allegheny County Fair.[22]

Three months after the South Park demonstration began and only weeks after President Lyndon Johnson signed a law to stimulate rapid transit in September, PAT took another essential step in the development of rapid transit for Allegheny County. In late October 1965 with money provided by the state, PAT engaged the engineering firm Parsons, Brinckerhoff, Quade & Douglas (PBQD) to prepare a plan for rapid transit and include an evaluation of the rubber-wheel Skybus system.[23] PBQD did the planning for the Bay Area Rapid Transit system (BART) under construction in the San Francisco Bay area. BART was the nation's boldest development in rapid transit at the time. PAT charged PBQD to investigate all possible options and routes and produce estimates of feasible alternatives with the final report due in 1967. The results of this study and a number of others would strongly influence the fate of Skybus.

PAT had been contemplating a study of rapid transit before fall 1965. In early 1964, half a year after it had entered into the Skybus experiment, PAT board members informed the Conference executive committee of their consideration of rapid transit and distributed a reprinted article about BART and PBQD.[24] In summer 1964 PAT decided to end commuter railroad operations, allowing the Pennsylvania Railroad's remaining trains to stop running ninety days later. PAT's own hasty study of the Pennsylvania Railroad's service convinced Leland Hazard, chairman of PAT's Rapid Transit Committee, of the need for a comprehensive master plan for rapid transit in Allegheny County. As a member of PAT's board and the corporate community, Hazard was a tireless, outspoken advocate for rapid transit.[25]

At the initiation of the PBQD study, PAT officials claimed that they had not yet determined the appropriate technology for rapid transit in Allegheny County despite participation in the Skybus demonstration at South Park. Perhaps this was true, but by fall 1965 PAT already had a two-year relationship with Westinghouse and Skybus. Further, the discussion of futuristic solutions, the recommendation for automated transit in 1962 in the Golden Triangle Master Plan, the canceling of commuter rail service in 1964, the concurrent targeting of the local rapid transit industry (discussed below), and HUD's interest in the Skybus technology surely had PAT board members favorably disposed to Westinghouse's rubber-wheel vehicles when they engaged PBQD.[26]

Skybus picked up momentum in early 1966 when PAT asked the Transportation Research Institute (TRI) at Carnegie Mellon University to study a distribution loop within downtown, which would use a similar design concept. In December 1966, PAT also contracted with TRI to conduct studies of other technological aspects of Skybus.[27] Then in 1967, when PBQD was still completing its work, confirmation of the technical feasibility of

Westinghouse's system came from the local MPC Corporation's positive evaluation of the South Park demonstration, favorable results of TRI's studies, and a supportive evaluation by the consulting engineering firm Richardson, Gordon, and Associates. Early in 1967 MPC concluded that the Transit Expressway system was a feasible technology for medium density markets and that the public, at least at South Park, accepted the concept of unmanned vehicles. MPC recommended additional design and engineering refinements and continuation of the demonstration.[28] In April 1967 Allegheny County and Westinghouse each put up two hundred thousand dollars to extend the testing of Skybus at South Park with the expectation that these investments would leverage two million dollars from state and federal sources for additional engineering and design work. In September 1967, PAT board member Leland Hazard announced the recommendation by his Transit Committee for building a Skybus demonstration line to the South Hills, underscoring the unsuitability of steel rails for Pittsburgh's terrain.[29] Hazard's release of his committee's report before the release of the nearly completed PBQD study may have reflected rumors that the prestigious engineering firm favored steel-wheel technology.

PBQD released its long-awaited report in December 1967. The firm proposed rapid transit corridors to the eastern suburbs, North Hills, the Ohio valley, and two to the South Hills, encompassing sixty miles and estimated costs of over seven hundred million dollars. PBQD did not expressly endorse one technological system, rubber tire or steel wheels. Although newspaper articles about the report emphasized the choice between the two technologies, PAT's intention to adopt Skybus seemed reasonably clear from the preceding studies and projects.[30] Two days after the release of PBQD's report, Westinghouse received HUD's first Urban Transportation Award. The *Pittsburgh Press* noted that "This commendation is particularly encouraging because the Allegheny County Port Authority Transit (PAT) hopes to receive $300,000 from HUD for a feasibility study of a plan to operate Skybus between the South Hills and downtown Pittsburgh. If all goes well, the next step would be construction of a $60,000,000 test line to be completed by 1970."[31]

PAT's formal acceptance of PBQD's report in March 1968 positioned PAT to apply for federal financial assistance in designing and building a rapid transit system. In August, PAT's Transit Committee submitted to the PAT board a twenty-eight-mile Early Action Program and proposed Westinghouse as the system manager for the engineering study that would apply the Skybus design to the recommended South Hills demonstration line (this became known as TERL, the Transit Expressway Revenue Line).[32] With

Westinghouse in place, PAT applied to the Department of Transportation for a technical study grant, which was approved on November. Conditions of the grant made it clear that Westinghouse was not to participate in the final decision on the rapid transit technology used on the TERL corridor.[33]

Despite more than five years of close interaction with Westinghouse, PAT was not yet formally committed to the Skybus technology until the following summer when the technical grant was completed and PAT was ready to seek additional federal funding. In July 1969 PAT ignored the last minute submission of an alternative steel-wheel scheme, approved the Early Action Program to include Skybus on the South Hills line, and filed an application with the Urban Mass Transportation Administration of HUD (UMTA). In September 1969 after public hearings, the Allegheny County Commissioners approved the program and agreed to the financial commitments it engendered. In June 1970 UMTA approved $8,700,000 for the project and added an additional $60,000,000 in September 1971.[34]

Although Westinghouse's Skybus now seemed certain to be built in Pittsburgh and to become a model for other medium-density markets, a discordant note to this process had appeared in the newspapers in early 1968. A major fracture in civic unanimity surfaced and widened during the approval process in summer 1969. At the time, however, few of Skybus's proponents realized how serious this fracture would turn out to be.

DETROIT OF THE TRANSIT INDUSTRY

The strategy to make Pittsburgh the center of the rapid transit industry was closely entwined with the region's efforts to construct an innovative rapid transit system. The same coalition of public and private leaders that had orchestrated the city's Renaissance after the Second World War targeted the rapid transit industry for special attention. Corporate leaders with the essential support of R. K. Mellon worked through nonprofit organizations and partnered with PAT to promote a rapid transit system and industry.

Public officials at all governmental levels who participated actively in the development of a rapid transit system (including Skybus) shared the industry targeting goals; but they were apparently, and quite logically, less involved in the targeting strategy itself. This distinction proved in the end to be a fatal weakness in the private-public coalition for the industry targeting objective. Viewing targeting as a private sector program, some public officials who came into office late in the process felt little commitment to Skybus, especially as central to the targeting program, and for political expediency were willing to accept an alternative technology.

At the same time, the Skybus plan opened a fracture within the corporate community. Without the leadership of R. K. Mellon to hold it together, the private sector faded away from the fray when conflict over Skybus erupted in the public arena. The reasons are unclear for the corporate community's failure to continue its promotion of a local rapid transit industry after 1972, but the federal government's weak financial support of urban mass transit in the 1970s more than likely deflected the interest of corporate executives toward greener pastures.[35]

The idea that Pittsburgh might become the center of the rapid transit industry followed logically from the region's contemporary experience and industrial history. The desire to diversify the region's industrial structure and extend the progress of Renaissance with rapid transportation fit comfortably with the corporate strengths in transportation engineering and manufacturing and with the civic leadership's confidence in effecting change. Just as aircraft manufacturers saw opportunities for new markets in the federal government's postwar goals to develop missile and space programs, corporations with ground transportation capabilities perceived growth potential in the government's emerging policy to encourage rapid transit across the nation.

In a 1965 demonstration of rapid transit equipment for the future, US Steel president Leslie Worthington cited the Census Bureau's projection that 75 percent of the nation's anticipated population would live in three hundred metropolitan areas.[36] After examining forty-two cities that were the most likely to build systems, the company estimated construction costs of "more than $8 billion dollars over the next 15 years. . . . These systems offer a potential market for steel of about six million tons."[37] Westinghouse Electric Corporation and Westinghouse Air Brake Company (WABCO) had been developing their transit capabilities for several years, undoubtedly in consultation with federal authorities. Three top Westinghouse Electric executives stood among the invited dignitaries who witnessed President Lyndon Johnson sign the 1965 rapid transit bill authorizing ninety million dollars for research, development, and demonstration projects. One month later Westinghouse president Donald C. Burnham brought his board of directors to South Park to see Skybus because he felt rapid transit systems would become an important factor in the company's future.[38]

Even though Pittsburgh's reputation rested on steel production, the area had a long involvement in various transportation industries. Boatbuilding along the banks of the three rivers began in the early years of the nineteenth century. The boatyards initially turned out simple wooden rafts and keelboats but then graduated to more complicated steamboats that plied the inland waterways for the rest of the century.[39] Long after the steamboat industry disappeared, local boatyards such as Dravo Corporation produced river barges and military landing craft for the Second World War, and area steel mills forged massive armor plates for US Navy warships.

In the midnineteenth century, the rapid expansion of railroads across the continent triggered the transformation of Pittsburgh's iron rolling mills into a mass production steel industry that dominated the nation's production for decades. In order to compete for the burgeoning railroad rail market, many local ironmasters, most notably Andrew Carnegie and his associates, installed new technologies, vastly expanded the scale of production, and eventually adopted modern management techniques. Carnegie's Edgar Thomson works, which opened in Braddock in 1875, became the prototype integrated steel rail mill for the industry.[40] At the same time, dozens of local foundries produced railroad wheels, axles, and frogs as well as the mining cars required by the region's hundreds of coal mines and coke works. By the early twentieth century Pittsburgh manufacturers had become major suppliers of railroad equipment. Besides rails and spikes, local firms produced locomotives (e.g., H.K. Porter), railroad cars (e.g., Pullman Standard in Butler and Pressed Steel Car in McKees Rocks), wheels, axles, couplers, boilers, engines, valves, and numerous other products. There were more than a dozen major railroad repair shops. Of special note were the air brake and switching companies in George Westinghouse's empire. In the 1860s Westinghouse devised the railroad air brake and then followed, over the next several decades, with a succession of switching and signaling innovations. These developments resulted in the formation of the Westinghouse Air Brake Company as well as the Union Switch and Signal Company.[41]

Many Pittsburgh corporations and engineering firms were by the early 1960s deeply involved in designing products for the anticipated growth of the rapid transit market. They established transit research centers within their own corporate structures and joined with other corporations, often local ones, in creating new products. By 1962 WABCO brought several divisions together in its Mass Transit Center, including its Union Switch and Signal Division. It worked on automated controls, braking gears, and other experimental equipment for Montreal's Expo '67, Newark's interterminal transit system, and San Francisco's BART. In 1965 the Pullman Company established a Transportation Systems Center at its Pittsburgh rolling stock division in Butler and entered into a relationship with the Swindell-Dressler engineering and equipment group. In cooperation with ALCOA, Edgewater Steel created an aluminum- centered steel wheel, which it tested with the Chicago Transit Authority and supplied to BART for experimental purposes. In turn, ALCOA worked with railroad car manufacturers to devise increased uses of aluminum in the transit industry, some of which was tested by the Long Island Railroad. US Steel participated with other local companies such as PPG Industries and Midland Ross, an electronics equipment producer, in fashioning its demonstration car called SCOT (Steel Car of Tomorrow). Westinghouse Electric had been testing propulsion designs with BART and, of course, launched its Skybus demonstration project in August 1963. Among other local companies, Rockwell Manufacturing produced transit meters and compressor units, and Koppers Company sold railroad ties and plastics for car interiors.[42]

Whoever initially recognized the advantages of a coordinated promotion of Pittsburgh's rapid transit industrial capabilities is not known. The June 1963 agreement to build the South Park Skybus loop may have been the initial step in a coordinated effort, for it brought together public entities and several private companies in addition to Westinghouse. County Commissioner Dr. William D. McClelland explicitly supported the Skybus demonstration because he believed it would lead to new local industry and would revitalize the industrial valleys. Comments by McClelland and Westinghouse executive George W. Jernstedt in 1967, four years after the agreement, suggest that Skybus was an initial step in a strategy to help Westinghouse win contracts with BART. At the January 1964 meeting of the Conference's executive committee, Robert Ryan, then head of the nonprofit Regional Industrial Development Corporation (RIDC), averred that, in light of "the opportunities in the field of rapid transit," the implementation of the Golden Triangle Master Plan of 1962 (which recommended an automated rapid transit system) held "great potentialities for the area in terms of increased employment and economic growth." Ryan, once described as "an established troubleshooter for the Mellon interests," may have merely reflected ideas that were commonly under discussion at the time in business circles, but he had brought them to the attention of the one organization, the Allegheny Conference, with the inclination, corporate perspective, and power to formulate an industry targeting effort.[43]

Whatever the inception date, the targeting strategy was publicly acknowledged and put into action by mid-1965. In the typical Renaissance manner, the Chamber of Commerce under the auspices of the Conference and with the participation of public officials launched a new organization to spearhead the effort only a month before Westinghouse began operating its Skybus demonstration at South Park. At a June luncheon chaired by R. K. Mellon at the prestigious Duquesne Club, Chamber of Commerce president Henry Avery announced the formation of the Urban Transportation Development Council (later simply called the Urban Transportation

Council or UTC).[44] Mayor Barr, corporate presidents, and representatives of the newspapers attended the luncheon. J. Stanley Purnell, an assistant to the president of T. Mellon & Sons, chaired the new council of sixteen business and civic leaders, including representatives from PAT, trade associations, and engineering, metal, and material firms. He described the UTC's mission as bringing worldwide attention to Pittsburgh "as a center of mass transit production and design," conducting events that would bring local companies into contact with potential customers and thereby creating jobs with the subsequent expansion of business. Moreover, Purnell added the objective to "push solution of Pittsburgh's own mass transit . . . problems."[45] As its first effort to achieve these goals, the UTC scheduled an international conference on mass transportation for early February 1966.

By the beginning of the conference, the construction of rapid transit in Allegheny County and the development of the local industry had been publicly linked as complementary elements of the targeting strategy. Upon President Johnson's signing of the transportation bill in late September 1965, both corporate leaders and PAT officials predicted to local newspapers that the targeting strategy would be a stimulus to the local transit industry. Local politicians such as State Senator Robert D. Fleming as well as the daily newspapers urged the region not to fall behind other cities and to keep Renaissance moving forward.[46] PAT officials presented their hopes for rapid transit at the annual Conference dinner meeting; their prominence on the meeting's agenda reflected the Conference's support for not only a rapid transit system but also the local transit industry.[47] In a 1966 presentation to the Kiwanis Club, Gene R. Schaefer, director of WABCO's Mass Transit Center, linked the construction of a rapid transit system in Pittsburgh with the promotion of the local industry. Schaefer predicted that by the early 1970s Pittsburgh would be building a rapid transit system because of the capabilities of local industry. Pittsburgh would "become the most prominent city in mass transit—not only as a supplier but also from an operating standpoint."[48]

Momentum for the targeting strategy continued to mount. One week after Schaefer's speech, two hundred industrial and civic leaders attended the formal dedication of Skybus at South Park. Both PAT chairman Judge Loran L. Lewis and County Commissioner McClelland told reporters that this experiment could result in an important new industry for the region.[49] A little more than two weeks later, on the eve of the initial UTC conference, the *Pittsburgh Post-Gazette* editors expressed confidence that "Pittsburgh will demonstrate through the construction of its own rapid transit system just what its industries are capable of doing. Nothing is more persuasive than a going concern."[50] RIDC's Ryan claimed that developing a rapid transit system for Pittsburgh was a critical part of an industry targeting strategy. Because his organization was created in 1955 to help diversify the local economy, he may have been in the best position to be a spokesman. According to the *Pittsburgh Press* report, Ryan warned that "this city can become an urban transportation center only by demonstrating its own capabilities in the industry on its own home grounds. This will require total commitment by public officials and agencies."[51] Ironically, at this early date Ryan also noted both weaknesses in the region's targeting strategy when he recognized the corporate competition among local firms for these markets and the need for total public commitment to rapid transit among the region's transit producers.

With the convening of the First International Conference on Urban Transportation on February 1, 1966, the city made its pitch. As conference organizer, the UTC hoped to further the cause of urban rapid transit nationwide and focus attention on Pittsburgh as a center for the research, design, and production of transit equipment and systems.[52] More than one thousand people from around the nation attended the three-day affair. Topics and speakers reflected the national agenda for rapid transit. The local agenda was made explicit by an exhibit of local companies' transit capabilities—almost a trade fair as one participant observed—and tours of Skybus at South Park and local industrial plants.[53] Indeed, some participants complained to the *New York Times* that they were "tricked into attending a local chamber of commerce promotion," a lament that was partially correct.[54]

The announcement at the conference of the formation of the Transportation Research Institute at Carnegie Institute of Technology (soon to be renamed Carnegie Mellon University) emphasized the city's commitment to the rapid transit industry. Supported by an initial grant of three hundred thousand dollars by R. K. Mellon through the A. W. Mellon Educational and Charitable Trust, TRI aspired to become an international center for transit research and information.[55] The Pennsylvania governor William Scranton, Mayor Barr, and other local public officials participated in the conference. County Commissioner McClelland reportedly commented that county voters would support a referendum on rapid transit funding, signaling political commitment to local transit policy and to targeting the local industry.[56] The indomitable Ryan captured the general satisfaction with the conference's outcome when he surmised it had given the city a boost toward becoming the "Detroit of the transit industry," an industry expected to be worth billions of dollars.[57]

Over the next two years, the Detroit analogy became a common refrain.

PAT moved toward the seemingly inevitable adoption of a rapid transit plan with the Skybus technology, and the corporate community pursued its goal of promoting the local rapid transit industry. Three weeks after the first transportation conference, members of the downtown Golden Triangle Association and the Building Owners and Managers Association visited Toronto to inspect its transportation system.[58] In the spring of 1966, the state awarded WABCO a grant to study high-speed railroad service between Pittsburgh and Harrisburg. In announcing the grant, Pennsylvania secretary of commerce John K. Tabor allowed that even if WABCO were to determine such a rail route to be infeasible, the study would help establish Pennsylvania's capabilities in the transportation industry. Having missed the automobile, radio, aviation, missile, electronics, and space industries, the state, he argued, could not be allowed to miss this new one.[59]

As with the initial symposium, the Second International Conference on Urban Transportation acted as a lightning rod for announcements intended to publicize the city's march toward becoming the capital of the rapid transit industry. UTC Chairperson Purnell told the Conference that the April 1967 event would focus on solutions to rush-hour congestion and would highlight industry's research and development role.[60] During the week preceding the conference, several announcements seemed timed to impress the conferees, the industry, and the city with the progress achieved toward the industry targeting goal. Mellon made a second grant to the TRI, this one for $700,000. WABCO revealed that it had received a $370,000 grant from HUD to examine all types of mass transit, including Skybus.[61] But most dramatically, Westinghouse announced the decision to locate its new corporate transportation center in the nearby suburb of Forest Hills because of, General Manager Jernstedt explained, the cooperation and commitment of Allegheny County and other public officials toward Skybus in South Park. That commitment, he added, helped Westinghouse win the Tampa airport transit business and a $26,000,000 contract with BART, which would result in one hundred new local jobs. Consequently, the county and the corporation agreed to commit more funds toward Skybus.[62] Then, on the first day of the conference, the new Pennsylvania governor, Raymond P. Shafer, called for a ten-year $300,000,000 commitment by the state for intercity and mass transportation and named PAT's Hazard to head a governor's committee on transportation.[63]

Pittsburgh Post-Gazette reporter Thomas M. Hritz laid out the targeting strategy in an article on the second conference. Hritz identified Mellon, Purnell, Hazard, John W. Dameron (PAT's executive director), and ALCOA chairman Frederick J. Close as "key figures behind the conference and transportation here." Hritz saw the conference as a means to harness the city's "vast industrial powers" toward a common end. He quoted Purnell as saying, "In order to insure success, the power structure was pulled out." Even competing local companies realized they had much to gain by joining forces behind the conference.[64] As if to secure this corporate cooperation and that of public officials, the UTC filed for incorporation later in the year. While the incorporators were the familiar figures of US Steel's Worthington, ALCOA'S Close, PAT's Hazard, RIDC's Ryan, and Mellon's Purnell, the directors included the presidents of many other major corporations (most of whom were the Conference executive committee members as well); I. W. Abel of the United Steelworkers; the chairmen of PAT, RIDC, and the chamber of commerce; the president of Carnegie Mellon University; and key public officials, Governor Shafer, Mayor Barr, and County Commissioner Leonard Staisy.[65] The successful Renaissance formula of public and private cooperation orchestrated by the Mellon interests and the Conference was being repeated.

Events of 1968—as noted earlier, PAT's acceptance of the PBQD report, submission of the Early Action Program by PAT's rapid transit committee, and Washington's approval of the technical grant to study TERL with Westinghouse as systems manager—all seemed to confirm that rapid transit with the Skybus technology and industry targeting of the transportation industry were moving smoothly toward a successful conclusion. Only a few weeks after PAT applied for the technical grant in September 1968, public officials joined representatives of fifteen local firms, including both Westinghouse and WABCO, to inspect the different transit technologies operating in Montreal and Toronto.[66] Thus, during the waning months of 1968, the public-private partnership appeared firmly in place and rapid transit securely a part of the county's future. The strategy for targeting the local rapid transit industry looked like a winner.

THE STRATEGY FALTERS

Cooperation among the rapid transit players, however, was not to be long-lived; in fact, it did not survive the decade. A few key public officials broke ranks from the generally broad-based political support and shattered the partnership with private organizations, objecting to the elite bias of their interests and behind-closed-doors style of decision making. At the same time, WABCO's challenge to the Early Action Program and Westinghouse's Skybus technology broke the unanimity of the corporate community. Both fractures revealed weaknesses in the longstanding Renaissance formula, which now appeared because of changes in leadership and political context.

When the omnipotent old leaders of the public-private partnership died (both Mellon and Lawrence), stresses in the coalition could not be contained. Moreover, the public's growing distrust of elite forms of power in the late 1960s, violence following Martin Luther King's assassination, and intensification of civil rights and neighborhood activism provided the opportunity for new political leaders to discredit and attack the Renaissance partnership.

By 1967 the Democratic Lawrence/Barr era was coming to an end, and the consensus among business and political leaders began to unravel. Lawrence died in 1966. A few public leaders with different agendas began to seek power. Although in 1967 the Democratic organization managed to elect two new county commissioners who were faithful to the rapid transit program (Leonard Staisey of the Monongahela valley and former state representative Tom Foerster), a less friendly Republican William L. Hunt defeated Blair Gunther for the minority commissioner position. Hunt was an aggressive partisan from the Monongahela valley who united with elected officials from the valley's industrial towns, especially Republican Mayor Zoran Popovich of McKeesport, to oppose the Early Action Program on the grounds that the valley had been left without planned routes. The McKeesport mayor's opposition to Skybus along with that of several other municipalities reflected the acrimonious debate over creating a countywide mass transit system in 1963. McKeesport's mayor at the time, Andrew J. Jakomas, had feared that consolidating local transit companies (bus and streetcars) was a step toward the creation of a metropolitanwide government at the expense of municipal autonomy. Suburban communities throughout Allegheny County had feared metropolitanism since the beginning of the century. The opposition should have been anticipated.

In 1967 the Barr administration's attention was being diverted from physical redevelopment. Many factors caused this reorientation, including the demands of the civil rights and welfare rights movements, anti–Vietnam War protests, the increasing number of categorical grants available to cities from the federal government for the development of new organizations to manage federal money, and the community's growing hostility toward past renewal efforts.[67] By 1969 the Barr administration had experienced explosive riots, a revenue crisis, and strident strikes. The riots following the assassination of Martin Luther King Jr. on April 4, 1968, shocked the city and Barr. He decided not to run for reelection. Sixty-three years old, he had spent thirty years in public life and was prepared to step aside. In a public statement Barr said: "To be mayor of a major city means to be involved in the period of the greatest social challenge and change in our nation's history.

Never before has there been greater ferment and social conflict in our urban centers."[68]

In the spring 1969 Democratic primary, Pittsburgh city councilman Pete Flaherty defeated the organization's candidate, Judge Harry Kramer, to be the Democratic candidate for mayor. Flaherty attacked the Lawrence/Barr organization and the public-private partnership symbolized by the Conference, which he described as "a top down elitist operation" that was inefficient, lacked fiscal soundness, and neglected Pittsburgh neighborhoods, especially African American ones. He ran as "nobody's boy," without endorsement of the Democratic organization, labor, or the business community. Once mayor, Flaherty replaced the directors of all departments, including the planning department and the Urban Redevelopment Authority, rupturing the important staff relationships that had implemented the public-private partnership of Renaissance.[69]

While the political leadership was being transformed, the Conference also experienced change. In the closing years of the decade Richard K. Mellon adopted a passive role in civic affairs; then he died in June 1970. After the civil rights riots and demands that followed the assassination of Martin Luther King Jr., the new Conference executive director, Robert Pease, presided over a change in the organization's focus to "human renewal," emphasizing social and economic development, education, and employment training. The Conference's annual report in 1968 expressed concern for social issues: "An urban crisis, more challenging and even more difficult of solution than the physical crisis of the 1940s, confronted Pittsburgh—the problems of the urban poor, the black and white citizens in the deprived neighborhoods of our community where poverty, unemployment, crime, delinquency, poor housing, alienation and other corrosive forces of ghetto existence sap the vitality and strength of our urban life."[70] The Conference resolved to help bring the urban poor into the mainstream of community life so that the city could realize its full potentialities. This new focus on human renewal diverted energies from physical redevelopment and rapid transit, although it did not end the Conference's commitment to them.

In this changing political environment, WABCO disrupted the unity of the business community and smooth progress toward PAT's and the UTC's goals with the submission in July 1969 of an alternative rapid transit plan. There had been little public warning of this rupture earlier in the spring, when the Renaissance partnership seemed still to be functioning routinely. In March 1969, at the Fourth International Conference on Urban Transportation, Allegheny County Commissioner Staisey announced that Skybus would be constructed. His announcement drew public support from the heads of PAT, RIDC, and the Pittsburgh Chamber of Commerce, who all believed that the UTC's original goals were now within sight. In early April, Westinghouse chairman of the board Donald Burnham assured stockholders at the corporation's annual meeting that they were ready to build Skybus since no technical problems remained. These claims by Staisey and Burnham seemed to dispel nagging concerns about the steel-rails versus rubber-wheels technological issue that had been left unresolved in the PBQD report and simmering during 1968. Two other concerns recognized in a January 1968 *Post-Gazette* editorial—high construction costs and the long time frame for completion of the new system—still loomed in the background.[71]

At an evening closed-door executive session of the PAT board in July 1969, WABCO officials presented their PATMETRO rail transit plan for Allegheny County as an alternative to the Early Action Program. PAT was ready to adopt formally the Early Action Program in order to proceed with a grant proposal to the Department of Transportation. The board had anticipated only limited revisions to the proposed South Hills Skybus line. Instead, it faced a proposal for a complete system that differed from the Early Action Program in many significant respects. WABCO proposed a twenty eight-mile steel-wheel-on-steel-rail line from East Liberty in the city's East End through downtown to the South Hills. Company officials emphasized that the plan could be implemented without disrupting current trolley service, depended on proven technology, employed modern Metro cars that could be operated either automatically or manually, and used extant rights-of-way with no grade level crossings and no overhead concrete Skybus structures (see Figure 8.2). Most important, the WABCO system would cost only $114,000,000, half of the Skybusbusway program.[72] Despite a telegram from Democratic mayoral candidate Pete Flaherty urging no action until the WABCO plan could be studied, the board approved the Early Action Program on a 7–2 vote only two days later at its regularly scheduled meeting, filed the grant application with HUD, and asked for Allegheny County's commitment to the required $4,000,000 supplement to the $8,700,000 HUD proposal.[73]

Allegheny County commissioner Thomas Foerster, a Skybus proponent, scheduled a public hearing on PAT's request for the county's financial commitment because such a commitment was, in effect, public policy. The hearing provided the opportunity for those opposed to Skybus to air their case against the Early Action Program. WABCO did not wait for the hearing scheduled in August and instead released its plan to the press the day after its presentation to the PAT executive committee. The controversy had now migrated to the public arena. WABCO's indiscretion angered PAT board

FIG. 8.2 View of the elevated Skybus track, indicating its visual impact on the built landscape (Harold Corsini Collection, courtesy of the Archive Services Center, University of Pittsburgh).

chairperson William Henry, senior vice president of Gulf Oil Corporation. He declared the $114,000,000 figure grossly underestimated.[74] On behalf of PAT, he engaged the local engineering firm Michael Baker Jr. Incorporated to evaluate the WABCO plan before the hearing, especially the cost projections. Michael Baker adjusted the figure upward by $104,000,000, making Skybus's estimated cost competitive. The consulting firm submitted its report immediately before the hearing, leaving WABCO little opportunity to examine the methodology and respond effectively.[75]

For Pittsburgh and Allegheny County a lot rode on the outcome of the commissioners' hearing when it began on August 20, 1969. The Department of Transportation in Washington, DC, expressed concern over the rift in the community, threatening the millions of dollars it was predisposed to award for local rapid transit and jeopardizing the existence of rapid transit in the region. The technologies of the region's two major rapid transit manufacturers, WABCO and Westinghouse, were pitted against each other in this public forum. More than the transit futures of these two key corporations were at risk; the community's industry targeting strategy had also arrived at a perilous juncture. As one transportation official ironically noted: "The industry wants to see if the community that bills itself as the transit capital of the world can solve its own mass transit problems."[76]

Led by mayoral candidate Flaherty and Republican County Commissioner Hunt, the opposition raised technological, financial, and social concerns and attacked the elite nature of the PAT board. Recognizing the new "power to the people" atmosphere of the late 1960s and riding the populist wave that was propelling his mayoral campaign, Pete Flaherty charged the PAT board as being representative of the business community, because two-thirds of its members were corporate executives. In his view, the board was a creature of the Renaissance public-private partnership with a propensity for decisions made in secret that reflected business interests and perspectives. Since tax revenues would build rapid transit, the public had the right to full disclosure and participation in the process through publicly elected representatives. However, as an authority and not an elected body PAT, Flaherty charged, operated paternalistically and without accountability. He argued that such a position could no longer be tolerated: "In short, the whole issue of rapid transit up until now has been . . . a private affair of the PAT Board. My own experience at the PAT Board meetings . . . was not one of welcome receptivity. The tone of the Board toward public suggestions was to look upon such suggestions as minor intrusions. In my own case it was as though I were interrupting the usual order of business. . . . Their tone is not one of 'the public be damned' but rather—'We know best.'"[77]

Although a respected and active member of the corporate community, WABCO buttressed Flaherty's position by complaining that PAT had not allowed time for a proper response and had tried to muzzle WABCO's Metro plan. Flaherty concluded that "an emotional commitment by the majority of the PAT Board and the Pittsburgh industrial establishment to the Skybus plan" precluded change to the plan filed in Washington.[78] In turn, Flaherty attacked the technology of Westinghouse's rapid transit system. Despite the various engineering studies that certified Skybus, Flaherty revived doubts about the safety and reliability of automated, unmanned trains. More than twenty years later (now as county commissioner) Flaherty offered the following scenarios to illustrate his fears:

> Picture, if you will, a young, female office worker in downtown Pittsburgh who finishes her workday and afterwards goes shopping or to a restaurant, and about 9:00 p.m. goes to the Skybus Station for her trip home to Mt. Lebanon. A Skybus car pulls into the station, automatically operated by a computer. Doors open automatically after the car stops and a voice from a cassette says "Please enter." The young woman sees only two men on the car. If she gets on, she will be alone with two strangers through the tunnel and up into the first stop in Beechview. An older couple in their seventies get on at South Hills Junction to go downtown. On the way, an electrical storm or electrical malfunction causes a power failure. The car stops on the concrete piers 40 feet or so above ground level. How do they get out? It's somewhat like being on an elevator between floors without power. Vandals throw old tires and junk on the track. The train, which has no operator, plows into the debris and is jammed to a stop. Passengers on board are placed in an unsafe situation. Ice and snow storms have similar hazards if heavy enough. There are no snow plows up there (on the elevated routeway).[79]

Flaherty argued further that the proposed routes did not serve enough of the poor and working-class people of the county and city. Neither the Monongahela valley nor most of the city's neighborhoods had access to the South Hills route. Some studies agreed that the most densely populated corridor was to the east, running through the city to the near suburbs. If Skybus or any fixed route system were to be built, the eastern route was the logical choice. However, this route would traverse at least one and most likely two of the largest African American neighborhoods in the region. In contrast, the proposed route to the South Hills connected white middle-class suburbs to the city's downtown. In the context of populism and civil rights militancy of the late 1960s, it was difficult to defend this apparently biased choice of route.[80]

Flaherty predicted that PAT's and the 's commitment to Skybus was too strong to change. The county commissioners split along party lines to approve the Early Action Program at their meeting on September 23, 1969. The majority reasoned that an innovative rapid transit system would likely attract federal aid, which was at a "premium," and would "lay the groundwork for Allegheny County to become the rapid transit center of the world."[81]

The targeting vision was still intact, but relationships among the strategy's partners had changed. The 1969 hearings might have been seen as merely an irritant to the plans of PAT and the UTC because funding, design work, and even some construction on the Early Action Program went ahead for the next two years. But the opposition had found its voice in the summer of 1969 and drove the publicity and controversy-shy business community into the shadows at a time when its former leader, R. K. Mellon, was no longer available to enforce corporate unity. The presentation and acrimonious public discussion of WABCO's Metro plan disrupted, and in the end doomed, the industry targeting strategy. Further, the election of Democrat Flaherty as mayor ruptured the essential partnership between public officials and private leaders.

After the hearing, civic leaders moved to shore up support for the Early Action Program, although discordant notes reappeared at awkward moments. With Barr still as mayor for a few more months and a supporter of PAT's plans, his chairman of the City Planning Commission, David Olbum, addressed one criticism of PAT in a letter to the county commissioners. He wrote that "there has been better coordination among the various agencies on this project than on any other development within the memory of the Planning Commission," and he urged "prompt approval on the Early Action Program."[82] In October longtime Skybus proponent and close Mellon associate Robert Ryan was appointed chairman of the UTC, replacing former US Steel president Leslie Worthington who had originally taken the post at Mellon's urging. The contract of UTC's executive director, former US Steel executive Robert Hardin, was not renewed. These steps signaled the UTC's continued advocacy of Skybus, which it endorsed "minutes after Ryan's election." Worthington and Hardin had not publicly endorsed either of the competing technologies. US Steel was believed to be sympathetic to WABCO's steel-wheel technology, while ALCOA supported Westinghouse's Skybus. The changes indicated deepening disharmony within the business community over the issue.[83] At PAT's request, consulting engineers Richardson, Gordon, and Associates issued a report in January 1970 stating that Skybus was "not only entirely feasible but very practical." Then, in February the Conference executive committee voted to endorse the Early Action Program after listening to reports on it and to Commissioner Hunt's opposition.[84]

During the week following the Conference's endorsement, however, concern over Skybus as a federally financed project was expressed in the US Senate, and a delegation from McKeesport presented its opposition to the legal department of the Department of Transportation (DOT). The Transport Workers Union also expressed disapproval.[85] While these remonstrations delayed approval of PAT's application for funds, DOT did finally grant the $8,700,000 in June 1970. Still, DOT requested its Bureau of Public Roads and the NASA Electronics Research Center to evaluate the technical issues of the proposed system. Although Kaiser Engineers on behalf of Los Angeles and Baltimore had rejected the Skybus technology, DOT's reviews "concluded that there was no engineering basis to raise significant questions." In summer 1971 DOT awarded an additional $60,000,000 to PAT.[86] By the end of the year, the Pittsburgh City Council and other appropriate municipalities expressed support, and both the county and the state pledged commitments of capital expenditures for which they were responsible. Moreover, PAT had undertaken eminent domain proceedings, land purchase agreements, and some initial construction contracts.[87]

Just as Skybus, and possibly also Pittsburgh's industry targeting project were poised to become reality, the opposition filed a preliminary injunction in January 1972 to stop construction. Mayor Flaherty used legal delaying tactics, such as not issuing construction permits to renovate the tunnel through Mount Washington, blocking the sale of city land to PAT for its Midtown Plaza station, and vetoing the plan in city council (which it then reversed). Finally, Flaherty and Mayor Peter Page of suburban Bethel Park marshaled the mayors of several municipalities to join with them and Commissioner Hunt in filing suit against PAT's Early Action Program. After six months of hearings and legal procedures, Judge Anne X. Alpern issued the injunction. The opposition had taken a costly step, for as Secretary of Transportation John Volpe informed Flaherty, the federal funds had been granted only for the Early Action Program. New applications would have to be filed for a different proposal. When Pennsylvania Governor Shapp, a newly elected Democrat, withdrew his support in the fall of 1972 (and hence the state funding), the strategy of promoting a local rapid transit industry on the back of a local rapid transit system that employed the Skybus technology then foundered.[88] The injunction underscored the collapse of the public-private partnership. In suing PAT public officials also indirectly attacked the Conference, which was committed to PAT's Early Action Plan and enhancing the local rapid transit industry.

Although Judge Alpern's decision was reversed on appeal by the Pennsylvania Supreme Court in early 1973, the Skybus program was hopelessly deadlocked. Federal support remained for Skybus, but the intense controversy led to an evaluation of alternatives. The county commissioners formed a transit task force in 1972. Winning both the Democratic and Republican primaries, Flaherty easily won reelection in November 1973. The new Conference president, Dravo Corporation chairman Robert Dickey III, recognized that a working relationship with the mayor was essential for resuming redevelopment of the region, and therefore, that the conference might have to diminish its support for Skybus.[89]

Task force members came from all levels of government and the Port Authority. PAT board member John P. Robin chaired the task force. Robin, the first executive of the Urban Redevelopment Authority and a central figure in Pittsburgh's Renaissance, had not been involved in the development of the rapid transit strategy or in the controversy. Widely respected by all parties, he was the ideal person to seek a compromise for transit. Under the specter of losing federal funds, the task force selected a consultant through a method that dispelled concerns of a biased process. In 1976 the consultant recommended abandoning Skybus and opting for less controversial exclusive bus lanes, the upgrading of streetcars to a light rail system to the South Hills, and construction of a downtown subway loop. Construction of the light rail system began five years later.

CONCLUSION

The Skybus struggle generated so much animosity within Pittsburgh's business and political communities that the industry targeting strategy became untenable and was abandoned. In the end, the "new center" for the design, promotion, and production of rapid transit systems could not produce its own local system. Although in the beginning optimism prevailed, Pittsburgh's industry targeting effort failed because political support waned for the centerpiece of the strategy, the building of an innovative rapid transit system for the region. Political opponents of the city's traditional civic leadership found in the Skybus program opportunities to press an attack. The feasibility of Skybus technology with respect to topography, weather, and particularly safety remained in question despite the numerous studies supporting the system. A decision to run the demonstration line on an active route rather than under controlled conditions at South Park might have proved its viability, won over the public, and quieted critics who used the technical doubts to arouse public fears.[90]

Suburban communities feared in a countywide mass transportation system the threat of metropolitanism, by which they could lose their municipal autonomy. This long-standing concern had been aroused during the 1963 controversy over the decision by the county commissioners to consolidate transit into a single system, and it had not had time to dissipate.[91] Moreover, the industrial towns of the Monongahela valley and the African American communities of the city's East End, which were not served by the Early Action Program's proposed route, felt neglected once again by the region's powerbrokers and gave their support to the Skybus opponents. Finally, the United Steelworkers union registered displeasure with a technology that did not use steel rails.

In the twenty years after the Second World War, political opposition to Renaissance projects could not overcome the power of David Lawrence's Democratic Party organization working in an alliance with Richard K. Mellon and the corporate community and supported by a cheerleading media. However, the civil rights movement, rising populism, and increasing community activism in the 1960s undermined the party organization and encouraged challenges to the elite-based, top-down decision-making structure that characterized postwar redevelopment in Pittsburgh. The death of David Lawrence further weakened the party. The public-private partnership was slow to appreciate the changing political landscape. Confident in their power to push through the transit program, as they had with other Renaissance programs, civic leaders failed to build a broad-based consensus behind Skybus. PAT, for example, never studied the likely positive impact of building and operating a rapid transit system on employment and income in the region. Nor did PAT adequately justify its selection of the South Hills route over the more obvious eastern corridor. Comprehending this new political environment, nonorganizational Democratic candidate for mayor Pete Flaherty and Republican county commissioner William Hunt used the Skybus program as an example of backroom secretive decision-making to attack (successfully) their opponents in the 1969 election year.

In attacking Skybus, they also were attacking the Conference at its most vulnerable time. Late in the approval process key companies decided to no longer subordinate their self-interest for the larger regional industry targeting strategy. Westinghouse and WABCO's fight over rubber-wheel or steel-wheel technology brought a private fight into the public fray, while a few other companies, in particular US Steel, also failed to unite behind the strategy. Previously, Richard K. Mellon had enforced corporate unity for Renaissance goals, but by the late 1960s the ailing business leader had withdrawn from civic engagement. Further, the private partners of the Renaissance alliance, used to getting their way, misjudged the power of the emerging opposition. They failed to heed the warning signs of municipal dissent and corporate disagreement and did not take the steps necessary to neutralize the opposition. When Flaherty won the mayoral election, he ended the partnership between the mayor's office and the Conference. The region could no longer present a united front when applying for funds at the state and federal levels.

Pittsburgh's efforts to target the rapid transit industry in the 1960s underscore the inherently political nature of industry targeting as a regional economic development strategy. Whatever the methodological problems in selecting a targeted industry, implementation of a development program for that industry requires supportive public policies. Pittsburgh's strategy of showcasing the local rapid transit industry by holding promotional conferences and, most critically, building its own rapid transit system linked industrial development to local infrastructure needs and, therefore, to a local political decision-making process. Policies that favor some companies over others within the local industry, such as occurred in Pittsburgh, may open rifts that weaken private sector support. Changes in civic leadership as well as in the local political landscape like those that occurred in the city in the late 1960s may undermine the ability of public officials to deliver necessary public policies. Thus, the public part of a targeting strategy may fall victim to political fights that may not be essentially concerned with the merits of industry targeting. Division within the private sector and conflicts among politicians, in turn, can prevent a region from presenting the unified civic front that is often a requisite in obtaining state and federal financial commitments.

The Skybus technology never really disappeared from the national transportation marketplace. It is used in a few communities, such as Morgantown, West Virginia, and many airports. Its demise as a rapid transit system in Pittsburgh also spelled the collapse of the regional effort to target the local rapid transit industry for development. Ironically, twenty years later, some in the Pittsburgh region again proposed targeting a local transit industry based on the innovative magnetic levitation technology, tied it to the construction of public infrastructure, and depended on obtaining federal funds. This effort, known as MAGLEV, quietly dissolved in the face of numerous policy hurdles laden with political challenges mostly at the national level. The light rail line that did go to the South Hills was extended as a subway in downtown and then much later under the Allegheny River to the north shore stadiums, Carnegie Science Center, and surrounding development. Although transit equipment manufacturing remains, the region never became the global production center that was envisioned in the 1960s.

NOTES

Originally accessed by Edward K. Muller, Morton Coleman, and David Houston, "Skybus: Pittsburgh's Failed Industrial Targeting Strategy of the 1960s" (Pittsburgh: Center for Industry Studies, University of Pittsburgh, 2002), www.industrystudies.pitt.edu.

1. Michael P. Weber, *Don't Call Me Boss: David L. Lawrence, Pittsburgh's Renaissance Mayor* (Pittsburgh: University of Pittsburgh Press, 1988), 263; Shelby Stewman and Joel A. Tarr, "Four Decades of Public-Private Partnerships in Pittsburgh," in R. Scott Foster and Renee A. Berger, eds., *Public-Private Partnerships in American Cities* (Lexington, MA: D. C. Heath, 1982), 59–127.

2. Kenneth Voytek and Larry Ledebur, "Is Industry Targeting a Viable Economic Development Strategy?" in Richard D. Bingham and Robert Mier, eds., *Dilemmas of Urban Economic Development: Issues in Theory and Practice*, Urban Affairs Annual Reviews, no. 47 (Thousand Oaks, CA: Sage Publications, 1997), 171–94.

3. Edgar M. Hoover, *Economic Study of the Pittsburgh Region. Volume 1. Region in Transition* (Pittsburgh: University of Pittsburgh Press, 1963).

4. The term "mass transportation" refers to a system of public transportation that involves the daily mass movement of people about an urban area, while the term "rapid transit" refers to a specific aspect of mass transportation, which involves "the mass movement of people in wheeled vehicles on exclusive right(s)ofway" in order to free the vehicles of surface street congestion. MPC, *Report on Testing and Evaluation of the Transit Expressway* (MPC Corporation, Pittsburgh, PA., 1967), 3. The MPC Corporation was a nonprofit organization owned by the Mellon Institute, University of Pittsburgh, and Carnegie Institute of Technology (later renamed Carnegie Mellon University).

5. Donald T. Iannone, "Commentary on Industry Targeting," in Bingham and Mier, *Dilemmas of Urban Economic Development*, 195–97; Sabina E. Deitrick, "Commentary on Industry Targeting," in Bingham and Mier, *Dilemmas of Urban Economic Development*, 197–201.

6. Weber, *Don't Call Me Boss*, 228–76; Stewman and Tarr, "Four Decades"; Roy Lubove, *Twentieth-Century Pittsburgh, Vol. 1: Government, Business, and Environmental Change* (New York: John Wiley and Sons, 1969), ch. 6.

7. Frank Giarratani and David B. Houston, "Economic Change in the Pittsburgh Region," in J. J. Hesse, ed., *Regional Structural Change and Industrial Policy: An International Perspective* (BadenBaden: NomosVerlag, 1988), 59, 70.

8. Hoover, *Economic Study*. The population of the metropolitan area peaked in the 1960s.

9. Mark H. Rose, *Interstate: Expressway Highway Politics, 1939–1984*, rev. ed. (Knoxville: University of Tennessee Press, 1990); Kenneth T. Jackson, *Crabgrass Frontier: The Suburbanization of the United States* (New York: Oxford University Press, 1985), ch. 14.

10. John F. Bauman and Edward K. Muller, *Before Renaissance : Planning in Pittsburgh, 1889–1943* (Pittsburgh: University of Pittsburgh Press, 2006); Lubove, *Twentieth-Century Pittsburgh, Vol. 1*; Tarr, *Transportation Innovation*.

11. Weber, *Don't Call Me Boss*, 288–89; Lubove, *Twentieth-Century Pittsburgh, Vol. 1*, 127.

12. David L. Lawrence, "Rebirth," in Stephen Lorant, *Pittsburgh: The Story of an American City* (New York: Doubleday Press, 1961), 383; Roger Ahlbrandt and Morton Coleman, *The Limits of a Corporate Civic Responsibility* (Pittsburgh: University Center for Social and Urban Research, University of Pittsburgh, 1987); Sherie R. Mershon, "Corporate Social Responsibility and Urban Revitalization: The Allegheny Conference on Community Development" (PhD diss., Carnegie Mellon University, 2000).

13. *Pittsburgh Post-Gazette*, December 1959 (clipping).

14. Morton Coleman, "Interest Intermediation and Local Urban Development" (PhD diss., University of Pittsburgh, 1983), 85–103.

15. Coleman, "Interest Intermediation," 88.

16. Stewman and Tarr, "Four Decades," 92.

17. Interview with Walter Geisey, in *The Pittsburgh Renaissance Project: The Staunton Balfour Oral History Collection, Final Report* (Pittsburgh: Buhl Foundation, 1974), 44, in AIS 1973.24, Archives & Special Collections, University of Pittsburgh Library System, Pittsburgh, PA.

18. Quoted in *Flaherty v. Port Authority of Allegheny County, PA 299 a.sd*, 613; Mershon, "Corporate Social Responsibility," 591–93.

19. Brief for Defendant, Port Authority of Allegheny County, Supreme Court of Pennsylvania, Western District, No. 41 March Term, 1973, 4–5; "Mass Transit Up to County as Authority Unveils Blueprint," *Pittsburgh Post-Gazette*, March 13, 1963. See *Pittsburgh Press*, March 15, 1963, for an example of the controversy over the referendum. Also "Mass Transit Backers, Foes in Bitter Clash," *Pittsburgh Press*, April 19, 1963; "Judge Blasts Jakoma's Stand on Transit Plan," *Pittsburgh Press*, April 18, 1963; "Transit Plan Speeded after Okay by County," *Pittsburgh Post-Gazette*, April 24, 1963. Mershon, "Corporate Social Responsibility," 568–91.

20. Minutes of the Allegheny Conference on Community Development Executive Committee, February 17, 1964 (MSS #285, Records of Allegheny Conference on Community Development, Detre Library & Archives, Senator John Heinz History Center, Pittsburgh). The Pittsburgh Regional Planning Association was closely linked to the Conference throughout the Renaissance years. Former Westinghouse executive George W. Jernstedt recalled that his company came up with the automated design in response to a 1963 request by Allegheny County through the Conference for solutions of the transportation problem (a request open to all local corporations). However, the 1963 partnership between PAT and Westinghouse for a demonstration project and the earlier Golden Triangle Master Plan suggest that the idea had been under consideration for some time. Interview with George A. Jernstedt, April 18, 1994, notes in possession of author.

21. MPC, *Report on Testing*, 3–4.

22. MPC, *Report on Testing*, 1–10 and cover letter.

23. *PAT News* 11, no. I (February 1966).

24. Minutes of the Allegheny Conference on Community Development Executive Committee, February 17, May 10, 1964.

25. "Pittsburgh: Rail Rapid Transit in the Cards?" *Railway Age Weekly*, November 1, 1965; Leland Hazard, *Attorney for the Situation* (Pittsburgh: Carnegie Mellon University, 1975). In April 1963 Hazard made a speech in which he argued for both metropolitanism and mass transportation as solutions to Pittsburgh's problems. He was appointed to PAT's board in June 1963, the same month PAT entered into the Skybus partnership. Former vice president of PPG Industries and a member of the Conference, Hazard enjoyed access to the corporate leadership.

26. "Rail Rapid Transit," *Railway Age Weekly*, November 1, 1965. Hazard claimed he was selected by PAT board chairman Loren Lewis because of his penchant for innovative solutions. He said that, as chair of PAT's transit committee, he was convinced of Skybus's possibility and pushed for its construction. "Hazard Gets County Port Authority Job," *Pittsburgh Post-Gazette*, June 26, 1963; "Will Pittsburgh Live or Die? Hazard Offers Answer," *Pittsburgh Press*, April 21, 1963; Interview with Leland Hazard by Joel A. Tarr and James Romuoldi, Pittsburgh, 1979, notes in possession of author.

27. "Much Deeper Study of Rapid Transit Authorized by PAT," *Pittsburgh Post-Gazette*, December 17, 1966; "Transit Loop Downtown Envisioned," *Pittsburgh Press*, February 2, 1967.

28. MPC, *Report on Testing*, 1–10 and cover letter.

29. PAT news release, September 18, 1967; "City Wins Shot at Transit Title," *Pittsburgh Press*, April 13, 1967. While claiming impartiality as early as December 1966, Hazard seemed infatuated by the innovative aspect of Skybus and its potential for solving the engineering problems presented by Pittsburgh's topography. *Pittsburgh Post-Gazette*, December 17, 1966.

30. Parsons, Brinckerhoff, Quade, & Douglas, *Allegheny County Rapid Transit Study* (Pittsburgh, 1967); "County Given 'Choice' of Rapid Transit Rides," *Pittsburgh Press*, December 29, 1967; "Transit Pros and Cons: Steel vs. Rubber; Time Will Tell Which One PAT Picks," *Pittsburgh Press*, December 31, 1967.

31. "Skybus: New Hope for Cities," *Pittsburgh Press*, December 20, 1967.

32. *Flaherty v. Port Authority of Allegheny County, PA 299 a.sd*, 616.

33. Exhibits and Testimony Pages, cited in *Flaherty v. Port Authority*, Brief for Defendant Port Authority of Allegheny County, Supreme Court of Pennsylvania, Western District, No. 41, March Term, 1973 (hereafter *Flaherty v. Port Authority*, Exhibits and Testimony Pages, with page), 634a.

34. *Flaherty v. Port Authority*, Brief for Defendant, Port Authority of Allegheny County, 8–9; *Flaherty v. Port Authority*, Exhibits and Testimony Pages, 406a.

35. Roger Biles, *The Fate of Cities: Urban America and the Federal Government, 1945–2000* (Lawrence: University Press of Kansas, 2011), 194–97.

36. "US Steel Cites Needs in Future of Transit," *Pittsburgh Post-Gazette*, August 11, 1965.

37. "Rail Rapid Transit," *Railway Age Weekly*, November 1, 1965.

38. "LBJ OKs $90 Million for High Speed Transit," *Pittsburgh Post-Gazette*, September 30, 1965; "Transit Bill Seen Benefit for County," *Pittsburgh Post-Gazette*, October 1, 1965; "Westinghouse Directors to Meet in South Park," *Pittsburgh Post-Gazette*, October 27, 1965.

39. Leland Baldwin, *Pittsburgh: The Story of a City* (Pittsburgh: University of Pittsburgh Press, 1937), 129–44.

40. Joseph Frazier Wall, *Andrew Carnegie* (New York, 1970); David Nasaw, *Andrew Carnegie* (New York: Penguin Press, 2006).

41. David A. Hounshell, Mark D. Samber, and Joel A. Tarr, "Technology and Transformation: The Railroad as a Shaper of Regional Space, Natural Resources, Industrial Practice, and Economic Development in Pittsburgh, 1830s–1920s" (unpublished paper presented at the Symposium entitled "Localized Production Systems and the Formation of Metropolitan Areas: The Pittsburgh Metropolitan Industrial District 1870–1930," Center for Social History, Pittsburgh, November 1994).

42. "Rail Rapid Transit," *Railway Age Weekly*, November 1, 1965.

43. The description of Ryan was made by the reporter Thomas M. Hritz in "Ryan Heads PUTC: Skybus Endorsed," *Pittsburgh Post-Gazette*, October 21, 1969. See also "South Park 'Skybus' Could Revitalize Area," *Pittsburgh Post-Gazette*, June 10, 1963; "City Wins Shot at Transit Title," *Pittsburgh Press*, April 13, 1967; "Westinghouse Making Area Transit Hub," *Pittsburgh-Post Gazette*, April 14, 1967; Interview with Robert Hardin, October 7, 1991 (Pittsburgh), notes in possession of author; Minutes of the Allegheny Conference on Community Development Executive Committee, January 20, 1964, 2. RIDC was another nonprofit organization that grew out of Renaissance and the efforts of the Conference. See Stewman and Tarr, "Four Decades."

44. Interview with Robert Hardin, notes in possession of author.

45. "Transit Industry Plug Due Here," *Pittsburgh Press*, June 18, 1965. Purnell was also secretary of the Conference at the time.

46. *Pittsburgh Press*, October 20, 1965; "Rapid Transit Progress," *Pittsburgh Post-Gazette*, November 16, 1965; "Transit Bill Seen Benefit for County," *Pittsburgh Post-Gazette*, October 1, 1965.

47. "Super Agency for Transit Urged Here," *Pittsburgh Press*, November 16, 1965. The Conference executive committee had been briefed earlier in the fall on the UTC's upcoming initial conference.

48. "Rapid Transit Setup Predicted for City," *Pittsburgh Press*, January 6, 1966.

49. "New Industry Hailed," *Pittsburgh Post-Gazette*, January 13, 1966.

50. "World Transit Capital," *Pittsburgh Post-Gazette*, January 31, 1966.

51. "Build Transit 'Showpiece,' City Told," *Pittsburgh Press*, February 6, 1966.

52. "World Transit Capital," *Pittsburgh Post-Gazette*, January 31, 1966.

53. "Transit Experts Heading for City," *Pittsburgh Press*, January 30, 1966; "Transit Experts to Meet," *Pittsburgh Post-Gazette*, January 31, 1966. The description of a trade fair was made by Robert Hardin. Interview with Robert Hardin, notes in possession of author.

54. "Technology and U.S. Aid Raise Mass Transit Industry's Hopes," *New York Times*, February 4, 1966.

55. "City Seeking Role of Transit Leader," *Pittsburgh Post-Gazette*, February 4, 1966.

56. "County Vote Called For on System," *Pittsburgh Post-Gazette*, February 2, 1966.

57. "Build Transit 'Showpiece,' City Told," *Pittsburgh Press*, February 6, 1966.

58. "County Vote Called For on System," *Pittsburgh Post-Gazette*, February 2, 1966.

59. "State OKs Survey of Speed Road," *Pittsburgh Post-Gazette*, April 22, 1966.

60. Minutes of the Allegheny Conference on Community Development Executive Committee, March 13, 1967, 2.

61. "Air Brake to Tell Transit Plans," *Pittsburgh Post-Gazette*, April 13, 1967.

62. "City Wins Shot at Transit Title," *Pittsburgh Press*, April 13, 1967; "Westinghouse Making Area Transit Hub," *Pittsburgh Post-Gazette*, April 14, 1967.

63. "90Minute Trip Feasible WABCO Says," *Pittsburgh Press*, April 17, 1967.

64. "City Eyes Transit Capital Crown," *Pittsburgh Post-Gazette*, April 13, 1967.

65. "Transit Council Seeking Charter," *Pittsburgh Post-Gazette*, November 14, 1967.

66. Untitled, *Pittsburgh Post-Gazette*, September 23, 1968.

67. Coleman, "Interest Intermediation," 42.

68. Interview with Joseph M. Barr, July 14, 1972, in *Pittsburgh Renaissance Project*, 5. See also Joe W. Trotter and Jared N. Day, *Race and Renaissance: African Americans in Pittsburgh since World War II* (Pittsburgh: University of Pittsburgh Press, 2010), 103–40; Alyssa Ribeiro, "'A Period of Turmoil': Pittsburgh's April 1968 Riots and Their Aftermath," *Journal of Urban History* 39, no. 2 (2012): 147–71.

69. Stewman and Tarr, "Four Decades," 89–90; Morton Coleman, personal recollections, January 1991.

70. The Conference, *Annual Report, 1968* (MSS#285, Records of the Allegheny Conference on Community Development, Detre Library & Archives, Senator John Heinz History Center, Pittsburgh, Pennsylvania), 2.

71. "Skybus Route 'Boom' Studied," *Pittsburgh Press*, March 16, 1969; "Civic Leaders Hail Rapid Transit Push," *Pittsburgh Press*, March 16, 1969; Untitled, *Pittsburgh Post-Gazette*, April 3, 1969; "NonRapid Transit Plan," *Pittsburgh Press*, January 11, 1968.

72. "PAT Given Cheaper Rail Plan," *Pittsburgh Press*, July 9, 1969.

73. *Flaherty v. Port Authority*, Exhibits and Testimony Pages, 374a.

74. Gulf Oil Corporation grew out of Mellon investments at the turn of the century and was run for years by W. L. Mellon. Its chief executives had been closely allied with the Mellon interests for years. David E. Koskoff, *The Mellons: The Chronicle of America's Richest Family* (New York: Thomas Y. Crowell, 1978).

75. *Flaherty v. Port Authority*, Exhibits and Testimony Pages, 373a; "Wabco Cites Low Cost of Transit Plan," *Pittsburgh Press*, July 9, 1969.

76. "City's 'Transit Capital' Claim at Stake in PAT Hearings," *Pittsburgh Press*, August 17, 1969.

77. *Flaherty v. Port Authority*, Exhibits and Testimony Pages, 375a–88a. See also interview with Leland Hazard, notes in possession of author.

78. *Flaherty v. Port Authority*, Exhibits and Testimony Pages, 375a–88a. Flaherty also noted that, although WABCO presented its plan at the hearings, PAT and not Westinghouse discussed the Early Action Program and Skybus.

79. Peter Flaherty, letter to Morton Coleman, dated August 21, 1991, in possession of author. Westinghouse's Jernstedt concurred that the technological issues all boiled down to concerns for safety and that by 1968 PAT knew these concerns would be discussed. Hazard believed that WABCO's attack on the technology was really instigated by a "feud" between the Westinghouse "siblings" over their traditional policy of not competing in certain fields of business. WABCO felt that Westinghouse was encroaching on their transportation business. Interview with George W. Jernstedt, and interview with Leland Hazard, notes in possession of author.

80. Interview, Peter Flaherty, Pittsburgh, August 13, 1991, notes in possession of author.

81. *Flaherty v. Port Authority*, Exhibits and Testimony Pages, 395a–97a; *Flaherty v. Port Authority*, Brief for the Defendant, 9.

82. David Olbum, letter to Leonard C. Staisey, chairman of the Board of County Commissioners, dated August 25, 1969, in *Flaherty v. Port Authority*, Exhibits and Testimony Pages, 393a–94a.

83. "Skybus Endorsed," *Pittsburgh Post-Gazette*, October 21, 1969. See also "Urban Post for Ryan: Skybus Boost," *Pittsburgh Press*, October 21, 1969. Hazard believed that US Steel executives disliked the rubber-wheel technology because it did not use as much steel as the steel-rail alternative and that they used their considerable influence against Skybus. Interview with Leland Hazard, notes in possession of author.

84. Minutes of the Allegheny Conference on Community Development Executive Committee, February 9, 1970. See also *Flaherty v. Port Authority*, Exhibits and Testimony Pages. Hazard viewed Hunt as a political opportunist who represented the negative position of the railroad unions in the Skybus debate. Interview with Leland Hazard, notes in possession of author.

85. *Pittsburgh Post Gazette*, February 11, 1970; "DOT May Delay Skybus Approval," *Pittsburgh Post-Gazette*, February 18, 1970.

86. *Flaherty v. Port Authority*, Exhibits and Testimony Pages, 400a, 406a. See also *Pittsburgh-Post Gazette*, July 17, 1969; *Pittsburgh Press*, November 19, 1970; *Flaherty v. Port Authority*, Brief for the Defendant, 9.

87. *Flaherty v. Port Authority*, Exhibits and Testimony Pages, 407a, 41la–12a, 438a; *Flaherty v. Port Authority*, Brief for Defendant, 9–13.

88. *Flaherty v. Port Authority*, 616–17; *Flaherty v. Port Authority*, Exhibits and Testimony Pages, 653a; interview with John P. Robin, July 9, 1969, Pittsburgh, and interview with Robert B. Pease, August 3, 1991, notes in possession of author.

89. Interview with Robert B. Pease, January 11, 1995, in *The Pittsburgh History Project: The Staunton Balfour Oral History Collection, Final Report* (Pittsburgh: Buhl Foundation, 1974), AIS 1973 24, Archives a–d Special Collections, Collections, University of Pittsburgh Library System, University of Pittsburgh.

90. Interview with Robert B. Pease, January 11, 1995, in *The Pittsburgh History Project.*

91. "Super Agency for Transit Urged Here," *Pittsburgh Press*, November 16, 1965; "Joint Transit Agency Urged by Judge Lewis," *Pittsburgh Post-Gazette*, November 16, 1965.

III ENERGY, THE ENVIRONMENT, AND THE MODERN CITY

Throughout its history Pittsburgh has been closely related to various energy sources and to the environmental burdens posed by exploitation of these sources. Perhaps best known is the city's reliance on coal and its title "The Smoky City," as it suffered countless overcast days, heavy particle pollution, and buildings darkened with black carbon deposits. And, as the following articles make clear, the coal-burning steel industry also had a devastating effect on both water and land.[1]

Less familiar is the cycle of energy transitions that the city has gone through as it passed through periods of natural gas supply from both local sources in the late nineteenth century and distant sources after the Second World War as is reflected in the chapter on Pittsburgh as an Energy Capital. The positive effects on air quality of the substitution of natural gas for coal at various times in the city's history have overshadowed the damage that extensive drilling for natural gas and oil have had upon the state and the region both in the past and in the present. The next chapter in this section on Pittsburgh's first natural gas boom and its environmental effects uses a template that back casts the environmental effects of the state's recent natural gas boom (the Marcellus and Utica shales) on to the past. In this chapter we query if a better understanding of past natural gas development would have helped us avoid some of the environmental effects of the present boom.

In these energy cycles, the coal and coke industries played critical roles in supplying fuel to the steel industry and in negatively impacting air and water quality. The coke industry underwent a major transition of its own in the late nineteenth and early twentieth centuries, with the shift from coke being produced in beehive coke ovens located near the coking coal fields to the development of by-product coke ovens located close to the mills and urban areas. This shift resulted in major efficiencies for the steel industry and the capture of valuable chemical by-products that had formerly been wasted. However it also resulted in a shift in the air and water pollution resulting from the coking process to expose the urban population near by-product coke plants to hazardous water and air emissions. This essay focuses on the pollution of the drinking water supply of the city of McKeesport by a major by-product coke plant and the city's suit against US Steel that resulted in one of the first legal cases successfully brought against a major industry.

The fourth essay in this section explores the metabolism of Pittsburgh over time and the region's air, water, and land environmental histories. Pittsburgh has suffered extensively from the environmental effects of pollution and has also seen major improvements. The environmental history of the city, as Joel Tarr has characterized it, has been marked by devastation and renewal. But, as those who reside in the city know, the pollution effects of extensive industrial development and of issues surrounding water infrastructure are still with us.

NOTE

1. Because Joel Tarr has written extensively on Pittsburgh air quality and water issues in his other books, the decision was made not to include articles specifically on these subjects here. Articles on Pittsburgh smoke and water and wastewater issues can be found in Joel A. Tarr, *The Search for the Ultimate Sink: Urban Pollution in Historical Perspective* (Akron: University of Akron Press, 1996).

9 PITTSBURGH AS AN ENERGY CAPITAL

PERSPECTIVES ON COAL AND NATURAL GAS TRANSITIONS AND THE ENVIRONMENT

Joel A. Tarr and Karen Clay

Throughout most of its history Pittsburgh has been closely identified with the fossil fuel coal as a source of both industrial progress and environmental degradation. With the city located on top of the high quality bituminous coal seam, Pittsburgh's businesses, industries, residents, railroads, and steamboats benefited from the high-energy and easily available fuel. Coal has shaped the pattern of industrial development, settlement, population, and labor force composition. Its mining and consumption also drove profound environmental contamination and the physical alteration of land and water, as well as seriously polluting the air. Without coal and the advantages of its location, Pittsburgh would not have become one of the world's great industrial powers in the late nineteenth and early twentieth centuries.[1] The tentacles of the city's industrial and financial interests and its ecological footprint spread throughout the region, tying its hinterland ever closer to the city.

The full energy history of Pittsburgh, however, encompasses more than coal. The city, for instance, played a prominent role in the coal-oil industry in the late 1850s and early 1860s and in the petroleum industry soon after that, becoming the nation's oil refining center for approximately fifteen years. More recently, in the post–Second World War decades, it played a prominent role in the development of nuclear energy.[2] But the most significant aspects of Pittsburgh's energy history are those involving transitions between coal and natural gas. The first of these transitions was relatively short-lived, taking place approximately between 1880 and 1890 (see "The Pittsburgh Region's First Natural Gas Boom" in this volume). The second has been more lasting; it began in the years after the Second World War and continues today.

These energy transitions had significant impacts upon the city's population, industries, and environment. They also shaped public policy and public health.[3] The transitions were primarily driven by costs and supply factors, but they were aided by the city's attempt to devise policies to escape from coal's environmental externalities and to find a substitute that would provide its energy needs. Today extensive debates about both coal and natural gas development in terms of their effects on both the environment and the public health have reemerged, reminding us of the importance of understanding our energy history.

This chapter is organized in the following manner. The first section, "The Landscapes of Coal," will consider the development of coal mining, infrastructure necessary for its operation, and the evolution of transportation systems for moving coal to national and international markets. The second section, "The Landscapes of Industry," will examine those industries most tightly linked to coal, especially iron and steel. The third section, "The Environmental Effects of Coal and Coal Consumption," will explore coal from mining through consumption. The fourth section will discuss the "First Transition to Natural Gas." The fifth section will consider the "Environmental Effects of Natural Gas." And the sixth section, "The Second Transition to Natural Gas," will examine the shift from coal to natural gas that occurred from 1945–1960 and its impacts on the city and the region from different perspectives.

THE LANDSCAPES OF COAL

The Pittsburgh coal seam before its exploitation was approximately 14,200 square miles in area, covering parts of twelve counties. The seam extended northward from the southwest corner of the state to Lake Erie and the southern New York State boundary and to the Allegheny Front on the east, and was composed of a number of different beds (see Map 9.1). The bituminous coal lay primarily in horizontal seams approximately three–four feet thick, located on the side of hills and at the bottom of valleys, with relatively little deep mining initially required to extract it.[4] The coal seam was first exposed on Pittsburgh hillsides, and further rich deposits were soon

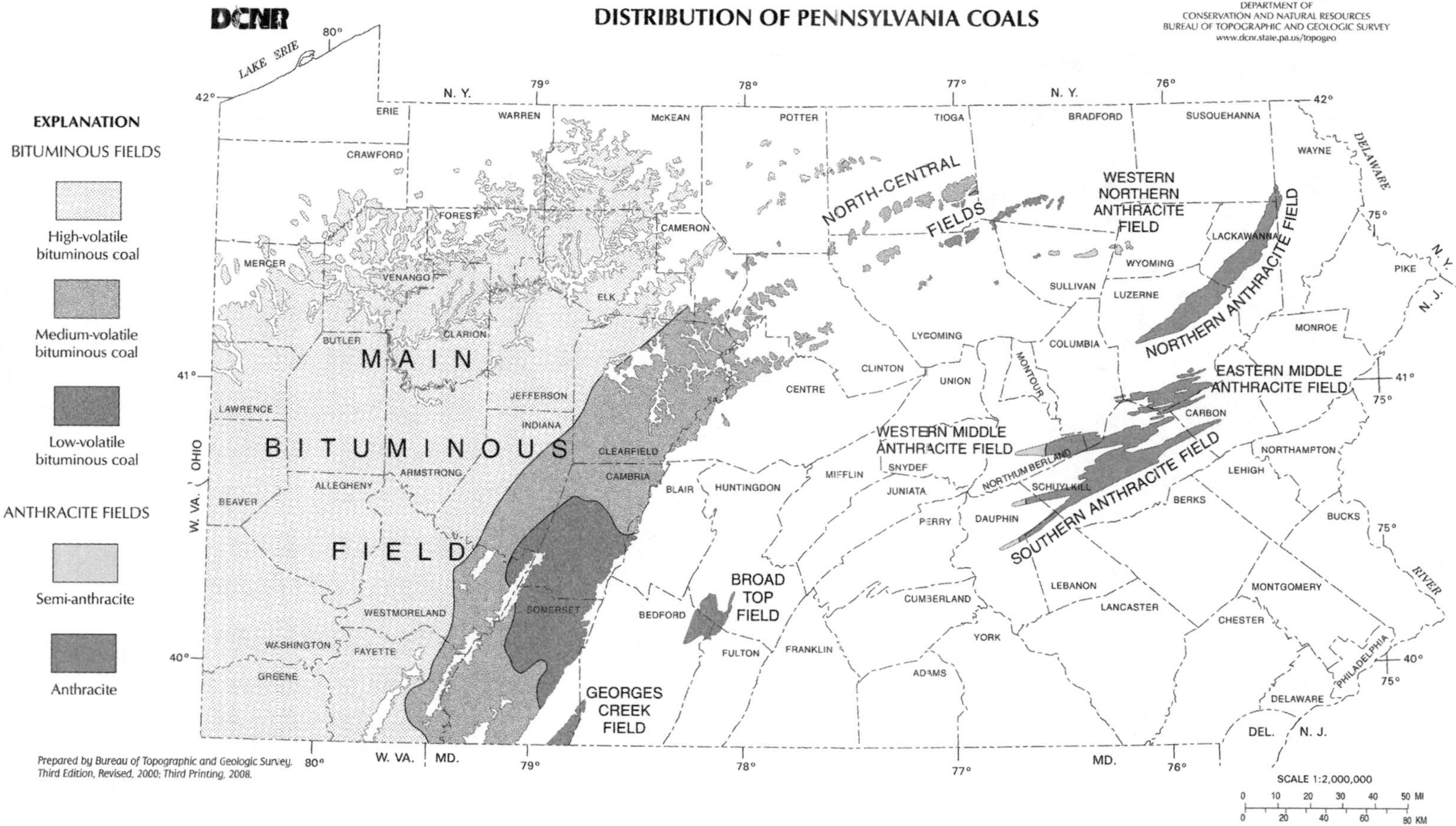

Map 9.1 Coalfields of Pennsylvania (Pennsylvania Department of Conservation and Natural Resources, "Distribution of Pennsylvania Coals," http://www.dcnr.state.pa.us/topogeo/coal/index.aspx).

Fig. 9.1 Coal tipple and tug—infrastructure for coal was critical on land and river, 2002 (photograph by Joel A. Tarr).

discovered extending into the city's hinterland along the Monongahela and Allegheny Rivers and their tributaries.[5] Bituminous production expanded greatly after the Civil War, as water and rail connections improved.[6] During the nineteenth and early twentieth centuries, Pennsylvania was the leading producer of bituminous coal, most of it coming from the Pittsburgh coal seam.

The center of the Western Pennsylvania coal district was the city of Pittsburgh. Mining and local consumption in Pittsburgh had begun as early as 1784.[7] The four key counties that produced bituminous coal in the nineteenth century were Allegheny, Fayette, Washington and Westmoreland Counties. The peak of bituminous coal production in the four-county region came in 1918, when 101,959,000 tons of coal was produced from over one thousand mines. In the twentieth century the counties of Cambria, Clearfield, Indiana, and Somerset joined these four as major bituminous coal producing areas.[8]

Over time the industry became increasingly mechanized; in 1924 about one-third of Pennsylvania's bituminous coal was produced by hand and about two-thirds by machine. In the years from 1920 to 1924 the number of employees in Pennsylvania's bituminous coal mines averaged over 170,000.[9] In 1960 the number of miners remained about the same, but because of mechanization they produced four times as much coal.[10]

Throughout the Pittsburgh region a landscape developed that was devoted to the mining of coal. Its most recognizable feature was the coal tipple and the head frame, located near the mine entrance and protruding from riverbanks and/or standing above railroad tracks. Here the coal was sorted, weighed, and loaded for transport. Other buildings comprising the mining complex included a hoist house for deep mines to lower miners into the coal shafts, a boiler house and electrical powerhouse, and a repair shop, a fan house for ventilation, a mine office, a lamp house, and storage sheds. A large "gob" pile or dump of slate and other refuse from coal cleaning usually overlooked the mine complex (see Figure 9.1).

Coal companies built "patch towns" in order to house their workers near isolated mine sites and to provide a stable and controllable labor supply. They erected rows of identical semidetached wooden houses for workers and their families on unpaved roads leading to the mine or on a grid plan across from the railroad tracks serving the mine. The companies operated company stores; they provided water through hydrants or outdoor pumps and open sewers for wastes and storm water. One writer described them in 1946 as being "pretty much alike, springing out of the fields, creeping up to slate dumps, climbing hilltops in rows of identical double houses with narrow frame porches divided in half, fenced back yards, and outdoor toilets."[11]

Bituminous coal from Western Pennsylvania found important markets in the region itself as well as nationally and internationally. Pittsburgh's network of rivers, including the major bodies of water, the Allegheny, Monongahela, and Ohio Rivers and tributary streams such as the Beaver, Clarion, and Youghiogheny, were the primary avenues used for the transportation of coal before railroads entered the region in the 1850s (see "Pittsburgh's Rivers: From Urban Industrial Infrastructure to Environmental Infrastructure" in this volume). Many of the mines were located on their banks, and millions of tons of coal were shipped by barge to the city. In 1855, for instance, the city itself consumed 935,714 tons while exporting 570,649 tons. In 1917, 60,441,000 tons or 52.6 percent of the coal mined in Western Pennsylvania were sold to markets in Pennsylvania (many in the Pittsburgh district).[12]

Most coal shipments were on the Monongahela, but until the private Monongahela Navigation Company completed a system of locks and dams to Brownsville, Pennsylvania (sixty miles away) in 1846, coal transport was limited by both low water conditions and freezing rivers.[13] Navigation on the Ohio River improved in 1885 with the opening of the Davis Island Locks and Dam. Major improvements on Pittsburgh's third river, the Allegheny, came more slowly and had to wait until the city and county raised thirty-two low-lying bridges in the 1920s.

In 1852 the Pennsylvania Railroad linked Pittsburgh with Philadelphia, providing the first through rail route over the Alleghenies. Other mainline trunk roads followed, as did a number of small feeder roads that penetrated into the coalfields. Many of the region's railroad carriers such as the Pittsburgh Chartiers & Youghiogheny, the Montour, the Monongahela Southern, and the Unity Railroads owned mines and were dedicated solely to the transport of coal and coal products. Coal companies also invested directly in railroads as feeder lines. These lines grew rapidly, from five in 1860 to seventy-eight in 1898, about two-thirds of which were connected to mainline railroads.[14] All mainline railroads were located on flat ground along the major rivers. Feeder lines tended to hug the shores of tributary streams.

Coal had a special relationship with the nation's railroads but especially those in the Pittsburgh region. It was the largest single item of revenue tonnage for the roads, constituting about 20 percent of loaded freight cars. By 1880 bituminous made up over 90 percent of railroad fuel, peaking in 1918 at 34,210,000 tons for all carriers. It remained at that level through the 1920s. The onset of the depression brought sharp operating cutbacks, and coal consumption declined until wartime demands generated a revival. In the postwar period, however, the adoption of the diesel-electric locomotive produced an even sharper decline, and within a decade coal consumption by railroads was negligible.

Railroad transport of bituminous coal was typically greater than that by water. The best year for rail transport during the first half of the twentieth century was 1918, when railroads carried 128,518,000 tons of bituminous and barges carried only 8,985,000 tons. From the 1920s onward, coal shipment by water encroached on rail, with an especially sharp drop in rail shipments after 1949 when coal consumption fell sharply. The cost of water transport, although slower, was usually about 18 percent of the rail rate. The margin over rail was most marked when the coal could be moved entirely by river from origin to destination, such as for mills and utilities sited directly on the rivers.[15]

THE LANDSCAPES OF INDUSTRY

Coal provided the necessary energy source to power Pittsburgh's growing industrial sector in the nineteenth and twentieth centuries. As the writer Willard Glazier wrote in 1883, all of Pittsburgh's industry was "rendered possible by the coal which abounds in measureless quantities in the immediate neighborhood of the city."[16] Cheap fuel provided energy not only for the iron and steel industries but also for glassworks, textiles, breweries, machine shops and saltworks. Iron and steel were the signature products manufactured by Pittsburgh industry. By the 1830s iron products had emerged as the young city's leading industry, with eighteen iron foundries and nine rolling mills; in twenty-five years the total number of plants had more than doubled. These iron manufacturing works initially depended on supplies of pig iron that came from charcoal blast furnaces based on rural iron plantations. By the late 1850s, however, for pig iron they had shifted to iron furnaces using bituminous coal located in or near the city.[17]

The shift to coke as an iron-making fuel was made possible by the adoption in southwestern Pennsylvania of the beehive coke oven, a technology in which bituminous coal was baked in brick ovens for approximately forty-eight hours to drive out the oils, gases, and tars (see "Searching for a Sink for an Industrial Waste" in this volume). The process produced a hard porous coke of silvery luster with few impurities. The best coking coal, known as Connellsville Coke, was found in a narrow forty-mile-long seam located about thirty-five miles south of the city. The ovens were usually located close to the coal mines, and the resulting coke was shipped by water or rail to the Pittsburgh blast furnaces. By the end of the 1870s coke had become the preferred fuel to produce pig iron; by 1900 ninety coke plants with nearly twenty-one thousand ovens operated in the coke district; by 1920 this number had almost doubled.

An urban network arose to service the coal coke industry. Coke district towns like Greensburg, Connellsville, and Uniontown contained administrative offices, financial, retail, and wholesaling services, and associated manufacturing firms like foundries, machine shops, or mining equipment producers. The rivers and rails tied the district physically to Pittsburgh, while the steel corporations and allied financial interests connected it to the city through ownership of the major mines, coke plants, and coke ovens.[18]

The large integrated iron and steel mills that consumed the coke first emerged in the 1870s. They were initially formed by the entrepreneur Andrew Carnegie and his partners as well as by several independent managers with long experience in the iron industry.[19] In the early 1880s Henry Clay Frick, the dominant figure in coke production, joined Carnegie Steel as a partner, providing a vital link between their complementary coke and steel interests. This alliance guaranteed Carnegie an uninterrupted flow of the high quality coke necessary to the making of steel.[20]

Furnaces, rolling mills, and steelworks were located both within the city and along the Monongahela River (see Map 9.2). Because of the greater availability of large sites on the bends or meanders of the Monongahela, the largest plants were first located there. As these sites filled up, the steel companies built mills along the Alleghany and its tributaries and down the

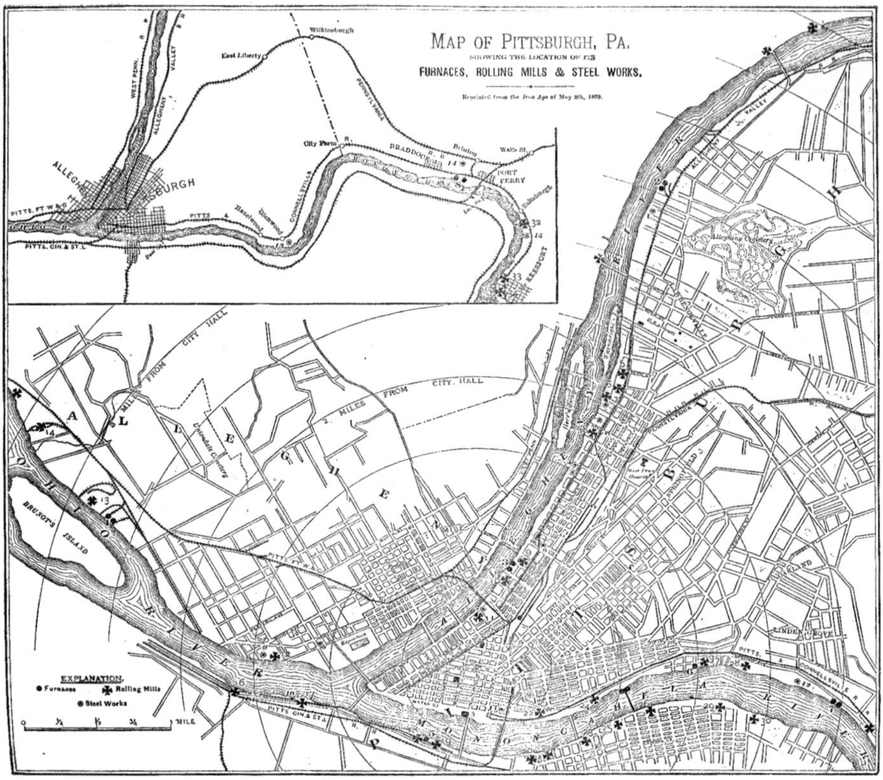

Map 9.2 Map of Pittsburgh, showing the location of its furnaces, rolling mills, and steelworks (reprint from the *Iron Age*, May 8, 1879, in *Report on the Social Statistics of Cities*, compiled by George E. Waring Jr. [US Census Office, Part 2, 1887]; Perry-Castaneda Library Map Collection—U.S. Historical City Maps, http://www.lib.utexas.edu/maps/historical/pittsburgh_iron_steel_1879.jpg).

Ohio River. The map also shows the extensive railroad network that linked Pittsburgh to regional coal mines and coke plants, and to national markets.

A brilliant manager, Andrew Carnegie believed in the importance of economies of scale for production and pricing as well as for the efficient movement of materials throughout the integrated plants. These values were reflected in the large integrated mills covering hundreds of acres of ground that sometimes occupied both banks of the rivers on which they were sited, with hot metal bridges connecting the blast furnaces on one bank and the Bessemer and open-hearth ovens on the other. Carnegie and other ironmasters and steelmakers such as Jones and Laughlin and the National Tube Works built their plants in the flat land in the Monongahela River valley. As these sites filled up, the steel companies built mills along the Allegheny and Ohio Rivers (see "Pittsburgh's Industrial Corridors" in this volume). The major integrated iron and steel mills were joined by dozens of more independent metals firms in the river valleys and an array of specialized enterprises, including sintering plants, bridge fabricators, machine shops, and barge builders to form industrial corridors.[21]

Many of the steel operations presented a chaotic assemblage of huge brick and metal sheds, towering blast furnaces, hot ovens, Bessemer converters, open-hearth furnaces, rolling mills, giant ore loaders, and ore and coal yards, all framed by river and rail. Connecting the mills to neighboring towns and the city was a matrix of pipelines, electric, telegraph, and telephone wires, railroad lines, extensive gas pipelines, and mile-long river barge tows that dominated the river valleys.[22] Railroads and rivers were key elements in this matrix. Rails, like industrial plants, were located largely on flat land, in the floors of the river valleys, and mills were sited between railroad and river. This positioning facilitated the easy movement of goods both in the region and to and from the East Coast and the ever-expanding western markets. It also provided managers such as Carnegie with the opportunity to play off the rivalry between the two modes of transport to secure cheaper rates. By the First World War six major trunk lines and sixteen industrial and switching railroads served the city and its industries.[23]

In the first decades of the twentieth century, by-product coke ovens, which were sited close to the mills rather than near the mines, added to the industrial assemblage. In 1916 US Steel opened the first full by-product coking plant in the region, at Clairton on the Monongahela River, twenty miles south of Pittsburgh. These works occupied a riverfront site measuring fifty-two hundred feet long and eighteen hundred feet in width; it was the world's largest plant at the time of its construction. The Jones and Laughlin Iron & Steel Corporation constructed a major by-product plant in 1918–1920 in the Pittsburgh neighborhood of Hazelwood to serve its adjoining iron- and steelworks. Before the First World War more than 20 percent of the bituminous coal mined in Pennsylvania was made into coke at the mine by beehive ovens, but the substitution of the by-product for the beehive oven caused the percentage to drop to 5 percent in 1929 and below 1 percent in 1958 (see "Searching for a Sink for an Industrial Waste" in this volume).[24]

The iron and steel industry and allied coke works were the greatest users of coal in the Pittsburgh region, but other manufacturing and transportation activities also consumed large amounts of the fuel (see Chart 9.1). These activities included the glass industry, metal products manufacturers, and cement and brick makers. Electrical utilities became major coal consumers, especially after the First World War. Quantities for retail sales of

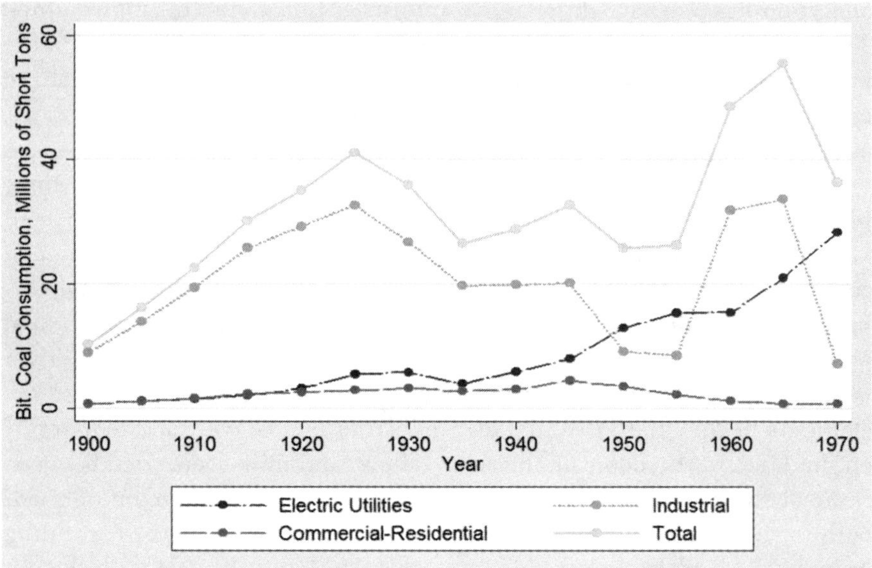

CHART 9.1 Coal consumption in Pennsylvania by type, 1900–1970 (G. Gschwandtner, K. Gschwandtner, and K. Eldridge, "Historical Emissions of Sulfur and Nitrogen Oxides in the U.S. from 1900–1980," EPA report, October 1983).

coal, primarily domestic, were available only on a national basis. At that time they constituted about 16 percent of national consumption, but one can estimate that they probably exceeded that in the Pittsburgh region.[25]

THE ENVIRONMENTAL EFFECTS OF COAL

In spite of the economic benefits of the cheap fuel, coal had large environmental and human costs at every stage of its development. Thus, its cost and benefits should be evaluated from the point of its removal from the ground through different mining processes and to its end use. Environmental damages in the coal mining areas represent an extension of Pittsburgh's footprint because of the linkages between the mines and the city's industrial and domestic consumption. Coal mining, by its very nature, whether surface or deep, alters the land, impacts geological strata, groundwater, and vegetation. Before 1977 coal mining had disturbed approximately 220,000 acres of Pennsylvania land. A smaller acreage had serious safety and environmental hazards.[26] Environmental problems included disrupted water supplies, streams filled with mining debris, and land subsidence. Mining left huge heaps of mining wastes or gob piles near the mines that loomed over the patch towns, occasionally collapsing with considerable loss of life.[27]

The formation of acid mine drainage was a particular problem with long-lasting and difficult-to-remedy consequences. Mine acid results when iron sulfates interact with the sulfides found in coal and with groundwater entering the mine so as to form sulfuric acid. These acidic waters contaminated aquifers, often coming to the surface in rivers many miles from the original source. The high acidity of the water eradicated aquatic life and vegetation; often the iron oxide imparted a deep red or brown color to the streams. Fish populations disappeared, ending stream use by commercial and recreational fishermen. Public health agencies worried that acid wastes in disinfected urban water supplies might force consumers to unknowingly drink from infected sources.[28] Water authorities were concerned with the corrosive nature of the contaminated water, which damaged pumps and pipes and forced the authorities to seek out new and protected sources. High acid concentrations damaging boilers, pipes, and infrastructures also had large costs for industry. Industries that needed clean water for their processes constructed treatment facilities to ensure supplies, and railroads built reservoirs in protected watersheds.[29]

Although mine acid drainage severely impacted a multitude of water users, no legal remedy existed for many decades. In the 1870s, in the landmark case of *Sanderson v. the Pennsylvania Coal Company* involving mine acid damages to private property, the Pennsylvania Supreme Court ruled that the inconvenience of an individual landowner must give way to the greater community's economic interests. The court maintained that the production of acid drainage was a "natural and necessary result" of coal mining and that the plaintiff could not collect damages for harm. The court further argued that burdening mine owners with the costs of limiting mine acid drainage would hamper economic development by raising the price of coal. The Sanderson precedent remained in force in Pennsylvania from the 1870s through the 1920s, when legal and societal attitudes toward industrial pollution shifted and the courts began holding coal companies legally responsible for damages from mine acid.[30] Mine acid, however, especially from abandoned mines, was difficult to halt and still continues to be a major problem today.

The Connellsville coke region experienced particularly severe environmental damage as thousands of beehive ovens roasted coal and emitted volumes of smoke and fumes. "Cloud by day and fire by night" was a phrase used to characterize the region (see Figure 9.2). In 1900 a Pennsylvania state botanist noted that the region's most conspicuous feature was "the general wretchedness of everything of the nature of shrub or tree," as sulfur fumes and hydrocarbons killed and stunted trees and crops and left layers of ash

FIG. 9.2 Smoke from Strip District industrial plants, 1906 (courtesy of the Carnegie Library of Pittsburgh).

on surrounding land surfaces. Operators at coke works dumped coal wastes into the nearby creeks, damming their flow, damaging stream ecology, and causing flooding (see "Searching for a Sink for an Industrial Waste" in this volume).[31]

Pittsburgh itself had been plagued with heavy smoke resulting from coal consumption since early in its history (see "The Metabolism of the Industrial City" in this volume). Because of its easy availability and low costs, coal served as the city's primary fuel for domestic heating, commerce, and manufacturing. When railroads entered the city in the 1850s they added to its smoke burden. Meteorological conditions also contributed to reducing air quality, since the city was subject to atmospheric inversions, a process in which warm air prevents the upward movement of air below and the dispersal of emissions. Conditions were especially severe in the river valleys where industries, railroads, and riverboats were concentrated.[32] In 1868 James Parton published an article in the *Atlantic Monthly* in which he named Pittsburgh the "Smoky City," where "every object is black. Smoke, smoke, smoke, everywhere smoke."[33] Nineteenth-century writers, however, often talked about the "salubrity" of the city's environment, arguing that the smoke possessed "anti-miasmatic" qualities. As late as the 1870s and 1880s the Pittsburgh Board of Health linked the city's low death rate from consumption to the healthfulness of Pittsburgh's smoky air.[34]

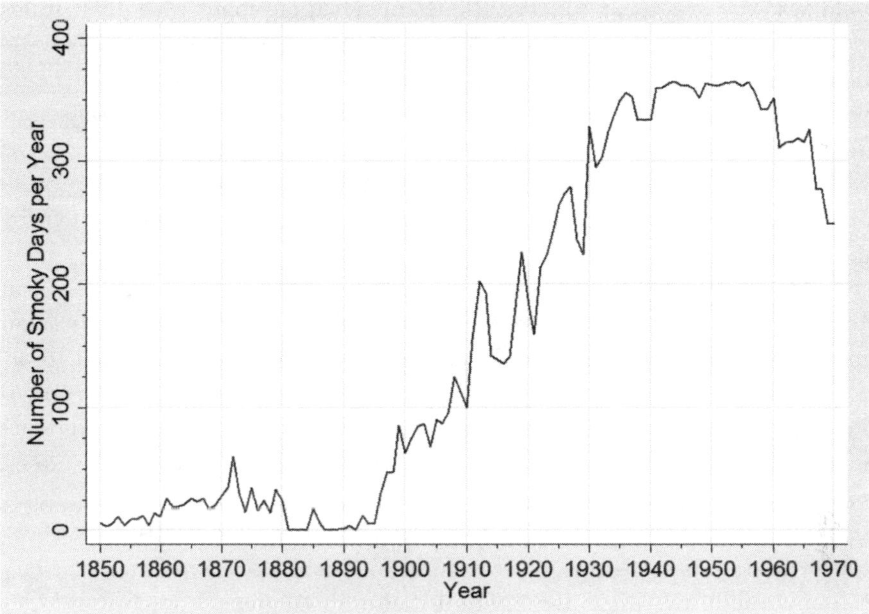

CHART 9.2 Number of smoky days per year, 1850–1970 (Cliff I. Davidson, "Air Pollution in Pittsburgh: A Historical Perspective," *APCA Journal* 29 [October 1979]:1035–41).

Compared to its very earliest days and the surrounding countryside, Pittsburgh was indeed getting smokier over the course of the 1860s and 1870s (see Chart 9.2). Public officials took little action against the smoke. In 1816 the city councils enacted an ordinance to control smoke from domestic sources and workshops by regulating chimney heights; in 1864, they banned construction of coke ovens within the city's boundaries; and in 1869 they forbade locomotives burning either bituminous coal or wood from entering the city. These were weak and ineffective laws that were poorly enforced, and smoke density continued to increase.[35]

THE FIRST TRANSITION TO NATURAL GAS

It was a transition to natural gas rather than public policy that produced the city's first clean air period. This fuel shift occurred in the years from approximately 1880 to the early 1890s, when the substitution of natural gas for coal gave Pittsburgh a decade of clean air.[36] Driving the transition was the cheapness of natural gas, its ease of combustion, its cleanliness, and its high Btu value. Natural gas had been discovered in the northwestern corner of the state during the oil boom of the 1860s, and in the mid-1870s a major field was discovered at Murrysville, Pennsylvania, about seventeen miles outside of the city. In 1875 and 1876 gas was piped in from the Murrysville field to several Pittsburgh area ironworks, and in 1883 Andrew Carnegie began substituting gas for coal at his Union Mills, Edgar Thomson Bessemer Works, and Homestead Steel Works.[37] That year Pittsburgh Plate Glass as well as other several glass manufacturers also shifted to gas.[38] During the 1880s and 1890s the city was able to draw gas from several relatively nearby gas fields as well as from wells within the city.[39]

Development of gas resources in Pittsburgh for domestic use began in 1884, when George Westinghouse sunk a productive well on his homestead in the Point Breeze section of Pittsburgh. Westinghouse proceeded to organize the Philadelphia Company to supply gas to homes and industries in Pittsburgh and its outlying areas.[40] A number of other entrepreneurs formed companies to compete for the Pittsburgh market; by 1886 sixteen natural gas companies operated in the city, supplying thousands of domestic and industrial consumers. Numerous derricks erected throughout Pittsburgh altered its landscape while natural gas standpipes throughout the city flared through the night (see "The Pittsburgh Region's First Natural Gas Boom" in this volume).[41]

The widespread substitution of natural gas for coal, as natural gas replaced dirty coal in industries and homes, resulted in a sharp reduction in the number of days of heavy smoke. Coal production went down by twenty million tons in Pittsburgh region mines, causing widespread unemployment in the minefields.[42] Writers in newspapers and magazines marveled at the city's cleaner air and changed appearance, noting "Fresh green shade trees . . . , newly painted buildings [and] cream colored granite walls" that were contrasted with "dingy-looking" buildings covered with "years of soot and smoke and . . . dyed to a uniform black."[43] In 1889 a county history applauded the benefits of natural gas and the disappearance of the "black pall-like cloud" that had previously hung over the city, and an article in *Harper's Weekly* in 1892 observed that a "peaceful revolution" had taken place in Pittsburgh because of natural gas; the city had lost its "Smoky City" title.[44] City boosters lauded the benefits of natural gas and boasted about its "almost incomprehensible quantities" and "inexhaustible" nature.[45]

THE ENVIRONMENTAL EFFECTS OF NATURAL GAS

The development of natural gas, like coal, had marked environmental impacts on its points of consumption and production and along its pipeline routes (see "The Pittsburgh Region's First Natural Gas Boom" in this volume).[46] Most noted was the reduction in the smoke burden that had plagued

Pittsburgh because of the city's heavy coal use. This was a major accomplishment (although, as will be seen, it was of relatively short duration). On the negative side, however, for several years after the introduction of gas, the city experienced a number of explosions resulting in deaths, fires, and the destruction of property. These were because of pipeline leaks and a lack of consumer familiarity with the inflammability of the fuel. A *Pittsburgh Daily Post* editorial titled "Death in the Streets" warned that "save in a state of war we don't believe any large city in the world was ever in a more perilous situation than Pittsburgh is today owing to the dangers of natural gas explosions."[47] Protest meetings were held throughout the city, and the city councils appointed the Natural Gas Commission to investigate the causes of the explosions. Testimony from gas company officials before the commission revealed that gas pipes were inadequately tested for leaks. In response to the commission's findings, in 1885 the councils passed the Natural Gas Act, which made the transportation and supply of natural gas for public consumption a public service open to regulation. Later in the year the councils passed an act setting specific standards for the laying and testing of pipe, for required pressures, for pressure gauges, and for a system of safety pipes. In 1886, however, Peoples Natural Gas challenged those ordinances that gave the city engineer control over the manner in which pipes were laid, their location, and by whom, and the Pennsylvania Supreme Court declared these sections invalid because of conflict with state natural gas legislation.[48]

In addition to the wells drilled within the city, during the late nineteenth and into the twentieth century thousands of additional natural gas and oil wells were sunk throughout the Western Pennsylvania region. Similarly to coal, natural gas and oil wells could cause environmental damages at various stages of their development, and these damages represented a further extension of Pittsburgh's environmental footprint.[49] Unfortunately, only a partial record exists of the effects of these wells during their operations. Aside from wells with known locations, today there are many thousands of abandoned or so-called orphan wells whose locations are unknown. Many wells were abandoned when they were exhausted, and an unknown number were not properly plugged. These orphan wells often leak gas, presenting an explosion hazard, and can be a conduit for salt brine that pollutes ground and surface waters.[50]

Those fragmentary records that do still exist concerning the environmental effects of past well operations suggest some of the problems that were created. For instance, in 1908, the Pennsylvania Department of Health (DOH) noted that operations at gas and oil wells often polluted water bodies with substances such as "sand pumpings," oil and grease wastes, and "burnt glycerine." The DOH warned that contaminated wastewater ("brine") leaking from wells that had not been properly cased or from abandoned wells that had been left unplugged could contaminate surface streams and endanger urban water supplies, explaining that the problem often ensued when well owners removed the casing for use elsewhere when wells became dry. In addition, it warned that if wells were not properly plugged surface and subsurface water could both fill up other gas and oil reservoirs and pollute water bodies.

The threat posed by these wells both to water quality and to other producing wells was reflected in a series of statutes passed by the Pennsylvania legislature, first in 1878 and then in successive years, requiring operators to plug the wells that ceased to be productive. In 1885 the legislature approved a statute formalizing "the incorporation and regulation of natural gas companies," which included specific regulations concerning the plugging of abandoned wells. The act stipulated a two-hundred-dollar fine in case of violations, but there was no enforcement mechanism specified. In 1891 the legislature passed new regulations requiring that abandoned wells be plugged in order to "prevent the pollution of springs, water wells and streams by water escaping from abandoned oil wells and gas wells." Violators of the law were guilty of a misdemeanor; they were required to pay fines of up to one thousand dollars or face up to six months imprisonment. In 1907 the legislature approved further statutes that required the clearing of brush and trees around natural gas and oil wells in order to prevent fires. A 1921 act provided more specific information about the manner to which wells were to be plugged and existing wells protected from water entering the gas strata from new well drilling.[51]

The passage of these laws reflects an awareness of the environmental problems these wells posed, and the need for conservation, but enforcement of the laws appears to have been inconsistent. It appears that some companies, when abandoning wells, plugged them following state law, but many others probably did not. The Pennsylvania DOH was responsible for enforcing the law in cases of water pollution but was largely reactive to complaints rather than regularly inspecting well sites. The reports of the DOH and of the Sanitary Water Board between 1923 and 1971 note various complaints about gas and oil pollution of water supplies from runoff from drilling and sites.[52]

In 1906, for instance, the Clarion Water Company in Clarion County complained that the development of natural gas and oil wells in the watershed had polluted the sources of water from which they supplied the town; they asked for permission to extend their water-gathering area to a clean source. The DOH investigated and found the company's supplies indeed to be polluted and "prejudicial to the public health." The department reported that the "waste material produced in the operation of drilling the wells, in shooting them, and in cleaning them out, is deposited on the surface of the ground round about and eventually gets into the main stream of the water supply." The DOH ordered the water company to either filter the water or find a new source. It ordered the company not to allow any gas or oil drilling on its lands and to regularly inspect the wells in the vicinity of the borough so as to prevent saltwater from the wells to contaminate water supplies.[53]

In addition to state enforcement of the statutes relating to natural gas and oil statutes, the courts considered nuisance cases generated by gas and oil pollution of private drinking water wells. Few of these cases got to the courts, but when they did they were usually decided in the favor of the plaintiffs. In an 1890 case the Pennsylvania Supreme Court affirmed damages against a natural gas company for permitting saltwater to contaminate a private drinking water well because of inadequate casing, noting that, "when the salt water is allowed to mingle with the fresh, it will spoil the whole neighborhood." The court also held that the 1870s Sanderson opinion on mine acid drainage did not apply because the driller knew that such contamination could occur and did not take actions to prevent it.[54] Other pollution cases of private wells appear to have been settled out of court by the gas companies. The Pew Papers at the Hagley Museum and Library, for instance, contain several letters to Joseph N. Pew, president of the People's Natural Gas Company, from attorneys representing clients complaining of injuries to their water supplies and livestock from gas well leaks and pipe lines; these complaints appear to be have been settled.[55] The Peoples Natural Gas Company was aware that problems ensuing from poor casing could cause water pollution. It required contractors to ensure that casing be inspected and if water was found "the well . . . be thoroughly drained and sand pumped until all drillings and sediments are removed."[56] It is unknown, however, if other gas companies—and especially the smaller and fly-by-night drillers—followed the regulations.

RETURN TO COAL AND SMOKE

Natural gas produced cleaner air but, contrary to popular belief, it was not inexhaustible. In addition, the "rule of capture" (*ferae naturae*)—a common law principle maintaining that any gas coming into your well, even if it originated from a neighbor's land, was yours—was upheld by the Pennsylvania Supreme Court in 1889 in the case of *Westmoreland & Cambria*

Natural Gas Co. v. De Witt. The law of capture produced an emphasis on digging multiple wells and pumping at a rapid rate to ensure your neighbor did not capture your gas.[57] By 1890 fluctuating and declining supplies negatively affected industrial users, and they began shifting back to coal.[58] The depletion of natural gas supplies was a constant concern of the utilities, and they unsuccessfully experimented with methods to produce manufactured gas from bituminous coal cheaply enough to compete with coal.[59] In 1892 a speaker at a meeting of the Western Pennsylvania Engineering Society woefully observed: "We are going back into the smoke. We had four or five years of wonderful cleanliness for Pittsburg [*sic*], and we have all had a taste of knowing what it is to be clean. We all felt better, we all looked better, we all were better. But we are back into the smoke. It is growing worse day by day."[60]

The return of the smoke caused the city's first major smoke control effort. The Ladies Health Protective Association of Allegheny County, an organization composed mostly of upper-class women, drove the campaign. Recruiting allies from among the engineering and business communities, the anti-smoke forces pushed for effective regulatory legislation in succeeding years. In 1892 and 1895 the city councils passed smoke control ordinances but they were only weakly enforced. In 1902, the courts declared the 1895 ordinance unconstitutional.[61] During the following years, as smoke pollution increased in severity, reformers drove the city council to approve new ordinances.

Several research efforts contributed to the pressure for such legislation. The Pittsburgh Survey, conducted by the Russell Sage Foundation in 1907–1908, aroused Pittsburgh to various social and environmental issues that affected the quality of life in the industrial city, and these included smoke.[62] Following this, between 1911 and 1914, the Mellon Institute of Industrial Research conducted a smoke investigation, which published ten bulletins written by experts on the effects of smoke on architecture and building materials, weather, vegetation, human health, psychology, and Pittsburgh's economy. These studies showed the smoke's negative impacts on many aspects of the city's life, but they were inconclusive in regard to its effect on health. Still, the reports contained enough information concerning the costs of smoke to drive the city council in 1914 to approve the toughest smoke control ordinance enacted up to that time.[63]

Enforcement of the ordinance plus an increase in natural gas availability via pipelines from West Virginia wells improved Pittsburgh air quality during the immediate prewar years, but this source was also depleted in several years by wastage and overuse. Between 1914 and 1921, for instance, the amount of gas produced by the Equitable Gas Company, Pittsburgh's largest provider drawing from its West Virginia wells, declined from 43,189 to 13,359 million cubic feet.[64] The war years brought a further deterioration of air quality because of increases in industrial emissions. In addition, a collapse in rail transportation beginning in late 1916 and extending into the early 1920s generated a fuel crisis putting pressure on coal and natural gas availability. The US Fuel Administration, created in 1917, imposed natural gas rationing on some communities and industries and forbade natural gas delivery without a license.[65] A hearing held in Pittsburgh in 1919 by the Pennsylvania Public Service Commission of the Commonwealth of Pennsylvania emphasized the great waste in natural gas production, transport, and consumption.

The uncertainty of gas supplies caused major industries, especially in the metals sector, to shift back to coal in the 1920s, repeating the pattern of the 1890s.[66] Consumption by the iron and steel industry was sharply reduced because of the lower price of coal and concern about the consistency of gas supply. Domestic consumers were the largest natural gas users, constituting about 15–20 percent of total Pittsburgh households. The glass industry also continued to rely on natural gas because of its high caloric content and the absence of ash and dust, which provided special advantages for quality glassmaking.[67] Although thousands of new wells were drilled in Pennsylvania in the 1920s and 1930s, total gas production did not increase as older wells lost pressure.[68]

During the 1920s engineers and smoke regulators involved in smoke control concluded that domestic smoke from coal consumption as well as that from industries and railroads had to be controlled. They argued that residential chimneys emitted smoke at low height levels where it could not be dispersed by the winds.[69] How to devise and implement a policy to raise stacks, however, was politically difficult and involved both technological and fuel issues. But before the new strategy could take effect, the Great Depression hit, and Pittsburgh experienced sharp industrial slowdowns and high unemployment. Households and industries cut back on fuel expenditures; railroads and steel, coke, and coal industries as well as other manufacturers reduced production and cut coal and gas use. The air became cleaner, but clear skies and unemployment was a combination that Pittsburghers found unacceptable.[70] Many wished for a return to smoking stacks and productive mills, as the old equation between smoke and jobs was reinforced. In a defiant reflection of this belief, in 1939 the city council voted to eliminate the Smoke Control Bureau.[71]

SMOKE CONTROL, THE SECOND TRANSITION TO NATURAL GAS, AND RAILROAD DIESELIZATION

While Pittsburgh was reducing its efforts to control smoke, another smoky city, St. Louis, was moving to improve its air quality. The mayor of St. Louis had appointed Raymond R. Tucker, a combustion engineer and former faculty member at Washington University of St. Louis, his secretary with the responsibility of devising a means to "clarify the air." Tucker hit on a strategy requiring the use of either clean fuel or smokeless mechanical equipment. He gradually achieved his goal by persuading the board of aldermen to approve a series of regulatory ordinances targeting different polluters. The final success came in April 1940, after several years of especially heavy smoke palls, when the St. Louis Board of Aldermen approved an ordinance requiring domestic users to use clean fuel or smokeless combustion technology. The result was a series of smokeless days that city officials claimed was the result of the smoke ordinance.[72]

Pittsburgh officials and representatives of smoke control groups visited St. Louis and returned with glowing reports. The press demanded that the Pittsburgh City Council pass similar legislation. In response, Mayor Cornelius Scully appointed the Mayor's Commission for the Elimination of Smoke with wide representation from steel and coal corporations, labor unions, the health professions, the media, and civic groups. A technical advisory subcommittee provided necessary advice and information about fuel availability and combustion equipment. The commission recommended a procedure similar to St. Louis's procedure requiring the use of smokeless fuels or the utilization of smokeless mechanical equipment. While the act contained provisions for regulating railroad and industrial smoke, the focus of the ordinance was on domestic coal consumers.

The Pittsburgh City Council approved the smoke control ordinance by a vote of eight to one in early July, but its full implementation would have to wait until the end of the Second World War. The willingness of the representatives of the coal corporations and of the mine workers union on the mayor's commission to support the ordinance can be explained by the belief that bituminous coal could serve as the basis for new industries processing local coal for smokeless fuel, coal tar, and for coal gasification. Many of the smaller mine operators were skeptical, however, and warned that creation of an industry to manufacture processed coal was "wishful thinking." Instead, they pushed for the use of better combustion technology to reduce smoke emissions from bituminous consumption. Their doubts were to be borne out in the postwar period when inadequate supplies of smokeless coal threatened the success of the ordinance.[73]

Implementation of the Smoke Control Act in the postwar period focused first on domestic users—considered to be inefficient energy consumers whose emissions were harder to disperse because they were closer to ground level. Individual householders could choose among several alternatives in order to meet the law's requirements. One was to purchase smokeless combustion equipment that would permit the continued use of high-volatile coal. A second was to install combustion equipment using alternative fuels such as natural gas or oil or to retrofit existing equipment to burn these fuels. A third alternative was to utilize smokeless coal in existing stoves and furnaces. Because the last option required the least capital outlay, most working-class households preferred it. From the perspective of enforcement, however, this alternative posed the most difficulties.

There were approximately one hundred thousand homes using hand fired coal burning stoves and furnaces in Pittsburgh, including about sixty-nine thousand that depended on coal stoves for cooking as well as heating. To enforce against the individual domestic consumer was an impossible task for the Bureau of Smoke Prevention's twelve inspectors. The bureau solved the enforcement problem by focusing on the coal distribution yards (approximately thirty) and the coal truckers. It forbade yards to sell high-volatile coal for use in hand-fired equipment and forbade truckers to deliver it. Truckers hauling coal for consumption in the city had to be licensed and to have license numbers painted on the side of the truck for easy identification. Those caught hauling illegal high-volatile (or bootleg) coal were subject to fines, as were the dealers who made illegal sales.[74]

Popular Pittsburgh history attributes the success of the city in cleaning up its air to the Smoke Control Ordinance and its implementation. Smoke control is pictured as the important first step in the Pittsburgh Renaissance, brought about by a public-private partnership spearheaded by the mayor David Lawrence, the banker Richard King Mellon, and the nonprofit Allegheny County Conference on Community Development composed of the city's major CEOs. Undoubtedly the Smoke Control Ordinance and the reduction of air contamination was a major step in reforming the industrial city. Some decision makers chose to believe that clean air could be achieved without major harm to the coal and related industries, however. Coal had been the major element in the rise of Pittsburgh to industrial prominence, and many of the city's industrialists expected that it would remain a major factor in the city and region's economy.

The Smoke Control Ordinance was implemented at a time when the nation was already in the middle of an energy transition. Coal had suffered during the 1920s and the Great Depression as the competing fuels of oil and natural gas cut into its markets. Rising incomes after the depression caused the sales of consumer appliances and improved home heating equipment to rise, as natural gas and fuel oil companies greatly expanded their marketing campaigns. Household oil burners increased in sales more than sixfold between 1929 and 1941, and the sale of gas home heating units and other gas-using appliances greatly increased where pipelines made natural gas newly available. Even Pittsburgh's local gas utilities saw increases in demand from domestic and industrial users.[75]

Confronted by their vulnerable market position, the Pittsburgh regional coal companies fought hard to protect their interests. There were limits to their influence. Probably the key reason for their inability to weaken stringent municipal smoke control regulations was the influence of Richard King Mellon, who exercised enormous economic power through his leadership of the Mellon banking interests and linked energy corporations such as the Pittsburgh Coal Company, Koppers Coke, and Gulf Oil. Mellon had a keen interest in smoke control, both because his father had sponsored the original Mellon Smoke Investigation and because he believed that cleaner air was vital to Pittsburgh's economic future. In 1945 he helped engineer a merger between the United Smoke Council, the leading anti-smoke organization, and the Allegheny Conference on Community Development, the pivotal group that brought about the Pittsburgh Renaissance.[76]

Control of smoke, however, in the eyes of corporate decision makers and politicians, did not necessarily mean the end of coal's dominance in Pittsburgh for domestic heating, industrial uses, and railroad fuel. Because of issues surrounding the uncertain availability of competing fuels, especially natural gas, decision makers and politicians were confident that treated coal and mechanical stokers would sustain coal production as well as stimulate new industries producing smokeless coal, stoves, and furnaces after the war. In 1943, for instance, the US Bureau of Mines noted: "Lower cost to consumers and availability at all times . . . are the principal factors favoring the use of coal."[77] In addition, restrictions on the availability of oil and natural gas and limited production of new furnaces during wartime suggested that coal would continue to dominate. The coal industry therefore looked forward with some confidence to continued control of markets in the postwar period.[78]

Significant developments in the area of natural gas availability, however, boded ill for the future of coal especially in Pittsburgh domestic markets.

In 1945 the Texas Eastern Transmission Corporation purchased the twenty-four-inch ("big inch") and the twenty-inch ("little inch") pipelines—constructed by the federal government during the war to transport oil from the Southwest to industrial markets—and converted them to natural gas. In 1947 these pipelines reached the Pittsburgh region and supplied clean, cheap natural gas to local gas utilities.[79] A second major factor was the expansion of underground storage pools for natural gas, which allowed the gas industry to transport and store gas from the Southwest in the summer and withdraw it during the winter to satisfy residential needs, thereby eliminating a serious problem that had led to winter gas shortages particularly for industrial users. Between 1944 and 1954, the capacity of national underground storage pools increased from 135 billion to 1,859 billion cubic feet. In Pittsburgh, the Equitable Gas Company, the largest Pittsburgh based natural gas utility, increased its storage from 8,943 million cubic feet in 1947–1948 to 25,064 million cubic feet in 1952–1953. Peoples Natural Gas Company, another major Pittsburgh utility, expanded its storage inventory from 4,600 million cubic feet in 1945 to 13,920 million cubic feet in 1950.[80]

Retail prices of coal increased in the immediate postwar years, while natural gas prices in Pittsburgh remained stable (see Chart 9.3). In Pittsburgh, as well as in other cities such as Chicago and Cleveland, gas became cheaper than bituminous coal in 1947, and customers began to switch to the cleaner fuel. Discussions of heating fuel and furnaces appeared in newspapers and popular magazines, along with advertisements for gas and conversion units, as utility companies launched extensive sales campaigns. A series of strikes by coal miners, particularly in 1946 and 1949–1950, undoubtedly accelerated the pace of change as the price of coal increased in response to the work stoppages.[81]

In Pittsburgh the high price of coal and the advantages of natural gas combined with the requirements of the smoke control ordinance to encourage customers to switch fuels and purchase new combustion equipment. The increased use of gas is reflected in changes in domestic heating apparatus. In 1940 the US Census reported that 81 percent of Pittsburgh households burned coal and 17.4 percent burned natural gas; by 1950, the numbers were 31.6 percent for coal and 66 percent for natural gas.[82] Large numbers of homeowners and commercial users installed either new gas boilers or conversion units for gas in their coal-burning boilers. Some also installed mechanical stokers. In the same period Equitable Gas and Peoples Natural Gas reported that their residential and commercial sales had doubled while their industrial sales had increased by over one-third.[83]

The winter of 1947–1948 was critical for the new statute. Some of the

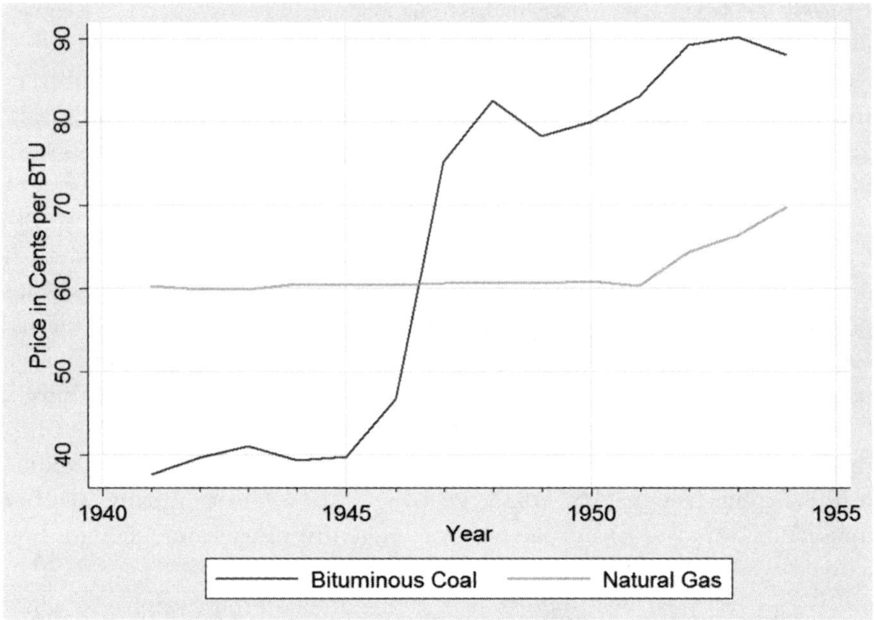

CHART 9.3 Coal and gas prices in Pittsburgh, 1941–1954 (American Gas Association, *Historical Statistics of the American Gas Association 1966–1975* [Washington, DC: AGA], table 231, 3).

more dire predictions of the ordinance's critics were borne out. Supplies of smokeless fuels proved inadequate and prices were inflated. In 1948, bituminous coal was $10.70 a ton while "Disco" or treated coal was $17.10. The ordinance fell hardest on coal-burning low-income families, because fuel costs composed a larger percentage of their budget than for higher income groups. They often purchased their coal by the week in bushel lots from itinerant truckers, since they had neither the cash nor the storage space to buy larger amounts. Because of a lack of familiarity with the characteristics of low-volatile coal, as well as the sale of low-grade mixtures, many Pittsburghers had serious problems keeping warm. Complaints about the regulation poured into city hall, newspaper offices, and radio stations, and several city councilmen attempted to have it suspended. "Undoubtedly," an important city official later admitted, "some very real difficulties were imposed on many people."[84]

In spite of the many difficulties with fuel supply, the heating season of 1947–1948 showed a considerable improvement in air quality compared to previous years. An unusually mild winter aided in reducing the smoke palls. "PITTSBURGH IS CLEANER" reported the *Pittsburgh Press*. The worst smogs

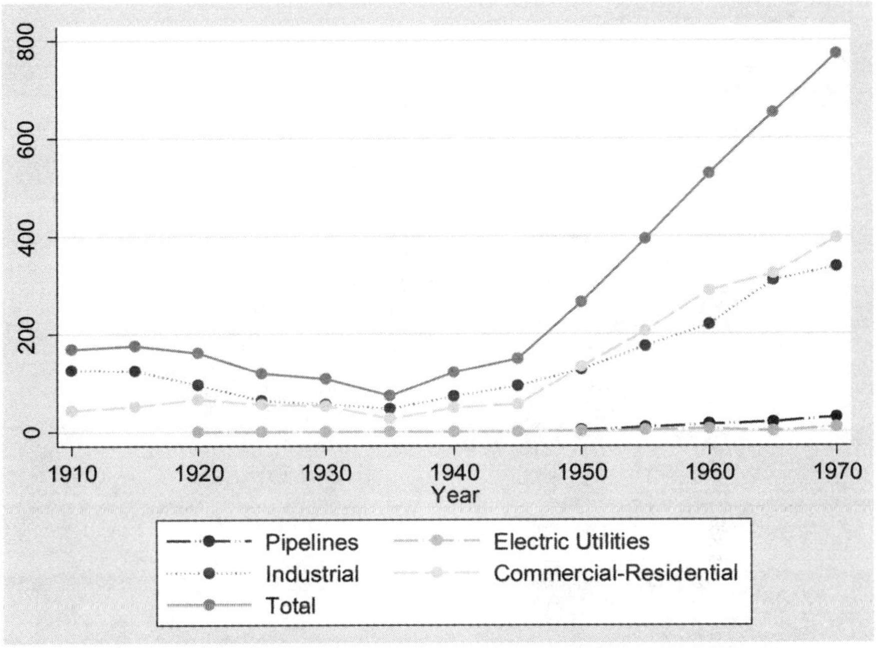

CHART 9.4 Natural gas consumption by type, 1910–1970 (G. Gschwandtner, K. Gschwandtner, and K. Eldridge, "Historical Emissions of Sulfur and Nitrogen Oxides in the U.S. from 1900–1980," EPA report, October 1983).

were gone, homes were cleaner, and white shirts did not develop black rings around the collars. The United Smoke Council boasted in a publication entitled "The New Look in Pittsburgh," that it was losing its reputation as "the Smoky City."[85] Soaring natural gas adoption for residential purposes in the coming years (see Chart 9.4) ensured that the smoky city was gone (see Figure 9.3).

Another major fuel change that further reduced Pittsburgh's smoke burden in the 1950s was the railroads' conversion from coal-burning steam locomotives to diesel electrics. Smoke investigators often pinpointed locomotives as offensive smoke generators, responsible for a large fraction of the city's smoke burden; they were considered especially polluting because of their mobile nature. Railroads were concerned with coal not only because of fuel availability and costs but also because it was their largest single item of revenue tonnage.[86] The Pittsburgh Smoke Control Ordinance of 1941 was the nation's strictest; in 1947 the Pennsylvania House of Representatives approved a bill giving the Allegheny County Commissioners jurisdiction over railroad smoke, but coal-burning locomotives remained a problem.[87]

Fig. 9.3 Celebrating "Cleaner" air in Pittsburgh, 1952 (courtesy of the Senator John Heinz History Center).

Improvement would come with a major change in technology—from coal burning to diesel-electric locomotives. In the 1930s railroads had used diesels as switching engines in some cities and substituted them for steam locomotives on long-distance passenger runs, but railroads had resisted the capital costs involved in adopting the new technology, and locomotive manufacturers largely remained wedded to the steam locomotive. The coming of the Second World War further retarded the transition and 39,592 steam locomotives were in service in 1946 compared to 5,008 diesels. The change to diesel locomotives, however, occurred with great swiftness after this date. By 1951 there were almost as many diesels as steam locomotives in the nation, and by 1960 there were 30,340 diesels and only 374 steam locomotives.[88] Pittsburgh railroads were part of this transition. By 1952 the Pennsylvania Railroad, which operated the city's largest number of passenger and freight trains in the city, had replaced almost all its steam locomotives with diesel electrics. The same pattern was true for Pittsburgh's other roads—in its 1955 report the Bureau of Smoke Regulation observed, "The Diesel locomotive has solved the smoke problem of the railroads."[89]

EFFECTS OF THE ENERGY TRANSITION

The shift from coal to natural gas as a fuel for domestic and commercial heating and the replacement of the steam locomotive with the diesel electric had significant effects on environmental quality, on the health of Pittsburghers, and on Pittsburgh's civic ambience. The most evident environmental improvement was the reduction in the number of hours of heavy smoke that began in the winter of 1947–1948. Some of the reduction is attributable to declines in industrial production and the implementation of more efficient combustion technologies in the immediate postwar period, but the magnitude and timing of the change suggests that the shifts in heating and railroad fuels also played key roles.

In regard to health, a large epidemiological literature links exposure to air pollution to higher morbidity and mortality. Pittsburgh was particularly subject to particle pollution, which is associated with higher winter mortality. Such pollution was especially generated by the coal that was burned for home heating and discharged from chimneys at relatively low levels. Throughout the twentieth century public health investigators had sought to link coal use with specific medical problems, but they were met with limited success. The 1909–1914 Mellon Smoke Investigation, for instance, produced a series of papers on the influence of smoke on health that were inconclusive. Later studies of the relationship between smoke and pneumonia by the Pittsburgh Department of Public Health and the Air Hygiene Foundation of the Mellon Institute for Industrial Research also failed to establish a strong causal connection.[90]

The availability of stronger data and means of analysis today makes it possible to shed better light on the relationship between coal burning, health, and the positive effects of the transition to natural gas for home heating. In a national study of the effects of retail coal use on mortality, we show that the monthly mortality rate is related to retail sales of coal. A 1 percent increase in retail coal sales caused a 0.06–0.10 percent increase in the overall monthly mortality. Other studies have found that declines in TSP (total suspended particles) cause declines in infant mortality.[91] These conclusions concerning the positive health effects of banning the consumption of bituminous coal in urban areas were supported by a study of Dublin, Ireland. Dublin's air quality had deteriorated in the 1980s after a switch from oil to cheaper and more readily available fuels, especially bituminous coal for domestic space and water heating. Greater air pollution, however, increased in-hospital respiratory deaths and on September 1, 1990, the Irish government banned the marketing, sale, and distribution of bituminous coals within the city. A 2002 study of these effects concludes that the control of particulate air pollution in Dublin had "led to an immediate reduction in cardiovascular and respiratory deaths."[92]

Many of the benefits of smoke control in terms of improved air quality, increased sunshine, and health were difficult to quantify, but the Pittsburgh Bureau of Smoke Prevention did attempt to put a dollar figure on savings resulting from "greater cleanliness." In 1950 the bureau calculated the total savings at $26,808,000—or forty-one dollars per capita per year. This included savings on cleaning costs, reduced building depreciation, laundry bills, injury to vegetation, and fuel costs. These calculations do not include the fuel cost savings and improvements in industrial efficiency that took place in industries that substituted natural gas for coal.[93]

From the perspective of the civic culture, smoke control played a critical role in the Pittsburgh Renaissance, the first attempt by a major industrial city to renew itself. A *National Geographic* article on the city's renewal in 1949 noted that "Smoke elimination has become a dramatic symbol of the whole powerful impetus toward civic improvement." A *Newsweek* article in the same year claimed that smoke control had cut the smoke pall by half and that the "result has been a revelation to the city's dwellers," because it had convinced Pittsburghers that "better things, somehow, can get done," giving them faith in the whole Renaissance redevelopment program. There is no doubt that without smoke control the Pittsburgh Renaissance would never have been accomplished.[94] The city's boosters now heralded it as a Renaissance city that was no longer dependent on coal and its noxious byproducts, smoke and dust fall.

CONCLUSION

Although Pittsburgh is famous within the annals of energy history for the fortunes derived from exploitation of the Pittsburgh coal seam and for its "smoky city" nickname, it has actually experienced several energy transitions. Among the most significant of these transitions were those involving coal and natural gas. The first transition occurred in the late nineteenth century, and the second took place in the decades after the Second World War.

Issues relating to supply and demand, fuel prices, labor issues, and technology shaped these transitions, as did forecasting failures, unexpected events, and public policies in regard to smoke control.

The discovery of natural gas in the Pittsburgh region was an unexpected event, although gas was known to exist in the oil fields in the northwest corner of the state. The first transition period was marked by exaggerated forecasts in regard to the extent of the local natural gas supply. By approximately 1890 supplies began to fail, which resulted in a return to coal for many domestic and industrial users. The second and longer transition was driven by the arrival in the region of extensive gas supplies from the Southwest provided by the inch pipelines. This had unanticipated elements as well, since authorities had thought the transition would be driven by cleaner processed coal and not a different fuel. Public authorities also failed to anticipate the rapidity of the replacement of coal-burning locomotives with diesel electrics in the 1950s, even though the technology had been available for some years.

Each of these transitions had significant effects on labor, on public health, on the economy, on the environment, and on concepts of civic improvement. In the first transition, natural gas availability stimulated the growth of the iron, steel, and glass industries. The city's downtown experienced a commercial building boom as industries and banks constructed new headquarters. Production in the mining areas, however, was reduced, and large numbers of miners were put out of work. When natural gas supplies declined, industries and households returned to coal, bringing back heavy smoke palls. In turn, this stimulated a movement toward the achievement of clean air through regulation and fuel change. It would be approximately fifty years before success was achieved, and it would at best only partially be attributable to public policy. Finally, the transition from coal to natural gas in both periods resulted in improvements to the public health as the smoke burden was reduced. But while the smoke pollution of the past has been eliminated, present-day air quality measures make it clear that Pittsburgh still suffers from poor air quality because of continued industrial use of coal and other fossil fuels. Whether a transition to nonfossil fuels will bring further public health improvements has still to be determined.[95]

NOTES

This essay was originally published as Joel A. Tarr and Karen Clay, "Pittsburgh as an Energy Capital: Perspectives on Coal and Natural Gas Transitions and the Environment," in Joseph A. Pratt, Martin V. Melosi, and KathleenA. Brosnan, eds., *Energy Capitals: Local*

Impact, Global Influence (Pittsburgh, PA: University of Pittsburgh Press, 2014), 5–28, 199–208, and reprinted with permission. The authors would like to thank Chris Jones, Austin Mitchell, Edward K. Muller, and Werner Troesken for their helpful comments on the manuscript and Paula Levin at Heinz College, CMU, for her aid in data processing.

1. Pittsburgh Regional Planning Association, *Region in Transition, Report of the Economic Study of the Pittsburgh Region* (Pittsburgh: University of Pittsburgh Press, 1963), 226.

2. The petroleum came from the oil fields in the northwest corner of the state, the nation's first major oil producing area. In the 1860s oil was shipped down the Allegheny River on barges and other forms of river transport, with rail transport becoming increasingly important in the following decades. Pittsburgh became a petroleum warehouse and a refining center, and in 1866 it had eighty-six refineries. In the late nineteenth century, however, the refining industry played a diminishing role in the city's economy because of railroad-freight-rate discrimination and competition from Cleveland refineries, which had superior transport options for the crude. See A. Michael Sulman, "The Short Happy Life of Petroleum in Pittsburgh," *Pennsylvania History* 30 (January 1966): 50–69; Harold F. Williamson and Arnold R. Daum, *The American Petroleum Industry: The Age of Illumination, 1859–1899* (Evanston, IL: Northwestern University Press, 1959), 55–60, 165–231. The environmental impacts of oil exploitation in northwestern Pennsylvania are explored in Brian Black, *Petrolia: The Landscape of America's First Oil Boom* (Baltimore: Johns Hopkins University Press, 2002).

3. For energy transitions, see Vaclav Smil, *Energy Transitions: History, Requirements, Prospects* (New York: Praeger, 2010). For a study of the role of different energy sources in the American economy, see Sam H. Schurr and Bruce C. Netschert, *Energy in the American Economy, 1850–1975: An Economic Study of Its History and Prospect* (Baltimore: Johns Hopkins University Press, 1960).

4. E. V. d'Invilliers, *Report on the Pittsburgh Coal Region, Annual Report of the Geological Survey of Pennsylvania for 1886, Part 1* (Harrisburg: Board of Commissioners, 1887), 119–256.

5. Susan J. Tewalt et al., "Chapter C-A Digital Resource Model of the Upper Pennsylvania Pittsburgh Coal Bed, Monongahela Group, Northern Appalachian Basin Coal Region," USGS Professional Paper 1675, http://pubs.usgs.gov/pp/p1625c/.

6. For discussions of coal in Pennsylvania, see Frederick Moore Binder, *Coal Age Empire: Pennsylvania Coal and Its Utilization to 1860* (Harrisburg: Pennsylvania Historical and Museum Commission, 1974); John N. Hoffman, "Major Economic Changes in the Mining and Distribution of Pennsylvania Bituminous Coal" (PhD. diss., Pennsylvania State University, 1961); Howard N. Eavenson, *The First Century and a Quarter of American Coal Industry* (Pittsburgh: Privately printed, 1942), 138–226.

7. Howard N. Eavenson, "The Pittsburgh Coal Bed: Its Early History and Development," *American Institute of Mining Engineers, Transactions* 130 (1938): 55.

8. Eavenson, *The First Century*, 485–90, table 49; John J. Schanz, "Historical Statistics of Pennsylvania's Mineral Industries, 1759–1955" (Paper 1, no. 69, College of Mineral Industries, Pennsylvania State University, March 1957), 19; Hoffman, "Major Economic Changes," 64; Wilbert G. Fritz and Theodore A. Veenstra, *Regional Shifts in the Bituminous Coal Industry with Special Reference to Pennsylvania* (Pittsburgh: Bureau of Business Research, 1935), 15–24. The four coal-mining counties composed a region where 77 percent of Pennsylvania's coal was mined although they occupied only 14.7 percent of the state's land area.

9. Fritz and Veenstra, *Regional Shifts*, 65–66; US Bureau of Mines, *Mineral Resources, 1924*—Part 2 (Washington, DC: GPO, 1925), 471, 481, 490.

10. National Coal Association, *Bituminous Coal Facts, 1966* (Washington, DC: NCA, 1966), 60.

11. See V. Price Fishback, *Soft Coal, Hard Choices: The Economic Welfare of Bituminous Coal Miners, 1890–1930* (New York: Oxford University Press, 1992).

12. Fritz and Veenstra, *Regional Shifts*, 25–35.

13. Shera A. Moxley, *From Rivers to Lakes: Engineering Pittsburgh's Three Rivers, A Report from 3 Rivers 2nd Nature* (Pittsburgh: Carnegie Mellon University Studio for Creative Inquiry 2001), 16–17.

14. Pittsburgh was also an important manufacturer of railroad equipment such as rails, locomotives, and freight cars. For the impact of railroads on the Pittsburgh economy, see Hounshell et al., "Economic Impact of Rail Transportation."

15. Hoffman, "Major Economic Changes," 109–12, 125; Pittsburgh Regional Planning Association, *Region in Transition*, 213–14.

16. Willard Glazier, "The Great Furnace of America," reprinted in Lubove, *Pittsburgh*, 22–29.

17. Warren, *The American Steel Industry*, 15–28.

18. Muller and Tarr, "Interaction of Natural and Built Environments," 21.

19. Ingham, *Making Iron and Steel*, 47–95.

20. Warren, *Triumphant Capitalism*, 21–268.

21. Warren, *The American Steel Industry*, 114–15, 135–36; Ingham, *Making Iron and Steel*, 140–51; Edward Muller and Joel A. Tarr, "Pittsburgh's Industrial Corridors," in Barbara Jones, ed., *Born of Fire: The Valley of Work* (Pittsburgh: University of Pittsburgh Press, 2006), 15–35.

22. Edward K. Muller, "River City," in Tarr, *Devastation and Renewal*, 41–63.

23. Warren, *The American Steel Industry*, 137.

24. Hoffman, "Major Economic Changes," 137.

25. Pittsburgh Regional Planning Association, *Region in Transition*, 229–33.

26. Coal was obtained primarily by room and pillar deep mining before the 1950s, when longwall mining and strip mining or surface mining became common. Both of these newer techniques produce large environmental damages, but they reduce the human risks in coal mining. The volume of material involved in strip mining made its environmental impacts especially severe. For strip mining, see Mark Squillace, "The Environmental Effects of Strip Mining," chapter 2 of *Strip Mining Handbook*, http://sites.google.com/site/stripmininghandbook/chapter-2-1/. For longwall mining, see the Center for Public Integrity, *The Hidden Costs of Clean Coal: The Environmental and Human Disaster of Longwall Mining*, http://www.publicintegrity.org/investigations/longwall/pages/documents/.

27. The Surface Mining Control and Reclamation Act (SMCRA) of 1977 defined abandoned mine land (AML) as lands that were mined, left in an inadequate reclamation status, and abandoned before August 3, 1977, with no continuing reclamation responsibility attributed to any individual or company under state or federal laws. Many sources deal with the environmental impacts of coal use. See, for example, "Coal Mining," http://wiki.dickinson.edu/index.php/Coal_mining; "Environmental Effects of Coal Mining and Burning," Wikipedia, http://en.wikipedia.org/wiki/Environmental_effects_of_coal; Source Watch, "Environmental Impacts of Coal," http://www.sourcewatch.org/index.php?title=Environmental_impacts_of_coal/.

28. Some health authorities were reluctant to counsel the complete exclusion of mine acid drainage from streams because the acid waste had a germicidal effect on sewage pollution.

29. Nicholas Casner, "Acid Mine Drainage and Pittsburgh's Water Quality," in Tarr, *Devastation and Renewal*, 89–109.

30. Tarr, *Devastation and Renewal.*

31. Joel A. Tarr, *The Search for the Ultimate Sink: Urban Pollution in Historical Perspective* (Akron: University of Akron Press, 1996), 390–91.

32. "Inversion (meteorology)," in Wikipedia, http://en.wikipedia.org/wiki/Inversion_percent28meteorologypercent29.

33. See Eavenson, "The Pittsburgh Coal Bed," 20–21. See also John O'Connor, "The History of the Smoke Nuisance and of Smoke Abatement in Pittsburgh," *Industrial World*, March 14, 1913.

34. Angela Gugliotta, "How, When, and for Whom Was Smoke a Problem in Pittsburgh?" in Tarr, *Devastation and Renewal*, 110–14.

35. A. B. Bellows, O. R. McBride, and A. A. Straub, *Some Engineering Phases of Pittsburgh's Smoke Problem, Vol. 6: Mellon Smoke Investigation* (Pittsburgh: University of Pittsburgh, 1914), 12; Angela Gugliotta, "Hell with the Lid Taken Off: A Cultural History of Air Pollution—Pittsburgh" (unpublished doctoral dissertation, University of Notre Dame, 2004), 32–36, 58–59, 118, 122.

36. For a list of gas wells in the Pittsburgh region before 1885, see Francis C. Phillips, *Report on the Composition and Fuel-Value of Natural Gas, Part II, Annual Report, Geological Survey of Pennsylvania 1886* (Harrisburg, Board of Commissioners for the Geological Survey, 1887), 690–92.

37. The plants were the ironworks of Spang, Chafant & Company, the Isabella Blast Furnace, and the iron mills of Graff, Bennett & Company.

38. See "Glass: Pittsburgh as a Center," in Engineers' Society of Western Pennsylvania, *Pittsburgh* (Pittsburgh: The Society, 1930), 365–74.

39. "Report of a Committee, on Natural Gas, May 21, 1884," *Proceedings of the Engineers' Society of Western Pennsylvania, Pittsburg [*sic*]* 2 (September 1882–1884). The new gas well fields were located in Butler, Westmoreland, and Washington Counties as well as in the township of Tarentum in Allegheny County.

40. Westinghouse also patented a number of improvements in gas distribution technology including the use of double piping to avoid leaks. In 1886 he formed the Safety Appliance Company to manufacturer gas meters and regulators. See Quentin R. Skrabec Jr., *George Westinghouse: Gentle Genius* (New York: Algora Publishing, 2007), 71–75.

41. For the early growth of the Philadelphia Company, see George H. Thurston, *Pittsburgh's Progress, Industries and Resources* (Pittsburgh: A. A. Anderson & Son, 1886), 13. Thurston claimed that 3,000 families, 34 iron and steel mills, 60 glass factories, and 300 small factories and hotels used natural gas by the late 1880s. By 1885 the Philadelphia Company piped in gas from 45 wells, had laid 331 miles of pipe, and supplied 2,637 homes. Stanley Paul Wagner, "Natural Gas Comes to Pittsburgh" (MA thesis, University of Pittsburgh, 1947), 50–56. In 1890, *Brown's Directory of American Gas Companies* listed seventy-eight gas companies in the Pittsburgh region. See *Brown's Director of American Gas Companies* (Duluth, MN: Harcourt Brace Jovanovich, 1890), 143–44.

42. E. V. d'Invilliers, *Report on the Pittsburgh Coal Region*, 18–19; "Natural Gas vs. Coal at Pittsburg [*sic*]," *National Labor Tribune*, July 24, 1886.

43. Gugliotta, "Hell with the Lid Taken Off," 129–39.

44. "The City of Pittsburg [*sic*]," *Harper's Weekly* 36 (February 27, 1892): 202–3. See the discussion of this article in Gugliotta, "Hell with the Lid Taken Off," 143–47.

45. See, for instance, Thurston, *Pittsburgh's Progress*, 6–8, published in 1886, where he repeats and reiterates optimistic comments about the gas supply that he originally had made in 1876. See also Thurston, *Allegheny County's Hundred Years* (Pittsburgh: A. A. Anderson & Son, 1888), 92–95, 202–9; Gugliotta, "Hell with the Lid Taken Off," 128–31.

46. Regulations regarding natural gas pipeline construction and routes were specified by the state legislature in "An Act to Provide for the Incorporation and Regulation of Natural Gas Companies," *No. 32: Laws of Pennsylvania, Session of 1885*, 33–35.

47. Quoted in Wagner, "Natural Gas Comes to Pittsburgh," 42.

48. See W. W. Thomson, *A Digest of the Acts of Assembly Relating to the General Ordinances of the City of Pittsburgh from 1804–1886* (Harrisburg, 1887), 369–725; Hiram Schock, comp. and ed., *Digest of the General Ordinances and Laws of the City of Pittsburgh to March 1, 1938* (Pittsburgh: The City, 1938), 728–37; see 729n1, for the void of parts of the 1885 ordinance by the courts.

49. The Penn State Extension website reports that a Pennsylvania study found that the average volume of water produced during shallow gas well drilling in western Pennsylvania was 25,000 gallons during drilling, 50,000 gallons during stimulation, and 150 gallons per day during production. See "Water Issues," Penn Sate Extension, http://extension.psu.edu/naturalgas/issues/environmental/resources/water.

50. Pennsylvania Department of Environmental Protection, *Orphan Oil and Gas Wells and the Orphan Well Plugging Fund*, http://www.portal.state.pa.us/portal/server.pt/community/abandoned___orphan_well_program/20292.

51. See An Act No. 80, *Session of 1878*, 57 (plugging oil wells); An Act No. 122, *Session of 1881*, 110–11 (plugging abandoned oil wells); An Act No. 54, *Session of 1883*, 61–65 (oil pipeline regulations); An Act No. 32, *Session of 1885*, 29–37 (act for the incorporation and regulation of natural gas companies); An Act No. 114, *Session of 1885*, 145–46 (an act to protect oil, gas, and water wells); An Act No. 199, *Session of 1887*, 310–13 (right of gas companies to eminent domain); An Act 114, *Session of 1891*, 122–23 (an act to prevent the pollution of springs, water wells, and streams by water from abandoned oil and gas wells); An Act No. 322, *Session of 1921*, 912–14 (an act to regulate the drilling, operating, and abandoning of oil and gas wells); all acts in *Laws of Pennsylvania*. See also Blakely M. Murphy, ed., *Conservation of Oil & Gas: A Legal History, 1948* (Chicago: American Bar Association, 1949), 429–35.

52. For the history of the Sanitary Water Board, see http://www.portal.state.pa.us/portal/server.pt?open=514&objID=588469&mode=2. Issues/.

53. See *Annual Report of the Pennsylvania Department of Health, 1908* (Harrisburg, 1908) 2:486–88 (Google Books, at com/books/about/Report.html?id=0xdNAAAAMAAJ).

54. *Nannie R. Collins v. Chartiers Valley Gas Co.* 139 Pa. 111 (1890–1891).

55. J. M. T Carpenter to J. N. Pew, November 17, 1892; E. T. Bouser to the Peoples Natural Gas Company, July 19, 1900; E. Robbins to Peoples Natural Gas Company, November 22, 1894; Moorhead and Head to Peoples Natural Gas Company, May 19, 1899; all in Pew Papers, Hagley Museum and Library, Wilmington, Delaware. The Pew Papers also contained a "Proposal and Specifications for Drilling Wells," dated July 22, 1901.

56. The Peoples Natural Gas Company, "Proposal and Specifications for Drilling Wells," July 22, 1901, Pew Papers.

57. *Westmoreland & Cambria Natural Gas Co. v. De Witt*, 18 A, 724 (Pa. 1889); Ross H. Pifer, "The Rule of Capture in Pennsylvania Oil and Gas Law" (PennState The Dickinson School of Law, August 17, 2009 (www.law.psu.edu/aglaw). For a valuable discussion of the development of this case and oil and gas case law and legislation in Pennsylvania compared with those of Colorado, see Thomas A. Mitchell, "The Future of Oil and Gas Conservation Jurisprudence: Past as Prologue," *Washburn Law Journal* 49 (Winter 2010): 379–422.

58. Wagner, "Natural Gas Comes to Pittsburgh," 73–74. By 1891 Carnegie's Edgar Thompson Works was using only coke for fuel, and in 1893 the Philadelphia Company terminated its contract with the mill. See Edgar P. Allen, "Natural Resources of Pittsburgh," *Proceedings of the Engineer's Society of Western Pennsylvania* 7 (1891): 11–13. Gugliotta analyzes labor's position on the use of natural gas in "Hell with the Lid Taken Off," 183–266.

59. Gugliotta, "Hell with the Lid Taken Off, 151–58.

60. *Proceedings of the Engineer's Society of Western Pennsylvania* 8 (1892): 42–43. The speaker was Dr. R. Stansbury Sutton, a prominent physician. See also Gugliotta, "Hell with the Lid Taken Off," 200.

61. The best discussion of the role of the Ladies Health Protective Association and the consequent agitation for smoke control can be found in Gugliotta, "Hell with the Lid Taken Off," 132–43.

62. Joel A. Tarr, "The Pittsburgh Survey as an Environmental Statement," in Maurine W. Greenwald and Margo Anderson, eds., *Pittsburgh Surveyed: Social Science and Social Reform in the Early Twentieth Century* (Pittsburgh: University of Pittsburgh Press, 1996), 179–81.

63. Tarr, "The Pittsburgh Survey," 374–404; Tarr, *Ultimate Sink*, 241.

64. Samuel S. Wyer, *Gas Situation of the Philadelphia Company's Natural Gas Properties in West Virginia and Pennsylvania* (Columbus, Ohio, July 7, 1920); John Gates Jr., "Domestic and Industrial Use of Natural Gas," *Gas Age* (May 1, 1919): 470–71; Eugene D. Thoenen, *History of the Oil and Gas Industry in West Virginia* (Charleston, WV: Education Foundation, 1964), 361. The peak of gas production from Appalachian fields was in 1917. See Arion R. Tussing and Connie C. Barlow, *The Natural Gas Industry: Evolution, Structure, and Economics* (Cambridge: Ballinger, 1984), 32. In 1919 and 1920 a brief local boom occurred when drillers discovered gas near the city of McKeesport, fifteen miles from Pittsburgh, but the wells soon turned dry. See Meredith E. Johnson, *Geology and Mineral Resources, Topographic and Geologic Atlas of Pennsylvania No. 27, Pittsburgh Quadrangle* (Harrisburg: Bureau of Publications, 1929), 122–32; Joel A. Tarr. "There Will Be Gas," *Pittsburgh Post-Gazette*, August 2, 2009.

65. John G. Clark, *Energy and the Federal Government: Fossil Fuel Policies, 1900–1946* (Urbana: University of Illinois Press, 1987), 51–109.

66. See Public Service Commission of the Commonwealth of Pennsylvania, *Supply and Conservation of Natural Gas in the State of Pennsylvania, Proceedings at Pittsburgh, Pennsylvania, Jan. 8, 1919* (Harrisburg: 1919); F. F. Schauer (vice president and general manager, Equitable Gas), "A Resume of the History, Organization, Operation and Present Day Problems of the Equitable Gas Company Pittsburgh & West Virginia Gas Company, Philadelphia Oil Company" (unpublished ms., Pittsburgh, February 15, 1932), 6–7; Johnson, *Geology and Mineral Resources*, 110–11; James H. Reed, "Pittsburgh and the Natural Gas Industry," in Greater Pittsburgh Chamber of Commerce, *Pittsburgh and the Pittsburgh Spirit: Addresses at the Chamber of Commerce, 1927–28* (Pittsburgh: Robert L.

Forsythe, 1928), 126–27, 134. From 1922 to 1927 Equitable Gas manufactured coal gas that it mixed with natural gas to supplant the decline in natural gas supplies.

67. Johnson, *Geology and Mineral Resources*, 110. For glass, see Charles R. Fettke, *Glass Manufacture and the Glass Sand Industry of Pennsylvania*, no. 12, Pennsylvania Topographic and Geological Survey Commission (Harrisburg: L. L. Kuhn, 1919), 97.

68. Natural gas production in Pennsylvania (mostly western Pennsylvania counties) ranged from approximately 125,787,000 million cubic feet in 1920 to 101,951,00 in 1929. Production figures were sharply reduced during the Depression. See Schanz, "Historical Statistics of Pennsylvania's Mineral Industries, 1759–1955," 37.

69. Gugliotta, "Hell with the Lid Taken Off," 501–9; Clark, *Energy and the Federal Government*, 145.

70. A national study done in 1931–1933 found that winter particulate levels remained among the worst in the nation but the general trend during the Depression was for a decline in smoky days. See James E. Ives et al., *Atmospheric Pollution of American Cities for the Years 1931–1933, with Special Reference to the Solid Constituents of the Pollution*, Public Health Bulletin no. 224 (Washington, DC: GPO, 1936).

71. Tarr, *Ultimate Sink*, 232–33.

72. Joel A. Tarr and Carl Zimring, "The Struggle for Smoke Control in St. Louis. Achievement and Emulation," in Andrew Hurley, ed., *Common Fields: An Environmental History of St. Louis* (St. Louis: Missouri Historical Society, 1997), 199–220.

73. Tarr, *Ultimate Sink*, 240–41, 246–47; Gugliotta, "Hell with the Lid Taken Off," 595–97.

74. Tarr, *Ultimate Sink*, 243–51.

75. Clark, *Energy and the Federal Government*, 254–57, 349. Natural gas pipelines were extended to many parts of the country in the 1930s, but not to the Pittsburgh area or other parts of Pennsylvania, New York, and New England. See John H. Herbert, *Clean Cheap Heat: The Development of Residential Markets for Natural Gas in the United States* (New York: Praeger, 1992), 91–92; Pittsburgh and West Virginia Gas Company and Equitable Gas Company, *Annual Reports 1940 and 1941* (Pittsburgh, 1940, 1941), 15–16 (1940) and 15–19 (1941).

76. Tarr, *Ultimate Sink*, 244–45. Other influential Pittsburgh businessmen besides Mellon, such as J. H. Hillman, had interests in both coal and competing fuels. Hillman owned Pittsburgh Coke and Chemical and controlled several coal, coke, and iron companies, and he served as president of the Texas Gas Transmission Corporation. In 1948, in return for gas supplies for his industrial interests, he made scarce steel piping available for the pipeline expansion of Texas Eastern, the firm that converted Little Inch and Big Inch to natural gas. See Christopher J. Castaneda and Joseph A. Pratt, *From Texas to the East: A Strategic History of Texas Eastern Corporation* (College Station: Texas A&M Press, 1993), 84–85.

77. Castaneda and Pratt, *From Texas to the East*, 252.

78. "Caution Urged on County Smoke Law," *Pittsburgh Press*, December 21, 1945; "Coal Industry Opens Drive on Air Pollution," *Pittsburgh Press*, February 3, 1946. The coal industry created the Western Pennsylvania Conference on Air Pollution to study combustion equipment, fuels, prices, and methods to reduce smoke. This later evolved into Bituminous Coal Research.

79. For the story of the "Inch" lines, see Castaneda and Pratt, *From Texas to the East*, 13–74.

80. Equitable Gas Company and Subsidiaries, *Annual Report, 1952*, 19; Peoples Natural Gas Company, "Peak Storage Inventory, 1943–1957," *Annual Gas Sales Volume*, 20A, in author's files.

81. Herbert, *Clean Cheap Heat*, 91–103.

82. The projected industry to manufacture treated coal (Disco) never became a success although one plant was constructed. To meet the ordinance's requirements, the Bureau of Smoke Prevention permitted a mixture of 50 percent high volatile coal and 50 percent low volatile coal to be used. See City of Pittsburgh Bureau of Smoke Prevention, *Report 1953* (Pittsburgh, 1954), 12. Discussions of Disco can be found in C. E. Lesher, "Disco, A Smokeless Fuel," and Caleb Davies Jr., "Tar and By-Products from the Disco Process," *Industrial and Engineering Chemistry* 33 (July 1941): 858–64.

83. The Bureau of Smoke Inspection reported that 4,173 domestic natural gas conversion units, 1,283 commercial conversion units, and 1,743 domestic gas boilers were installed between 1948 and 1955. In addition 1,257 domestic mechanical coal stokers and 628 commercial stokers were installed. Domestic household and commercial interests installed new boilers and gas-consuming conversion units at a declining but still high rate through 1955, while stoker installations had declined to almost zero by that date. See Bureau of Smoke Prevention, *Report 1955* (Pittsburgh, 1955), n.p. For Equitable sales increases, see Equitable Gas Company, *Annual Reports, 1949 and 1956* (Pittsburgh: the Company, 1949 and 1956); for Peoples sales increases, see Peoples Natural Gas Company, *Annual Gas Sales Volume*, 1943–1957. The Peoples's compilation includes comparative fuel prices.

84. Sherie R. Mershon and Joel A. Tarr, "Strategies for Clean Air: The Pittsburgh and Allegheny County Smoke Control Movements, 1940–1960," in Tarr, *Devastation and Renewal*, 160. For comparative costs of competing fuels, see Peoples Natural Gas Company, *Operating and Financial Statistics Years 1943–1972* (Pittsburgh, 1973), 23a. While there had been considerable discussion in both the 1941 and 1946 hearings about special provisions for the poor, cash subsidies of a limited amount were only provided for public assistance recipients. In enforcing the statute the Bureau of Smoke Prevention attempted to educate low-income consumers as to the proper measures of firing smokeless coal rather than fining them for smoke violations.

85. Tarr, *Ultimate Sink*, 250.

86. Tarr, *Ultimate Sink*, 262–82.

87. Mershon and Tarr, "Strategies for Clean Air," in Tarr, *Devastation and Renewal.* The railroads hated the city smoke control ordinance and opposed any serious county regulation. In 1943 they used their political influence to secure exemption from a state-enabling law that empowered Allegheny County to regulate smoke, but in 1947 the Pittsburgh anti-smoke interests, including corporate leaders such as Richard King Mellon, were able to secure state authorization for county legislation.

88. For a study of the dieselization of American railroads, see Albert J. Churella, *From Steam to Diesel: Managerial Customs and Organizational Capabilities in the Twentieth-Century American Locomotive Industry* (Princeton, NJ: Princeton University Press, 1999).

89. Pittsburgh Bureau of Smoke Prevention, *Report, 1955*, n.p. In 1955 the Pennsylvania Railroad had 602 diesel units in service and only 18 steam engines. Pittsburgh Bureau of Smoke Prevention, *Report, 1952*, 12, *Report, 1953*, 14–18, *Report, 1954*, 20, and *Report, 1955*, 16–20. Diesels could "smoke," but the bureau reported that no violations had been recorded for Pittsburgh railroads.

90. Pittsburgh Department of Public Health, Bureau of Smoke Prevention, "Pneumonia and Atmospheric Dust," *Report, 1954*, 12; Gugliotta, "Hell with the Lid Taken Off," 404–15. For an earlier study that also found no significant relationship, see Ewald Tomakek and Edwin B. Wilson, "Pneumonia in Pittsburgh," *Proceedings of the American Philosophical Society* 53 (1924): 279–319.

91. Clay and Tarr, "Coal, Smoke, and Death," working paper (2011); Kenneth Y. Clay and Michael Greenstone, "The Impact of Air Pollution on Infant Mortality: Evidence from Geographic Variation in Pollution Shocks Induced by a Recession," *Quarterly Journal of Economics* 118 (2003): 1121–67; Janet Currie and Matthew Neidell, "Air Pollution and Infant Health: What Can We Learn from California's Recent Experience?" *Quarterly Journal of Economics* 120 (2005): 1003–30.

92. Luke Clancy, Pat Goodman, Hamish Sinclair, and Douglas W. Dockery, "Effect of Air-Pollution Control on Death Rates in Dublin, Ireland: An Intervention Study," *Lancet* (2002): 1214.

93. Pittsburgh Bureau of Smoke Prevention, *Report on Stationary Stacks* (Pittsburgh, 1951), 13.

94. Roy Lubove, *Twentieth-Century Pittsburgh, Vol. 1: Government, Business, and Environmental Change* (New York: John Wiley, 1969), 16–41; Tarr, *Devastation and Renewal*, 173.

95. See, for instance, Jakob Lazzaro, "Pittsburgh's Air Quality Better than the Past but not yet Clean," August 1, 2018, at https://www.wesa.fm/post/pittsburghs-air-quality-better-past-not-yet-clean.

10

BOOM AND BUST IN PITTSBURGH NATURAL GAS HISTORY

DEVELOPMENT, POLICY, AND ENVIRONMENTAL EFFECTS, 1878–1920

Joel A. Tarr and Karen Clay

Pittsburgh and Western Pennsylvania have a rich energy history involving the development and utilization of the natural resources of coal, oil, and natural gas (see "Pittsburgh as an Energy Capital" in this volume). Within the last ten years the region has been experiencing a boom in natural gas production because of a rise in gas prices and the application of the technology of hydro fracking horizontal drilling of the Marcellus shale deposit that extends throughout the state. This natural gas boom, however, is not the region's first but, rather, its second—and it mirrors in many ways a natural gas boom that occurred in the region from approximately 1878 to 1920. This period of initial discovery involved many of the same generic issues of policy formulation, expected lifetime of supply, and environmental costs discussed with regard to today's Marcellus gas boom. This article, therefore, will discuss the development of the first Pittsburgh region boom, the evolution of natural gas policy, and impacts on the environment.

BRIEF HISTORY OF THE PITTSBURGH REGION'S FIRST NATURAL GAS BOOM

The Early Years

Natural gas was first discovered in the northwestern corner of Pennsylvania in the 1860s by drillers seeking oil and salt; the gas was often flared but occasionally it was used to heat boilers and to power drilling equipment. In the early 1870s gas was found in Butler, Armstrong, and Clarion Counties and gas from these wells was piped to several Pittsburgh area iron mills. The discovery of gas generated a wave of drilling in these and surrounding counties. Wells were sunk throughout the region, and gas was often ignited with spectacular landscape effects. A description of an 1883 Butler County well, for instance, observed that the "flame of this natural torch is about 40 feet long and fifteen feet wide, and keeps at these dimensions night and day with striking regularity."[1] By 1884 ten counties had over a hundred producing gas wells, and within the next three years four hundred new wells were drilled and hundreds of new gas companies were organized (see Figure 10.1).[2]

Gas was first used in the iron, steel, and glass industries. In the late 1870s the mills of Spang, Chafant & Company in Etna and those of Graff, Bennett & Company in Millvale pioneered in the use of gas for iron making from wells in Butler County.[3] Other mills soon followed, and in September 1883 Andrew Carnegie began the process of substituting gas for coal at his three Pittsburgh area plants: the Edgar Thomson Bessemer Works, the Homestead Steel Works, and the Union Mills.[4] Natural gas also rapidly became the preferred fuel in the making of glass because it was so much cleaner than coal, resulting in a superior product.[5]

Natural gas, however, was not used in the city of Pittsburgh until the early 1880s. Gas had been discovered in the Murrysville region about twenty miles east of the city in the late 1870s, but entrepreneurs were initially reluctant to pipe gas to untested markets because of required investment in expensive and untried infrastructure.[6] In 1882, however, the Fuel Gas Company and the Penn Fuel Company—both incorporated under the Pennsylvania Corporation Act of 1874 and both drawing on wells in the Murrysville field—received charters from the city council to provide natural gas to the city.[7] Based on the timing of its charter, the Fuel Gas Company claimed that it had the exclusive right to distribute gas in the city, and it constructed eight miles of wrought iron pipe to supply gas to the mills in Pittsburgh's South Side.

Shortly after, in February 1884, the inventor and entrepreneur George Westinghouse began drilling on his estate "Solitude," located in Pittsburgh's Point Breeze neighborhood seeking fuel for his hot house and conservatory. On May 29, 1884, the drill struck gas, resulting in a "roarer" estimated to flow at about twenty million C/F per day. The pressure of the gas was so great that it blew a large wooden plug and drilling apparatus—together weighing about thirty-six hundred pounds—many feet in the air. The gas ignited and burned for days, and a torch one hundred feet high lit the

FIG. 10.1 Pittsburgh's first natural gas boom from "Natural Gas in Pennsylvania," *Harper's Weekly*, January 14, 1885.

neighborhood until Westinghouse brought it under control with a stopcock. Within several weeks the Westinghouse well was drowned out by water, a common problem with gas wells in western Pennsylvania, but the realization that there was gas under the city "started a perfect furore [*sic*] in gas drilling" throughout Pittsburgh.[8] Numerous derricks sprouted up in the city and altered the Pittsburgh landscape while gas standpipes flared through the night.

Westinghouse drilled seven more wells in Pittsburgh's Point Breeze and Homewood neighborhoods and acquired land in the Murrysville area, a proven gas reserve. He also proceeded to organize the so-called Philadelphia Company, under an old state charter to supply gas to homes and industries in Pittsburgh and its outlying area, aggressively acquiring industrial and domestic customers and competing firms.[9] In addition, Westinghouse developed and patented technical innovations in the transport of natural gas, in gas regulators, and in meters.[10]

During the first half of 1884, a number of natural gas explosions occurred throughout the city as well as in other parts of the region. Westinghouse moved quickly to emphasize the safety of his distribution system, and he developed a system of double piping that was designed to prevent leakage from gas being distributed under high pressure.[11] He also arranged for his city council allies to introduce an ordinance ("the Westinghouse Ordinance") specifying the use of his double piping innovation in any pipeline installed in the city. Warning that "the extension of weak and imperfect pipes through the city" meant its inhabitants were "living on a powder magazine," the *Pittsburgh Post* demanded that the Westinghouse ordinance be passed. On July 31, 1884, the council approved the ordinance and several months later approved a more detailed ordinance for the Philadelphia Company.[12]

The winters of 1884 and 1885, however, brought another wave of natural gas explosions with resulting property destruction and deaths. The competition between the gas companies resulted in rapid pipe construction throughout the city, often without proper attention to natural gas risks. The distribution of the fuel to city consumers, most of whom were inexperienced in its use (the gas was odorless), involved a relatively new and uncertain technology. Questions existed about the proper material—cast or wrought iron—to use for pipelines, the behavior of pipes under severe winter conditions, the proper sealing to avoid leaks in joints, and the determination of safe amounts of gas pressure. Frequent newspaper articles about gas explosions causing injuries, deaths, and property destruction stimulated alarm and protest meetings throughout the city. On February 2, 1885, the

Pittsburgh Daily Post ran an editorial entitled "Death in the Streets," warning that "Save in a state of war we don't believe any large city in the world was ever in a more perilous situation than Pittsburgh is [in] today owing to the dangers of natural gas explosions."[13]

Regulation

The city council appointed the Natural Gas Commission, which in March, 1885, took extensive testimony from gas company personnel, technicians, and city officials to determine the cause of the explosions. Expert testimony before the commission revealed that pipelines were inadequately tested for leaks, especially at the joints, and were frequently not placed far enough underground to prevent freezing and breakage.[14] Seeking to take advantage of the public outcry over gas explosions, the worst of which had involved his competitors' systems, Westinghouse ran newspaper ads throughout 1885 and 1886, boosting that his Philadelphia company had "facilities equaled by no other company for the safe and economical use of this fuel" and possessed reserves that would guarantee uninterrupted gas supply.[15]

In August 1885, the Pittsburgh City Council passed a general natural gas ordinance that made the transportation and supply of natural gas for public consumption a public service open to regulation; later in the year the council passed an act setting specific standards for the laying and testing of pipe under the direction of the city engineer. A number of the features in this ordinance, such as requiring double piping for safety, involved Westinghouse's patented improvements in gas transmission. The passage of this ordinance, however, was to bring Pittsburgh into a legal collision with the Commonwealth of Pennsylvania.[16]

The Penn Fuel Company had challenged the Fuel Gas Company's monopoly claim to distribute natural gas in Pittsburgh, and the Allegheny County Court of Common Pleas had upheld its monopoly in 1883. In February 2, 1885, however, in the case of *Emerson and the Penn Fuel Company v. the Attorney General*, the Pennsylvania Supreme Court ruled that neither company had an exclusive right to distribute natural gas because the Corporation Act of 1874, under which they had been incorporated, authorized the provision of only manufactured gas. This ruling also invalidated any city ordinance conferring legal rights in regard to natural gas distribution and left in legal limbo the standing of all companies formed to provide natural gas to customers.[17] The problem could only be solved by having the state legislature formulate a natural gas act.

After a spirited debate had taken place in the state house and senate regarding the risks relating to natural gas, on February 4, 1885, Senator John

Upperman of Allegheny County presented a bill to "provide for the incorporation and regulation of natural gas companies."[18] Extensive debates over the terms of the natural gas legislation occupied house and senate for weeks. The primary areas of contention were the terms of the natural gas act, the extent to which one company could monopolize the market and the extent to which Pittsburgh could regulate and control the terms of the entrance of natural gas into the city. Companies organized under the act had the right of eminent domain. The act contained specific terms regarding the sealing and plugging of abandoned wells with a two-hundred-dollar fine if the regulations were not followed. While no governmental agency was tasked with its enforcement, the act provided that if a well was left unplugged an owner of adjacent lands or "in the neighborhood" of the well could plug it at the cost of the original owner. The motivation for this feature appears to have been both to avoid waste and to prevent flooding of adjacent wells. Governor Robert E. Pattison signed the act on May 29, 1885.[19]

By 1885 the Philadelphia Company had become the city's largest natural gas distributor, having consolidated with twenty other smaller natural gas firms. Peoples Natural Gas sought to enter the city with its pipeline from Murrysville, but it was blocked by the terms of the council's natural gas ordinance. In January 1886, in the case of *The People's Natural Gas Co. v. The City of Pittsburgh*, brought in the Allegheny County Court of Common Pleas, the company challenged the act's constitutionality. A master appointed by the court decided in favor of Peoples, agreeing that parts of the city's ordinance were in conflict with the Natural Gas Act.[20] The city appealed to the Pennsylvania Supreme Court, but the high court supported the master's opinion, finding that several sections of the Pittsburgh ordinance were invalid because they conflicted with the newly enacted state Natural Gas Act. State preemption of the local ordinance permitted Peoples Natural Gas to enter and distribute gas throughout the city.[21]

By 1886 six companies had received municipal charters and were piping gas into the city as an industrial and residential fuel.[22] In addition, a number of iron and steel firms drilled wells on their own property, although most did not find gas.[23] The Philadelphia Company remained the largest distributor of gas in the city, and by 1888 it was supplying seven hundred mills, factories, and commercial establishments and twenty-five thousand homes with fuel—as well as rapidly consolidating with other companies.[24]

The Postregulation Climate

In the decades following the passage of the state Natural Gas Act of 1885, the only laws relating to natural gas that were enacted by the legislature involved environmental issues and gas conservation. The picture of natural gas in Pennsylvania after the decade of the 1890s is largely one of increasing domestic and industrial demand, fluctuating production, exploration for new sources, and rising prices. By the end of the period between 1878 and 1920, Pennsylvania natural gas production was sharply down. A report at the end of 1918 on the situation by Samuel S. Wyer, conservation chief of the US Fuel Administration, noted that 43 percent of Pennsylvania's gas consumption was imported from other states, largely West Virginia; that fewer new wells were being drilled; that the reserve of gas lands were declining; that 72 percent of the state's consumption was used by industry, but that domestic demand was growing; and that costs for all gas services were rising.[25]

Reduced production was not the only cause of the crisis. The natural gas industry was well known for its wasteful practices. Wells were drilled and gas erupted, but weeks of delay could occur before the wells were connected to pipelines or plugged. Pipelines often leaked badly. Both manufacturers and household appliances used gas inefficiently. Standpipes illuminated towns and cities with light throughout the night, and open flame or flambeaux torches were common. In its initial decades gas for domestic use was often sold at flat rates by fixture, and low rates encouraged unnecessary use. As the Bureau of Mines noted in 1913, the history of the natural gas industry was "an appalling record of incredible waste."[26] A report in 1920 by the state geologist George H. Ashley on the "Future of Natural Gas in Pennsylvania" warned of an uncertain future for natural gas production in Pennsylvania and a need to prevent waste, explore new sources, and balance industrial and domestic needs. By 1920 it appeared that Pennsylvania's natural gas industry was following the path of decline that had been experienced half a century before by its oil producers.[27]

THE ENVIRONMENTAL EFFECTS OF NATURAL GAS

Air Pollution

Like the present, natural gas had both positive effects on air pollution, because it was substituted for coal, and generally unknown negative effects, because of the extensive release of methane. The most dramatic effect of the substitution of natural gas for coal occurred in the period from about 1885 to 1895, especially in the reduction of the number of Pittsburgh's days of heavy smoke. Estimates of the amount of coal displaced by natural gas ranged from six to twenty million tons, with resulting widespread unemployment in the minefields.[28] National as well as local publications applauded the benefits of natural gas and the disappearance of the "black pall-like cloud" that had hung over the city; natural gas, said *Harper's Weekly*, had produced a "peaceful revolution."[29] City boosters lauded the benefits of natural gas and boasted about its "almost incomprehensible quantities" and "inexhaustible" nature.[30]

Unfortunately, declines in supply—and growth in the city industry more generally—led to the return of smoke. And this produced major smoke control efforts by reform groups with allies from the engineering and business communities. After several failed efforts, in 1914 the city council approved the toughest smoke control ordinance to be enacted up to that time. But coal use increased because of the defense effort, and the war increased the smoke burden. It would be several decades until Pittsburgh air became relatively smoke free. Although natural gas would be the primary cause, it was gas provided by pipelines from the Southwest rather than local supplies that provided the clean fuel.[31]

A major concern today relates to methane leakage from well sites, pipelines, and other gas appliances. Today's focus on methane relates to the fact that it is a potent greenhouse gas. Concern in the past related primarily to the fact, as the 1927 *Natural Gas Handbook* noted, "gas leaking into the atmosphere mean[s] a continual loss in money," although as recorded earlier, gas explosions were also an issue.[32] Leakage from site operations occurred because of excessive blowing of water from a well, from irregular or too rapid lowering of rock pressure because of rapid production, and from the waste of gas in order to secure oil from a well. According to one expert writing in 1919: "This is the principal cause of the depletion of many gas fields, and is responsible for a greater volume of gas waste than probably all other causes put together." One study of West Virginia oil wells showed that the amount of natural gas wasted from the state's more than sixteen thousand oil wells was an amount "equivalent to about one-third of all the natural gas used for domestic consumption in the United States."[33] In addition to the waste from wells, considerable leakage occurred along pipelines. The Bureau of Mines conducted numerous studies of pipeline leakage, and summaries of their findings can be found in their reports in natural gas publications.[34]

Leakage has also proved a serious problem in natural gas fields located near or even in residential areas. One of the most famous cases of problems created by gas leakage from old wells occurred in McKeesport, Pennsylvania, in the post–Second World War period. Between the years from 1919 to 1921, a natural gas boom occurred in what was known as the McKeesport Gas Field, drawing from the Speechley sandstone at a depth of about three thousand feet. Over a thousand wells were drilled, often on small residential lots. Wildly exaggerated predictions had been made about the extent of the field, but, as state geologists predicted in 1920, its production declined rapidly. Many well bores that were never properly plugged were covered over by structures or filled by landowners. There appears to have been some surface leakage in the 1930s, but the most serious problem occurred after the Second World War when many casings were removed to be sold as scrap metal and methane leaked into structures, creating air pollution and explosion hazards. According to a 2007 study by the National Energy Technology Laboratory: "Abandoned and improperly plugged wellbores appear to be the primary vertical migration pathways for . . . stray hydrocarbon gas" (see Figure 10.2).[35]

Wells were especially dangerous in coal mining areas because methane could leak into the mines and cause explosions. In 1913 the Bureau of Mines held a conference in Pittsburgh that dealt with this issue. The report of the conference warned that leakage from abandoned gas wells had caused many coal mine explosions and suggested a number of regulations in regard to well drilling, abandonment, and plugging to reduce the risk. The report also concluded that "it would be useless to enact laws without a special officer to carry them into effect" and recommended that states create a well inspection department. Surveyors who draw surface maps for coal companies were careful to indicate the presence of gas and oil wells.[36]

Landscape Effects

The extensive drilling that took place in Western Pennsylvania damaged and fragmented the landscape through deforestation and the construction of well pads, roads, pipelines, surface reservoirs and other structures. Between 1880 and 1920 the number of productive wells rose rapidly, reaching almost fifteen thousand in 1917. The total number drilled was higher, because some wells were nonproducing.

The extent of these landscape disturbances in the past was not recorded, but recent US Geological Survey studies have devised a set of landscape metrics using geographical information systems (GIS) and other instruments to understand the dynamics of these disturbed natural systems. Using these studies for counties in southwestern Pennsylvania, we can get a general sense of its likely historical magnitude. In Allegheny County between 2004 and 2010, conventional (non-Marcellus) wells took up 0.4 hectares per site, and the disturbed hectares were 0.7 per site. Further, each well was associated with 0.3 kilometers of road. In Washington County, which is also in Western Pennsylvania and was an early producer, wells took up 0.8 hectares, disturbed 2.0 hectares, and were associated with 0.3 km of road.

FIG. 10.2 The McKeesport Natural Gas Boom, 1919 (courtesy of the McKeesport Historical Society).

There were 17,262 wells drilled in Pennsylvania over the period. If the values for Allegheny County are extrapolated to the state, 17,000 acres were used for drilling, 30,000 acres were disturbed and 3,100 miles of road were constructed from 2004 to 2010. If the values for Washington County are extrapolated to the state, 34,000 acres were used for drilling and 85,000 acres were disturbed. Even these numbers may be conservative. By 1917 gas companies controlled 2.5 million acres in Pennsylvania through lease and outright ownership and their impact may have extended well beyond the 30,000–85,000 acres suggested by modern studies.

Surface and Water Well Pollution

The reports of the Department of Health and Sanitary Water Board (1923–1971) note various complaints about gas and oil pollution of water supplies from runoff from drilling sites.[37] In 1906, for instance, the Clarion Water Company in Clarion County complained that the development of natural gas and oil wells in the watershed had polluted the sources of water from which they supplied the town and asked for permission to extend their water gathering area to a clean source. The DOH investigated, finding the company's supplies indeed to be polluted and "prejudicial to the public health." The department reported that the "waste material produced in the operation of drilling the wells, in shooting them, and in cleaning them out, is deposited on the surface of the ground round about and eventually gets into the main stream of the water supply." The DOH ordered the water company to either filter the water or find a new source. It also ordered the company not to allow any gas or oil drilling on its lands and to regularly inspect the wells in the vicinity of the borough in order to prevent salt water from the wells to contaminate water supplies.[38]

In addition to state enforcement of the statutes relating to natural gas and oil statutes, the courts considered nuisance cases generated by gas and oil pollution of private drinking water wells. In an 1890 case the State Supreme Court affirmed damages against a natural gas company for permitting salt water to contaminate a private drinking water well because of inadequate casing, noting that, "when the salt water is allowed to mingle with the fresh, it will spoil the whole neighborhood."[39] Other pollution cases of private wells appear to have been settled out of court by the gas companies. The Pew Papers at the Hagley Museum and Library, for instance, contain several letters to Joseph N. Pew, president of the People's Natural Gas Company, from attorneys representing clients complaining of injuries to their water supplies and livestock from gas well leaks and pipe lines. These complaints appear to be have been settled.[40] The Peoples Natural Gas Company was aware that problems ensuing from poor casing could cause water pollution. It required that contractors insure that casing be inspected and if water was found "the well . . . be thoroughly drained and sand pumped until all drillings and sediments are removed."[41] It is unknown, however, if other gas companies and especially, smaller and fly-by-night drillers, followed the regulations.

Many wells that were drilled came in dry, were quickly exhausted, or were overwhelmed by water within a short time. Gas experts and engineers were aware that unless wells were plugged they could become conduits for brine and water that would overwhelm neighboring wells and pollute nearby surface waters and groundwater. The 1885 state Natural Gas Act had a requirement that wells be plugged after the gas was exhausted, but the law was poorly enforced, if enforced at all. In 1891 the state legislature again passed an act requiring the plugging of wells that were abandoned or not operating. Especially interesting is the environmental focus of the plugging requirement—plugging was required "in such manner as to prevent water from any such well injuring or polluting any spring, water well or stream which is or may be used for the purposes aforesaid." Violation of the act was made a misdemeanor.[42]

The drilling of gas wells and their abandonment also polluted water bodies and threatened surface waters and other gas and oil reservoirs.[43] The threat that these wells posed to both water quality and to other producing

NOVEMBER 7, 1885. HARPER'S WEEKLY. 733

OUTLET OF A NATURAL GAS WELL, NEAR PITTSBURGH.—DRAWN BY W. P. SNYDER.—[SEE PAGE 731.]

FIG. 10.3 "A Pittsburgh Standpipe, 1885" (*Harper's Weekly*, "Outlet of a Natural Gas Well Near Pittsburgh," November 7, 1885).

wells was reflected in a series of statutes passed by the Pennsylvania legislature in the late nineteenth century and after, requiring operators to plug their wells when they ceased to be productive. The 1885 state Natural Gas Act, as noted, included specific regulations concerning the plugging of abandoned wells. In 1891, also as previously noted, the legislature passed new regulations with an environmental focus requiring that abandoned wells be plugged in order to "prevent the pollution of springs, water wells and streams by water escaping from abandoned oil wells and gas wells." Violators of the law were guilty of a misdemeanor and required to pay fines of up to $1,000 or face up to six months imprisonment. A 1921 Act provided more specific information about the manner to which wells were to be plugged and existing wells protected from water entering the gas strata from new well drilling.[44] The legislature's passage of the laws reflects an awareness of the environmental problems these wells posed and the need for conservation, but enforcement appears to have been inconsistent or even nonexistent.

CONCLUSIONS

The Pittsburgh region's first natural gas boom and its environmental effects from approximately 1878 to 1920 have been the focus here. Although they occurred about a century ago, the developments in this period are analogous in many ways to those in the current Marcellus Shale natural gas boom. During the earlier period there was uncertainty and overoptimism about the extent of the gas deposit, concern about the risks and hazards from gas use, the passage of municipal and state legislation regarding natural gas, and issues regarding local versus state authority.

There are also close similarities in regard to environmental effects. Landscape impacts from well pads, roads, and pipelines were extensive although at this point their full extent is not known. In regard to water pollution, while the record is fragmentary, it still indicates that drilling had substantial polluting effects on both surface water and groundwater. The passage of legislation in 1891 aimed at such pollution is further evidence of its existence. Concern over abandoned wells and the necessity to plug them adequately was recognized as early as 1885 and was reiterated in later state legislation. The potential danger of these wells to other gas wells, to coal mines, and to methane leakage is a matter of serious concern today as it was a century ago.

From the public and legislative discussions going on today regarding the Marcellus Shale boom, its effects, and the proper means of regulating them, it is clear that little attention has been paid to lessons that could be learned from the historical record. The development of natural gas, like coal, had marked environmental impacts at its points of production and distribution in its first period of development. Attention to the past record, therefore, can help Pennsylvania avoid another legacy of environmental damage.

APPENDIX 10.1

Aspects of Natural Gas Production, 1880–1920

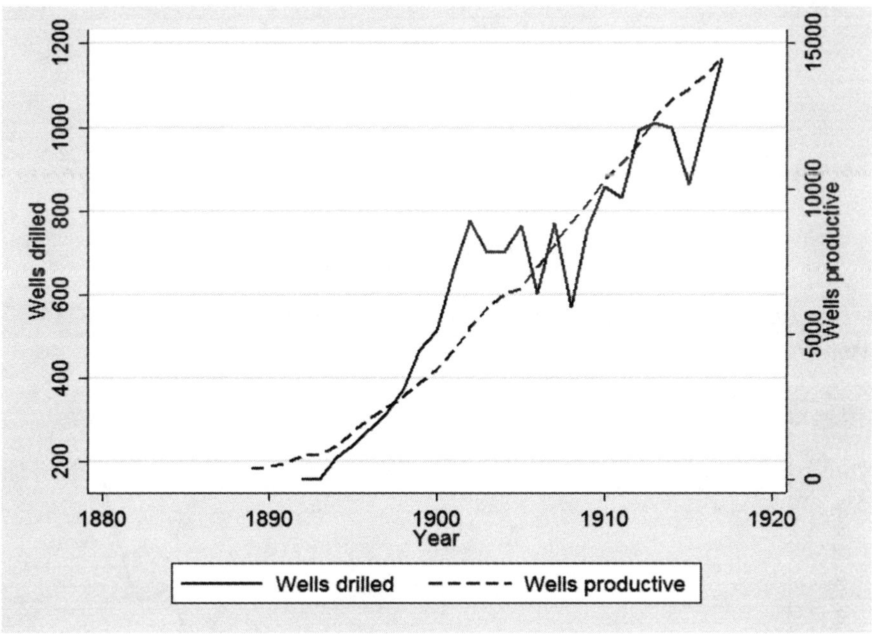

Chart 10.1 The number of wells drilled and the number of productive wells in the state, 1880–1920. The number of productive wells rose rapidly, reaching almost fifteen thousand in 1917. Roughly 20–25 percent were dry or otherwise unproductive (USGS, *Mineral Resources of the U.S.*).

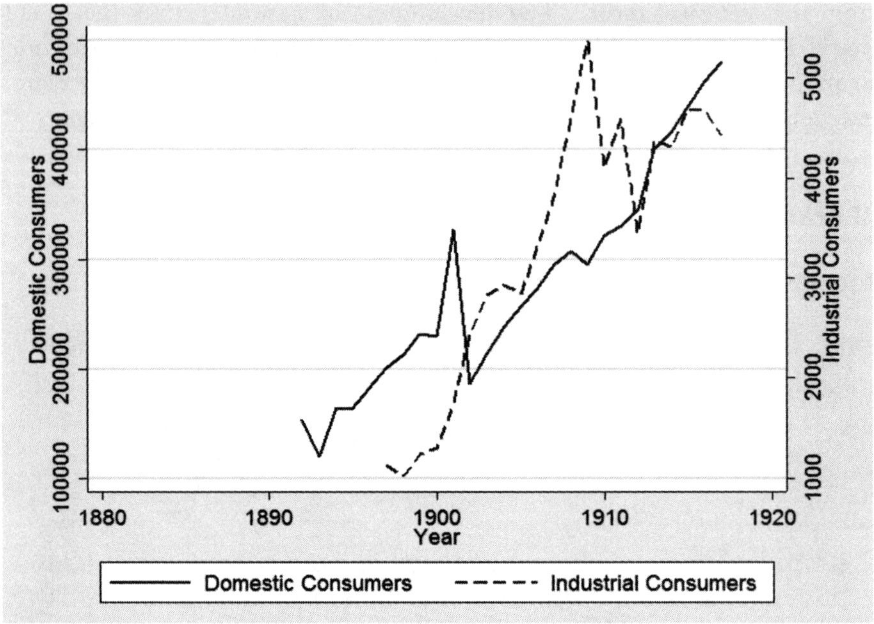

CHART 10.2 Domestic and industrial natural gas customers, 1890–1917 (USGS, *Mineral Resources of the U.S.*).

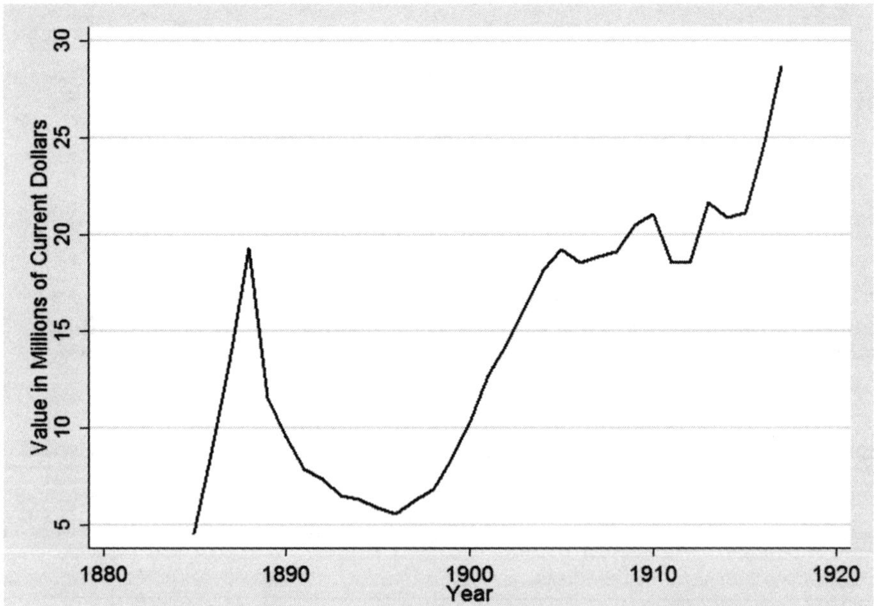

CHART 10.3 The value of gas produced in Pennsylvania from 1885 to 1917. The value is measured by the price at which retail and industrial consumption occurred. (USGS, *Mineral Resources of the U.S.*).

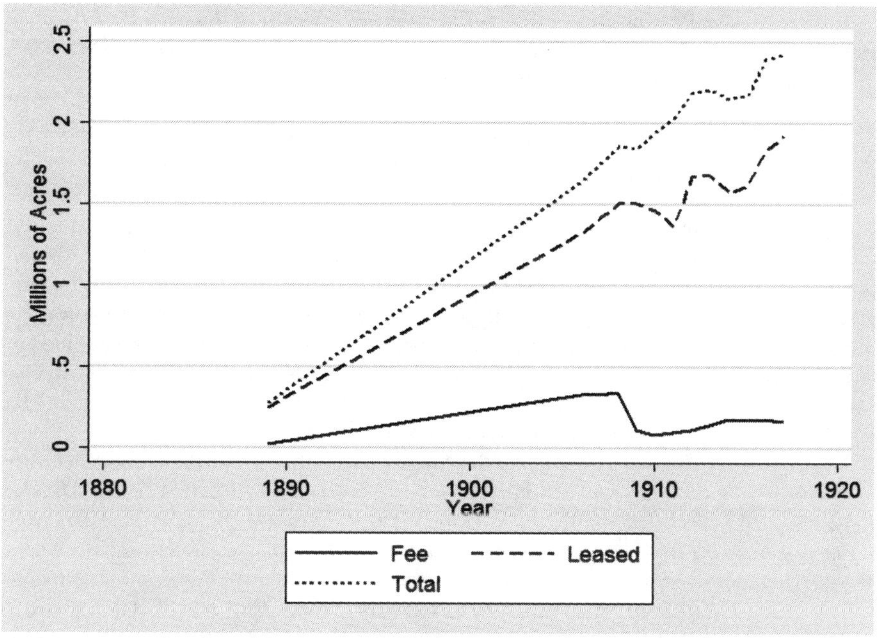

CHART 10.4 The number of acres controlled by gas producers. The vast majority of acres were leased, not owned by gas companies in fee (USGS, *Mineral Resources of the U.S.*).

NOTES

This essay was originally published as "Boom and Bust in Pittsburgh Natural Gas History: Development, Policy, and Environmental Effects, 1878–1920," *Pennsylvania Magazine of History and Biography* 139 no. 3 (October 2015): 321–40, and reprinted with permission.

Research for this paper was generously supported by the Carnegie Mellon Steinbrenner Institute for Environmental Education and Research.

1. John B. Pearse and Franklin Platt, "A Report on the Use of Natural Gas in the Iron Manufacture," in *Special Report on the Coke Manufacture of the Youghiogheny River Valley in Fayette and Westmoreland Counties, Second Geological Survey of Pennsylvania, 1875* (Harrisburg, 1876), 183–84.

2. *Annual Report of the Geological Survey of Pennsylvania for 1886, Part 2: Oil and Gas Region* (Harrisburg, 1887), 603–4.

3. Pipelines were forced to follow a winding route, "due to the hostility of the farmers, who, fearing conflagrations, refused the right of way, and compelled the location of the line along the township roads." *Pennsylvania Geological Report, 1876*, 183.

4. Pearse and Platt, "Natural Gas in the Iron Manufacture," 161–216; George B. Hill & Company, *Pittsburgh: Its Commerce and Industries, and the Natural Gas Interest* (Pittsburgh, 1887), 8–9. The use of gas at the Edgar Thompson Works resulted in the reduction of four hundred tons of coal a day. *Geological Survey for 1886*, 676.

5. See "Glass: Pittsburgh as a Center," in *Engineers' Society of Western Pennsylvania, Pittsburgh* (Pittsburgh, 1930), 365–74; US Bureau of Mines, *Mineral Resources, 1883–1884*, 242 (hereafter cited as *Mineral Resources* with date).

6. Andrew Carnegie, "The Natural Oil and Gas Wells of Western Pennsylvania," in *The Empire of Business* (1902), 264–80; *Geological Survey of Pennsylvania, 1889*, 16; George H. Thurston, *Allegheny County's Hundred Years* (Pittsburgh, 1888), 205.

7. *Mineral Resources, 1883–1884*, 239; *Pennsylvania Geological Survey, 1886*, 674–75. The Fuel Gas Company had been incorporated for the purpose of "supplying heat to the public from gas," originally thought to be coal gas although the company soon shifted to providing natural gas. The Penn Fuel Company was chartered a month later "for the purpose of supplying heat to the public within the city of Pittsburgh by means of natural gas conveyed from such adjoining counties as may be convenient." The two firms combined in late 1884. See "A Natural Gas Deal," *Milwaukee Sentinel*, November 19, 1884, 2. A further firm, the Chartiers Valley Gas Company, was organized on July 31, 1883, also receiving its charter under the Pennsylvania Corporation Act of 1874.

8. James H. Reed, "Pittsburgh and the Natural Gas Industry," in Pittsburgh Chamber of Commerce, *Pittsburgh and the Pittsburgh Spirit* (Pittsburgh, 1928), 127–29; *Mineral Resources, 1883–1884*, 238–40; David A. Waples, *The Natural Gas Industry in Appalachia: A History from the First Discovery to the Maturity of the Industry* (Jefferson, NC, 2005), 48–49.

9. *Annual Report of the Philadelphia Company, 1886–1887*, 16–17. For the early growth of the Philadelphia Company, see George H. Thurston, *Pittsburgh's Progress, Industries and Resources* (Pittsburg, 1886), 13. Thurston claimed that by the late 1880s 3,000 families, 34 iron and steel mills, 60 glass factories and 300 small factories and hotel used natural gas. Stanley Paul Wagner, "Natural Gas comes to Pittsburgh" (masters thesis, University of Pittsburgh, 1947), 50–56.

10. For a full list of Westinghouse's natural gas patents, see Henry G. Prout, *A Life of George Westinghouse* (New York, 1921), 362–65.

11. "Gas Pipes," *Pittsburgh Post*, August 8, 1884. This article quotes the Westinghouse patent language. There is a description of the Westinghouse two-pipe system in *Mineral Resources, 1886*, 193–94.

12. The Westinghouse ordinances are in the "Appendix," Court of Common Pleas No. 2 of Allegheny County, *The Peoples Natural Gas Co. v. the City of Pittsburgh*, no. 438, January 1886, 357–60.

13. Quoted in Wagner, "Natural Gas Comes to Pittsburgh," 42.

14. The commission's findings are discussed in Court of Common Pleas, *The Peoples Natural Gas Co. v. The City of Pittsburgh*, no. 438, January Term, 1886, 309–19; Wagner, "Natural Gas Comes to Pittsburgh," 45–47.

15. See, for instance, *Pittsburgh Daily Post*, March 6, 1885; *National Labor Times*, May 15, 1886.

16. *A Digest of the Acts of Assembly Relating to, and The General Ordinances of the City of Pittsburgh 1804 to Sept. 1, 1886* (Harrisburg, 1887), 369–75. Discussions of the ordinances can be found in Court of Common Pleas No. 2 of Allegheny County, *The People's Natural Gas Co. v. the City of Pittsburgh*, no. 438, January 1886, and "History of the Case" in *Appeal of City of Pittsburgh*, Pennsylvania Supreme Court, November 11, 1886, 3–5.

17. *Emerson and the Penn Fuel Company v. Attorney General*, Pennsylvania Supreme Court, *Weekly Notes of Cases*, vol. 15, no. 27, February 12, 1885, 425–31.

18. "Natural Gas," *Daily Legislative Record*, February 3, 1885, 142–43, February 4, 1885, 166, 170, February 23, 1885, 311. On the same day the senate approved a bill to prohibit damage to "oil, gas or water wells, tanks, pipes and machinery connected therewith" and to impose a fine or imprisonment if the perpetrator was found guilty.

19. "An Act to Provide for the Incorporation and Regulation of Natural Gas Companies," *Laws of Pennsylvania, Session of 1885*, 29–37.

20. *The People's Natural Gas Co. v. the City of Pittsburgh*, Court of Common Pleas No. 2 of Allegheny County, no. 438, January term, 1886.

21. See W. W. Thomson, *A Digest of the Acts of Assembly Relating to the General Ordinances of the City of Pittsburgh from 1804–1886* (Harrisburg, 1887), 369–725; Hiram Schock, comp. and ed., *Digest of the General Ordinances and Laws of the City of Pittsburgh to March 1, 1938* (Pittsburgh: The City, 1938), 728–37; see n. 1, 729, for the voiding of parts of the 1885 ordinance by the courts.

22. *Mineral Resources, 1883–1884*, 239–41; *Mineral Resources, 1884–1885*, 172–73; *Geological Survey, 1886*, 692–94; *Geological Survey, 1889*, 20–21.

23. *Mineral Resources, 1883–1884*, 241; *Mineral Resources, 1888*, 486; *Geological Survey, 1886*, 692–94.

24. *Annual Report of the Philadelphia Company, 1885–1886* (Pittsburgh, 1886); George H. Thurston, *Allegheny County's Hundred Years* (Pittsburgh, 1888), 207.

25. Samuel S. Wyer, *Present and Prospective Supply of Natural Gas Available in Pennsylvania* (Washington, DC, December 28, 1918), 3–4.

26. Samuel S. Wyer, *Natural Gas: Its Production, Service, and Conservation*, Bulletin no. 102, part 7, Smithsonian Institution (Washington, DC: GPO, 1918), 52–57.

27. George H. Ashley, "Future of Natural Gas in Pennsylvania," Bulletin no. 17, Bureau of Topographic and Geological Survey, December 18, 1920.

28. *Mineral Resources, 1888*, 482–83, E. V. d'Invilliers, *Report on the Pittsburgh Coal Region*, 18–19; "Natural Gas vs. Coal at Pittsburg [*sic*]," *National Labor Tribune*, July 24, 1886.

29. "The City of Pittsburg [*sic*]," *Harper's Weekly* 36 (February 27, 1892): 202–3.

30. See, for instance, Thurston, *Pittsburgh's Progress*, 6–8, published in 1886, where he repeats and reiterates optimistic comments about gas supply he originally made in 1876,and Thurston, *Allegheny County's Hundred Years* (Pittsburgh: 1888), 92–95, 202–9.

31. Tarr, *Ultimate Sink*, 241.

32. John C. Diehl, *Natural Gas Handbook* (Erie, Pennsylvania, 1927), 330.

33. Wyer, *Natural Gas*, 53–54.

34. See section on "Leakage," in Diehl, *Natural Gas Handbook*, 330–41.

35. National Energy Technology Laboratory, *Methane Emissions Project Borough of Versailles, Pennsylvania, Executive Summary*, Pittsburgh, October 31, 2007, 1–2. The McKeesport boom actually covered a much larger area than Versailles, but methane leakage appears to have been not as problematic since the wells were more distant from each other. For the state geologist's perspective on the boom, see George H. Ashley, *The McKeesport Gas Boom, Allegheny County, Pennsylvania*, Bulletin no. 5, 2nd ed., January 12, 1920.

36. George S. Rice, O. P. Hood, et al., *Oil and Gas Wells through Workable Coal Beds*, Bureau of Mines Bulletin no. 65, *Petroleum Technology* 7 (Washington, DC, 1913). The Consol Energy Collection at the University of Pittsburgh Archives Center contains many maps drawn by surveyors of surface conditions including gas and oil wells above coal mines.

37. For the history of the Sanitary Water Board, see http://www.portal.state.pa.us/portal/server.pt?open=514&objID=588469&mode=2. Issues.

38. See *Second Report of the Commissioner of Health* (Harrisburg, 1908), 486–88. Google Books, at com/books/about/Report.html?id=0xdNAAAAMAAJ, accessed November 10, 2011.

39. *Nannie R. Collins v. Chartiers Valley Gas Co.* 139 Pa. 111 (1890–1891).

40. J. M. T Carpenter to J. N. Pew, November 17, 1892, Pew Papers, Hagley Museum and Library, Wilmington, Delaware, E.T. Bouser to the Peoples Natural Gas company, July 19, 1900, E. Robbins to Peoples Natural Gas Company, November 22, 1894, Pew Papers, and Moorhead and Head, to Peoples Natural Gas Company, May 19, 1899, Pew Papers. The Pew papers also contain a "Proposal and Specifications for Drilling Wells, dated July 22, 1901.

41. The Peoples Natural Gas Company, "Proposal and Specifications for Drilling Wells," July 22, 1901, Pew Papers.

42. "An Act To prevent the pollution of springs, water wells and streams by water escaping from abandoned oil wells and gas wells," Act 114, *Laws of Pennsylvania* (May 26, 1891), 122–23.

43. *Second Annual Report of the Commissioner of Health* (Harrisburg, 1908), 486–89.

44. See An Act No. 80, *Session of 1878*, 57 (plugging oil wells); An Act No. 122, *Session of 1881*, 110–11 (plugging abandoned oil wells); An Act No. 54, *Session of 1883*, 61–65 (oil pipeline regulations); An Act No. 32, ibid, Session of 1885, 29–37 (act for the incorporation and regulation of natural gas companies); An Act No. 114, ibid, Session of 1885, 145–46 (an act to protect oil, gas and water wells); An Act No. 199, ibid., Session of 1887, 310–13 (right of gas companies to eminent domain); An Act 114, ibid, Session of 1891, 122–23 (an "Act to Prevent the Pollution of Springs, Water Wells and Streams by Water from Abandoned Oil and Gas Wells"); An Act No. 322, Session of 1921, 912–14 ("An act to Regulate the Drilling, Operating, and Abandoning of oil and Gas Wells"); all in *Laws of Pennsylvania.* See also Blakeley M. Murphy, ed., *Conservation of Oil & Gas: A Legal History, 1948* (Chicago: American Bar Association, 1949), 429–35, for a discussion of numerous attempts to enact legislation regarding the conservation of natural gas in Pennsylvania.

11 SEARCHING FOR A SINK FOR AN INDUSTRIAL WASTE

IRON-MAKING FUELS AND THE ENVIRONMENT

Joel A. Tarr

The creation of wastes from any process, be it a natural, consumer, or production process, requires location of a place of deposit or a "sink" for disposal. Much of the history of industrial waste disposal, as well as the disposal of wastes from other sources such as an urban population, involves the search for a "sink" in which wastes could be disposed of in the cheapest and most convenient manner possible.[1] Often, however, such sinks proved only temporary, and substances placed in them created severe pollution, interacted with other substances to produce serious nuisance and health consequences, or leaked out and migrated into other media. Society reacted against such pollution problems in various ways, depending upon the severity of the problem, the existence of a technological means to reduce or control the pollution, the prevailing legal and legislative norms relating to the environment, and the existence and availability of other possible sinks. Often, action or policy intended to remove a polluting waste from one environmental sink resulted in its deposition in another sink.

Several pollution problems and environmental damages result from the production of fuel to be used in the smelting of iron. In the United States iron makers first used charcoal as a metallurgical fuel in their furnaces but began switching to mineral fuels in the 1830s and 1840s. Anthracite coal was used initially, but in the post–Civil War decades iron and steel manufacturers increasingly replaced anthracite with coke—the solid residue of almost pure carbon that is left when heat is used to drive out the volatile matter from bituminous coal. By 1911 coke fueled the smelting of 98 percent of the nation's pig iron. From about the 1850s through the First World War, the technology used to produce coke was the beehive oven, but after that date there was a rapid transition to the by-product coke oven, the technology in use today.

All processes for the making of fuels for iron manufacturing were (and are) polluting to a degree, but changes in the technology and in its location resulted in significant differences in the environments and populations affected. The transition from the beehive to the by-product oven and the resultant shift in location of much of the nation's coke-making facilities from rural to urban sites was a change that moved the pollution burden to different environmental media and which resulted in the harming of drinking water quality in a number of metropolitan areas. Different policy options were followed by government and the courts at a time when industrial waste disposal was of limited public concern.

IRON-MAKING FUELS BEFORE COKE

Mineral fuel, in either the form of anthracite or bituminous coal, did not become important in the making of iron and steel in the United States until the mid-nineteenth century. Before this time the fuel most commonly used was charcoal, an ideal furnace fuel because it was relatively free from sulphur and phosphorus impurities and because its ash furnished part of the flux required to smelt the ore. Charcoal manufacture usually took place on what was called an iron plantation, a large forested tract of land that also contained an iron furnace, a charcoal "pit" or "hearth," casting beds, and workers' housing. On the plantation, bundles of cordwood in six to ten feet lengths were stacked in a cone with a base measuring about twenty-five feet in diameter, covered with damp leaves and turf, and burned for between three and ten days. No attempt was made to condense any of the by-product wood chemicals vented from the stack during the charcoaling process.[2]

Charcoal production had major environmental effects both because of the amount of timber consumed and because it involved the slow burning of wood with no emissions control. The geographer Michael Williams estimates that it took 150 acres of woodland to produce 1,000 tons of pig iron, the annual output of an average iron furnace. Plantations ranged in size from the 3,000 acres of woodland usually required for a profitable iron plantation to more than 10,000 acres. In 1862, a year of low production, 25,000 acres were cleared, while in the peak year of charcoal-iron production, 1890, 94,000 acres (147 square miles) were cleared. While timber harvested for iron production constituted only 1.3 percent of the land cleared for agriculture, it was heavily concentrated in certain states such as Ohio, Pennsylvania, and West Virginia.[3]

In addition to forest depletion, the charring process produced severe local air pollution effects. While the timber was being charred, the smoking piles of wood covered with wet leaves gave off a dark heavy smoke with a disagreeable odor that gathered over the stream valleys where the operations of the iron plantations were often located. Many Pennsylvania boroughs passed ordinances prohibiting charcoal manufacture within town limits. The iron furnaces themselves were also heavy polluters, as the opening at the top of the furnace permitted heat, smoke, and carbon monoxide to escape creating great clouds of smoke and fumes.[4]

As technological improvements that improved productivity were gradually made in both charcoal-making and iron furnaces during the course of the nineteenth century, growing demand for iron depleted conveniently located timber supplies. Beginning in the 1830s, however, the pressure on fuel supply was relieved by the increasing substitution of anthracite coal for charcoal. Anthracite possessed almost pure carbon content and burned with a small blue flame that produced intense heat and little smoke. A ton of anthracite was equal in heat energy to two hundred bushels of charcoal, giving it a strong cost advantage. The primary deposits of anthracite were in the rugged mountainous areas of northeastern Pennsylvania, making access difficult, but in the 1830s the construction of three major coal canals sharply reduced the cost of transportation and permitted large-scale production.[5]

Iron makers had seldom used anthracite in their blast furnaces before the 1830s because the fuel was difficult to ignite. In the middle of that decade, however, it was discovered that the "hot blast," an innovation developed in Great Britain in 1828 for use in charcoal furnaces, facilitated the use of anthracite as a fuel. Anthracite had greater strength than charcoal and could be burned in larger furnaces with higher thermal efficiency. Furnaces utilizing the mineral fuel sprang up along the established coal trade routes close to urban areas, with the Lehigh Valley of Pennsylvania becoming the center of the anthracite iron industry. By 1853 there were 121 anthracite blast furnaces in eastern Pennsylvania, the nation's center of iron manufacture.[6]

From the 1850s until the end of 1870s, anthracite served as the dominant fuel in the making of iron. The shift to anthracite from charcoal partially shifted the environmental burden of providing fuel for iron making from the forests to the coal-bearing lands of eastern Pennsylvania.[7] But although anthracite retained its position as a desirable fuel in manufacturing and in domestic heating until the middle of the twentieth century, its importance in the iron-making industry was relatively short-lived. In 1852 the railroad crossed the Appalachian Mountains, opening the rich bituminous coalfields of Western Pennsylvania to extensive exploitation and development. In the process, some of the most fertile valleys in Western Pennsylvania were exposed to widespread environmental damages from the mining of coal, the making of coke, and the smelting of iron.

BITUMINOUS COAL AND COKE

The bituminous coal located in the Connellsville fields of Western Pennsylvania (part of the Pittsburgh seam) was the world's richest coking coal—it was the critical factor in making the Pittsburgh region the nation's iron and steel center in the late nineteenth century. "Coking," noted John Fulton in 1895, "is the art of preparing from bituminous or other coal a fuel adapted for metallurgical and other special purposes." It involves using heat to expel volatile matter such as water, sulphur, and hydrocarbons from the coal, leaving a solid residue consisting primarily of fixed carbon, ash, and the non-volatilizable sulphur. The best coking coal was a coal with few impurities such as sulphur or phosphorus, a sufficient proportion of volatile or gaseous matter to supply the necessary heat in coking, and one that would produce a coke with a porous structure and strong physical strength.[8]

Coke was low in cost compared to anthracite and ideal in structure for blast furnace use. It possesses a porous structure that permits it to be burned at a rapid rate and also ample strength at high temperature to carry the burden of the blast furnace charge. These advantages of cost and quality led to coke's rapid displacement of anthracite and charcoal in the iron-making process. In 1854, for instance, charcoal iron composed about 47.5 percent of the nation's total pig iron production, anthracite pig iron 45 percent, and bituminous pig iron 7.5 percent. By 1880, however, the percent of pig iron made with bituminous coal and coke had risen to 45 percent and charcoal had dropped to 13 percent. In 1911 bituminous coal and coke provided the fuel for 98 percent of the pig iron manufactured in the nation, and charcoal had practically disappeared as a source of fuel for the process.[9]

Coke was initially produced following a technique borrowed from charcoal preparation: bituminous coal would be placed in piles or rows about fourteen feet wide on level ground surfaced with coal dust; wood was interspersed to ignite the mass. In the most effective process, the coal was burned slowly in a moist smoldering heat, driving off the sulphur and the hydrocarbon gases and leaving a silvery white coke high in carbon. When the burning of the gaseous matter had ceased, the heap was smothered with a coating of dust or duff, followed by application of a small quantity of water. No attempt was made to capture any of the escaping gases. The time necessary for coking a heap was usually between five and eight days, with a yield of approximately 59 percent of coke.[10]

The so-called beehive coke oven manufactured most of the coke produced in the nation from about 1850 to 1920. These ovens were first constructed in the 1850s in Western Pennsylvania, and by the late nineteenth century most coke makers had adopted the technology. The oven consisted of a circular domelike chamber, lined with firebrick and with a tiled floor. Although there were improvements in oven design over the years, changes were relatively minor. The ovens were first preheated by a wood and coal fire and then charged with coal from a car (a "Larry") running on tracks above the oven. The coke was leveled by hand with a scraper and the front opening bricked up with clay, with a two- or three-inch opening at the top. The coking process proceeded from the top downward, with the burning of the volatile by-products escaping from the coal producing the required heat. The coking process was complete when all the volatile material was burned. The brickwork was removed from the door, the coke was cooled by a water spray from a handheld hose and then removed from the oven by hand or by mechanical means. On average, it took about 1.5 tons of high quality bituminous coal "coked" over a period of forty-eight hours to produce a ton of coke, the composition of which was between 85 and 90 percent carbon.[11]

In 1855 there were 106 beehive ovens in the nation; by 1880 the total had increased to over 12,000 ovens in 186 plants; by 1909 there were almost 104,000 ovens in 579 plants, the maximum number ever to exist. Initially almost all of the beehive ovens were located in the Connellsville coke region of western Pennsylvania, and as late as 1918 more than half the country's ovens were still in this area. Beehive ovens were normally arranged in banks of single or double rows, often built into a hillside in order to conserve heat. Normally, they were constructed in banks of about 300, considered the optimum scale for efficient operation. Numerous small operations were scattered over the countryside in coking areas. Some installations, however, were much larger, with between 600 and 900 ovens. The J&L Iron and Steel Company beehive coking plant in the Hazelwood area of Pittsburgh was the world's largest, with 1,510 ovens. The J&L ovens were also unusual in that they were located close to the blast furnaces of an integrated mill, whereas

Fig. 11.1 Beehive coke ovens and workers in Pittsburgh. Coke was produced primarily in beehive coke ovens until well into the twentieth century ("Coke Workers and Their Dwellings at Pittsburgh Coke Ovens," *Harper's Weekly*, July 1, 1888).

FIG. 11.2 Jones & Laughlin Pittsburgh beehive coke works, 2003.

most beehives were sited in proximity to coal deposits in order to reduce transportation costs (see Figure 11.1).[12]

The uncontrolled emissions vented from the beehive ovens had a devastating impact on the nearby environment. The ash, fumes and various hydrocarbons released by the coal distillation process killed and stunted trees and crops within the locale of the ovens and often left a layer of coal dust, ash, and particles on the surrounding fields. Writing in 1900, a Pennsylvania state botanist observed that "the most conspicuous feature in coke oven surroundings is the general wretchedness of everything of the nature of shrub or tree, either individual or collective." In those areas where there were large numbers of ovens scattered over the countryside, he wrote, "the district becomes almost continually one of a highly vitiated air, seldom without the overhanging clouds of smoke."[13] In 1905 and 1906 the US Forest Service, interested in the possibility of reclaiming "waste lands," conducted studies at the request of the H. C. Frick Coke Company concerning possible reforestation of some of their Western Pennsylvania lands. These studies, both performed by Samuel N. Spring, a graduate of the Yale forestry program, emphasized the extreme effect of the "sulphur smoke" from the coke ovens on vegetation around the ovens and on vegetation on hills some distance downwind of the ovens (see Figure 11.2).

"Cloud by day and fire by night" was the phrase often used to characterize the coke region. But while the damage from the sulfurous fumes did the most environmental damage, solid wastes from the coking process also caused injuries. Coke oven operators often dumped materials such as coal wastes and ashes into nearby creeks, damming their flow, causing flooding, and undoubtedly damaging stream ecology. Local courts heard several cases in the early twentieth century brought by farmers suing for damages because their lands had been damaged by flooding and the silting up of bottomlands caused by the dumping of coking wastes.[14]

In several cases in the late nineteenth and early twentieth centuries Pennsylvania courts held that beehive coke plants, like other manufacturing firms, were liable for damages caused by their operations. In these cases the courts made a clear differentiation between responsibility for injuries from coking operations and those resulting (as they held in the *Sanderson* cases of the 1880s) from the "natural and necessary result of the development of his own land by the owner." Since the manufacture of coke was not the "natural and necessary use" of property, even on coal lands, individuals whose property was injured by such operations were entitled to compensation.[15]

But although judges might award damages, they seldom issued injunctions that would close down a firm's operations. Rather, they usually performed a rough type of cost-benefit analysis that Christine Rosen has called "private" or "social cost" balancing. In such a situation, judges weighed the benefits the victims would receive from an abatement of pollution with the economic injury either the firm (in private balancing) or society (with social cost balancing) would suffer if the court required the polluter to reduce its pollution.[16] Invariably, in late nineteenth-century Pennsylvania, the courts found the projected costs to society of an injunction to be too high, even though they awarded compensation for property damages to individuals. These awards, however, were usually relatively small since most coking operations were in rural areas, and the cost of damages to surrounding farmers were minor compared to the potential cost of pollution-control equipment such as tall stacks.

Because of the heavy pollution produced by beehive ovens, cities were reluctant to allow them to operate within their boundaries. In 1869, for instance, a Pittsburgh ordinance forbade the construction of coke ovens within the city limits and assessed a penalty of one hundred dollars per day for operating an oven. The ordinance, however, was probably not enforced, since the 1884 Sanborn maps for Pittsburgh show well over a hundred coke ovens within the city boundaries. In 1892 the city revised its policy and enacted a new ordinance permitting coke oven construction if the ovens were supplied with "smoke control devices" approved by the chief of the Department of Public Safety. The Jones & Laughlin Steel beehive oven plant in Hazelwood (constructed between 1899 and 1907), for instance, was fitted with tall stacks to burn and disperse the oven gases and smoke away from nearby residential areas.[17]

While these stacks undoubtedly reduced the emissions flow compared to the average beehive oven, the pollution was still substantial. In 1914 the Mellon Institute "Smoke Investigation of Pittsburgh" reported that coke ovens located in the Pittsburgh district (but not specifically naming J&L) smoked "almost constantly, although the smoke . . . is no denser than 60 percent black," a figure probably derived from the smoke measurement device known as the Ringlemann Chart. Although by today's standards this would be considered very substantial air pollution, the level was not unusual for industrial emissions in Pittsburgh in the first decade of the twentieth century. The city passed several smoke control ordinances in this period, but either they exempted iron and steel mills or they were unenforceable. Court records show no lawsuits that specifically referred to the urban coke operations.[18]

Another drawback of the beehive process was the waste of the valuable coal by-products that were vented during coking. For instance, in 1910, the maximum year for beehive production, 53 million tons of coal were processed into coke. One study suggests that this amount of coal had the potential of producing approximately 530 billion cubic feet of gas, 400 million gallons of coal tar, nearly 150 million gallons of light oils, and 600,000 tons of ammonium sulfate. A few attempts were made to construct beehive ovens in which the by-products could be captured, but engineers had little success except in regard to waste heat. Even if the by-products were recovered, aside from the coal gas, few markets existed in the United States in the late nineteenth century for other coal distillation by-products.[19]

In addition to wasting valuable by-products, the beehive oven had other disadvantages as a production technology. Most important was that it required very high quality bituminous coal in order to produce good coke, and it was a difficult technology with which to achieve scale economies. The beehive's principal advantage over alternatives was its low cost and ease of construction and operation. As long as high quality bituminous supplies existed and markets for coal distillation by-products were limited, there was little incentive to alter the technology.

The primary alternative coke-making technology to the beehive oven at the turn of the century was the retort or by-product oven, developed by Belgian, French, and German engineers because of the absence of good coking coal in Europe. The by-product or retort oven was a narrow slot oven constructed in batteries in which coking chambers alternated with heating

FIG. 11.3 Clairton works smoke plume. The by-product coke industry has been a major cause of polluted air in the region since its inception (photograph by Joel A. Tarr).

chambers. Coal was charged through openings in the top of the oven and the coke pushed out by a power-driven ram at the end of the combustion process, to be quenched outside the oven. The gas evolving from the coal supplied the heat required for distillation and was also used for other purposes throughout the mill.[20]

The by-product oven had the advantage of capturing the volatile elements freed by the coking process. The yield of by-products was determined by the quality and quantity of coke desired. The freed gases were collected by a system of pipes at the top of the oven and then cooled, resulting in condensation of tar and water vapor into a liquid of about 70 percent tar and 30 percent of ammonia in water. The ammonia underwent further separation at a still and was eventually transformed into various ammonium compounds. Other by-products from the coking process included benzene, toluene, naphtha, and xylene. Because it salvaged useful materials that might otherwise be wasted, one engineer observed that the by-product oven was "a part of the movement for the conservation of our natural resources," an interesting attempt to place this development in industrial technology in the conservation movement of the early twentieth century (see Figure 11.3).[21]

The by-product oven had several other advantages over the beehive oven in addition to capturing the coal distillation products: it could produce high grade coke using blends of various qualities of coal; it produced a higher coke yield per ton of coal (average of 70 percent compared to 64.5 percent); and it provided for more rapid coking. But the technology also had serious disadvantages. One involved the concern of pig-iron furnace men that by-product coke, because of its smaller size and dull black color, was actually inferior to the silvery beehive coke. The second, and probably the most critical, was the high capital and operating costs involved in producing by-product coke. Markets for by-products could, in principle, make up some of this differential, but the United States were largely without a well-developed chemical industry capable of utilizing coal distillation products such as tar, ammonia, and benzene. Coal tar products produced in Germany dominated the American markets. These factors, plus the availability of large supplies of superior coking coal, retarded the technology's widespread adoption in this country.[22]

Coal, iron, and steel firms did construct several by-product ovens at the beginning of the century, transferring and adopting different versions of the European technology, but more rapid development did not occur until after 1914. One important factor stimulating change was the discovery by US Steel that coke oven gas and tar could produce important fuel efficiencies in the integrated steel mills. In addition, the cutting-off of organic chemical supplies from Germany by the war provided an especially strong impetus for rapid development. Faced by the loss of synthetic dyes, drugs, and solvents, as well as benzene, toluene, and phenols for the production of explosives, the United States had to rapidly create a chemical industry largely based on aromatic compounds.[23]

Many by-product plants were constructed to take advantage of the new markets. They were most frequently located at integrated steel mills, where the coke could be used in the blast furnaces and the gas and tar could be used as fuel to provide heat in the iron- and steelworks. In addition, a number of cities, including St. Paul, St. Louis, Baltimore, and Jersey City, began obtaining their municipal gas supplies from by-product ovens. By 1929, in what was a "revolutionary" industrial change, the new technology was supplying 75 percent of the coke manufactured in the United States. Between 1909 and 1940, the number of beehive ovens in the country shrank from nearly 104,000 to about 15,000, located in 75 different plants and consuming 4,802,996 tons of coal. By the same year, the number of by-product ovens had increased to 12,734 in 89 plants, consuming 76,582,780 tons of coal.[24]

THE BY-PRODUCT COKE OVEN AND DRINKING WATER SUPPLIES

By-product coke ovens were customarily located on the banks of rivers or lakes, usually in close proximity to the blast furnaces of an integrated steel mill. The water bodies provided them with the water necessary for their operations, with cheap barge transportation for the coal, and with a place to dispose of their liquid wastes. These locations were usually in or near urban areas, in contrast to the mostly rural locations of the beehive ovens. Although the by-product oven produced fewer air emissions than did the beehive oven, it still had a heavy pollution flow both to the air and to the water. Its wastewater stream, for instance, contained heavy concentrations of ammonia, cyanide, and phenolics, as well as various acid, base, and neutral hydrocarbons. All of these substances could damage stream life and the quality of water supplies, but the phenol-containing effluent stream discharged by the ammonia stills had the most noticeable impact, creating severe taste and odor problems in drinking water. The volumes discharged were extremely large; one chemical engineer estimated in 1923 that by-product coke plants discharged approximately thirty-eight million tons of still wastes in that year.[25]

While phenols would produce obnoxious tastes and odors in any water supply, the effect on drinking water was especially severe if the receiving waters were chlorinated. During the late nineteenth and early twentieth centuries, a number of American cities with centralized water systems attempted to protect their supplies from infectious sewage wastes by adopting filtration technology or chlorinating their supplies. The first successful use of chlorination occurred in 1908, when Jersey City proved the effectiveness of the technique in protecting its water supply from pathogens. A number of other municipalities, also faced by the threat of sewage pollution of their water supplies, adopted the technology. As chlorination spread to various industrialized areas, however, waterworks managers observed that the water supply often developed strong medicinal tastes and odors. This was initially blamed on the chlorine alone, but in 1918 chemists from the Milwaukee Department of Health and the city waterworks determined that the tastes and odors were the result of interaction between the chlorine and the coal-tar wastes.[26]

Cities in the Ohio River Basin were particularly subject to these problems because of their heavy use of chlorine to protect their water supplies (drawn from sewage-polluted rivers) and the concentration of by-product coke ovens in the region. In the mid-1920s, the US Public Health Service (USPHS) identified twenty-five cities in the Ohio River valley where the interaction of chlorine with phenol wastes made the water almost undrinkable. Other cities in different watersheds such as Chicago, Cleveland, Detroit, Milwaukee, Rochester, and Troy also experienced similar problems.[27] In this case, two new technologies had interacted chemically to produce harmful results for drinking water quality.

Aside from the taste and odor nuisances, public health officials worried about the health effects of the phenols in water supply. They had four principal concerns: phenols could injure the health of persons drinking the polluted water; the offensive tastes and odors might discourage individuals from drinking sufficient water for good health; they might drink biologically contaminated water; and, because phenols reacted with chlorine, waterworks managers might reduce the amount of chlorine treatment, thereby increasing the risk of exposure to infectious disease. These fears were highlighted by a typhoid outbreak in 1925 in Ironton, Ohio (eighteen cases, three deaths), which was attributed to the fact that "choloro phenol" tastes in the municipal water supply were so offensive local residents were forced to drink unprotected water.[28]

The focus on the health risks presented by the phenol wastes—rather than upon their injuries to property—represented a shift in concern in regard to pollution from coke manufacture. The emissions from beehive ovens were viewed as producing primarily private property damages that could be compensated for monetarily, but the threat to water supply threatened the public good. Public authorities had several courses of action to choose from, the most available of which, given the absence of specifically applicable state statutory industrial waste regulations, was to use the courts to secure relief under the common law.[29] Here state authority in regard to the police power was a well-established basis for court action to protect the public health.

The most important court action occurred in McKeesport, Pennsylvania, an industrial city of approximately fifty thousand people located at the junction of the Youghiogheny and Monongahela Rivers about fifteen miles above Pittsburgh. From 1881 until 1916, McKeesport obtained its water supply from the Youghiogheny River, but increased pollution by mine acid drainage and other industrial wastes caused the city to shift to the Monongahela River in 1916. Although the Monongahela was also polluted by industrial wastes, its waters required less treatment than those from the Youghiogheny, significantly lowering the city's treatment costs.[30]

Approximately eighteen months after McKeesport had moved to the Monongahela for its supplies, the Carnegie Steel Corporation (a subsidiary of the US Steel Corporation) brought on line the world's largest by-product coke operation, located at Clairton, Pennsylvania. This plant was sited on the banks of the Monongahela River about two miles above the McKeesport water intake and was meant to provide coke for the US Steel integrated steel mills in the Monongahela valley. The plant initially had 768 ovens, each of which had a capacity of 13.2 tons of coal per charge and produced about 9.0 tons of coke. In addition, the plant produced large quantities of coal by-products such as gas, tar, benzene, and ammonium sulphate.[31]

The Carnegie by-product works at Clairton discharged the liquid wastes from their plant through a pipe into Peters Creek, a stream that ran through their property and into the Monongahela River. The city of McKeesport charged that in the river the wastes "permeated" the water and caused "foul" odors and "offensive and nauseating taste" in its water supply. In September 1918, McKeesport sued in the county courts for an injunction to prevent the Carnegie Steel from discharging these polluting wastes, charging that the plant's discharges rendered McKeesport's water "unwholesome, unpalatable and unfit for drinking purposes and domestic uses, as well as injurious to health." The courts, following the well-established precedent that the police power could be used to protect the public health, granted the injunction, observing that the city's "duty to supply its inhabitants reasonably pure and palatable water cannot be questioned; nor can the right of its inhabitants to such quality be injuriously affected by foul and noxious fluids." If it wanted to continue operations, Carnegie Steel would have to find a different means to dispose of the wastes from its by-product coke plant.[32]

The Clairton decision reflected the fact that, by 1918, legal precedent existed under the police power to prevent the pollution of water supplies by industrial wastes if those wastes clearly injured the public health. In the case of by-product coke oven wastes, cause and effect were usually clearly definable and the courts were willing to act. In regard to other industrial wastes, however, cause and effect were less obvious and therefore the courts and municipal and state health authorities were much more reluctant to use the police power to take action.[33]

Another strategy to deal with industrial pollution was to push for new legislation to enlarge the power of state health departments over industrial wastes. In most states, control over water pollution originally rested in the health departments because of the relation between pollution and infectious disease and (aside from in Massachusetts) little attention was paid to industrial pollution in the first decades of the twentieth century. In the 1920s, such pollution increasingly became a matter of concern, and several states enacted legislation to attempt to regulate its discharge. In Pennsylvania, for instance, the legislature established the Sanitary Water Board in 1923 to determine the proper use of streams in the Commonwealth and to control pollution. In 1924 the deputy state attorney general ruled that the Sanitary Water Board had the power to prevent the pollution of public water supplies by industrial wastes (such as phenols) that could cause the public to avoid drinking the water because of tastes and odors. In Ohio, in 1925, the legislature approved a bill that gave the State Health Department the authority to zone sources of water supplies and to require new industries, or industries developing new processes, to file plans for satisfactory treatment plants. The state director of health called it "the most advanced piece of public health legislation bearing on the subject of stream pollution prevention in the country."[34]

In both Pennsylvania and Ohio, the directors of the relevant administrative bodies argued that cooperation rather than legal action was the proper strategy to follow in regard to industrial pollution, an approach to regulation that was typical of the 1920s. Underlying this strategy in the case of industrial pollution was a belief that "no existing satisfactory and economically possible means of treatment existed for the wastes of many important industries" and that legal action could drive industry out of the state rather than produce environmental improvement.[35] State authorities believed that firms themselves wished to find a means to deal with pollution and would be willing to cooperate in seeking means of remedial action.

Pennsylvania pioneered in the area of cooperative agreements and during the 1920s made compacts with industries such as pulp and paper and tanning to achieve voluntary pollution reduction. This strategy was also used in regard to phenol pollution, and by 1928 the Sanitary Water Board had reached agreements with all Pennsylvania by-product coke operators to prevent taste- and odor-producing substances from reaching state waters. In Ohio, similar agreements between the state and industry were reached during the decade. In spite of these agreements, however, state authorities worried about the limitations on their ability to secure action by firms located on interstate streams such as the Ohio River. Without such agreements, it would be difficult to secure voluntary compliance by intrastate firms because of their fear of being at a disadvantage in competitive markets.[36]

Dr. John E. Monger, director of the Ohio Board of Health, in a 1923 letter to US Surgeon General Homer S. Cummings argued that the problem of interstate pollution required federal leadership, since "it is apparent that any particular State is powerless to secure a remedy." The federal government, however, had limited authority in regard to water pollution. In 1912 the US Congress had assigned the USPHS the task of "investigating" the relationship between health and water pollution. The USPHS was concerned with industrial wastes primarily because of their relation to the quality of drinking water supplies. Beginning in 1913, it launched a series of stream pollution investigations centering on the Ohio River that were directed from what later became its Center for Pollution Studies in Cincinnati. In February 1923, after having received considerable complaints about phenol pollution of water supplies, the USPHS launched a national survey of the problem.[37]

Dr. Monger of the Ohio State Board of Health urged the USPHS to take a leading role in addressing the interstate problem, but the surgeon general, Cummings, was extremely cautious about overstepping his authority. It was only after considerable urging that he agreed to take the minimal step of sponsoring a national conference on the phenol question. This conference, held in Washington on May 18, 1923, was attended by representatives from fifteen state health departments, as well as federal agencies such as the USPHS, the Bureau of Mines, and the Bureau of Standards. Although the federal role remained limited, the meeting served important organizational and informational purposes.[38]

A second national conference, also called by the surgeon general, was held in Washington in January 1924, and this led to the formal organization of the Ohio River states. Three months later, in April 1924, health department officials from the Ohio River states met in Pittsburgh with representatives of the basin's by-product coke firms to see if they could reach agreement to control phenol wastes in the Ohio River. The tone of the meeting was cooperative rather than confrontational. By this time, many of the firms had already signed agreements with the Ohio and Pennsylvania departments of health to control their phenol wastes, and now the remainder agreed to take similar action.[39]

At the Pittsburgh meeting, the health department representatives from Ohio, Pennsylvania, and West Virginia also signed the Ohio River Interstate Stream Conservation Agreement. In this compact, the signatories agreed upon uniform policy in regard to the protection of water supplies from phenols and other tarry acid wastes. The chief engineers of the three departments of health were constituted a "Board of Public Health Engineers of the Ohio River Basin," with the responsibility for protecting the watershed from industrial pollution. The prominent role of the engineers rather than the public health physicians (the directors of state public health departments were required to be physicians in almost all states)—in this case reflects both the rise to prominence of engineers in public health activities and the extent to which industrial pollution was viewed as a technical problem (see Figure 11.4).[40]

By 1929 seventeen of the nineteen basin firms had installed phenol

Fig. 11.4 CITE sign at the Clairton Works, 1997. The coke industry has attempted to control air emissions but with limited success (photograph by Joel A. Tarr).

elimination devices, sharply reducing the most severe taste and odor problems. The procedure utilized by fourteen of the plants having 88 percent of the nation's coke-making capacity was to use the phenolic wastewater to quench the glowing coke, vaporizing the wastewater into the atmosphere rather than disposing of it in waterways. The Carnegie Steel Corporation had adopted quenching at its Clairton Works in 1918 after the McKeesport injunction, and it was to become the model for most of the other by-product plants, actively pushed by Judge E. H. Gary, chairman of the board of directors of the US Steel Corporation. Having themselves installed a quenching system, US Steel directors were anxious to persuade their competitors to adopt a technology at least as costly as the one they were utilizing. After a visit to the Clairton Works to examine their quenching operation, Monger wrote to coke plant managers urging them to adopt the technique. "We trust," he said in a thinly veiled warning, "that voluntary action will be taken by various coke producing companies in Ohio without formal order by this department."[41]

Quenching with the phenolic wastewater was an expensive environmental control technology, especially for companies not used to expenditures on pollution control. The capital costs of installing such a system at one plant of the Youngstown Sheet and Tube Company with a five-thousand-ton daily capacity in the mid-1920s was $250,000, with much higher costs at larger plants. The companies disliked quenching, not only because of its capital costs but also because it greatly increased the rate of equipment and structural corrosion. US Steel's maintenance costs at its Clairton works (thirty-thousand-ton capacity) in the mid-1920s were over $60,000 per year. The phenolic wastewater used in the quenching system also imparted an odor to the coke, limiting its use for home heating. The coke manufacturers, however, had little choice, since alternative approaches such as phenol recovery or chemical treatment were either uncertain or prohibitively expensive.[42] In the absence of other more cost-effective recovery methods, and under pressure from the threat of lawsuits, the companies voluntarily (and reluctantly) adopted the quenching technique.

The importance of the threat of legal action in achieving "cooperation" from industry was illustrated in the case of phenol pollution in the Chicago area. Chicago, as well as other smaller cities in Illinois and Indiana, drew their water supply from Lake Michigan. In 1927 phenolic wastes from coke ovens in the Calumet region of Indiana, located on the lake, so badly polluted the water supply that it was undrinkable for a week. As in the Ohio River basin, conferences were held between industry representatives and the state health authorities. On June 13, 1928, representatives of the health departments of states bordering the Great Lakes (Illinois, Michigan, Wisconsin, Indiana, Minnesota, Ohio, Pennsylvania, and New York), signed the Great Lakes Water Covenant, an agreement similar to that in the Ohio River basin in regard to reducing phenol pollution.

At the time of the signing of the agreement, the involved industries gave the health authorities "verbal assurances" that they would control their phenol wastes within a two-year period. In spite of the "assurances," however, no action was taken, and during the following year a number of episodes of tastes and odors in the water supply related to phenol wastes occurred. The Chicago health authorities "realized that unless pressure was exerted by the Department of Health in an unmistakable way, the citizens of Chicago might be forced to drink unpalatable water for many years to come," and the department threatened to obtain a court injunction shutting down the firms. Faced with the threat of legal action, the Indiana coke companies capitulated and installed quenching technology.[43]

Coke quenching with the phenol wastewater did not actually eliminate the waste stream; instead it shifted the burden of pollution from the water to the air. Engineers originally thought that quenching destroyed the pollutants in the wastewater, but it soon became apparent that the volatile components such as phenol, cyanide, and ammonia were actually being steam-distilled and discharged into the atmosphere. Some engineers considered this an undesirable solution. At the 1927 convention of the American Water Works Association, for instance, an engineer and chemist for the Rochester Gas & Electric Corporation, a firm that was itself having problems with its phenol wastes, commented that quenching was "one of the most objectionable things that could be inflicted on any community because we simply delay the time of getting them [the phenols] into the water supply." But this was a minority view, and most engineers and public health figures accepted quenching as the only option that came close to meeting both environmental and economic constraints.[44] In the absence of air pollution statutes, and with only a very limited understanding of the effects of airborne industrial pollutants, the air became a preferable sink to the water.

CONCLUSIONS

This study of the connection between the production of metallurgical fuels for the iron-making process, especially that of coke, and the creation of environmental damage and pollution, illuminates several aspects of the relationship between industrial technology, the environment, and public policy in the period before stringent local, state, or federal environmental legislation. As technologies, both the beehive and the by-product coke ovens were major polluters, but their effects on the environment were substantially different. Beehive coke oven operators made only very limited attempts to capture emissions, most of which went into the atmosphere, fouling the air and destroying nearby vegetation. Since these ovens were largely located in rural rather than urban areas (as were charcoal plantations), a somewhat smaller population was affected, but because the ovens were usually scattered over the landscape they impacted a larger geographical area. Air quality was notoriously bad, for instance, in the Connellsville coke area, with the largest concentration of beehive coke ovens in the world, was notoriously bad. A city such as Pittsburgh could either ban the ovens outright or attempt to impose pollution-control requirements, although enforcement was uncertain at best. The only recourse urban and rural dwellers often had was the common law—an option that was both expensive and cumbersome and which brought limited damages.

By-product coke ovens were most frequently located near heavily populated metropolitan areas where the potential existed for pollution impacts on a larger population. In contrast to the beehive ovens, the by-product ovens were viewed as an improvement in regard to air emissions. The Mellon Smoke Investigation of Pittsburgh, the first comprehensive study of the impact of smoke pollution on a major American city, for instance, found

FIG. 11.5 The Clairton by-product coke works, 2003. The change in mode from beehive to by-product ovens shifted coke production closer to the mills and the city (photograph by Joel A. Tarr).

it encouraging in 1914 that by-product coke ovens, "which give no [visible] smoke," would soon replace the city's "antiquated" beehive ovens.[45] Unanticipated, however, was the phenol waste stream's severe impact on chlorinated drinking water supplies. Thus, two new technologies—one that had produced significant public health improvements and the other which both improved productivity and reduced air emissions—had interacted to produce a health and nuisance-related environmental problem.

The quenching technology utilized to keep the phenol wastewater out of the waterways, and thus to protect drinking water quality itself, ultimately proved problematical from an environmental and health perspective. Quenching shifted the pollution burden from the water to the air, but it was not until the 1960s, at a time of growing environmental consciousness, that the technique received any serious challenge. Until this decade air pollution (because of uncertainties about health effects) clearly held a lower position on the environmental policy agenda than did water pollution.[46]

Policy making by government also reflected a tolerance for industrial pollution unless it had obvious health effects. The Ohio River basin agreement between coke producers and public health authorities, which removed the phenolic wastes from water supplies, was the result of a cooperative strategy (backed by the threat of court action) rather than a policy of command

and control. Such an approach became the norm in Pennsylvania and many other industrial states in regard to industrial pollution for most of the period from the 1920s through the 1960s. State government officials, as well as industrial managers, were concerned over possible federal inroads into their authority and uniform standard setting from a distance. In 1926, for instance, when Congress was considering national legislation to control stream pollution, the Ohio River Basin Association passed a resolution opposing federal control. The leadership of the USPHS, which had strong ties with the state health organizations, also held this position. Agreements such as the compact over phenols, said Dr. Wade H. Frost, director of the Cincinnati Research Station of the Public Health Service, gave "infinitely more promise of success than the enactment of federal laws to regulate the pollution of interstate streams." This skepticism about federal command and control regulation and a preference for interstate agencies and state standard setting remained the preferred line of attack on industrial pollution for Ohio River states through the 1970s.[47]

✦ ✦ ✦

The case of waste disposal from coke manufacturing highlights the extent to which, in the past, because of economic and technological factors, we have often shifted our pollution burdens from one medium and one sink to another instead of adopting a more holistic approach to the environment. Lack of knowledge and expensive control costs clearly limited choices at the time of the innovations, but company resistance to large expenditures for control technology often slowed progress in pollution control. Society attempted a range of options in attempting to cope with industrial pollution, including, in this example, local and county ordinances, state legislation, regional compacts, and eventual federal standards. The movement from one governmental level to another reflects the difficulties of regulating interstate pollution, the public's frustration over the slowness of state regulation and industry response, and a shift from concern over property damages to the environmental and health effects of pollution.

Today our society confronts the necessity of paying for past waste disposal practices that both affect environmental quality and pose potential health dangers. Many current environmental problems involve cross-media effects, such as groundwater pollution by runoff from hazardous waste dumps or sanitary landfills that reflect past disposal choices. The history behooves us, therefore, to sharpen our sensitivity to the interconnected nature of the environment and the implications of these connections for environmental policy (see "The Metabolism of the Industrial City" in this volume).

NOTES

Reprinted with permission from Char Miller and Hal Rothman, eds., *Out of the Woods: Essays in Environmental History* (Pittsburgh: University of Pittsburgh Press, 1997), 163–80.

1. For elaboration of this concept, see Joel A. Tarr, "The Search for the Ultimate Sink: Urban Air, Land, and Water Pollution in Historical Perspective," in J. Kirkpatrick Flack, ed., *Records of the Columbia Historical Society of Washington, D.C.* 41 (Charlottesville, VA, 1984): 1–29.

2. Arthur C. Bining, *Pennsylvania Iron Manufacture in the Eighteenth Century* (Harrisburg, PA, 1973), 19–38; Michael Williams, *Americans and Their Forests: A Historical Geography* (New York, 1989), 104–10; Paul F. Paskoff, *Industrial Evolution: Organization, Structure, and Growth of the Pennsylvania Iron Industry, 1750–1860* (Baltimore, 1983), 1–38, 91–105. Some charcoal kilns, developed shortly before the Civil War, attempted to capture wood chemicals; charcoal retorts, developed in the 1870s and 1880s, were specifically designed to capture volatile wood chemicals. See R. H. Schallenberg and D. A. Ault, "Raw Materials Supply and Technological Change in the American Charcoal Iron Industry," *Technology and Culture* 18 (July 1977): 453–54.

3. Peter Temin, *Iron and Steel in Nineteenth-Century America: An Economic Inquiry* (Cambridge, MA, 1964), 82–83; Paskoff, *Industrial Evolution*, 18; Williams, *Americans and Their Forests*, 147–50, 347–44.

4. Bining, *Pennsylvania Iron Manufacture*, 59.

5. Schallenberg and Ault, "Raw Materials Supply," 436–66. Alfred D. Chandler Jr., "Anthracite Coal and the Beginnings of the Industrial Revolution in the United States," *Business History Review* 46 (Summer 1972): 151–64. Chandler maintains that this substitution occurred not because of demand for new energy sources but because anthracite operators acquired the means to develop and make available the supply of anthracite.

6. Paskoff, *Industrial Evolution*, 101–2; Temin, *Iron and Steel*, 58–62.

7. The total production of charcoal iron rose until 1890, but the proportion made with the fuel diminished sharply as a fraction of total production. See Temin, *Iron and Steel*, 266–69; Williams, *Americans and Their Forests*, 337–44. For a discussion of the anthracite region, see Donald L. Miller and Richard E. Sharpless, *The Kingdom of Coal: Work, Enterprise, and Ethnic Communities in the Mine Fields* (Philadelphia, PA, 1985).

8. The Connellsville coke region was 42 miles long, an average of 3.54 miles wide, and it covered 147 square miles. John Fulton, *Coke: A Treatise on the Manufacture of Coke and Other Prepared Fuels and the Savings of By-Products* (Scranton, PA, 1906), 145. John Fulton, "A Report on Methods of Coking," in *Second Geological Survey of Pennsylvania, 1875* (Harrisburg, PA, 1876), 122–23; Raymond Foss Bacon and William A. Hamor, *American Fuels*, 2 vols. (New York, 1922), 1:6–9; Frederick Moore Binder, *Coal Age Empire: Pennsylvania Coal and Its Utilization to 1860* (Harrisburg, PA, 1974), 118–19.

9. Temin, *Iron and Steel*, 268–69; Kenneth Warren, *The American Steel Industry, 1850–1970: A Geographical Interpretation* (Oxford, England, 1973), 77–80, 110, 200–206; Chandler, "Anthracite Coal," 141–81.

10. Fulton, "A Report on Methods of Coking," 146–57.

11. Fulton, "A Report on Methods of Coking," 146–57. The process of drawing coke by hand was immensely difficult. Not only was the work heavy, but the laborers were also exposed to the heat of the ovens and dust and fumes. Workers willing to perform these

difficult tasks were hard to find, and attempts were made to develop mechanical coke drawers as well as mechanical levelers and watering devices. See Walter W. Macfarren, "Coke Drawing Machines," in *Proceedings of the Engineers Society of Western Pennsylvania* 23 (November 1907): 451–509; F. C. Keighly, "The Connellsville Coke Region," *Engineering Magazine* 20 (October 1900): 39. The yield of high class Connellsville coal coked in beehive ovens in 1875 was 63 percent. Franklin Platt, *Special Report on the Coke Manufacture of the Youghiogheny River Valley, Second Geological Survey of Pennsylvania: 1875*, 63; in 1911 the US Geological Survey reported the average yield nationally for beehive ovens was 64.7 percent. See F. H. Wagner, *Coal and Coke* (New York, 1916), 296–99. Higher quality coke could be produced by increasing the length of the coking process to seventy-two hours.

12. H. N. Eavenson, *The First Century and a Quarter of the American Coal Industry* (Baltimore, 1942), 380–84, 579–83; David Demarest and Eugene D. Levy, "A Relict Industrial Landscape," *Landscape* 29 (1986): 30–32; Muriel E. Sheppard, *Cloud by Day: The Story of Coal and Coke and People* (Uniontown, PA, 1947), 22–24; William L. Affelder, "Jones & Laughlin's Coke Plant," *Mines and Minerals* 29 (December 1908): 195–99.

13. W. A. Buckhout, "The Effect of Smoke and Gas upon Vegetation," *Annual Report of the Pennsylvania State Department of Agriculture* (Harrisburg, PA, 1900), 180–82. One observer of the beehive coke region wrote that the ammonia "thrown into the atmosphere . . . by coke ovens . . . no doubt add[s] materially to the fertility of our land; for nature never wastes anything, and it is in all probability precipitated." See John W. Boileau, *Coal Fields of Southwestern Pennsylvania. Washington & Greene Counties* (Pittsburgh. Privately printed, 1907), 56.

14. See Sheppard, *Cloud by Day*. Some accounts describe the whole Connellsville region as frequently blanketed with the fumes emitted from beehive coke ovens. See, for instance, William A. Metcalf, "On Smoke," *Proceedings of the Engineer's Society of Western Pennsylvania* 8 (1892): 29–30. Miners and coke oven workers often planted gardens close to the ovens but placed them downwind of the oven fumes. See John K. Gates, *The Beehive Coke Years: A Pictorial History of Those Times* (Uniontown, PA, 1990). Fumes and other emissions from the beehive ovens, as well as contact with the tarry coal wastes, almost certainly affected workers' health and possibly that of nearby residents, but the author has been unable to find a study documenting this.

15. For an interesting interpretation of common law rulings on pollution cases in the nineteenth and early twentieth centuries, see Christine Rosen, "A Litigious Approach to Pollution Regulation, 1840–1906" (unpublished paper, School of Business, University of California, Berkeley, 1990). In the *Sanderson* cases, the Pennsylvania Supreme Court held that injured parties could not collect damages because of harm done to their property from mine acid drainage, because mine acid was a result of the "natural and necessary use" of property. See *Sanderson v. Pennsylvania Coal Co.*, 86 Pa. 401 (1878) and 102 Pa. 370 (1883); *Pennsylvania Coal Co. v. Sanderson* 94 Pa. 302 (1880) and 113 Pa. 126, 146 (1886). See *Brown et al. v. Torrence* 7 Pa. *State Reports* 186 (1880); *Adam Robb v. Carnegie Bros. & Co.*, 145 Pa. 324 (1891); *Joseph Lentz v. Carnegie Bros. & Co.*, 145 Pa. 612 (1891); *Campbell v. Bessemer Coke Company*, 23 Pa. *Superior Ct.* 374 (1903).

16. Christine Rosen, "Cost Benefit Analysis in Pollution Nuisance Law 1840–1904" (unpublished paper, University of California at Berkeley, 1990). See, for instance, *Adam Robb v. Carnegie Bros. & Co.*, 145 Pa. 324 (1891).

17. J. F. Slagle, *A Digest of the Acts of Assembly and a Code of the Ordinances of the City of Pittsburgh* (Pittsburgh, PA, 1869), 269; Hiram Schock, comp. and ed., *Digest of the*

General Ordinances and Laws of the City of Pittsburgh to March 1, 1938 (Pittsburgh, PA, 1938), 384–85; Affelder, "Jones & Laughlin's Coke Plant," 197. No mention has been found of other attempts to control pollution from beehive ovens, although at the Continental No. 1 Plant of the H. C. Frick Coke Company, located near Uniontown, Pennsylvania, a system was developed that used a tall stack to burn by-products and generate steam. See also Charles Catlett, "Increasing the Coke Yield from Bee-Hive Ovens," *Cassier's Magazine* 24 (October 1903): 534–42.

18. Mellon Institute, *Some Engineering Phases of the Smoke Problem*, Bulletin no. 6, Mellon Institute Smoke Investigation (Pittsburgh, PA, 1914), 68–69. The report notes that, in these coke ovens, the gases were "conveyed by long passages to the stacks where they are discharged." Since most beehive coke ovens vented through the roof, the use of the stacks suggests that the J&L ovens were included in the observation. In 1904, however, in the case of *Sullivan v. Jones & Laughlin Steel Company*, the Pennsylvania Supreme Court sustained an injunction issued by a lower court that enjoined J&L Steel from operating its blast furnaces to cause substantial damage to nearby residential areas. The suit had been engendered by J&L's use of fine Mesabi ore, which produced severe dust fall problems. See *Sullivan, Appellant, v. Jones & Laughlin Steel Company* 208 Penn. State Reports 540 (1904). See also "Decision of the Supreme Court of Pennsylvania on the Use of Mesabi Ores," *Bulletin of the American Iron and Steel Association* (July 10, 1904): 100–101. Full compliance with the injunction, however, was difficult to achieve given the nature of the technology, and the courts held in 1908 that the modifications installed by J&L constituted adequate compliance with the decree, in spite of evidence that the plaintiffs were still suffering injury. See *Sullivan v. Jones & Laughlin Steel Co.*, 222 Pa 72 (1908).

19. Sam H. Schurr and Bruce C. Netschert, *Energy in the American Economy, 1850–1975* (Baltimore, 1960), 98n75; Fulton, *Coke*, 311–12; Catlett, "Increasing the Coke Yield," 534–42; William Gilbert Irwin, "Coke-Making in the United States," *Cassier's Magazine* 19 (January 1901): 205; Heinrich J. Freyn, "The Wastefulness of Coke Ovens," *Scientific American Supplement No. 1998* (April 1914), 246–47; Floyd W. Parsons, "Everybody's Business: Needless Coal Wastes," *Saturday Evening Post*, March 13, 1920, 36–38.

20. M. Camp and C. B. Francis, *The Making, Shaping and Treating of Steel*, 4th ed. (Pittsburgh, PA, 1919), 101–16.

21. Davis, "The Semet-Solvay By-Product Oven," in *Journal of the Engineers' Society of Pennsylvania* 2 (October 1910): 401. See also Camp and Francis, *Treating of Steel*, 101–2, 116–41; Wagner, *Coal and Coke*, 303–6. For the conservation movement, see Samuel P. Hays, *Conservation and the Gospel of Efficiency* (Cambridge, MA, 1959).

22. Quivik, "Industrial Pollution," 15; William H. Blauvelt, "The By-Product Coke Oven," *Engineering News* 60 (August 27, 1908): 218–23; Aaron J. Ihde, *The Development of Modern Chemistry* (New York, 1964), 454–61.

23. C. A. Meissner, "The Modern By-Product Coke Oven," in James T. McCleary, ed., *Year Book of the American Iron and Steel Institute* (New York, 1913), 118–78; Hyde, *The Development of Modern Chemistry* (New York, 1964), 614–17, 671–94.

24. Parsons, "Everybody's Business," 38. Wilbert G. Fritz and Theodore A. Veenstra, *Regional Shifts in the Bituminous Coal Industry with Special Reference to Pennsylvania* (Pittsburgh, PA, 1935), 116–20. Beehive ovens continued to be constructed in situations where the expense of a by-product plant could not be justified. See Warren, *American Steel Industry*, 112–15; Eavenson, *The First Century*, 582–85. During the Second World War, many beehive ovens were fired up to meet wartime demands. See G. S. Scott, J. A. Kelley,

E. L. Fish, and L. D. Schmidt, *Modern Beehive Coke-Oven Practice, Preliminary Report* (US Bureau of Mines R. I. 3738, Washington, DC, December 1943).

25. Richard G. Luthy, "Problems of Water Reuse in Coke Production," in E. Joe Middlebrooks, ed., *Water Reuse* (Ann Arbor, MI, 1982), 501–20. "Phenols" is the broad term applied to the monohydroxy derivatives of the benzene ring; it includes phenol, cresols, and xylenols. Coke oven waste includes a combination of all the phenols. See Ohio River Valley Water Sanitation Commission, *Phenol Wastes: Treatment by Chemical Oxidation* (Cincinnati, OH, 1951), 9; R. D. Leitch, "Stream Pollution by Wastes from By-Product Coke Ovens: A Review, with Special Reference to Methods of Disposal," *Public Health Reports* 40 (September 25, 1925): 2022.

26. Stuart Galishoff, "Triumph and Failure: The American Response to the Urban Water Supply Problem, 1860–1923," in Martin V. Melosi, ed., *Pollution and Reform in American Cities, 1870–1930* (Austin, TX, 1980), 50–54; H. P. Bohmann, "Find Causes of Obnoxious Tastes in Milwaukee Water," *Engineering News-Record* 82 (January 23, 1919): 181–82. H. R. Crohurst, a sanitary engineer with the USPHS, estimated in 1924 that one part of phenol waste to seventy million to one hundred million parts of chlorinated water would bring detectable tastes and odors. See E. S. Tisdale, "Cooperative State Control of Phenol Wastes on the Ohio River Watershed," *Journal of American Water Works Association* 18 (1927): 575; Wellington Donaldson, "Industrial Wastes in Relation to Water Supplies," *American Journal of Public Health* 11 (March 1921): 195. Interestingly, very high concentrations of chlorine would neutralize the phenol. See Ohio River Valley Water Sanitation Commission, *Phenol Wastes*, 9.

27. "Discussion of Report of Committee No. 6 on Industrial Wastes in Relation to Water Supply," *JAWWA* 12 (1924): 411–15; F. Holman Waring, "Results Obtained in Phenolic Wastes Disposal under the Ohio River Basin Interstate Stream Conservation Agreement," *AJPH* 19 (1929): 758–70; "Progress Report of Committee on Industrial Wastes in Relation to Water Supply," *JAWWA* 10 (1923): 415–30, and *JAWWA* 16 (1926): 302–3.

28. Waring, "Results Obtained, 758–70; "Progress Report on Recent Developments in the Field of Industrial Wastes in Relation to Water Supply," *JAWWA* 16 (1926): 310–11.

29. In 1912 the city of New Castle, Pennsylvania, sued the Carnegie Steel Company of Farrel, Pennsylvania, to stop it from polluting New Castle's water supply with phenolic wastes from its by-product coke oven. The company settled the case out of court and agreed to prevent further difficulties. See Waring, "Results Obtained," 759–61.

30. The Youghiogheny River waters were plagued by extreme hardness, acidity, and turbidity. See E. C. Trax, "A New Raw Water Supply for the City of McKeesport, Pennsylvania," *Journal of the American Water Works Association* 3 (1916): 947–53.

31. See Camp and Francis, *Treating of Steel*, 103–4, for a description of the Clairton by-product coke plant.

32. *McKeesport v Carnegie Steel Company* in 66 *Pittsburgh Legal Journal* 695 (1918); and 66 *Pittsburgh Legal Journal* 696.

33. E. B. Besselievre, "Statutory Regulation of Stream Pollution and the Common Law," *Transactions of the American Institute of Chemical Engineers* 16 (1924): 217–29; John H. Fertig, "The Legal Aspects of the Stream Pollution Problem," *AJPH* 16 (August 1926): 782–88.

34. Joel A. Tarr, "Industrial Wastes and Public Health: Some Historical Notes, Part 1, 1876–1932," *AJPH* 75 (September 1985): 1059–67. See also W. L. Stevenson, "Pennsylvania Sanitary Water Board," *Engineering News-Record* 91 (October 25, 1923): 684–85;

Almon L. Fales, "Progress in the Control of Pollution by Industrial Wastes," *AJPH* 18 (1928): 715–21. The board established three classes of streams: those that were relatively pure; those in which pollution needed to be controlled; and those that were already so polluted that they could not be used for public water supplies or recreational purposes and, therefore, were not worthy of pollution removal. Some conservationists criticized the Pennsylvania law as focusing too strongly on drinking water quality and not paying enough attention to larger environmental questions. See Tarr, "Industrial Wastes and Public Health," 1062; Philip P. Wells, Deputy Attorney General, to Charles E. Miner, MD, Secretary of Health, April 12, 1924, printed in 72 *Pittsburgh Legal Journal* 648; "Discussion of Report of Committee No. 6 on Industrial Wastes in Relation to Water Supply," *JAWWA* 12 (1924): 411, with comments of W. L. Stevenson; John E. Monger, "Administrative Phases of Stream Pollution Control," *AJPH* 16 (August 1926): 790–91. Existing plants were exempt from the requirement.

35. Ellis Hawley, "Herbert Hoover, the Commerce Secretariat, and the Vision of an Associative State, 1921–1928," *Journal of American History* 61 (1974): 116–40; Monger, "Administrative Phases," 792–94.

36. W. L. Stevenson, "The Sanitary Conservation of Streams by Cooperation," *Transactions of the American Institute of Chemical Engineers* 27 (1931): 13–21. The agreement also required the firms to notify state authorities immediately in case of an accident that threatened water supplies. John E. Monger to Homer S. Cumming, November 6, 1923 USPHS Archives, Record Group 90, National Archives, Washington, DC (hereafter USPHS Archives). Cooperation was sometimes slow in coming, and the threat of legal action was always in the background. See "Discussion of Report of Committee No. 6 on Industrial Wastes in Regard to Water Supply," *JAWWA* 12 (May 22, 1924): 411–12, with the comments of J. W. Ellms; Tisdale, "Cooperative State Control," 577–78.

37. Monger to Cummings, November 6, 1923, USPHS Archives. See also Tarr, "Industrial Wastes and Public Health," 1064; and a series of letters from various state departments of health to Surgeon General Cummings in USPHS Archives.

38. Monger to Cummings, February 7, 1923; H. H. Streeter to Cummings, December 24, 1923; Wade Frost to Cummings, November 19, 1923; all in USPHS Archives. See also Tisdale, "Cooperative State Control," 256–57. The state health officials officially requested that the USPHS conduct an investigation of the health effects of phenols and that the Bureau of Mines investigate its "industrial" aspects. Only the Bureau of Mines study was published. See Leitch, "Stream Pollution," 2021–26. Leitch was a chemical engineer employed by the Bureau of Mines.

39. See Tisdale, "Cooperative State Control," 256–57.

40. Waring, "Results Obtained," 764–66. The agreement was eventually signed by the states of Kentucky, New York, Maryland, Illinois, Indiana, Tennessee, North Carolina, and Virginia. This compact was an early example of a single-purpose basinwide agreement. For a discussion of such agreements, see Roscoe C. Martin et al., *River Basin Administration and the Delaware* (Syracuse, NY, 1960), 227–37. For the growing importance of engineers within the field of public health and their conflict with physicians, see Joel A. Tarr et al., "Disputes over Water Quality Policy: Professional Cultures in Conflict," *AJPH* 70 (April 1980): 427–35; Joel A. Tarr et al., "Water and Wastes: A Retrospective Assessment of Wastewater Technology in the United States, 1800–1932," *Technology & Culture* 25 (April 1984): 246–50.

41. Willard W. Hodge, "Waste Disposal Problems in the Coal Mining Industry," in Willem Rudolfs, ed., *Industrial Wastes: Their Disposal and Treatment* (New York, 1953), 312–418; Luthy, "Problems of Water Reuse," 501–20. The quenching ratio was about five hundred gallons of water to quench the coke produced by one ton of coal. Other methods such as biological treatment were also used but primarily for discharge to sewers. Monger to Cummings, August 6, 1923, and enclosures.

42. Waring, "Results Obtained," 761; Leitch, "Stream Pollution," 2021–2026. See also Luthy, "Problems of Water Reuse," 511.

43. Sanitary Engineering Division, Chicago Board of Health, "Water Contamination with Phenol Wastes," *Annual Reports, 1926–1930* (Chicago, 1930), 470–76, 492–504; Arthur E. Gorman, "Pollution of Lake Michigan: Survey of Sources of Pollution," *Civil Engineering* 3 (1933): 519–22; Craig E. Colten, *Industrial Wastes in the Calumet Areas, 1869–1970* (Champaign, IL, September 1985).

44. Norman F. Prince, chemist and engineer from the Rochester Gas and Electric Corporation, in "Discussion," *JAWWA* 18 (1927): 582–83. See also F. W. Sperr Jr., "Disposal of Phenol Wastes from By-Product Coke Plants," *AJPH* 19 (1929): 907.

45. Mellon Institute, *Some Engineering Phases*, 72. By-product ovens did produce fumes and steam but not necessarily heavy smoke pollution.

46. In 1969 Allegheny County, Pennsylvania, the home of US Steel's Clairton coke works, approved new air pollution rules and regulations requiring that "The water utilized for the quenching of coke, prior to use as a quenching agent, shall be of a quality as may be discharged into the nearest stream or river, in accordance with the Acts of the Commonwealth of Pennsylvania." Compliance with this act would have required water completely free of phenols, an almost impossible task, and the code was amended in 1970 to require that 99 percent of the phenol be removed. Since that time, the coke industry and the regulatory authorities have engaged in constant conflict and negotiation about control of coke plant emissions to the environment, with the primary concern focused on health damages to workers and county residents. For a discussion of these acts and of subsequent events, see Charles O. Jones, *Clean Air: The Policies and Politics of Pollution Control* (Pittsburgh, 1975). In 1929, for instance, a case was filed in Allegheny County by a group of plaintiffs trying to secure compensation for personal and property damage from coke-oven chimney wastes. The case was not disposed of until 1940, having been to the US Supreme Court, the Pennsylvania Supreme Court, and to the US Court of Appeals a number times on procedural grounds. The merits of the case were never dealt with, and the plaintiffs secured no relief. See J. Philip Bromberg, *Clean Air Act Handbook*, 2nd ed. (Rockville, MD, 1985), 16.

47. "Enforcement through persuasion and cooperation" was also characteristic of enforcement of the Allegheny County air pollution statutes from 1949 through the 1960s. See Jones, *Clean Air*, 94. In 1924 Congress had passed the Oil Pollution Act, but this only applied to coastal waters and made no reference to water supplies. Quoted in Tisdale, "Cooperative State Control," 580. The preferred vehicle for dealing with interstate river pollution problems was the Ohio River Valley Sanitation Commission (ORSANCO), an interstate compact founded by authority of Congress in 1936. See Edward J. Cleary, *The ORSANCO Story: Water Quality Management in the Ohio Valley under an Interstate Compact* (Baltimore, 1967), 249–83.

12 THE METABOLISM OF THE INDUSTRIAL CITY

THE CASE OF PITTSBURGH

Joel A. Tarr

The concept of *metabolism* has been adopted from biology and refers to physiological processes within living things that provide the energy and nutrients required by an organism as the conditions of life itself. These processes can be described in terms of the transformation of inputs (sunlight, chemical energy, nutrients, water, and air) into biomass and waste products. Although this is essentially a concept originating in science, I have found it useful as a mean to comprehend the environmental history of cities as well. Cities just as much as living things require the inputs of light, energy, nutrients, water, and air. That is, cities cannot exist without those inputs—urbanites require clean air, water, food, fuel, and construction materials to subsist, and urban industries need materials for production purposes. These materials may initially come from the area of the urban site itself, but increasingly over time they are derived from the urban hinterland or even further—that is, as the city grows, it extends its *ecological footprint* further and further into its hinterland.

The ecologist Eugene Odum has written that "the city is a parasite on the natural and domesticated environments," since it doesn't grow food, and it dirties its own air and water. One can also note that it reshapes and consumes the land. Odum observes that a parasite "does not live for very long

Fig. 12.1 Two men in daytime downtown smoke, c. 1940s (Pittsburgh City Photographer Collection, courtesy of the Archives Service Center, University of Pittsburgh).

if it kills or damages its host." Therefore, for a parasite to survive, it must develop systems of exchanges that benefit both its host and itself.[1] Some may object to characterizing the city as a "parasite" on the environment, thus raising the ancient specter of the evil city and the natural countryside, but from a purely descriptive perspective the concept is a valid one. Cities do consume their environments and cannot survive unless they reach a point of equilibrium with their sites and their hinterlands in regard to the consumption of air, water, and land resources.[2] Today we describe this goal of equilibrium as seeking a *sustainable city*.

Cities and their metropolitan areas since their first appearance have had major effects on the natural environment, but these impacts have accelerated over the past two centuries with the development of industrialism and rapid urbanization. In the United States urban development has advanced, and today a large majority of the population lives in sizable metropolitan areas. These metropolitan areas are growing not only populationwise but also in terms of aerial extent. In these habitats, city builders have reshaped and often destroyed natural landscapes and eliminated animal, bird, marine, and insect species, and urban demands for resources have profoundly affected hinterlands.

The relationship between the city and the natural environment has actually been interactive, with cities having massive effects on the natural environment, and the natural environment, in turn, has profoundly shaped urban configurations. Nature has not only caused many of the annoyances of daily urban life such as bad weather and pests, it has also produced natural disasters and catastrophes such as floods, fires, volcanic activity, and earthquakes. Often, however, the actions of urbanites—such as building on floodplains and steep slopes, under the shadow of volcanoes, or in earthquake prone zones—has exacerbated the dangers they are exposed to from natural hazards.[3]

The focus of this chapter is on the metabolism of one major industrial city—Pittsburgh—in the years from about 1880 to 2000. This entails an exploration of issues relating to the resources of water, air, and land, and the ways in which they were used, misused, and remediated. This also entails a consideration of the ways in which the city has moved from a lack of concern with environmental goods toward a more sustainable level (see Figure 12.1).

Pittsburgh is sited in southwestern Pennsylvania, west of the Allegheny Mountains. The physical geography of the region consists of an uplifted plateau of about twelve hundred feet in height that has been dissected by an extensive river and stream network flowing from the Allegheny Mountains. The cutting action of rivers and streams carved a complex topography of hills and steep valleys with a general relief of five hundred feet but also sharp variations. Human action as well as natural forces have shaped and reshaped the landscape. Development has taken place especially along the floodplains and terraces in the major valleys as well as in the interior valleys and hollows (see "The Interaction of Natural and Built Environments in the Pittsburgh Landscape" in this volume). The region's greatest mineral resource is bituminous coal, but it also has natural gas and petroleum deposits that were historically important. The city's population reached a high of approximately 676,000 in 1950, but in 2000 it was down to about half that total. The six-county metropolitan area is at a plateau of about two and one-quarter million, where it has remained for several decades. Territorially, through annexation, the city grew to fifty-five square miles during the nineteenth and twentieth centuries, but the area has remained stagnant since about 1930. Conversely, the urbanized area of the mature metropolitan region has continued to expand along its periphery. During this period, the city and the region's environment—its water, air, and land resources—have undergone dramatic changes.

WATER SUPPLY AND WASTEWATER DISPOSAL

Cities require freshwater in order to exist. These supplies fill a number of functions, such as domestic needs, commercial and industrial purposes, street flushing, and firefighting. One of the most serious environmental problems Pittsburgh has faced throughout its history is the pollution of its neighboring rivers. As a riverine city Pittsburgh has been both blessed by abundant supplies and cursed by the extensive pollution of these supplies. This pollution, from both domestic and industrial sources, has severely impacted the quality of the water drawn from the rivers for both drinking water and industrial uses as well as from wells. In addition, pollution has sharply curtailed the availability of the rivers for recreational purposes (see "Pittsburgh's Three Rivers" and "Searching for a Sink for an Industrial Waste" in this volume).

Like other urbanites at the beginning of the nineteenth century, Pittsburghers drew their water from local sources such as wells, rivers, and ponds as well as from rainwater gathered in cisterns. Both private and public water suppliers provided water to the city almost from its very beginnings. In 1802, for instance, the Pittsburgh Select and Common Councils passed an ordinance allowing the borough to construct four public wells and for the purchase of private wells "in useful and necessary parts of the Borough."[4] Private vendors peddled water in the streets, and the 1815 city directory listed five water carters. As the city grew, its water needs increased rapidly, requiring more ample sources.

The debate over improved water supply focused initially on the issue of public versus private provision. In 1818 the councils refused to approve an attempt by private interests to obtain a municipal water franchise, and in 1821 sixty-one prominent citizens successfully petitioned the councils to provide new wells and to make all existing pumps public. In 1822 citizens again petitioned the councils, requesting that the municipality build a waterworks to supply Allegheny River water to the city. The petitions maintained that municipal ownership was required to guarantee improved fire protection and to secure lower fire insurance rates, to service domestic and manufacturing needs, and to meet public health requirements.[5] The insistence on public rather than private provision highlights the widespread belief that water was too important to city life to be left to the private profit-making sector.

In 1826 the councils responded to citizens' demands and approved the construction of a waterworks that would, according to the councils president, provide protection against fire and "beneficial effects to every manufactory and . . . family in the city." The city completed the waterworks in 1828. The system utilized a steam pump to draw water from the Allegheny River and raise it to a million-gallon reservoir for gravity distribution throughout the city. Responding to new demands caused by a major fire and the annexation of contiguous towns, the councils expanded the system in 1844 and again in 1848. By the end of 1850 the city had laid 21 miles of water pipe, with the system serving 6,630 dwellings, stores, and shops. System expansion continued, especially after the major annexations of territory in 1868 and 1872. In 1879 the city opened a new waterworks, which pumped water from the Allegheny River and stored it in two reservoirs for gravity distribution throughout the city. From 1895 to 1915, the city expanded the water supply network from 268 to 743 miles.[6]

The funding of the waterworks was the single largest expenditure made by the city during its first fifty years. Pittsburgh was not unusual in the extent to which waterworks costs constituted a substantial part of the total municipal budget. The building of New York's Croton Aqueduct in 1842, for instance, increased the city's debt from five hundred thousand dollars to over nine million dollars and caused many citizens to predict financial disaster.[7] Pittsburgh's willingness to make such a large expenditure for a public good can be explained by the joining together of a variety of interest groups—merchants and industrialists, homeowners, fire insurance companies, and those concerned with the public health—to demand the construction of an adequate waterworks. Waterworks were ordinarily the most expensive capital project undertaken by nineteenthcentury American cities, a fact indicating their importance to urban metabolism.

Access to water services, however, was unevenly distributed throughout the city, an important issue of what today we call environmental justice. Working-class districts had poorer water supplies than the affluent neighborhoods did, often relying on local springs or wells subject to pollution. Piped water was frequently accessed through a spigot in the backyard (frequently located near the privy vaults) rather than through indoor plumbing. The infamous Painter's Row, tenements owned by US Steel on the South Side, had one spigot in the yard serving ninety-one families.[8]

An administrative ruling acerbated the situation with regard to water access. In 1872 the City Water Commission ruled that the size of the pipe laid on a particular street would be determined by the amount of potential revenue. This ruling resulted in either insufficient supply or no supply to poor neighborhoods. Such a policy, however, was not unusual for American cities. Robin L. Einhorn has called it the "segmented system"—a system that provided benefits to those who paid for them but which also "made

FIG. 12.2 Privies and water supply share back court in Homestead (Margaret F. Byington, *Homestead: The Households of a Mill Town* [New York: Russell Sage Foundation, 1910]).

the American urban landscape a physical expression of political inequality."[9] Typhoid death rates were high throughout the city but were highest in working-class immigrant and African American areas.[10]

A supply of potable water was only one part of the city's metabolic system—wastewater from households and industries as well as storm water had to be disposed of also. Household wastes and wastewater were usually placed in cesspools and privy vaults. These were a frequent source of problems (see Figure 12.2).[11]

Many portions of Pittsburgh's heavily industrialized South Side, for instance, for their water utilized springs that were located close to neighborhood privy vaults. Private scavengers under contract to the city were responsible for maintaining sanitary conditions by cleaning privy vaults and removing garbage. In the process of performing this task, however, they frequently fouled the streets and polluted the rivers. As the city grew, domestic waste disposal problems increased; in the late nineteenth century the Pittsburgh Board of Health identified privy vault nuisances as the major health issue facing the city.[12]

The provision of running water to homes and householders' adoption of water using appliances such as sinks, showers, and water closets exacerbated the nuisance problem. On the one hand increased water supply in the home was a benefit, but on the other hand it often had a devastating effect on public health. In many cases, in order to dispose of the wastewater, householders connected these appliances to the existing wastewater disposal sinks—the cesspools and privy vaults. In 1881, for instance, householders had connected four thousand of the city's sixty-five hundred water closets to privy vaults and cesspools; only about fifteen hundred were connected to street sewers.[13]

Increasingly it became obvious that only the construction of a sewerage system would alleviate wastewater disposal problems. A variety of public and private sewers existed. Until the 1840s all municipal sewers were above ground and made of wood or brick. These sewers were intended to provide street drainage and to eliminate pools of water that could breed miasmas, but the conduits often became receptacles for decaying wastes. Concern over epidemic disease, especially cholera, led the council in June 1832 to establish a sanitary board to "direct all such measures as they think necessary for averting the introduction of the frightful epidemics." The board had the power to "cause the streets, lanes, alleys, buildings, lots and shores of the rivers to be explored, cleansed and purified in an efficient manner." It proceeded to organize the city into sanitary districts and to exercise its sanitary duties. The councils also, in these crisis years, enacted ordinances to improve waste collection and to extend the water system.[14] But the city's response to the public health threat remained limited, and conditions soon reverted to their normal unsanitary state. Fear of epidemic disease alone could not persuade the councils to make the large expenditures necessary to build a sewerage system. In addition to costs, confusion over disease etiology as well as uncertainty about the technical and design requirements for an efficient system had a discouraging effect.

By midcentury, however, demands for improved services, particularly from the city's commercial interests, persuaded the municipality to construct underground sewers in the business district. By 1866 this district possessed a "fairly adequate" system of main sewers. Other sections of the city were provided with services in a more uneven and haphazard fashion. By 1875 the city had constructed about twenty-five miles of sewers, mostly for storm water drainage. These sewers, however, suffered from design faults and were often either undersized or oversized and subject to constant clogging. The city had no topographical maps until the 1870s, and sewers did not conform to topography; neither did they follow an overall engineering plan. Rather, the municipality built sewers as a result of council members' attempts to meet their constituents' demands. In addition, householders often constructed their own sewers, many of which went unrecorded. In 1881 a noted New York civil engineer, J. J. R. Croes, hired to consult on improving the system, commented to a meeting of the Engineers' Society of Western Pennsylvania that, "You have no sewers; you don't know where they are going, or where they are to be found." Without sewers, the great majority of households in the city continued to depend on cesspools and privy vaults for disposal of domestic waste.

Debate raged about possible designs of the sewer system. Should it be a separate small-pipe system that carried only domestic and industrial wastes (the technology advocated by the famous sanitarian Col. George E. Waring Jr.)? Or should it be a larger, combined system that could accommodate both wastewater and storm water (a design favored by many noted sanitary engineers)?[15] The city's public health and engineering professionals were divided over this question. Physicians argued that the separate system was preferable because it would protect health by removing wastes from the household before they had begun to generate disease-causing sewer gas. Storm water was a secondary matter and could be handled by surface conduits.

Sanitary engineers took a different position, maintaining that sanitary wastes and storm water were equally important and that a large pipe system that would accommodate both was more economical. The superior virtues of the combined system in terms of both health and storm-water removal convinced city officials, and by the late 1880s Pittsburgh had begun to build such a system.[16] Between 1889 and 1912, civil engineers from the new bureau of engineering of the Public Works Department constructed over 412 miles of sewers, almost all of the combined type. The construction of the planned centralized sewerage system signified a movement away from the "piecemeal, decentralized approach to citybuilding characteristic of the 19th century."[17] In constructing a large centralized combined sewer network, Pittsburgh was following the lead of other large American cities such as Boston, Chicago, and New York.[18]

Many citizens resisted connecting to the new sewer lines and attempted to keep their old privy vaults and cesspools. The board of health used the sanitary code to compel connection. In a series of acts in the late nineteenth and early twentieth centuries, the council barred the construction of cesspools where sewer service was available, outlawed water closets from draining into a privy vault, and prohibited the connection of privy wells to a public sewer. Resistance to connecting to the system continued, particularly in working-class areas, because of householder resistance to paying sewer assessments (see Figure 12.3).[19]

Building a sewer system reduced nuisances but increased contamination of the city's water supply. By 1900 most of the Pittsburgh population

Fig. 12.3 Combined sewer building in downtown, 1911 (Pittsburgh City Photographer Collection, courtesy of the Archives Service Center, University of Pittsburgh).

received its water from either the Allegheny or the Monongahela River, and over the years the watersheds of these streams had become increasingly populated. By 1900, for instance, more than 350,000 inhabitants in seventy-five upriver municipalities discharged their untreated sewage into the Allegheny River, the river that provided water supplies for most of Pittsburgh's population. Some of Pittsburgh's own sewers discharged into the river at sites located above the water-supply pumping stations. The resulting pollution gave Pittsburgh the highest typhoid fever death rate of the nation's large cities from 1882 to 1907—well over 100 deaths per 100,000 population. In contrast, in 1905 the average for northern cities was 35 per 100,000 persons.[20]

Typhoid fever death rates were highest in working-class immigrant and African American living areas. The health department advised that drinking water be boiled, but new immigrants often ignored such advice since they viewed the water as uncontaminated. "You cannot make the foreigner believe that Pittsburgh water is unwholesome," observed one physician, noting that roughly half of all foreign-born men sickened with typhoid within two years of arriving in the city.[21] Pittsburgh had one of the highest rates of bottled water consumption in the nation, but these supplies were out of reach for most working-class people. Thus, as a 1909 Pittsburgh survey article observed, "those who could not afford to buy bottled water continued to drink filth." According to the municipal health department, Pittsburgh appeared "as two cities, one old and congested with a high mortality, and the other new and spacious with a very low death rate."[22]

Beginning in the 1890s agitation increased among women's groups, engineers, and physicians about the need to protect the water supply from infectious disease. The new science of bacterial water analysis had convinced many of these citizens that mortality and morbidity from infectious waterborne disease could be prevented. In the 1890s engineers and civic groups cooperated to investigate the quality of the water supply using the new methods of bacterial science. These studies conclusively demonstrated the relationship between typhoid and water quality, and in 1896 the council approved an ordinance authorizing the mayor to create the Pittsburgh Filtration Commission to further study the matter and make public policy recommendations.[23]

The commission's investigations reconfirmed the link between contaminated water and disease, and its 1899 report recommended construction of a slow sand filtration plant as the most economical means of dealing with the threat to the public health. In 1899 voters approved a bond issue for plant construction, but factional political battles over control of the construction contracts and issues of technological choice necessitated a second vote in 1904 and delayed the final completion of the filtration plant until the end of 1907. Once in operation, the filtration system had dramatic effects, and by 1912 Pittsburgh's death rate from typhoid fever equaled the average for the largest American cities.[24]

Water filtration provided one safety net in regard to polluted water, but many sanitarians and public health physicians believed it was also necessary to treat the city's sewage for maximum protection. Professional, business, and medical groups protested against sewage disposal by dilution only. They demanded that municipalities treat their sewage, and they agitated for state laws against stream pollution.[25] In the years after the turn of the century, states such as Connecticut, Massachusetts, Minnesota, New Hampshire, New Jersey, New York, Ohio, Pennsylvania, and Vermont, responding to a series of unusually severe typhoid epidemics, gave state boards of health increased power to control sewage disposal in streams.[26]

The Pennsylvania act "to preserve the purity of the waters of the State for the protection of the public health," passed by the state legislature in response to the severe Butler typhoid epidemic of 1903, typified these laws. It forbade the discharge by new municipal systems of any untreated sewage into state waterways. Although it permitted cities already discharging to continue the practice, it required them to secure a permit from the State Health Commission if they wished to extend their systems.[27] Engineering opinion largely disagreed with these prohibitions. As the *Engineering Record* noted in 1909, "it is often more equitable to all concerned for an upper riparian city to discharge its sewage into a stream and a lower riparian city to filter the water of the same stream for a domestic supply, than for the former city to be forced to put in sewage treatment works."[28]

Although Pittsburgh was filtering its own water after 1907, the city continued to dump its untreated sewage into its neighboring rivers, thus endangering the water supply of downstream communities. In the beginning of 1910 the city requested the Pennsylvania Department of Health to grant it a permit allowing it to extend its sewerage system. The department, headed by a physician, Samuel G. Dixon, first responded by requesting a "comprehensive sewerage plan for the collection and disposal of all of the sewage of the municipality." In addition, the department argued that, in order to attain efficiency of treatment, the city should consider changing its sewerage from the combined to the separate system. F. Herbert Snow, the department's chief engineer, maintained that the plan was needed to protect the public health of communities who drew their water supplies from rivers downstream from Pittsburgh. "The baneful effect of Pittsburgh's sewage on the health of the brightest citizens at her door," wrote Snow, "admonishes city and state authorities alike of the futility of defying nature's sanitary laws."[29]

The city of Pittsburgh responded to Dixon's order by hiring the engineering firm of Allen Hazen and George C. Whipple to act as consultants for the required study. Hazen and Whipple were among the nation's most distinguished sanitary engineers and were already known for their espousal of water filtration as an alternative to sewage treatment to protect drinking-water quality. Hazen had actually served as chief consultant on the construction of Pittsburgh's sand filtration plants. The engineers based their study primarily upon an evaluation of the costs of building a treatment system and of converting Pittsburgh sewers to the separate system.

In their report, issued on January 30, 1912, Hazen and Whipple argued that Pittsburgh's construction of a sewage treatment plant would not free the downstream towns from threats to their water supplies nor from the need to filter them, since other communities would continue to discharge raw sewage into the rivers. The method of disposal by dilution, they maintained, sufficed to prevent nuisances, particularly if storage reservoirs were constructed upstream from Pittsburgh to augment flow during periods of low stream volume. Hazen and Whipple argued that there was no case "where a great city has purified its sewage to protect public water supplies from the stream below."[30]

Hazen and Whipple's most powerful argument concerned the lack of economic feasibility of converting Pittsburgh's sewerage system to separate sewers and building a sewage treatment plant. There was no precedent, they claimed, for a city replacing the combined system by the separate system "for the purpose of protecting water supplies of other cities taken from the water course below." They calculated that financing such a project would have caused the city to exceed its municipal indebtedness level and thus violate state law. Moreover, because the sewage treatment plant was intended for the protection of the downstream communities, it would not give Pittsburgh any direct benefits. Furthermore, downstream cities would still have to filter their water to protect against waterborne pathogens. No "radical change in the method of sewerage or of sewage disposal as now practiced by the city of Pittsburgh is necessary or desirable," they concluded."[31]

While the engineering press received the Hazen-Whipple report with enthusiasm, Pennsylvania Health Commissioner Dixon found it an insufficient response to his original instructions requesting Pittsburgh to develop a comprehensive sewerage plan based on long-range planning. He maintained that he had envisioned a report that would take a regional rather than a local approach to Western Pennsylvania water-pollution problems. He argued that water pollution had to be viewed from a health rather than a nuisance perspective, and that the immediate costs of sewage treatment would be outweighed by the long-range health benefits. The time had come, Dixon stated, "to start a campaign in order that the streams shall not become stinking sewers and culture beds for pathogenic organisms."[32]

Given the political context, however, and the financial limitations upon the city, Dixon had no realistic means by which to enforce his order. In 1913 he capitulated and issued Pittsburgh with a temporary discharge permit. The city continued to receive such permits until 1939, and it was not until 1959 that Pittsburgh and seventy-one other Allegheny County municipalities began treating their wastes and ceased discharging raw sewage into the abutting rivers.[33] Thus, nearly half a century was to pass before Dixon's vision of sewage-free rivers would even begin to be realized.

This particular case has implications larger than those that relate only to Pittsburgh. The dispute pitted public health physicians against sanitary engineers and illustrated their different conceptions of the choice dictated by the urban environment. Sanitary engineers believed that they had a superior conception of the relative needs and values of cities in regard to public health because of their understanding of municipal financial limitations—thus sewage treatment was a luxury, less critical than other urban public health needs. Many public health officials believed, on the other hand, that sewage disposal was not a proper use of streams, especially if drinking-water quality was involved.[34] From the perspective of urban metabolism and urban sustainability, the short-term nature of the engineering option is clear, but driven by fiscal necessities.

SMOKE AND AIR POLLUTION

A vital part of the urban metabolism is its access to clean air, but effective metabolism also requires a constant source of energy, which often conflicts with the goal of maintaining clean air. The primary air quality concern of cities before the Second World War was smoke pollution, which consisted primarily of particles generated by the burning of fossil fuels, especially bituminous coal. These particles blocked the sunlight, irritated the lungs, discolored clothing and other materials including building facades, and threatened the public health (see Figure 12.4).

Heavy smoke pollution was a problem for many cities, but especially for those like Pittsburgh and St. Louis that were located close to large deposits of bituminous coal. Smoke pollution in Pittsburgh resulted from a conjunction of the factors of topography, urbanization, industrialization, and the availability at low cost of large sources of high-volatile bituminous coal. The coal was used for domestic and commercial heating purposes, for processing raw materials and manufacturing goods, and for providing fuel for transportation systems.[35] Early in the nineteenth century, Pittsburgh gained the reputation as the "smoky city' (see "Pittsburgh as an Energy Capital" in this volume).

The increase of smoke pollution as Pittsburgh grew and industrialized compelled public authorities to make at least some gestures at control. In 1868 the city councils passed a statute banning the use of bituminous coal or wood by railroads within the city limits, and in 1869 they forbade the construction of beehive coke ovens. Neither statute, however, was strictly enforced. During the 1880s the discovery and exploitation of local supplies of natural gas provided the city with approximately six years of clean air. Exhaustion of the local gas supply, however, caused a return to soft coal as a fuel and a return to heavy smoke palls, stimulating various elite and professional groups to press for smoke control (see "The Pittsburgh Region's First Natural Gas Boom" in this volume).[36] The Woman's Health Protective Association joined with the Engineers' Society of Western Pennsylvania to push for smoke control statutes. The city council responded by passing a series of ordinances in the 1890s and the beginning of the twentieth century

FIG. 12.4 Smoke from the J&L Steel Corporation mill in Pittsburgh (Pittsburgh City Photographer Collection, courtesy of the Archives Service Center, University of Pittsburgh).

that regulated dense smoke from industrial, commercial, and transportation sources—but not from domestic sources. In 1911 the city council created the Pittsburgh Bureau of Smoke Regulation for enforcement purposes. The bureau's director believed that education—training firemen to operate furnaces and boilers more efficiently as well as retrofitting with various smoke-consuming devices—and not legal sanctions would persuade polluters to stop producing smoke. Fuel efficiency, it was argued, provided an incentive, since smoke was a sign of incorrect firing and fuel waste.[37]

Although it had some limited success, the smoke control movement failed to control the smoke nuisance to any appreciable degree during the first third of the century. During the 1920s and 1930s, therefore, smoke and fuel researchers and regulators redefined the problem. They agreed that industries and railroads had made advances in eliminating dense smoke through technological and fuel improvements, by care in firing methods, and through cooperation with smoke bureaus. The smoke problem persisted, smoke investigators held, because of a failure to control domestic furnaces. Experts argued that smoke from household furnaces was especially objectionable because "the amount of black smoke produced by a pound of coal is greatest when fired in a domestic furnace and that domestic smoke is dirtier and far more harmful than industrial smoke."[38]

Domestic furnaces had not been regulated for several reasons, the most important of which were the political and administrative problems involved in controlling the heating habits of a multitude of householders. In 1940 there were 175,163 dwellings in Pittsburgh, of which 141,788 burned coal and 30,507 consumed natural gas; 53,388 of those burning coal had no central heating plant and used stoves to heat their homes. Smoke regulators lacked an effective administrative mechanism to control domestic smoke without hundreds of smoke inspectors. Politically, the issue was difficult because control threatened to impose higher costs for capital equipment and fuel on the householders. And, because of a historical equation between smoke and prosperity in Pittsburgh and other industrial cities, it was difficult to develop a public consensus for stringent controls.[39] In short, the problem was one of devising a strategy to change individual behavior in regard to fuel use in the name of the collective social goal of clean air (see "Pittsburgh as an Energy Capital" in this volume).

The climate of opinion in Pittsburgh in the late 1930s, however, discouraged discussion of smoke control. A city dependent on heavy industry, Pittsburgh was badly scarred by the Great Depression; clear skies suggested closed factories and unemployed workers. In addition, many local businesses were related to the coal mining industry, which also suffered severely from the depression. As a sign of its belief that smoke equaled prosperity and its relief at the return of full employment, in 1939 the Pittsburgh City Council actually eliminated the Bureau of Smoke Regulation. "You'll never get elected again," said one politician to a member of the city council who supported anti-smoke legislation. "Don't you know, the poor people, they don't want smoke control. It's going to cost them more money." "We like to see smoke," added another politician; "it means prosperity."[40] Many working-class people held opinions such as these—although they found smoke a nuisance and an annoyance, they were concerned that smoke control would cost them jobs. Pittsburgh, therefore, appeared an unlikely environment for the passage of substantive legislation controlling smoke emissions from either industries or homes.

At the end of the decade, however, the Pittsburgh smoke control forces received a dramatic assist from the city of St. Louis, also an industrial center dependent on bituminous coal. During the period from 1937 to 1940, under the leadership of the smoke commissioner Raymond R. Tucker, the city took major steps to reduce its smoke pollution. Tucker realized that the key to solving the city's smoke problem was to persuade inhabitants to use either a smokeless fuel or improved combustion equipment.[41] In April 1940 the St. Louis Board of Aldermen approved an ordinance requiring the use of smokeless fuel or smokeless mechanical equipment by fuel consumers, including homeowners. The essential control mechanism was city licensing of fuel dealers in order to control the quality of fuel at the source. The result of the first test of the ordinance in the 1940–1941 heating season was a series of smokeless days that city officials claimed were the result of the smoke ordinance.[42]

In February 1941 the *Pittsburgh Press* began a concerted series of articles and editorials pointing to the success in St. Louis and asserting that Pittsburgh could also achieve clean air.[43] Most effective in mobilizing opinion were two pictures published on the front page of the *Pittsburgh Press* showing a smoke-darkened St. Louis street before smoke regulation and the same street sunlit after the control ordinances had become operative. Egged on by the paper, readers, especially irate housewives, began bombarding Pittsburgh mayor Cornelius D. Scully with hundreds of letters a day demanding action. Delegations of civic officials and politicians visited St. Louis on a "civic pilgrimage" to examine the administrative machinery of smoke control and to assess its potential political costs. Most returned convinced of its technical feasibility. Three individuals who might be called "entrepreneurs" for the collective social good—Abraham Wolk, a lawyer and city council member who supposedly became involved in the campaign because of the effect of the smoke on his asthmatic son's health; Edward T. Leech, editor of the city's most influential newspaper, the *Pittsburgh Press*; and Dr. I. Hope Alexander, director of the Pittsburgh Department of Public Health—provided leadership for smoke control efforts.[44]

The anti-smoke campaigners stressed the achievement of St. Louis in achieving clean air and emphasized that the benefits of smoke control would outweigh the costs both for the community and for its citizens. In February 1941, the mayor appointed the Commission for the Elimination of Smoke, which represented a broad spectrum of the community. In his charge to the commission, Mayor Cornelius D. Scully declared that "Pittsburgh must, in the interest of its economy, its reputation and the health of its citizens, curb the smoke and smog which has made this season, and many others before it, the winter of our discontent." The commission included representatives of business, labor, government, the media, the health professions, and voluntary associations with a civic and a welfare orientation; the inclusion of three women reflected the campaign leadership's perception of the importance of women in achieving smoke control. A technical advisory group stood ready to present recommendations concerning control of specific sources such as railroads and metallurgical companies and to gather information on questions such as the availability of smokeless fuel and smokeless equipment.[45]

While the commission was holding its hearings, the Civic Club and the League of Women Voters conducted a countywide campaign of public arousal and education through a network of voluntary associations. While voluntary organizations of all types were represented in the network, women's groups were the most numerous, reflecting the deep involvement of women in the smoke elimination campaign. As homemakers, women of all classes knew how much extra cleaning smoke necessitated, with the burden falling most severely on working-class women who lived close to the mills. Middle- and upper-class women in the Civic Club and the League of Women Voters coordinated luncheons and lectures and provided speakers to interested groups.[46]

Eventually the Mayor's Commission for the Elimination of Smoke held twelve closed meetings and four public meetings. The purpose of the public meetings was to give interested groups a chance to be heard, but even more to "get across to the public something which . . . still needs more hammering,—the need for smoke control. . . . It gives the papers and the Commission a show. It gives the people a chance to be part of [the] . . . meetings."[47] While the public meetings served the function of public arousal and information transmission about smoke's negative effects, the closed meetings provided information on the more policy-relevant questions such as smokeless fuel and technology supply, costs, effects of the policy on the coal industry, coal miners, and the poor, and possible administrative procedures and timetables for enforcement. The discussion within the commission clearly reflected the conviction of its members that, with the right policy, the socially desirable end of smoke elimination could be achieved without excessive costs to individuals or to industry. As Chairman Wolk noted early in the commission's proceedings, "We want to make this city smokeless without hurting anybody."[48]

Controlling smoke, however, would not be without cost. Among the groups who would be most effected were coal miners and low-income workers. The representative of the Mine Workers on the commission appeared to accept the argument that smoke control would not substantially impact mine employment because the need for smokeless coal would actually result in the mining of larger amounts of bituminous.[49] As for working-class consumers, the commission took the position that smoke control would bring more benefits than costs to the working class because that class suffered the most from the effects of smoke pollution.[50]

In spite of disagreements within the Commission for the Elimination of Smoke, all members, including coal industry and labor representatives, signed the final report. The report listed the names of two hundred voluntary organizations including fifty-six women's clubs, twenty-four business organizations, and many labor and civic groups as supporters of smoke control. The report held that smoke elimination would "bring about a new era of growth, prosperity and well-being" for the city and would impose "little or no additional burden on the low-income groups of the city."[51]

The commission report recommended a strategy based upon control of smoke at the source. Over a staged two-year period, all fuel users would have to either burn smokeless fuels or utilize smokeless mechanical equipment. By controlling the quality of the fuel inputs into the city's metabolic engine, air quality would improve.[52] -The commission also recommended the creation of the Bureau of Smoke Regulation to be housed within the Pittsburgh Department of Health and headed by a "qualified engineer" with the power to impose fines and to seal equipment in case of law violations. Only public opinion, concluded the report, would determine if the city would become smoke-free.[53]

After a delay caused first by the Second World War and then by a shortage of smokeless fuels, the smoke control ordinance was implemented in October 1947. The most critical question in terms of implementation continued to be enforcement against domestic consumers. The Bureau of Smoke Regulation solved the enforcement problem, as had St. Louis, by focusing on the coal distribution yards (numbering approximately thirty) and the coal truckers. The bureau forbade yards to sell high-volatile coal for use in hand-fired equipment and forbade truckers to deliver it. Truckers hauling coal for consumption within the city had to be licensed and to have license numbers painted on the side of the truck for easy identification. Those caught hauling illegal high-volatile (or bootleg) coal were subject to fines, as were dealers who made illegal sales.[54]

Successful implementation, however, would not have taken place without the support of the newly elected mayor, David Lawrence, and the efforts of two newly created and allied organizations—the United Smoke Council (USC), consisting of eighty allied organizations from Pittsburgh and Allegheny County, and the Allegheny Conference on Community Development, formed in 1943. The function of the USC was to continue public educational efforts about the need for smoke control.[55] The mission of the Allegheny Conference on Community Development was the development of "an over all community improvement program" for Pittsburgh, in which smoke control played a vital part. The Conference was especially critical because of its concentration of corporate power and its help in providing the planning that was essential for policy implementation.[56]

In spite of many difficulties with fuel supply, the heating season of 1947–1948 showed a considerable improvement in air quality compared to previous years. An unusually mild winter aided in reducing the smoke palls. "PITTSBURGH IS CLEANER" reported the *Pittsburgh Press* on February 21—the worst smogs were gone, homes were cleaner, and white shirts did not have black rings around the collars.[57] Because of the visible improvement in Pittsburgh air quality, public opinion shifted from limited to strong approval of the law.[58] During the next few years heavy smoke nearly disappeared from the Pittsburgh atmosphere. In 1955, for instance, the Bureau of Smoke Regulation reported only 10 hours of "heavy" smoke and 113 hours of "moderate" smoke as compared with 298 hours of "heavy" smoke and 1,005 hours of "moderate" smoke in 1946.[59]

The improvements in Pittsburgh air quality that occurred after the implementation of the smoke control ordinance, however, were not necessarily the result of the type of fuel and equipment substitutions projected by the 1941 policy makers. In 1941, and also to an extent in 1946–1947, those involved in formulating and implementing the ordinance assumed that coal would continue to be the city's dominant domestic heating fuel for some years. The price of natural gas and oil was higher than that of coal throughout the Second World War and supplies were erratic.[60] Clean air would thus result from the use of smokeless coal produced from local bituminous or the use of equipment permitting smokeless combustion of bituminous.

Although the use of low-volatile and processed coal (Disco) and smokeless coal-burning equipment did play a role in reducing smoke in 1947–1948, they steadily declined in significance. Increasingly, low-priced natural gas, furnished by pipelines from the Southwest and stored in underground storage pools, became the dominant fuel used for Pittsburgh domestic heating.[61] The rates of change for the city are striking. In 1940, 81 percent of Pittsburgh households burned coal and 17.4 percent burned natural gas (from Appalachian fields); by 1950, the figures were 31.6 percent for coal and 66 percent for natural gas. This represented a change in fuel type and combustion equipment by almost half the city households; most of the changes took place after 1945.[62] In addition, railroad conversion from steam to diesel-electric locomotives between 1950 and 1960 also greatly reduced the railroads' contributions to the city's smoke burden.

Because of the shift to natural gas in Pittsburgh the reduction in smoke pollution would undoubtedly have eventually occurred without the smoke control law. The price of natural gas made it competitive with coal from an economic perspective, and heating with gas was much more convenient. But, although not as critical as some Pittsburgh boosters would have one believe, the Pittsburgh smoke control ordinance undoubtedly accelerated the rate of change to clean fuel. Comparisons in rates of fuel change made between Pittsburgh and other cities make this clear. The clear air initiative was also important as a motivating factor in the famous Pittsburgh Renaissance, convincing Pittsburghers that positive change was possible.[63]

The movement for smoke control in Pittsburgh also produced a similar drive in Allegheny County. Here industry and the railroads played a much more prominent role in standard setting and timetables for implementation than in the city. The 1949 county law omitted some of the region's key industries, such as steel and coal, from having to meet any specific performance standards for air pollution. The Allegheny County Bureau of Smoke Regulation had only a handful of inspectors and was not capable of monitoring and enforcing air-pollution restrictions.[64]

The resulting system of business-government cooperation in the county brought uneven progress. While fuel substitution and improvements in technology reduced county air pollution, progress was negligible in several key areas. To a large extent emissions of fumes, gases, and odors, especially from by-product coke ovens and open-hearth furnaces, were not regulated, and high levels of industrial pollutants plagued steelmaking areas. It could be argued that the actual success in controlling visible smoke actually masked the importance of regulating other elements that were present in air pollution. By the 1960s it was obvious to clean air advocates that achieving clean air in the Pittsburgh region required control of all activities that affected the metabolism of the city and the region rather than a selected few.[65]

USES OF THE LAND

While water and air are commonly thought of as inputs into the metabolism of the city, the land also needs to be considered an input. The building of a city creates a new landscape fitted into and imposed upon a preexisting landscape. As the geographer Ian Douglas notes, while the foundations of the built environment have to be designed in congruence with the rock structures and soils beneath them, city development can drastically change conditions.[66]

Over the course of the nineteenth and twentieth centuries, industry usurped the Pittsburgh area riverbanks, building on the flat land along the floodplain. Integrated steel plants constituted the largest installations, sited especially on the flat land in the river meanders between river and rail lines. Some observers of the Pittsburgh scene such as Robert A. Woods, writing in the *Survey Magazine* in 1909, admired the development of the site—the "involved panorama of the rivers, the . . . long ascents and steep bluffs, the visible signs everywhere of movement, of immense forces at work,—the pillar of smoke by day, and at night the pillars of fire against the background of hillsides strewn with jets of light."[67] Others such as R. L. Duffus, writing in the *Harpers* in 1930, bemoaned the landscape alterations: "From whatever direction one approaches the once lovely conjunction of the Allegheny and the Monongahela the devastation of progress is apparent. Quiet valleys have been inundated with slag, defaced with refuse, marred by hideous buildings. Streams have been polluted with sewage and the waste from the mills. Life for the majority of the population has been rendered unspeakably pinched and dingy. . . . This is what might be called the technological blight of heavy industry."[68]

The devastation witnessed by Duffus was dramatically illustrated by the fate of the beautiful stream valley of Nine Mile Run, located at the city's eastern boundary. Nine Mile Run is one of Pittsburgh's major urban streams, named for its distance from the Pittsburgh Point. Its watershed, measuring 6.7 square miles, drains the city's East End and winds its way southward down steep slopes to the Monongahela River. Throughout the late nineteenth and early twentieth centuries the stream had some minor development, serving as the site for a saltworks, a few farms and houses, a golf course, and a natural gas field. Most significantly, it represented Pittsburgh's last remaining access point to the Monongahela River, since industry and railroads had already occupied the rest of the waterfront.[69]

Because of its beauty and its location close to densely populated mill areas, the valley attracted the attention of reformers concerned with

Pittsburgh's environmental quality and social stability during the first quarter of the twentieth century. These Progressive Period reformers were largely the same elite individuals who had driven the campaigns for water filtration and for smoke control. Along with other urban reformers, they embraced the philosophy of Frederick Law Olmsted that a healthy environment would directly improve the well-being of urban residents and reduce urban pathologies.[70] Their campaign was a part of a larger effort to exert control over the region's degraded environmental resources.

In 1909 George Guthrie, a Democratic reform mayor, appointed a civic commission composed of the city's leading business and professional leaders to deal with the deteriorating urban landscape. The commission interpreted its mandate broadly, embracing many aspects of urban and environmental reform. It employed landscape designer Frederick Law Olmsted, son of the great designer of Central Park, as one of the commission's three major consultants. Olmsted prepared a plan for the city entitled *Pittsburgh Main Thoroughfares and the Down Town District 1910*, which was published in 1911. He recommended a new system of downtown roads and made suggestions for riverfront improvement, steep slope development, and transportation improvements (see "The Automobile Comes to Pittsburgh" in this volume). He also explicitly noted the value of Nine Mile Run:

> Perhaps the most striking opportunity noted for a large park is the valley of Nine Mile Run. Its long meadows of varying width would make ideal playfields; the stream, when it is freed from sewage, will be an attractive and interesting element in the landscape; the wooded slopes on either side give ample opportunity for enjoyment of the forest, for shaded walks and cool resting places; and above all it is not far from a large working population. . . . [A]nd yet it is so excluded by its high wooded banks that the close proximity of urban development can hardly be imagined. If taken for park purposes, the entire valley from the top of one bank to the top of the other should be included, for upon the preservation of these wooded banks depends much of the real value of the park.[71]

Unfortunately, a new mayor, Chris Magee, ignored many of Olmsted's recommendations for land use changes. Although the city issued bonds throughout the 1910s for playgrounds and to maintain the city's four parks, it did not attempt to acquire Nine Mile Run, reflecting a preference for active recreation rather than open space.[72]

The next attempt to preserve Nine Mile Run for public use occurred in the early 1920s as a result of the activities of the Citizens Committee on Civic Plan for Pittsburgh, which originated in 1918 from the decision of a group of Pittsburgh elites to create a city plan and to develop "city planning in all its aspects in the Pittsburgh district." The committee established six task forces to examine a range of urban problems, including recreation. In 1923 the recreation subcommittee issued its report on the parks. The subcommittee noted that there was only one place in the whole Monongahela River valley—Nine Mile Run—that could serve as the location for a waterfront park since in all other locations either railroad tracks or industry blocked access to the river. The subcommittee recommended that Nine Mile Run become an active waterside attraction, with a botanical garden, an athletic field, camp and picnic grounds, tennis courts, a theater, and a lake with a small beach. Because the site was close to working-class residential locations, it would provide open space to groups who were otherwise distant from such amenities. By providing healthy recreation, the park could supply physical and moral stability within the community.[73]

The citizens committee also recommended that the city adopt a zoning ordinance to control land use, a recommendation that various civic groups had made several times in the past. In 1923 the city council approved legislation providing for zoning—including separate zoning for heavy and light industrial and commercial areas and for low-density and high-density residential areas. The legislation also limited building heights in certain zones. The riverbanks were largely zoned as heavy industrial, with light industrial in back of the heavy industrial. The zoning board, however, designated the 238 acres of Nine Mile Run valley as residential, providing an exceptional access to the river.[74]

But the zoning ordinance only provided limited authority to the community to control development, and it did not prevent spoliation of the valley. In September 1922, the Duquesne Slag Products Company had purchased ninety-four acres in Nine Mile Run valley for the purpose of disposing of the wastes of Pittsburgh area steel mills, especially those of the Jones and Laughlin Steel Company, located in the city several miles down the Monongahela River. This purchase grandfathered the industry in the valley, since it took place before the city council approved the zoning ordinance.[75] For the mills, the location of Nine Mile Run valley close to their operations was ideal, since it kept transportation costs low and provided them and Duquesne Slag with a competitive advantage.

Over the years from 1922 to 1962, Duquesne Slag acquired further land within the valley and gradually filled it with slag, often leaving sharp slopes as steep as 80 percent. The slag generated by the iron- and steelmaking processes and dumped by the company consisted of silica and alumina from the original ore. For every ton of iron, more than a half ton of blast furnace slag was produced, while steelmaking produced a quarter ton of slag for every ton of steel. By the time the dumping stopped, in 1972, over 17 million cubic yards of slag was deposited in the valley, forming a mountain of slag that was up to 120 feet high. Although the land was zoned residential, because Duquesne Slag had purchased property in the valley prior to the passage of the zoning ordinance, the company's industrial use of the land was categorized as a "non-conforming use" and was allowed to proceed. Protests over the years by neighboring residents did little to control the nuisances created by the slag deposition.[76]

When slag dumping ceased in 1972, city officials and developers began thinking of possibilities for site development. As one of the city's last undeveloped sites it had great potential, especially because of its location between Frick Park and the Monongahela River. The City Planning Department completed a site development plan in 1982. Following this, over the next decade, several private interests prepared development proposals suggesting a mix of residential, retail, light industrial, office, research and development, and parks development. The complexities of site development, however, were large, and funding and developers were hard to find. Issues relating to traffic and neighborhood opposition were especially significant, and none of these plans became a reality.[77]

In 1995, however, the Pittsburgh Urban Redevelopment Authority (URA), at the initiative of Mayor Tom Murphy, purchased the land in Nine Mile Run for $3.8 million for possible residential neighborhood development. Murphy believed that attracting a residential population back into the city from the suburbs was critical for urban revitalization. New homes in Nine Mile Run would be located next to the stable middle-class residential neighborhoods of Squirrel Hill and Point Breeze, providing a powerful magnet. Environmental assessments and planning soon began, and in 1996 Copper Robertson & Partners, a New York design consulting firm, released a master plan. This plan proposed creation of a new community with between 950 and 1,150 New Urbanism–type housing units (since reduced to 713 units) including a mix of stand-alone homes, townhouse type units, and apartment dwellings. The development, called Summerset at Frick Park, will also include 114,000 square feet of retail space, an elementary school, and 54 acres of open space. The plan was to be developed in four stages. Not only would the city's housing stock be substantially incremented by development, but it also involved converting a brownfield into a new residential neighborhood (see Figure 12.5).[78]

Community involvement in the city's design and management of the site increased after the original proposal. Public meetings on both the

Fig. 12.5 Grading the Nine Mile Run slag pile for residential housing development, Summerset, 1999 (photograph by Joel A. Tarr).

housing design and the extension of adjoining Frick Park were held. An important public-private partnership formed involving local groups, the developer, the city, the Heinz Endowments (a Pittsburgh foundation), and a team of experts from Carnegie Mellon University. A dramatic change in the original plan, driven by the ecological perspectives of an interdisciplinary group from Carnegie Mellon University's Studio for Creative Inquiry, provided for daylighting rather than culverting the Nine Mile Run stream and the creation of a green corridor reaching to the river (see Figure 12.6). Other changes were made to meet neighborhood concerns that were expressed at public meetings about construction and traffic nuisances and possible environmental hazards.[79]

The successful development of Nine Mile Run through a partnership involving the city, developers, the neighborhoods, and the Carnegie Mellon University reflects a sharp change in attitudes toward the urban environment and land restoration. Previous to the 1990s the history of Nine Mile Run had reflected a failure on the part of both civic and elite leadership to take steps to protect land and water resources. In addition, the history reflects the reluctance of the city to take steps to protect both natural areas and residential neighborhoods against industrial interests. As Andrew McElwaine notes, Pittsburgh favored industrial interests over ecological and preservation values.[80] Values do change, however, and today a new administration

FIG. 12.6 Nine Mile Run restored, 2005 (photograph by Joel A. Tarr).

and a city population that increasingly thinks in terms of urban ecology have moved to restore the site and to bring it to a state of environmental sustainability. Whether such ecological development will continue on other Pittsburgh brownfield sites has yet to be seen.

CONCLUSIONS

The concept of metabolism in relationship to the environmental history of the city of Pittsburgh has led us to examine the domains of water, air, and land in regard to their use, misuse, and attempted restoration. To a great extent, the use and misuse of environmental resources were predicated upon a value system that emphasized production and material progress rather than environmental protection. Reaction against abuses of the natural system began in the late nineteenth century, led particularly by women's groups and socially minded engineers. Progress, however, was slow and even nonexistent, as the forces of industrial development overwhelmed those whose priorities emphasized environmental protection and restoration.

The years since the end of the Second World War, however, have witnessed increasing momentum on the part of groups and individuals concerned with environmental quality. While some environmental improvements were stimulated primarily by concern over urban redevelopment rather than by environmental values, substantial improvements were accomplished. Improved air and river water quality as well as increased species and fish diversity are encouraging improvements. Environmental values are receiving more attention and have been embraced by a larger sector of the public. Progress, however, has been halting, and many aspects of the environment wait to be redeemed. In addition, even in areas where there has been partial land use change, new developments often have little design or aesthetic distinction and pay little homage to environmental qualities. Thus, although the metabolism of the city has begun to move toward a point of balance, many areas of the city and the region await action to help them reach sustainability.

NOTES

"The Metabolism of the Industrial City: The Case of Pittsburgh," *Journal of Urban History* 28, no. 5 (July 2002): 511–45.

1. Eugene P. Odum, *Ecology and Our Endangered Life-Support Systems* (Sunderland, MA: Sinauer Associates, 1989), 17.

2. Another way of expressing the concept of the society-nature interaction is to think of a society as making "colonizing interventions," where such an intervention is "the sum of all purposive changes made in natural systems that aim to render nature more useful for society." Thus, metabolism and colonization are "intricately interwoven," reflecting aspects of nature-society interactions. Verena Winiwarter, "Where Did All the Waters Go? The Introduction of Sewage Systems in Urban Settlements," in Christoph Bernhardt, ed., *Environmental Problems in European Cities in the 19th and 20th Century* (New York: Waxman, 2001), 107.

3. Mike Davis, *Ecology of Fear: Los Angeles and the Imagination of Disaster* (New York, 1998); B. R. Stephenson, *Visions of Eden: Environmentalism, Urban Planning, and City Building in St. Petersburg, Florida, 1900–1995* (Columbus, 1997); Theodore T. Steinberg, *Acts of God: The Unnatural History of Natural Disasters* (New York, 2000).

4. Richard C. Wade, *The Urban Frontier: The Rise of Western Cities, 1790–1830* (Cambridge, MA: Harvard University Press, 1959), 95. See also Catherine E. Reiser, *Pittsburgh's Commercial Development, 1800–1850* (Harrisburg: Pennsylvania Historical and Museum Commission, 1951), 129; Leland D. Baldwin, *Pittsburgh: The Story of a City* (Pittsburgh: University of Pittsburgh Press, 1937), 156.

5. Richard A. Sabol, "Public Works in Pittsburgh prior to the Establishment of the Department of Public Works" (research paper, Department of History, Carnegie Mellon University, 1980), 5; Frank Kern, "History of Pittsburgh Water Works, 1821–1842" (research paper, Department of History, Carnegie Mellon University, 1982), 1–4.

6. Erwin E. Lanpher and C. F. Drake, *City of Pittsburgh: Its Water Works and Typhoid Fever Statistics* (Pittsburgh: City of Pittsburgh, 1930), 23–25. Extensive waste and leaky pipes plagued the system resulting in frequent water shortages.

7. James H. Thompson, "A Financial History of the City of Pittsburgh, 1816–1910"

(PhD diss., University of Pittsburgh, 1948), 44–45; Paul Studenski and Herman E. Kross, *Financial History of the United States* (New York: McGrawHill, 1952), 13.

8. Susan J. Kleinberg, *The Shadow of the Mills: WorkingClass Families in Pittsburgh, 1870–1907* (Pittsburgh: University of Pittsburgh Press, 1989), 87–93.

9. Robin L. Einhorn, *Property Rules: Political Economy in Chicago, 1833–1872* (Chicago: University of Chicago Press, 1991), 104.

10. Clayton R. Koppes and William P. Norris, "Ethnicity, Class, and Mortality in the Industrial City: A Case Study of Typhoid Fever in Pittsburgh, 1890–1910," *Journal of Urban History* 2 (May 1985): 269–75.

11. Charles Davis, in discussion following Geo. H. Browne, "A Few of Pittsburgh's Sewers," *Transactions, Engineers' Society of Western Pennsylvania* 1 (January 1880–June 1882): 229; Terry F. Yosie, "Retrospective Analysis of Water Supply and Wastewater Policies in Pittsburgh, 1800–1959" (PhD diss., Carnegie Mellon University, 1981),14–16, 48–49. The nuisances they created led to municipal regulation of privies as early as 1816.

12. Charles Davis, in discussion following Browne, "A Few of Pittsburgh's Sewers," 229.

13. Yosie, "Retrospective Analysis of Water Supply," 49. Before the availability of piped-in water Americans had found various ways—such as cisterns, wells, and local ponds—to provide a water supply for household plumbing. See Maureen Ogle, *All the Necessary Conveniences: American Household Plumbing, 1840–1890* (Baltimore: Johns Hopkins University Press, 1996).

14. Jacqueline Corn, "Municipal Organization for Public Health in Pittsburgh, 1851–1895" (Unpublished Doctor of Arts Dissertation, Carnegie Mellon University, 1972), 15–16. See also John Duffy, "The Impact of Asiatic Cholera on Pittsburgh, Wheeling, and Charleston," *Western Pennsylvania Historical Magazine* 47 (July 1964): 205, 208–9.

15. Browne, "A Few of Pittsburgh's Sewers," and "Discussion," 214–49.

16. For a discussion of the conflict in Pittsburgh between engineers and the board of health, see Browne, "A Few of Pittsburgh's Sewers," 219–21.

17. Jon A. Peterson, "The Impact of Sanitary Reform upon American Urban Planning," *Journal of Social History* 13 (Fall 1979): 84–89.

18. Combined sewer overflow events are a frequent cause of bacterial pollution in the Pittsburgh area rivers today.

19. The socalled street acts, passed by the city councils in 1887–1889, provided that street and lateral sewer improvements would be made on the petition of onethird of the abutting property owners in a neighborhood. All abutters, however, would be assessed for improvements. In 1891 the state supreme court declared these acts unconstitutional. See Thompson, "Financial History," 178–79; Yosie, "Retrospective Analysis of Water Supply," 112–13.

20. *Fourth Annual Report of the State Department of Health* (Harrisburg, PA: 1911), 1476.

21. Quoted in Nancy Tomes, *The Gospel of Germs: Men, Women, and the Microbe in American Life* (Cambridge, MA: Harvard University Press, 1998), 189–90.

22. Quoted in Koppes and Norris, "Ethnicity, Class, and Mortality," 271. For a study of a similar situation in Pittsburgh's neighboring city of Allegheny, see Bruce W. Jordan, "The Allegheny City Water Works, 1840–1907," *Western Pennsylvania Historical Magazine* 70 (January 1987): 29–52. Pittsburgh annexed Allegheny in 1907.

23. *Report of the Joint Commission of the Chamber of Commerce of Pittsburgh,*

Engineers' Society of Western Pennsylvania, Allegheny County Medical Society, and Iron City Microscopical Society (Pittsburgh, 1894).

24. C. E. Drake, "Statistics of Typhoid Fever in Pittsburgh," in *City of Pittsburgh, Its Water Works* (Pittsburgh, 1931), 29–38.

25. See, for example, Pittsburgh Chamber of Commerce, *Sewage Disposal for Pittsburgh* (Pittsburgh, 1907); G. Soper, "The Sanitary Engineering Problems of Water Supply and Sewage Disposal in New York City," *Science* 25 (1907): 601–5; "Up Stream or Down Stream?" *New York Times*, September 25, 1910; C. D. Leupp, "To the Rescue of New York Harbor," *The Survey* (October 8, 1910), 89–93; Merchants Association of New York, *Committee on Pollution of State Waters, Protest against the Bronx River Valley Sewer* (New York, 1907); Merchants Association of New York, *The Battle of the Microbes: Nature's Fight for Pure Water* (New York, 1908).

26. "The Unusual Prevalence of Typhoid Fever in 1903 and 1904," *Engineering News* 51 (1904): 129–30.

27. F. H. Snow, "Administration of Pennsylvania Laws Respecting Stream Pollution," *Proceedings Engineers' Society West Pennsylvania* 23 (1907): 266–83.

28. "Sewage Pollution of Water Supplies," *Engineering Record* 48 (1909): 117.

29. "The Greater Pittsburgh Sewerage and Sewage Purification Orders," *Engineering News* 63 (1910): 179–80; "Pittsburgh Sewage Purification Orders," *Engineering News* 63 (1910): 70–71; "The Sewerage Problem of Greater Pittsburgh," *Engineering Record* 61 (1910): 183–84. See also G. Gregory, "A Study in Local Decision Making: Pittsburgh and Sewage Treatment," *Western Pennsylvania Historical Magazine* 57 (1974): 25–42.

30. "The Most Important Sewerage and Sewage Disposal Report Made in the United States," *Engineering Record* 65 (1912): 209–12; "Pittsburgh Sewage Disposal Reports," *Engineering News* 67 (1912): 398–402.

31. "Pittsburgh Sewage Disposal Reports," 400–401.

32. "The Pittsburg [*sic*] Sewage Purification Order: Letters from Commissioner Dixon and Mayor Magee," *Engineering News* 67 (1912): 548–52.

33. Pennsylvania Commissioner of Health, *Eighth Annual Report* (Harrisburg, 1913), 901–2; Gregory, "Study in Local Decision Making," 41–42.

34. "The Pollution of Streams," *Engineering Record* 60 (1909): 157–59.

35. Comments were made about smoke in Pittsburgh as early as 1800. For a review of nineteenth-century developments, see John O'Connor Jr., "The History of the Smoke Nuisance and of Smoke Abatement in Pittsburgh," *Industrial World* (March 24, 1913); Robert Dale Grinder, "From Insurgency to Efficiency: The Smoke Abatement Campaign in Pittsburgh before World War I," *Western Pennsylvania Historical Magazine* 61 (1978): 187–202.

36. Grinder, "Isurgency to Efficiency," 187–202.

37. See, for example, J. W. Henderson, Bureau Chief, Pittsburgh Bureau of Smoke Regulation, "Smoke Abatement Means Economy," *Power* (July 24, 1917); R. Dale Grinder, "The Battle for Clean Air: The Smoke Problem in Post–Civil War America," in Martin V. Melosi, ed., *Pollution and Reform in American Cities, 1870–1930* (Austin: University of Texas, 1980), 89.

38. Victor J. Azbe, "Rationalizing Smoke Abatement," in *Proceedings of the Third International Conference on Bituminous Coal* (Pittsburgh, 1931), 2:603.

39. Osborn Monnett, *Smoke Abatement, Technical Paper 273, Bureau of Mines*

(Washington, DC, 1923); H. B. Meller, "Smoke Abatement, Its Effects and Its Limitations," *Mechanical Engineering* 48 (November 1926): 1275–83.

40. Interview with Abraham Wolk, April 26, 1973, in "An Oral History of the Pittsburgh Renaissance," Archives of Industrial Society, University of Pittsburgh (hereafter cited as "Oral History"). Letters defending air pollution still appear in the Pittsburgh newspapers at times when tighter air pollution controls are discussed for industry.

41. Joel A. Tarr and Carl Zimring, "The Struggle for Smoke Control in St. Louis: Achievement and Emulation," in Andrew Hurley, ed., *Common Fields: An Environmental History of St. Louis* (St. Louis: Missouri Historical Society Press, 1997), 199–220; Oscar H. Allison, "Raymond R. Tucker: The Smoke Elimination Years, 1934–1950" (unpublished PhD. diss., St. Louis University, 1978).

42. "Cities Fight Smoke," *Business Week*, April 6, 1940, 33–34.

43. *Pittsburgh Press* and *Pittsburgh Post-Gazette*, February 3, 4, 12, 1941.

44. David L. Lawrence, "Rebirth," in Stefan Lorant, *Pittsburgh: The Story of an American City*, 2nd ed. (Lenox, MA, 1975). Lawrence himself was the boss of the county Democratic Party. Wolk noted that in 1941 "Dave Lawrence never said a word to me against it." Interview with Abraham Wolk, April 26, 1973, "Oral History." One commentator observed that it was important that Alexander, a physician, was prominently involved because "he was able to generate some real fear on the part of the people that maybe after all this was dangerous to health as well as being an economic proposition." Interview with William Willis, April 16, 1973, "Oral History." Dr. I. Hope Alexander noted that "The medical profession is in accord with the statement that smoke is a health menace of major proportions. . . . For the present, however, there are a few scientific facts to definitely establish a case of cause and effect." Alexander, "Smoke and Health" (United Smoke Council of Pittsburgh, 1941 [hereafter USC with date]).

45. *Pittsburgh Press*, March 13, 1941.

46. See, for example, *Pittsburgh Press* and *Post-Gazette*, March 13, April 30, June 24, 1941; M. Jay Ream to unknown recipient, April 3, 1941, Civic Club Records; "Notes Taken on Smoke at Annual Meeting," May 8, 1941, Civic Club Records. See also "List of Organizations Co-Operating with Civic Club on Smoke Elimination," Civic Club Records.

47. The comment is that of John P. Robin, the mayor's executive secretary, in "Fourth Meeting of the Mayor's Commission for the Elimination of Smoke," March 12, 1941, 74, Pittsburgh City Council Archives.

48. "Hearings before the Pittsburgh Smoke Commission," April 15, 1941, 49, in "Fourth Meeting of the Mayor's Commission."

49. "Hearings before the Pittsburgh Smoke Commission," April 15, 1941, 38–39, in "Fourth Meeting of the Mayor's Commission."

50. See, for instance, "Proceedings of the Fifth Meeting of the Pittsburgh Smoke Commission," March 31, 1941, 23, 69–78; "Proceedings of the Sixth Meeting," April 7, 1941, 38–39.

51. *Report of the Mayor's Commission for the Elimination of Smoke* (Pittsburgh, 1941), 19.

52. In addition to smoke, the suggested ordinance provided for enforcement against other air pollutants such as fumes, gases, fly ash, and noxious acids. This provision was also included in the St. Louis ordinance and represented an advance in air pollution control as compared to earlier ordinances that had focused on dense smoke only.

53. *Pittsburgh Press*, July 7, 1941.

54. There are discussions of methods of enforcement by Dr. Sumner B. Ely in "Minutes," United Smoke Council, December 13, 1945, and in *Report of Stationary Stacks* (Bureau of Smoke Regulation, Department of Public Health, Pittsburgh, 1948), 9–10. See also Interview with Albert Brandon, July 21, 1972, Pittsburgh Renaissance Project. Brandon was assistant city solicitor in charge of the enforcement of smoke control.

55. See "The United Smoke Council of the Allegheny Conference," USC Records, and "Minutes," Meeting of the United Smoke Council of Pittsburgh and Allegheny County, October 18, 1945, USC Records, in Records of the Allegheny Conference on Commnity Development, Heinz History Center.

56. "Minutes, Meeting of the United Smoke Council of Pittsburgh and Allegheny County," November 3, 1945, USC Records.

57. *Pittsburgh Press*, February 21, 1948; USC, *That New Look in Pittsburgh* (n.p., n.d.), Heinz History Center.

58. The ordinance fell the hardest on poor families, because fuel costs composed a larger percentage of their budget than for higher-income groups, and because of their fuel-buying habits. Instead of fining people for smoke violations the bureau attempted to educate low-income consumers as to the proper measures of firing smokeless coal. In 1948, for instance, only 15 persons were summoned before magistrates for smoke violations, as compared to 250 truckers' violations.

59. City of Pittsburgh, Department of Public Health, Bureau of Smoke Prevention, *Report 1955* (Pittsburgh, 1955), 6.

60. "Lower cost to consumers and availability at all times," noted the Bureau of Mines in 1943, "are the principal factors favoring the use of coal." Arno C. Fieldner, *Recent Developments in Fuel Supply and Demand* (US Department of the Interior, Bureau of Mines, November 1943), 11. For discussions of the high price and erratic supply conditions of natural gas in 1941, see transcripts of the Mayor's Commission for the Elimination of Smoke, March 12, 1941, 17–19, 60; March 28, 1941, 7–8; March 31, 1941, 74–76.

61. See "Jobs for Inches," *Business Week*, December 29, 1945, 19; "Natural Gas Is on the Up," *Business Week*, March 13, 1948, 26; Annual Reports of the Philadelphia Company (Equitable Gas Company), for 1946, 15, for 1948, 16–17, and for 1949, 21–22. See also Christopher James Castaneda, *Regulated Enterprise: Natural Gas Pipelines and Northeastern Markets, 1938–1954* (Columbus: Ohio State University Press, 1993), 75–89, 118.

62. Data on household fuel use are available from the 1940 and 1950 censuses of housing. See US Department of Commerce, Bureau of the Census, *Housing: Characteristics by Type of Structure, 16th Census of the U.S.* (Washington, DC, 1945) and *Census of Housing: 1950*, vol. 1: *General Characteristics 17th Census* (Washington, DC, 1953).

63. The evidence suggests that the coal producers and miners were correct in warning that the smoke control law would hasten the loss of their domestic markets and their jobs. Pittsburgh representatives of the United Mine Workers charged in the postwar period that there was a conspiracy in Pittsburgh to drive out coal in favor of natural gas. See *Pittsburgh Press*, December 21, 1945, March 8, 9, April 23, December 2, 5, 1947, July 3, 1948. In its 1950 annual report, Pittsburgh Consolidation Coal noted, "it was obvious five years ago that in many of the areas into which our coal normally moved there would be a gradual decrease in the amount of coal used for domestic heating as natural gas, with its greater convenience, found its way into their markets." In its 1949 annual report, the Equitable Gas Company, which served more households in Pittsburgh than any other gas utility,

observed that smoke abatement legislation and the high cost of coal were increasing their domestic sales.

64. Sherrie Mershan and Joel A. Tarr, "Strategies for Clean Air: The Pittsburgh and Allegheny County Smoke Control Movements, 1940–1960," in Joel A. Tarr, ed., *Devastation and Renewal: An Environmental History of Pittsburgh and Its Region* (Pittsburgh: University of Pittsburgh Press, 2003).

65. Tarr, *Devastation and Renewal*, 172–73, 33–39.

66. Ian Douglas, *The Urban Environment* (Baltimore: Edward Arnold, 1983), 93.

67. Robert A. Woods, "Pittsburgh: An Interpretation of Its Growth," quoted in Kellogg, ed., *The Pittsburgh District*, 19–20.

68. R. L. Duffus, "Is Pittsburgh Civilized"? *Harpers Monthly Magazine* 161 (October 1930): 537–45.

69. The following material dealing with the Nine Mile Run valley draws heavily on Andrew S. McElwaine, "History and Context: 'Slag in the Park,'" in Tarr, *Environmental History*, 174–92.

70. For a discussion of the effect of Olmsted's ideas about nature on Progressive Period reformers, see Paul Boyer, *Urban Masses and Moral Order in America, 1820–1930* (Cambridge, MA: Harvard University Press, 1978), 220–51.

71. Frederick Law Olmsted, *Pittsburgh Main Thoroughfares and the Down Town District* (Pittsburgh: Pittsburgh Civic Commission, 1911), 119–20.

72. Roy Lubove, *Twentieth-Century Pittsburgh, Vol. 1: Government, Business, and Environmental Change* (Pittsburgh: John Wiley and Sons, 1969), 53–56.

73. Citizens Committee on City Plan for Pittsburgh, *Parks: A Part of the Pittsburgh Plan* (Pittsburgh, September 1923), 64–71.

74. McElwaine, "Slag in the Park," 10–11; Anne Lloyd, "Pittsburgh's 1923 Zoning Ordinance," *Western Pennsylvania Historical Magazine* 57 (July 1974): 288–305; Janet R. Daley, "Zoning: Its Historical Context and Importance in the Development of Pittsburgh," *Western Pennsylvania Historical Magazine* 71 (April 1988): 99–125.

75. McElwaine, "Slag in the Park," 12–13.

76. See "The Development of Nine Mile Run: A Brownfield Site in Pittsburgh" (Pittsburgh: Carnegie Mellon University, March 20, 1997) for technical details concerning the site. For zoning and protests by neighbors of the site, see McElwaine, "Slag in the Park," 11–17.

77. City of Pittsburgh, Department of City Planning, *Nine Mile Run Development Proposal*, Pittsburgh, August 1982; City of Pittsburgh, Department of City Planning, *Nine Mile Run Major Development Project*, March 1987; GAI Consultants, *Nine Mile Run Development Traffic Study* (Pittsburgh, 1988).

78. John Paul and Molly Davidson-Welling, "Brownfield Development Case Study: Nine Mile Run" (unpublished report, Carnegie Mellon University, July 17, 1996). A description of Summerset at Frick Park can be found at http://www.ura.org/maj2.htm.

79. McElwaine, "Slag in the Park," 14–17.

80. McElwaine, "Slag in the Park," 18–19.

IV PLANNING THE MODERN CITY

Americans did not embrace comprehensive city planning until the early twentieth century and then only cautiously. They, especially members of the business community, viewed planning as intruding on the prerogatives of private enterprise and private property rights despite the inefficient, unhealthy, and unsafe consequences of unfettered free markets. With the exception of founding street layouts such as Pittsburgh's Woods-Vickroy plan of 1784, piecemeal development of urban infrastructure (e.g., streets, waterworks, sewers, parks, etc.) without overall guidance or a central vision shaped most American cities during the nineteenth century.[1] Under the auspices of the progressive reform-inspired Pittsburgh Civic Commission, the preeminent planner Frederick Law Olmsted Jr. produced the city's first comprehensive plan in 1911. In the same year the Pennsylvania legislature authorized Pittsburgh to have a planning commission—staffed by a department of planning but limited to an advisory role to the city council and mayor. Planning by the public sector and nonprofit civic organizations, sometimes in partnership with each other, has been a significant part of the region's development since Olmsted's 1911 report.[2]

The first chapter in this section reveals a web of elite Pittsburghers who hired the Olmsted brothers to plan the landscaping of their estates, lay out subdivisions, and design civic projects. This experience gave them confidence to entrust Frederick Law Olmsted Jr. with their city's first foray into planning. The second and third chapters explore some limitations, successes, and consequences of planning in this quintessential industrial city. Tracing the decades of planning proposals for the city's riverfronts highlights the dominance of industrial and utilitarian priorities for three-quarters of the century. In the years after the Second World War, however, aesthetic and recreational visions challenged the traditional priorities, laying the foundation for the remarkable transformation of postindustrial Pittsburgh's riverfronts. The third chapter examines downtown over two centuries to reveal its dynamic, ever-changing spatial patterns. The city and region's slowing and then stagnating economic vitality led to the partnering of public and nonprofit sector leaders with private sector leaders in shaping the Golden Triangle. The partnerships still remained far removed from the concerns of the city's neighborhoods. The final essay narrows the focus to the process of planning for the preservation of the region's industrial heritage and the efforts to help former industrial communities reimagine postindustrial futures.

NOTES

1. Jon A. Peterson, *The Birth of City Planning in the United States, 1840–1917* (Johns Hopkins University Press, 2003).

2. John A. Bauman and Edward K. Muller, *Before Renaissance: Planning in Pittsburgh, 1889–1943* (Pittsburgh: University of Pittsburgh Press, 2006).

13 THE OLMSTEDS IN PITTSBURGH

LANDSCAPING THE PRIVATE CITY

Edward K. Muller and John F. Bauman

On January 29, 1901, John C. Olmsted, the stepson of the great urban park creator Frederick Law Olmsted Sr., arrived in Pittsburgh from Boston, probably on the nine o'clock morning train. A carriage whisked him to William Larimer Mellon's downtown office for a nine-thirty meeting. Olmsted waited fifteen minutes before Mellon received him. The traction magnate in 1901 was building a new Pittsburgh home on three lush acres overlooking Schenley Park in the city's East End, and the Olmsted firm had been summoned to propose a plan for landscaping the estate. It was neither the first nor the last visit to the smoky city for Olmsted's firm. Although little has been written about such visits, it was typical of many that John C. Olmsted and his half brother, Frederick Law Olmsted Jr., made to Pittsburgh during the first quarter of the twentieth century.

The Olmsteds left behind a deep—albeit unheralded—mark on the private, civic, and public landscapes of Pittsburgh and its region. The focus of this chapter is primarily on the Brookline, Massachusetts, firm's long and sometimes strained association with Pittsburgh's elite and the private as well as the civic world it sculptured for the wealthy in the East End and the more peripheral Sewickley area. It probes the web of social and business relationships attracted private landscaping consultants such as the Olmsteds into the elegant, often sumptuous, world of the urban-industrial elite and perforce into the vortex of urban reform. Historians long ago confirmed the elite impetus behind twentieth-century urban planning; however, few historians have attempted to fathom the matrix of business, civic, and social relationships linking the worlds of landscape architecture, the urban elite, and early twentieth-century environmental reform (see Figures 13.1, 13.2).

We contend that despite their late-nineteenth-century retreat to leafy suburbs, the wealthy turn-of-the-century Pittsburgh families regarded the cityscape of streets, mills, department stores, rail yards, warehouses, courthouses, jails, and even the tangle of slum housing as their patrimony to be brought somehow into conformity with upper-class moral and aesthetic standards. The orderly landscaped suburban communities and civic settings that the Olmsteds helped shape palpably reflected those standards. Indeed, the charge to redesign the industrial city that Pittsburgh elites would convey to Frederick Law Olmsted Jr. in 1909 might be best comprehended as an extension or broadening of their collective individual ambition to mold, with the Olmsteds' help, a rational, safe, and beautiful private world.

EARLY PITTSBURGH COMMISSIONS

The Olmsted family's role in shaping the landscape and planning history of Pittsburgh and its region has remained unheralded. The Olmsted name is traditionally linked with Frederick Olmsted Jr.'s father, the renowned designer of New York's Central Park, where he blended an exhaustive knowledge of arboriculture and horticulture with a deep aesthetic sensitivity for nature as well as a certain foreboding about the social deterioration of urban America. Joined later in the nineteenth century by his sons, John C. and Frederick Jr., Olmsted Sr. creatively articulated the role of parks in urban society.[1] Despite Frederick Olmsted Sr.'s fleeting business acquaintance with Carnegie, circumstances seemingly precluded a role for the famed landscaper in Pittsburgh.[2] Olmsted's reputation resonated as a park planner, but among large cities Pittsburgh lagged behind on building public parks. Olmsted and Calvert Vaux prepared a plan for Allegheny City's modest West Park in 1867, but two decades elapsed before the City of Pittsburgh seriously entertained the idea of park development. When the city did acquire parkland in 1869, it was not Olmsted but an admirer, Pittsburgh public works director Edward M. Bigelow, who undertook the park design work.[3]

Moreover, the elite vogue for extravagantly landscaped estates, perhaps evoking the gardens of Europe, did not reach Pittsburgh until the late 1890s, too late for the elder Olmsted. While perhaps knowing of his fame as Central Park's creator, Pittsburgh elites were unaware possibly of Olmsted's

FIGS. 13.1 & 13.2 Frederick Law Olmsted Jr. (above, left. Courtesy of the National Park Service, Frederick Law Olmsted National Historic Site). Frederick's stepbrother, John C. Olmsted (above, right. Courtesy of the National Park Service, Frederick Law Olmsted National Historic Site).

talent as a private estate landscaper; or it may be that in no-nonsense Presbyterian Pittsburgh there was little thought of obtaining outside consultation for private landscaping.[4]

Boston architect H. H. Richardson, commissioned in 1884 to design the Allegheny County Courthouse, may have been the vehicle for Olmsted Sr. to become active in Pittsburgh. Olmsted and Richardson had a long professional relationship. Two of Richardson's young protégés, A. W. Longfellow and Frank E. Alden, had worked on the important courthouse project, and after Richardson's death in 1886 they spawned a new firm with Alfred Harlow. This firm forged another strong link between Boston's design community and wealthy Pittsburghers. Longfellow, Alden, and Harlow quickly landed commissions in Pittsburgh, which put them in touch with the people who would become Olmsted's first local clients. One of the architectural firm's early commissions was the residence of Andrew Carnegie's personal physician, Dr. James McClelland; Longfellow, Alden, and Harlow also won the competition for the Duquesne Club (1887), and the Vandergrift (1888) and Conestoga (1890) Buildings, both developed by J. J. Vandergrift, as well as Vandergrift's private estate in the East End.[5] These close connections between Boston and Pittsburgh by the end of the 1880s afforded bountiful opportunities for Pittsburghers such as Carnegie and Vandergrift to know of Olmsted and his work. In 1889 Carnegie asked Olmsted to survey a building site for the steel magnate's country estate at Cresson in the Allegheny Mountains near Altoona. Olmsted toured the estate grounds with Carnegie and recommended a site.[6]

More is known about a second contact with Pittsburgh some six years later—appropriately with the steel industry. In 1895 the treasurer of Pittsburgh's Apollo Iron and Steel Co., Wallace Bache, wrote Olmsted Sr. seeking a plan for a new model industrial company town on the Kiskiminetas River in Westmoreland County. J. J. Vandergrift was the major investor in Apollo Iron and Steel. The firm's president, George McMurtry, who was the moving force behind the new plant and town, maintained his office in the Vandergrift Building in Pittsburgh and named the town Vandergrift. Whether Vandergrift's Boston architectural associations led the company to contact Olmsted, or whether Olmsted's reputation and recent work at the 1893 Chicago World's Fair provided the impetus is unknown. On the heels of a bitter lockout at their Apollo mill in 1893 and in the general context of violent strikes at Homestead, Pullman, and elsewhere, McMurtry and Vandergrift purchased a farm a few miles downriver where they could build a more expansive, modern works and fashion a workers' community. Undoubtedly aware of George Pullman's celebrated industrial experiment near Chicago and the current discourse about model company towns, McMurtry embarked upon a plan to blend sound environmental planning and paternalism to fashion a more stable social order than the common southwestern Pennsylvania iron and steel town.[7]

At age seventy and already suffering severe lapses of memory, Olmsted deferred the Vandergrift matter to his partners, his stepson John C. Olmsted and Charles Elliot. The associates jointly crafted a socially and aesthetically pleasing plan for the town of Vandergrift. In contrast to Pullman and most other company towns, Vandergrift featured the naturalistic curvilinear design first seen in Olmsted and Vaux's plan for upper-class Riverside, Illinois, in 1856. McMurtry envisioned Vandergrift as a community of homeowners. Accordingly, Olmsted and Elliot arranged single family homes on unusually spacious lots and used restrictive covenants to control subsequent development. They placed picturesque miniparks at key street intersections and incorporated into their design a monumental central square anchored on one end by an impressive railroad station and on the other by an attractive town hall. As completed, Vandergrift reflected severe compromises that the penurious board of the steel company imposed upon Olmsted and Elliot's original plan. Nevertheless, publicity surrounding Vandergrift undoubtedly strengthened the reputation of the Brookline firm in Western Pennsylvania, and especially that of John C. Olmsted, who by 1900 with his half brother, Frederick Law Olmsted Jr., headed the firm called Olmsted Brothers.[8]

The Vandergrift commission soon led the Olmsteds directly into the city of Pittsburgh. During the summer of 1895 the treasurer of Apollo Iron and Steel requested the Olmsteds' advice on another of J. J. Vandergrift's real estate investments. Vandergrift and an associate, Charles Lockhart, owned ninety acres along Frankstown Road in Homewood, which they wanted to develop into residential lots. After a visit to the site, known as Homewood Driving Park, the Olmsteds recommended laying out the plan and providing improvements that would attract the "better class of occupation . . . [people] who are most likely to build, immediately, attractive suburban houses with all the modern conveniences and comforts and showing considerable individuality." Although the rectangular grid of extant city streets around the site prohibited a curvilinear plan, they believed that the widening of Frankstown and Homewood Avenues and the planting of curbside grass and shade trees would create an attractive environment. Further, the firm proposed landscaped center strips on some other streets, three-to-four-acre miniparks, and the planting of fruit trees and shrubbery on the lots in advance of the sale. For the "quickest and greatest profit," they urged the construction of all general improvements such as sewers, gutters, paved roads, and water and gas lines before selling the lots. While the Homewood Driving Park plan was filed with the city in a few years, the developers clearly did not implement the Olmsteds' suggestions, and a more prosaic subdivision of small lots, closely spaced houses, and a few landscaping amenities emerged.[9]

Within three years of beginning their Vandergrift commissions, another steel company asked Olmsted Brothers to consult on subdivision plans. In October 1898 L. C. Phipps, second vice president of the Carnegie Steel Company, solicited the Olmsteds' advice for landscaping the seventy-five-acre "Hill Subdivision" of the company's City Farm property adjacent to its Homestead Mill in Munhall Borough. Phipps may have sought out the Olmsteds because of their Vandergrift work; however, he was also a member of the investment group that two months earlier had engaged the firm for the Schenley Hotel project the group was developing. The industrialist not only accepted the Olmsted plan but requested suggestions for plantings and for trees. Through their work with L. C. Phipps and the Apollo Iron and Steel principals, especially J. J. Vandergrift, the Olmsted firm had the opportunity to become known among Pittsburgh's iron and steel elite.

ESTATE PROJECTS

Over the years many prominent Pittsburghers, communicating through their business contacts, civic roles, and private lives, recommended the Olmsteds to each other. In some cases either local or out-of-town architects suggested the Olmsteds to their clients. Although the eminence of the firm in landscape design and later urban planning would have alone commended the Olmsteds, surviving correspondence reveals a web of personal recommendations based on firsthand acquaintance with their landscaping work, which led to inquiries for consultation. This network of relationships produced for the Olmsteds important Pittsburgh commissions for landscaping private residences, planning subdivisions, and designing the grounds for various civic establishments.[10]

The landscaping firm that Frederick Olmsted Jr. and John C. Olmsted headed in 1901 had originated in the mid-nineteenth century under the senior Olmsted, who with Calvert Vaux had designed Central Park. In 1872 Olmsted Sr. ended his long and shaky partnership with Vaux and soon thereafter founded the firm of Olmsted Associates, headquartered in his home at 209 West Forty-Sixth Street in Manhattan. Although until 1877 he retained his job as head of the New York Park Department's Bureau of Design and Superintendence, Olmsted feuded endlessly with Tammany Hall bosses, mainly over the issue of professionalism versus patronage. In 1883 he moved his family and the firm to the more sedate and less socially fractious elite suburban world of Brookline. Here on the grounds of his small estate, "Fairstead," in a wing of his large residence, Olmsted established a full-scale professional landscaping firm, which emphasized the teaching as well as the practice of landscape architecture (see Figure 13.3).[11]

Olmsted's landscaping gems—his Central Park, the "Emerald Necklace" of parks bejeweling Boston, and the celebrated lagoon system informing the "White City" of Chicago's 1893 Columbian Exposition—secured the writer-horticulturist-planner a prominent niche in the pantheon of American landscape architects. Tragically, by 1895 premature senility forced Olmsted out of the public world. He died in 1903. However, the firm he founded survived, and prominently so. Indeed, by 1900, John C. Olmsted enjoyed a solid national reputation among the wealthy urban-industrial elite as a favorite architect for the landscaping of their large estates. And, at a time when the profession of city planner was fairly unknown, Frederick Olmsted Jr., a member of the prestigious body of architects and artists commissioned by Congress in 1901 to restore Washington, DC, to Pierre L'Enfant's original baroque design, boasted an equally distinguished career.

Fig. 13.3 Olmsted Brothers offices in Brookline, Massachusetts, in 1930 (courtesy of the National Park Service, Frederick Law Olmsted National Historic Site).

Until 1935 Olmsted Associates ranked among the top three landscape planning firms in America, listing among its clients, in addition to the US government, universities such as Stanford and Johns Hopkins and America's richest families.[12]

The turn of the century proved auspicious for the Olmsteds' debut in Pittsburgh. Beginning in the 1880s a sizeable segment of the city's wealthy began abandoning the din, pollution, and ethnic mottle of the industrial city for bucolic suburban retreats in the East End and Sewickley areas. After the pall of economic depression lifted in the late 1890s, home building boomed in the fashionable suburbs. Middle- and upper-middle-class Pittsburghers now joined the urban elites, making places such as the East End a crucible where a new, more cosmopolitan, upper-class culture was being created. Once caricatured as stern, self-abnegating Calvinists who shunned luxury as a sin, Pittsburgh elites increasingly immersed themselves in the cult of consumption, especially of a more beautiful residential environment. In the early 1900s they built pretentious estates that required professional landscaping.[13]

Between 1901 and 1902 four stalwarts of modern urban-industrialism (Howard J. Heinz, William Larimer Mellon, John Guffey, and F. T. Lovejoy) and one scion of the old order (Elizabeth Dohrman Thaw, widow of wealthy coal merchant William Thaw Jr.) approached the Olmsteds about landscaping their properties. Consistent with the firm's division of labor, John Olmsted usually handled private estate work while Olmsted Jr. busied himself with the firm's public and semi-public works, city parks, street and thoroughfare layouts, and civic spaces.

On January 14, 1901, the Olmsteds wrote W. L. Mellon at the suggestion of William Falconer, superintendent of Schenley Park, offering their services for planning the property of his projected residence near the Murdoch Street entrance of Schenley Park. Falconer knew of the Olmsteds' work on the Schenley Hotel and the Bigelow Boulevard entrance to the park in Oakland. Mellon obviously reacted positively for John Olmsted arrived by train in Pittsburgh on January 29, 1901, and after briefly visiting Mellon at his office, joined Falconer and adjacent property owner Leonard G. Woods in perambulating the site located at Darlington Road. A friend of Mellon since childhood and a partner in local street railway ventures, Woods had sold part of his property to Mellon for the residence. On his field inspection, and typical of his firm's procedures, Olmsted, notebooks in hand, carefully recorded the land elevations. He observed as well the vegetation of the park and adjoining properties, the house plan details, and (of utmost importance) Mr. Mellon's personal vision of the place. They discussed the residential plans of neighbors William Kay and Julian Kennedy, the latter a Yale classmate of John Olmsted's and a notable figure in the city's steel industry who had been superintendent of Carnegie Steel's Homestead Works. From his copious notes, Olmsted prepared and within a week submitted to Mellon an extensive ten-page report. In addition to exterior recommendations such as grading, retaining walls, steps, piazza, terrace, walkways, and plantings, the architect suggested changes in the siting and layout of the house so as to take greater advantage of the park view, to gain more sunlight, and especially to dissipate disagreeable cooking odors by enhancing natural air circulation. As the firm prepared a more formal preliminary plan during March 1901, Olmsted and his assistants coordinated land grading with respect to Mellon's neighbors' properties and proposed to Falconer the restructuring of the Murdoch Street connection with the park. Over the next eighteen months, the firm made several additional site visits, consulted regularly with Mr. and Mrs. Mellon, and worked closely with their architects, Boston's Alden and Harlow (see Appendix 13.2).[14]

Between February 1901 and April 1903 the Olmsted firm produced sixty-one topographic maps of Mellon's Darlington Road property. Depending on the physical size of the estate and its complexity, over time (years in many cases) the Olmsteds generated anywhere from ten to occasionally one hundred maps. These more or less highly detailed topographic maps invariably included one or more "preliminary" or conceptual plans and numerous cross-sectional studies showing the house in relationship to other main infrastructural and natural features such as drives, formal and informal walks, sewers, and clumps of trees to be removed or preserved. Grading maps followed, as well as the elaborate "planting plans," and finally, the piece de resistance, the "general plan." The orchestration of these topographic plans expresses magnificently the firm's syncretic relationship with its clients. Although both Olmsted Jr. and his half brother, John, inherited their father's affection for the romantic landscape, often incorporating serpentine stone paths, tree stands, and other naturalistic landscape motifs into their design, they were equally sensitive to the hubris of their powerful clients. French chateau-esque, Tudor, and Beaux Arts mansions demanded baroque elements, formal gardens and driveways, to complement the Olmsteds' signature romantic designs. Although their taste frequently exceeded the depth of their clients' pocketbooks, they mastered the fine art of massaging the well-developed ego.

Within days of inspecting of Mellon's property, John Olmsted received a letter from George S. Orth, the Pittsburgh architect who was designing Elizabeth Dohrman Thaw's new forty-four-room summer home, called "As You Like It," being built on forty-five acres in Sewickley Heights.[15] Orth had read in the newspapers about Olmsted's consultation on the Mellon and Kennedy properties and wondered if on his next visit to Pittsburgh Olmsted would tour and evaluate the Thaw property adjoining the B. F. Jones (of Jones & Laughlin Steel Corporation) estate near the new Allegheny Country Club. The firm did not customarily make preliminary visits merely on the speculation of obtaining business. Rather, for a set fee of $100 plus travel expenses, one of the principals would undertake an initial visit of the property and prepare a short report of his observations for a general landscaping plan. If the client wished to proceed, then for $150 the Olmsteds would prepare an elaborate preliminary plan for reshaping the topography, locating driveways and outbuildings, constructing walls, establishing proper drainage and planting trees, shrubs, and gardens. The client could keep the plan or contract with the Olmsteds to develop detailed grading and construction plans, implemented either under their supervision or by a contractor of the client's choice.

In late February of 1901 Elizabeth Thaw joined John Olmsted and her son at the Sewickley Heights property for a site visit, and by March 6 she received a twelve-page report. Thaw found the report pleasing enough to order the preparation of the preliminary plan, and she instructed her architect to mail Olmsted the requisite maps and topographical surveys of her property. He produced a plan by the end of April. Following additional site visits, discussions of the plan, estimates of charges, and concern over expenses, in August 1901 Thaw accepted a contract for carrying out the detailed plan. A year later Orth assumed supervision of further landscaping based on the Olmsted plan, but Thaw periodically consulted with the Olmsteds during the next fifteen years about the plantings (see Appendix 13.3).[16]

May 1901 was a busy month for John Olmsted in Pittsburgh. While he was discussing plans with W. L. Mellon and Elizabeth Thaw, he received an inquiry from Thaw's neighbor the Allegheny Country Club. Club vice president Henry R. Rea, a well-connected member of the city's iron and steel elite, and John Denniston Lyon, the club's secretary and a prominent city banker, asked Olmsted to consult on the building of cottages on the organization's grounds.[17] Even as Olmsted submitted his report at the end of the month, he had already agreed to visit H. J. Heinz's Penn Avenue estate, "Greenlawn," in Pittsburgh's East End. Heinz had recently toured the mansions lining Cleveland's fashionable Euclid Avenue, and after consulting with several landscape architects before 1901 on the recommendation of his friend, General Warner Washington, he invited Olmsted to his East End home. The strong-willed Heinz somewhat resisted Olmsted's magisterial approach. Heinz wished not only for English gardens but also for a grape arbor, tennis courts, stables, and a vegetable garden; but he limited Olmsted to problems of grading, shaping the front lawn, and defining an entrance to the property. Clearly vexed, Olmsted complained that the "mixed character of this record [his field notes] illustrates the skimpy way in which Mr. Heinz brought the facts and his ideas to my attention. He headed off all attempts on my part to plan the whole place." Despite their disagreements, including Heinz's fear of the consultant's steep traveling expenses, Olmsted produced a landscape plan with which Howard Heinz and his father were "much pleased." Howard Heinz wrote: "I told my father in a smiling mood that this was what Yale [both Olmsted and young Heinz graduated from Yale] did for a man. My father replied that the man must have been a good deal of a man even before Yale took hold of him." Heinz agreed to have the Brookline firm prepare plans for grading the property, and during 1902 Olmsted visited the Heinz property twice more in his efforts to create an acceptable plan for gardens and planting (see Appendix 13.1).[18]

Olmsted experienced less difficulty with his other two East End clients. Colonel Joseph W. Guffey, whom Olmsted described as a free-spending man, "good natured . . . [and] democratic in nature . . . [who] swears considerably and also chews tobacco," had made his fortune with Andrew W. Mellon wild-catting for Texas oil. The other East Ender, F. T. Lovejoy, struck gold in

J. P. Morgan's consolidation of Carnegie's steel empire into US Steel. A close friend of Henry Clay Frick, Lovejoy employed Alden and Harlow to design his new residence, called "Edgehill," located near Penn and Braddock Avenues on property adjoining Frick's extensive acreage near his Clayton mansion in Point Breeze. It was Lovejoy's architects who importuned Olmsted about the landscaping. Lovejoy neither completed nor occupied "Edgehill"; however, the stone walls, serpentine paths, and lush plantings that embodied Olmsted's landscaping plans for Lovejoy, Mellon, and others imparted a romantic ambience to the East End, reflecting the new wealth and cosmopolitanism of fin de siècle Pittsburgh.[19]

CIVIC LANDSCAPE DESIGNS

Not all of the Olmsted firm's early twentieth-century consulting work in Pittsburgh involved private estate landscaping, although that work kept them busy. In this era of rapid suburbanization, the Olmsteds found work platting new subdivisions and civic landscapes. The ongoing consultations with Elizabeth Thaw in Sewickley Heights during the early years of the century led to an important commission for designing a subdivision in the adjoining Edgeworth Borough. On the advice of Thaw, James B. Oliver of the Oliver iron and steel companies sought John Olmsted's advice in June 1905 about platting his wife's thirty-acre inheritance into lots with one-hundred-foot frontages. Oliver and his wife, Amelia Shields, disagreed on the merits of a prosaic rectilinear lot design versus the romantic curvilinear plan favored by Olmsted. A local engineering firm, Edeburn and Cooper, with whom Olmsted often worked in Pittsburgh, proposed a typical rectilinear style for the acreage. Oliver's wife favored a curvilinear street layout, which Olmsted described in a letter as picturesque, especially for those eager to "escap[e] from the strictly rectangular subdivision so universally adopted in the suburbs of Pittsburgh."[20]

Although Amelia Oliver loved Olmsted's plan, her businessman husband feared that it departed too radically from the gridiron tradition established in the East End and in nearby Ohio River suburbs such as Bellevue. Based on the advice of the local real estate community, he also worried that it would unduly raise development costs. Further, Oliver noted the objections of two neighbors who felt that curved roads looked good on paper but in time would degenerate into mere "crooked lines" because the borough would fail to maintain them. Oliver temporarily prevailed upon Olmsted to produce a rectangular plan, writing that it was "the best and most sensible one," even though his wife "still adheres to the curvilinear." In this last phrase, Olmsted saw his opportunity and quickly wrote back to argue his case. Normally, he averred, the curvilinear plan in large cities like New York and Philadelphia raised land values. "We judge, however, that in the vicinity of Pittsburgh a departure from the commonplace rectangular system of subdivision is much more a novelty, and therefore, much less likely to be appreciated by the majority of seekers for home sites." Nevertheless, he pleaded, the novelty itself in Pittsburgh may well attract many customers. Within a week Oliver capitulated, and Olmsted reproduced his picturesque albeit modest plan, replete with a long list of covenants controlling the character of development. Although Oliver died before the year ended, Amelia Oliver eventually recorded the plan as "Oliver Place" and incorporated Olmsted's restrictions establishing minimum house values and setbacks from the road, right-of-ways for electric and telephone wires, and clauses prohibiting chicken coops, pasturing of animals, and houses with flat roofs.[21]

The route the Olmsted brothers followed from being landscapers to the Thaws, Olivers, and other Pittsburgh elites to being framers of the city's first urban plan passed directly through the Progressive Era, specifically the "City Beautiful" movement. During this era in the late nineteenth and early twentieth centuries, Pittsburgh's wealthiest citizens extended their passion for environmental order and beauty beyond their private suburban world into the civic realm. Indeed, the historian John Peterson has traced the roots of the "City Beautiful" movement in America to this involvement of such people in municipal art, civic improvements, and outdoor art movements. Apostles of these civic crusades contended that, in an age of obsessive individual competition, the unkempt commonweal or public good would be well served by creating parks, erecting artistic fountains, building tree-lined boulevards, removing billboards, and in other ways beautifying and making orderly the public landscape. Indeed, a deep moral commitment to order and beauty infused the suburban ethos visible in Pittsburgh's East End. Appalled by the ugliness of the industrial landscape, elite and upper-middle-class reformers espoused a philosophy that equated environmental quality with elevated moral behavior. Little distance, therefore, separated the elite impetus for artistically landscaped private estates from the progressive crusade for civic betterment.[22]

In Pittsburgh many of these elite crusaders for civic beauty and moral environmentalism marched in the ranks of the Civic Club of Allegheny County (CCAC). Founded in October 1895 amid economic depression and the premonition of class warfare heightened by the violent Homestead and Pullman strikes, the CCAC mirrored the gamut of popular fears about the deterioration of the urban environment: the squalid, unhealthy living condition of the city's ethnic working class and the implications for the volatility of the urban social order. At the same time, the women and men who comprised the CCAC resonated with the millennial optimism about the depths of civic virtue, the inevitability of progress, and the power of environmental reform to restore social order and social justice.[23]

With a membership comprised of prominent upper-class women such as the organization's treasurer, Elizabeth D. Thaw, as well as leading businessmen and professionals, the CCAC investigated the dark dank corners of the urban industrial environment. Its agenda encompassed building public baths and playgrounds for the poor (the former a special interest of Thaw's), industrial education, prohibition of cigarette sales to minors, outdoor schools for tubercular children, smoke abatement, Arbor Day, tenement house laws, professionalization of social work, abolition of child labor, control of billboards, and the need for good government. Urban beauty ranked high among the club's objectives.[24] Its various departments included not only "Social Service" and "Public Health," but also "Art," the latter dedicated "to increasing the beauty of our parks and public places, and raising standards of taste."[25] At century's turn, the CCAC embodied the fervent progressive belief in the curative power of a beautified urban environment. Significantly, it listed among its leading members not only Elizabeth Thaw but also Howard Heinz, Andrew Mellon, and Mr. and Mrs. Franklin Nicola, all clients of Olmsted Associates.[26]

The CCAC's agenda placed the organization neatly within the civic improvement movement championed by Charles Mulford Robinson from Rochester, New York, the father of the "City Beautiful" movement. But prior to 1909, civic improvement in Pittsburgh, Rochester, and most of urban America involved more whimsy than planning. There was no coherent vision of environmental reform guiding action. Reformers planted trees here, monuments there; they eradicated unsightly roadside billboards, cleared rubble-strewn lots for a playground, transformed prosaic horse troughs into Grecian fountains, and campaigned for romantic urban parks.[27] For example, the three hundred acres of Oakland woodlands that city public works director Edward Bigelow in 1889 cajoled from Londoner Mary Schenley, and which he hoped to groom into an Arcadia for the social elevation of the lower classes, in actual fact lay beyond the pathways of the city's ethnic poor.[28] City Beautiful apostles such as CCAC member Franklin Nicola abjured the downtown for Oakland, where Nicola was developing an upper-middle-class subdivision and hotel near the planned main entrance to Bigelow's Schenley Park.

In 1898 Bigelow wanted an impressive neoclassical gateway for Schenley Park in Oakland. He envisioned this majestic entrance symbolically separating the brutal mechanized world of the city from the serene natural world of the park. Bigelow's distinguished superintendent of Schenley Park, the young English landscape architect William Falconer, recommended that the Olmsteds be commissioned to design the main park entrance, which would be located off Forbes Avenue near the new Carnegie Library. On Bigelow's behalf, Falconer enjoined John C. Olmsted to produce a Beaux Arts masterpiece by "magnificently, tastefully, artistically" designing an entrance, "the whole forming one grand harmonious picture."[29]

We know nothing about Olmsted's 1898 park entrance plan. Whatever its fate, the landscape architect's work there surely pricked the entrepreneurial imagination of Franklin Nicola. With his investment partners, including in Falconer's words "our most prominent friends, or, in plain English 'ring' men," Nicola in 1898 was building the Schenley Hotel as a cornerstone of his design for a Pittsburgh "White City" in Oakland, inspired by that built along Chicago's Lake Michigan as part of the 1893 Columbian Exposition. Nicola's Oakland tapestry already included Longfellow, Alden, and Harlow's Carnegie Library and Institute (1895). Working in concert with Bigelow and Falconer, Nicola engaged Olmsted to weave the park entrance and the Schenley Hotel grounds into one fabric. John Olmsted discussed his landscape design ideas with Nicola, as well as with the steel magnate L. C. Phipps and Colonel Albert J. Logan, a Pittsburgh mattress manufacturer keenly interested in planning. All three shared Nicola's Oakland vision. By 1902 planting and contouring progressed smoothly on Olmsted's hotel landscaping, but the park entrance plans languished. Olmsted continued to consult on the hotel's plantings through 1908.[30]

In late January 1901, within days of being approached by W. L. Mellon and Elizabeth Thaw for work on their estates, John Olmsted was asked by park superintendent Falconer to consider redesigning Allegheny Cemetery. Recall that Falconer had also been involved in Olmsted's consultation for the design of Mellon's Murdoch Street estate as well as for the Schenley Hotel and park entrance commissions. By the end of the nineteenth century, "rural" cemeteries like Allegheny, built in large cities during midcentury, were undergoing extensive renovations that embodied the era's environmental reform ideas. Reluctant to undertake the arduous work of cemetery revisions, Olmsted nevertheless agreed to conduct a preliminary visit in June and requested maps and notes from the cemetery's head gardener. Olmsted then made a second visit, and in the last days of 1901 submitted an extensive sixty-eight-page report on the cemetery. Presumably impressed, the board of managers for Allegheny Cemetery two years later lured Falconer from his city parks post to oversee the revamping. Over the next twenty-five years Falconer managed the massive reconstruction and rehabilitation of the cemetery, transforming it into one of the nation's finest and propelling himself into the top ranks of the Association of American Cemetery Superintendents.[31] Olmsted's report apparently formed the basis, at least initially, for Falconer's far-reaching work on Allegheny Cemetery.

In 1908, five years after Falconer had left his Schenley Park position, the Department of Public Works solicited Olmsted's services for the development of Arsenal Park. As customary, he refused to confer on speculation, but he agreed to draft a proposal of work based on blueprints forwarded by the city.[32] Nothing came of this matter, but the Olmsteds' involvement in civic design escalated considerably in 1909 when the Pittsburgh Civic Commission (PCC) engaged Frederick Law Olmsted Jr. to prepare a plan for the city. This public role of the Olmsteds in Pittsburgh is elaborated in our book *Before Renaissance: Planning in Pittsburgh, 1889–1943*.[33]

Nevertheless, Frederick Law Olmsted Jr.'s greater visibility attending his work on the city plan sparked a flurry of inquiries and commissions. PCC member Thomas E. Billiquist queried Olmsted in April 1910 about a planned real estate development in nearby Washington, Pennsylvania. No evidence confirms his working on Billiquist's subdivision, but several months later Olmsted began drafting reports for landscaping the grounds of Howard Heinz's Morewood Heights home and for F. S. Willock's estate in Sewickley. In both cases Edward C. Whiting, Olmsted's associate in Pittsburgh who coordinated the city plan work, conducted the site visits, collected appropriate maps and surveys, and offered suggestions for these residential reports. One Whiting note regarding the Willock estate and the peculiar environment of Pittsburgh informed Olmsted that "evergreen trees don't do well in smoky air. Can we use rhododendrons?"[34] In March 1911 the attorney William A. Way of Sewickley asked whether Olmsted, while visiting Pittsburgh on civic commission business, would consider advising on a street problem in Edgeworth Borough (where the Oliver subdivision was located).[35] Olmsted graciously declined. A month later the Civic Club and the Chamber of Commerce of Johnstown, Pennsylvania, cognizant of the firm's Pittsburgh work, requested Olmsted's services on a "general and set plan" for the city. However, unexplained delays postponed the actual competition until 1916, when Johnstown selected architect Henry Hornbostel as its consultant.[36]

After submitting the Pittsburgh plan in 1911 and completing residential reports for Heinz and Willock, the Olmsteds undertook no new local commissions until 1919. Frederick Olmsted Jr.'s interests broadened considerably between 1911 and 1920. In addition to his burgeoning reputation as one of the fathers of city planning, Olmsted Jr. fought to protect the national parks from commercial incursions and cultivated his role with John Nolen as the American authorities on industrial housing. During the First World War he moved to Washington, DC, where he initially served as town planner with the War Industries Board's Bureau of Industrial Housing. In 1918 he headed the town planning section of the US Housing Corporation and oversaw the building of several exemplary wartime government housing developments including Yorkship Village in Camden, New Jersey and one project in McKees Rocks.[37]

Olmsted Jr.'s wartime preoccupation with industrial housing aside, he managed to remain engaged in Pittsburgh civic affairs during the 1911–1920 period. When the City Art Commission in 1913 retained Edward H. Bennett to revise the plans for bridge approaches to the Point, Bennett contacted Olmsted, who naturally directed the Chicago planner to his two-year-old city plan.[38] In 1914, the art commission asked him to join a jury evaluating designs for the still unfinished main entrance to Schenley Park. Olmsted declined the appointment, primarily on the grounds that a competition was an inappropriate means to secure a quality design and that having already prepared a solution for the entrance years earlier, he could not be considered an impartial juror.[39] Two years later Olmsted did participate as a juror in a competition sponsored by the Beaux Arts Salon of Pittsburgh for design of the important intersection of Fifth Avenue and Craig Street in Oakland. The sponsors, members of Pittsburgh's elite such as Marvin F. Scaife and Mrs. Roy A. Hunt, hoped that a public square, circle, or some other solution would "add to the beauty of the avenue or street without in any way lessening its dignity or utility."[40]

POST–FIRST WORLD WAR COMMISSIONS

When the war ended the Olmsted brothers resumed their business as landscaping consultants for some of Pittsburgh's wealthiest citizens. After John C. Olmsted died in 1920, various associates, including the trusted Whiting, handled local site visits and reported back to the Brookline office and Frederick Law Olmsted Jr. Most commissions concentrated in Pittsburgh's East End and in the Sewickley area, though a few reflected the expanding residential horizons of the city's upper class. By October 1919 the firm had undertaken landscape planning for both Andrew W. Mellon's home on Woodland Road and Richard Beatty Mellon's Alden and Harlow–designed residence at 6500 Fifth Avenue. Olmsted's work for R. B. Mellon, which continued into the 1930s, involved redesigning his extensive gardens, including lavish plantings around the estate's lily pond.[41]

Other East End commissions and inquiries in this post–First World War period stemmed from the firm's past and ongoing work in the city. Whiting reported to the Brookline office in March 1921 on a site visit to the Georgian brick home of architect Frederick I. Merrick, who was the Morewood Heights neighbor of Howard Heinz, a client of the Olmsteds a decade earlier. A local architect, Stanley Roush, the nephew of a Mount Lebanon client, businessman J. C. Roush, had recommended the firm to Merrick. The Olmsted firm prepared a preliminary report, but Merrick terminated the relationship after deciding to carry out some aspects of the project himself and at his own pace.[42]

Frequently nothing at all happened following a rash of interest in the Olmsteds' services. For example, earlier in 1921 Longvue Country Club inquired about having Olmsted landscape the club's grounds. The Brookline office rushed a statement of terms, but the Longvue people failed to respond. Two years later architect Benno Jannsen wrote Brookline again on behalf of Longvue. Olmsted informed Jannsen of the aborted first inquiry and restated the firm's terms. Again, and for the last time, the matter died.[43]

As before the war, the residential attractiveness and development potential of the verdant Sewickley area attracted Pittsburgh elites, and they sought Olmsted's advice. The Tuxedo Land Company wrote Olmsted about a planned subdivision for two thousand Sewickley Heights acres near the Allegheny Country Club. Preoccupied with war work, Olmsted declined. But after the war ended, he began in the spring of 1920 a two-year commission for landscaping the James Park estate. Pittsburgh architect William Boyd designed the Park house and asked Olmsted to plan gardens, terraces, and the driveway as well as to design plantings for the property that abutted the country club. Olmsted's handpicked gardener, Jetson Dyer from Maine, lived on the Park estate and supervised the project. However, Olmsted's relationship with Park steadily deteriorated largely because Park objected to the expense. In laboriously written notes to the Brookline office, Dyer beseeched Olmsted for another assignment because of Park's unrelenting negative and penurious attitude.[44]

In fact, Olmsted had another job in mind for their loyal Maine gardener. Boyd recommended the firm to another one of his clients, Mr. and Mrs. Charles A. Painter, who were moving from Pittsburgh's East End into a French chateau–style house on eight acres in Sewickley Heights. During the summer of 1921, while wrangling with Park over expenses, Olmsted prepared a plan for the Painters and suggested Dyer as the gardener. Their consultation with the Painters ended with the submission of the plan, but Dyer informed them of the interest of another Heights landowner. Seeing that Olmsted was working on the Park and Painter estates, wholesale lumber dealer George Nicola requested that the firm landscape his property across the valley from Park. Following a discussion of the potential charges, Nicola demurred, and the Olmsteds' work in the Sewickley area ended.[45]

Throughout the 1920s and into the depression of the 1930s, the Olmsteds preserved their foothold in Western Pennsylvania, although by 1930 it had become somewhat strained. Year by year the work for R. B. Mellon, begun in 1919, continued. In the mid-1920s, Mellon also engaged Olmsted to landscape the grounds of his new Rolling Rock golf course and club house near Ligonier and to design the club's reflecting pool and cascade gardens. While employed on Rolling Rock in 1930, Olmsted entertained a request from Mrs. George M. Laughlin to consult on the placement of the family's main cabin and several smaller ones on her property adjoining the country club. Laughlin, who lived on Woodland Road near A. W. Mellon, had earlier employed the Olmsteds on a project for her Mount Lake, Florida property. Discussions about the cabins continued all summer, then in late August she put her plans on hold because of "difficulties."[46]

Indeed, by 1930 the Great Depression created "difficulties" even for the wealthiest Pittsburghers. Olmsted's consulting fees that R. B. Mellon had harped about as early as 1919 and the expense of proposed landscaping work, estimated for Mellon at twelve thousand dollars in 1931, proved less tolerable with the nation's economy in an abyss. In early 1931, while Olmsted's longtime associate E. C. Whiting, was still supervising R. B. Mellon's garden reconstruction, the Olmsted firm agreed to prepare plans for the adjoining Shady Avenue property of R. B. Mellon's son-in-law, Alan M. Scaife. Later that summer, having evaluated Olmsted's preliminary plans and detailed work sheets, Scaife (like his father-in-law had earlier done) bristled at the expense. He paid the outstanding bill, requested a copy of the report, and then (unlike his father-in-law) brusquely decided to do no further business with Olmsted.[47]

Not all of the Olmsted firm's postwar work in southwestern Pennsylvania concerned private residences and clubs. As before, some involved subdivision planning, especially for industrial housing. Despite their professional reservations about the Vandergrift plan as it was developed, the publicity about the Westmoreland Country industrial town had been extensive and highly favorable, especially in the writings of Ida Tarbell in 1915 and 1916.[48] Moreover, Olmsted Jr.'s directorship of the US Housing Corporation had brought him to McKees Rocks to oversee the war housing project there. After the war, in November 1919, Thomas J. O'Brien of the Fort Pitt Malleable Iron Company requested help with housing problems for employees at the McKees Rocks works. By the end of 1920 Olmsted had produced a plan "showing grades, storm drainage, sewerage, walks, and other details" able to support twenty-seven houses. Olmsted recommended a "four-room semi-detached house" model, which "though small, yet contains all the essentials and may properly be considered the minimum decent accommodation." Noting other recent examples of four-room company houses in the Pittsburgh area at Midland, Donora, and Clairton, Olmsted suggested that the firm could prepare sketches of houses "showing suitable groupings of various house elevations differing chiefly through the judicious handling of this feature that attractive general effects can be produced with little, if any, extra cost and without departing from the most serviceable floor plan." O'Brien found the plan satisfactory, but he felt front porches and central flues would improve the houses. He requested the plan's details be readied for implementation, though "the building will not be done for some time."[49] A visit to the site in late 1992 revealed that, contrary to Olmsted's recommendations, a number of small "detached" frame two-story worker's dwellings were built.

THE OLMSTED LEGACY

For thirty-five years the Massachusetts-headquartered Olmsteds actively participated in shaping the Pittsburgh region's environment. The focus here has been mainly on the landscaping work that the Olmsteds performed as consultants to the city's most prominent families and on smaller "civic" projects that flowed directly from their private work. In the late nineteenth century the Olmsted brothers, already renowned as America's preeminent landscape architects, erected an extensive network of Pittsburgh clients from among the cream of the city's urban-industrial elite, including the Heinzes, the Mellons, Vandergrift, Thaw, Oliver, and Phipps among others. On one important level the firm's presence in Pittsburgh mirrored the stature of the city as a national center of wealth-producing industrial capitalism. On another it reflected a growing cultural shift among the city's urban elite. Easing away from its abstemious Presbyterianism of the past, Pittsburgh's fin-de-siècle aristocracy embraced a new cosmopolitanism manifested in a passion for large, architecturally exquisite estates. The Olmsteds capitalized on this passion and exerted a profound influence in shaping the romantic suburban ethos of the East End, as well as the more pastoral environment of the Sewickley retreat. The stone gates, serpentine paths, graded lawns, and tastefully and elaborately planted gardens helped endow Pittsburgh with a signature of distinction.

Sadly, very little evidence of the Olmsteds' artistry remains. Seventy-five years later only a sharp observer can discern the imprint of the Olmsteds' vision on the private landscape of Pittsburgh. Over the decades, new owners and new gardeners have sculptured and redecorated the land to fit their own visions and the different styles of new eras. Many of the trees, shrubs, and plants carefully selected by the Olmsteds have died from old age and neglect. When grand mansions such as "As You Like It" were pulled down, developers subdivided the properties and built new homes, reconfiguring the estate grounds sometimes beyond recognition. Yet, the graceful contours of former driveways, now serving as roadways of new subdivisions, recall the Olmsteds' plans, as do the remnants of age-darkened stone walls and gates, the quiet repose of ponds, and the majesty of stately trees exotic to Western Pennsylvania. Vandergrift and the diminutive Oliver Place, with their signature curved streets, landscaped roadside edges, and public spaces at street intersections, still retain an ambience that affords further evidence of the Olmsteds' work and vision.[50]

However, the Olmsted legacy is greater. In addition to the new cosmopolitanism, the firm's presence among the Pittsburgh urban elite reflected another profound social change transforming urban society. Fearful of the growing and increasingly noisome immigrant slums, dreading the labor unrest and other forms of social disorder that marked the late nineteenth century, early twentieth-century urban elites pushed the boundaries of their concern for order and environmental beauty beyond their safe private world and into the larger urban community. The civic realm of public parks and squares, cemeteries, boulevards, and main thoroughfares became an important domain of young landscape architects such as the Olmsteds, who with their elite and upper-middle-class patrons believed that an antidote to urban violence and disorder existed in civic art and civic improvement.

The reform agenda of Pittsburgh's elite and upper middle class transcended the building of parks, playgrounds, and fountain-bedecked public squares. In their quest for urban order and urban redesign, Pittsburgh's reform community targeted the city's boss-controlled political machinery and sought to gain regulatory control over decisions regarding the use of urban space. From 1906 to 1910 the tide of urban reform in the city crested, as was evidenced by the election of the reformer George Guthrie as mayor. At the height of this reform intensity, Mayor Guthrie appointed the Pittsburgh Civic Commission, which in turn enlisted Frederick Law Olmsted Jr. to draft a plan for the city. Olmsted Jr. and his team studied the city intensely during 1910, communicating frequently with the PCC and the new mayor, William A. Magee. Reflecting the PCC's narrow charge, Olmsted titled his

1911 plan *Main Thoroughfares and the Down Town District*. He advocated not a blueprint or a master plan but a permanent mechanism for rationally planning the continuous development of the city, which emphasized the importance of routinely collecting and maintaining an extensive archive of data as a scientific foundation for future planning and decision making. The Olmsted report lent credence to several long-standing Pittsburgh development conversations: cutting further Grant's Hill (known locally the Hump cut), erecting a new South Hills bridge and tunnel (eventually the Liberty Bridge and Tunnel), reclaiming and celebrating the Point, widening key downtown streets, and building a new artery to the East End (the future Boulevard of the Allies). The plan also delved into topics such as parks and a transformed Monongahela Wharf not specifically requested by the PCC. Many of the recommendations were ultimately acted upon in ways that still affect the Pittsburgh landscape, although not necessarily in ways he proposed.

The planning euphoria of 1911 nurtured a budding public sector planning ethic for the city. The state authorized the establishment of the Pittsburgh City Planning Commission staffed by the Department of City Planning. Politics intervened with the election of Mayor Magee's successor, who defunded the planning commission. But a voluntary planning sector endured and helped to revive public sector planning in the 1920s, which endeavored to impose order on the industrial city's landscape. Strong elements of continuity link the planning of the Olmsted years and the post–Second World War Renaissance years. Readers wishing to pursue the emergence and development of planning prior to the emergence of the Renaissance years are encouraged to read our book *Before Renaissance: Planning in Pittsburgh, 1889–1943*.[51]

A century after the Olmsteds designed landscapes for Pittsburgh's elite and public areas, one can see striking continuities with the language and goals of their various reports. The Bostonians beseeched Pittsburghers to appreciate and exploit the natural beauty of their hilly and riverine topography. In particular, Frederick Law Olmsted Jr. saw Pittsburgh as endowed with spectacular natural advantages comparable to Edinburgh, Paris, and Lyon. The Olmsteds' appeal that early twentieth-century residents should realize the extraordinary potential as a place of beauty resonates today with the Pittsburghers' efforts to fashion a postindustrial city.

FIG. 13.4 H. J. Heinz's "Greenlawn" residence, circa 1901 (Olmsted Brothers, courtesy of the National Park Service, Frederick Law Olmsted National Historic Site).

APPENDIX 13.1

Howard J. Heinz's "Greenlawn"

In 1901 H. J. Heinz commissioned Frederick Law Olmsted Jr. to landscape his estate called Greenlawn. The home on the grounds was a magnificent French chateau–style mansion, fronting Penn Avenue between Lang and Murtland Streets in the Point Breeze section of the city. Heinz wanted Greenlawn to include a greenhouse and a large stable behind the mansion (in his general plan). Heinz adopted most of Olmsted's landscaping ideas but positioned the stable (also a large chateau-style building) to the right of and set back from the main house. To display his renowned collection of Oriental porcelain, Heinz later added a museum, which flanked the mansion on the left. On a regular basis the Pittsburgh industrialist invited city schoolchildren to tour his museum (see Figures 13.4, 13.5). Olmsted's plan for Greenlawn featured a low stone wall ringing the estate and topped by a wrought iron fence (which is still there). Richly planted serpentine gardens featuring more than sixty varieties of flowering plants and shrubs and other flora bordered the wall on the inside. A graceful circular drive approached

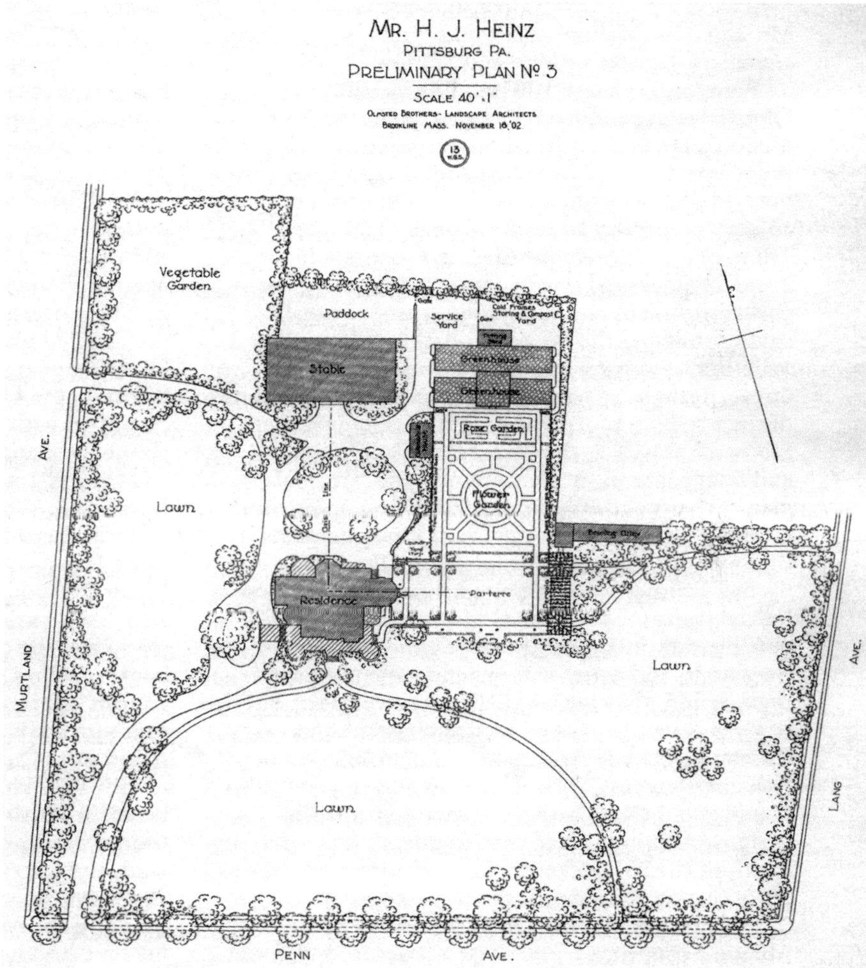

FIG. 13.5 Preliminary Plan No. 3 for H. J. Heinz, 1902, (Olmsted Brothers, courtesy of the National Park Service, Frederick Law Olmsted National Historic Site).

the front of the house, from which a stone staircase led onto the large manicured lawn.

Between 1900 and 1919, the year H. J. Heinz died, the museum building was added and other changes were made, most noticeably the removal of the stunning, broad front porch with its Greek-inspired columns. However, Olmsted's landscaping remained intact.

Tragically, Greenlawn survived its master's death by only four years. None of the children—John, Howard Jr., Clifford, or Irene—chose to reside at the estate after Heinz's death. Seeking to memorialize him, and at the same time save ten thousand dollars in inheritance taxes, the family in 1922 offered the Penn Avenue property, including the greenhouse, to the city as a park site. Contending that the structures would be too expensive to heat and maintain, the city's mayor rejected the offer.

To generate revenue while the fate of the property awaited resolution, the family used the rich Santo Domingo mahogany trim, carved doors, boilers, and bathroom and electrical fixtures from the mansion to convert the garage and museum buildings into the Greenlawn Apartments. In 1923 the great home was demolished, and the estate was subdivided into a plan of lots called Meade Place. The plan extended Meade Street, which ran between Penn and Fifth, two-thirds of the way into the center of the Greenlawn parcel, creating a cul-de-sac called Meade Place. Anxious to assert its power to control urban form, the Pittsburgh Planning Commission demanded that Meade Place be cut through and used as a public thoroughfare. The ensuing battle tested the breadth of the city's authority over lot plans, but the commission yielded two years later.

Today a mere shadow of Greenlawn's early twentieth-century glory remains. A prominent cartouche adorning the center bay of the two-story Greenlawn Apartments—once Heinz's carriage house—provides a glimpse of the extravagant architrave of the demolished mansion. Likewise, the low stone wall, the traces of wrought iron fence, as well as some unkempt vestiges of Olmsted's plantings hint at the mastery of the original estate landscaping. Most passersby, however, little suspect that, in its early twentieth-century heyday, this Penn Avenue address epitomized the fabulous prosperity enjoyed by Pittsburgh's industrial elite.

APPENDIX 13.2

W. L. Mellon's "Ben Elm"

For the first half of the twentieth century W. L. Mellon's estate, Ben Elm ("Ben" meaning "home" in Scottish), graced the Murdoch Street entrance to Schenley Park. The grayish brown sandstone mansion fronted Darlington Road, looking west over the park toward Oakland. The Olmsteds called for dignified thirty-inch-thick stone walls between the Darlington Road entrances of the curving driveway to the porte cochere and along the northern border of the property, adjoining the bend of Forbes Avenue where it heads toward the Squirrel Hill shopping district. Stairs still there today at the northeast corner of the property allowed direct access to the trolley stop at the park's entrance (see Figures 13.6, 13.7).

William Larimer Mellon, born in 1868, was the son of James Ross Mellon, an older brother of A. W. and R. B. Mellon. After graduating from

Fig. 13.6 W. L. Mellon's "Ben Elm" residence (courtesy of Carnegie Library of Pittsburgh).

Pennsylvania Military Academy, he joined the family banking business and worked closely with his famous uncles in building the Mellon family's extensive financial empire. Toward the century's end, he entered two of the nation's newer growth industries, electric street railways (trolleys) and oil, becoming president of the Monongahela Street Railway Company and a founder and president of Gulf Oil Corporation.

In 1901 and 1902, the Olmsteds consulted frequently with Mellon, his architects (Alden and Harlow of Boston), and his contractor, while the house was being built on the hourglass-shaped grounds extending five and a half acres. Their plans called for expansive lawns that sloped gently away from the house to the north and west and a great variety of trees, shrubs, and flowers. They scouted the city's East End for mature trees to replant, to be interspersed with evergreens as a protective barrier along busy Forbes Avenue. In contrast, elaborate and sinuous flower beds and widely spaced, decorative trees framed the view of the park and city from the house's front terrace and piazza. The Olmsteds, at Mary Mellon's request, eschewed highly formal gardens. On the utilitarian south side and rear of the property, they used poplar trees to screen the laundry yard from the house, proposed vegetable garden, and children's playground, and they erected a high stone wall to separate the stable from neighboring properties.

The forty-five-room house was lavishly equipped with thirteen baths, a dozen or more fireplaces, stained-glass windows, carved wood paneling, gold-stamped leather wall coverings, and an interroom telephone system. Such grandeur, however, did not last much beyond Mellon's death in 1949. The Squirrel Hill builder Jacob Simon purchased the estate and demolished the house in 1951. He ran a cul-de-sac from Darlington Road into the property and subdivided the grounds into many smaller house lots. Today, the stone walls along the property lines and stairs to Forbes Avenue remind one of the Olmsteds' part in Pittsburgh's princely past.

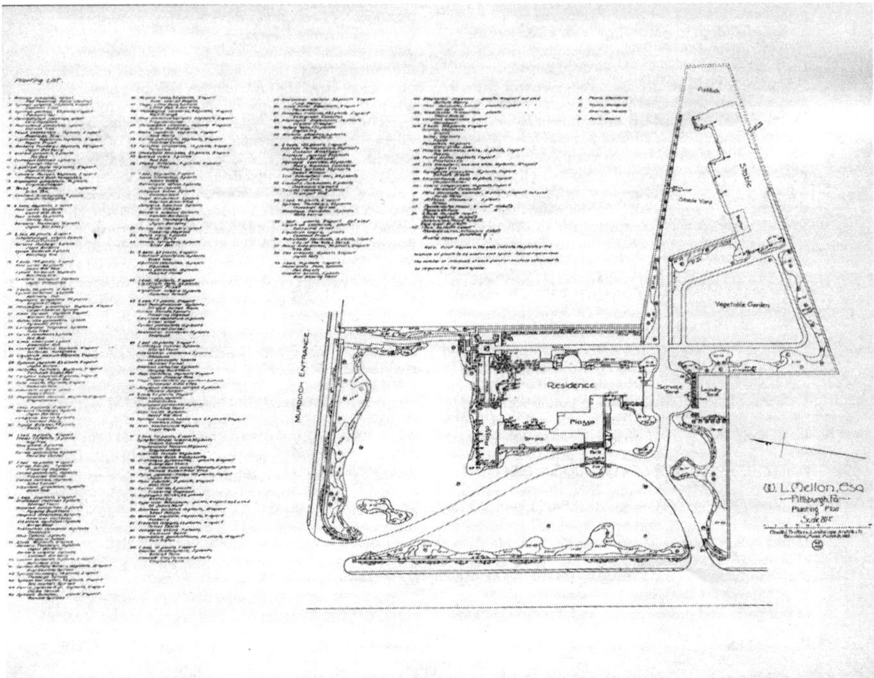

Fig. 13.7 Planting plan for W. L. Mellon, 1902 (Olmsted Brothers, courtesy of the National Park Service, Frederick Law Olmsted National Historic Site).

APPENDIX 13.3

Elizabeth Thaw's "As You Like It"

When John C. Olmsted in 1901 commenced landscaping Elizabeth D. Thaw's summer estate in Sewickley Heights, its mansion, designed by George S. Orth, was only half complete. Finished in 1902, the stucco-faced Tudor Revival mansion boasted forty-four lavishly appointed rooms. One hundred Oriental carpets adorned the hardwood floors, and mounted on the walls of Thaw's game and sitting rooms were elk, buffalo, and deer trophies.

Elizabeth Dohrman Thaw was the widow of William Thaw Jr. He was a Pittsburgh coal merchant, the son of the late steamboat and railroad tycoon William Thaw Sr., and stepbrother of Harry Thaw, made notorious in the Stanford White shooting. William Thaw Jr. died suddenly, leaving his young wife, Elizabeth, to fashion a remarkable career as one of the brightest of Pittsburgh's late-nineteenth and early twentieth-century civic reform luminaries. A founder and treasurer for forty years of the Civic Club of Allegheny County, and instrumental in establishing Pittsburgh's League of

FIG. 13.8 Summer estate, "As You Like It," of Elizabeth Dohrman Thaw, 1902, architect George S. Orth (courtesy of the National Park Service, Frederick Law Olmsted National Historic Site).

Women Voters, Thaw was also active in the women's suffrage and birth control movements of the period. A stalwart of the Civic Club of Allegheny County, the far-ranging civic reform organization dedicated both to the City Beautiful Movement and to bettering the condition of the urban-industrial poor, Thaw financed the building of Pittsburgh's first public bathhouse, and she campaigned vigorously against the "civic smallpox" of billboards, and for the display of art in public schools.

The frenetic pace of Elizabeth Thaw's involvement slowed somewhat when she traded the winter responsibilities of life on Pittsburgh's Forbes Avenue for the rural pleasures of her summer estate called "As You Like It" (see Figure 13.8). In landscaping it, Thaw gave the Olmsteds carte blanche, and John C. Olmsted used it to imprint the acreage with a rich panoply of landscape delights. Indeed, over the years, Olmsted introduced more than sixty different topographical maps showing elevations, grading, and planting schemes, and general plans (see Figure 13.9). The final plan included a long sweeping carriage road ascent, which culminated in a circular driveway approach to the hilltop mansion's port cochere. A serpentine "stepping stone" path afforded an alternate romantic route to the home. As the final touch, Olmsted incorporated both classical and baroque motifs in a magnificent vine-covered pergola, which adjoined an Italianate garden luxuriantly planted with ferns, shrubs, and annual and perennial flowers. All told, Olmsted scheduled eighty-three different varieties of shrubs, plants, and evergreen, flowering, and nonflowering trees for the estate. Behind the main residence, near the large stables and the caretaker's house, Olmsted located a large vegetable garden—a fixture in most estate landscaping plans of the era.

Inexplicably—the Depression may have been reason enough—Elizabeth Thaw in 1939 ordered her summer house demolished and the site carved into a subdivision called Thawmont. Just as likely is that, at age eighty-five, she no longer could muster the energy to entertain summer guests or

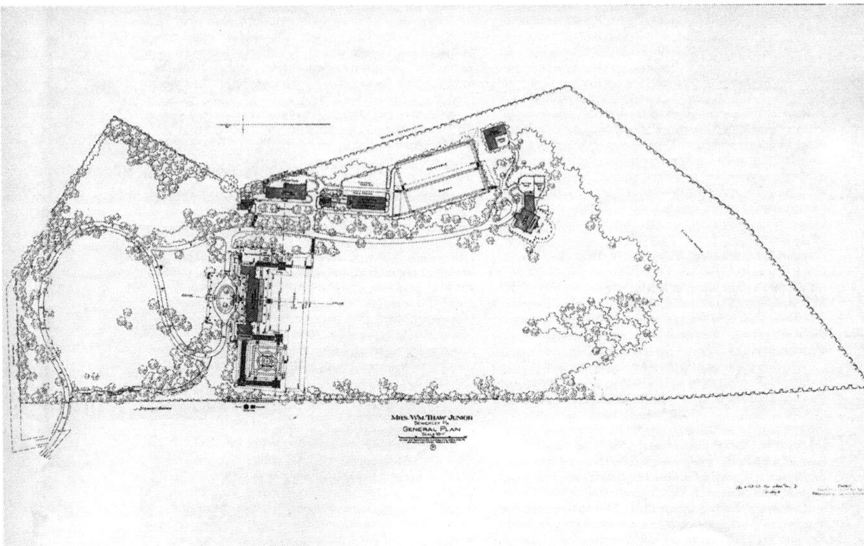

Fig. 13.9 General Plan for Mrs. Wm. Thaw Jr. (Elizabeth Dohrman Thaw), 1902 (Olmsted Brothers, courtesy of the National Park Service, Frederick Law Olmsted National Historic Site).

perambulate her gardens. At the same time, however, Thaw remained active in Pittsburgh civic affairs as a staunch member of the Pittsburgh Orchestra Association and the treasurer of the Civic Club. She resigned that post in 1946, and later that same year was seriously injured when a car struck her chauffeured vehicle from behind. She died two years later.

Although wreckers destroyed Thaw's great Tudor mansion fifty-four years ago, evidence of its splendor and Olmsted's work remain. Olmsted's carriage drive still approaches the hilltop, and buried beneath the weeds are the crumbling remains of the baroque garden wall adjoining the pergola. The caretaker's house and stables also remain—all faint reminders of a fleeting but lavish and unforgettable epoch in American aristocracy.

NOTES

Reprinted with permission from *Pittsburgh History* 76, no. 3 (1993–1994): 122–40. In this research on the Olmsteds' influence in Pittsburgh, the authors gratefully wish to acknowledge the generous assistance of Frederick W. Bauman Jr. and Jeffery M. Flannery, senior manuscript librarians of the Library of Congress; Joyce Connolly, reference archivist at the Frederick Law Olmsted National Historic Site, Brookline, Massachusetts; Audrey Iacone, librarian at the Historical Society of Western Pennsylvania; Professor Roy Lubove of the University of Pittsburgh; Mary Beth Pastorious of the Sewickley Valley Historical Society;

and the staffs of the Pennsylvania Room of the Carnegie Library, Pittsburgh and the University of Pittsburgh's Archives of Industrial Society. This project was supported by a grant from the Faculty Professional Development Council of the State System of Higher Education of the Commonwealth of Pennsylvania.

1. Laura Wood Roper, *FLO: A Biography of Frederick Law Olmsted* (Baltimore: Johns Hopkins University Press, 1974), 319–474; Witold Rybczynski, *A Clearing in the Distance: Frederick Law Olmsted and America in the Nineteenth Century* (New York: Scribner, 1999); David Schuyler, *The New Urban Landscape: The Redefinition of City Form in Nineteenth Century America* (Baltimore: Johns Hopkins University Press, 1986).

2. This statement is based upon an examination of the subject files of the papers of Frederick Law Olmsted Sr. in Olmsted Associates Papers, Manuscript Division of Library of Congress, Washington, DC (hereafter cited as OAP).

3. Jim Stuart, "The History of the Pittsburgh Park System from 1867 to 1893" (unpublished seminar paper, Carnegie Mellon University, 1981). Industrial cities other than Pittsburgh did plan parks. Schuyler, *The New Urban Landscape*, 129–33. For Richardson and Olmsted, see Roper, *FLO*, 319; Walter Kidney, *Landmark Architecture: Pittsburgh and Allegheny County* (Pittsburgh: Pittsburgh History & Landmarks Foundation, 1985), 167–68. On parks, see Barbara Judd, "Edward M. Bigelow: Creator of Pittsburgh's Arcadian Parks," *Western Pennsylvania Historical Magazine* 58 (January 1975): 53–67.

4. For a discussion of the vogue for landscaped gardens among America's industrial elite where the authors attempt to trace the phenomenon to the elite's yearning for Europe and a European class structure, see Marc Griswold and Eleanor Weller, *The Golden Age of American Gardens: Proud Owners, Private Estates, 1890–1940* (Garden Club of America, 1991). The caricature of the elite as no-nonsense Presbyterians comes from John Ingham, *Making Iron and Steel: Independent Mills in Pittsburgh, 1820–1920* (Columbus: Ohio State University Press, 1991); see also Frances Couvares, *The Remaking of Pittsburgh: Class and Culture in an Industrializing City, 1877–1919* (Albany: State University of New York Press, 1984); Joseph F. Rishel, *Founding Families of Pittsburgh: The Evolution of a Regional Elite, 1790–1910* (Pittsburgh: University of Pittsburgh Press, 1990).

5. Longfellow and Alden split from Harlow in 1896. On the architectural firm, see Margaret Henderson Floyd, *Architecture after Richardson: Regionalism before Modernism: Longfellow, Alden, and Harlow in Boston and Pittsburgh* (Chicago: University of Chicago Press and Pittsburgh History & Landmarks Foundation, 1993).

6. Roper, *FLO*, 319; Kidney, *Landmark Architecture*; James Howard Bridge, "Carnegie at Cresson: Daily Life at Braemar Cottage," *Carnegie Magazine* 8 (1934): 38.

7. Anne E. Mosher, *Capital's Utopia: Vandergrift, Pennsylvania, 1855–1916* (Baltimore: Johns Hopkins University Press, 2004).

8. Mosher, *Capital's Utopia*, 73–93.

9. J. J. Vandergrift and C. J. Lockhart File, Box 101, OAP.

10. The Carnegie Steel job was apparently misfiled in Box 101. On the Olmsted firm's relationships with wealthy clients, see Roper, *FLO*, 383–424. See job files for various prominent Pittsburgh families—the Heinzes, Thaws, Mellons, Scaifes, etc.—in OAP.

11. Roper, *FLO*, 319–474.

12. Roper, *FLO*, 319–474.

13. Robert J. Jucha, "The Anatomy of a Streetcar Suburb: A Development History of Shadyside, 1852–1916," *Western Pennsylvania Historical Magazine* 62 (1979): 302–19; Margaret Marsh, *Suburban Lives* (New Brunswick, NJ: Rutgers University Press, 1990).

Also on suburban ethos, see Michael H. Ebner, *Creating Chicago's North Shore* (Chicago: University of Chicago Press, 1988); Ann Durkin Keating, *Building Chicago: Suburban Developers and the Creation of a Divided Metropolis* (Columbus: Ohio State University Press, 1988).

14. See W. L. Mellon File, Box 28, File 271, in OAP; note that the firm of Longfellow, Alden, and Harlow had by now split up. Floyd, *Architecture after Richardson.* In 1992 only the stone walls and gateposts on Murdoch and Darlington Streets attest to Olmsted's extensive work on the Mellon property.

15. Mrs. William Thaw File, Box 16, OAP. On Elizabeth Thaw, see *Pittsburgh Press*, January 30, 1946, and "Mrs. William Thaw Dies at 94: Was Society Leader for 50 Years," *Pittsburgh Press*, October 4, 1948, both in Thaw File, Pennsylvania Room, Carnegie Library, Pittsburgh, Pennsylvania.

16. See Mrs. William Thaw File, Box 16, OAP. Today Olmsted's elegant drives still grace the "As You Like It" site. However, casual inspection indicates that only a few moldering, vine-covered brick pillars recall the elaborately landscaped grounds of the early twentieth-century Thaw estate. The mansion was demolished in 1939, and the grounds were converted into a subdivision called "Thawmont." See Thaw obituary, *Pittsburgh Press*, October 4, 1948; also note that in 1929 the Olmsteds prepared landscaping plans for her burial plot in Allegheny Cemetery. See Thaw Burial Plot File, Box 479, OAP.

17. Allegheny Country Club File, Box 150, OAP. John Denniston Lyon was related to the Thaws through his mother. He was a trustee of the Allegheny Cemetery, a future Olmsted client. Henry R. Rea was the son-in-law of the steel magnate Henry W. Oliver.

18. H. J. Heinz File, Box 16, File 133, OAP.

19. Colonel Joseph W. Guffey was a leading figure in the state Democratic Party; see Joseph Guffey, *Seventy Years on the Red Fire Wagon: From Tilden to Truman, through New Freedom and New Deal* (privately printed in Pittsburgh, 1952). See also Colonel Joseph W. Guffey File, Box 12, OAP; John C. Olmsted notes from the site visit, July 11, 1901, in F. T. Lovejoy File, Box 30, OAP; James D. Van Trump, *Life and Architecture in Pittsburgh* (Pittsburgh: Pittsburgh History & Landmarks Foundation, 1983), 277–81.

20. John C. Olmsted to James B. Oliver, August 21, 190, in James B. Oliver File, Box 200, OAP.

21. See John C. Olmsted's Site Visit Report, July 21, 1905; John C. Olmsted to James B. Oliver, August 21, 1905. See also Oliver to Olmsted, August 26, September 4, 6, 1905, all in James B. Oliver File, Box 200, OAP. For a contemporary but hyperbolic view of "Oliver Place," see the promotional brochure "Oliver Place in Sewickley Valley" (Sewickley Valley Historical Society, Sewickley, Pennsylvania, n.d.). James B. Oliver was the younger brother and active partner of Henry W. Oliver, who was the driving force behind the Oliver iron and steel empire.

22. Jon A. Peterson, "The City Beautiful Movement: Forgotten Origins and Lost Meanings," *Journal of Urban History* 2 (1976): 415–30; Jon A. Peterson, *The Birth of City Planning in the United States, 1840–1917* (Baltimore: Johns Hopkins University Press, 2003); William H. Wilson, *The City Beautiful Movement* (Baltimore: Johns Hopkins University Press, 1989). On the suburban ethos, see Ebner, *Creating Chicago's North Shore*, 195–240; Marsh, *Suburban Lives*; Keating, *Building Chicago.*

23. On the depression of the 1890s, the middle-class concern for social order, and the roots of Progressive reform, see David Thelen, "Social Tensions and the Origins of Progressivism," *Journal of American History* 56 (1970): 323–41; Arthur S. Link and Richard

L. McCormick, *Progressivism* (Arlington Heights, IL: Harlan Davidson, 1983); Paul Boyer, *Urban Masses and Moral Order in America, 1820–1920* (Cambridge, MA: Harvard University Press, 1978). See, especially, Civic Club of Allegheny County (CCAC), *Fifteen Years of Civic History* (Pittsburgh: CCAC, 1915); CCAC, *Annals of the Civic Club of Allegheny County, 1897–1921* (Pittsburgh: CCAC, 1921).

24. CCAC, *Annals of the Civic Club*, 7. Elizabeth Thaw was the treasurer of the Civic Club for forty-three years. She served as treasurer of the Pittsburgh Housing Association and helped found and was first president of the Birth Control League. She was also instrumental in founding the Equal Franchise League, later the League of Women Voters. See *Pittsburgh Press*, January 30, 1946, in Thaw File, Carnegie Library.

25. CCAC, *Fifteen Years*, 2.

26. CCAC, *Fifteen Years.*

27. Peterson, "City Beautiful Movement," 426; Mel Scott, *American City Planning since 1890* (Berkeley: University of California Press, 1969), 85–109. The definitive study of the City Beautiful Movement and its critics is Wilson, *The City Beautiful Movement.*

28. Kristin Szylvian Bailey, "Fighting 'Civic Smallpox': The Civic Club of Allegheny County's Campaign for Billboard Regulation, 1896–1917," *Western Pennsylvania Historical Magazine* 70, no. 1 (1987): 3–28; Judd, "Edward Bigelow," 62–67.

29. Falconer to Messrs. Olmsted, Brookline, January 10, 1898. See also William Falconer to John C. Olmsted, Brookline, January 15, 1898, both in Box 24, OAP.

30. Letter from William Falconer to Frederick Law Olmsted Jr., August 29, 1898, Box 24, OAP. Franklin Toker, *Pittsburgh: An Urban Portrait* (Pennsylvania State University. Press, 1986) attributes the rebuilding of Beechwood Boulevard to Frederick Law Olmsted Jr., but we have not been able to verify his involvement. In Frederick Law Olmsted Jr.'s 1911 plan for Pittsburgh, he proposed two plans for an entrance to Schenley Park.

31. See Roy Lubove, "Pittsburgh's Allegheny Cemetery and the Victorian Garden of the Dead," *Pittsburgh History* 75 (1992): 148–56; Roy Lubove, "Falconer: Horticulturist, Editor, Park Cemetery Executive," *The Cemeterian* (1975): 26–32; both in Allegheny Cemetery File, Box 11, OAP.

32. Arsenal Park File, Box 240, OAP.

33. John F. Bauman and Edward K. Muller, *Before Renaissance: Planning in Pittsburgh, 1889–1943* (Pittsburgh: University of Pittsburgh Press, 2006).

34. E. C. Whiting to John C. Olmsted, December 12, 1910, Box 285, OAP. See also T. E. Billiquist File, Box 274, OAP; Howard Heinz File, Box 283, OAP; F. S. Willock File, Box 285, OAP.

35. William A. Way to Frederick Law Olmsted Jr., Edgeworth File, Box 289, OAP.

36. Letter from William B. Howland to Frederick Law Olmsted Jr., April 6, 1911, Johnstown File, Box 290, OAP.

37. For example, see Frederick Law Olmsted Jr. to Frank A. Waugh, Forest Service, Department of Agriculture, October 1, 1917, Olmsted to Horace McFarland, December 19, 1917, Olmsted to A. W. Crawford, September 24, 1918, all in Horace McFarland Papers, Pennsylvania State Archives, Harrisburg, Pennsylvania; also see Scott, *American City Planning*, 170–74.

38. Frederick Law Olmsted Jr. to J. D. Hailman, secretary of the Department of City Planning, December 10, 1913, Box 243, OAP.

39. Schenley Park Entrance File, Box 327, OAP.

40. Quote from "The Beaux Arts Salon Announces an Architectural Competition for

a Municipal Improvement," 1916, in Beaux Arts Salon File, Box 353, OAP. Marvin Scaife was a partner in the successful Scaife family iron business. Mrs. Hunt was married to the grandson of the founder of the Aluminum Company of America (ALCOA), Alfred Hunt, and the son of a future president of the corporation, Roy A. Hunt.

41. A. W. Mellon and R. B. Mellon Files, Box 373, OAP.

42. Frederick I. Merrick File, Box 385, OAP; Stanley J. Roush File, Box 381, OAP.

43. Longvue Country Club File, Box 383, OAP. Similarly, in 1926 Mrs. Roy A. Hunt, who had been secretary treasurer of the Beaux Arts Salon on the occasion of the 1916 competition that Olmsted Jr. had juried, importuned the firm about consulting on her Amberson Place property in Shadyside. Here too, nothing followed. See Mrs. Roy Hunt File, Box 438, OAP.

44. Sewickley Heights Estates (Tuxedo Land Company) File, Box 343, OAP; James Park File, Box 378, OAP. Despite the fact that part of the estate was sold off for building lots, evidence of Olmsted's work remains visible in the still thriving exotic trees, gardens, and long curving driveway leading to the hilltop location of the Park mansion.

45. On Boyd's recommendation of the Painters as clients, see Stanley Roush File, Box 381, OAP. On Painter and Nicola, see Charles A. Painter Jr. File, Box 386, OAP; George Nicola File, Box 387, OAP.

46. See Rolling Rock Country Club File, Box 373, OAP; Mrs. George M. Laughlin File, Box 381, OAP.

47. Scaife File, Box 494, OAP.

48. See Mosher, *Capital's Utopia*, 83–93, 174–175.

49. For quotations, see J. O'Brien to Olmsted Brothers, January 27, 1921, Olmsted Jr. to J. O'Brien, December 6, 1920, Fort Pitt Malleable File, Box 373, OAP.

50. Definitive assessment of the Olmsteds' impact on the region's private landscape awaits a careful and painstaking comparison of the original drawings, plans, and planting instructions with contemporary features and an examination of their influence, if any, on the local landscape architecture profession.

51. Bauman and Muller, *Before Renaissance*.

14 "'IN SPITE OF THE RIVER' OUGHT TO BE A PITTSBURGH TOWN-SLOGAN"

RIVERFRONT PLANNING IN PITTSBURGH, 1900s–1970s

Edward K. Muller

Pittsburgh, like many cities around the world, has over time discovered the scenic, recreational, touristic, and residential values of its miles of rivers and riverfronts. For more than a century, these lands and bodies of water were the scene of intense industrial development and environmental degradation. Only the massive deindustrialization of the 1980s and its aftermath could inspire civic leaders and developers to overturn the long held perception of the rivers and riverfronts as first and foremost integral parts of the region's urban industrial infrastructure. During the past twenty-five years, environmentalists, river advocates, planners, and eventually both developers and civic leaders have proposed various ideas and implemented projects, which manifest the reconceptualization and redevelopment of the riverfront lands. In recreational activity, scenic enjoyment, and ecological restoration these projects emphasize physical and visual access to the rivers such that they have become a significant contributor to the city's revitalization.[1]

Pittsburgh's postindustrial discovery of the aesthetic and recreational qualities of its rivers follows a long history of riverfront planning. Several times during the twentieth century, locally and nationally prominent planners, architects, and landscape architects advanced plans for improving the central riverfronts, especially for the historic Point where the three rivers converge. Their ideas for scenic and recreational uses of Pittsburgh's waterfronts reflected widely circulated plans for cities such as Harrisburg, Seattle, and Chicago.[2] The proposals ran counter to the prevailing conception of these lands as being primarily essential to the Pittsburgh's industrial economy. To most civic leaders, improvements meant upgrading the central wharves for commerce and erecting flood walls to protect downtown. Businessmen and public officials shared this utilitarian view, even when community-oriented visions emanated from civic organizations dominated by business leaders. Fiercely probusiness, pragmatic, and conservative, these leaders and their public sector allies set limited parameters within which planners and architects could draw up nonindustrial riverfront plans. Despite Pittsburgh's adoption of city planning in 1911, the utilitarian perception of the rivers and riverfronts endured for several decades. Thus, Frank Lloyd Wright felt amply justified in 1935 in rendering his pejorative judgment that "'In spite of a river' ought to be a Pittsburgh town-slogan."[3]

Decline of the region's industrial economy inspired some Pittsburgh civic leaders to rethink the utilitarian role of the central riverfronts. The Great Depression stimulated renewed efforts in the 1930s to turn the badly degraded Point area into a historic and monumental park. Little came of these efforts. Dire predictions of dismal post–Second World War prospects for the city, however, led to the path-breaking creation (at least for Pittsburgh) of Point Park in the postwar era through the leadership of a powerful public-private partnership. The park plan suggested a new outlook for the rivers and riverfronts, for it explicitly took advantage of the site's scenic potential.[4] But, they viewed Point Park more as the lynchpin to revitalizing downtown and a symbol of modernizing the city than the beginning of transforming the riverfronts. With commercial and industrial activities already declining along the central riverfronts, opportunities to transform these lands increased. Although civic leaders held tightly to the utilitarian perspective, a few espoused improving the rivers as part of the city's celebrated Renaissance. By the 1960s those few enthusiastically spoke of a River Renaissance and plans for an invasion of greenery on the riverfronts.[5] Unfortunately, plans for a renaissance of the riverfronts came during the final years of Pittsburgh's postwar redevelopment when both social and political events foreclosed carrying out substantial riverfront improvements.

In the 1970s, when cities such as Boston, Baltimore, and Portland, Oregon, were famously redefining their waterfronts, most Pittsburgh leaders had not fully grasped the great potential of the rivers for improving the city's quality of life and contributing to its economic development. Two signature public projects erected during the decade—the Convention Center and Three Rivers Stadium—ignored the rivers, despite their being located on central riverfronts. Yet the utilitarian view no longer solely commanded the perception of the rivers and riverfronts. Building on plans promoted during Renaissance I, scenic and recreational ideas for transforming the riverfronts reappeared in the second half of the 1970s, being advocated as an essential part of what urban experts considered the new postindustrial American city to be. Here I look at the history of riverfront planning in Pittsburgh before the crisis of deindustrialization in the 1980s finally overwhelmed the utilitarian view and inspired the recent river and riverfront transformation. I trace the roots of postindustrial riverfront revitalization to the early years of the twentieth century and situate its beginnings in the city's postwar Renaissance, when an anticipated economic crisis caused civic leaders to reexamine long-held beliefs and practices.[6] The early years of Renaissance II revived these beginnings such that, when the economic crisis fully hit in the 1980s, the city was in a better position to transform its riverfronts.

PROGRESSIVE PLANS

During the nineteenth century Pittsburgh's rivers, river edges, and riverfronts increasingly became integral components of the area's rapid industrialization. Because of the region's challenging topography, most development sought the flat, accessible floodplains of the three major rivers and their tributary streams. Despite the nuisance of frequent high water events and occasional devastating floods, industry and working-class neighborhoods lined the riverfronts by the beginning of the twentieth century (see "Pittsburgh's Industrial Corridors" in this volume). Little concerned with flooding, the US Army Corps of Engineers erected locks and dams in order to enhance commercial navigation. By 1929 the three rivers, indeed the entire Ohio River to Cairo, Illinois, had become a series of slackwater pools between the dams. Enormous tows of coal barges plied Pittsburgh's central pool and tied up along the riverbanks. Shippers and manufacturers hardened river edges with bulkheads, erected giant circular mooring terminals, and in places extended the banks with fill. Both industry and local municipalities depended on the rivers for water supplies and disposal of wastes. Junk and trash littered underused riverbanks. Engineered and intensely developed, the three rivers and their floodplains had become part of the urban industrial infrastructure (see "Pittsburgh's Three Rivers" in this volume).[7]

Pittsburgh's dismal landscape at the turn of the century—smoke-laden skies, soot-covered buildings, polluted rivers, and deforested and billboard-covered hillsides—spurred progressive reformers, design professionals, and civic leaders to advocate measures for beautification and improving public health. Public works director Edward M. Bigelow, for example, established a park system in the 1890s. Andrew Carnegie erected his cultural complex adjacent to Schenley Park in 1895, and his business partner and boyhood friend Henry Phipps donated a botanical conservatory for the park.[8] The city even erected its first water treatment plant in 1907. In this reform milieu the Pittsburgh Architectural Club pressed for municipal improvements of downtown. Beginning around 1900 the architectural club held competitions and exhibits with particular attention to the design of a downtown civic center of municipal buildings adjacent to architect H. H. Richardson's renowned Allegheny County Courthouse. Reporting on its first competition, the club also advocated improving the central waterfronts and the Point. The Point had deteriorated into a bleak area of railroad tracks, warehouses, and old deteriorating residences. The adjacent Monongahela Wharf, once the heart of Pittsburgh's commercial life, had been declining for years as a result of the railroad's ascendancy. Although not the first recognition of the unkempt character of the riverfront, the club's competition inaugurated a century-long discussion of these important central spaces.[9]

Aware of the nascent national planning movement, progressive reformers dreamed of bringing order and beauty to the Smoky City through planning. Inspired by the 1893 World's Columbian Exposition in Chicago and the fashionable City Beautiful movement, a center of public and not-for-profit institutions was emerging in the city's Oakland section. At the same time, the Chicago architect Daniel Burnham, the Chicago exposition's acclaimed director and a leading proponent of City Beautiful planning, designed an office tower for Henry Clay Frick (1901), a grand terminal for the Pennsylvania Railroad (1902), and fourteen other buildings in Pittsburgh. During the months that Burnham was finalizing his grand plan for Chicago, sponsored by that city's Commercial Club, Pittsburgh reform mayor and prominent lawyer George Guthrie and other civic leaders moved decisively toward creating a plan for Pittsburgh. Although there is no evidence that Burnham suggested Pittsburgh initiate city planning, local leaders likely knew of his several projects in the city. Evidence of such conversations might be the Chicagoan's appointment to the Pittsburgh Civic Commission's advisory board, which advocated planning.[10]

In June 1909, one month before the publication of Burnham's *Plan of Chicago*, the Pittsburgh Civic Commission (PCC) invited Frederick Law Olmsted Jr. to consider preparing a plan for the city's main streets and downtown. Departing Mayor Guthrie charged the PCC, to which he appointed eighteen leading private citizens, to address a number of social, political, and environmental problems highlighted by the embarrassing investigation of the Pittsburgh Survey. The PCC's decision to hire Olmsted arose from extensive discussions about the value of planning by the Civic Club of Allegheny County and the Chamber of Commerce. After a year of intense research and consultation with PCC members, the mayor, and other public officials, the landscape architect produced his plan for Pittsburgh at the end of 1910. Olmsted observed that Pittsburgh like many American river ports had neglected the main wharf, leaving it a "primitive" cobblestone bank. Presciently comprehending the central problem in planning the riverfronts for most of the twentieth century, Olmsted deplored "the false impression spread abroad that economical and useful things were normally ugly; and the vicious idea which followed, that beauty and the higher pleasures of civilized life were to be sought only in things otherwise useless. Thus, the pursuit of beauty was confounded with extravagance." He asserted that Pittsburghers, "familiar with the present neglected aspect" and "not familiar with the finer European quays," simply accepted the unsightliness of the riverfronts as the price of doing business and could not conceive of the benefits of aesthetic improvements.[11]

Olmsted identified three uses for the riverfronts that with proper planning, he averred, could coexist. All improvements would have to be coordinated with the recommendations of the Flood Commission, which was established after the devastating flood of 1907 and had yet to issue its report on mitigating the effects of such events. However, he did not consider the commission's probable recommendation of a flood wall to be a problem for his proposals. Based on precedents in European cities such as Paris, Lyon, and Berlin, Olmsted envisioned modernizing the river quays in order to attract additional packet boat trade, which he believed to be the riverfront's primary function. For the Monongahela Wharf, he proposed ramps from street level down to wide floating quays outfitted with cranes (see Figure 14.1). A flood wall at the landward edge of the wharf would protect the downtown and create a base for a broad street on its top. This street, the second use of the riverfronts, would be part of a traffic circuit around the edge of downtown, what he defined as "a wide marginal thoroughfare for the relief of traffic congestion . . . [by] diverting some of the main streams of heavy teaming from the older streets."[12] The idea of a circuit or loop for traffic around downtown along the riverfronts would become a persistent theme in the city's planning and eventually an awkward reality.

With an improved quay and wide thoroughfares, the city could concurrently develop the waterfront's third function of its "value for recreation and as an element of civic comeliness and self-respect." Olmsted advocated

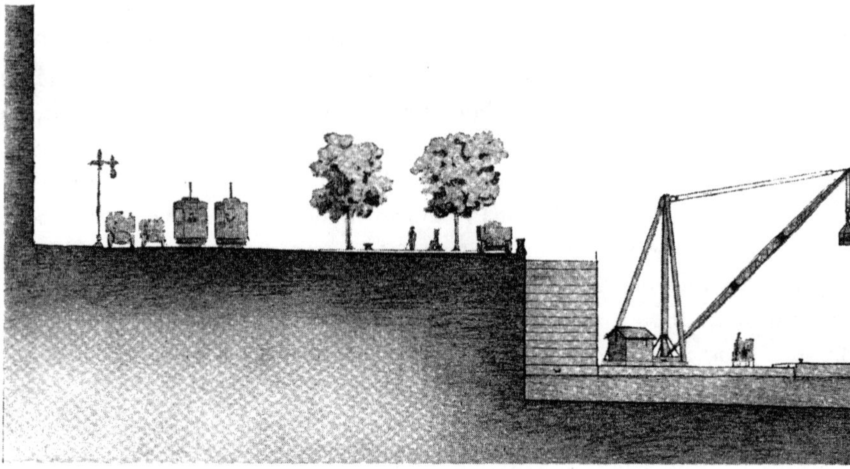

FIG. 14.1 One proposal for improving the Monongahela wharf and the street above it (Frederick Law Olmsted Jr., *Pittsburgh Main Thoroughfares and the Down Town District* [Pittsburgh: Pittsburgh Civic Commission, 1911], courtesy of the Archive Services Center, University of Pittsburgh).

a tree-lined promenade along the circuit streets with benches and overlooks from which to "enjoy . . . the natural beauty of the river valley and the always interesting activities of which it is a stage." Although Mount Washington across from the Monongahela Wharf was scarred and eroded, the planner pictured its reforestation such that in combination with the rivers and their incessant hum of activity, the city's "spacious and impressive landscape" would be restored. He urged the city to treat its landscape "with the respect it deserves."[13]

Having presented his plans for riverfronts Olmsted turned to the Point. He reviewed the geographical and historical meanings of this space and concluded: "Poetically, this spot, at the meeting of the rivers, stands for Pittsburgh." Although offering only a vague vision of its redevelopment, he implored civic leaders to consider the Point as a whole and in conjunction with bridges and traffic that converged there. Olmsted had underscored the problem that would stymy acceptable plans for the Point until the 1940s. But, whatever would be decided in the future for the Point, a plan must be, he advised, monumental, dignified and designed with the "best artistic skill."[14]

Bitter political fights relegated most of Olmsted's plan for riverfronts to dusty shelves. Whereas some influential members of Chicago's business community championed Burnham's plan for their city, Pittsburgh businessmen did not undertake a similar role. The riverfront proposals never progressed far enough to engender conflict with business and industry. However, as a creature of the city's privately sponsored reform movement, the PCC and thus the Olmsted plan as well soon became embroiled in political squabbles with the Republican machine mayor, William A. Magee. Objecting that Magee cherry-picked a few proposed projects rather than viewing them as part of a comprehensive plan, the PCC strenuously fought the mayor's large bond issue put to the voters as a referendum on paying for them. Nevertheless, the mayor did support planning, and he engineered through the state legislature in 1911 enabling legislation for establishing a city planning commission and staffing it with a planning department. Unfortunately, he also battled with a political rival, Joseph G. Armstrong, the public works director whom he eventually fired. Armstrong succeeded Magee as mayor and eviscerated the new Department of City Planning. In short, politics scuttled the harmony among civic leaders that was necessary for obtaining public support for implementing Olmsted's proposals, including those for the riverfronts.[15]

Over the years, planners wrestled with many issues, which Olmsted addressed. Although some of his recommendations eventually became part of the landscape, albeit configured differently, the flood wall, circuit thoroughfares, and the Point remained central to planning concerns through the 1930s. Olmsted's proposal for a promenade and the reconstruction of the wharves foundered on the pervasive business utilitarian view of the riverfronts. Before he left office in 1913, Mayor Magee received an annual report from the Department of City Planning, which recommended waterfront improvements that would create "a great inland harbor." Written by an engineer, the report bemoaned the "antiquated and inadequate" terminal facilities and emphasized the need for a flood wall and for the modernization of freight-handling and storage services. It gently rejected Olmsted's aesthetic proposals, saying "There would be opportunity for making all this improvement attractive as well as useful, although there may not be the desire to carry attractiveness to the lengths it has been carried in some cities of Europe."[16] Fortuitously, plans to upgrade the wharves for commerce failed to move forward because the river packet trade never revived along the Ohio River to warrant the expenditures. The Flood Commission's recommendations became entangled in federal politics and did not materialize until after the Great Depression.

In the wake of the Department of City Planning's diminished status after Magee's departure, the new municipal Arts Commission and the Civic Club of Allegheny County kept the idea of planning alive, particularly for the Point, until another elite organization could revive it. In 1913 the Arts Commission engaged Edward H. Bennett, former partner of the late Daniel Burnham, to prepare a plan for the Point. Completed a year later, Bennett's report echoed Olmsted's suggestions, proposing a small park at the tip of the Point and wide highways parallel to the riverfronts with promenades for recreation. Like more reports to come, it was never implemented. The city's brief flirtation with planning before the First World War did not alter either the utilitarian view of the riverfronts or their outmoded and unseemly condition.[17]

INTERWAR UTILITARIANISM

At the end of the First World War, a group of business leaders formed the Citizens Committee on the City Plan (CCCP) at the instigation of a local planner, Frederick Bigger. The men undertook a six-part plan as a means to reinvigorate the planning process and bring some order to this haphazardly growing industrial city. The six reports, together called *The Pittsburgh Plan*, targeted specific aspects of the city: playgrounds, parks, major streets, railroads, transit, and waterways. This second effort at comprehensive planning only ten years after Olmsted's plan confirmed that his vision of the scenic qualities of the central riverfronts had faded. The renewed advocacy of a traffic circuit loop around downtown in *The Pittsburgh Plan: Major Street* report foresaw the streets paralleling riverfronts as the best places to build highways to relieve congestion. This version of the circuit loop ignored Olmsted's promenade and overlooks. The plan's *Waterways* report published in 1923 emphatically stated that the riverfronts themselves were to remain primarily commercial infrastructure.[18]

The CCCP subcommittee charged with preparing the *Waterways* report defined the principle underlying recommendations for the riverfronts as the necessity of nurturing extant industries and attracting new ones. Men from shipping, coal, steel, and other interests comprised the committee. An engineer from the office of St. Louis planning consultant Harland Bartholomew provided technical expertise. The committee members declared "it to be undisputed, that navigation interests have a prior right to the use of those portions of the City's waterfront which can be advantageously used for water transportation." They predicted that the anticipated completion of the US Army Corps of Engineers improvements to the Ohio River would generate large increases in barge and packet freight traffic. Consequently, they recommended the retention of city-owned riverfront lands for freight handling and services. Community uses of these public properties, the men emphasized, must not prevent the tying up of commercial craft or the erection of hoisting equipment. Committee members wanted the Monongahela Wharf left open for packet freight traffic and proposed the construction of several rail-to-river freight terminals elsewhere along the central riverfronts. It advocated the conversion of the deteriorating and infrequently used exposition buildings on the Allegheny River side of the Point to such a terminal. Foreclosing public access to the rivers, these prominent businessmen supported the erection of substantial flood walls along the central riverfronts.[19]

Instead of the anticipated growth of packet boat commerce, however, Pittsburgh experienced an enormous increase in motor vehicle traffic, especially coming into and through downtown, which deflected planners' attention away from commercial riverfront improvements (see "The Automobile Comes to Pittsburgh, 1910–1935" in this volume). In the 1920s, traffic congestion in the compact downtown, which had always been a serious problem, became a nightmare. Between 1920 and 1927, the number of automobiles and trucks entering downtown daily increased 71 percent to more than ninety thousand. Streetcars, buses, and horse-drawn wagons pushed the total number vehicles to over one hundred thousand.[20] The rejuvenated Department of City Planning ignored calls for commercial upgrades of the wharves and focused on designing the circuit loop for automobiles. It targeted the paths of least resistance and expense—the Golden Triangle's underused riverfronts. During the 1920s and 1930s, several proposals by both the city and county planning departments, as well as private groups, advocated turning Water Street along the Monongahela and Duquesne Way along the Allegheny into high-volume high-speed by-pass routes. They variously advanced schemes for six-lane boulevards, elevated highways, and double-decked roads. Most envisioned parking on the wharves. Some included streetcar rights-of-way and one even included subways. Infrastructure, not aesthetics and recreation, remained the top priority for the riverfronts.[21]

Although civic leaders generally agreed on the necessity of by-pass highways, conflicts among public agencies, the complexity of easing traffic congestion at the Point, and existing private uses on the wharves prevented any consensus on the details of a traffic plan into the 1930s. Proposals struggled with the confounding presence of the old Baltimore & Ohio Railroad station on the Monongahela Wharf, Pennsylvania Railroad tracks on the Allegheny riverfront, and the deteriorating Exposition Hall near the Point. Bigger, the chief planner, supported an elaborate traffic circle to coordinate converging traffic from the Point's two bridges. The Western Pennsylvania Exposition Society's efforts in the 1930s to revive its membership with a new multipurpose civic center threatened Bigger's plans. River businesses held out for commercial wharf improvements, while the Lower Downtown

Businessmen's Association lobbied for an additional bridge from the South Hills into downtown, which would complicate traffic patterns near the Monongahela waterfront. Finally, the city and county planning departments acrimoniously squabbled about the designs for the loop around downtown.

Most of the proposals for riverfront boulevards incorporated flood walls and embraced minimal riverfront amenities such as landscaped river edges, tree-lined esplanades, or small parks. The department of planning's "Report on River Front Development" in 1932, for example, displayed tree-lined boulevards skirting the edges of downtown, reminiscent of Olmsted's 1911 proposals. But Bigger, who shared Olmsted's view of city planning and was a founding member of the visionary Regional Planning Association of America at the time of preparing the *Pittsburgh Plan*, still granted priority to commercial and transportation uses along the riverfronts. As author of the CCCP's report on *Parks*, the fourth volume of the comprehensive plan, Bigger propounded the wisdom of some park development on the public waterfront for the recreational use of downtown workers and "the substitution of an embellishment in lieu of unimaginative neglect and ugliness." However, he proposed only small "rest parks" adjacent to bridge ramps, simply landscaped and furnished with benches. This minor concession to recreational and contemplative use would come only after the "utilitarian" needs of streets, terminals, and transportation identified elsewhere in the city plan had been addressed. He wrote that "no irreconcilable conflict exists between the predominant commercial requirements and the minor requirements for recreation. . . . All reasonable utilitarian needs for many years to come can be provided for and still leave a modest residue of river front area which may be wisely developed for recreation." Although Bigger argued that human needs outweighed automobile "storage" on the waterfront, his principle did not hold sway, and parking soon occupied the publicly owned Monongahela Wharf. In his usual pragmatic manner, Bigger had raised and brushed aside the conflict between utilitarian and recreational uses that, along with budgetary issues, would bedevil riverfront development for several more decades.[22]

After thirty years of discussion and several plans, the conditions of the riverfronts had not improved, whether from a utilitarian or recreational perspective. In a 1935 interview for the *Pittsburgh Sun-Telegraph*, Frank Lloyd Wright denounced the condition of the city's river lands. The previous fall, department store magnate and civic leader Edgar J. Kaufmann invited the architect to visit the city with the prospect of several commissions, including a possible Civil Works Administration multimillion-dollar package of projects that involved wharf improvements and a flood wall. The commissions never materialized for him. The ever prickly Wright dismissed the official committee, with which he met, as being too conservative. Wright glimpsed the depressing reality and great potential of the riverfronts.[23] In developing Pittsburgh, he observed, the principle must have been "to hell with nature and we'll get what we want in spite of her." He described the city as huddled uncomfortably on both sides of the rivers, vainly trying to hold "together with bridges, more bridges, and again bridges. . . . 'In spite of the river' ought to be a Pittsburgh town-slogan." Although he suggested how the river valleys might have been sculpted for beauty, he saw little hope of improvement for years to come: "In all probability, [Pittsburgh] will have to be abandoned some day, a rusty ruin to tumble into the river, keeping the river waters still stained with oxide of iron for another half century, meanwhile serving, at least, to mark the spot where one great phase of human endeavor, centralization, ended."[24]

Despite Wright's remarks and the city's years of inaction, civic leaders and planners had not given up, however. Learning that thirty-eight acres of St. Louis's riverfront had been designated as Jefferson National Park, a few civic leaders exhumed the dream of a national park for Pittsburgh's Point. The city council heeded their request for a Point Park Commission to prepare a plan for the area and pursue National Park Service recognition. Bigger weighed in with a brief report on the idea, not just for the tip of the peninsula but for a more expansive area with raised ground levels that would offer views of the rivers. He wanted to screen the bridges and ramps with landscaping and emphasize the Point's historical importance. At the same time, articles in the chamber of commerce publication, *Greater Pittsburgh*, predicted increased recreational use of the rivers and acknowledged the need to clean up and improve the riverfronts. The National Park Service's stipulations for recommending historic status were too rigid and expensive.[25] However, unlike with earlier plans that received little sustained support, some civic leaders were gradually beginning to envision the important role that a park and improved riverfronts might have on revitalizing downtown and the city.

After a depression-induced hiatus, the revival of the private, voluntary planning body that had sponsored the 1920s *Pittsburgh Plan* marked a watershed in both planning and ultimately the implementation of city redevelopment plans. Frustrating stalemates on a few long-standing projects would be overcome in the ensuing years as the private planning body assumed an activist role. In 1936 Howard Heinz reopened the offices of the Municipal Planning Association (formerly the CCCP) and renamed it the Pittsburgh Regional Planning Association (PRPA). He retained Bigger as a consultant and hired as executive director the hyperactive Wallace Richards, who had been working on the New Deal's Greenbelt housing project in Washington with Bigger. After courting New York's master planner of parks and parkways Robert Moses for several months, Heinz finally secured his consent in 1939 to prepare a report on solving the long-standing problems of traffic in downtown.[26]

Moses's planning team encountered renewed energy for redeveloping the Point into a historical park and constructing the highway circuit loop. The vision of a large complex involving some combination of monument, museum, restored forts, and parking, while simultaneously accommodating traffic, had remained alive despite the National Park Service's negative decision. Moreover, Heinz and Richards's persistent pressure to forge a consensus among planners and officials resulted in construction of the Water Street improvement, parallel to the Monongahela Wharf, as one leg of the loop around downtown. The opportunity to obtain Public Works Administration funds, along with Washington's concern to upgrade Pittsburgh's infrastructure for defense purposes, drove Heinz to push the unusual, sunken, two-level Water Street design. The new configuration (today Fort Pitt Boulevard and the Parkway East's infamous bathtub) incorporated the long awaited flood wall. Other components of the typical roster of downtown improvements, including Duquesne Way and the Point, still languished.[27]

Moses's plan—a slim document issued in November 1939—did not break new ground, as even he forewarned. The New York power broker reiterated the overriding priority of mitigating traffic congestion; all plans for the Point and the waterfront boulevards had to yield to this concern. In considering the Point, he declared that "traffic rather than history must be the decisive factor in the reconstruction of the apex of the Pittsburgh Triangle and in the establishment of Point Park." Despite this emphasis, Moses did recommend landscaping the slivers of land sandwiched between the highways and the rivers near the Point and proposed a large park nestled between the large highway ramps to the bridges (see Figure 14.2). The ramps as they rose to the bridges would have blocked the views of the rivers from the park, however. He urged removal of the railroads and automobile parking from the waterfronts. Once the by-pass boulevards with flood walls were in place, he envisioned attractively landscaping the river edges and putting an esplanade on top of the wall along Duquesne Way. In keeping with the traffic priority, he proposed bringing the much discussed Pitt Parkway (Parkway East) into downtown from the nearly completed Pennsylvania Turnpike along the Monongahela north shore to connect with the new Water Street paralleling the wharf. In a concession to proponents of

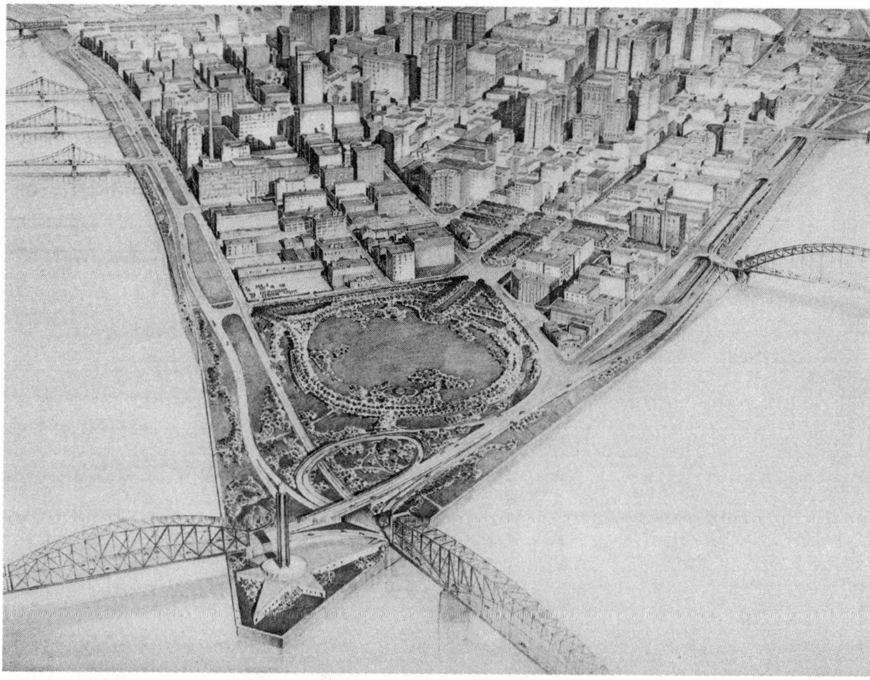

Fig. 14.2 Robert Moses's proposal for a Duquesne Boulevard, Pitt Parkway, a Point Park, and a Shaft of black Pennsylvania granite signifying the historic Point (Robert Moses, *Arterial Plan for Pittsburgh* [Pittsburgh: Pittsburgh Regional Planning Association, 1939], courtesy of the Archive Services Center, University of Pittsburgh).

recreational uses, Moses suggested putting a small parklet with handball courts and a boat landing next to the Brady Street Bridge about one mile upstream from the Monongahela Wharf.[28]

Moses's plan did not threaten the prevailing utilitarian view of the primary importance of the rivers and riverfronts as infrastructure. Nor did it advance the modest aesthetic and recreational proposals for these lands. In the minds of most leaders, the large park at the Point and the softening of the river edges would come only after the flood and traffic problems had been addressed. The newly formed Golden Triangle Division of the chamber of commerce, for example, never mentioned the riverfronts in its assessment of necessary steps for improving downtown. Moses's report did alter the planning and development process, however. Heinz and PRPA's Wallace Richards were delighted, even surprised, at the favorable publicity attending its publication. They resolved to take the lead, rather than remaining ineffectual advisors, in forging consensus and moving plans from the drawing board to construction. The recently revived dream of a signature Point Park and eventually even upgrading the riverfronts for recreation would benefit from this new determination by civic leaders.[29]

RENAISSANCE RIVERS

Although the Second World War energized the Pittsburgh region's industries, it shelved public improvement projects. Civic leaders and planners in Pittsburgh and across the nation nonetheless continued to discuss solutions for urban problems. The business community's determination to revitalize Pittsburgh resulted in the twenty-five-year post–Second World War redevelopment program known as Renaissance. A new partnership between public officials and business leaders established a redevelopment process by which a number of environmental, infrastructural, and downtown projects were completed (see "Downtown Pittsburgh" in this volume").[30] It changed the city's relationship to the rivers, riverfronts, and the Point. At the outset, Point Park signaled the city's revitalization and became a springboard for modernizing downtown. Simultaneously, civic leaders attacked the long-standing air and water pollution. Even so, with steel and coal industries still the region's economic foundation, most leaders continued to embrace the utilitarian perception of the riverfronts. As the success of Renaissance became apparent, pressure mounted for incorporating scenic and recreational aspects of the rivers and riverfronts into the modern city image rapidly replacing the old Smoky City reputation. However, only Point Park of various riverfront ideas began to take shape before Renaissance's momentum collapsed at the end of the 1960s.

A new nonprofit organization orchestrated Pittsburgh's Renaissance redevelopment program. Formed in 1943, the Allegheny Conference on Community Development (the Conference) was dominated by the city's major corporate leaders; it was led by Richard King Mellon, the Republican scion of the Mellon financial interests. Unlike earlier nonprofit groups involved in planning and promoting public policies, Mellon and the Conference forged an effective partnership with the head of the Democratic political machine, David L. Lawrence. Working through subcommittees, it drew up the redevelopment agenda, coordinated with other nonprofit organizations, and tasked the Pittsburgh Regional Planning Association with much of the planning. The Conference exercised considerable influence at all governmental levels, especially with Pennsylvania Republican governors, to obtain funding and legal authority for implementing projects. Lawrence brought along essential political support, local governmental authorizations, and some public funding. Mellon and Lawrence kept the historically fractious business community and politicians in line, respectively, overcoming the fragmentation that had parallelized past redevelopment efforts.[31]

Renaissance was a multipronged economic development strategy to retain locally based corporations and attract new ones by cleaning up the environment and modernizing infrastructure and downtown. Smoke control ordinances and the increasing availability of natural gas markedly brightened skies in the 1950s (see "Pittsburgh as an Energy Capital" in this volume). Federal flood control construction resumed after the war, and the new Allegheny County Sanitation Authority began treating sewage in 1959 for the first time in the area's history with notable improvement in the rivers' water quality. Before these actions could have significant results, the Conference registered little recognition of the potential aesthetic and recreational qualities of the rivers and riverfronts for economic development. Instead, the chamber of commerce in 1943 again promoted an intermodal freight terminal on the north shore of the Allegheny River for the port of Pittsburgh. The Conference supported the proposal in keeping with the business community's long-standing support for upgrading the wharves. The two groups also successfully lobbied the state for funding a plan of the port. Business leaders could not yet picture the rivers and riverfronts as scenic and recreational assets in view of the industries still lining the riverfronts, the fleets of massive coal tows plying the rivers, and the visibly degraded riverine environment. They doggedly pursued completion of the long-discussed circuit loop of highways and flood walls along the rivers and parking on the Monongahela Wharf.[32] Consequently, downtown waterfronts were not accessible to the public. Neither did Renaissance programs make the industrial and abandoned riverfront lands across from the Golden Triangle more inviting.

Point Park represented an important exception to the utilitarian perspective. The prewar advocacy of a large park at the Point limped along during the war, but it gained momentum in 1945 as Pittsburgh leaders revisited plans to modernize downtown. Given the impossibility of a national park at the Point, the Conference turned to the state for assistance. With the state already involved in redesigning the highway interchange at the Point, it made sense to fold a park proposal into the highway solution. Conference leaders convinced the governor to create a state park at the Point, and in turn state officials delegated their planning role to the PRPA and the Conference. Park plans also became coupled with a proposal for redevelopment of an adjacent rundown area into a modernist-style office complex, which emerged as Gateway Center in the 1950s. Critical private investment for the ambitious office project depended on the state's commitment to develop the adjacent Point Park scheme. Complicated financial, political, and infrastructural issues delayed the park's final plans.[33] A design controversy simmered between those desiring a historical emphasis and others like the chair of the Conference's architectural and design subcommittee Edgar J. Kaufmann, who promulgated a bold innovative architectural statement. Kaufmann again engaged Frank Lloyd Wright, who sketched a futuristic scheme in 1946. Wright's vision of an enormous three-story, beehive-like structure set at the Point incorporated entering and exiting traffic at different levels with spiral ramps to circulate the vehicles and included a mélange of entertainment, business, and government uses. The Conference's delegation to Wright's studio at Taliesan West in Arizona blanched at the architect's radical and, in their opinion, impractical proposal. By spring 1948 even Kaufmann had given up on his architect's design.[34]

The following year the Conference Point Park Committee hired the New York landscape architecture firm of Clarke, Rapuano, and Holleran (who were experienced in working with Robert Moses) along with the local firm of Ralph Griswold and Associates to devise a traffic interchange at the Point as an alternative to the scheme favored by the state highway department. The interchange had always been an obstacle to designing a park appropriate for this historically and geographically significant site. Three years earlier the Pennsylvania governor Edward Martin boldly approved the PRPA's proposal to remove the existing Point bridges and erect two new ones a little farther upstream so as to provide more land for the park. This unprecedented decision allowed designers to create an acceptable interchange solution and a park plan that embraced the scenic qualities of the rivers and riverfronts. With the highway interchange moved eastward from the Point's apex, Griswold and Rapuano's plan emphasized an open westward view of the Ohio River punctuated by a symbolic fountain. Further, their design provided pedestrian access to the rivers' edges. Making alterations as construction progressed, planners extended the riverbanks by fifty feet and hardened them, embedded boat mooring rings in the new river walls, built a strolling trail around the Point, and placed a stepped seating space along the Allegheny for spectator viewing of water events. Although critics doubted the efficacy of the recreational use of a downtown park, activities in subsequent years justified the architects' intentions. Groundbreaking for Point Park began in 1953, but construction proceeded slowly because of numerous problems. The park's dedication finally occurred in 1974, but the design and ongoing construction of the symbolic project from the beginning helped to change perceptions of the role of the rivers and riverfronts in Pittsburgh's Renaissance.[35]

During the second half of the 1950s, a few Pittsburgh civic leaders reconsidered the contribution of the rivers to Pittsburgh's revitalization efforts. The anticipated benefits of a sewage treatment plant and the new federal flood control system, plus the emerging footprint of Point Park, suggested cleaner rivers that people could enjoy and that would enhance the modern urban landscape that had been unfolding since the Second World War. The 1947 exhibit *Pittsburgh in Progress* sponsored by Kaufmann's Department Store had presented futuristic imaginings of a "City for Tomorrow," which among many other fanciful ideas envisioned a tremendous expansion in the use of the rivers for "educational and recreational purposes." A few ventures at the end of the decade reflected the exhibit's musings. Entrepreneur John E. Connelly launched the Gateway Clipper Fleet in 1958 for river tours; and the Conference, enthused by the improving rivers, obtained funds to construct a waterborne musical stage for concerts.[36]

A city-sponsored plan at the end of the 1950s set forth the most ambitious riverfront goals to date. Acknowledging the city's improving environmental conditions, the Pittsburgh Parks and Recreation Department engaged Griswold's firm to prepare a concept plan for the riverfronts and hillsides. Director Robert J. Templeton believed that, despite its accomplishments and acclaim, Renaissance had ignored the potential beauty of the city's dramatic topographical features. As a result of the new park arising at the Point and the city's desire to be modern, he and Griswold detected an "awakening to the recreational and aesthetic value of its rivers and riverfronts." The purpose of the study was to redress the long-standing neglect of the city's natural setting by creating "a unified program of adequate recreation and conservation." In *A Master Plan for the Development of Riverfronts and Hillsides* published in 1959, Griswold noted that public purchase of some waterfront properties would stop the general depreciation of riverfront lands and offer opportunities for public access. He predicted increased recreational boating and demand for leisure facilities resulting from greater free time for local workers benefiting from successful unionization. Griswold recommended that one-fifth of the city's riverfronts be devoted to walks and drives, marinas, boat-launching ramps, picnic landings for boaters (see Figure 14.3), riverbank landscaping, and even an elaborate double-deck structure with docks, restaurants, swimming pool, terraces, and a rooftop garden. In what surely must have seemed like an incredible flight of fancy, Griswold imagined a great festival park on industrialized Herr's Island (two miles above downtown in the Allegheny River, today named Washington's Landing) like Skansen in Stockholm or Tivoli in Copenhagen. He proposed a two-mile-long walk and drive along the north shore of the

FIG. 14.3 Ralph Griswold's suggestions for riverside picnic landings (*A Master Plan for the Development of Riverfronts and Hillsides in the City of Pittsburgh*, prepared by Griswold, Winters, and Swain [Pittsburgh: Department of Parks and Recreation, 1959], courtesy of Archive Services Center, University of Pittsburgh).

Ohio and Allegheny Rivers from Manchester to the Heinz plant like those along the Charles River in Boston and the Potomac in Washington. Even modest suggestions for riverfront walks on the north shore of the Monongahela near an enormous slag dump and on the South Side near the Jones & Laughlin Steel Corporation's mill must have struck readers as far-fetched in the industrial climate of 1959. In retrospect, Griswold was in fact remarkably prescient.[37]

At first glance, Point Park and Griswold's *Master Plan* signaled a major shift in the city's perception of its rivers and riverfronts. The new park at the Point did represent a departure from the old perceptions in its recognition of the rivers as scenic assets and in the expensive adjustment of traffic infrastructure to meet the park's goals. The 1959 *Master Plan* also embraced scenic possibilities and proposed several recreational opportunities. The *Pittsburgh Post-Gazette* dubbed it the "Renaissance of Riversides." With the improved condition of the rivers, recreational boating did experience growth during the Renaissance years.[38]

Despite the enthusiasm surrounding the development of Point Park, a truly new day for the rivers and riverfronts had not yet arrived. Civic leaders still accepted the priority of industrial and infrastructural river uses. Even the "City for Tomorrow" left the Monongahela and Ohio riverfronts to the industry prevalent there and focused on the Allegheny River's north shore for recreational development. Point Park with its unprecedented accessibility to the river edges represented only a small portion of the still largely inaccessible central waterfronts, where automobile infrastructure obstructed pedestrian use, except for a few hardy runners out for lunchtime exercise. The 1959 *Master Plan* itself began by reiterating that most flat riverfront property must remain the province of the industry that supported the region. The objective was to find a "balance among the diverse interests" and, accordingly, the plan proposed making 20 percent of the shore within the City of Pittsburgh, not just the central riverfronts, available for scenic and recreational uses. Without the Conference's adoption of the plan, little concrete was accomplished.[39] In 1963, Patrick Horsbrugh, a consultant hired by the city to make design recommendations with respect to the area's dramatic topography, proposed the renovation of Pittsburgh's "waterfrontages to re-establish industrial activities along the banks." A year earlier the PRPA in its extensive Golden Triangle plan only allowed for a modest pedestrian pathway to a vaguely stated waterfront development.[40]

However, public planning often sparks conversation and additional planning. Events in the mid-1960s indicated that ideas for a "Renaissance of Riversides" remained alive. Allegheny County engaged the landscape architecture firm of Simonds and Simonds (today named EPD) to plan a recreational park for Twelve Mile Island, named for its distance in the Allegheny River from the Point. The firm's ambitious plan for reforestation, trails, and water amenities of various kinds generated excitement among some leaders of this industrial region. Unfortunately, the sand and gravel company that owned the property rebuffed county proposals to purchase it. Years later the principal planner of the project, John Ormsbee Simonds, thought that the defeat ignited "a region-wide campaign" for riverfront improvements.[41]

Possibly in response to the collapse of the Twelve Mile Island plan and the languishing of riverfront improvement, representatives from city planning, the Allegheny County Commissioners, the state senate, the Conference, and private industry announced in November 1966 the formation of the Three Rivers Action Development Committee (TRIAD), with the goal of promoting a River Renaissance. TRIAD intended to be a coordinating body and catalyst for cleaning up the rivers, developing recreational uses, and making them attractive "to encourage and lead the people of Western Pennsylvania to want to live, work, and play along the rivers." At the initial meeting, city planning director John Mauro identified several ideas "on the drawing board." In particular, he mentioned a North Shore Park that would include a proposed sports stadium and would stretch for two miles opposite downtown and Point Park. By this juncture the stadium idea had been under consideration for several years. TRIAD mostly brought attention to the rivers by advocating their beautification, a term widely in vogue since President Lyndon Johnson and his wife, Lady Bird, advocated for the beautifying of American landscapes. TRIAD president Arthur Harris, a Gulf Oil executive, believed the nonprofit organization was "channel[ing]" a long-standing desire of Pittsburghers to improve the rivers. The organization implored property owners, mostly businesses, to clean up their riverbanks, paint their buildings, and landscape the river edges. With the city, it sponsored the River Clean Up Week in April 1968, a River History Week in May, and a Three Rivers Renaissance Week in June, culminating in a carnival weekend of water sports and programs. TRIAD continued its promotional activities until it ran out of financial support and closed its doors in 1978.[42]

Riverfront planning during Renaissance peaked the year of TRIAD's initial river festival. In the same year (1968), with Three Rivers Stadium taking shape, the Department of City Planning hired Simonds to plan an adjacent riverfront pedestrian walkway from the Sixth Street Bridge to the stadium, as well as a larger north shore park between the West End and

Sixteenth Street bridges, identified in its earlier North Shore Park Study. In 1963, city planning consultant Patrick Horsbrugh had complained about the "disassociation" between the river and the proposed stadium, despite its eventual name. John Simonds was already part of the team designing the stadium site. His early discussions with team members posited a marina, motel, and floating restaurant. But the city stuck with the limited walkway idea. For the narrow strip allotted for the walkway, he proposed a combination of rip-rap edge, hard river walls, a public dock for the Gateway Clipper's water taxi, lighting, and landscaping. In its final constructed form, it was named Roberto Clemente Park.[43]

The stadium, named Three Rivers Stadium, was part of the Renaissance effort to modernize downtown, remake the Smoky City image, and capture tourism dollars. The original design of a horseshoe to provide views of Point Park and downtown crashed, like Simonds' river edge plans, because of excessive cost predictions. In the end the stadium failed to attract surrounding development, which in part confirms Horsbrugh's earlier assessment of dissociation from the river.[44]

Recognizing that extant US Steel and railroad properties west of the stadium impeded a linear park along the entire riverfront as originally proposed, Simonds and the Department of City Planning agreed to design parks for limited areas. Near the West End Bridge, they focused on the adjacent community, for which the landscape architect envisioned ball fields, basketball courts, and other recreational facilities. For the stretch of the north shore from the Ninth Street Bridge to the Heinz plant opposite downtown, Simonds advanced an ambitious multilevel development that he called Allegheny Riverside. Near the river, he drew up public recreational activities from picnicking and fishing to a boat-launching area and swimming pool that would be convertible to ice-skating in the winter. He included private businesses from the motel and restaurants (which were deleted from the stadium walkway proposal) to a yacht club and marina with motor boating, canoeing, and rowing. Back from the riverside on higher land, Simonds foresaw opportunities for high density residential and office development with views of downtown and pedestrian connections to the river.

Allegheny Riverside held out the promise of being Pittsburgh's first waterfront complex. It would have put the city in the forefront of the emerging national trend for waterfront development, which swept across the nation after 1980. It would have also added to the city's reputation for innovative redevelopment like postwar Renaissance redevelopment had done. Unfortunately, Simonds submitted the proposal in early 1970, when changed political and social conditions conspired to bring Renaissance to an end. Toward the end of the year, the city planning department informed the consultants that "no active recreation [could] be added to the riverfront." Allegheny Riverside joined the many riverfront studies before it got lost in a file cabinet. The idea for north shore improvement went dormant, however, not dead.[45]

PRELUDE TO POSTINDUSTRIAL RIVERFRONTS

The opening of Three Rivers Stadium in 1970 with its modest riverside walkway across from the nearly completed Point Park with its majestic fountain appeared to showcase at last the long-desired contribution of the central riverfronts to Pittsburgh's postwar Renaissance. In fact, the election of Peter Flaherty as mayor in 1969 signaled city government's withdrawal from the public-private partnership and the end of Renaissance. By the middle of the 1970s, however, a looming fear of industrial decline and a sense that the city needed to regain momentum—especially downtown—rekindled interest in the riverfronts. As the industries located on the riverfronts weakened or closed, private entities saw opportunities for redevelopment, and the city dusted off its north shore plans. The stage was set for the postindustrial transformation of the riverfronts when the deindustrialization crisis of the 1980s undermined the utilitarian perspective and spurred civic leaders to search for new economic drivers.

Riverfront development ambitions ground to a halt at the end of the 1960s. African American civil rights protests intensified with anger at the injustices of urban renewal projects, most infamously in the lower Hill District. The riots following Martin Luther King's assassination on April 4, 1968, spurred the Conference and city officials to shift their agendas from physical redevelopment to social issues. Pete Flaherty capitalized on the anger of minorities and the resentment of the white working class toward the public-private partnership that, they believed, had neglected them in favor of the large corporations and downtown redevelopment. Flaherty severed relations with the Conference and shifted city policy and federal funds from downtown to the neighborhoods. He instituted austere budgets and a moratorium on further urban renewal projects. Riverfront development did not fit into his vision. Frustrated by Flaherty's inaction, state and federal officials threatened to cancel pending long-delayed grants for a convention center and rapid transit. Civic leaders had to reach a consensus on them or lose the funds. Flaherty reluctantly resumed cooperation with the Conference on the projects. The resulting decision to locate the Convention Center between Tenth and Eleventh Streets in downtown, but orient its backend and loading docks toward the Allegheny River, indicated that besides Point

Part the development potential of downtown's riverfronts was not yet fully appreciated.[46]

Despite these difficult years for river enthusiasts such as TRIAD, prospects for revived interest in the riverfronts picked up during the second half of the 1970s. With financial backing from Richard Mellon Scaife and his Allegheny Foundation, in 1976 the Pittsburgh History & Landmarks Foundation purchased the passenger terminal of the moribund Pittsburgh & Lake Erie Railroad (P&LE) located along the Monongahela River at the south end of the Smithfield Street Bridge. City planners had long targeted the P&LE's declining railroad yards and buildings as a site for future redevelopment. Landmarks president Arthur Ziegler refurbished the stunning interior of the terminal's waiting room into a sumptuous, successful restaurant and rehabbed the upper-floor offices, all without assistance from city government. Naming it Station Square, Ziegler later with the city's assistance expanded the preservation project to other buildings on the site and constructed a riverside hotel facing downtown. He intended the ambitious rehabilitation of the railroad terminal to bring attention to Pittsburgh's waterfronts as the acclaimed Ghirardelli Square project did for San Francisco.[47]

Station Square's success spotlighted the great potential of the riverfronts opposite downtown, which were less encumbered by highway infrastructure. Civic leaders once again showed interest in the central riverfronts. In its 1976 Six Year Development Program, the city resurrected plans for the north shore of the Allegheny River as part of a ninety-one-acre renewal project. The following year Flaherty resigned to assume a position in President Carter's administration. Incoming mayor Richard Caliguiri recognized that the region's unfolding industrial crisis and the stagnation of downtown required the administration's active involvement both in development and in revival of the public-private partnership that had propelled the postwar Renaissance. In a speech at the Allegheny Conference's annual meeting, its chairman and Dravo Corporation CEO Robert Dickey took note of Station Square and with hyperbole foresaw the prospect of turning the Allegheny's north shore into Pittsburgh's Left Bank. He declared that a new renaissance was at hand.[48]

Mayor Caliguiri believed that the city needed to reinvent itself once more, although he did not have a fully formed picture of what that new city might be. Calling for a second Renaissance, he moved aggressively with private partners to foster new downtown development and to expand the Golden Triangle's boundaries to adjacent eastern areas such as the Strip District and across the rivers. In 1979 the Urban Redevelopment Authority reported it had received state funds to acquire property for a possible north shore development of residences, offices, and a park. Searching for a site of a new headquarters building, Duquesne Light Company investigated north shore properties. As riverfronts opposite downtown sprang to life, downtown riverfronts also started attracting attention. The Conference's 1979 proposal for a cultural district in a fourteen-square-block area between Liberty Avenue and the Allegheny River mentioned a riverfront promenade. In its headquarters search, Mellon Bank seriously considered creating a campus at the site of the old Baltimore & Ohio Railroad terminal on the Monongahela Wharf. Farther west along Fort Pitt Boulevard at Stanwix Street, plans were solidifying for a twenty-story office building overlooking the river.

At the beginning of the 1980s, with Caliguiri's Renaissance II gaining momentum, Pittsburgh finally seemed poised to redevelop its riverfronts for their potential aesthetic and recreational attributes. The groundwork for a postindustrial river renaissance had been laid with the first Renaissance's establishment of Point Park and the surge of riverfront planning that did, however, collapse along with the public-private partnership's brief demise. Riverfront enthusiasm resurfaced in the late 1970s such that older ideas would finally flower in the following decade with the Allegheny Landing sculpture park on the north shore and the Washington's Landing development on old Herr's Island.

CONCLUSION

A sudden conversion to comprehensive riverfront redevelopment had not yet taken place, despite Pittsburgh's "golden" era of industrial power and prosperity having come to an abrupt end with deindustrialization. Over more than a hundred years of industrialization and concomitant urbanization, civic leaders had turned the rivers and riverfront lands into essential components of the region's industrial infrastructure. In so doing, Pittsburghers generally lost access to and contact with these signature geographical features. Polluted, crowded with enormous coal tows, and made inaccessible with muddy trash-strewn banks and foreboding railroad tracks to be negotiated, the rivers did not seem either natural or scenic to most people.[49] Moreover, the highways with flood walls built decades earlier as part of the circuit loop around downtown—Fort Pitt Boulevard and the Parkway East along the Monongahela River and Duquesne Way and the Tenth Street Bypass along the Allegheny—deterred ambitious waterfront improvements.[50] Civic leaders' initial panic to replace as soon as possible the employment of closed mills and factories along the rivers with industrial jobs conflicted with the ideas of those wanting to reinvent the riverfronts with postindustrial retail, office, residential, and recreational uses. Even though the reason underlying the century-long utilitarian priority for riverfronts was rapidly unraveling, its stranglehold on perceptions dissipated more slowly.

Nevertheless, the economic crisis of deindustrialization did generate a more broadly shared and fundamental rethinking of the rivers and riverfronts' appropriate roles in the emerging postindustrial Pittsburgh. Civic leaders and private developers were finally relinquishing their utilitarian views of the rivers and riverfronts so that scenic, recreational, and even residential uses promulgated in years past by a few planners and farsighted leaders could eventually flourish.[51] At each stage of planning, Pittsburgh's leaders had feared the consequences for economic growth of not improving traffic circulation with a circuit loop and failing to upgrade the commercial utility of the waterfronts. Proposals to caste at least part of the riverfronts in a different light failed to penetrate prevailing utilitarian priorities. Prior to the Second World War neither private leaders nor public officials showed a commitment to work on behalf of modest riverfront proposals in the manner that Charles Wacker and Walter Moody had for Burnham's Chicago plan.[52] Only after the war did private leaders, alarmed by dire predictions of dismal economic prospects, assume active roles in bringing about some change on the waterfronts.

Pittsburghers did not reevaluate their self-defined industrial identity until deindustrialization left that self-perception in tatters. Deindustrialization allowed alternative futures for the rivers and riverfronts to materialize. The process since the 1980s of recovering the region's riverine character has been complicated, multifaceted, contentious, exciting, and slow. The process has built on the foundation laid during the Renaissance years. Point Park most importantly, plans for the north shore, the Griswold report, TRIAD, and Allegheny Riverside all pointed to the possibilities inherent in the city's ample river frontage. While Olmsted, Moses, and others could not have envisioned the commercial and residential development now taking place along the rivers, they did foresee in broad terms the linear trails, parks, boating facilities, and ecological regeneration transforming the rivers and riverfronts. But even here, they would be amazed at the extent of the transformation, for in their day the industrial imperative was just too dominant.

NOTES

This essay was originally published as "Riverfront Planning in Pittsburgh, 1900s–1970s," *Proceedings*, Thirteenth Biennial Conference, International Planning History Society, 2008, 1440–52.

1. Edward K. Muller and Joel A. Tarr with Timothy M. Collins, "Pittsburgh's Three

Rivers: From Industrial Infrastructure to Environmental Assets," in Christof Mauch and Thomas Zeller, eds., *Rivers in History: Perspectives on Waterways in Europe and North America* (Pittsburgh: University of Pittsburgh Press, 2008), 41–62, and in this volume; http://www.riverlifepgh.org; http://www.friendsoftheriverfront.org.

2. Jon A. Peterson, *The Birth of City Planning in the United States, 1840–1917* (Baltimore: Johns Hopkins University Press, 2003); Carl Smith, *The Plan of Chicago: Daniel Burnham and the Remaking of the American City* (Chicago: University of Chicago Press, 2006). In this chapter I define the central riverfronts of Pittsburgh as generally those of downtown, the two river neighborhoods immediately to the east of downtown, and across the three rivers from downtown.

3. Frank Lloyd Wright, "Broadacres to Pittsburgh," *Pittsburgh Sun Telegraph*, June 24, 1935. For an overview of planning in Pittsburgh before the Second World War, see John F. Bauman and Edward K. Muller, *Before Renaissance: Planning in Pittsburgh, 1889–1943* (Pittsburgh: University of Pittsburgh Press, 2006).

4. The park on Pittsburgh's point is officially a state park and therefore named Point State Park. I refer to it here as Point Park as most Pittsburghers do. See also Roy Lubove, *Twentieth Century Pittsburgh, Vol. 1: Government, Business, and Environmental Change* (1969; repr., Pittsburgh: University of Pittsburgh Press, 1996), 106–41; Sherie R. Mershon, "Corporate Social Responsibility and Urban Revitalization: The Allegheny Conference on Community Development, 1943–1968" (PhD diss., Carnegie Mellon University, 2000); Shelby Stewman and Joel A. Tarr, "Four Decades of Public-Private Partnerships in Pittsburgh," in R. Scott Fosler and Renee A. Berger, eds., *Public-Private Partnerships in American Cities* (Lexington, MA: Lexington Books, 1984), 59–127.

5. Robert C. Alberts, *The Shaping of the Point: Pittsburgh's Renaissance Park* (Pittsburgh: University of Pittsburgh Press, 1980).

6. In situating the roots of the postindustrial transformation of Pittsburgh in the postwar Renaissance period, I am following the argument of Tracy Neumann, *Remaking the Rust Belt: The Postindustrial Transformation of North America* (Philadelphia: University of Pennsylvania Press, 2016), 2. In general, the term "postindustrial" stands for the transformation of many American cities once based on an industrial economy to ones focused on financial and business services, educational and medical services and research, advanced technology, and amenities.

7. Joel A. Tarr and Terry F. Yosie, "Critical Decisions in Pittsburgh Waste and Waterwater Treatment," in Joel A. Tarr, ed., *Devastation and Renewal: An Environmental History of Pittsburgh and Its Region* (Pittsburgh: University of Pittsburgh Press, 2003), 64–88; Edward K. Muller, "River City," in Tarr, *Devastation and Renewal*, 41–57; Muller and Tarr with Collins, "Pittsburgh's Three Rivers."

8. Roy Lubove, *Twentieth-Century Pittsburgh, Vol. 1*, chs. 2–3; Bauman and Muller, *Before Renaissance*, ch. 2.

9. *Catalogue of the First Annual Exhibition of the Pittsburgh Architectural Club* (Pittsburgh: Pittsburgh Architectural Club, 1900).

10. Thomas S. Hines, *Burnham of Chicago: Architect and Planner* (New York: Oxford University Press, 1974), 371–83; Bauman and Muller, *Before Renaissance*, chs. 2–3.

11. Frederick Law Olmsted Jr., *Pittsburgh Main Thoroughfares and the Down Town District* (Pittsburgh: Pittsburgh Civic Commission, 1911), 20, 21, 28. See also Bauman and Muller, *Before Renaissance*, ch. 3.

12. Olmsted, *Main Thoroughfares*, 20–28. The Flood Commission of Pittsburgh under the chairmanship of H. J. Heinz was established in 1908 by the Chamber of Commerce of Pittsburgh after the devastating 1907 flood. The publication of its report four years later made many recommendations, several of which were eventually implemented decades later. See *The Report of the Flood Commission of Pittsburgh, Penna.* (Pittsburgh, 1912).

13. Olmsted, *Main Thoroughfares*, 21, 23, 25.

14. Olmsted, *Main Thoroughfares*, 29–30. Olmsted's concern for the relationship between the rivers and the uses of riverfronts is seen in his many letters written during the year of research and preparation of the plan of 1910. See Olmsted Associates Papers, Manuscript Division of the Library of Congress, Washington, DC.

15. John F. Bauman and Margaret Spratt, "Civic Leaders and Environmental Reform: The Pittsburgh Survey and Urban Planning," in Maurine W. Greenwald and Margo Anderson, eds., *Pittsburgh Surveyed: Social Science and Social Reform in the Early Twentieth Century* (Pittsburgh: University of Pittsburgh Press, 1996), 164–69.

16. Albert J. Logan, *Report of the Department of City Planning for Year Ending January 31, 1913* (Pittsburgh: Department of City Planning, 1913), 60–65.

17. Roland M. Smith, "The Politics of Pittsburgh Flood Control, Part 1, 1908–1936," *Pennsylvania History* 42, no. 1 (1975): 5–24; Bauman and Muller, *Before Renaissance*, 98.

18. Bauman and Muller, *Before Renaissance*, ch. 4.

19. *Waterways: A Part of the Pittsburgh Plan, Report No. 6* (Pittsburgh: Citizens Committee on the City Plan of Pittsburgh, 1923), 13.

20. Joel A. Tarr, *Transportation Innovation and Changing Spatial Patterns in Pittsburgh, 1850–1934* (Chicago: Public Works Historical Society, 1978), 28–31.

21. Bauman and Muller, *Before Renaissance*, chs. 6–8.

22. *Parks: A Part of the Pittsburgh Plan*, report no. 4 (Pittsburgh: Citizens Committee on the City Plan, 1923). See also Bauman and Muller, *Before Renaissance*, 131–33.

23. Franklin Toker, *Fallingwater Rising: Frank Lloyd Wright, E. J. Kaufmann, and America's Most Extraordinary House* (New York: Alfred A. Knopf, 2003), 118–26, 157.

24. Frank Lloyd Wright, "Broadacres to Pittsburgh," *Pittsburgh Sun Telegraph*, June 24, 1935. See also James A. Raubie, "Frank Lloyd Wright Ridicules Pitt Shaft," *Pittsburgh Sun Telegraph*, June 30, 1935.

25. Alberts, *The Shaping of the Point*, 42–46; Dr. James H. Greene, "Our Rivers," *Greater Pittsburgh* 20, no. 3 (July 1939): 3; no author, "Master Regional Plan," *Greater Pittsburgh* 24, no. 2 (June 1938): 19, 35.

26. Bauman and Muller, *Before Renaissance*, 231–36; John F. Bauman and Edward K. Muller, "The Planning Technician as Urban Visionary: Frederick Bigger and American Planning, 1915–1963," *Journal of Planning History* 1, no. 2 (2002): 124–53.

27. Bauman and Muller, *Before Renaissance*, 232–50.

28. Robert Moses, *Arterial Plan for Pittsburgh* (Pittsburgh: Pittsburgh Regional Planning Association, 1939), 12–22.

29. No author, "To Boost Golden Triangle," *Greater Pittsburgh* 20, no. 5 (November 1939): 3, 24; no author, "Golden Triangle Division," *Greater Pittsburgh* 22, no. 3 (February 1940): 11–12; Bauman and Muller, *Before Renaissance*, 250–67.

30. Jon Teaford, *The Rough Road to Renaissance: Urban Revitalization in America, 1940–1985* (Baltimore: Johns Hopkins University Press, 1990); Lubove, *Twentieth-Century Pittsburgh, Vol. 1*; Stewman and Tarr, "Four Decades of Public-Private Partnerships."

Because civic leaders declared the revitalization of Pittsburgh in the 1980s, particularly of downtown, as a second Renaissance, most people have now identified the post–Second World War redevelopment as Renaissance I.

31. Mershon, "Corporate Social Responsibility," 242–90; Michael P. Weber, *Don't Call Me Boss: David L. Lawrence, Pittsburgh's Renaissance Mayor* (Pittsburgh: University of Pittsburgh Press, 1988), 228–53.

32. Mershon, "Corporate Social Responsibility," 257–60, 399, 489.

33. Alberts, *The Shaping of the Point*, 68–90.

34. Alberts, *The Shaping of the Poiny*, 91–97; Mershon, "Corporate Social Responsibility," 426–35; Toker, *Fallingwater Rising*, 337 40.

35. Alberts, *The Shaping of the Point*, 110–28, 152–54, 184–205; Mershon, "Corporate Social Responsibility," 436–42.

36. *Pittsburgh in Progress*, exhibition brochure (Kaufmann's, 1947), not paginated. See also Mershon, "Corporate Social Responsibility," 648. The exhibit took its design cue from the then fashionable Le Corbusier view of the modern city.

37. *A Master Plan for the Development of Riverfronts and Hillsides in the City of Pittsburgh*, prepared by Griswold, Winters, and Swain (Pittsburgh: Department of Parks and Recreation, 1959), 2, 5.

38. "City Plans Renaissance of Riversides," *Pittsburgh Post-Gazette*, October 2, 1959.

39. *A Master Plan for the Development of Riverfronts and Hillsides in the City of Pittsburgh*, 2 3, 5, 7.

40. Patrick Horsbrugh, *Pittsburgh Perceived: A Critical Review of Form, Features, and Feasibilities of the Prodigious City* (Pittsburgh: Department of City Planning, 1963), 199; PRPA, *A Plan for Pittsburgh's Golden Triangle* (Pittsburgh: PRPA, 1962), 113–23. Ira Lowry suggests that the plan also saw some apartments for the riverfront. Ira S. Lowry, *Portrait of a Region* (Pittsburgh: University of Pittsburgh Press, 1963), 152.

41. "A Study of Twelve Mile Island: Water, Water, Everywhere" (1963), Twelve Mile Island, Pennsylvania, Box 165, John Ormsbee Simonds Collection, Special and Area Studies Collections, George A. Smathers Libraries, University of Florida, Gainesville, Florida (hereafter cited as JOS Collection). See also "Commentary, C/P 40," Item #3, Box 187, JOS Collection.

42. "A New Life for Our Rivers through TRIAD," press statement, TRIAD, n.d.; "TRIAD Charts Course for River Beauty," *Pittsburgh Press*, November 17, 1968, n.p. (Mauro); "Fete Will Hail River Benefits," *Pittsburgh Press*, February 18, 1968, n.p. (Harris); "Statement of Purpose," press statement, TRIAD, n.d.; all of the TRIAD newspaper articles and press statements can be found in "Pittsburgh: Riverfront Studies," Box 51, JOS Collection. The Three Rivers Action Development Committee was later renamed the Three Rivers Improvement and Development Corporation or TRIAD. For a brief overview, see "Three Rivers Improvement and Development Corporation (TRIAD)," *Western Pennsylvania History* 99, no. 1 (Spring 2016), 18–19.

43. Horsbrugh, *Pittsburgh Perceived*, 240b. See also Meeting notes, April 26, July 18, August 18, 1968, in "Pittsburgh: Riverfront Studies," Box 51, JOS Collection. The landscape architecture firm of Simonds and Simonds worked with the architecture firm of Dieter, Richey, Sippel on the design of Three Rivers Stadium and its site.

44. Aaron Cowan, *A Nice Place to Visit: Tourism and Urban Revitalization in the Postwar Rustbelt* (Philadelphia: Temple University Press, 2016), 101–26.

45. Meeting notes, September 17, 1969 (quote), January 22, August 7, 1970, Box 51,

JOS Collection. Simonds and Simonds submitted a proposal to the Department of City Planning for the riverfront titled "Allegheny Riverside—A Development Proposal."

46. Joe W. Trotter and Jared N. Day, *Race and Renaissance: African Americans in Pittsburgh since World War II* (Pittsburgh: University of Pittsburgh Press, 2010), 90–118; Stewman and Tarr, "Four Decades of Public-Private Partnerships," 89–94; Tracy Neumann, "Renaissance and Retrenchment in the 1970s," *Journal of Urban History* 41, no.1 (2015): 39–43; *Pittsburgh 80: A Report of the Urban Redevelopment Authority of Pittsburgh* (Pittsburgh: Urban Redevelopment Authority, 1980), 19.

47. Roy Lubove, *Twentieth-Century Pittsburgh, Vol. 2: The Post-Steel Era* (Pittsburgh: University of Pittsburgh Press, 1996), 218–21; Richard Moe and Carter Wilkie, *Changing Places: Rebuilding Community in the Age of Sprawl* (New York: Henry Holt, 1997), 135–38.

48. Neumann, *Remaking the Rust Belt*, 110–11.

49. Edward K. Muller, "The Legacy of Industrial Rivers," *Pittsburgh History* 72, no. 2 (1989): 64–75. Renaissance diligently worked to remake Pittsburgh's image as modern, no longer the old industrial city.

50. URA, *Pittsburgh 80*, 19; Lubove, *Twentieth-Century Pittsburgh, Vol. 2*, 57–61; Neumann, *Remaking the Rust Belt*, 118–20; Robert McLean, *Countdown to Renaissance II: The New Way Corporate America Builds* (Pittsburgh: Urban Marketing Associates, 1984), 66–84; Franklin Toker, *Pittsburgh: An Urban Portrait* (University Park: Pennsylvania State University Press, 1986), 29.

51. Lubove, *Twentieth-Century Pittsburgh, Vol. 2*, 201–7.

52. Smith, *The Plan of Chicago*, chs. 7–8.

15 DOWNTOWN PITTSBURGH

RELENTLESS CHANGE

Edward K. Muller

Petula Clark's popular mid-1960s song *Downtown* extolled the excitement and bustle of the American downtown, even as these emblematic places of any city were struggling to maintain their prominence. From the inception of a town, businesses, transportation facilities, and civic institutions concentrated at the center of the city, often at the waterfront. The ensuing central business districts were sites of economic power, substantial property investment, and civic authority. They evolved in response to major economic, technological, and social changes. For more than half of the twentieth century, downtowns (the popular name of central business districts) symbolized the modern American city. The iconic features of skyscrapers, opulent department stores, grand railroad terminals, luxurious hotels, and theater palaces signified modernity in the American imagination, even as suburban developments in the second half of the century challenged downtown's primacy.

Pittsburgh's Golden Triangle—the approximately 255-acre peninsula bounded by hills to the east and the converging Allegheny and Monongahela Rivers that meet at the western tip—grew and changed in ways similar to downtowns of other American industrial cities. Starting as a small settlement on the Monongahela River's north bank, Pittsburgh became the bustling gateway to the west centered on the Ohio River valley. In the mid-nineteenth century, Pittsburgh's business district began the transformation to become a modern downtown. The railroads challenged the city's commercial raison d'être at the head of the Ohio River. Merchants, manufacturers, and entrepreneurs turned their attention to manufacturing, particularly iron and glass. By the early twentieth century, massive iron and steel, coal and coke, and glass industries, along with several other prominent new industries, spread across six counties. Further, Pittsburgh had become a leading center of corporate finance. The urban industrial complex with Pittsburgh at its core ranked among the nation's ten largest metropolitan regions. The wharf, manufacturing, and residences of the original business district all declined, while financial, legal, and corporate offices, department stores, and entertainment venues replaced them and congregated in specialized functional districts in downtown, increasingly called just "town" by residents throughout the region.

Slowing industrial growth and then deindustrialization challenged the region for much of the century after 1920. Simultaneously, suburban expansion imperiled downtown retail, entertainment, and even office activities. These trends, common to industrial cities, forced civic leaders to reimagine the region's economy and its downtown and to intervene in private development processes.[1] Over several decades after the Second World War, a postindustrial downtown emerged in Pittsburgh, featuring additional skyscrapers, a cultural district, riverfront amenities, tourism destinations, educational institutions, and a resurgence of residences. Moreover, downtown finally escaped the tight boundaries of the original triangular site.

Pittsburgh's downtown evolved through various stages. Fundamental shifts in the region's economy altered firm size, workforce composition, the role of finance, and the involvement of government and not-for-profit organizations. New technologies in communication and transportation, office work, and building construction contributed to downtown's changing spatial patterns and appearance. The rise of a thriving middle class and new marketing methods increased the consumption of goods, changed the geography of retailing, and altered entertainment venues. Throughout these changes, downtown remained a prime site of real estate investment and regional power, often displayed architecturally.

Despite 250 years since the first plan for Pittsburgh, the Golden Triangle is still a work in progress. Relentless change has been the most consistent characteristic of Pittsburgh's downtown. American capitalism's constant search for investment opportunities and the redeployment of capital have resulted in a persistent process of "creative destruction," by which demolition and construction have continually remade the Triangle's landscape.[2] Private enterprise, private property, and market forces dominated the process, especially throughout the nineteenth century. Local government opened and paved the streets, oversaw the wharf, built water and sewer infrastructure, erected government buildings, and franchised and feebly regulated services such as street lighting. Nonetheless, downtown reflected foremost the private market and business aspirations at work.

By the turn of the twentieth century, unfettered growth threatened the Triangle's economic welfare and caused increasingly unhealthy conditions. Reluctantly, local government, often under pressure from voluntary organizations, took modest steps to influence private development and encourage growth by building bridges and improving highways, engaging in some planning, and adopting zoning. Only after the Great Depression and the Second World War, when the region's economic future looked dismal, did a powerful public-private partnership intervene and promote the modernization of downtown in order to retain corporations, attract new businesses, and alter the city's national image. In the last quarter of the century, with deindustrialization ravaging the region's manufacturing, the public sector increased its role in the partnership in order to revitalize downtown and rebrand Pittsburgh and the Golden Triangle as postindustrial. Private investment remained central to the city-building process, but government agencies, a historic preservation organization, and foundations also participated in downtown's development.

The Golden Triangle experienced forces and changes common to most downtowns of America's industrial cities. Yet, it always was a distinctive place. The sharp boundaries formed by the rivers and the bordering hills worsened traffic congestion, inhibited horizontal expansion, increased density, and heightened visual qualities. In the mid-twentieth century, Pittsburgh's redevelopment success and the publicity promulgated by the public-private partnership stamped Pittsburgh as innovative and attracted imitators. While many visitors to the city can identify features that are shared with other American downtowns, the Golden Triangle set apart from most adjacent development by its rivers has been distinctive and easily recognizable as Pittsburgh.

PART 1: THE PRIVATE CITY

The Gateway City's Mercantile Triangle

Located at the head of the Ohio River, late eighteenth-century Pittsburgh seemed destined to become the transfer point between eastern overland routes and the main river route to the western frontier. Surveyors Colonel

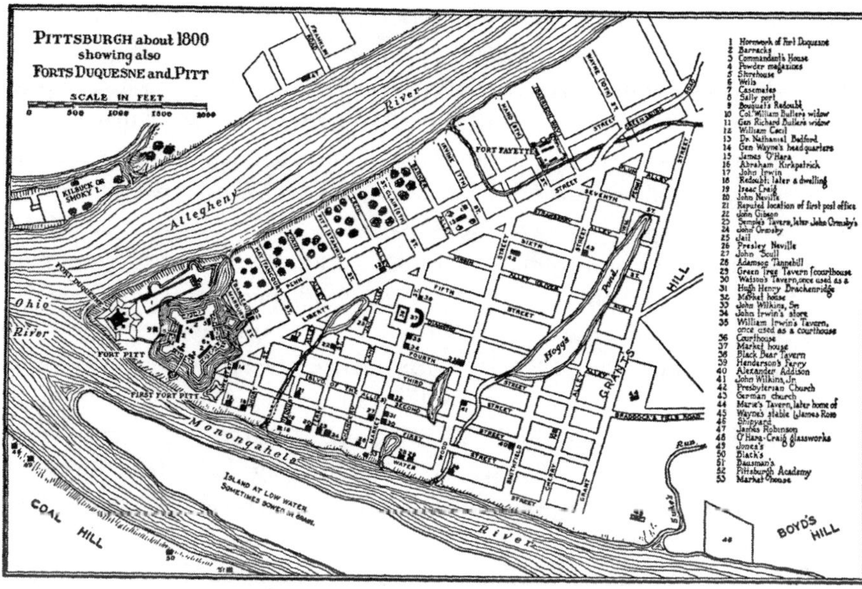

FIG. 15.1 The Woods-Vickroy plan of Pittsburgh (Leland D. Baldwin, *Pittsburgh: The Story of a City, 1750–1865* [Pittsburgh: University of Pittsburgh Press, 1937], courtesy of the Archive Services Center, University of Pittsburgh).

George Woods and Thomas Vikroy recognized this prospect when they laid out the street plan for the town in 1784 (see Figure 15.1). With a few alterations in the ensuing two centuries, their plan would remain the basic framework for downtown Pittsburgh. They designed a gridiron pattern like Philadelphia's, which was the model for many new towns in early America. The surveyors oriented the long base of the plan, Water Street, to be parallel to the waterfront along the Monongahela River. They projected Market Street perpendicular to Water Street northward to a public square, Market Square—or the Diamond as Pennsylvanians commonly called such squares. They extended the plan from Fort Pitt on the Point east for nine blocks to Grant's Hill, where they laid out Grant Street northward from the river over the hill to Liberty Avenue.[3]

Pittsburgh's plan differed from Philadelphia's in a couple of important ways, however. It was much smaller in spatial extent. Further, Woods and Vikroy had to accommodate existing houses and narrow streets and recognize the deteriorating Fort Pitt. In 1764 Colonel John Campbell had laid out four square blocks east of the fort, bounded in the 1784 plan by Water and Second Streets running east to west and Ferry and Market Streets going south to north. The later surveyors extended Campbell's small grid across most of the Triangle, but to accommodate existing settlement that had spread beyond the initial plan they designed the blocks east of Market Street to be considerably larger than Campbell's blocks. Unlike Philadelphia where the Delaware and Schuylkill Rivers flow roughly parallel to each other at the center of Franklin's original plan, the Allegheny River rushes to meet the Monongahela at a sharp angle, cutting awkwardly across the surveyors' gridiron design. Woods and Vikroy reasoned that because trade depended on river transportation, they oriented a second smaller gridiron plan to the Allegheny with only two streets, Penn and Liberty, parallel to the river. The two gridiron plans met at Liberty Avenue where the junctions of the streets created oddly shaped blocks. With rivers on two sides of the Triangle and Grant's Hill on the east, entry to the relatively small peninsula that for a few decades encompassed the entire town of Pittsburgh was accomplished by landing at the Monongahela wharf, by crossing the rivers from opposing shores, or by traveling along the floodplain strips of land at the southeastern and northeastern corners.[4]

The economic life of early Pittsburgh focused on the Monongahela wharf and Market Street north to the Diamond. Merchants conducted the city's vital trade from the wharf, a mudflat stretching between Ferry (Stanwix today) Street and Smithfield Street. The proliferation of steamboats on western rivers following the long 1819–1823 depression and the Pennsylvania state turnpikes that improved overland travel stimulated a rapid increase of trade. As a result, city officials appointed a wharf master in 1825 to bring order among the numerous crafts landing at the wharf. Westward destined migrants stopped over for supplies, information, and recuperation before striking out on the trail again. Local manufacturers found western markets for glass wares and iron goods, especially bars and nails. Boat builders, steam engine makers, wheelwrights, saddlers, and others serviced transporters. Pittsburgh shops carried on a lively business in goods and services for the town's residents and for those from small communities along the south shore of the Monongahela River and Allegheny City to the north. Toll bridges opened in 1818 and 1819 that connected those communities to Pittsburgh. Population had grown to 12,568 by 1830, the majority residing within the Triangle west of Grant's Hill.[5]

Despite the spread of population across the Triangle, most businesses remained heavily focused on the wharf and Market Street. Leland Baldwin recognized this concentration when he wrote: "Until about 1840 most of the business activities of Pittsburgh were confined to the Triangle bounded by the rivers and Wood Street. Market Street was the hub of the town." Business directories in 1815 and 1826 bear out his generalization. Businesses of many different kinds and residents, including many prominent families, existed shoulder to shoulder in the small area west of Wood Street. Two- and three-story buildings predominated, yielding a low skyline penetrated most prominently by the belfry of the county courthouse on the Diamond.[6]

Samuel Jones, compiler of the 1826 city business directory, offered an unflattering picture of the frontier city's appearance. He found it loud, filthy, smoky, without charm. He complained that "the loud strokes of the hammer, and the lumbering of wheels, are heard within its borders, from the rising to the setting of the sun, and when winter comes to rule the varied year often long after." A traveler, he asserted, "looks [a]round, with commendable disgust, on the dark and melancholy aspect of man and things. Lines of low, plain brick houses, not continuous, but broken, ever and anon, by unseemly vacancies, or interspersed with wooden fabrics, of every size and shape, meet his disappointed eye." He judged the streets as "narrow, roughly paved, filthy, beyond compare, and filled with hogs, dogs, drays and noisy children." Because residents, businesses, steamboats, and manufacturers all burned coal that was readily accessible in the surrounding hills, smoke often hung over the Triangle. Pittsburgh, Jones observed, "is darkened with a 'sulphurous [*sic*] canopy' which nearly conceals the place from view; seems to shut it out from the light of the sun, and hangs over the valley."[7]

In a manner similar to other American cities at the time, and despite a seemingly chaotic jumble of activities, Pittsburgh evidenced a discernible spatial pattern of land uses. This underlying geography resulted from locational efficiencies warranted by specific businesses, varying real estate values, and a sense of how a city should be organized that derived from experiences in established commercial cities. Businesses of commercial cities typically located across a triangular framework of a long waterfront and a main perpendicular retail street leading to the site of civic functions.[8] This pattern captures the spatial sorting of businesses in 1820s Pittsburgh. With trade at the heart of their businesses commission merchants, forwarding firms, and warehouses crowded near the Monongahela wharf on Water Street, Front Street, and the initial blocks of perpendicular streets from Ferry to Wood. With the shipping season in full swing, the city's commercial energy converged on this humble mudflat. Even after discounting for booster rhetoric, an 1838 newspaper description conveyed the scene:

> The whole of our broad levee, from the bridge to Ferry Street, is closely dotted with drays and wagons, hurrying to the margin of the river from every point of access, burdened with the valuable products of our facto-

> ries or with Eastern goods. Some half a dozen of the steamers are puffing away ready to start. The margin of the wharf is absolutely covered to the height of a man with freight in all its varieties, while higher up on the footwalks and streets the fronts of the great forwarding houses are blocked by piles of boxes, bales and barrels in beautiful disorder. Shippers, porters, draymen and steamboat clerks lend their hurried voices at once—one is actually deafened with their cheerful din and rush.[9]

Although many retail stores, artisan shops, personal services, and residences were located among the trading activities, they appeared most frequently in the vicinity of Market Street, Market Square, and adjacent blocks of Third, Fourth, and Diamond (later renamed Forbes) Avenues. Public markets at the intersections of Market Street with Water Street, Second Street, and the Diamond emphasized that street's centrality. The market at the Diamond drew a profusion of wagons, carts, and drays that detracted from its functioning as a central public square despite the presence of the county courthouse there.[10]

The town's larger manufacturing firms found the less developed, less expensive land parcels near the Point and east beyond Grant Street suitable for their purposes. Foundries, an iron rolling mill, steam engine works, grist mills, and a brewery located in the vicinity of the Point in 1826. Similar manufacturers congregated around Grant Street and eastward along the Monongahela (a district called Kensington and later Pipetown). The McClurg foundry at the corner of Fifth and Smithfield indicated that even this site was distant from the city's business core. Several manufacturers located in the blocks that faced the Allegheny River. In contrast to the more heavily capitalized manufacturing establishments, small wood, leather, cloth, and metal artisan shops scattered throughout the business area. Little wonder Jones complained about the incessant noise.[11]

By 1830 a few businesses had drifted eastward from Market Street toward Wood Street, Smithfield Street, and Liberty Avenue. Many served the estimated three–five thousand wagons that entered the city annually from the east using the state turnpikes and Liberty Avenue through Bayardstown (the Strip District). Traffic from Allegheny City and points north crossed the bridge at St. Clair Street (Sixth Street). Sites along Liberty, Penn, Wood, and Smithfield, the latter two streets traveled by teamsters to the wharf and Market Street, attracted some businesses and population, foreshadowing the inevitable expansion of the growing central business district.[12]

In the second quarter of the century, steamboats and the Pennsylvania Canal together greatly enhanced Pittsburgh's gateway role and opened an additional focus of commercial activity on the other side of the Triangle. The tonnage of goods recorded at the Monongahela wharf rose seventeen-fold from 1826 to 1848. As many as eighteen hundred steamboats arrived in 1837, a representative commercial season.[13] The river trade also benefited from improved cross state transportation via Pennsylvania's Main Line Canal, which connected Philadelphia and Pittsburgh in 1834. The canal ran parallel to the Allegheny River along its north shore with terminal basins in Allegheny City and another between Penn and Liberty Avenues reached by an aqueduct over the river at Eleventh Street. The canal improved trade with eastern markets such that toll revenues had risen sevenfold by mid-century. Packet boat companies ran from thirty to thirty-five boats in and out of Pittsburgh daily, carrying agricultural and extractive products as well as merchandise of all kinds. The large movement of pig iron, iron blooms, castings, sheet, and nails to and from Pittsburgh on the canal reflected the growth of the city's iron industry. There were thirteen rolling mills and thirty foundries at midcentury. As historian Catherine Reiser wrote, "every turn of the factory machine, every stroke of the hammer, strengthened Pittsburgh's commerce."[14]

During the 1830s and 1840s, the city's trade and transport interests flourished. Dozens of commission merchants, forwarders, wholesalers, brokers, and auctioneers flocked to the waterfront area and expanded it eastward to Smithfield and one block northward to Second Avenue. This concentration of river trading businesses attracted dry goods and hardware merchants and the warehouses of iron and glass manufacturers. Market Street and the Diamond continued to be a retail and service area. The city built a city hall and market house on the Diamond in 1854, reinforcing the area's traditional centrality.[15]

However, the canal basin at Liberty Avenue and Eleventh Street and the bridge from Allegheny City at St. Clair Street created a second commercial node in the central business district. The offices of canal boat firms, warehouses, small hotels, and rooming houses clustered near the basin. Many more wholesale grocers, liquor, and pork dealers located here than at the wharf district. Because timber products from northwestern Pennsylvania came down the Allegheny River, lumber merchants chose the area, although woodworkers, saddlers, harness makers, and boots and shoe shops split between the two business nodes.[16]

Shops and services of various kinds located between the canal basin and the wharf and Market Square district. Attorneys in particular moved eastward from the Market Street area, pulled by the grand 1841county courthouse on the elevated site of Grant's Hill. Half of the eighty-five attorneys recorded in the *Harris' Pittsburgh Directory of 1844* listed addresses in the blocks between Smithfield and Grant Streets, notably along Fourth Avenue. Another third gave addresses between Wood and Smithfield. The blocks east of Smithfield also housed the most residents and churches in the Triangle. Two imposing churches, St. Peter's Episcopal and St. Paul's Catholic Cathedral, were erected at Grant and Fifth in the 1850s and the first high school at Smithfield and Fifth.[17]

With the robust growth, civic leaders acted to upgrade the Triangle, where investment was most intense and many elites still lived. Often using a mix of private and public funding, they followed the model of eastern cities in beginning to provide much needed infrastructure. Toll bridges replaced ferries. In 1826 the city councils authorized constructing a waterworks with a reservoir on Grant's Hill to supply water to businesses and residents. The city paved streets, illuminated them with manufactured coal gas, and created street numbers. Despite a subsequent expansion of the waterworks in 1844, the water system was inadequate to extinguish the terrible fire of April 1845 that burned twenty blocks from Ferry to Grant and from the Monongahela River to Fourth Avenue. The fire destroyed the gasworks, the Smithfield Street Bridge, goods piled on the wharf, and adjacent warehouses. In all one thousand buildings were lost, and thousands of people left homeless. Reconstruction commenced almost immediately.[18]

Floods, poor drainage, and inadequate sanitation remained serious issues. At least ten times in the first half of the century, floodwaters flowed through the Triangle, damaging property and exacerbating sanitation problems. Unable to mitigate flooding, city leaders filled low-lying water areas with dirt from digging the canal basin and a tunnel through Grant's Hill for an unproductive canal connection with the wharf. In the 1840s, two cuts of Grant's Hill failed to remove this obstacle to a smooth flow of traffic, but they did provide additional fill for leveling the peninsula's topography. With cholera epidemics in the 1830s and sanitary conditions worsening, the councils designated a barge at the foot of Grant Street as a dump and finally commenced construction of underground sewers to replace open gutters in the street. Although the new infrastructure improved conditions in the central business district, the smoke, dirt, and noise that Samuel Jones found so disconcerting in 1826 still alarmed visitors such as Charles Dickens and Anthony Trollope when they encountered Pittsburgh.[19]

The Iron City's Incipient Downtown

The arrival of railroads at midcentury first challenged and then ended Pittsburgh's gateway role, but they also ushered in the ambitious, successful pursuit of manufacturing as a new foundation of the city's economy. The city and adjacent towns grew so rapidly, despite the withering 1870s depression, that by 1880 the population of the urban area totaled 235,000, a threefold increase since 1850.[20] The number of businesses, shops, and legal and financial services swelled in the central business district as the transactional and power center for this emerging industrial region. While the land use pattern of the gateway city era remained visible, the railroads and industrializing economy were remaking the central business district into more clearly defined functional areas.

The spread of railroads across the eastern half of the nation between 1840 and 1880 abruptly altered Pittsburgh's economic course. First, the Pittsburgh, Fort Wayne, and Chicago Railroad reached Allegheny City from the west in 1851, and then Pittsburgh celebrated the Pennsylvania Railroad's arrival a year later. By the late 1870s half a dozen railroads serviced the city. Pittsburgh's river trade faltered as the railroads moved goods to distant destinations bypassing the local merchants and middlemen. Increasingly, steamboats served only nearby ports such as Wheeling and Steubenville on the Ohio River, while powerful towboats pushed barges laden with bulk products such as coal, coke, sand, and gravel. The age of the steamboats was winding down. Perspicacious canal boaters saw that the canal era was also rapidly ending and shifted to other businesses.[21]

Merchants, businessmen, and local manufacturers with capital resources concentrated on manufacturing iron, glass, and railroad equipment. Railroads presented an immense market for iron, needing iron rails, bridges, and equipment such as locomotives, cars, wheels, axles, and air brakes. Civil War materiel, oil wells, pipelines, and city building itself all demanded iron products. The thirteen rolling mills in 1850 ballooned to thirty-eight iron and crucible steel mills thirty years later. Blast furnaces, forges, and foundries rounded out the robust iron industry. In turn, iron manufacturing depended on the development of the coal and coke industries. Regional glass manufacturing grew into another nationally prominent industry. By 1880 Pittsburgh had completed the transition to an industrial city.[22]

The rise of these industries depended on financial, legal, and information services, stalwarts of the transaction economy. The heavily capitalized iron industry required access to financial resources that far exceeded those of earlier merchants. Some wealthy men such as Andrew Carnegie and James Laughlin formed partnerships with other capitalists to raise funds. Others turned to a new breed of bankers such as Judge Thomas Mellon to arrange the necessary capital. Investments in land development, home construction, and transportation underwrote the city-building process.[23] Financial, real estate, and industrial transactions required the services of attorneys, brokers, insurance agents, and purveyors of information. These professionals grew markedly in number by 1880, signaling the emergence of the transactional economy in Pittsburgh's Triangle. According to the 1880–1881 business directory, the number of banks had increased from barely a handful in 1850 to forty. Similarly, insurance companies, insurance agents, and realtors mushroomed to several dozen, while attorneys and notaries rose fourfold to 360. The number of newspapers doubled, and the number of printers and publishers tripled.[24]

The several hundred financial businesses, attorneys, and other professionals needed offices from which to conduct their business. Proximity to each other and critical institutions was a priority. A decade after Allegheny County moved its courthouse to Grant's Hill in 1841, a new federal courthouse and post office opened on Smithfield between Third and Fourth Avenues, and in 1872 the city erected a large city hall at Fifth and Smithfield. Prior to the 1880s most firms were small, lot parcels were narrow, and buildings were walkups of three to five stories. Consequently, the central business expanded horizontally rather than vertically as would happen in ensuing decades. Elaborating the eastward shift toward Grant Street that began before 1850, attorneys, notaries, and real estate agents rented offices between Wood and Grant along Fourth, Diamond, and Fifth Avenues. Printers and publishers located in close proximity to them. Banks and brokers established a financial district centered on Fourth Avenue between Market and Wood, although the center of gravity for them was moving toward Wood Street with several banks on Wood and even some on Smithfield. Insurance companies and agents claimed addresses that mixed in both the banking and legal areas, reflecting both their business connections and, for some, multiple roles as insurance representatives, bankers, and/or attorneys.[25]

The spatial legacy of the Gateway era influenced the evolving central business district in other ways. Even though railroads diminished the salience of the wharf and canal basin, they reinforced the attraction of these two areas for specific activities. The Pennsylvania Railroad entered downtown on tracks parallel to Liberty Avenue through the Strip District. At Union Station where Grant Street and Liberty intersect, the railroad split in three directions to freight depots: south a short way to sheds on either side of Grant to Seventh Avenue, another to the yards where the canal basin once existed between Tenth and Eleventh Streets and where tracks of two subsidiary railroads crossed the river from Allegheny City, and the third west the length of Liberty Avenue to a freight depot near the Point. Thus, the Pennsylvania Railroad replaced the canal in the northeast corner of the

Triangle. The Baltimore & Ohio Railroad established its presence on the Monongahela waterfront with yards, freight depots, and a passenger terminal all stretching west from Try Street to the foot of Grant. Both railroads roughly followed the failed canal line across the back of the Triangle by running short distances along Try Street from their depots. Wagons and drays clogged traffic in serving these depots, while the trains added to the noise, smoke, dirt, and danger of the central business district, especially along Liberty Avenue.[26]

Adding to the tumult, the railroads directly served a few industries at the three corners of the Triangle. Wayne Iron and Steel, for example, lay adjacent to the railroad yards on the former canal basin. George Westinghouse established his new switch and signal venture in nearby Garrison Alley. The Point district still contained foundries, machine shops, and steam engine and boiler works among other industrial enterprises. The Baltimore & Ohio facilities served the Pittsburgh Steel Works as well as the Pennsylvania Tube Works and Jones & Laughlin's warehouses.[27]

Despite its waning importance, the Monongahela wharf area continued to house steamboat agents, a dozen surviving commission merchants, and a sprinkling of wholesale grocers and liquor dealers. In much greater abundance along Water Street were dozens of towboat offices and 60 percent of the city's fifty-four coal and coke dealers bunched around the Coal Exchange at Water and Smithfield. The offices of iron commission merchants and manufacturers mingled with the coal dealers. Together, the growth of towboat offices, coal dealers, and iron merchants and the decline of steamboat agents and general commission merchants underscored the city's shift to industry from its earlier commercial role.[28]

The Penn-Liberty commercial area became increasingly differentiated from the wharf, while the lower Triangle retail area expanded. With access to the Pennsylvania Railroad's freight facilities, the blocks from Sixth to Eleventh Streets became a locus for many wholesalers and brokers. Two-thirds of the city's general commission merchants and merchandise brokers now located to this area. Offices of grain brokers, pork packers, and leather and hide dealers were there too, along with half of the city's liquor wholesalers, oil dealers, and tea brokers. Market Street, the Diamond, and the blocks of lower Fourth and Fifth Avenues became more clearly a retail district, with the decline of the wharf and with financial and legal professionals moving into more distinct areas. There, retailers and a few wholesalers of fancy goods, notions, trimmings, and dry goods appealed to women in particular. Jewelers, engravers, and hosiery, glove, and hat shops attracted men and women. Joseph Horne and Rosenbaum's had shops on Market near the Diamond, precursors to their later existence as department stores. Although stores and dealers could be found in most parts of the Triangle, the basic spatial sorting of activities was well underway by 1880.[29]

The four wards that comprised the central business district lost population during the three decades of the Iron City period. Their population peaked at midcentury, and by 1880 the number and density per acre of residents in the wards had dropped by nearly 40 percent. The growth of business and continued deterioration of the environment pushed many folks to separate their residence from their work by moving to homes elsewhere in the city and region. The adoption of the horsecar after 1859 with lines extending to the East End, South Side, and Allegheny City encouraged commuting from a few miles beyond the Triangle (see "The Omnibus, Commuter Railroad, and Horsecar" in this volume). Wealthier commuters rode steam railroads to points more than five miles away, places such as East Liberty, Wilkinsburg, and Sewickley. Thus, with population declining and business growing and spreading out across the peninsula into more clearly defined functional districts, Pittsburgh's central business district was developing the presence of a modern twentieth-century downtown.[30]

The Steel City's Golden Triangle

In the half century after 1880, the central business districts of American industrial metropolises became downtowns in the popular imagination. Population and industry sprawled outward for miles from central cities along railroad and electric streetcar lines in an unprecedented fashion. At the same time corporate headquarters, financial institutions, professional offices, and civic authority remained centralized in downtowns. There, urbanites found bustling railroad terminals, magnificent department stores, breathtaking skyscrapers, glittering amusement palaces, and brilliantly illuminated streets and buildings. Contemporaries dubbed this new place "downtown," the "heart" of the metropolis, the visible symbol of modernity. In Petula Clark's words, "everything's waiting for you" in downtown.[31]

Pittsburgh's peninsula—the Golden Triangle, as boosters called it—shared these hallmarks of American downtowns. While the Pittsburgh industrial region spread out for as much as thirty miles and the metropolitan population surged past the one-million mark by 1920, the compact central business district grew ever more congested, buildings rose majestically upward, and brightly lit streets and shops beckoned men and women to the excitement.[32] Downtown's residential population plummeted further, but the numbers of businessmen, working women, patrons, and visitors coming to downtown skyrocketed. Even the smoke laden atmosphere could not mask that downtown was the powerful center of one of America's largest metropolitan regions.

Pittsburgh's ironmasters resolutely turned to the mass production of steel and steel products after 1880. In the wake of Andrew Carnegie's remarkably successful new Edgar Thomson Bessemer steel rail works, owners of iron mills felt challenged to compete, and many of them did. By 1900 the production of wrought iron slumped, while in contrast local Bessemer and open-hearth steel output led the nation. Pittsburgh had become the Steel City.[33]

The huge iron and steel mills were only the centerpiece of a massive regional industrial complex (See "Industrial Suburbs and the Growth of Metropolitan Pittsburgh" in this volume). Many smaller mills specialized in semifinished products such as pipe and wire. Steel construction and bridge companies worked around the world. Coal mines and coke plants fueled the mills' furnaces. Railroad, mining, oil, electrical, and steel-making equipment firms flourished. Aluminum, glass, and even food processing manufacturers also developed international capabilities. Railroad, river, and telegraphic networks tied the many industrial components into an interconnected regional complex.[34]

Downtown was the command center of the industrial region. Changes in the size and character of industrial firms—notably large integrated corporations—along with the region's elaborate communication infrastructure facilitated the separation of management from production sites. Many manufacturers moved production to undeveloped level sites beyond the city where they built much larger mills and factories. In addition, firms often operated multiple plants.[35] The industrialists developing large and multiple facilities had to find additional investors and raise funds from banks, investment houses, and other financial intermediaries. They often arranged deals at private downtown clubs such as the Duquesne, Pittsburgh, and Union Clubs. Downtown provided easy access to financial and legal services. The telegraph companies connected managers to their regional operations until telephone networks emerged around the turn of the century. Railroads offered managers the ability to visit and inspect their plants.[36]

Corporations, financial institutions, and professional firms employed clerical staff and middle managers to generate, file, and retrieve the burgeoning paperwork of modern bureaucracies and the transactional economy. Janitors, elevator operators, and myriad other support personnel swelled the downtown daytime population. An estimated eighty-seven thousand people worked in downtown in 1917. As the working population skyrocketed, the residential population fell by 35 percent to under nine thousand in the

Fig. 15.2 Construction of the Union Arcade (Union Trust Building) in 1916, revealing the steel-frame construction, which in the 1880s breached the traditional height limits of masonry buildings (courtesy of the Archive Services Center, University of Pittsburgh).

1890s, and dwelling units dropped by 26 percent. Consequently, the number of workers commuting to downtown rose rapidly. Executives, lawyers, and bankers could afford the time and cost of commuting by railroad. In 1917 the railroads ran two hundred commuter trains daily, carrying thirty-one thousand passengers. These numbers continued to grow until railroad commuting peaked in the early 1920s. The more numerous elevator operators, clerks, typists, and white-collar workers rode to town in electric streetcars, which had replaced the horsecars in the 1890s ("The Cable and Electric Streetcar Networks," in this volume). By 1902 the Pittsburgh Railways Company's trolleys operated 470 miles of track; ridership had increased more than threefold since 1890. In 1909 alone trolleys leaving downtown daily had seats for twenty-four thousand passengers. The diurnal rhythm and crush of rush hours had been firmly established.[37]

The compact space of the Golden Triangle limited horizontal expansion to accommodate the unprecedented demand for office space. Vertical growth of tall office buildings solved the problem and remade downtown's skyline. Steel-frame construction and elevators freed buildings from walkup constraints on their height (see Figure 15.2).

A few industrialists, bankers, and other wealthy businessmen saw in skyscrapers the opportunity to advertise their business and erect symbols of their success. However, the potential to generate profit spurred many to invest in this new type of building type. The banks and corporations could not use all or even the majority of a skyscraper's offices, but the general proliferation of professionals and office staffs warranted speculation in rentable space, capitalizing on soaring land values.[38]

The tall buildings of commerce replaced the steeples and shafts of religious and civic authority as downtown's dominant visible feature. In 1885 the tower of architect H. H. Richardson's new Allegheny County Courthouse, erected on the site of its predecessor that had burned down, briefly loomed above the central business district. The location on Grant's Hill accentuated its presence. Within a few years several industrialists and businessmen erected office buildings ranging from seven to thirteen stories high. George Westinghouse, Jacob Jay Vandergrift (oil and steel, two buildings), businessmen Samuel Hamilton (music), and Christopher L. Magee (streetcars and politics) built five of the ten masonry towers that arose between 1885 and 1895. Fittingly, Carnegie erected the first steel-frame tower in memory of his brother Tom, exposing the steel skeleton for the public to admire for nearly a year before cladding it in 1895. Steel men David E. and William G. Park similarly used a steel frame for their fifteen-story tower. The lingering 1893 depression slowed this initial burst of tall buildings, but the nineteenth century's low skyline had been eclipsed forever.[39]

After the depression, industrial corporations and powerful financial institutions underwrote a boom in skyscrapers, several over twenty stories, before the 1907 flood and financial panic again depressed the region's economy.

Banks led the way putting up ten towers with the Farmers Deposit National Bank the tallest at twenty-four stories. Industrialists Henry Clay Frick and Carnegie's longtime associate Henry Phipps accounted for two each, while the Dravo Corporation, Crucible Steel's Herbert DuPuy, and Jones & Laughlin Steel Corporation each erected a tower. Besides the Pennsylvania and Wabash railroad terminals with several floors of offices above the passenger stations, additional new skyscrapers brought the total in this brief period to twenty-six. The removal of the Pennsylvania Railroad tracks from Liberty Avenue in 1904–1905, along with Phipps's two thirteen-story buildings that bracketed the Sixth Street entrance to downtown, enhanced the appeal of the Penn-Liberty corridor between the Pennsylvania and Wabash terminals, where ten of the era's towers arose. Only the Fourth Avenue financial district rivaled this profusion of skyscrapers.[40]

After 1908 the construction of skyscrapers focused more on the center of downtown. Before he died in 1904, Henry Oliver had begun purchasing property along Virgin Alley and Sixth Avenue between Wood and Smithfield Streets. His executors completed his plans by erecting the twenty-five-story Oliver Building, while the city widened the alley and renamed it Oliver Avenue. Once Frick agreed to the city's lowering Grant's Hill by sixteen feet, he went ahead with the Union Arcade (later called the Union Trust) and William Penn Hotel projects on Grant Street to complement his earlier Frick and Allegheny Buildings. Local government added to Grant Street's growing importance by putting up the City County office building next to the Richardson courthouse. Altogether, fourteen tall buildings were built between 1908 and 1920.[41]

A final flurry of eleven new towers arose in the 1920s and early 1930s, completing the remaking of downtown in the Steel City era. The removal of the Pennsylvania Railroad's freight sheds on the north end of Grant Street led to its completion as a corporate and civic street. Mellon family interests erected at this northern end the thirty-four-story Koppers Building and the forty-four-story Gulf Building (the city's tallest) across Grant from a new federal complex of courthouse, post office, and federal reserve buildings. The Bell Telephone tower completed the cluster. The forty-story Grant Building complemented the Frick Building at the street's southern end.[42]

The approximately five dozen tall office buildings built from the late 1880s to the early 1930s reinforced the trend of clustering activities by function that was already underway and altered other trends. The concentration of financial institutions and professionals on Fourth Avenue became more pronounced. With the Pittsburgh Stock Exchange, which became essential to the city's impressive corporate growth after 1895, situated on Fourth

Avenue, over 80 percent of investment bankers, mortgage providers, and real estate agents listed their addresses on this regional Wall Street. Although retail bank offices spread widely about downtown, a majority of brokers of various kinds, accountants, and insurance agents also located in Fourth Avenue's tall buildings. More than three hundred attorneys filtered throughout the financial district, most notably in the Berger Building on Fourth Avenue. But many more attorneys flocked to the established legal node of the county courthouse and Grant Street. The attraction of Grant Street for attorneys, especially in the new Frick and Allegheny Buildings and smaller ones such as the Bakewell and St. Nicholas Buildings, only increased with the construction of the city-county, state, and county office buildings, along with the mortuary and federal buildings. Together, they constituted a civic nucleus on Grant and Ross Streets, around which approximately half of the nearly one thousand attorneys in downtown were located.[43]

The transactional economy grew so large that some lawyers, financial intermediaries, and other professionals established offices in several tall buildings that were not part of the Fourth Avenue and Grant Street clusters. The twenty-four-story Farmers Deposit National Bank building at Fifth and Wood attracted more than half of the natural gas agents and companies along with several oil companies. The offices of railroad companies, coke firms, iron manufacturers, and iron and steel brokers also clustered in the Farmers Deposit Bank and the fifteen-story Park Building at Fifth and Smithfield. Many offices of the same industries located in the Carnegie and the two Frick buildings where proximity to other offices of these corporations seemed to be an inducement. In contrast, architects, advertising agents, and engineers—all newly listed professionals since 1880—scattered about downtown's office buildings.[44]

With the elaborate Pennsylvania and Wabash railroad terminals opening around the turn of the century, one at each end of Liberty Avenue, the grid of streets formed by Penn and Liberty with seventeen tall buildings tightened its grip on the offices of wholesalers and reinforced the trend away from the Monongahela wharf that was evident before 1880. Once the traditional focus of the business district the wharf area still had some brokers, wholesalers, and supply houses. But the Penn-Liberty corridor had become dominant. Two-thirds of general merchandise brokers and importers agents were located in the corridor in 1907, and 78 percent of fabric and clothing wholesalers, handling woolens, dry goods, hats, millinery, and shoes, also did business from offices there. The core of the twentieth-century jewelry district had formed there, with two-thirds of the jewelry manufacturers and suppliers. More than 60 percent of wholesalers in food stuffs such as groceries, teas, coffees, and sugar, also located to the area, with grain dealers congregated in and around the Grain Exchange near Tenth and Penn.[45]

The development of department stores, the new emporiums for middle-class female consumers, anchored the expansion of the older Market Square and lower Fifth Avenue retail area northward into the Penn-Liberty corridor and eastward to Smithfield Street. Becoming a department store, Horne's moved from Market Street into a six-floor store at Penn and Stanwix Street in the 1890s and subsequently expanded the building twice. Rosenbaum's at Sixth Street and Penn, Spear and Company on Penn, and Jonassasson on Liberty at Oliver Avenue also operated department stores in the western half of the Penn-Liberty corridor. The construction opposite Horne's of the eight-story Jenkins Arcade in 1912 with three floors of retail shops and offices arrayed around a main hall added to the retail cluster. At the same time, Kaufmann's, Kaufmann and Baer (later Gimbels), and Frank and Seder opened their department stores on Smithfield, while five-and-ten chain stores McCreery's on Wood and Murphy's (1930) at Market Square rounded out robust shopping opportunities. The seven department stores and five-and-tens of the Steel City era formed the peak moment for downtown retailing.[46]

Shoppers, travelers, and businessmen and their customers patronized live theaters and movie houses near the retail hubs. Several theaters such as the Gayety and the Alvin located around Sixth Street. In the 1920s the palatial Penn Theatre (Heinz Hall) and Stanley Theatre (Benedum Center) arose in the Penn-Liberty corridor, while movie mogul James B. Clark built his twenty-five-story Clark Building adjacent to the Stanley. The Nixon Theater, the Grand Opera House, and several movie houses enlivened the Smithfield Street vicinity. Altogether in 1929, there were sixteen live and film theaters in downtown, which like retailing was a peak for entertainment for half a century.[47]

Beyond the creation of a civic nucleus on Grant Street, the city and county governments as well as civic groups increased their efforts to enhance the success of downtown. The worsening congestion and environmental conditions drew the different groups into an expanded role. The Chamber of Commerce, the Civic Club of Allegheny County, and the reform-inspired Pittsburgh Civic Commission addressed these issues by sponsoring studies with national experts. Rather than ending the debates about solutions, the studies often provoked additional controversy. The foremost controversy was about how to ease access to downtown and then mitigate the ensuing traffic congestion within the compact Triangle. The termination of tolls on bridges and the replacement of older inadequate bridges with new ones after 1910 demonstrated the public officials' determination to promote the Golden Triangle. The removal of railroad tracks from Liberty Avenue and the leveling of Grant's Hill (the Hump cut) significantly improved the attraction of these two parts of downtown. Complaints about streetcar service fomented public debate over the wisdom of public ownership of the Pittsburgh Railways Company and the construction of a subway system. The proliferation of motor vehicles complicated the debate and diverted the various governments' attention to alleviating congestion on streets originally built for horse-powered technologies (see "The Automobile Comes to Pittsburgh" in this volume). A few major improvements were accomplished such as the widening of Second Avenue (renamed the Boulevard of the Allies), extending the boulevard to Schenley Park, and building the Liberty Tunnels and Bridge. However, parking, regulating traffic, and fashioning a highway circuit around the perimeter of downtown dominated discussion through the 1920s.[48]

Similar to concerned citizens in other cities across the nation, businessmen and progressive reformers in Pittsburgh despaired over the deteriorating environment of the Golden Triangle. Floodwaters often muddied downtown, and smoke still choked the pedestrians and blackened the masonry-clad buildings. The presence of railroads on the riverfronts, the Point, and a few streets posed the classic dilemma of economic growth versus a healthy environment. Many reformers decried the deleterious impact of tall buildings on the streetscape, unsightly litter and billboards, and downtown's unkempt appearance. Crusaders for city beautification—led by the Civic Club of Allegheny County, often women calling themselves municipal housekeepers—locked arms with health professionals, social workers, and the Chamber of Commerce to advocate regulations and city planning. The mayor and other public officials adopted some reform measures. But when reforms threatened business interests or posed considerable expense, they rarely gained approval or, if they were passed, were weakly enforced. The Pittsburgh Flood Commission's proposal to erect flood walls for the protection of downtown, for example, waited decades before adoption, and a smoke control ordinance failed to diminish the sooty burden produced by railroads and steel mills.[49]

City planning had a similarly mixed record. The renowned planner Frederick Law Olmsted Jr. drew up plans for dignifying the Point, designing a City Beautiful–style civic plaza and building complex near the courthouse, and developing a European-style promenade above a revamped Monongahela quay. The plans garnered very little interest from public officials. Commercial interests claimed priority over public use of the riverfronts, which deteriorated into rundown borders of downtown. Politicians, planners, and reformers did unite in 1923 behind the adoption of land use zoning, a policy viewed nationally as a panacea for much that ailed cities. Pittsburgh's zoning ordinance limited the height of skyscrapers to 256 feet, double what local planner Frederick Bigger promoted. But it allowed towers to rise on top of buildings above the limit. Architects circumvented the height restriction by setting back upper stories as towers; the Grant, Koppers, and Gulf Buildings used this strategy. The spotty record of planning and transportation achievements reflected diverse downtown stakeholders, a prevailing laissez-faire view of government's role, and public officials' inability to embrace a long-term vision. With planning proposals on the public agenda, downtown businesses and property owners organized to promote their interests and then fragmented into separate groups. Frequent zoning variance proposals to city council frustrated the planners. In short, business as usual dominated development.[50]

The transformation of Pittsburgh's business district into a modern downtown accompanied the region's remarkable industrialization, rapid population increase, and ascent to become a national urban power. The Golden Triangle housed the region's financial and industrial powerbrokers in numerous skyscrapers clustered in functional subdistricts. Managers, professionals, support staff, and service workers commuted via mass transit and steam railroad. The architecture of these buildings confirmed to Pittsburghers their national prominence. The region's burgeoning middle class enjoyed numerous shopping and recreational choices. Ornate railroad terminals welcomed travelers. Despite the eminence of the business community and a powerful Republican political machine, city leaders failed to address adequately downtown's problems because of their inability to forge a shared vision and a partnership for the implementation of proposals.

PART 2: THE PARTNERSHIP CITY

Renaissance Redevelopment

In the wake of the Second World War, cities across America faced the necessity of revitalizing their downtowns. After nearly fifteen years of deterioration because of depression and war and with renewed suburbanization of industry, retail, entertainment, and residents, civic leaders worried that the "hearts" of their metropolitan regions would decline and so would both tax revenues and private investment.[51] Pittsburgh's Golden Triangle was no exception. In addition to the twin scourges of deterioration and decentralization, smoke pollution, periodic floods, and severe congestion added to downtown's dismal condition and prospects. One month after the devastating St. Patrick's Day flood in 1936, private leaders revived their planning organization, renamed it the Pittsburgh Regional Planning Association (PRPA), and set out to address the problems of downtown and the region. They adhered closely to the national consensus of downtown problems and solutions. After a pause during the war, private and public leaders joined forces to enact a Pittsburgh program of economic, infrastructural, environmental, and downtown redevelopment. They called the program Renaissance. The civic partnership proved to be the key to modernizing downtown over the following twenty-five years, finally accomplishing changes that had been debated since 1900. Some trends evidenced as early as the 1920s continued to challenge the Golden Triangle, however.

The deterioration of Pittsburgh's downtown during the long years of depression and war distressed property owners, businesses, and civic leaders alike. Office vacancies persisted. Little used railroad sheds, the decaying exposition buildings, debris-strewn riverbanks, and rundown residences debased the Point area. Dark, particulate-laden smoke often blanketed the Golden Triangle, and the 1936 flood swamped downtown in ten feet of water. Assessed valuations declined by 27 percent after the flood. Severe congestion snarled traffic. The *Wall Street Journal* predicted little growth for the city, and a few iconic corporations explored relocating their headquarters to New York. Such moves would be devastating to the city's image and confidence, Pittsburgh leaders fretted.[52]

If the deterioration was not cause enough for worry, the decentralization of businesses and residents to the suburbs also troubled downtown stakeholders. Manufacturers began choosing regional sites after 1880. Railroads and streetcars had enabled people to move to outlying communities for decades, and automobiles accelerated the trend after the First World War. The city's proportion of Allegheny County's population peaked at 52 percent in 1910 and dropped below half by 1940. Pittsburgh's population peaked in 1950 and began a steady decline. Twenty years later it constituted only one-third of the county's population.[53]

Well before the Second World War, the growth of population in outer city neighborhoods and suburban communities supported new stores, movie houses, and professional offices, which competed with downtown businesses. The secondary business district of East Liberty especially posed a challenge. Although department store sales remained healthy in the 1920s, retailers feared that traffic congestion and inadequate parking would deter suburban shoppers from venturing downtown. Then department store sales plummeted in the 1930s. Throughout these prewar decades, organizations such as the Lower Downtown Businessmen's Association led by Joseph Horne department store's Albert Burchfield vigorously advocated for solutions to the traffic question. The organizations advanced schemes for a subway, a loop road around the Triangle along the riverfronts, and even double-deck highways. Despite considerable discussion, little had been accomplished by 1946 to lessen congestion, and suburbanization was poised to resume. Retailers in the Golden Triangle and downtowns across America anticipated a postwar recession and competition from new suburban shopping centers with abundant parking and modern store appearances.[54]

Pittsburgh's planners, real estate interests, and civic leaders joined the national conversation about downtown problems and solutions. They participated in national conferences, made presentations, and read the publications emanating from this conversation. They believed that freeways would ease access to downtown and that parking facilities would relieve parking anxieties. They advocated cleaning up the streetscapes, modernizing building facades, and demolishing vacant structures in order to present a safe and attractive environment for white middle-class female shoppers. Finally, experts stressed that "blighted" adjacent commercial districts and low-income (often African American) neighborhoods detracted from downtown and occupied land to which it could expand. In short, local civic leaders adopted the national consensus for revitalizing downtown with improved access, plentiful parking, modernization, and removing blight.[55]

In the prewar years, the PRPA and the Chamber of Commerce with several prominent men holding leadership roles in both organizations took the initial steps to address downtown's problems. The peripheral loop of highways received a boost with the construction of a new Water Street and flood wall parallel to the Monongahela wharf. In 1939 the PRPA engaged Robert Moses, the heralded builder of New York's parkways, to prepare an arterial plan for downtown. The media enthusiastically praised Moses's report. The PRPA created parkway and Triangle commissions to capitalize on the momentum. Simultaneously, the chamber formed the Committee of One Hundred chaired by Richard K. Mellon to study the Golden Triangle. In addition to cleaning up the streets and older buildings, the committee emphasized improving mass transit, vehicular access, traffic control, and parking. It engaged the national expert W. S. Menden to study mass transit. Amid this flurry of activity, a few organizations approached the National Park Service with a proposal for a national park at the Point. The Park Service's rejection of the proposal and the stalling of highway projects because of the war dashed current hopes for revitalizing downtown.[56]

During the war, however, civic leaders strived to overcome the fractured relations between city and county agencies and to prepare for postwar redevelopment. Frustrated by years of limited progress they organized the

Allegheny Conference on Community Development in 1943 as a means to unite the community. The Allegheny Conference (or simply the Conference) was comprised of 150 community leaders, but it was dominated by Richard K. Mellon of the powerful Mellon family financial interests and an executive committee of the largest corporation presidents. The Conference established an agenda for the city's revitalization, engaged planning consultants, orchestrated private sector consensus, and coordinated the involvement of public agencies and private organizations. In the words of Mellon: "We expedite." The Republican, Protestant, and blue-stocking Mellon of Ulster descent acknowledged the necessity of cooperating with the Democratic Party boss and mayor, the Irish Catholic David L. Lawrence, who came from humble origins. Communicating mostly through aides, Mellon and Lawrence formed a public-private partnership of enormous clout, which bulldozed inconvenient opposition and engineered twenty-five years of redevelopment. Unabashed in the wielding of power, these two leaders appointed interlocking members to the essential authorities and committees, who then represented their wishes.[57]

Plans for revitalizing Pittsburgh addressed four broad concerns: economic overspecialization, a degraded environment, outdated infrastructure, and an aging downtown. Although other cities were preparing for postwar redevelopment along similar lines, Pittsburgh initiated its program before the federal acts of 1949 and 1954 jump-started urban renewal in most cities.[58] Although environmental and infrastructural reforms did not solely focus on the Golden Triangle, they were essential for its redevelopment. Congress authorized multi-state dam and reservoir construction for flood control. At times civic leaders applied their political clout to keep construction moving forward. In contrast, enforcement of the city's 1941 smoke abatement ordinance tested the public-private partnership's resolve. Mellon employed pressure tactics to obtain the compliance of companies, and Mayor Lawrence risked the support of coal miners opposed to reduced coal consumption and members of his working-class electorate who were facing the costs of converting to natural gas or using expensive "smokeless coal." Enforcement began in October 1946; the partnership secured a countywide law in 1949. Then consumers shifted increasingly to natural gas as supplies via pipelines from the Southwest rapidly reduced prices for the fuel. Pittsburgh's skies brightened during the ensuing decade. The creation of a multi-community sewer authority and the completion in 1959 of the sewage treatment plant began the process of cleaning up the rivers. With flood control, smoke abatement, and sewage treatment in place, Renaissance leaders assuaged environmental concerns deterring investment in downtown.[59]

The Allegheny Conference, PRPA, and Golden Triangle businessmen fervently advocated building expressways and the circuit loop around downtown. They worked to overcome years of controversy over routes for the circuit loop, the Penn-Lincoln Parkway, and the Crosstown Boulevard along the eastern edge of downtown between the Liberty Bridge and a proposed Eleventh Street bridge over the Allegheny River. The parkway and most of the circuit loop became a reality. Although the bridge over the Allegheny was not built until the 1980s, the Crosstown Boulevard did allow traffic from the South Hills to avoid the Triangle, and it expanded downtown's boundary a few blocks eastward from Grant Street. It also established a barrier to the Hill District.[60]

The prospect of more cars arriving downtown, many correctly predicted, would exacerbate the parking shortage. The number of vehicles entering downtown daily grew by 21 percent between 1947 and 1955. In 1946 the PRPA proposed creating a public parking authority to meet anticipated demand. The proposal and pending state authorizing legislation ignited acrimonious debate between private parking operators, along with many who felt that government was unconstitutionally meddling in the private market and those, including the Renaissance leadership, who doubted that private operators could meet the demand. In 1947 the legislature established the Pittsburgh Public Parking Authority. The parking authority built seven garages by 1960, providing 80 percent of the six thousand parking spaces that were new since the war. Private operators mostly added surface lots in downtown's periphery for commuters. The parking authority located its garages centrally for short-term parkers, especially female shoppers. Kaufmann's and Horne's department stores erected their own multilevel garages in cooperation with the parking authority. Demand still outpaced supply, however, and parking around new suburban shopping centers was more convenient and less expensive.[61]

Civic leaders maintained that improved mass transit would also enhance downtown's attraction and retain its regional centrality. They lamented the financially distressed and outdated Pittsburgh Railways Company (the streetcars), the railroads' disinterest in operating commuter trains, and the uncoordinated service of independent bus lines. In typical Renaissance fashion, the Conference with its political allies promoted a countywide public authority to consolidate the private transit companies into a unified publicly owned transit system. After another long debate about government's appropriate role, the state legislature passed a bill in 1959, which empowered the Port Authority of Allegheny County to operate mass transit. During the 1960s the Port Authority consolidated the private companies into a mass transit system, though it failed to construct a rapid transit line (see "Skybus" in this volume).[62]

While addressing freeways, parking, and mass transit, the Conference tackled the issue of blight in and near downtown. The sullied historic Point area was ripe for redevelopment. Since the turn of the century many plans, including those of illustrious planners Frederick Law Olmsted Jr., E. H. Bennett, Robert Moses, and Frank Lloyd Wright, had been advanced to reclaim the Point in order to celebrate its geographical and historical significance. But infrastructure requirements complicated planning. Proposed circuit loop highways with flood walls would converge on the Point's two bridges, forming a complex interchange. Ramps rising to the bridges left little room for a commemorative park and blocked views of the river. The Conference obtained the governor's commitment to make the area a state park. The design solution came with the governor's bold approval to demolish the two extant bridges and erect new ones a short distance upstream in order that more of the Point would be available for a park (see Figure 15.3). Construction began immediately, although disputes and engineering problems periodically arose and delayed completion of Point Park until 1974.[63]

The civic partners fretted over blight adjacent to the new park's eastern boundary. The abandoned Wabash Railroad terminal, railroad sheds, warehouses, and several businesses populated the twenty-three acres between the park and Stanwix Street. They argued that redevelopment for skyscrapers would create a proper neighbor for the thirty-six-acre Point Park and a modernist transition to downtown's central core. Fire destroyed the railroad buildings and several warehouses in early 1946, hastening the opportunity for redevelopment. The Conference appointed the Point Redevelopment Committee to shepherd the renewal project and coordinate interagency, multigovernmental relationships. The project involved overcoming a legal challenge to using eminent domain for private commercial purposes, razing ninety-three buildings, and obtaining the commitment of the Equitable Life Assurance Society of New York as developer. Equitable Life saw the state's commitment to the adjacent Point Park project as key to its positive decision. However, before proceeding with financing for Gateway Center, as the project was named, Equitable Life needed assurance of tenants for the skyscrapers. R. K. Mellon, other Conference leaders, and Mayor Lawrence pressured nine of the city's major corporations to sign leases. Construction began in 1950 on the three original cruciform-shaped towers nestled in a park-like setting in the style advocated by modernist designers. By the mid-1960s, four more office buildings arose in Gateway Center and joined the handsomely landscaped Equitable Plaza, a Hilton Hotel, and an apartment

Fig. 15.3 Aerial view of the Golden Triangle with the Point Bridge (right foreground) spanning the Monongahela River, the Fort Duquesne Bridge (second bridge on the left), and the Manchester Bridge (left foreground) spanning the Allegheny River. Both the Point Bridge and the Manchester Bridge were demolished in 1970 to make way for the fountain at the Point.

tower. With Point Park, Gateway Center, new bridges, and the Penn-Lincoln Parkway, Pittsburgh had totally reconstructed the western fifty-nine acres of the Golden Triangle and energized further investment.[64]

Point Park and Gateway Center symbolized the city's rejuvenation. The partnership turned to the center of the Golden Triangle with the announcement that the Mellon foundations would give the city a park comprising an entire block. As part of the deal, the Pittsburgh Parking Authority committed to constructing a garage beneath the park. The block had housed Mellon Bank's early buildings. With San Francisco's Union Square located over a parking garage and New York's Rockefeller Center apparently in mind,

FIG. 15.4 The cleared site of the lower Hill District urban renewal project, showing its massive extent (courtesy of the Carnegie Library of Pittsburgh).

R. K. Mellon envisioned an elegant open space around which two of his corporations could erect skyscrapers for their headquarters. Mellon Bank moved into a forty-one-story tower adjacent to the square's south side in 1952, which it shared with US Steel. Alcoa constructed an aluminum-clad thirty-story showcase facing the square's north side. Mellon Square—with a stunning modernist design by landscape architect John O. Simonds—opened in 1955 as "integral to reimagining Pittsburgh as a place of commerce and innovation." Mellon Square and Gateway Center positioned the Golden Triangle as a major locus of corporate headquarters in America.[65]

The civic partnership considered the old neighborhood immediately adjacent to Grant and Ross Streets, the lower Hill District, a blighted drag on downtown's image and an obstacle to expansion. Although construction of the Crosstown Boulevard cleared thirty acres and buffered downtown from this neighborhood, planners eyed the lower Hill for federal urban renewal funds and redevelopment with higher value uses appropriate to a central location. After a rancorous controversy about use of the cleared land, local officials and Conference leaders settled on the erection of a huge cultural auditorium centered in a modernist parklike development. Clearing of ninety-five acres of the former immigrant community—now largely impoverished yet lively African American—began in 1955 (see Figure 15.4). The renewal project displaced more than fifteen hundred households and four hundred businesses. Initially a symbol of revitalization, the Civic Arena (1961) became the target of African American protest of urban renewal. The domed facility with a retractable roof was conceived as a combination sports arena and cultural venue. It failed to attract much investment in the renewal area beyond the Crosstown Boulevard. Instead, surface parking for Arena patrons and downtown office workers surrounded the behemoth, while the long-planned Crosstown Boulevard isolated it from downtown. With the exception of two apartment buildings and a hotel, little additional development took place on the site for several decades. The lower Hill District represented the failure of urban renewal in Pittsburgh.[66]

In a 1954 speech at Harvard, Conference executive director Park H. Martin declared, "What has been accomplished in Pittsburgh to date should in a large measure deter decentralization of the Triangle." Some indicators supported Martin's assertion (see Figure 15.5). Despite construction of tall office buildings, the vacancy rate in top grade office space stood at 1 percent in 1960. Assessed valuations rose dramatically after 1947, reversing a long decline since the onset of the Great Depression. Similarly, the number of people entering downtown each day increased steadily during the 1950s. More than one hundred thousand worked in the Triangle, and an additional fifty thousand came daily to shop or on personal business. The demand for short-term parking spaces still outstripped the parking authority's and private operators' ability to provide spaces. When the PRPA launched its Golden Triangle study in 1958–1959, work was underway on Point Park, another parking garage, the Hilton Hotel in Gateway Center, the Civic Arena, and the Fort Pitt Bridge. Renaissance redevelopment did seem to restore downtown's vibrancy.[67]

Despite this sense of renewal, the inexorable development of Pittsburgh's suburbs and the city's weakness in the region's industries undermined some of downtown's traditional functions. The population of the City of Pittsburgh declined by 23 percent between 1950 and 1970. Not only were people moving from the city to the suburbs, but a major study in the 1960s estimated that 120,000 people had left the region altogether.[68]

In her contrarian manner, urban planning critic Jane Jacobs believed more than suburbanization was weakening America's downtowns. In her 1961 seminal book *The Death and Life of Great American Cities*, Jacobs argued that modernist planning that sought the separation of land uses and

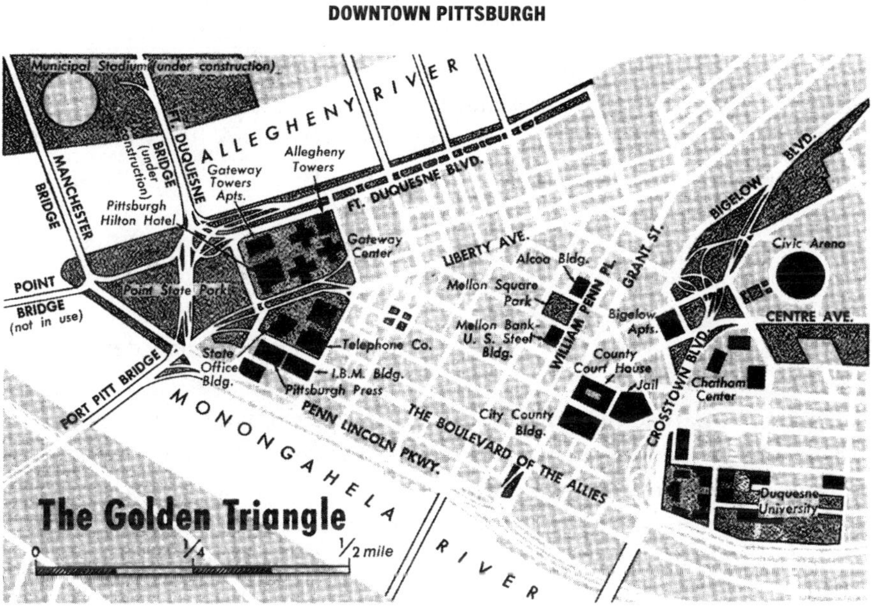

FIG. 15.5 Map showing the Renaissance I projects in downtown (Roy Lubove, *Twentieth Century Pittsburgh, Vol. 1. Government, Business, and Environmental Change* [Pittsburgh: University of Pittsburgh Press, 1996]).

homogeneous streetscapes for a more "orderly" environment eroded the diversity and density of small businesses. For example, the Gateway Center skyscrapers set in an expansive, parklike setting created "dead" pedestrian space, while civic leaders' obsession with majestic office buildings fostered an extreme imbalance between daytime and nighttime populations. Planners, Jacobs asserted, needed to rethink what made downtowns successful.[69]

Pittsburgh's retailers felt the full force of suburbanization and modernist planning. Between 1948 and 1958, downtown retail sales declined 9 percent, while sales across the region rose 38 percent. Department store sales shrank by two million dollars; and Frank and Seder and Rosenbaum's closed. By 1963 suburban department stores occupied more square footage than the three remaining downtown stores—Kaufmann's, Horne's, and Gimbels. Downtown sales of apparel, furniture, and appliances as well as variety stores decreased. Some specialty shops such as jewelers, stationers, and booksellers did increase sales. Predictions for the future, however, did not foresee a reversal of these downward trends, though optimists predicted stability at some point.[70]

A few other downtown activities also did not fare well in the face of suburbanization. With the closing of the Nixon Theater in 1950, quality live theater disappeared. Movie houses, bowling alleys, pool halls, and strip shows presented an undistinguished array of entertainment for visitors and shoppers. Wholesaling and manufacturing—largely, printing and publishing—employed less than seven thousand workers. They located primarily in loft buildings of the Penn-Liberty corridor and the Monongahela waterfront, where there was a 17 percent vacancy rate. These once lively areas had become marginal fringes. Like manufacturing, which had been leaving downtown since the late nineteenth century, residences maintained only a minimal presence. New units at Gateway Center, the Bigelow Apartments, and the Carlton House (also a hotel) filled the small demand for downtown living.[71]

Offices remained the bright spot in the Golden Triangle's revitalization. Renaissance leaders explicitly emphasized the construction of skyscrapers with the projects at Gateway Center and Mellon Square as dignified settings for corporate offices. The excitement around these projects, the sense that the old industrial city was becoming modern, and the postwar economic boom that major Pittsburgh corporations enjoyed encouraged investment in downtown offices. With the completion of the US Steel and PNC Bank Buildings in the early 1970s, twenty office towers had risen since the Second World War. The PRPA estimated that nearly sixty-eight thousand (two-thirds of downtown's employment) were office workers. Major corporations, both local and regional offices of national corporations, soaked up 30 percent of the office space. Government occupied 22 percent of downtown office space, professional and business services 19 percent, and financial firms 13 percent. Gateway Center had become a new locus of offices, while the long-standing Fourth Avenue and Grant Street nodes expanded. Renaissance leaders' intention to retain and attract major corporations meant that the Golden Triangle would be a modern center of corporate headquarters.[72]

The Pittsburgh Regional Planning Association's 1962 plan for the Golden Triangle built on the success of the initial fifteen years of Renaissance. The redevelopment projects, plus the positive impacts of environmental and infrastructural improvements, had in their minds stabilized downtown, accelerated the pace of new development, expanded its boundaries beyond Grant Street for the first time, and removed a blighted adjacent neighborhood. Now they intended to complete the remaking of the Golden Triangle. They proposed modernizing the old district that was bounded by Wood and Stanwix Streets. To stabilize retailing, the plan envisioned making Fifth Avenue a pedestrian mall west of Wood and improving its streetscape east of Wood, as well as the streetscape of Smithfield, by widening sidewalks and planting trees. The success of Mellon Square inspired planners to propose a square at Penn and Seventh Street to revitalize the old entertainment area, a courthouse plaza, and a square on the southern end of Grant Street between Third and Fourth Avenues. In addition to improving the streetscape of Grant, the 1962 plan designated the Penn-Liberty corridor east of Seventh Street as the Allegheny Housing Renewal Area for high density housing. It also suggested redesigning the blocks between Grant and the Crosstown Boulevard into an attractive area for future development. Except for redevelopment west of Stanwix Street and Mellon Square, changes during the initial phase of Renaissance had left intact the general land use pattern of the earlier industrial era. The 1962 plan imagined broader changes in that spatial framework, but it did not address Jane Jacobs's critique of sustaining a dense mix of small businesses along downtown streets.[73]

As the public-private partnership planned to extend its ambitious redevelopment agenda, obstacles arose because of changes in its leadership, internal tensions within each of the partners, community resistance to urban renewal, and a gloomy economic forecast for the region's future. Urban renewal projects, especially the lower Hill District, galvanized African Americans, white neighborhood groups, and small business owners to oppose slum clearance and top-down planning. Deaths, retirements, and new public officials in the city and county governments weakened the partnership, while the fight over the proposed Skybus rapid transit system exposed fractures in the corporate community. Amid these changes, a multivolume economic study criticized the region for failing to diversify its industrial base and predicted slow growth followed by substantial declines in manufacturing employment.[74] Activists even challenged Renaissance's signature success of smoke control by demanding regulation of air pollution, not just visible smoke. By the end of the 1960s the PRPA's plan for the Golden Triangle seemed like a nonstarter.

Postindustrial Renaissance II

Renaissance I represented a turning point in Pittsburgh's development history. It established the efficacy of public-private partnerships, improved the environment, modernized infrastructure, and reversed the downward trajectory of the Golden Triangle. The impact of Renaissance I was not only visible in the landscape but also palpable in the spirit of partnership, action, and success, which civic leaders invoked during the deindustrialization crisis. Dubbed Renaissance II in 1977, the second period of redevelopment lasted a little more than a decade. The public-private partnership built on changes to downtown accomplished during Renaissance I and instituted new trajectories consonant with postindustrial ideas. Renaissance II involved greater initiative by local government than in the previous period; it spread projects more widely about the Golden Triangle, expanded downtown's boundaries, and had a greater effect on the landscape. Under the leadership of Mayor Caliguiri, the Urban Redevelopment Authority (URA) and his Mayor's Development Council nurtured downtown redevelopment. They courted private investors, shepherded projects through governmental agencies, and leveraged public funds. The public sector upgraded downtown infrastructure to encourage private investment, welcomed historic preservation-inspired redevelopment, and cooperated with a nonprofit initiative to develop cultural attractions.

Renaissance I ended with the installing of Pete Flaherty as mayor in 1970. Capitalizing on civil rights and anti-urban renewal sentiments, Flaherty attacked the Allegheny Conference for elitism and the public-private partnership for excessive focus on downtown and neglect of the neighborhoods. He terminated the partnership, deflated Allegheny County's innovative Skybus rapid transit proposal, instituted budgetary austerity, reduced city government's workforce, and shifted half of the city's federal aid to the neighborhoods. Meanwhile, the Conference appointed a new executive director, Robert Pease, and turned its attention to social programs in response to African American unrest and the riots following Martin Luther King's assassination. Flaherty and the Conference no longer focused on the Golden Triangle.[75]

Despite the contentious relationship between the former partners and the diminished concentration on downtown, development continued during the Flaherty years because of the momentum of the postwar Renaissance. In the late 1960s Westinghouse Electric completed its headquarters tower along Fort Pitt Boulevard. Oliver Avenue was vacated west of Wood Street for a plaza in which a thirty-eight-story skyscraper, one Oliver Plaza, opened in 1968. Seven years later Equibank moved into a second tower there, while Pittsburgh National Bank built its headquarters on the plaza's Fifth Avenue side. US Steel topped off its sixty-four-story headquarters on Grant Street in 1971, which symbolically towered over downtown. Disappointed that the Civic Arena project failed as a satisfactory cultural venue, the Heinz Foundation under the leadership of Heinz family scion, H. J. (Jack) Heinz II, funded the renovation of old Penn Theater on Sixth Street into a concert hall for the Pittsburgh Symphony and other arts performances. The new office towers finished the remaking of the lower Triangle and accentuated the Grant Street importance, while Heinz Hall reflected the PRPA's 1962 plan for revitalizing the Penn Avenue entertainment area.[76]

However, these developments in the first half of the 1970s could not dispel the sense of pending crisis for the city and downtown. Civic leaders fretted over gloomy prospects for the steel industry, continued racial unrest, and mounting population loss. Manufacturing employment as a percentage of the total labor force declined from 44 to 33 percent during Renaissance I. The closing of many industrial facilities would soon follow. Although Flaherty produced a small budget surplus, the fiscal distress of cities around the country, acrimony between city hall and the Conference, the much publicized failure of the Skybus transit proposal, and inaction on a new convention center all contributed to anxiety about the future. Even with new office buildings, downtown seemed to need assistance. The districts paralleling the rivers had underutilized older buildings, too many surface parking lots, and little new investment. A vice trade added to the tired feel of the once vital Penn-Liberty corridor. The department stores struggled to compete with suburban malls, as white flight from the city accelerated, especially after the 1968 riots. The Fifth Avenue retail corridor between the Horne's and Kaufmann's department stores looked shabby and catered increasingly to low income shoppers, including African Americans from the Hill District whose neighborhood business district had vanished from urban renewal.[77]

Efforts to resolve the stalled rapid transit and convention center projects helped to resuscitate the public-private partnership and create Renaissance II. When the state threatened to withhold funding for the convention center in 1974, Flaherty and the Conference cooperated in selecting a site between Tenth and Eleventh Streets. In the same year, with waning federal commitment to rapid transit, the mayor appointed the Transit Task Force to end the impasse over the proposed system's mode. In 1976 the task force selected a traditional light rail system over the rubber wheel and elevated concrete track of Skybus. Construction soon began on both projects and was completed in the 1980s. A joint effort to have corporate executives work with county officials to make government more efficient elicited additional cooperation. By the mid-1970s, new Conference chairperson Robert Dickey of Dravo Corporation announced the organization's renewed interest in downtown and foresaw a second Renaissance.[78]

Succeeding Flaherty, who resigned in 1977 to join President Carter's administration, Richard Caliguiri announced that a second Renaissance was at hand. He did not have a clear vision of this new Renaissance, but Caliguiri (1977–1988) soon understood that Pittsburgh had to reinvent itself. Population plummeted another 150,000 by 1990. Factories and mills closed across the region, shedding more than 100,000 jobs. Reminiscent of Renaissance I, the second Renaissance that included downtown was central to a strategy for transforming Pittsburgh, which he wished to rebrand as a postindustrial city. In addition to promoting education, research, advanced technology, and health care, civic leaders wanted to retain the city's status as a major center of corporate headquarters, finance, and professional services. Even as production facilities closed or left the region, corporate headquarters in Pittsburgh, the leaders reasoned, could function as command and control centers of their far-flung operations, if business and living conditions met their needs. To this end, Renaissance II leaders worked to upgrade downtown's infrastructure, office buildings, and amenities.[79]

Infrastructure projects mostly involved improving access between downtown and the region. Once the Transit Task Force decided on the mode for rapid transit, the light rail system from downtown to the South Hills moved forward.[80] As it opened in the 1980s, the completion of a busway to the East End replacing unused railroad tracks and the long delayed Parkway North through the East Street valley to the North Hills addressed earlier complaints of a sole focus on the South Hills. Civic leaders bet on a convention center to generate hospitality business and promote the region. Undersized, poorly sited, and austere, it had to be extensively renovated and reoriented toward the Allegheny River in the early 2000s. Finally, the 1985 decision to build a new airport aimed not only to attract businesses in its vicinity but also to offer air service commensurate with a headquarters city.

When Caliguiri moved into the mayor's office in 1977, the demand for top grade office space was rising; the occupancy rate would soon approach 99 percent. However, with local production facilities closing, Pittsburgh's global corporations had less reason to keep their headquarters in the city. The region and downtown could not afford to lose major corporate citizens. PPG Industries had already begun an assessment of whether to remain in Gateway Center or erect a new skyscraper to "showcase" its worldwide brand. Duquesne Light Company announced its desire for new offices, and US Steel searched for a developer of the five-acre Grant Street East site, for which the city had reconfigured streets and assigned subsurface rights for a light rail subway station.[81]

Caliguiri seized the opportunity to accommodate PPG Industries and other corporations considering office expansion in order to burnish the corporate headquarters component of his postindustrial strategy to reinvent Pittsburgh. Unlike during the Flaherty years, he refocused city government on the Golden Triangle, although he wisely never ignored the neighborhoods. He revived the partnership with the Allegheny Conference, but in this second iteration of the partnership Caliguiri's administration assumed a prominent role. He directed the URA to cooperate with corporations in their development planning. Caliguiri established the Mayor's Development Council (MDC) of directors of several city agencies and appointed his executive secretary as chair. The MDC met weekly to coordinate city efforts on behalf of downtown projects. Thus, during this deindustrialization period when corporate leaders had less time for community affairs as they struggled to keep their companies profitable and independent, the mayor established the mechanisms and spirit of cooperation to retain and enhance their presence. He made it easier for the executives to, in their words, "do the right thing" and stay in the city in which their firms had prospered for decades.[82]

During the dozen years of Caliguiri's administration, eight more skyscrapers joined the skyline of downtown, along with a twenty-eight-story hotel. The URA and MDC worked closely with the developers of several of these projects. Initially PPG Industries sorted through nine sites, including two across the rivers. The company especially liked a Market Square site, but extensive city cooperation was needed before the Philip Johnson–designed complex of five low-rise buildings, a plaza, and a forty-story tower could come to fruition (see Figure 15.6). City agencies declared property blighted, used eminent domain powers to assemble land, relocated businesses, addressed parking issues, provided a tax break, and promised to upgrade Market Square. As the 1970s ended, Dravo Corporation assessed three locations before settling on the Grant Street East property, which necessitated the demolition of the twenty-one-story Carlton House Hotel. The city also helped Mellon Bank evaluate locations for erecting a headquarters. Although the bank initially favored the site of the old Baltimore & Ohio Railroad terminal along the Monongahela River and additional property near the airport, it engineered an intricate deal when Dravo ran into financial difficulties in the early 1980s. The bank took over Dravo's incomplete fifty-four-story skyscraper at Fifth and Grant. The privately developed forty-story Oxford Center on Grant Street between Third and Fourth Avenues lured Duquesne Light as a primary tenant.[83]

Even as these three projects moved forward, the URA shopped for a developer of a site where Liberty and Grant intersected across from the Convention Center. The URA envisioned this location, calling it Liberty Center, as an anchor along with the Convention Center for redevelopment of the Penn-Liberty corridor and the eastern terminus of Grant, the city's grand corporate avenue. Simultaneously, the Conference submitted a plan for improving Grant's streetscape, which the city implemented. The twenty-seven-story Federated Investors Tower and a companion Vista International Hotel arose on the Liberty Center site. Together, the new streetscape and the Oxford, Mellon, and Federated Investors skyscrapers on Grant Street projected the headquarters image that the public-private partnership desired.[84]

Fig. 15.6 The forty-story glass tower anchors the complex of several smaller glass buildings and a central plaza known as PPG Place, 2005. The complex represents the close working partnership of the city government and local corporations in Renaissance II (photograph courtesy of Joel A. Tarr).

Similarly, the PPG complex emphasized the modernization of the lower Triangle begun during the first Renaissance with Gateway Center and the complementary three Oliver Plaza towers. The new twenty-story Riverfront Center at Stanwix and Fort Pitt Boulevard bolstered the southern end of Stanwix Street. At the other end, the thirty-one-story Fifth Avenue Place (1987) occupied the intersecting block of Fifth, Liberty, and Stanwix on the site of the former Jenkins Arcade. A few blocks east on Liberty, Consolidated Natural Gas erected a skyscraper. Renaissance II's skyscrapers filled out the lower downtown and Grant Street office complexes, as proposed in the 1962 Golden Triangle plan, and upgraded the older Penn-Liberty corridor. Overall, the second Renaissance added more than six million square feet of high quality office space in the fashionable, historicized postindustrial architectural styles of the period. The daily workforce of downtown rose to 140,000 with another 80,000 people coming to "town" for personal business or entertainment.[85]

New skyscrapers were not the only means for redeveloping downtown. Like many American cities in the last third of the century, Pittsburgh believed regionally distinctive cultural and entertainment activities could compete with suburban venues and appeal to the white-collar workers employed in corporate headquarters and advanced technology cities. The success of Heinz Hall (1971) and the adjoining Heinz Plaza (1979) suggested the potential of a cultural district, but the concert hall's location was marginal to downtown's Renaissance I redevelopment, embedded amid warehouses, wholesalers, and vice activities. In keeping with the Golden Triangle plan, the Conference proposed in 1979 a culture district for the Penn-Liberty corridor between Stanwix and the Convention Center. Justifying the clustering of arts organizations and theaters as an economic development strategy, the Conference incorporated the Pittsburgh Cultural Trust in 1984 and charged it with developing the requisite properties, attracting and coordinating cultural organizations, and managing the venues.[86]

With critical funding from the Heinz Endowments and cooperation by the city, corporations, and other foundations, the Cultural Trust became the central actor in the redevelopment of the Penn-Liberty corridor. Between 1984 and 1987 it shepherded the conversion of the old Stanley Theatre into the Benedum Center for Performing Arts and construction of CNG Tower, from which the Trust received income. It encouraged new art galleries, restaurants, and loft residences in addition to more theaters. While the skyscraper boom of Renaissance II ended with the national recession at the end of the 1980s, the Trust continued redeveloping the Cultural District. In 1991 it converted the old Fulton Theater into the Byham Theater for small arts companies, turned an X-rated movie theater into the Harris venue for foreign and specialty films, opened an art gallery, constructed the O'Reilly Theater for the popular Pittsburgh Public Theater, and built a large parking garage. The city and the Trust obtained the designation of a sizable portion of the corridor as a National Historic District; with this in place they sponsored a street and building facade improvement program. Rehabilitation of some historic buildings for loft apartments and the conversion of the Fulton office building into an upscale hotel demonstrated the transformative impact of the culture strategy for this old part of town.[87]

Despite the extensive redevelopment since the Second World War, many older buildings with architectural merit and entire blockfronts of pre–First World War structures remained intact. With federal tax incentives for the rehabilitation of commercial buildings legislated in the 1970s and 1980s, historic preservation became an important factor for downtown redevelopment. Although preservation advocacy for buildings in the path of projected construction often irritated public officials, they willingly encouraged preservation that promised to upgrade buildings or areas not inhibiting new projects. Preservation advocates targeted the ten-block area paralleling the Monongahela wharf, which contained some of the oldest mercantile, warehouse, and office buildings. It had been a backwater since investment moved from the wharf to other parts of the Golden Triangle in the late nineteenth century. Acknowledging the wharf area as the earliest commercial center, the city renamed it Firstside, supported its designation as a National Historic District, discouraged the creation of more surface parking lots, and encouraged rehabilitation of many lofts into professional offices and residences. A few blocks north toward the heart of downtown, the city cooperated in retaining the historical character of Pittsburgh's "little Wall Street." Once the center of financial institutions, Fourth Avenue suffered from the consolidation of the financial industry and the movement of financial firms to new skyscrapers located elsewhere in downtown. Demolition diminished the number of historic buildings, particularly west of Wood Street; but the National Historic District designation helped preserve an impressive collection of turn-of-the-century architecture and the Manhattan "canyon-like" streetscape. Elsewhere in downtown preservation incentives led to the rehabilitation of scattered individual buildings such as the former Romanesque-style Old German Savings Bank on Sixth Avenue and the Daniel Burnham–designed Pennsylvania Railroad terminal, which was turned into an apartment building. The success of preservation held off some of modernism's deleterious effects and maintained the high density and diverse building fabric that is critical for a vital downtown.[88]

The rehabilitation of older buildings also played a role in expanding the boundaries of downtown to the east and across the rivers. Pittsburgh History & Landmarks Foundation's (PHLF) decision in the mid-1970s to turn the Pittsburgh & Lake Erie Railroad's elegant passenger terminal into a restaurant and office building, named Station Square, alerted the Conference's Robert Dickey to the possibilities of an expanded downtown. With private funding, PHLF demonstrated the viability of its preservation development strategy. Although the mayor did not initially cooperate with the Station Square project for fear it would compete with downtown businesses, the administration grudgingly obtained grant money to aid its expansion to four more repurposed buildings and a new Sheraton Hotel during the 1980s. The Smithfield Street Bridge and light rail transit tied the complex's offices, shops, and hotel to downtown.[89]

The URA and city planners eyed additional expansions of downtown's traditional boundaries. The city had long wanted to develop ninety-one acres of the Allegheny River's north shore as part of the Three Rivers Stadium project (see "In spite of the river ought to be a Pittsburgh town-slogan" in this volume). Mayor Flaherty delayed the plans; but by the end of the 1970s, the URA again promoted it. The city built a three-acre sculpture park called Allegheny Landing, which in turn complemented two new low-rise office buildings. In the 1990s two rehabbed buildings plus the Carnegie Institute's Warhol Museum and Alcoa's new six-story headquarters joined this north shore complex. West of the stadium, the Carnegie opened a science center in 1991. The old wholesale businesses and warehouses of the Strip District also seemed ripe for development, although the city had little funding resources left to devote to the area. It did assist the Historical Society of Western Pennsylvania's conversion of an old ice warehouse at Twelfth and Smallman Streets into its new museum. At the same time, lawyers and speculators transformed small shops and lofts into offices along Fifth Avenue a few blocks east of the courthouse.[90]

Mayor Caliguiri hoped, in 1977, that a second renaissance would breathe life into a city experiencing long-term decline, and in the mid-1980s he crowed that Renaissance II was achieving the goal. Caliguiri declared that downtown's new office towers, streetscapes, cultural amenities, rapid transit, and historic rehabilitation were crucially aiding the transformation of the city and the region to a vigorous new economy of education, health care, advanced technology, and professional and business services. Indeed, Pittsburgh had adopted strategies for the postindustrial era shared by other cities. Caliguiri actively pursued private and nonprofit developers with tax abatements, land assembly, low interest loans, and street improvements. By

1990 large sections of downtown had undergone substantial redevelopment, and office occupancy rates remained healthy. A few new skyscrapers included clusters of retail stores and public open spaces such as the PPG Winter Garden.[91] Large plazas around office buildings such as the US Steel building and the PPG complex remained empty and windswept space in concert with modernist visions, as Jacobs had worried. National experts such as William H. Whyte Jr. urged cities to nudge private developers to "reweave" these "dead" spaces into the streetscape by making them pedestrian friendly. PPG, US Steel, and several other property owners did just that, contributing to downtown's increasing vibrancy. Nevertheless, problems remained in the retail sector highlighted by the closing of Gimbels in 1986. Although improving, nightlife was still minimal and concentrated in the emerging cultural district, while too few residential opportunities existed.

Post-Renaissance Developments

Mayor Caliguiri's untimely death in 1988 coincided with the end of Renaissance II. The accumulating problems of sustained population loss, plant closings, high unemployment, strained tax revenues, and a national recession caused the next administration under Sophie Masloff to become less entrepreneurial. Development in downtown subsided, although a few new skyscrapers added to downtown's robust skyline. Pressure mounted for completing the cultural district, upgrading the dilapidated Fifth Avenue retail corridor, expanding convention business, and stimulating more nightlife and residences. By the mid-1990s the rebounding national economy renewed demand for office space. With his election as mayor in 1994, Tom Murphy addressed these issues with the full satchel of governmental tools and the initiation of some new projects. The planned projects in an expanded downtown area had observers talking about a third renaissance.[92]

Mayor Murphy's major downtown initiative at century's end involved a scheme to revive retailing in the Fifth Avenue corridor. The city invested heavily in persuading Lazarus to close its old (formerly Horne's) department store adjacent to Gateway Center and construct a smaller but showy store on Fifth Avenue. Farther up Fifth at Smithfield, the city enticed Lord & Taylor to repurpose the historic Mellon Bank Building (1924) into a store. In a controversial move, the URA negotiated a deal with a Chicago developer to assemble several blocks of the lower Fifth area, demolish more than sixty buildings, displace approximately 125 businesses, and develop a mall-like complex of national retail shops and entertainment attractions called Market Place at Fifth and Forbes. Led by PHLF, preservationists protested the proposed destruction of downtown's older fabric. Small business owners in the path of demolition railed against the city's secretive planning process. They and PHLF doubted the wisdom of attracting chain stores that duplicated those found in suburban malls. They feared downtown would lose its distinctive character. Others objected to using eminent domain for taking property and reselling it to private interests. The opponents favored an incremental process for revitalizing the Fifth and Forbes retail area, in which historic preservation would play a central role.[93]

The Market Place plan collapsed in 2000. The city relented and in cooperation with small businesses and preservationists forged a set of development principles. It contracted with a new developer for reviving some of the Market Square area. Rehabilitation of historic buildings and facades proceeded with PHLF in the lead role. Even as the city and PHLF poured their energies into the Fifth-Forbes retail area, Lazarus and Lord & Taylor's closed their stores. Saks decided to end its presence in downtown, and Macy's closed the iconic former Kaufmann's store. The department stores' long postwar efforts to compete with suburban retailers yielded to specialized shops in downtown.[94]

Concurrently, the city worked to sustain redevelopment momentum in the Penn-Liberty area, as the 1962 plan had proposed. With public and private money, some raised by Mayor Murphy for two development funds, the city supported the repurposing of the former Horne's store into an office building called Penn Avenue Place. At the other end of Penn Avenue, the city coordinated with the state in doubling the size of the convention center with an award-winning architectural design and reorienting it toward the Allegheny River. These two projects—along with continued development of the Cultural District, the conversion of lofts to residential units, and Renaissance II's skyscrapers—realized revitalization of the Penn-Liberty corridor.[95]

Additional developments significantly impacted the Golden Triangle in the post–Renaissance II years. The city helped both Mellon Bank and PNC Bank find downtown locations for large back-office functions. The small, business-oriented Point Park University weathered a financial crisis in the mid-1990s, and enrollments soon soared. Accordingly, the university embarked on developing a campus spread among downtown buildings. From its two initial buildings on Wood Street near Third Avenue, it renovated several more from the Boulevard of the Allies to Fifth Avenue, always on or close to Wood Street. Students now comprise a substantial downtown residential population.[96]

In keeping with the residential preferences of many young professionals and empty nest couples, downtown experienced a 20 percent increase of its residential population between 2000 and 2010. The demand for residences resulted in converted lofts in Firstside and the Penn-Liberty corridor, the eighteen-story Encore apartments on Seventh Street, and many projected units in the center of downtown. This modest residential growth was the first significant increase in the Triangle since the late nineteenth century.[97]

Although renovation of the Point from a shabby rundown area into Point Park symbolized the renewal of Pittsburgh, it failed to stimulate a rethinking of the Golden Triangle's riverfronts. The success of Station Square and the 1980s' conversion of industrial Herr Island two miles up the Allegheny River into trendy Washington's Landing suggested the possibilities of viewing riverfronts as environmental assets rather than abandoned wastelands (see "Pittsburgh's Three Rivers" in this volume). However, the postwar completion of the Parkway and the Tenth Street Bypass along downtown's riverfronts, also functioning as flood walls, appeared to foreclose their repurposing. A small group formed at the end of the 1980s to promote biking and hiking trails along the city's riverfronts. Then state representative Tom Murphy helped to fund the group named Friends of the Riverfronts; as mayor he made the trails a city priority. In 1999 some civic leaders established a task force with the ambitious goal of reclaiming the central riverfronts collectively as a park. Incorporated as Riverlife, the organization restored Point Park after thirty years of use, constructed trails and waterfront parks such as one at the Convention Center, and promoted river recreation.[98]

The long desired expansion of downtown's traditional boundaries proceeded after the initial steps taken in the 1980s. Murphy advocated continued development of the Allegheny River's north shore. He envisioned replacing the outdated Three Rivers Stadium with two new ones. Despite vigorous opposition, he cobbled together funding for PNC Park (baseball) and Heinz Field (football); they opened in 2001. In contrast to Three Rivers Stadium's failure to stimulate surrounding development, Murphy and successor administrations attracted hotels, offices, restaurants, and the Rivers Casino (2009) to complement the new stadiums and the Carnegie Science Center (1991). More development arose near Allegheny Landing. Eventually, light rail transit was extended under the river to the stadium complex. With the three sister bridges over the Allegheny, the north shore and Cultural District enjoy a synergy that adds to downtown's excitement and regional centrality.[99]

Completed and proposed projects to the east of downtown may create a similar synergy in the future. The Civic Arena in the lower Hill District renewal area failed to generate development; a sea of parking lots surrounded it. The Arena's demolition, the erection of Consol Energy Center (renamed PPG Paints Arena), and commitment of the development rights to a private entity portend additional offices and housing. When covering over the Crosstown Boulevard materializes (as a park), the lower Hill development may connect with downtown. Finally, developers have their eyes on the Strip District as being favorable for condominiums and offices, especially for technology firms, with access to riverfront trails and small parks. Whether this vision becomes part of downtown or remains a complementary fringe area is unknown.

New office towers, the filling out of the Cultural District, and the incremental development strategy to revitalize retail activities in the years since Caliguiri's death continued Renaissance II's trajectory. More than three decades after Caliguiri's resuscitation of the public-private partnership, the Golden Triangle displays the hallmarks of postindustrial American downtowns featuring waterfront amenities, entertainment with cultural and sports attractions, alternative transportation focused on separate bicycle lanes, and growing residential opportunities.

CONCLUSION

Powered by industrialization, shaped by new transportation and building technologies, and buffeted by centrifugal forces, Pittsburgh's nineteenth-century business center evolved into a modern America downtown. Skyscrapers, a financial district, a civic cluster, department stores, and movie palaces replaced manufacturing, wholesaling, and residences. However, the vitality and excitement of the industrial era downtown deteriorated in a few decades. Challenged by the Depression, degraded by smoke, flooding, and steam railroads, choked by automobiles, and improved only minimally by planning, downtown entered the post–Second World War era in need of massive new investment and imaginative redevelopment. Suburbanization, a declining metropolitan population, contentious race relations, deindustrialization, and the loss of several corporate headquarters over the second half of the century added further pressure on downtown. Adopting current fashions in planning, architecture, and redevelopment after the Second World War, the proactive public-private partnership managed to stabilize the Golden Triangle, enhance its accessibility, and position it for renewed success in postindustrial decades. Mistakes in design, demolishing historic buildings, and traffic planning were made along the way, but without the engagement of local government, foundations, and nonprofit organizations in initiating redevelopment, nurturing private investment, and obtaining state and federal financial support, the creative destruction of the Golden Triangle would probably not have been so golden at the outset of the twenty-first century.

Pittsburgh's Golden Triangle still reflects its origins as an eastern American downtown. It is densely developed with many skyscrapers, relatively few surface parking lots creating gaps in the block fronts, and narrow streets and sidewalks. A marvelous mix of different architectural styles, building facade textures and colors, and ornamental sculptures provides visual variety in the landscape. The awkward, angular junction at Liberty Avenue of the two original street plans disrupts the gridiron monotony for pedestrians, while giving traffic engineers headaches. Weekdays the sidewalks bustle with people, the streets fill with cars and buses. At night, theatergoers patronize Cultural District venues. The intensity of activity says this is downtown.

Two and a half centuries of constant change in Pittsburgh's downtown will not abate any time soon. Private investors and public officials relentlessly attempt to stay abreast of national and increasingly international trends to keep downtown relevant and profitable. In the words of Jane Jacobs: "The only way that dynamic systems can stay alive is constant self-renewal."[100] Relations among the private and public sector members of the powerful partnership will shift with political and economic changes. Technologies, economic activities, and social relationships inexorably change such that spatial patterns of land use reflect new imperatives. The earliest Pittsburghers would have found the downtown of the early twentieth century inconceivable, just as Pittsburghers from that era would find today's Golden Triangle disorienting. Legacies of earlier periods informed subsequent ones, but changes wrought by constant creative destruction most characterize Pittsburgh's downtown through the years.

NOTES

1. Civic leaders include both private and public sector leaders.

2. See also Max Page, *The Creative Destruction of Manhattan, 1900–1940* (Chicago: University of Chicago Press, 1999), 5–11.

3. Leland D. Baldwin, *Pittsburgh: The Story of a City, 1750–1865* (Pittsburgh: University of Pittsburgh Press, 1937), 103; Verna L. Cowan, *Pittsburgh Archaeological Resources & National Register Survey* (Pittsburgh: Carnegie Museum of Natural History, 1985), 51–52; James E. Vance, *The Continuing City: Urban Morphology in Western Civilization* (Baltimore: Johns Hopkins University Press, 1990), 263–68.

4. Cowan, *Pittsburgh Archaeological Resources*, 46–53.

5. Baldwin, *Pittsburgh: The Story of a City*, 129–53, 184–217; Richard C. Wade, *The Urban Frontier* (Chicago: University of Chicago Press, 1959), 39–49, 177–97; Catherine

Elizabeth Reiser, *Pittsburgh's Commercial Development, 1800–1850* (Harrisburg: Pennsylvania Historical and Museum Commission, 1951), 125–40.

6. Baldwin, *Pittsburgh: The Story of a City*, 231; John Swauger, "Pittsburgh's Residential Pattern in 1815," *Western Pennsylvania Historical Magazine* 68, no. 2 (1978): 265–77; J. M. Riddle, *Pittsburgh Directory for 1815* (Pittsburgh, 1815); Samuel Jones, *Pittsburgh in the Year 1826* (Pittsburgh, 1826).

7. Jones, *Pittsburgh in the Year 1826*, 38–39.

8. Martyn J. Bowden, "The Internal Structure of the Colonial Replica City" (unpublished paper, presented to the annual meeting of the Association of American Geographers, Kansas City, 1972); Diane Shaw, *City Building on the Eastern Frontier: Sorting the New Nineteenth-Century City* (Baltimore: Johns Hopkins University Press, 2004), 28–36. Shaw demonstrates that preindustrial Boston, Baltimore, and Philadelphia, as well as the new "western" cities of Rochester and Syracuse, displayed this general triangular pattern.

9. Reiser, *Pittsburgh's Commercial Development*, 133.

10. Cowan, *Pittsburgh Archaeological Resources*, 83–294.

11. Jones, *Pittsburgh in the Year 1826*, 49–85.

12. Reiser, *Pittsburgh's Commercial Development*, 69–83.

13. Reiser, *Pittsburgh's Commercial Development*, 44–49.

14. Reiser, *Pittsburgh's Commercial Development*, 193, also 84–111. See also Cowan, *Pittsburgh Archaeological Resources*, 73–74.

15. Based on an analysis of *Harris' Pittsburgh Directory of 1844* (Pittsburgh, 1844) and Cowan, *Pittsburgh Archaeological Resources*, 83–294.

16. *Harris' Pittsburgh Directory of 1844*.

17. Walter C. Kidney, *Landmark Architecture: Pittsburgh and Allegheny County* (Pittsburgh: Pittsburgh History & Landmarks Foundation, 1985), 33, 44; *Harris' Pittsburgh Directory*.

18. Baldwin, *Pittsburgh: The Story of a City*, 228–30; Michael Fitzgibbon Holt, *Forging a Majority: The Formation of the Republican Party in Pittsburgh, 1848–1860* (New Haven: Yale University Press, 1969), 28–35; Joel A. Tarr, "Infrastructure and City-Building in the Nineteenth and Twentieth Centuries," in *City at the Point: Essays on the Social History of Pittsburgh*, ed. Samuel P. Hays (Pittsburgh: University of Pittsburgh Press, 1989), 216–28; Donald E. Cook Jr., "The Great Fire of Pittsburgh in 1845," *Western Pennsylvania Historical Magazine* 51, no. 2 (1968): 127–53.

19. *Report of the Flood Commission of Pittsburgh, Penna.* (Pittsburgh: 1912), 44–45; Tarr, *Infrastructure and City Building*, 223–25; Baldwin, *Pittsburgh: The Story of a City*, 194, 231–32.

20. James C. Holmberg, "The Industrializing Community: Pittsburgh, 1850–1880" (PhD diss., University of Pittsburgh, 1981), ch. 2, viii.

21. The Pennsylvania Railroad purchased the Pennsylvania Main Canal in 1857, ending its usefulness. See Glenn Porter and Harold Livesay, *Merchants and Manufacturers: Studies in the Changing Structure of Nineteenth-Century Marketing* (Baltimore: Johns Hopkins University Press, 1971), 65–69, for a description of Benjamin F. Jones's shift from running canal packets to becoming an iron manufacturer.

22. John N. Ingham, *Making Iron and Steel: Independent Mills in Pittsburgh, 1820–1920* (Columbus: Ohio State University Press, 1991), 27–51.

23. Harold C. Livesay, *Andrew Carnegie and the Rise of Big Business* (Boston: Little,

Brown, 1975), 77–92; Kenneth Warren, *Triumphant Capitalism: Henry Clay Frick and the Industrial Transformation of America* (Pittsburgh: University of Pittsburgh Press, 1996), 11–19; Henry Oliver Evans, *Iron Pioneer: Henry W. Oliver* (New York: E. P. Dutton, 1942), 38–54, 115–30; David Cannadine, *Mellon: An American Life* (New York: Alfred A. Knopf, 2006), 43–44. Judge Mellon and his sons offer prime examples of private investment bankers, as they were central to the development of the city's growing East Liberty section.

24. Larry R. Ford, *America's New Downtowns: Revitalization or Reinvention?* (Baltimore: Johns Hopkins University Press, 2003), 25; *J. F. Diffenbacker's Business Directory, 1880–1881* (Pittsburgh: G. H. Thurston, 1880). Some of these professionals performed multiple services and thus cause some overcounting from the directories.

25. *Diffenbacker's Business Directory*; *Atlas of the Cities of Pittsburgh and Allegheny, Pennsylvania* (G. M. Hopkins, 1882), plates 1–3; Kidney, *Landmark Architecture*, 46–47.

26. *Diffenbacker's Business Directory*; *Atlas of the Cities of Pittsburgh and Allegheny*.

27. *Diffenbacker's Business Directory*.

28. *Diffenbacker's Business Directory*.

29. *Diffenbacker's Business Directory*.

30. Joel A. Tarr. *Transportation Innovation and Changing Spatial Patterns in Pittsburgh, 1850–1934* (Chicago: Public Works Historical Society, 1978), 1–14; US Bureau of the Census, *Eighth Census, 1860: Population of the United States* (Washington, DC: USGPO, 1864), 413, table 3.

31. There are several excellent general syntheses of the evolution of American downtowns since the late nineteenth century. See Robert M. Fogelson, *Downtown: Its Rise and Fall, 1880–1950* (New Haven: Yale University Press, 2001) and Alison Isenberg, *Downtown America: A History of the Place and the People Who Made It* (Chicago: University of Chicago Press, 2004).

32. Although the origin of the name Golden Triangle is not certain and one story places it after the fire of 1845, the name was commonly used after 1900 in referring to "the wealthy downtown banks and corporations and the thriving commercial climate." See Martin Aurand, *The Spectator and the Topographical City* (Pittsburgh: University of Pittsburgh Press, 2006), 209n63. For an overview of industrial suburbanization and the growth of the Pittsburgh metropolitan region at the turn of the century, see Edward K. Muller, "Industrial Suburbs and the Growth of Metropolitan Pittsburgh, 1870–1920," in Robert Lewis, ed., *Manufacturing Suburbs: Building Work and Home on the Metropolitan Fringe* (Philadelphia: Temple University Press, 2004), 124–42.

33. Ingham, *Making Iron and Steel.*

34. One of the best overviews of the regions industrialization is Mark David Samber, "Networks of Capital: Creating and Maintaining a Regional Industrial Economy in Pittsburgh, 1865–1919" (PhD diss., Carnegie Mellon University, 1995).

35. See Alfred D. Chandler Jr., *The Visible Hand: The Managerial Revolution in American Business* (Cambridge, MA: Harvard University Press, 1977).

36. Joel A. Tarr with Thomas Finholt and David Goodman, "The City and the Telegraph: Urban Telecommunications in the Pre-telephone Era," *Journal of Urban History* 14, no. 1 (1987): 38–80. Carnegie chose to locate his Edgar Thomson mill well beyond the city in Braddock, while George Westinghouse moved his air brake, electrical equipment, and switch and signal plants east of the city along the Pennsylvania Railroad tracks. The Jones & Laughlin Steel Corporation constructed a new works and town at Aliquippa, twenty-six miles beyond downtown on the Ohio River. Frick used the telegraph to keep in

close touch with the supervisor of his firm's many mines and coke works scattered about the Connellsville Coke District. For inspections he rode the railroad, which he could board either downtown or at the Homewood Station near his home. Similarly, his neighbor George Westinghouse found his Homewood residence convenient for commuting by railroad to his downtown office and his Turtle Creek plants or attending meetings in New York City. Warren, *Triumphant Capitalism*; Quentin R. Skrabec, *George Westinghouse: Gentle Genius* (New York: Algora Press, 2007).

37. Tarr, *Transportation Innovation*, 14–24; Howard V. Storch Jr., "Changing Functions of the Center-City: Pittsburgh, 1850–1912" (seminar paper, University of Pittsburgh, 1966); W. Schusler, "The Economic Position of Railroad Commuting Service in the Pittsburgh District: Its History, Present, and Future" (PhD diss., University of Pittsburgh, 1958).

38. Carol Willis, *Form Follows Finance: Skyscrapers and Skylines in New York and Chicago* (New York: Princeton Architectural Press, 1995); Larry R. Ford, *Cities and Buildings: Skyscrapers, Skid Rows, and Suburbs* (Baltimore: Johns Hopkins University Press, 1994), 28–40; Gail Fenske and Deryck Holdsworth, "Corporate Identity and the New York Office Building, 1895–1915," in David Ward and Olivier Zunz, eds., *The Landscape of Modernity: Essays on New York City, 1900–1940* (New York: Russell Sage Foundation, 1992), 129–59; James D. Van Trump, "The Skyscraper as Monument," in James D. Van Trump, *Life and Architecture in Pittsburgh* (Pittsburgh: Pittsburgh History & Landmarks Foundation, 1983), 243–48; Evans, *Iron Pioneer*, 299–303. Executors and family members constructed an imposing tower, still known today as the Oliver Building, as a monument to the deceased industrialist Henry W. Oliver.

39. Valerie S. Grash, "The Commercial Skyscrapers of Pittsburgh Industrialists and Financiers, 1885–1932" (PhD diss., Pennsylvania State University, 1998), 23–75; Franklin Toker, *Pittsburgh: An Urban Portrait* (University Park: Pennsylvania State University Press, 1986), 19–78; Aurand, *The Spectator and the Topographical City*, 10–89.

40. The temporal pattern of tall building development was largely compiled from Grash, "Commercial Skyscrapers"; Toker, *Pittsburgh*; Kidney, *Landmark Architecture*. Henry Phipps built seven buildings, not all tall, in downtown. See Grash, "Commercial Skyscrapers," 145–51.

41. Evans, *Iron Pioneer*, 209–303; Grash, "Commercial Skyscrapers," 76–107. For H. C. Frick's correspondence in relation to the Hump cut, see letters in Folders 11 and 12, Box 1, Hump Series, Helen Clay Frick Foundation Archives, Archives Service Center, University of Pittsburgh, Pittsburgh, PA.

42. Grash, "Commercial Skyscrapers," 161–82; Toker, *Pittsburgh*, 60–78. Mellon Bank built its exquisite four-story bank at Fifth and Smithfield in 1924. See Kidney, *Landmark Architecture*, 158.

43. Data compiled from R. L. Polk & Company and R. L. Dudley's, *Business Directory of Pittsburgh and Allegheny, 1907* (Pittsburgh, 1907). For a good overview of the regional economy, see Samber, "Networks of Capital." Both Samber ("Networks of Capital") and Grash ("Commercial Skyscrapers," 131) point out that Pittsburgh ranked among the top five financial centers in 1907, before the panic of 1907 that devastated the city's financial strength.

44. *Business Directory of Pittsburgh and Allegheny, 1907.*

45. *Business Directory of Pittsburgh and Allegheny, 1907.* An emerging shift of food wholesalers to the Strip District was evident in the nearly three dozen commission

merchants and several fruit and produce wholesalers in the vicinity of Twenty-First Street and Penn Avenue. At the same time, the city's erection of the new Diamond Market in 1916 retained a cluster of produce and meat retailers in Market Square.

46. *Business Directory of Pittsburgh and Allegheny, 1907*; Grash, "Commercial Skyscrapers," 159. The Kaufmanns expanded from their original location in the South Side to their Fifth and Smithfield location in 1885. See Toker, *Pittsburgh*, 42–43.

47. Toker, *Pittsburgh*, 56.

48. Tarr, "Infrastructure and City Building"; John F. Bauman and Edward K. Muller, *Before Renaissance: Planning in Pittsburgh, 1889–1943* (Pittsburgh: University of Pittsburgh Press, 2006), 51–193; Roy Lubove, *Twentieth-Century Pittsburgh, Vol. 1: Government, Business, and Environmental Change* (Pittsburgh: University of Pittsburgh Press, 1996), 1–58; Walter C. Kidney, *Pittsburgh's Bridges: Architecture and Engineering* (Pittsburgh: Pittsburgh History & Landmarks Foundation, 1999); Grash, "Commercial Skyscrapers," 41.

49. Maurine W. Greenwald and Margo Anderson, *Pittsburgh Surveyed: Social Science and Social Reform in the Early Twentieth Century* (Pittsburgh: University of Pittsburgh Press, 1996); Lubove, *Twentieth-Century Pittsburgh: Vol. 1*, 1–40; Bauman and Muller, *Before Renaissance*, 1–101; Isenberg, *Downtown America*, 13–77.

50. Bauman and Muller, *Before Renaissance*, 51–136; Grash, "Commercial Skyscrapers," 164–66; Ann Lloyd, "Pittsburgh's 1923 Zoning Ordinance," *Western Pennsylvania Historical Magazine* 53, no. 3 (1974): 289–305; Janet R. Daley, "Zoning: Its Historical Context and Importance in the Development of Pittsburgh," *Western Pennsylvania Historical Magazine* 71, no. 2 (1988): 99–125; John F. Bauman and Edward K. Muller, "The Planning Technician as Urban Visionary: Frederick Bigger and American Planning, 1915–1954," *Journal of Planning History* 1, no. 2 (2002): 124–53.

51. Fogelson, *Downtown*, 218–48; Jon C. Teaford, *The Metropolitan Revolution: The Rise of Post-Urban America* (New York: Columbia University Press, 2006), 9–20.

52. Robert C. Alberts, *The Shaping of the Point: Pittsburgh's Renaissance Park* (Pittsburgh: University of Pittsburgh Press, 1980), 57–59. Phillip M. Hauser of the US Census Bureau conducted the survey and classification of metropolitan areas in 1944, which predicted that Pittsburgh had poor prospects for postwar growth. His report appeared in publications such as the *Wall Street Journal* and *Business Week*.

53. Tarr, *Transportation Innovation*, 10–39; Roy Lubove, ed., *Pittsburgh* (New York: Franklin Watts, 1976), 266–71.

54. Fogelson, *Downtown*, 199, 219; Bauman and Muller, *Before Renaissance*, 194–226. In their efforts to expand markets, department stores built branch stores in secondary city centers and suburban shopping complexes. See Richard Longstreth, *The American Department Store Transformed, 1920–1960* (New Haven: Yale University Press, 2010), 2, 109–35, 178.

55. Bauman and Muller, *Before Renaissance*, 227–69.

56. The concern for change is made clear in several issues of the Chamber of Commerce's publication *Greater Pittsburgh*. See especially articles in issues of January and November 1939, February 1940, and March 1941. See also Alberts, *The Shaping of the Point*, 43–46, 70; Bauman and Muller, *Before Renaissance*, 250–60.

57. Sherie R. Mershon, "Corporate Social Responsibility and Urban Revitalization: The Allegheny Conference on Community Development, 1943–1968" (PhD diss., Carnegie Mellon University, 2004), 397, also 153–221; Michael P. Weber, *Don't Call Me Boss: David L. Lawrence, Pittsburgh's Renaissance Mayor* (Pittsburgh: University of Pittsburgh

Press, 1988), 233–37. Reportedly, the two men rarely met. For a critical look into these types of postwar public-private partnerships, see "Business Leadership Coalitions and Public-Private Partnerships in American Cities: A Business Perspective on Regime Theory," *Journal of Urban Affairs* 24, no. 1 (2002): 35–54.

58. Jon C. Teaford, *The Rough Road to Renaissance: Urban Revitalization in America, 1940–1985* (Baltimore: Johns Hopkins University Press, 1990), 46–47, 61, 108.

59. Joel A. Tarr, "Changing Fuel-Use Behavior and Energy Transitions: The Pittsburgh Smoke-Control Movement, 1940–1950," in Joel A. Tarr, ed., *The Search for the Ultimate Sink: Urban Pollution in Historical Perspective* (Akron, OH: University of Akron Press, 1996), 227–61; Sherie R. Mershon and Joel A. Tarr, "Strategies for Clean Air: The Pittsburgh and Allegheny County Smoke Control Movements, 1945–1960," in Joel A. Tarr, ed., *Devastation and Renewal: An Environmental History of Pittsburgh and Its Region* (Pittsburgh: University of Pittsburgh Press, 2003), 145–73; Mershon, "Corporate Social Responsibility," 291–395; Weber, *Don't Call Me Boss*, 238–40, 244–54.

60. Mershon, "Corporate Social Responsibility," 562–68. For a discussion of the national development of freeways and interstate highways, see Mark A. Rose and Raymond A. Mohl, *Interstate: Highway Politics and Policy since 1939* (Knoxville: University of Tennessee Press, 2012).

61. *A Plan for Pittsburgh's Golden Triangle* (Pittsburgh: Pittsburgh Regional Planning Association, 1962), 90–97. Crying socialism, opponents thought that the parking authority legislation was an unconstitutional intervention of government in the private marketplace. Mershon, "Corporate Social Responsibility," 450–63; Longstreth, *The American Department Store*, 105.

62. Mershon, "Corporate Social Responsibility," 568–93; Edward K. Muller, Morton Coleman, and David Houston, "Skybus: Pittsburgh's Failed Industrial Targeting Strategy of the 1960s," Center for Industry Studies, University of Pittsburgh, 2002, www.industrystudies.pitt.edu/, and in this volume.

63. Alberts, *The Shaping of the Point*; Mershon, "Corporate Social Responsibility," 397–405, 426–50. Because it is a state park, its official name is Point State Park, but it is commonly called Point Park. In 1945 the state passed a law authorizing municipalities to form their own redevelopment authorities. Under this legislation, certification of an area as blighted gave a redevelopment authority the legal basis for undertaking redevelopment, including the use of eminent domain to take private property for a project. However, the definition of blight was very broad, giving considerable leeway to the local authority to apply the term. See Brian Robick, "Blight: The Development of a Contested Concept" (PhD diss., Carnegie Mellon University, 2011).

64. Mershon, "Corporate Social Responsibility," 406–27; Shelby Stewman and Joel A. Tarr, "Four Decades of Public-Private Partnerships in Pittsburgh," in R. Scott Fosler and Renee A. Berger, eds., *Public-Private Partnerships in American Cities* (Lexington, MA: D. C. Heath, 1982), 73–75.

65. Susan M. Rademacher, *Mellon Square: Discovering a Modern Masterpiece* (New York: Princeton Architectural Press, 2015), 10. See also Stewman and Tarr, "Four Decades," 75–76; Mershon, "Corporate Social Responsibility," 463–68.

66. Lubove, *Twentieth-Century Pittsburgh, Vol. 1*, 106–41; Mershon, "Corporate Social Responsibility," 500–520, 740–44; Laura Grantmyre, "Conflicting Visual Representations of Redevelopment in Pittsburgh's Hill District, 1943–1968" (PhD diss., University of Pittsburgh, 2013).

67. Park H. Martin, "Redevelopment of Pittsburgh's Golden Triangle" (speech available at Harvard City Planning and Landscape Architecture Library, Harvard University, Cambridge, MA, n.d.); Pittsburgh Regional Planning Association, *A Plan for Pittsburgh's Golden Triangle, 1962*, 22, 32, 51; Mershon, "Corporate Social Responsibility," 475. A short report by the Allegheny Conference on Community Development in 1957 assessed the progress of downtown during Renaissance and concluded that the Golden Triangle had been stabilized and the office sector had flourished; but with mass transit in disarray and parking still not adequate, retail activity was in trouble and not likely to grow in the future. The report anticipated some of the recommendations made by the PRPA in 1962. Allegheny Conference on Community Development, *Golden Triangle Study, 1957*, in Park H. Martin Papers, 1935–1958, AIS 1971.1628, Archives & Special Collections, University of Pittsburgh, Pittsburgh, PA.

68. Ira S. Lowry, *Economic Study of the Pittsburgh Region, Vol. 2: Portrait of a Region* (Pittsburgh: Pittsburgh Regional Planning Association, University of Pittsburgh Press, 1963).

69. Jane Jacobs, *The Death and Life of Great American Cities* (New York: Random House, 1961), 106, 164–74, 263. She wrote: "Gateway Center is a Radiant City office and hotel project with the buildings set here and there in empty land" (106). She also decried that "They [downtowns] are being witlessly murdered, in good part by deliberate policies of sorting out leisure uses from work uses, under the misapprehension that this is orderly city planning" (171).

70. *A Plan for Pittsburgh's Golden Triangle*, 38–45, 23–26; Mershon, "Corporate Social Responsibility," 683.

71. *A Plan for Pittsburgh's Golden Triangle*, 58–64, 70–72.

72. *A Plan for Pittsburgh's Golden Triangle*, 48–53; Toker, *Pittsburgh*, 22–78.

73. *Prelude to the Future* (Pittsburgh, PA.: Pittsburgh Regional Planning Association, 1968); *A Plan for Pittsburgh's Golden Triangle*, 100–123; Jacobs, *Death and Life*, 175–76.

74. Mershon, "Corporate Social Responsibility"; Hoover, *Economic Study of the Pittsburgh Region.*

75. Roy Lubove, *Twentieth-Century Pittsburgh, Vol. 2: The Post-Steel Era* (Pittsburgh: University of Pittsburgh Press, 1996), 58–60; Tracy Neumann, *Remaking the Rust Belt: The Postindustrial Transformation of North America* (Philadelphia: University of Pennsylvania Press, 2016), ch. 4; Stewman and Tarr, "Four Decades," 89–91; Alyssa M. Ribeiro, "A Period of Turmoil: Pittsburgh's April 1968 Riots and Their Aftermath," *Journal of Urban History* 39, no. 2 (2013): 147–71.

76. Toker, *Pittsburgh*, 50–51, 64; Stewman and Tarr, "Four Decades," 91–94.

77. Gregory J. Crowley, *The Politics of Place: Contentious Urban Redevelopment in Pittsburgh* (Pittsburgh: University of Pittsburgh Press, 2005), 92; Stewman and Tarr, "Four Decades."

78. Neumann, *Remaking the Rust Belt*, 190–91; Stewman and Tarr, "Four Decades," 86–88, 91–93.

79. Lubove, *Twentieth-Century Pittsburgh, Vol. 2*, 29, 59–61, 297–98nn15–16; Crowley, *The Politics of Place*, 93; Stewman and Tarr, "Four Decades," 96.

80. The light rail transit system becomes a subway when it enters downtown.

81. Robert McLean III, *Countdown to Renaissance II; The New Way Corporate America Builds* (Pittsburgh: Urban Marketing Associates, 1984), 3–25; Stewman and Tarr, "Four Decades," 94–94, 97.

82. Roger S. Ahlbrandt Jr. and Morton Coleman, *The Role of the Corporation in Community Economic Development as Viewed by 21 Corporate Executives: Final Report* (Pittsburgh: University Center for Social and Urban Research, University of Pittsburgh, 1987); McLean, *Countdown to Renaissance II*, 26; Crowley, *The Politics of Place*, 102; Stewman and Tarr, "Four Decades," 94, 96, 107–12.

83. McLean, *Countdown to Renaissance II*, 28–79; Lubove, *Twentieth-Century Pittsburgh, Vol. 2*, 62–63; Stewman and Tarr, "Four Decades," 94–99.

84. Lubove, *Twentieth-Century Pittsburgh, Vol. 2*, 79; Neumann, *Remaking the Rust Belt*, 195; "Pittsburgh 80: Renaissance II in Action" (Urban Redevelopment Authority of Pittsburgh, City of Pittsburgh, 1980), 14–15.

85. Lubove, *Twentieth-Century Pittsburgh, Vol. 2*, 62–63, 300n31; Toker, *Pittsburgh*, 26–27, 29, 55.

86. Lubove, *Twentieth-Century Pittsburgh, Vol. 2*, 194–96; Neumann, *Remaking the Rust Belt*, 197–201. For an overview of the arts and city development before 1970, see the review essay by Julia L. Foulkes, "Dancing in the Streets: The Arts in Postwar U.S. Cities—Introduction," *Journal of Urban History* 41, no. 6 (2015): 955–61.

87. Lubove, *Twentieth-Century Pittsburgh, Vol. 2*, 196–201; Neumann, *Remaking the Rust Belt*, 203–4.

88. Lubove, *Twentieth-Century Pittsburgh, Vol. 2*, 65; Toker, *Pittsburgh*, 33–41, 48.

89. Lubove, *Twentieth-Century Pittsburgh, Vol. 2*, 218–23; Neumann, *Remaking the Rust Belt*, 203–4.

90. "Pittsburgh 80: Renaissance II in Action," 19; Neumann, *Remaking the Rust Belt*, 201–3; Lubove, *Twentieth-Century Pittsburgh, Vol. 2*, 55–56, 205, 294–95n2, 295n4.

91. Mclean, *Countdown to Renaissance II*, 83; Lubove, *Twentieth-Century Pittsburgh, Vol. 2*, 61.

92. Lubove, *Twentieth-Century Pittsburgh, Vol. 2*, 67.

93. Crowley, *The Politics of Place*, 109, 112–39; Lubove, *Twentieth-Century Pittsburgh, Vol. 2*, 68, 300n33; Jane Jacobs, "Downtown Is for People," in William H. Whyte Jr., ed., *The Exploding Metropolis* (New York: Doubleday, 1957), 140–68.

94. Pittsburgh Downtown Partnership, Pittsburgh, PA, "State of Downtown Pittsburgh 2012," http://www.DowntownPittsburgh.com, 16–18.

95. *A Plan for Pittsburgh's Golden Triangle*, 109–20.

96. For an overview of Point Park University, see https://en.wikipedia.org/wiki/Point.Park.University/; "State of Downtown Pittsburgh 2012," 28.

97. "State of Downtown of Pittsburgh 2012," 12–15.

98. Lubove, *Twentieth-Century Pittsburgh, Vol. 2*, 201–7.

99. "State of Downtown Pittsburgh 2012," 25.

100. Robert Kanigel, *Eyes on the Street: The Life of Jane Jacobs* (New York: Alfred A. Knopf, 2016), 11.

16 PRESERVING INDUSTRIAL HERITAGE LANDSCAPES AND COMMUNITY REVITALIZATION

Edward K. Muller

Driving through the river valleys of the Pittsburgh region in the early twenty-first century, one encounters few visible reminders of the once powerful and vibrant steel industry that once lined the river banks for miles. Gone are US Steel's mammoth mills at Homestead, Duquesne, and McKeesport; J & L Steel Corporation's works at the South Side, Hazelwood, and Aliquippa; and many more. US Steel's still operating Clairton coke works and its Edgar Thomson steel mill in Braddock convey some vestige of the illustrious industrial past. But the shopping centers, office parks, manufacturing incubator complexes, shuttered buildings, and forlorn brownfields that replaced mills and factories underscore both deindustrialization's devastation in the last quarter of the twentieth century and the uneven transformation of the Steel City into a postindustrial metropolis. Industrial neighborhoods in the City of Pittsburgh have experienced varying degrees of revitalization, and most former industrial towns in the region struggle to slow decline and find a path to recovery.[1]

As the driving force of the Pittsburgh region in the nineteenth and twentieth centuries, the once massive steel industry has demanded by its significance both commemoration and some form of historic preservation. Since the 1980s several nonprofit organizations with the aid of foundations and a few governmental agencies have endeavored to preserve aspects of the region's industrial heritage. Museum exhibits, documentary films, theatrical performances, landmark signage, heritage tours, and repurposed industrial buildings sprinkled about the region have achieved mixed success in preserving a sense of the past. Many obstacles challenge the preservation of industrial heritage. The large scale of industrial facilities proves expensive to preserve, and in the case of steel mills the buildings are not well suited for repurposing. Efforts focused on a specific industrial building and site do not adequately convey the region's industrial heritage and fail to attract governmental recognition and funding. Lingering environmental problems, the bitter legacy of labor conflicts, and weak political will in the face of development demands deter even the most dedicated preservationists. Although creating some economic opportunities, heritage tourism does little for downtrodden industrial communities and sometimes avoids them altogether.

Advocates of preserving industrial heritage in southwestern Pennsylvania and several other regions have adopted the strategy of large landscape conservation to accomplish their goals. When applied to historical resources, industrial heritage landscapes or heritage areas encompass multiple industrial sites as well as associated businesses, services, and workers' communities. Unlike designated national and state parks, heritage areas usually have vaguely defined boundaries; they include private property and living communities and depend on a mix of private and public funding sources and management structures. Designated as state heritage areas and often also recognized as national heritage areas authorized by Congress and part of the National Park Service, heritage landscapes emerge and operate with community involvement, the participation of heritage professionals, and public-private partnerships. This inclusive process frequently incurs discord among competing stakeholders, but it also presents opportunities for community empowerment and revitalization.[2]

I argue that, despite daunting obstacles, the process of preserving and managing industrial heritage landscapes has the potential to rebuild community pride and identity and contribute to imagining a revitalized future by connecting people to the past through remembering places. In recent years public historians, preservationists, and urban scholars have suggested, and in a few instances described, the possibilities of preservation for redeveloping inner city neighborhoods. The scattering of former industrial facilities and their adjacent communities around industrial regions poses preservation difficulties that are distinct from those of inner cities. However, similar to preservation in city neighborhoods, potential contributions to community redevelopment exist in the process of establishing industrial heritage areas. Heritage tourism is the most common contribution to development. Repurposing restored historic buildings for office, retail, and residential uses provides another path for redevelopment. Both paths have long been recognized and developed. However, a third contribution derives from participants in preservation projects who become inspired to extend their activism to their communities in projects and politics beyond the realm of preservation.[3]

I draw on the example of the Rivers of Steel National Heritage Area in the Pittsburgh region to illustrate the argument and indicate the problems of revitalization associated with large landscape preservation in comparison to preservation of bounded, self-contained sites. Rivers of Steel (ROS) emerged as a congressionally designated national heritage area in 1996 through an eight-year evolution from a group of volunteers determined to commemorate the Pittsburgh region's steel heritage. Members of the Steel Industry Heritage Task Force, begun in 1989, represented preservation interests, nonprofit organizations, labor unions, educational institutions, and state agencies, among other entities. The National Park Service advised the task force throughout the early years of its preservation effort. Based in a historic rehabilitated building in Homestead, ROS today includes and works in eight counties of southwestern Pennsylvania and is managed by the nonprofit Steel Industry Heritage Corporation.

CHALLENGES TO PRESERVING INDUSTRIAL HERITAGE

In spite of initial enthusiasm and dedication to preserving a community's industrial heritage, preservationists commonly faced crippling problems even before seriously engaging in the preservation process itself. Well into the 1990s the federal, state, and local governmental officials who designated historic status to properties often did not acknowledge industrial and labor buildings and sites as worthy of recognition and, therefore, funding support. Places associated with famous people and seminal events of our national saga such as Mount Vernon, Hyde Park, or Valley Forge presented little difficulty for gatekeepers. But resources as mundane as factory buildings, railroad yards, and workers' housing did not inspire similar sentiments. Officials' reluctance reflected the traditionalist origins of the preservation movement, the elite background of many preservationists, and the divisions of race, gender, and class in American society. As a result of concentrating on traditional preservation subjects, gatekeepers, in the words of landscape historians Arnold Alanen and Robert Melnick, "have generally not possessed suitable knowledge and direction to identify, evaluate, and manage, historic industrial resources."[4] Under political pressure, preservation officials eventually broadened their view to acknowledge a more diverse, inclusive national history and thus now approve sites that represent the significance of minorities, women, the working class, labor organizations, and industry. The easing of official barriers to historic status has diminished but has not entirely removed this obstacle to preserving industrial heritage.[5]

Weak political will for preservation on the part of civic leaders and the community at large has often frustrated preservation efforts. Civic leaders and former workers have pressed for redeveloping closed industrial sites in order to replace jobs and tax revenues as quickly as possible. They have disparaged preservation as being desirable but impractical and a low priority. In Homestead, for example, some workers advocated using eminent domain to take control and reopen parts of the steel mill, despite the dubious legality of the strategy and reputable studies emphasizing its lack of economic feasibility. In 1991 the mayor of Homestead supported demolishing the mill site, saying "Anything that goes down there is going to create jobs . . . be it housing, industrial, commercial. . . . I need a tax base at this point. I have nothing."[6] The more impoverished the community, the more eagerly civic leaders have embraced proposed developments, even if these required ignoring the poor quality of jobs, the inappropriateness of design, or the long-term deleterious consequences for quality of life. Commercial development has taken precedence, whether proposals called for such uses as a trash-compacting operation, warehousing that would employ few workers, or a suburban-style shopping center in an urban location, none of which would notably enhance the adjacent community. Only after economic priorities have been addressed would leaders consider preservation plans.

Other challenges have deterred the preservation of industrial heritage. The enormous scale of significant twentieth-century industries has presented questions concerning what to preserve that would convey a sense of the past and still be financially feasible. Production sites were large and buildings not easily conserved. US Steel's Homestead Works covered more than three hundred acres; Ford Motor Company's River Rouge complex encompassed twelve hundred acres. In an interview with journalist Carolyn Kitch, August (Augie) Carlino, the executive director of Rivers of Steel National Heritage Area, acknowledged that "You have to choose what you save and what you leave behind." Even after the selection of a limited number of extant buildings within such large plants, the estimated costs of stabilizing and rehabilitating them mount into millions of dollars. Modern building codes and standards—such as removing asbestos and remediating other lingering environmental toxins—pose additional financial burdens. ROS projected the expense of renovating its complex of two historically significant blast furnaces, the Carrie Furnaces numbers 6 and 7, at more than one hundred million dollars (see Figure 16.1).[7]

In addition to the large scale and daunting costs, the preservation of the industrial past may encounter the divisive issue of interpreting capitalism. While the business community has wished to celebrate industrial achievements, former workers and their unions have wanted to memorialize the sacrifices and conflicts of labor's struggles. The emotional power of past conflicts frequently has resonated with such depth that civic leaders avoid the issues surrounding industrial capitalism altogether by eschewing preservation. Further, civic leaders have not wanted to address the fundamental issues raised by shuttered plants about the negative effects of capital mobility and its uneven impacts on workers and communities.[8] These issues challenging industrial heritage preservation at the outset have led some to adopt an alternative strategy of large landscape conservation.

LANDSCAPES AND INDUSTRIAL HERITAGE

In 1984 John Brinckeroff Jackson wrote: "the longer I look at landscapes and seek to understand them, the more convinced I am that their beauty is not simply an aspect but their very essence and that that beauty derives from the human presence. . . . The beauty that we see in the vernacular landscape is the image of our common humanity: hard work, stubborn hope, and mutual forbearance striving to be love."[9] J. B. Jackson, as he was fondly known, was an iconic scholar of American cultural landscapes. In this quote he captured the essence and rationale for preserving large landscapes, including landscapes of industrial heritage. We celebrate the *hard work* of industrial workers who toiled (sometimes with great skill) under dangerous conditions, the *stubborn hope* of a better life for themselves and their children, and the *mutual forbearance* of the diverse peoples who lived out their lives in industrial communities. Forbearance was often fragile, but it was at the heart of the American industrial experience. The various sites within a large landscape reveal the rich humanity of the industrial experience.

In the last quarter of the twentieth century, preservationists discovered that the conservation of large landscapes for the protection of cultural and environmental resources offered several advantages for preserving industrial heritage. Beginning with authorization of the Cape Cod National Seashore in 1961, large landscapes with a mix of privately and publicly owned property became part of the nation's efforts to manage important and diverse resources. By the late 1980s large landscape conservation included historical resources, notably the innovative Lowell (Massachusetts) National Historical Park in 1978. The designation of the Illinois and Michigan Canal Heritage Corridor in 1984 and of the Blackstone River Valley National Heritage Corridor in 1986 provided models for the formulation of national and state heritage areas. By 2015 Congress had authorized forty-nine national heritage areas, typically with broad conservation missions. Reflecting its authorization, for example, the bylaws of the Steel Industry Heritage Corporation (the management organization for ROS) state that its purpose is "to conserve, interpret, develop and promote the historical, cultural, natural and recreational resources related to the colonial, industrial and cultural heritage of western Pennsylvania."[10]

The designation of heritage landscapes can turn the challenges of preserving large industrial resources into opportunities. Heritage landscapes are inclusive. They encompass multiple former and still operating industrial sites, associated industrial activities, and living communities that are integral to the industrial enterprise. In the words of the historical geographer Richard Francaviglia: "Heritage landscapes are associated with recognized patterns of activity in place and time. . . . They are manifestations of human activity in space . . . the essence of what gives character to and defines places." In contrast to simply recognizing a building or a group of buildings of a former mill or factory complex, landscapes expand the conception of industrial preservation to manifest more fully the industrial experience.[11]

The success of an industry depended not only on its primary production facilities but also on associated businesses, workers' communities, and the environment that together constituted an industrial system. The landscape designation may include land consumed by (in the case of southwestern Pennsylvania) transportation services such as rail yards, canals, river landings, and harbor facilities; linked manufacturers such as foundries and machine shops critical to the steel and coal industries; industrial waste operations such as slag dumps; and adjacent industrial communities where workers and their families resided, played, shopped, worshiped, and grieved (see "Searching for a Sink for an Industrial Waste" in this volume). Production sites and communities were inseparable because work so powerfully defined and shaped life. The story of the Homestead Works is incomplete without including Homestead the community; without the hole in the wall where workers were paid, and where their spouses hurried to rescue the pay envelopes; without the string of taverns trying to intercept thirsty workers and their pay envelopes; without the many churches nurturing the spiritual needs of families; without the rows of workers' housing; without Eighth Avenue, the community's once lively main street; and without Andrew

Carnegie's controversial library qua community center. The story of one cannot be conveyed and appreciated without the others.[12]

National heritage areas explicitly involve conserving environmental and recreational resources. Industries altered the environment to suit their purposes (see "The Interaction of Natural and Built Environments in the Pittsburgh Landscape" in this volume). In addition to harvesting natural resources by logging, drilling, or mining, industries cleared and leveled building sites and built drainage and sewer infrastructure. Water was critical for production. In the case of iron and steel mills, companies chose sites along water bodies from which they pumped water and returned wastes for dissolution. Water transportation required erecting docking facilities, ramps, bulkheads, and raised shorelines. Locks and dams controlled river flow for navigation. Sand and gravel companies dredged river bottoms for these essential construction materials. Industrial operations generated waste that to varying degrees polluted water, air, and land. Coal mining's gob piles, iron and steel's slag heaps, and waste water holding ponds altered and polluted land and water.[13]

The development of adjacent communities also shaped the environment. Homebuilders graded, filled, and drained land for streets and building sites. Wells tapped underground aquifers; privies sent human waste into underground vaults that were often poorly maintained. Water pumped from rivers, lakes, and bays returned to freshwater sources and ravines via sewer outflows, runoff, and industrial waste discharges. For the convenience of urban infrastructure and development, municipalities and private concerns buried streams and rerouted, straightened, and channeled water in culverts.

As industrial facilities and urban settlement endured for decades, people became inured to the altered physical properties of their towns. They accepted things as they were, and accordingly the preservation of buildings ignored the interpreting of the physical environment as well. However, preserving environmental resources in the context of industrial heritage areas embraces understanding what the environment was like before development took place and what alterations occurred. They must be recognized and interpreted as integral elements of the industrial past.[14]

Restoration of the environment in both industrial and urban contexts may not be feasible, but in some instances restoration can be introduced with remarkable results. Culverted streams may be "daylighted," wetlands nurtured back to health, and denuded hillsides reforested. Preparation of industrial buildings and brownfield sites for reuse requires remediating toxic problems. In addition to remediation, ROS works with a bioethicist for the ecological reclamation of the Carrie Furnaces site (see Figure 16.1). Rather

FIG. 16.1 Carrie Furnaces looking east, including the ore yard (courtesy of the Rivers of Steel National Heritage Area).

than simply removing invasive vegetation that recolonized the abandoned site and installing ornamental plantings, ROS follows a landscape plan, a work in progress called the "Iron Garden" that demonstrates the recolonization and succession of plants. In accordance with the recreational charge, environmental resources in a heritage area such as ROS may take the form of parks, hiking and biking trails on former railroad rights-of-way, or river landings for boating and fishing.[15]

Expanding industrial preservation to large landscapes allows the incorporation of vernacular architectural elements. Traditional preservationists assumed that industrial sites and adjacent workers' communities lacked architectural distinction. With the exception of a few buildings, the resources generally appeared ordinary—the stuff of ordinary life. Cultural and architectural historians have argued successfully for the importance of vernacular styles and elements. "Ordinary or vernacular landscapes," Alanen and Melnick believe, "are fundamental to our very existence."[16] Over many years residents, local business owners, and municipal officials haphazardly built, or minimally designed, workers' communities that emerged as an accumulation of individual decisions. In contrast, mills and factories were intentionally designed. Company owners and their engineers built, expanded, and altered industrial production sites to achieve specific outcomes. Some industrialists, either with or without engineering or architectural consultants, also planned and built communities as company towns. When companies sold the homes and new owners altered them, the intentionality of original designs diminished and a vernacular landscape appeared. The ordinary houses and commercial buildings of workers' communities, whether haphazardly developed or intentionally planned, give in Francaviglia's words "character to and define places." In their external appearance and interior compositions, they express with the aid of historical interpretation the everyday conditions that people experienced and that shaped their lives.[17]

Landscape conservation also addresses the difficult issue of change over time. Industrial landscapes are comprised of multiple layers of economic and cultural activity. Unlike isolated, often rural and scenic landscapes that seem appealingly frozen in time, they are inherently and recognizably dynamic. Needing to compete in the marketplace, industrialists turned to new products, adopted new technologies and processes, and abandoned unprofitable functions. Factories had to be reconfigured, new machines erected, and facilities demolished and replaced. New groups of workers, businesses, services, and entertainment fads changed industrial communities. Similarly, industrial decline and disinvestment led to boarded-up shops, decaying infrastructure, an influx of less desirable businesses, abandoned homes, and lower-income residents. Some older elements disappeared; others remained alongside new features. Commemoration of a former industry, labor conflict, or significant building by an isolated historical marker, a plaque on the side of a building, or a sculpture points to a past time. In contrast, designated large landscapes encompass these industrial changes. They provide a complex and dynamic pastiche of historical and living resources, rather than being fixated on a moment. Thus, the historic preservation of landscapes avoids preservationists' tendencies to, as the geographer David Lowenthal observes, "arrest change rather than accommodate transition."[18]

By accommodating change, industrial heritage landscapes record social changes that are the essence of the American experience. Just as a particular building, artifact, sound, or smell may spark a poignant memory, industrial landscapes are "storehouses" of memories that are clues to peoples' identities. They indicate, as Francaviglia avers, the "restless search for the identity that characterizes Americans as they [made] transition[s]" to new places, new technologies, and new economic activities. They evoke the travails of immigrants and migrants finding their way in adopted communities, adapting to American culture, and creating a coherent social order. They speak to the inherent contradictions of American capitalism in the contrasts of race and class that are evident in the built environment.[19]

For an example of a historic industrial landscape that projects identity, Alanen discusses Congress's authorization of the Keeweenaw National Historical Park in 1992—a dreary, abandoned, and wasting copper-mining and smelting landscape of Michigan's Upper Peninsula jutting into Lake Superior. The authorization confounded National Park Service (NPS) observers who saw Yellowstone, Yosemite, Gettysburg, or perhaps even Frederick

Law Olmsted's home and office in Fairstead, Massachusetts, as proper NPS units. A *Wall Street Journal* writer called Keeweenaw the bleakest of the NPS system's 378 units. Yet Alanen points out that the Keeweenaw National Historical Park resonated with people about "the grittiness of industrial and mining history. . . . These activities include the effects of technological changes, the role of numerous European immigrant groups in mining, the vagaries of corporate paternalism, the distinctive architectural and landscape features associated with mineral extraction and processing, and the boom-and-bust cycles characteristic of many natural resource areas."[20] This story—or more accurately as Dolores Hayden has written, "the many stories [landscapes] have to tell"—powerfully convey the Upper Peninsula's identity to Keeweenaw residents and to visitors.[21] Simultaneously, it reveals the themes of mining communities throughout the United States, whether in northeastern Pennsylvania's anthracite coal fields, the Appalachian bituminous coal region of Pennsylvania, West Virginia, or Kentucky, or Arizona's copper pits.[22]

As seen in Keeweenaw National Historical Park, the conservation of large industrial landscapes offers the opportunity to address complicated themes. The inclusion of varied and interconnected industrial activities, environmental changes, and ordinary communities—along with emotion-inspiring sites of innovation and conflict—reveals the many faces of America's industrial past. Because landscapes do not focus on a single period or place and encompass living communities, preservationists encounter the various phases of growth, conflict, civic development, and disinvestment. They must deal with the pride, hopes, and disappointments of those living in the landscape, as they strive to put together an interpretive program for a large area. In short, they cannot simply impose a viewpoint and program on a living landscape. They must establish partnerships and coordinate with a community's planning for its future, or if planning has not begun, they have to be a party to stimulating the envisioning of a future.[23]

CONTESTED SPACE, CULTURAL INTERPRETATION

The potential of historic landscapes for celebrating and understanding America's industrial past lies in fashioning an evocative and effective cultural interpretation. Landscape architecture professor Catherine Howett argues that "the quality and importance of any preservation project is determined not by the integrity of the site, but [by] the quality of what is made of the site through interpretation of its history. That is added value that can turn even a precious few evocative fragments, transformed by intelligence and imagination, into significant history; without it, even historic sites of exceptional integrity will remain sterile."[24] Arriving at an effective interpretation, however, challenges stakeholders to overcome emotional and practical issues. The diversity of American society and imperatives of capitalism along with the desire of stakeholders to celebrate their own pasts render industrial heritage landscapes contested space.

At the heart of conflict over interpreting industrial heritage landscapes lies the question of whose view of the past will be foregrounded, whose story will be told. Stakeholders in any historic industrial landscape bring to deliberations of preservation their special interests, ideological perspectives, and anger toward some participants, particularly those who belong to other social groups or who represent capital entities. The stakeholders can be many and varied, ranging from displaced workers and despairing community members to developers, industry managers, representatives of public agencies, historical experts, and preservationists.[25] Choosing a viewpoint for interpretation inherently risks not telling other stories and offending those who feel left out. Workers of industries not included in the story and the minorities and women whose historical contributions are often overlooked often feel slighted.

In an industrial heritage landscape, members of management and labor commonly eye each other warily across the table after decades of distrust and conflict. Disinvestment and shuttered factories exacerbate longstanding mutual hostilities. Workers blame management for disinvesting; managers blame workers and unions for inflexibility and excessive labor costs. At ROS, the steel companies, notably US Steel, and workers, particularly the United Steel Workers of America, feared that their story would not be told or that it would be told from the wrong perspective.[26]

Disagreements commonly divide stakeholders. In Homestead, local labor groups felt they had proprietary ownership over parts of the story and the landscape. Factions split workers over what should be preserved and how to do it. They all distrusted ROS as academics and outsiders. One labor group called ROS carpetbaggers, even though some of its members were part of the preservation organization. They further disliked ROS for its ability to partner with and raise funds from "downtown" foundations and companies, as well to obtain grants from state and federal sources. These entities symbolized for workers more than a century of struggle with the companies, the enemy in battles that characterized labor relations in the Pittsburgh industrial district. The journalist William Serrin portrayed ROS as a creature of Pittsburgh's power structure, "a continuation of the paternalism and authoritarianism that had existed for a century." Trust among most stakeholders and with the heritage area staff grew, and then only slowly, through working together on special projects. Some participants who were unable to resolve their differences quit ROS.[27]

Difficulties and conflicts arise from the depressed state of the communities and the diversity of social groups that live in designated heritage landscapes. People become depressed not just economically but also psychologically. The industrial communities that remain after plant closings feel tossed aside on the scrapheap of capitalism's "creative destruction." To the media and to themselves they seem to be failed communities. Often already in decline because many workers and their families had taken advantage of unionization's success and various public policy incentives to leave for the suburbs, once the plant was shuttered industrial communities suffered further weakening of local shops and services, tax bases, civic capacity, and their sense of place. In some places, new racially diverse and lower-income groups replaced departing working-class families. The demographic turnover, in the words of historian Robert Archibald, causes memory to lose "its moorings" and "imperils the bonds of civic life."[28] Those who had links to the adjacent industries before disinvestment and were experiencing the decline of their communities as they knew them engage preservation planning with little desire to participate. Many in Homestead projected their despair and anger on ROS. They saw preservation as being the project of outsiders. The mayor expressed these sentiments when she said, "These people don't know what working class people are all about. They're all college experts. They never got their hands dirty. . . . These people don't even know nothin' about it." Moreover, she and others anticipated only the development of parks, trails, and other aesthetic embellishments instead of manufacturing jobs that might bring back the good old days. The 1988 Remaking Cities Conference with England's Prince Charles in attendance and hosted in Pittsburgh reinforced this perception of preservation. A design team studied the Monongahela valley communities and particularly Homestead over the course of a few days and recommended among other things using some mill buildings for flower exhibitions. The reaction of the mayor and labor activists was visceral and negative.[29]

Although a landscape embraces multiple time periods and communities for potential interpretation, its designation as a heritage area may not initially satisfy the various voices at the table. For one thing, some stakeholders argue for a most important period. Advocacy of a period, when other periods present reasonable alternatives, stems from the proponent's desire for the landscape to reflect a specific legacy. Dissension ensues. The distrust, the cacophony of voices, and at times the hostility evinced by some participants and outside in the community make public historians and members from public agencies uncomfortable. The messy time-consuming grassroots process of sorting out viewpoints and periods may clash with the experts' assumptions of what is important. Even though declarations of national significance by historians may be impressive, local participants tend to foreground stories that emphasize local importance. The stakeholders must search for a balance in viewpoint and periods that accommodates their diverse perspectives.[30]

Choices of viewpoint and period depend in part on adequate documentation of historical authenticity. Over time cherished, sometimes metaphorical, stories take on the semblance of truth. David Lowenthal points out that the preserved past is an artifact of the present. People's memories become selective. They romanticize past events, places, and individuals, leaving out negatives that counter their stories. They shape the past to fit psychological or political purposes. In addition to the bias of memory, text materials and landscapes that are read as texts are inherently ambiguous and subject to readers' interpretations. Documentation helps sort out myth from fact and partial truths from more accurate views of the past. Historical scholarship that addresses ambiguity and that grounds interpretation in fact helps preservationists obtain the commitment and cooperation of governmental and civic partners, as well as that of the community, for an interpretive program.[31]

The success of interpretation for preservation rests not only on adequate documentation but also on the historical integrity of the buildings, sites, and landscapes under consideration. While the landscape approach aids in overcoming the problems of viewpoint, change over time, and inclusivity, it can work against favorable assessments of historical integrity. The NPS views integrity as "the ability of a property [or landscape] to convey its significance. . . . The physical record must be sufficiently intact . . . to allow the visitor to experience an environment that existed at a specific time in the past."[32] The NPS and state officials have often adhered to a strict definition of integrity, meaning a resource's being unimpaired and complete. However, as we have seen, industrial sites and landscapes are dynamic and layered with resources of more than one period. Alterations were inevitable. At ROS, for example, NPS officials deemed the site at the pump house and water tower, where the Pinkerton detectives landed to take control of the mill in the infamous Homestead Strike of 1892, lacked integrity and therefore was ineligible for landmark status. Despite depictions of these two structures in the contemporary imagery of the day, their merit was compromised in NPS's judgment by the company's having replaced the sloping mudflat of the riverbank with a vertical hard-edged bulkhead sometime after 1892. That the alteration had occurred was not contestable. However, iconic status of the pump house and water tower failed to outweigh the loss of the mudflat. Determination of acceptable integrity that is "sufficiently intact" is frequently a subjective judgment, making integrity a handy criterion with which to reject an application for other less transparent reasons.

The large scale of many industrial sites raises the question with respect to integrity as to how many and which structures must remain to convey significance. In the case of the Homestead Works, an industrial salvaging company demolished nearly all of the mill buildings on the three-hundred-acre site. Only a very small portion of the historic resources remained intact. In some ways demolition rendered the site similar to revered battlefields that sustained substantial physical and land use alterations before being designated and preserved for their historical significance.[33] The argument became whether the remaining elements of the steelworks and especially the rich built environment of the adjacent community offered sufficient resources for an effective interpretation of the industrial landscape that could convey a sense of the past.

Cultural traditions growing out of communities' ethnic background and intimate connections to local industry contribute to the integrity of industrial heritage. Dolores Hayden has asserted that "the cultural landscapes [including industrial ones] tell us who we are, as Americans, far more effectively than most architecture or exhibits in museums ever can."[34] Such a statement triggers debate among public history professionals, but it does point out the necessity of assessing cultural traditions in determining historical integrity. The physical resources of communities, which are associated with the broader understanding of the American past that includes race, gender, and class, are often vulnerable to change because of their ordinary architecture, low economic value, and/or disinvestment. Many stores on the main commercial street may be empty, some churches closed because of too few congregants, and homes abandoned or entire streets of former neighborhoods deemed "blighted" and cleared of buildings. Struggling industrial communities testify to the mobility of capital just as industrial ruins do, but people carry on with the cultural and folk-life traditions of their working class and their ethnic cultures, which provide solace, continuity, and coherence. The culture of living communities adapts to altered circumstances and "transcend[s] the physical remains." Because the factory and community form "an industrial-cultural system," the question of historical significance and integrity for industrial heritage landscapes should consider not only the built environment but also the community's "cultural beliefs, values, practices, and institutions."[35]

Cultural traditions can be surveyed, evaluated, and protected in much the same manner as physical resources. The Pennsylvania Heritage Affairs Commission urged ROS from its early days to include cultural conservation in its preservation planning. With funding from state and federal programs and the participation of multiple partners, during the 1990s ROS conducted ethnographic fieldwork and studies as a means to survey living cultural traditions across its several counties. The ROS director of cultural conservation archived numerous photographs, videos, and audio tapes of interviews, crafts, and performances. In 1999 the state designated ROS as the Regional Folklife Center for Southwestern Pennsylvania. ROS believed that cultural traditions warranted conservation in their own right and that together cultural conservation and physical preservation underscored historical integrity and significance and contributed to community revitalization.[36]

The standards for integrity must be less tied to rigid applications of physical completeness and flexible enough to accommodate the inherent difficulties of the enormous scale of sites, change in them over time, multiple periods of significance, and the integral character of a community and its culture. Otherwise, official gatekeepers can wield the standard of integrity to trump significance despite, as Howett argues, the development of an evocative, imaginative, and intelligent interpretation of history.[37] A negative review can jeopardize the preservation enterprise in the eyes of civic leaders and the community.

PRESERVATION PROCESS AND COMMUNITY REVITALIZATION

The process of fashioning, in the face of the many challenges, a successful cultural interpretation for a historic industrial landscape introduces possibilities of thinking beyond the preserving of buildings or sites to imagine a future for communities. The discussions and negotiations through which community members connect with their history and place, in the words of Hayden, "enhance the possibilities of creative practice."[38] Even if the process collapses with the failure to arrive at a mutually acceptable and successful interpretation, the struggle awakens memory; renews community self-esteem, identity, and pride; uncovers opportunities for projects; and subsequently contributes to community empowerment and envisioning a constructive future. Rivers of Steel offers an example of dedicated stakeholders engaging in the process of preserving the industrial heritage of a large and complicated industrial region. During the course of years of hard work, the process produced solid, though mixed, results in preservation and community revitalization.

When it formed in 1988, the Steel Industry Heritage Task Force undertook four interrelated efforts: development of a preservation plan, establishment of state and national recognition and funding, creation of the organizational capacity to pursue its goals, and contributions to community revitalization. Precedents that inspired the task force ranged from the early federal industrial preservation model of Lowell (Massachusetts) National Historical Park to the Southwestern Pennsylvania Heritage Preservation Commission centered on Johnstown and Altoona. However, a formal federal national heritage area program did not exist, and Pennsylvania had only just initiated its Heritage Area Program in 1989. Without a federal program in place, the task force did not have a clear view of what final form the preservation effort might take. Further difficulties arose when some NPS officials questioned the significance of industry and labor themes and resources for their programs. Additionally, the diverse members of the task force engaged in animated discussions as they sorted out the issues of viewpoint and labored to forge trust within the group. Nonetheless, with help from state and NPS officials, along with federal government funding, the task force groped toward a preservation plan.[39]

Challenged by the ongoing demolition of historic industrial resources across the region, the task force needed to formulate a preservation plan as soon as possible, raise funds, and establish credibility with civic leaders and depressed industrial communities. Initially without staff, the task force did not have the capacity to carry out any necessary studies, build relationships with key leaders and agencies, and implement early projects. Eventually, funding from local foundations and the federal government enabled the task force to hire staff and tackle more effectively the many issues facing it.

In 1990 the task force entered into a memorandum of understanding with the City of Pittsburgh, several counties and state agencies, the NPS, the Mon Valley Initiative (MVI), and a regional planning commission to undertake "a cooperative planning effort for the purpose of developing a broadly supported Mon Valley Steel Heritage Concept Plan/Feasibility Study and Action Plan." Funded under Pennsylvania's new Heritage Park Act and by a federal grant, the study and subsequent concept plan was an important step in obtaining designation as a state heritage park and a national heritage area. The 1993 plan advanced an overview of the Pittsburgh region's industrial past; itemized extant industrial, cultural, and natural resources; identified significant themes; and proposed three alternative preservation plans. Because of its varied activities and acceptance of funds, the task force reorganized as a nonprofit corporation, called the Steel Industry Heritage Corporation (SIHC). Based on the concept plan, SIHC initiated a final planning process with the aid of consultants and extensive public participation.

The process resulted in the 1996 management action plan and the proposal to the state and Congress for designation as the Rivers of Steel National Heritage Area. The plan envisioned "Making the region a national and regional destination" through heritage tourism and recreational projects that would create economic development opportunities.[40]

Although ROS grew from the fervor for historic preservation, it always embraced the additional goal of contributing to community development beyond just heritage tourism. Within months of the task force's inception, its leadership promoted preservation as one additional way to stimulate revitalization of the region's industrial communities. Redevelopment projects competed for limited financial and political resources, and preservation proposals were not high priorities of civic leaders. In response to the economic devastation of deindustrialization, political, private, and nonprofit leaders considered any and all strategies for some recovery. But they believed that heritage tourism would at best modestly contribute to revitalization efforts. In contrast, a few task force members saw that connecting people to their past and place had the potential to energize the communities to imagine a different future and empower them to take action.[41]

When Jo DeBolt agreed to voluntarily chair the task force in 1988, she was the executive director of the Mon Valley Initiative, an umbrella community development assistance organization for more than a dozen depressed industrial communities in the Monongahela River valley. An experienced community organizer, she believed historic preservation had the potential to complement MVI's community development mission. The organizers of the task force—and later SIHC—went into dispirited industrial communities to awaken pride in their past and demonstrate that outsiders from local as well as state and federal organizations valued their industrial achievements, labor struggles, and ethnic cultures. Further, efforts to preserve historical resources and cultural traditions reconnected some workers and their families who had moved to the suburbs ("over the hills and across the bridges," as they say in Pittsburgh) with their industrial and cultural roots. Reawakening bonds of ethnicity, work, and place, preservation established a sense of common history, fate, and purpose within and across some communities. It also added political and sometimes financial support.[42]

The preservation of the forty-eight-inch rolling mill of the Homestead Works exemplified the importance of tackling a significant and recognizable project for arousing community interest. Iconic images of the past, writes Francaviglia, "re-affirm the community . . . asserting durability, dependability, and traditional values."[43] For steel communities, blast furnaces, ladles that poured tons of molten steel, or physical reminders of labor's

Fig. 16.2 Dismantling the forty-eight-inch rolling mill of the Homestead Works (courtesy of the Rivers of Steel National Heritage Area).

struggles to improve working conditions provide such comforting images in the face of the catastrophic changes and enormous challenges presented by deindustrialization. Preserving the forty-eight-inch mill became part of the community's rediscovery of its past. The industrial salvaging company that bought the entire Homestead site from US Steel slated the mill and its shed for demolition. However, Smithsonian experts determined that the rolling mill was an outstanding example of late nineteenth-century steelmaking technology. With the aid of staff from the Historical American Engineering Record of NPS, SIHC documented the mill. It advertised for workers who had tended the mill and conducted oral interviews with them. ROS hired a rigging company with industrial strength cranes, trucks, and appropriate experience to take apart the roll stand, rolling tables, and power engine. Former workers and ROS staff marked and greased the disassembled parts, and ROS stored it at considerable expense for future restoration and interpretation (see Figure 16.2). The process took several weeks, generated community interest and publicity, and resulted in ten years of annual reunion celebrations of workers at the Homestead Carnegie Library. The resulting goodwill within the community established valuable momentum for subsequent preservation and development efforts.[44]

A successful preservation plan for a living industrial heritage landscape cannot be devised and imposed by a committee comprised of only historians, preservation planners, governmental advisors, and civic leaders. In the words of historian David Schuyler and landscape architect Patricia O'Donnell, "Physical planning that lacks broad support will remain a report rather than a renewed landscape."[45] In order to elicit grassroots buy-in for preservation, ROS conducted endless meetings, community organizing events, lectures, fieldtrips, and interviews. Initially, staff members went into communities to identify individuals interested in preservation and revitalization. Then they organized meetings to collect, share, and discuss the community members' photos, tapes, heirlooms, and stories (see Figure 16.3).

Regardless of how historically accurate, stories have special power in reviving community self-esteem and identity. SIHC's staff reworked the materials into presentations of community history for follow-up meetings, often in conjunction with groups such as Rotary or Kiwanus Clubs. The contrast between the past and the present frequently led to discussions of what could be saved to honor this history and to help construct a positive future for the community. SIHC midwifed dozens of preservation and recreational projects across the region, identifying funding opportunities and providing technical advice and review of applications. Beyond sparking interest in projects for main streets, trails, and riverfront rehabilitation, the meetings developed a network of people for initiating discussions about community needs and building local political support.[46]

Examples of Rivers of Steel's preservation efforts can be found in a couple of older Monongahela River towns. ROS assisted a group of concerned citizens to preserve the closed W. A. Young & Sons Foundry and Machine Shop in Rice's Landing Borough in Greene County. Located on the Monongahela River, the decades-old business repaired steamboat engines, mining machinery, and agricultural equipment. The owners padlocked the doors in the 1960s, leaving intact a veritable museum of similar shops that filled vital niches throughout the region. Community members and ROS raised funds and hired a contractor to stabilize the resource. In addition, ROS helped the town with comprehensive planning, signage, and the development of a riverfront trail and trailhead as part of a large county trail project.[47]

Several miles north of Rice's Landing, Brownsville had once thrived as a river port and a stop on the National Road (later US Route 40). But the small city had declined in recent decades, as evidenced by an intact, though deteriorating, collection of multistory buildings in its compact downtown. ROS assisted the Brownsville Area Redevelopment Corporation and the Mon Valley Initiative in restoring the Flat Iron Building with the goal of igniting the adaptive reuse of several more buildings. After the initial enthusiasm

Fig. 16.3 Typical industrial community meeting for the sharing of memories, photographs, and artifacts (courtesy of the Rivers of Steel National Heritage Area).

of attracting new tenants, however, downtown did not experience a rebirth. It languished. A speculator bought up downtown property in hopes of winning a casino license and benefiting from subsequent development. Lawsuits and the state's failure to legalize casino gambling left downtown in limbo. Meanwhile, ROS helped Brownsville obtain funding for riverfront improvements. Preservation and community assistance stabilized Rice's Landing, while adaptive reuse in Brownsville floundered amid speculative and political forces the small city could not control.[48]

At the same time, ROS promoted community participation and redevelopment through preserving historical resources. It encouraged cultural conservation activities to enhance these goals. Folk arts such as music, quilting, painting, and foodways brought people together, conveyed a sense of community stability, and suggested other means to address a sustainable future. Coordinating with the preservation staff, ROS's director of cultural conservation Doris Dyen initiated surveys of community cultural assets, organized school programs, conducted oral histories, ran grant workshops, and obtained grants from, for example, the Pennsylvania Folk Arts Council. The cultural program fostered many projects such as craft demonstrations, musical performances, ethnic cookbooks, preservation of murals in social halls and churches, and "inside-out" tours. These latter bus, boat, and walking tours brought outsiders to a site or community with insiders recruited from former mill workers, ethnic groups, or other community organizations to lead the tours. For example, "Babuskas and Hard Hats" tours explored "the magical mix of immigrants and industry." Local guides established authenticity to the tours, engaged in informal dialogue with the outsiders, and built pride among community members who now understood that outsiders valued their traditions.

One of the more unlikely—but hugely successful—programs was "Kitchen Tables Stories," in which four older women onstage at the Frick Art & Historical Center reminisced about their lives in Homestead. That Homestead women would be willing to go to the former home of the historically bitter enemy of mill workers, Henry Clay Frick, and that the Frick would welcome the women astonished both the audience and the women. ROS also established an ongoing, fruitful relationship with the Bulgarian Macedonian National Educational and Cultural Center in West Homestead. ROS helped the center obtain grants for planning, for building restoration, and for establishing archives. The center grew in membership, attracted younger members, and greatly expanded its programming. It has become an active community institution. After several years of the cultural conservation, ROS published a small book titled *Routes to Roots*, which identified seven self-guided tours of cultural sites throughout the region. Together the preservation and cultural conservation programs constructed a grassroots foundation of community participation that belied the lip service to public participation often touted by preservation and governmental agencies.[49]

In order to establish credibility and obtain governmental recognition and funding, ROS had to forge relationships with civic leaders, politicians, and officials of state and federal agencies. The inherently political nature of preservation activity required lobbying and constant nurturing of constructive, respectful, enduring, and personal relationships. In a 2003 interview with Constance Bodurow, Carlino emphasized the point. "If you think merit will win out, you are naïve. You need the political support—not only in Washington, it has to be something the region supports." ROS worked assiduously to turn these relationships into strong partnerships, especially with the NPS, Congress, the Pennsylvania Department of Conservation and Natural Resources, local foundations, and business and labor leaders. At moments of sharp disagreement with agency officials and with crises in state and federal budgeting processes, the web of partnerships provided the political access, support, and leadership that were crucial for obtaining favorable decisions to implement aspects of the preservation plan.[50]

Some community members became empowered by participating in

the planning process and the development of partnerships. Because ROS included multiple local jurisdictions, the preservation process brought together members from communities with similar industrial heritages. In the course of sorting out a plan and discussing how to build political support, they developed a rapport and more of a common perspective in contrast to the region's legendary parochialism. As Brenda Barrett, the former national coordinator for heritage areas in the NPS, explained: "The heritage area strategy is based on working collaboratively across boundaries to develop common vision based on a region's shared heritage. What that gives communities is a sense that they can in some way determine their future."[51]

Although the staff and board of directors had the primary responsibility to establish and maintain partnerships, ROS bussed community members to Harrisburg to meet with state legislators and agency personnel. Community members also met politicians and private leaders at local events. The experiences informed them how to engage the political process, for both its possibilities and its limitations. To paraphrase one local participant after a visit by a touring US senator, "he treated me just like I was a real person!"[52] Participation gave them the tools and the confidence to work for community redevelopment.

Inspired by preservation and cultural programs and/or participation in the planning process, some community members transferred their desire to improve their communities to projects not directly involving preservation. ROS could not be the vehicle for advocacy that was unrelated to its mission, but these newly active folks connected with their local community development organizations and with the Mon Valley Initiative. They advocated for housing policies, transportation enhancements, and career training. They formed a network of individuals identified through ROS's organizing activities, which spanned several communities and could be tapped to apply political pressure on legislators, agency officials, and local leaders. A few individuals, often women, became politically active in their communities and challenged the entrenched leadership.[53]

The success or failure of industrial heritage landscape preservation in contributing to the revitalization of communities depends not only on the typical problems challenging preservation but also on factors beyond the control of preservationists. In sorting out the issues of viewpoint, period, documentation, and integrity, preservationists confront the necessity of reaching consensus on an effective interpretation. Failure to do so results in what Carolyn Kitch calls "interpretive paralysis," which dooms the effort. Once over the interpretive hurdle, preservationists must fashion strategies to address multiple sites and communities and to cover high costs. The large scale and dispersed character of industrial heritage landscapes diminish the collective impact of successful projects and hinder collaborative efforts on nonpreservation issues. Those feeling that their sites have not received proper attention may become disaffected and drop out of the preservation effort. In this sense, strategic planning may exacerbate traditional parochialism, even as the planning process works to combat the fragmentation of communities across the heritage area. While one community celebrates a restored historic main street building or the completion of a trail segment and a river landing, other communities remain myopically focused on their own issues. They may not recognize a neighbor's good fortune as a success for the broader effort. Mainstream media's spotty reporting on depressed communities (other than for crimes or fires) renders successes nearly invisible to the region as a whole.[54]

While the heritage area's management organization wrestles with the myriad sites, communities, and personalities encompassed in its territory, national and state political and economic trends can overwhelm implementation strategies. Economic downturns in the years 2000 and 2008 stressed governmental budgets and private sector earnings and diminished funding opportunities for ROS and other national heritage areas. Once reduced or eliminated, budget lines for heritage and community revitalization programs are difficult to restore. With or without a declining economy, political power shifts in Washington and state governments alter public policy. Carefully constructed and nurtured partnerships can lose their political efficacy as elections either change the party in power or simply defeat key politicians. New administrations and legislative leaders have different priorities and may appoint agency directors who are less favorably disposed to preservation, heritage areas, or even particular regions. The retreat of government from preservation and revitalization after the 2008 economic crisis has forced heritage areas and communities to depend more on private and foundation funding sources. Relationships and partnership-building remain critical, but the depth of financial resources and opportunities for leveraging funds has diminished. The spinoff effects of preservation for community revitalization have suffered accordingly.

The vicissitudes of economic and political trends do not necessarily doom the enterprise, however. A heritage area and its community partners must be patient, persistent, innovative, and agile in order to continue their work. The ROS plan to turn the Carrie Furnaces into a major exhibit of iron production foundered initially on the lack of cooperation from the industrial salvaging company that owned the site. Subsequently, local political machinations over the redevelopment of the large brownfield that envelops the furnaces delayed transfer of them to ROS. The politics of federal budgeting and the budgetary impact of the 2008 recession presented additional problems. Despite these formidable obstacles, ROS has stabilized the Carrie Furnaces, slowly improved them (with plenty more to accomplish), obtained the valuable participation of volunteers, and programmed the furnaces successfully beyond expectations. Tours, workshops, programmed events, and numerous event rentals such as filming venues and weddings packed the annual event schedules. Fees and taxes from the revenue-producing programs went to the local municipality. Strategies and methods have changed to meet new circumstances, but restoration has continued and has inspired individuals from several communities.[55] Although the impact of a single project for a community can be determined, the collective impact of preservation projects for the heritage area is difficult to evaluate. More difficult yet is to determine the impact for communities of inspired community activism beyond preservation.

CONCLUSION

The preservation of America's industrial past presents difficult challenges for those wishing to convey a visceral sense and understanding of this once defining feature of the nation while contributing to the revitalization of adjacent industrial communities. Rehabilitation of a factory building, coal mine site, or worker's house has succeeded in interpreting a specific industry and generated some heritage tourism with modest economic benefits. A few comparatively self-contained, large industrial sites such as Lowell National Historical Park have succeeded in combining restoration and adaptive reuse of former industrial buildings. These mixed-use postindustrial redevelopment projects marry heritage sites with entertainment venues to create attractions for tourists and regional consumers. Planning for them may have been participatory and initially contested; but whether privately owned or under governmental control, a single entity or commission orchestrated the development. In contrast, large industrial complexes that shaped entire urban regions, which remain iconic images of twentieth-century America, defy straightforward development as heritage entertainment destinations. Preservation of large steelworks or automotive factories is simply impractical. Consequently, preservationists have turned to defining and working with living landscape areas formally designated as national heritage areas.

The number of living communities, industrial sites, and governmental entities in a national heritage area complicates the preservation planning process. Industrial heritage landscapes share with more site-specific preservation efforts the goal of connecting people with the past and places in order to revive pride in previous generations' achievements, skills, and struggles. But the complexity of living landscape preservation emphasizes the necessity of negotiated interpretations, community participation, and strong partnerships with public and private entities. In addition to preserving historical resources, the broad mission of national heritage areas to also conserve cultural, natural, and recreational resources lends itself to initiating projects that usually fall outside the goals of community and economic development organizations. National heritage areas partner with communities and a broad array of governmental agencies and organizations to identify projects and generate funding for them. The planning process sparks community activism among some participants and imparts confidence to work on a brighter future for their communities. The many former industrial communities in large industrial heritage landscape areas scatter projects across a region, diminishing the perception of an overall economic impact. However, within communities, projects have visibility and may become part of a larger transformative effort. Simultaneously, activists understand the importance of working with folks in other communities on shared political goals. While commemorating the industrial past and growing heritage tourism, industrial heritage landscape preservation becomes another platform for revitalizing industrial communities.

NOTES

1. The mills at Homestead, Braddock, and Duquesne were part of Andrew Carnegie's iron and steel empire until he sold them in 1901 as part of the formation of US Steel. For Pittsburgh as a postindustrial city, see Roy Lubove, *Twentieth-Century Pittsburgh, Vol. 2: The Post-Steel Era* (Pittsburgh: University of Pittsburgh Press, 1996); Allen Dieterich-Ward, *Beyond Rust: Metropolitan Pittsburgh and the Fate of Industrial America* (Philadelphia: University of Pennsylvania Press, 2016); Tracy Neumann, *Remaking the Rust Belt: The Postindustrial Transformation of North America* (Philadelphia: University of Pennsylvania Press, 2016).

2. Brenda Barrett, "Roots for the National Heritage Area Family Tree," and Constance C. Budurow, "The Vehicle for Conserving and Interpreting Our Recent Industrial Heritage," both in *The George Wright Forum* 20, no. 2 (June 2003): 41–49, 68–88. If defined, boundaries for industrial heritage areas usually are local municipal or county boundaries. I use the term "preservationists" in a broad sense to include not just preservation professionals but also those engaged in preserving a historical resource. An older brochure of the NPS defines national heritage areas in a manner that reveals the NPS bias toward physical geography: "A National Heritage Area is a place where natural, cultural, historic, and scenic resources combine to form a cohesive, nationally distinctive landscape arising from patterns of human activity shaped by geography. These patterns make National Heritage Areas representative of the national experience through the physical features that remain and the traditions that evolved in them." *National Heritage Areas* (Washington, DC: National Park Service, 2005), n.p.

3. Dolores Hayden, *The Power of Place: Urban Landscapes as Public History* (Cambridge, MA: MIT Press, 1995); Andrew Hurley, *Beyond Preservation: Using Public History to Revitalize Inner Cities* (Philadelphia: Temple University Press, 2010); Ned Kaufman, *Place, Race, and Story: Essays on the Past and Future of Historic Preservation* (New York: Routledge, 2009); Chloe E. Taft, *From Steel to Slots: Casino Capitalism in the Postindustrial City* (Cambridge, MA: Harvard University Press, 2016). In various publications and interviews, the cofounder of Pittsburgh History & Landmarks Foundation Arthur P. Ziegler has stated his belief that historic preservation of homes in working-class and low-income neighborhoods was another form of urban renewal. See Lubove, *Twentieth-Century Pittsburgh, Vol. 2*, 223–24.

4. Arnold R. Alanen and Robert Z. Melnick, "Introduction: Why Cultural Landscape Preservation," in Arnold R. Alanen and Robert Z. Melnick, eds., *Preserving Cultural Landscapes in America* (Baltimore: Johns Hopkins University Press, 2000), 12. Even today many gatekeepers are reluctant to consider recognizing industry and labor nominations and do so sometimes only under pressure. Bodurow, "Vehicle for Conserving," 82.

5. Hurley, *Beyond Preservation*, 1–46.

6. Daniel Holland, "Historic Preservation of Industrial Worksites: Homestead, Pennsylvania, A Case Study" (unpublished senior thesis, Carnegie Mellon University, 1991), 43.

7. Bodurow, "Vehicle for Conserving," 73–82; Carolyn Kitch, *Pennsylvania in Public Memory: Reclaiming the Industrial Past* (University Park: Pennsylvania State University, 2012), 175; Eleanor Mahoney, "Industrial Heritage at Risk: How National Heritage Areas Have Preserved the Landscape of Labor and Why This Capacity Is Now in Jeopardy," http://www.livinglandscapeobserver.net, 3; Anne E. Mosher, e-mail message to author, July 13, 2015. For an overview of the difficulties involved in preserving large industrial sites, see Daniel Campo, "Historic Preservation in an Economic Void: Reviving Buffalo's Concrete Atlantis," *Journal of Planning History* 15, no. 4 (2016): 318–23. Built in 1907, the Carrie Furnaces are the two remaining blast furnaces of a complex begun in the 1890s. They sit on thirty-three acres of land on the south shore of the Monongahela River. They produced iron that was transported across the river to the Homestead Works. Closed in 1978, they stand ninety-two feet high and were designated a national historic landmark. The hundred-million-dollar estimate presumes restoration to a pristine condition; ROS is programming the furnaces today in a state more as "rustic ruins," even as ongoing improvements are made.

8. Mahoney, "Industrial Heritage at Risk," 3; Holland, "Historic Preservation," 25–31.

9. John Brinckerhoff Jackson, *Discovering the Vernacular Landscape* (New Haven: Yale University Press, 1984), xii.

10. *By-Laws of Rivers of Steel National Heritage Corporation*, as amended; effective 01/23/14 (a Pennsylvania nonprofit corporation), 1, in the possession of Rivers of Steel National Heritage Area, Homestead, Pennsylvania. See also J. Glenn Eugster, "Evolution of the Heritage Area Movement," *The George Wright Forum* 20, no. 2 (June 2003): 50–59; Barrett, "National Heritage Area Family Tree," 41–49. The best example of preserving a large steel and coal industrial landscape is Germanv's Emscherpark in the Ruhr valley. See http://www.doc.dk/en/doc-cities/sustainable-cities/.

11. Richard V. Francaviglia, "Selling Heritage Landscapes," in Alanen and Melnick, *Preserving Cultural Landscapes*, 49.

12. See Margaret Byington, *Homestead: The Households of a Mill Town* (New York: Russell Sage Foundation, 1910), 37, 171; William Serrin, *Homestead: The Glory and*

Tragedy of an American Steel Town (New York: Vintage Books, 1993), 16–25, 55–65; Doris J. Dyen and Edward K. Muller, "Conserving the Heritage of Industrial Communities: The Compromising Issue of Integrity," *Historic Preservation Forum* 81, no. 4 (1994): 38. Homestead as commonly referred to is comprised of three municipalities—Homestead, West Homestead, and Munhall. Carnegie's gift of a grand multifunctional library, potentially serving as a community center, was controversial for many in Homestead because of the company's harsh working conditions and treatment of its mill workers as well as the violent repression of workers in the Homestead Strike of 1892.

13. Edward K. Muller and Joel A. Tarr, "The Interaction of Natural and Built Environments in the Pittsburgh Landscape," in Joel A. Tarr, ed., *Devastation and Renewal: Perspectives on the Environmental History of Pittsburgh and Its Region* (Pittsburgh, PA: University of Pittsburgh Press, 2003), 11–40; Edward K. Muller, "River City," in Tarr, *Devastation and Renewal*, 41–63.

14. S. J. Kleinberg, *The Shadow of the Mills: Working-Class Families in Pittsburgh, 1870–1907* (Pittsburgh, PA: University of Pittsburgh Press, 1989), 65–99.

15. Hurley, *Beyond Preservation*, 120–45; August Carlino, e-mail to author, April 12, 2016, in which he cites http;//www.post-gazette.com/life/homes/2011/08/20/Natural-look-advocated-for-Carrie-Furnaces-site/stories/201108200218; Nine Mile Run Watershed Association, http://www.ninemilerun.org.

16. Alanen and Melnick, "Introduction," 5. See also D. W. Meinig, "Introduction," in D. W. Meinig, ed., *The Interpretation of Ordinary Landscape: Geographical Essays* (Oxford: Oxford University Press, 1979), 6.

17. Francaviglia, "Selling Heritage Landscapes," 49.

18. Lowenthal quoted from Alanen and Melnick, "Introduction," 9. See also David Lowenthal, "Age and Artifact: Dilemmas of Appreciation," in Meinig, *Ordinary Landscapes*, 103–28; Kirk Savage, "Monuments of a Lost Cause: The Campaign to Commemorate Steel," in Jefferson Cowie and Joseph Heathcott, eds., *Beyond the Ruins: The Meaning of Deindustrialization* (Ithaca, NY: Cornell University Press, 2003), 237–56.

19. Francaviglia, "Selling Heritage Landscapes," 69. See also Mahoney, "Industrial Heritage at Risk," 3.

20. Arnold R. Alanen, "Considering the Ordinary: Vernacular Landscapes in Small Towns and Rural Areas," in Alanen and Melnick, *Preserving Cultural Landscapes*, 136.

21. Dolores Hayden, "Foreword: In Search of the American Cultural Landscape," in Alanen and Melnick, *Preserving Cultural Landscapes*, ix.

22. Richard V. Francaviglia, *Hard Places: Reading the Landscapes of America's Historic Mining Districts* (Iowa City: University of Iowa Press, 1991); Geoffrey L. Buckley, *Extracting Appalachia: Images of the Consolidated Coal Company, 1910–1945* (Athens: Ohio University Press, 2004); Margaret M. Mulrooney, *A Legacy of Coal: The Coal Towns of Southwestern Pennsylvania* (Washington, DC: HABS/HAER, National Park Service, 1989).

23. Author's interview with Jo Debolt, February 1, 2016, notes in possession of the author; Bodurow, "Vehicle for Conserving," 84–86; Miles Orvell, "Ruins," in Miles Orvell and Klaus Benesch, eds., *Rethinking the American City: An International Dialogue* (Philadelphia: University of Pennsylvania Press, 2014), 71–92.

24. Catherine Howett, "Integrity as a Value in Cultural Landscape Preservation" in Alanen and Melnick, *Preserving Cultural* Landscapes, 207.

25. Kitch, *Pennsylvania in Public Memory*, 13; Kristin Louise Bauersfeld, "The

Challenges and Complexities of Landscape Planning and Exhibition Design at a Commemorative Site: The Homestead Pumphouse" (masters thesis, University of Pittsburgh, 1998); Taft, *From Steel to Slots*, 158–66.

26. Serrin, *Homestead*, 329–72: John P. Hoerr, *And the Wolf Finally Came: The Decline of the American Steel Industry* (Pittsburgh: University of Pittsburgh Press 1988).

27. Serrin, *Homestead*, 405. See also Holland, "Historic Preservation," 25–36, 43–45.

28. Quotes from Robert D. Archibald, *A Place to Remember: Using History to Build Community* (Walnut Creek, CA: Altamira Press, 1999), 16. See also John Russo and Sherry Lee Linkon, "Collateral Damage: Deindustrialization and the Uses of Youngstown," in Jefferson Cowie and Joseph Heathcott, eds., *Beyond the Ruins: The Meanings of Deindustrialization* (Ithaca, NY: Cornell University Press, 2003), 218; Serrin, *Homestead*, 368–69, 378–87.

29. Holland, "Historic Preservation," 31, 45. See also Serrin, *Homestead*, 406–7.

30. Kitch, *Pennsylvania in Public Memory*, 129, 154–63; also see David Lowenthal, *The Heritage Crusade and the Spoils of History* (London: Viking, 1996).

31. Hayden, *Power of Place*, 13. For Lowenthal, see Howett, "Integrity as a Value," 200.

32. Howett, "Integrity as a Value," 188–89.

33. Edward K. Muller, "Homestead," unpublished paper presented to the National Park Service, Washington, DC, 1990, on behalf of the Steel Industry Heritage Task Force.

34. Hayden, "Foreword," ix. Hayden defines a cultural landscape as "that combination of natural landforms and buildings that defines a particular place or region." Hayden, "Foreword," ix.

35. Dyen and Muller, "Conserving the Heritage," 41, 39, 39. Some communities that are victims of plant closures do collapse and are unable to carry on cultural traditions successfully despite the strenuous efforts of community leaders and institutions. See, for example, S. L. Price, *Playing through the Whistle: Steel, Football, and an American Town* (New York: Atlantic Monthly Press, 2016).

36. Author's interview with Doris Dyen, ROS's director of cultural conservation, on April 18, 2016.

37. Howett, "Integrity as a Value," 205–7: Bodurow, "Vehicle for Conserving," 85.

38. Hayden, "Foreword," vii.

39. This brief overview of ROS's early development is based on the author's interviews with August Carlino, February 24, and Jo Debolt, February 1, 2016, and also on the author's memory as a participant of the development. See also Doris J. Dyen, "Forging Communication Links: Cultural Conservation Planning in Pennsylvania's Steel Region," *Folklore in Use: Applications in the Real World* 1, no. 1 (1993): 71–72; Lubove, *Twentieth-Century Pittsburgh, Vol. 2*, 245–51.

40. "Mon Valley Steel Heritage Project Memorandum of Understanding," September 4, 1990, in the possession of Rivers of Steel National Heritage Area; *Management Action Plan*, Steel Industry Heritage Corporation, 1996, consultants, UDA Architects, Pittsburgh, Pennsylvania. See also Dyen, "Forging Communication Links," 72; *Final Concept Plan: Steel Industry Heritage Project*, Steel Industry Task Force and the National Park Service, 1993, consultants, Rhodeside & Harwell, Incorporated.

41. Author's interview with Jo DeBolt, February 1, 2016; Lubove, *Twentieth-Century Pittsburgh, Vol. 2*, 249–54.

42. Author's interviews with Jo DeBolt, February 1, and August Carlino, February

24, 2016. For a useful summary of the Mon Valley Initiative's and DeBolt's perspective on community participation and economic development, see Lubove, *Twentieth-Century Pittsburgh, Vol. 2*, 168–69, 250.

43. Francaviglia, "Selling Heritage Landscapes," 45.

44. Author's interview with August Carlino, June 14, 2016.

45. David Schuyler and Patricia M. O'Donnell, "The History and Preservation of Urban Parks and Cemeteries," in Alanen and Melnick, *Preserving Cultural Landscapes*, 93.

46. Author's interviews with Jo DeBolt, February 1, and August Carlino, February 24, 2016; Lubove, *Twentieth-Century Pittsburgh, Vol. 2*, 250–51; Kitch, *Pennsylvania in Public Memory*, 11; Kaufman, *Place, Race, and Story*, 1; *Momentum: The First Ten Years, 1996–2007* (Rivers of Steel National Heritage Area, 2007), 2; Sharon Ann Holt, "Mill Stories: Deindustrialization as Public History," *Cross Ties*, November, 12, 2015 (Mid-Atlantic Regional Center for the Humanities, Rutgers University-Camden, Camden, NJ).

47. Author's interview with Carlino, June 14, 2016. Rice's Landing was placed on the National Register of Historic Places.

48. August Carlino, e-mail to author, June 21, 2016.

49. Author's interview with Dyen, April 18, 2016; Dyen and Muller, "Conserving the Heritage," 40–41. For a list of cultural conservation projects, see *Momentum: The First Ten Years*, 9. See also "Cultural Conversations," a publication of Rivers of Steel National Heritage Area (Autumn 2000, Spring 2001, and Summer 2001); "Making Strides: Focus on Heritage Partners," *Chronicle* 12, no. 1 (Spring 2005); author's interview with August Carlino, June 14, 2016; *Routes to Roots: A Driving Guide/Rivers of Steel National Heritage Area* (Homestead: Steel Industry Heritage Corporation, 2004); "2016 Tours and Workshops," www.riversofsteel.com; Patricia Lowry, "Women Recall Homestead's Her Story," *Pittsburgh Post Gazette*, March 21, 2006, C-3.

50. Carlino quoted from Bodurow, "Vehicle for Conserving," 82. See also Mosher, Mosher, e-mail to author, July 13, 2015, 3; Mahoney, "Industrial Heritage at Risk," 2, 6–7; Barrett, "National Heritage Area Family Tree," 46–54.

51. Brenda Barrett and Augie Carlino, "What Is in the Future for the Heritage Area Movement," *Forum Journal* (Summer 2003): 51.

52. Author's interview with Jo DeBolt, February 1, 2016.

53. Interview with Jo DeBolt, February 1, 2016; Hayden, *Power of Place*, 49–50. The Mon Valley Initiative reported that "Probably the most difficult to explain, but the most satisfying to experience, is the empowerment of individuals. Seeing someone speak at a public meeting for the first time, or press an elected official for an answer, or demand action on a community problem is something that has happened over and over again the past few years. . . . The lesson learned here is that the key to success in rebuilding the Valley is in developing people." Lubove, *Twentieth-Century Pittsburgh, Vol. 2*, 173.

54. Kitch, *Pennsylvania in Public Memory*, 148 (also 139–40, 170–76); author's interview with Jo DeBolt. February 1, 2016, notes in possession of author.

55. Author's interview with August Carlino, February 24, 2016, notes in possession of author; www.riversofsteel.com. Also see Campo, "Historic Preservation in an Economic Void," 316–17. Noting several different preservation efforts, Campo writes, "they generally share a do-it-yourself (DIY) approach that emphasizes thrift, amateur-based restoration practices, and evolving outcomes; and prioritizes public arts and cultural programming over more permanent adaptations that might enable higher and more consistent revenue streams." Campo, "Historic Preservation in an Economic Void," 316–17.

ADDITIONAL WORKS ON PITTSBURGH BY THE AUTHORS

WORKS BY EDWARD K. MULLER

"Ash Pile or Steel City? H. L. Mencken Helps Mold an Image." *Pittsburgh History* 74, no. 2 (1991): 51–61.

The Atlas of Pennsylvania. Editor with Ronald Abler, David J. Cuff, William J. Young, and Wilbur Zelinsky. Philadelphia: Temple University Press, 1989. Includes a section on Pittsburgh.

Before Renaissance: Planning in Pittsburgh, 1889–1943. With John F. Bauman Pittsburgh: University of Pittsburgh Press, 2006.

"Conserving Industrial Heritage: The Compromising Issue of Integrity." *Historical Preservation Forum* 81, no. 4 (1994): 37–44. With Doris Dyen.

"Coordinator's Introduction to the Forum," 3–5. Editor of "Forum: Pittsburgh's Renaissance Revisited." *Journal of Urban History* 41, no. 1 (2015): 3–46.

"A County Revisited." Introduction to reprinted edition of *Atlas of the County of Allegheny* (original publication by G. M. Hopkins, Philadelphia, 1876, reprinted by the Historical Society of Western Pennsylvania, 1988), i–iii.

"The Development of a Pittsburgh Museum of Industrial Society: A Concept Planning Document." Discussion paper prepared with John F. Bauman for the Committee on Pittsburgh Archaeology and History and the Historical Society of Western Pennsylvania, 1986.

"Downtown Pittsburgh: Renaissance and Renewal." In *A Geographic Perspective of Pittsburgh and the Alleghenies: From Precambrian to Post-Industrial*, edited by Kevin J. Patrick and Joseph L. Scarpaci Jr., 17–27. Washington: Association of American

Geographers, 2000. Revised and published in *Pittburgh and the Appalachians: Cultural and Natural Resources in a Postindustrial Age*, edited by Kevin J. Patrick and Joseph L. Scarpaci Jr., 7–20. Pittsburgh: University of Pittsburgh Press, 2006.

Exhibit Review, "Designing Oakland." *Journal of Planning History* 1, no. 3 (August 2002): 262–65.

"Foreword." In *Seeing Pittsburgh*, edited by Ron Baraff and Tiffani Emig, i–ii. Pittsburgh: Rivers of Steel National Heritage Area, 2008.

"The Formation of the Pittsburgh Region." In *Guidebook to the Pittsburgh Region*, edited by Christopher H. Marston, 3–10. Issued for the Twelfth Annual Conference of the Society for Industry Archeology, Morgantown, West Virginia, 1993.

"Frederick Bigger: The Planning Technician as Urban Visionary, 1881–1963." *Planning History Studies* 19, nos. 1–2 (1996): 21–39. With John F. Bauman. Revised and published as "The Planning Technician as Urban Visionary: Frederick Bigger and American Planning, 1915–1954," *Journal of Planning History* 1, no. 2 (2002): 124–53.

"Historical Aspects of Regional Structural Change in the Pittsburgh Region." In *Regional Structural Change and Industrial Policy in International Perspective: United States, Great Britain, France, Federal Republic of Germany*, edited by Joachim Jens Hesse, 17–48. Baden-Baden, West Germany: Nomos-Verlag, 1988.

"The History of the Pittsburgh Point." Exhibit introduction, *Get to the Point.* Hillman Library, University of Pittsburgh, 2015.

"Industrial Integrity and NHL Nominations: Homestead, PA." Discussion paper prepared for the National Park Service, 1990.

"'In spite of the river' ought to be a Pittsburgh town-slogan.'" *Proceedings*, 1440–52. Thirteenth Biennial Conference, International Planning History Society, 2008.

"The Legacy of Industrial Rivers." *Pittsburgh History* 72, no. 2 (1989): 64–75. Winner of the 1989 Solon J. Buck Award for Western Pennsylvania History.

"Lubove's Pittsburgh." *Pennsylvania History* 68, no. 3 (2001): 336–53.

"Metropolis and Region: A Framework for Enquiry into Western Pennsylvania." In *City at the Point: Essays on the Social History of Pittsburgh*, edited by Samuel P. Hays, 181–211. Pittsburgh: University of Pittsburgh Press, 1989.

"The Olmsteds in Pittsburgh: "Part II, Shaping the Progressive City." *Pittsburgh History* 76, nos. 3 and 4 (1993/1994): 191–205. With John F. Bauman. (Winner of the 1993 Solon J. Buck Award for Western Pennsylvania History).—(Part I is included in the collection).

"Pittsburgh." In *The City and Urban Life*, edited by Jan Rogozinski. Armonk, NY: M. E. Sharpe.

"Pittsburgh" and "Mencken, H. L." *Encyclopedia of American Urban History*, edited by David Goldfield, 2:457–58, 575–76. Thousand Oaks, CA: Sage Publications, 2007.

"Pittsburgh 1896–1929." In *Cities in American History: A Reference Guide.* Washington, DC: CG Press, 2011.

"Pittsburgh's Many Landscapes." *Western Pennsylvania History* 85, no. 1 (Spring 2002): 14–22.

"The Pittsburgh Survey and Greater Pittsburgh: A Muddled Metropolitan Geography." In *Pittsburgh Surveyed: Social Science and Social Reform in the Early Twentieth Century*, edited by Maurine W. Greenwald and Margo Anderson, 69–87. Pittsburgh: University of Pittsburgh Press, 1996.

"Pittsburgh's Waterfront Lands." A final report for the Urban Redevelopment Authority of Pittsburgh, 1983.

"The Point." In *Geographical Snapshots of North America*, edited by Donald G. Janelle, 231–34. Publication commemorating the Twenty-Seventh Congress of the International Geographical Union and Assembly. New York: The Guilford Press, 1992.

"Preserving Industrial Landscapes and Community." In *Alloy Pittsburgh 2013*, 12–13. Indiana, PA: Indiana University of Pennsylvania Printers, 2014.

"River City." In *Devastation and Renewal: Perspectives on the Environmental History of Pittsburgh and Its Region*, edited by Joel A. Tarr, 41–63. Pittsburgh, PA: University of Pittsburgh Press, 2003.

"The Steel Valley." In *A Geographic Perspective of Pittsburgh and the Alleghenies: From Precambrian to Post-Industrial*, edited by Kevin J. Patrick and Joseph L. Scarpaci Jr., 79–86. Washington: Association of American Geographers, 2000. Revised and published in *Pittsburgh and the Appalachians: Cultural and Natural Resources in a Postindustrial Age*, edited by Kevin J. Patrick and Joseph L. Scarpaci Jr., 36–48. Pittsburgh: University of Pittsburgh Press, 2006.

"Tribute: Roy Lubove, 1934–1995." *Journal of Urban History* 22, no. 6 (1996): 675–86.

An Uncommon Passage: Traveling through History on the Great Allegheny Passage Trail. Editor. Pittsburgh: University of Pittsburgh Press, 2009.

"Urban Pioneer: Essays in Honor of Roy Lubove, 1934–1995." Guest editor of the special issue of *Pennsylvania History* 68, no. 3 (2001), including "Introduction: Roy Lubove, 1934–1995," 269–77, and "A Roy Lubove Bibliography," 363–66.

"Was Pittsburgh's Economic Destiny Set in 1815?" *Indiana Magazine of History* 105, no. 3 (September 2009): 203–18.

"Western Pennsylvania and the Second Industrial Revolution." *Congressional Record*, September 28, 1993, E2260–61. With Richard O'Connor.

"Westmoreland County Historical Overview." In *Westmoreland County: Pennsylvania. An Inventory of Historic Engineering and Industrial Sites*, edited by Gray Fitzsimons and Kenneth D. Rose, 1–28. Washington: Historic American Engineering Record, National Park Service, 1993.

WORKS BY JOEL A. TARR

"Anatomy of a Fine Mess: Pittsburgh Sewerage History." *Pittsburgh Post-Gazette*, May 26, 2002. With David Dzombak.

"Carnegie Tech's On-Campus Gas Rig." *Pittsburgh Post-Gazette*, November 6, 2011.

"Changing Fuel Use Behavior and Energy Transitions: The Pittsburgh Smoke Control Movement, 1940–1950: A Case Study in Historical Analogy." *Journal of Social History* 14 (Summer 1981): 561–88. With B. Lamperes.

"The Changing Nature of Environmental History: An Interview with Joel A. Tarr." *Pennsylvania History, Special Issue: Environmental Histories of the Mid-Atlantic* 79 (Autumn 2012): 331–45. With Allen Dietrich-Ward.

"Coal and Natural Gas: A Century of Fuel Alteration in the Pittsburgh Region." *Energy History Report-4* (February 1980).

"Coal and Natural Gas: Fuel and Environmental Policy in Pittsburgh and Allegheny County, PA: 1940–1960." *Science, Technology, and Human Values* 5 (Summer 1980): 19–21. With G. D. Goodman and K. Koons.

"Critical Decisions in Pittsburgh Water and Wastewater Treatment." In *Devastation and Renewal: An Environmental History of Pittsburgh and Its Region*, edited by Joel A. Tarr, 64–88. With Terry F. Yosie. Reprinted in *A History of Water*, edited by T.Tvedt and E. Jakobsen, vol. 1: *Water Control and River Biographies*. London: I. B. Tauris, 2006).

Devastation and Renewal: An Environmental History of Pittsburgh and Its Region. Editor and contributor. Pittsburgh: University of Pittsburgh Press, 2003; paperback, 2005.

"Disputes over Water Quality Policy: Professional Cultures in Conflict, 1900–1917." *American Journal of Public Health* 70 (April 1980): 427–35. With Terry Yosie and James McCurley III.

"Food for Thought." *Legacies: Pennsylvanians and Their Environment* (May 2010): 40–41.

"Four Decades of Public-Private Partnerships in Pittsburgh," In *Public-Private Partnerships in American Cities*, edited by S. Fosler and R. Berger, 59–127. Lanham, MD: Lexington Books, 1982. With S. Stewman.

"The Greatest Bridge Never Built." *American Heritage of Invention and Technology* 5 (Fall 1989): 25–29. With Steven J. Fenves. Reprinted in the *Pittsburgh Press Sunday Magazine*, January 14, 1990.

"History Can Be an Asset in Revitalizing Industrial Towns." In *Remaking Cities: Proceedings of the American Institute of Architects International Conference*, edited by Barbara Davis, 140–42. Pittsburgh, PA, 1989. With Robert Gleeson.

"The Horse Era in Pittsburgh." *Western Pennsylvania History* (Summer 2009): 28–41

The Impact of Transportation Innovation on Changing Spatial Patterns: Pittsburgh, 1850–1934, Essays in Public Works History. Chicago: Public Works Historical Society, 1978.

"Infrastructure and City Building in the 19th and 20th Centuries." In *City at the Point: Essays in the Social History of Pittsburgh*, edited by Samuel P. Hays, 213–64. Pittsburgh: University of Pittsburgh Press, 1989.

"Lessons from Pittsburgh's Energy History: From Westinghouse to Marcellus." *New America*, February 15, 2015, https://www.newamerica.org/new-america/learning-from-pittsburghs-energy-history-from-westinghouse-to-marcellus.

"Life, Liberty and the Pursuit of Infrastructure." *Pittsburgh Post-Gazette*, December 15, 1990. With Stephen J. Hoffman.

"The Mill Town in the Industrial City: The Case of Hazelwood." *Urbanism Past and Present* 7 (Winter–Spring 1982): 1–14. With D. DiPasquale.

"Mon Valley's History Can Be A Vital Asset." *Pittsburgh Post-Gazette*, May 7, 1988. With Robert E. Gleeson.

"The Nation's Most Livable City: The Transformation of Pittsburgh." In *The Future of Winter Cities*, edited by Gary Gappert, 173–95. Los Angeles: Sage Publications, 1987. With Brian Berry, Susan Sanderson, and Shelby Stewman.

"Pedestrians at Risk." *Pittsburgh Post-Gazette*, October 5, 2014.

"Pittsburgh: The Transition from Steel to Healthcare." *Approach: Special Report*, autumn 2012 (in Japanese).

"Pittsburgh and the Manufactured Gas Industry." *Pittsburgh Engineer* (Winter 2006): 12–14.

Pittsburgh-Sheffield: Sister Cities Editor and contributor. Pittsburgh: CMU, 1986.

"Pittsburgh's Illuminating History." *Pittsburgh Post-Gazette*, August 6, 2016. With Anna Rosenberg.

"Pittsburgh's Industriekorridore." In *Feuererlander—Regions of Vulcan Malerei um Kohle und Stahl*, 357–72. Gegleitbuch zur Sonderausstellung: Aschendorff, 2010. With E. K. Muller.

"The Pittsburgh Survey as an Environmental Statement." In *Pittsburgh Surveyed: Social Science and Social Reform in the Early Twentieth Century*, edited by Maurine W. Greenwald and Margo Anderson, 170–89. Pittsburgh: University of Pittsburgh Press, 1996.

"The Plume Is Gone, But We Can't Forget Hazelwood." *Pittsburgh Post-Gazette*, May 27, 1998.

"Public-Private Partnerships in Pittsburgh." *Pittsburgh and Sheffield: Sister Cities*, edited by in Joel A. Tarr, 141–82. Pittsburgh: CMU 1986. With S. Stewman.

"Railroads Should Join Civic Groups to Improve Air Quality." *Pittsburgh Post-Gazette*, October 11, 2015.

"Realizing a Fantasy: Pittsburgh as a Sustainable City." *Pittsburgh Post-Gazette*, October 8, 1994.

"Strategies for Clean Air: The Pittsburgh and Allegheny County Smoke Control Movements, 1940–1960." *Devastation and Renewal: An Environmental History of Pittsburgh and Its Region*, edited by Joel A. Tarr, 145–73. With Sherie R. Mershon.

"There Will Be Gas: A Look at Western Pennsylvania's Other Natural Gas Drilling Booms (and Busts)." *Pittsburgh Post-Gazette*, August 2, 2009.

"Weekend Perspectives: Pittsburgh's History in a Stroll Schenley Park, a Marvel Itself, Shows the Layers of Our Legacy." *Pittsburgh Post-Gazette*, November 29, 2003.

"What to Do about Urban Floods." *Pittsburgh Post-Gazette*, October 2, 2004. With Tim Collins.

"When the Streets Ran with Gas." *Pittsburgh Post-Gazette*, October 28, 2012.

INDEX

Note: Page numbers in *italics* refer to illustrative materials, including charts, figures, and tables.